Bridging the Sea Islands' Past and Present, 1893–2006

Bridging the Sea Islands' Past and Present, 1893–2006

The History of Beaufort County, South Carolina, Volume 3

Lawrence S. Rowland and Stephen R. Wise

THE UNIVERSITY OF SOUTH CAROLINA PRESS

Published by the University of South Carolina Press
Columbia, South Carolina 29208

www.sc.edu/uscpress

Manufactured in the United States of America

23 22 21 20 19 18 17 16 15   10 9 8 7 6 5 4 3 2 1

Library of Congress Cataloging-in-Publication Data
can be found at http://catalog.loc.gov/.

ISBN: 978-1-61117-545-5 (cloth)

The book was printed on recycled paper with
30 percent postconsumer waste content.

In memoriam:
Gerhard Spieler, 1920–2012
George C. Rogers Jr., 1922–1997
Mary Gaffney Allen, 1930–2006

Contents

List of Illustrations

Acknowledgments

Many minds and many memories contributed to the completion of *The History of Beaufort County,* volume 3, *1893–2006.* Thanks go, first and foremost to my coauthor, Stephen R. Wise, who has been the director of the Marine Corps Museum on Parris Island since 1983 and an adjunct professor of history at the University of South Carolina Beaufort. Most important, he is a national expert on the naval history of the Civil War and is, therefore, the lead author of *The History of Beaufort County,* volume 2, *1861 to 1893.* We have guest-lectured in each other's courses and team-taught many lecture series on local history. Together we have led numerous historical tours of the lowcountry, afloat and ashore. Without his scholarship, friendship, and professional counsel, this book would not have been completed.

Two other individuals have shepherded both manuscripts from beginning to end. Since 1999, when work on this manuscript began, Mary Katherine Webb has provided technical, organizational, and editorial assistance. She placed both manuscripts on the computer and prepared the final drafts for presentation to the University of South Carolina Press. She was the first reader of both these books. Her perseverance, wise counsel, patience, and encouragement were crucial to advancing the manuscript. This book would not have continued without her friendship and support.

When the initial manuscript arrived at the press, it became the personal responsibility of Alexander Moore, acquisitions editor of the University of South Carolina Press, who is also co-author of *The History of Beaufort County,* volume 1. On his own time, he read, edited, and vastly improved the manuscripts of volumes 2 and 3. He also wrote forewords to both volumes, which elegantly link the three volumes of *The History of Beaufort County.* Without his knowledge of South Carolina history and editorial skill, the value of volumes 2 and 3 would be greatly diminished. The professionalism and patience of the staff of the USC Press, particularly Linda Fogle, Elizabeth Jones, and Suzanne Axland, was essential in ushering this project to its conclusion. The concluding tasks of indexing and final changes were expertly and cheerfully assisted by Barbara Thomas Crow. The authors gratefully acknowledge the help of all these professionals.

Many others contributed directly or indirectly to this book. The Beaufort County Public Library operates the "Carolina Room" at its main branch in Beaufort. The Carolina Room houses a treasure trove of historical documents, including the collections of the Beaufort County Historical Society (begun in 1939) and the microfilm archives of the *Palmetto Post* (1888–1907) and the *Beaufort Gazette* (1898–present). Ms. Grace Cordial, director of the Carolina Room, made these resources available to the authors and arranged for the county government to make microfilm copies of the *Beaufort Gazette* for my personal use. Particularly helpful was my former student and friend of many years, the late Hillary Barnwell, Beaufort County assistant librarian.

The late Gerhard Spieler's work on the history of Beaufort County began more than forty years ago. For twenty years he was a title researcher for the Beaufort County government. This career gave him a unique view of local history and kindled his interest in further scholarship. He began his own archival collection in the 1960s. His home, the historic DeTreville House in downtown Beaufort, has become one of the great repositories of local history. He shared his knowledge of local history by publishing articles in local magazines and a weekly column in the *Beaufort Gazette*. Specifically, he shared his expertise and his huge personal archive with the authors.

For many months, I haunted the back room of the University of South Carolina Beaufort library. Their microfilm reader became my personal office, and they often locked me in the library and told me to turn out the lights when I left. Former head librarian Ellen Chamberlain and assistant librarians Mae Mendoza and Jeannie Flowers provided hours of assistance, service, friendship, and humor that made the years of research for this book enjoyable. When the final manuscript was prepared, two USC Beaufort staff members were particularly helpful. Professor of Mathematics and Computer Science Tom Odom and staff member Jake Holmes both made important contributions.

The venerable repositories of South Carolina's historical record provided invaluable support for this book. At the South Caroliniana Library in Columbia, Robin Copp, Beth Bilderback, and director Dr. Alan Stokes were always helpful. At the South Carolina Historical Society in Charleston, former executive director Eric Emerson, current publications director Matt Lockhart, and archivist Mike Coker were particularly accommodating. Former publication director, editor, and author of several books on lowcountry history Stephen Hoffius has shared his knowledge on many lowcountry topics. At the South Carolina Department of Archives and History (SCDAH), Steve Tuttle, director of the search room, was always helpful, and Dr. Charles Lesser cheerfully shared his seemingly endless knowledge of South Carolina's historical records. Lynne Parker, graphics designer with USC Press, created the original maps for volumes 2 and 3. Another steady friend of this project is former SCDAH search room director, Alexia Jones Helsley, a native Beaufortonian, whose own history of Beaufort is cited often in this volume.

Another institution whose support advanced the progress of this book is the Institute of Southern Studies at the University of South Carolina. Its director, Dr. Walter B. Edgar, has made contributions to South Carolina history too numerous to mention. The institute provided me with a research fellowship in Columbia that allowed me to do much of the initial research for *The History of Beaufort County,* volumes 1 and 3. Walter Edgar's friendship and support was a great aid to the advancement of this project. The institute's assistant director, Bob Ellis, was also helpful throughout the years of scholarship on this book.

One of the institutions whose support was crucial to this endeavor is the U.S. Marine Corps Museum on Parris Island, whose director is this book's coauthor. In addition to Stephen R. Wise, assistant director and archaeologist Dr. Bryan Howard has been a steady friend. The remarkable photographic collection of the Parris Island Museum is the source of many of the illustrations in this book. The museum staff is the custodian of the archaeological site of the Spanish city of Santa Elena and the French Huguenot colony of Charlesfort, both featured prominently in volume 1.

The Beaufort County government also made significant contributions to this book. Ian Hill, county historic resource planner and a friend of many years, provided important historical census data and assisted in copying some of the larger photographs and maps.

The authors of *The History of Beaufort County* have spent many hours over many years speaking to local historical societies about the history of the lowcountry. The members of these societies have been our warmest and most enthusiastic patrons. First among them is the venerable Beaufort County Historical Society, founded in 1939. Thanks also go to the Historic Beaufort Foundation, the Jasper County Historical Society, the Hampton County Historical Society, the Bluffton Historic Preservation Society, and the Hilton Head Historical Society and Heritage Library.

In recent years, the charms of historic Beaufort have enticed historians of national and regional note to make Beaufort a part-time residence. Most of them have become personal friends and unofficial advisors to this book. Daniel K. Littlefield, author of *Rice and Slaves* (1981), has a home in Beaufort to which he often escapes. John M. McCardell, author of *The Idea of a Southern Nation* (1979) president emeritus of Middlebury College, and current president of the University of the South at Sewanee, Tennessee, has become a close friend and enthusiastic lecturer on local history. The closest and most constant consultations have been with John Martin Davis of Fort Davis, Texas, and Beaufort, South Carolina. A lawyer and certified public accountant in Dallas, Marty is also the author of a book-length manuscript on Civil War–occupied Beaufort from which grew articles in the *South Carolina Historical Magazine* on the Freedmen's Bank of Beaufort, the Port

Royal Railroad, and the Reconstruction phosphate industry. His encyclopedic knowledge of Reconstruction Beaufort is a regular reference. His humor and friendship have been among the pleasures of this work.

Local history cannot be written without intimate knowledge of local families, and in this regard I have been uniquely fortunate. Many old friends shared the records, stories, and memories of their families, adding immeasurably to the texture of this book. First among them are my friends from childhood, Richard Guerrard Pollitzer Jr. and his wife, Ann Christensen Pollitzer. Rick is the great-great grandson of Moritz Pollitzer, progenitor of the American family, and Ann is the granddaughter of Senator Niels Christensen. Through sailing on St. Helena Sound, swimming in Edings Creek, collecting bushels of lowcountry oysters, and raising our seven children together on their island paradise, they relived and contributed to each chapter of both volumes, sharing their families' genealogies and private histories. Rick's cousin, Henry Chambers, former mayor of Beaufort, and Ann's cousin Paul Summerville, current county councilman, were also generous in sharing their family records. Ruby Ellis Danner Hryharrow, known in Beaufort as "Dee," shared the stories and records of the Johnson, Danner, and Dale families. Local artist Nancy Ricker Rhett was generous in sharing priceless stories and letters of her Ricker ancestors. Anthropologist Laura Von Harten, also a current county councilwoman, and her father, H. H. "Bubba" Von Harten, shared not only their family records but also Laura's original research on the origin of Beaufort County's shrimping industry. Others who shared their family histories were W. F. "Bill" Marscher; Claude McLeod; Hope McLeod Cappleman; Dan Harrell; F. W. "Willie" Scheper; Julian Levin, Esq.; Joe, Hymie and Neil Lipsitz; Talbird Reeve Sams, Esq., and his sister Jean Sams Aimar; and Harriett, Billy, and Paul Keyserling. Future historians of Beaufort County will all be indebted to the late Dr. Herbert Keyserling for publishing his own family memoir, *Doctor K* (1999).

Full disclosure compels this author to acknowledge that George Waterhouse and Joseph O'Hear Sanders are my great-grandfathers. As a consequence, many cousins on both sides of my family contributed stories, records, and memories. On the Waterhouse side, Eleanor Waterhouse Hoyler, Maguerite Waterhouse Broz, and Molly Hoyler Gray and her husband, Dr. John W. Gray III, all made substantial contributions. Recently Molly Gray donated 170 years of Waterhouse and Crofut family papers to the South Carolina Historical Society for the benefit of future scholars. On the Sanders side, my cousins Margaret Witsel Lesesne, Daniel Lesesne Jr., and Ann Lesesne Ackerman, on whose sea island farm I spent part of my youth, all contributed to the substance of this book. My late cousin Susan Sanders of New York City added facts and memories of those who left Beaufort and a rare scrapbook of our great-grandmother. My mother, Elizabeth "Libby" Sanders Rowland, first taught me how history can stimulate the imagination, and though she died in 1965, she made me write this book.

On Friday, December 19, 2008, a building fire consumed my office, research library, and all the original notes for this manuscript. Fortunately, a nearly finished draft with footnotes was backed up on electronic files. By the following Monday morning, my friend and business partner, Claude N. Dinkins, had arranged space with a computer in the office suite of Millennium Partners in Port Royal, South Carolina. For two and a half years, they graciously tolerated my irregular hours and occasional guests. I am deeply indebted to the partners, Landon K. Thorne, Dean Morrissey, and Claude Dinkins, and their very talented office manager, Linda Freeman, for their hospitality.

I am particularly indebted to my three grown children—Captain Lawrence Sanders Rowland Jr. of Orange Beach, Alabama; Katherine R. Peabody, CPA, of Charleston, South Carolina; and Margaret R. VerStraten of Alexandria, Virginia—for growing up, graduating from college, and finding their own careers while Steve Wise and I wrote this book. The most profound gratitude goes to our wives, Margot Hunter Rowland and Alice Parsons Wise, for their support, good humor, patience, and perseverance, without which this lengthy endeavor would never have been concluded.

LAWRENCE S. ROWLAND

Foreword

No foreword can recapitulate the contents of the book it introduces, especially one that encompasses nearly 113 years of history. Hence, these few pages must pursue some other goals. First, they should convince a reader to enter the book. Then, they must provide some roadmap to the volume's contents and important themes. Given the success of the two previous volumes of Beaufort County history, the first task is a simple one. Readers are anxious to take up again the nearly five-hundred-year history of that locale and perhaps even find their own Beaufort stories in this concluding volume. The second task is more daunting because the contents of volume 3 are so various and the "important themes" of frontiers and revolution—if not always progress—that gave contexts to the previous volumes have unfolded at a dizzying pace in the aptly named "long twentieth century" that stretched from the 1890s into the twenty-first century. Lawrence S. Rowland and Stephen R. Wise have accomplished in volume 3 a considerable feat of scholarship: They have brought intelligible order to the last century of Beaufort history. In doing so, they have enlightened readers on critical epochs in the history of South Carolina and the nation. Beaufort County's microcosmic, representative character has been the chief theme of volumes 1 and 2 but has never been so well demonstrated as in the present volume.

Volume 3 succeeds two previous volumes of Beaufort County history and concludes a nearly thirty-year publishing enterprise. Volume 1, written by Lawrence S. Rowland, George C. Rogers, and Alexander Moore and published in 1996, recounted the history of that small corner of South Carolina from 1514, its first known appearance in recorded history, to November 7, 1861, the "Big Gun Shoot" that brought the American Civil War home to the state where that war had begun. Volume 2 by Stephen R. Wise and Lawrence S. Rowland began with the Union capture and occupation of Port Royal Sound and Beaufort County. A distinguished Civil War scholar, Wise took the lead role. He made that volume a powerful, original, and eminently readable study of occupied Beaufort and of the famous Port Royal Experiment. Rowland took up the story of postwar Beaufort and described the county's rise from abject poverty and social chaos to a New South vision of prosperity and political equality in 1890.

In volume 3 the authors have reversed their order of precedence. Rowland composed the majority of the volume, and Wise was a steady collaborator.

This final volume begins in 1893 with the Great Hurricane that devastated coastal South Carolina. The storm directly struck Port Royal Sound on August 27, 1893. It killed more than two thousand people and shattered the region's economy, which was based upon agriculture and phosphate mining. So great was the loss of life and devastation that Lawrence Rowland perceived the hurricane to have wrought a revolution nearly as great as that of the American Civil War and Reconstruction. Themes explored in the previous volumes—Beaufort as a frontier and a site of revolutions in politics, economics, and culture—are examined in volume 3, but these themes take on new meanings in the long twentieth century.

By any standards of judgment, the twentieth century was a hurricane of violence, political and social revolution, economic chaos, and religious and ideological turmoil. Paradoxically, it was also an epoch of nearly unbroken scientific and medical progress, technological innovation, cultural experimentation, and expansion of democratic institutions throughout the world. To assist modern readers in comprehending the century just past and the one we now inhabit, the authors of volume 3 have elaborated historical contexts that are of sufficiently small scale to perceive order amid storms of events and kaleidoscopes of personalities.

For starters, the political revolutions of volumes 1 and 2 are augmented in volume 3 by demographic ones. The Great Exodus of African Americans away from Beaufort County and the post-1960s Sunbelt immigration were cultural revolutions. These demographic changes transformed Beaufort County from a 90.5 percent majority black population in 1900 to a 61 percent majority white majority population in 1960. This population revolution had obvious political and cultural dimensions but took on environmental dimensions as well in the later twentieth century as resort and service economies supplanted agriculture and maritime industries. In South Carolina and Beaufort County, women's suffrage and the century-long struggle of African Americans to secure their share of the civil rights of all Americans have gone hand in hand with the expansion of democracy throughout the world. But progress in Beaufort and the state has not been steady, timely, or even complete. Rowland and Wise recount the practical effects of the undemocratic ratification of the state's 1895 constitution, the impact of a 1913 town council race in Beaufort, and the long struggle of African Americans to recover a modicum of the political clout they possessed at the end of the nineteenth century.

Twentieth-century warfare caught up with Beaufort County in the training and mobilization of troops in conflicts that began with the Spanish-American War in 1898 through two world wars, the Korean and Vietnam conflicts, and present-day military violence in Iraq and Afghanistan. Primary evidence of Beaufort County's importance in the nation's defense is found in the Marine Corps Training Center at Parris Island and other bases in the region. More subtle evidence of Beaufort's role in America's military culture has been the steady stream of retirees from military service who have settled in the region. Stationed there on active duty, retired men and women find the locale congenial to their martial culture and retirement interests. They continue to arrive in Beaufort County undiminished in number into the twenty-first century. Transients became immigrants in patterns first observed in volume 1 among the Yamasee Indians and Carolina colonists in the seventeenth century and Saint Peter's Parish planters in the eighteenth. In volume 2 northern philanthropists of many stripes came to Beaufort County to take part in the Port Royal Experiment. Duncan Campbell Wilson, John J. Dale, George Waterhouse, and the Christensens made the county their home after the Civil War and sought to revolutionize the region's economy as they had revolutionized its politics. They were Republicans and Democrats, industrialists and corporate farmers. They invested northern capital and made their homes in a second New South, based less on political than on economic revolutionary notions. By 1890 they had transformed a former Confederate and Democratic stronghold into a model of biracial democracy that survived into the worst years of Jim Crow political tyranny.

Perhaps the most representative immigrant experience has been that of retirees and resort home owners, a group that has flocked to the region from throughout the nation and the world because of the climate, carefully crafted lifestyle, and relatively low-cost economy. This phenomenon began in the late nineteenth century as wealthy northerners—financiers, industrialists, and industrial farmers—began purchasing former plantations and transformed them into private hunting preserves. Duck and quail hunters and seekers of quiet in nature restored thousands of acres of abandoned rice lands and cotton fields back into productive uses. They were among the first conservationists, and the impact of their stewardship has had powerful impact into the twenty-first century. Military retirees and members of golf and tennis resorts succeeded the hunting plantation owners. Their impact has been a mixed blessing for the region as large areas are taken out of cultivation and turned to recreational use. Suburban infrastructures as well as transportation issues are considerable challenges to modern civic leaders. For a century, resort developers Kate Gleason, Charles Fraser, and Bobby Ginn sought to orchestrate this specialized immigration. In the environmental revolution that has resulted, two elements are prominent: one is the rapid commercial and residential development that threatens the natural world; the other is the rise of a homegrown conservation ethic that includes land, water, wildlife, and historic preservation.

Rowland deftly utilizes the "names, not numbers" approach of his mentor George C. Rogers to make coherent the fast pace and the multiplicities of change that swept throughout Beaufort County during the long twentieth century. With his vast personal knowledge of the place and people—his forebears include Waterhouses, Sanderses, and Rowlands—he selects the most apt occurrence or identifies the representative person to transform complex phenomena into well-wrought stories. For example, the author leads the reader on walking tours of Bay Street, the commercial heart of the town and county of Beaufort in 1890, 1907, 1920, and 2006. By naming the retail shops, offices of professionals, and cultural landmarks, he offers *dulce et utile* lessons in the history of immigrations, persistence, and success and failure. This simple device reveals the economic, social, and racial composition of the area at critical junctures: 1890 preceded the Great Hurricane; 1907 recorded the devastation of the "Red Saturday" fire of January 19, 1907; 1920 demonstrated the growing depression in the South and set the stage for the collapse of the People's Bank of Beaufort in 1926. Finally, the 2006 tour reveals a region probably too dependent upon tourism and resort living.

Of course, monumental political events—the retrograde state constitution of 1895, the 1913 election that ended Beaufort's fusion political compromise between whites and blacks, the 1926 collapse of the Beaufort Bank, the civil rights revolution—are fully addressed from an insider's point of view. But amid all the frontiers, storms, and demographic revolutions, Rowland has subtly transformed volume 3 into a business history of the American South. Enterprise and entrepreneurship, whether successful or failed, link together all the themes and unite all the actors found in this work.

Volume 3 is a cornucopia of persons' names. Lists of individuals—baseball players, wartime casualties, harbor pilots, hunting plantation owners—identify through naming some of the powerful forces of change that have passed over Beaufort County. Well-crafted portraits of representative individuals fill this volume. Robert Smalls, Thomas E. Miller, George Waterhouse, Niels Christensen, Thomas Talbird, Tillie O'Dell, Isabella Glen, William Keyserling, Kate Gleason, Harriet Keyserling, Charles Fraser, and Bobby Ginn were active agents of change in politics, business, and culture. Indeed, Rowland and Wise have not only chronicled the stories of these people but have also been active participants in the stories they tell. Their own experiences as scholars and civic leaders are the stuff of the history that unfolds in the volume.

ALEXANDER MOORE

Chapter 1

The Great Sea Island Hurricane of 1893 and Its Aftermath

As Beaufort County entered the last decade of the nineteenth century, it was at the peak of its postwar prosperity. The previous twenty years had seen steady growth and economic transformation. The Port Royal and Augusta Railroad had linked the sea islands to the mainland, ending centuries of isolation. The phosphate and lumber industries brought regular wage-paying jobs to native sea islanders, and the economic spinoff supported a thriving commercial community in Beaufort. Port Royal had enjoyed twenty years as the premier deep-water port on the South Atlantic Coast, and the U.S. Navy had made it the permanent station of its South Atlantic Squadron.

In 1890 Beaufortonians had no reason to doubt that their progress and prosperity would continue into the future. In 1888 Beaufort County exported 257,385 tons of phosphate rock and 59,659 tons of processed fertilizer from the port of Port Royal. Nearly 80 percent of this produce went to foreign markets. The next year was the apex of South Carolina phosphate production. Beaufort County produced nearly 80 percent of the United States domestic production of phosphates, half of it made by the giant Coosaw Mining Company.

A visitor to Bay Street in the spring of 1890 would have found the street buzzing with commerce and full of optimism. Two old anchor stores at each end of Bay Street commanded the commercial district. At the east end, next to the ferry landing, was the ship chandlery and grocery store of F.W. Scheper, who confidently boasted that he "keeps the best stock in town." That stock included "fresh mincemeat, apple butter, evaporated apples, pigs feet, mackerel, corned beef . . . a complete line of canned goods . . . fine liquors, Irish whiskey, gin and brandy." Scheper had spent twenty years building his business into a local institution, buying and developing real estate all over Beaufort and Port Royal. From immigrant beginnings, he had made himself one of the wealthiest men in the county.

At the west end of Bay Street, by the steamboat landing, stood the multiple enterprises of George Waterhouse. The grocery and furniture store of

Waterhouse and Danner was on the street. On the riverbank were the wharf, storage shed, and cotton gin of Waterhouse and Ricker. Both were thriving businesses in 1890. Waterhouse had bought the Lewis Reeve Sams mansion at the east end of Bay Street, and there he raised a large family of two sons and three daughters. From humble beginnings in Kennebunkport, Maine, George Waterhouse had also made himself one of the richest men in the county. At the corner of Bay and Carteret Streets stood the hardware store of Captain Niels Christensen, who, like Scheper and Waterhouse, had begun multiple business enterprises and had grown wealthy.

Up and down Bay Street, other businesses were thriving. William H. Lockwood was the president of the Bank of Beaufort, and B. B. Sams, son of the Datha Island planters, was the cashier and chief operating officer. Dr. Henry Middleton Stuart Jr. followed in the footsteps of his father, the town doctor, to become a "Druggist and Pharmacist . . . offering toilet articles, perfumery and etc." Dr. J. Allen Patterson was the town dentist and surgeon who kept his office in room 21 of the Sea Island Hotel. Dr. Patterson customarily spent two weeks of each month in Beaufort and then made the rounds to Port Royal, Coosaw Mines, and the islands. The Sea Island Hotel was one of the enduring institutions of the age, operated by James O'Dell and his wife, Alice, the famous confectioner. J. Q. Allison's Bay Street "furniture and stove house" sold the expensive appliances of the day on "easy weekly and monthly terms."

W. H. Calvert sold "stoves, tinware, ironware and Japanned ware." John Franz, the town butcher, advertised "beef, pork, veal and mutton" and specifically noted that fresh meat was always available so that "Ship Masters and others can be supplied." C. G. Tolley, a "custom boot and shoemaker," kept his shop on Port Republic Street. William Roberts was a "dealer of groceries, liquor, and tobacco" on Bay Street, while J. F. Hutchings sold only food, candy, and necessary household supplies at his family grocery. Two new stores opened on Bay Street in 1890. H. F. VonHarten began a "new store with new stock" selling "groceries, liquor and tobacco," and the Libbey brothers from Charleston started another grocery and liquor store.

Several Bay Street businesses marketed luxury goods and services, a testimony to the prosperity of the town. Mrs. T. P. Buckley sold fine "French Millinery" and other feminine products at her Bay Street shop. Whitman and Bristol advertised gold and silverware at the Beaufort Jewelers. The Johnson brothers offered portrait services and sold photographs and ferrotypes at their photography shop "just back of the post office." Even yachts were sold in Beaufort. In 1890 Robert E. Jenkins advertised the "splendid yacht YumYum" for sale. It was fully equipped, ready to sail, and lying at the docks at Port Royal. James Gibbes operated the Beaufort News Depot on Bay Street offering daily newspapers from major cities, magazines, and schoolbooks.

Even more indulgent businesses were operated by Charlie Seeman, "manufacturer of soda water, ginger ale and sarsaparilla," and R. Milner Smith, the proprietor of the Club House Saloon. For those who indulged too much at the sarsaparilla shop or the Club House Saloon, they could always visit Ceasar Cousin's Bathing Salon, which offered "hot and cold baths [and] a shave and a haircut."[1]

Business had been good for those who had rebuilt Beaufort after the war. Colonel Duncan Campbell Wilson, now over sixty, had turned over the operation of his Port Royal Sawmill on Pidgeon Point and his Sea Island Chemical Company on Spanish Point to his son D. C. Wilson Jr. and retreated to an honored retirement at the Cuthbert mansion on Bay Street. Moritz Pollitzer, over seventy, had sold his grocery and dry goods business and turned over his sizable real estate holdings and cotton gin to his son Henry "Hal" Pollitzer. Moritz Pollitzer bought the old Verdier mansion at the east end of Port Republic Street, where four generations of Pollitzers were raised over the next century.

While Beaufort's commerce was booming in 1890, a few of Beaufort's more visionary leaders saw signs of trouble ahead. D. C. Wilson, lumber and phosphate pioneer, former president of the Port Royal and Augusta Railroad, and sage of the Beaufort's commercial elite, noted publicly the discovery of large deposits of 80 percent pure phosphate rock near Tampa, Florida. With a nearby deep-water harbor and rail connections to the Atlantic ports of Jacksonville and Fernandina, these new deposits would be stiff competition for Beaufort's biggest industry. George Waterhouse, who had become rich by packing and selling Beaufort's dominant agricultural product, sea island cotton, noticed the gradual decline of world cotton prices in the late 1880s. He observed the rising production of high-grade cotton from Egypt and India and concluded that sea island cotton was also facing stiff competition in the future. In addition, Beaufort's state senator, William J. Verdier, the county's leading white politician, an architect of "fusion politics" and the county's "People's Ticket" of 1888, was alarmed at the rise of a radical young farmer from Edgefield named Benjamin Ryan Tillman. Verdier thought this new brand of upcountry populism would be harmful to Beaufort's carefully crafted political balance, so he withdrew from the 1890 Democratic state convention.[2]

None of these business and political leaders took note of the increasingly unstable weather that was spinning off the sands of North Africa and into the warm waters of the eastern Atlantic. They did not have the scientific tools in 1890 to track such meteorological trends. The South Carolina coast had not experienced a major tropical storm for twenty years. They had no way of predicting that Beaufort County would be struck by five major hurricanes in the next ten years, 1893, 1896, 1898 (when two storms struck), and 1899.

The worst was the first. In fact, along with the Johnstown Flood of 1889, the Great Storm of 1893 was up to that time the worst natural disaster, in terms of lives lost, in the nation's history: estimates are that the hurricane took the lives of nearly two thousand people on the sea islands between Savannah and Charleston. Since that time, only the Galveston hurricane of 1900 has cost more human lives; approximately six thousand people died in that disaster.

The mortality from the storm of 1893 was high because on the isolated sea islands there was little warning of the approaching tempest. In Charleston first word of the storm came from Nassau, Bahamas, on Friday, August 25, where there were reports of a violent tropical cyclone "of huge proportions" located southeast of the Abacos. On Saturday, August 26, word reached Charleston that the storm was off the central coast of Florida. On Sunday morning, signal staffs at pilot stations from Tybee Island, Georgia, to Fort Sumter in Charleston harbor raised the dreaded double-gale warning flags. Small vessels scurried in to seek cover. Large ships in Savannah, Charleston, Port Royal, and St. Helena Sound began to lay out more cable and set additional anchors. By late Sunday afternoon, August 27, the dark, ominous cloud of the leading edge of the hurricane was clearly visible offshore from the barrier islands. Torrential rains and high winds pounded the coast from Savannah to Charleston. As night fell, barometers along the coast began to fall rapidly, and the hurricane wind began its constant howl. By 8:50 P.M. the barometers in Charleston harbor had fallen to 29.325 inches of mercury, and the wind was a steady seventy-two miles per hour from the northeast. A train of picnic excursionists from Savannah to Charleston could not return home via the Charleston and Savannah Railroad because the bridges and causeways to the south were nearly underwater. Ominously, all telegraph communication with Beaufort and the sea islands had fallen silent by 5:00 P.M.

In Beaufort, nestled among the sea islands eleven miles from the frothing ocean, some locals seemed blithely unconcerned, while others began to worry. They worried about the ships at anchor at Port Royal, three miles downriver, but they worried more about the phosphate works, dredges, and barges on the Bull River, completely exposed to the wide, treacherous waters of St. Helena Sound. St. Helena Sound was dangerous for large ships even on calm days. The Spanish in the sixteenth century had called it the "Bay of Shoals" and learned to avoid it at all costs. With a hurricane bearing down on it, St. Helena Sound became a monster that could smash the largest ships afloat. Out on Lady's Island, St. Helena Island, and the smaller islands, farmers had no warning of the storm until the rains and winds began to strengthen on Sunday afternoon. By nightfall, the steady gale and torrential rain forced most island families to huddle together in their shuttered cabins.

Low tide in the sea islands was at 2:00 P.M. on Sunday. For the next six hours, the incoming flood tide roared in with a force never seen before or since in Beaufort County. By high tide at 8:00 P.M., twenty-one bridges had been destroyed, and all the major connecting ferries had been smashed. There was no escape for thousands of people trapped on the low-lying sea islands. After high tide, the disaster became worse. The tide never ebbed. It just kept rising, driven by winds that by 10:00 P.M. exceeded 100 miles per hour. The eye of the hurricane passed near Beaufort about midnight. At 12:45 A.M. wind speed in Charleston harbor, sixty miles north of the eye of the storm, was a sustained 97 miles per hour. The barometer on the tug *Weymouth* in the Beaufort River read 27.60 inches of mercury. Winds to the east of Beaufort reached 120 miles per hour, but the wind was not the worst. Before midnight a storm surge came ashore on top of a double tide. In downtown Beaufort the surge was fifteen feet above a normal high tide. To the east of Beaufort, on Lady's, St. Helena, Warsaw, Coosaw, and Datha Islands, the tidal wave reached nearly twenty feet. It drove across the low-lying islands like a scythe.

August 27–28 was a night of incalculable terror. Houses were lifted from their foundations and whole families were swept away. Many sea islanders survived only by clinging to the tops of the giant live oaks. Many more drowned. Their bodies, scattered across the marshes and creeks, were not discovered for weeks. One mother and five children on St. Helena Island perished when their cabin was swept away by the flood. She never learned that her husband, a fisherman, had capsized his boat and drowned in Station Creek while trying to go for help. Another St. Helena man, seeing the rising water enter his house, lifted his two small children from the floor onto the bed. He wrapped his sick wife in a blanket and carried her to safety on higher ground, wading through waist-deep water. When he turned to rescue his children, the house collapsed and was swept away with his children in it. "Bitterly his poor wife cried when she found he had saved her instead of the children," noted one account. The man commented tearfully, "It was a hard thing to choose." Another St. Helena family of four struggled to hold their house together through the night. The teenage son clung to his four-year-old brother all night and saved his life. When the house gave way under the storm surge, a wave knocked the mother unconscious. The father turned to grab her but watched her as she was swept away. As the teenager recalled, "We ain't seen her no more." The appalling tragedy broke the father's spirit. The boy commented, "Pa, he most broken down all to geder."

The ingenuity of the sea islanders saved many others from certain death. One father put his family in a boat "that was driven upon the waves and guiding it into a thicket, kept them safe til morning." Another man, "feeling his house quiver and lift, took his ax and cut a hole in the floor, let the water in to weight down his house." This act saved the lives of twenty people who had sought refuge in his home. A third islander "put ox chains out one window, round a tree stump, in at another window, fastened them together, so saving his family and his house."

The great live oaks were the only trees strong enough to withstand the storm surge. They saved many sea islanders. On Cane Island, Captain H. D. Elliott saved his family by tying them into the branches of a giant live oak. From this perch above the raging water, they watched the whole island submerge and their house float away. On St. Helena Island, Viola Chaplin recounted that "one man took his wife and children on his back, one by one, and put them in a big oak tree and there they remained until morning."[3]

As dawn broke on the morning of Monday, August 28, 1893, the scene of destruction was like nothing known in Beaufort County's five hundred years of recorded history. Witnesses described the sea islands as if they had been burned over or scorched by fire rather than inundated by flood: "The Sea Islands appeared as if a conflagration had swept the earth and destroyed or withered everything." As news seeped out of Beaufort, the tragedy gripped the nation. On August 30 a headline in the *Boston Herald* read, "An Appalling Rumor: 500 Lives said to be Lost: Sea Islands Swept by Waves: The Terrible Report not Verified." Charleston reported much destruction of property but only six deaths. Savannah reported the worst damage in forty years. But from Port Royal, where the huge storm had unleashed its greatest fury, there were rumors of "many deaths . . . but only meager reports." By September 1 the estimate of deaths in Beaufort County had risen to seven hundred. The September 3 *Boston Herald* headline read, "Fifteen-Hundred Dead! It's Terrible! 1,500 dead and 15,000 starving!"

In the week following the "Great Storm of 1893," personal stories of terror, destruction, survival and death began to emerge from the wreckage of Beaufort County. During the storm the steamer *City of Savannah,* owned by the Savannah and Boston Steamship Line, "went to pieces about six miles from the St. Helena light." The women and children were sent ashore to St. Helena Island in life rafts. The men hung in the rigging of the sunken vessel for fifty hours without food or water. Boats from the SS *Birmingham,* which was following the storm, rescued the survivors. Remarkably, no lives were lost in the wreck of the *City of Savannah.*

Captain Niels Christensen wrote to his wife, Abbie Holmes Christensen, who was in Boston, of the damage to their home, their farm, their hardware store, and their lumberyard on East Street. The storm blew the roof off their home on East Street, broke out all the windows, and filled the house with water, ruining everything within. Their barn on Pidgeon Point was blown down, and all the cows were killed. Captain Christensen's two-hundred-dollar horse was drowned. Much of the stock in the hardware store was destroyed or damaged when the store filled with nearly two feet of seawater. Lumber stacked in the yard was scattered all over town. The tidal wave crushed the tabby seawall at their home and flooded the garden on the lower terrace, killing two hundred varieties of roses and a half-dozen fig trees. Christensen estimated his loss to be ten thousand dollars, a huge sum in 1893. F.W. Scheper and George Waterhouse sustained greater losses because their businesses on the riverbank were exposed to the storm's full fury. F.W. Scheper's loss was estimated at twenty thousand dollars. Waterhouse and Ricker's wharf and warehouse full of cotton were entirely gone. Their cotton-ginning machinery was in the bottom of the river. The paddle-wheel steamer *Pilot Boy,* lying at Waterhouse and Ricker's wharf, "parted her hawsers as though they were twine" and was driven high and dry against the bluff along the shell road. The tugs *Reliance, Juno,* and *Kinkora* were also high and dry along the bluff. The *Weymouth* was against the bluff in front of D. C. Wilson's house. The schooner *Alma Cummings,* which had been tied to Scheper's wharf, was a mile away, stuck in mud. Every dock and wharf on Bay Street was gone.

On the outer islands, stories of terror, death and survival began to filter in. On Parris Island, the quarantine doctor, Gowan Hazel, drowned while trying to rescue two African American boys caught in the flood. I. I. Densler's house floated away, and he and his wife survived by spending the night in the top of a live oak tree. It was reported in the *Boston Herald* that there were "no buildings on St. Helena Island . . . all had floated away." It was only a slight exaggeration.

The worst destruction wrought by the Storm of 1893 was the enormous loss of life. A week after the storm struck, specific casualty reports began to reveal the extent of the tragedy: on St. Helena Island, 200 killed; on the Savannah River plantations, 150 killed; on Kean's Neck, 60 killed; on Coffin Point, 80 killed; on Warsaw Island, 47 killed; on Dataw Island, 37 killed; on Lady's Island, 27 killed; on Parris Island, 24 killed; and on Chisholm Island, 26 killed.[4] As appalling as these numbers were, they were only preliminary figures.

In the week after the hurricane, relief organizations were formed to assist the suffering sea islands. Local leaders formed the Sea Island Relief Committee to seek outside assistance and organize the reconstruction. The committee represented the political balance of fusion politics. The members were George Holmes, mayor of Beaufort; Robert Smalls, collector of customs; W. H. Lockwood, president of the Bank of Beaufort; Niels Christensen; George W. Ford; Charles E. Danner; Thomas F. Walsh; and E. F. Courvoisier. The first help to arrive came from Columbia, the state capital. Governor Ben Tillman immediately dispatched one of the highest-ranking medical officials in the state to assess the loss and recommend relief measures. Dr. James W. Babcock, superintendent of the State Hospital in Columbia, arrived in Beaufort and traveled to the outer islands to calculate the damage. On September 4, 1893, he submitted his first report to Tillman. When he visited Lady's Island and St. Helena's Island, he noted, "Previous reports from there have not been exaggerated." At Eustace Place on Lady's Island, 21 of 31 buildings had been swept away; 51 people were killed; and 44 bodies buried in a single mass grave. "On account of the water logged soil," Babcock wrote, "graves could not be dug more than two feet deep." The cotton and corn crops were destroyed, and the potatoes had all been "burned" by the salt water. At Land's End there had been a settlement of 21 houses and 85 residents. The storm washed away 13 houses and severely damaged all the rest. All the crops were lost. One child was killed, and several people were still missing. At Tombee, with 25 houses and 102 people, only 4 houses were left standing. At Dr. Jenkins's on Land's End, where 19 houses had been home for 64 people before the storm, 10 remained standing. Three houses had collapsed, and 6 had been washed away. Fifty-one people were homeless and all crops had been destroyed. At Jane Pritchard's place on Seaside Road, only 11 of 28 houses remained standing, 83 people were homeless, all crops and provisions had been lost, and "the only food since the storm was half rotten sweet potatoes." At Scott Place 9 houses were flattened and all the rest damaged. At Eddings Point 18 houses were wrecked and 3 washed away. Of the 11 buildings at the Mary Jenkins's Place on Eddings Point, 9 had been washed away. At Croft and Corner Place, 5 people drowned, 13 houses were destroyed and all crops and provisions were ruined. At the Oaks Plantation, 20 houses were wrecked, 2 washed away, and the remaining 11 houses were damaged. On Wassaw Island, 15 people were killed and 36 houses were wrecked. On the whole island, only 3 houses were left standing. At the Lawrence Fripp Place, the Oliver Fripp Place, and Caper's Place, 5 buildings were washed away, all the remaining structures were damaged, and 1 person was killed. Across St. Helena Sound at the Chisolm Settlement Place, 6 houses had been destroyed and 41 people were living in one building. Quarantine Officer Allan Stuart reported from the naval station on Parris Island that 24 people were killed and "almost every house was destroyed." At the naval station itself, the roof blew off the officers' quarters, the massive, heavily timbered wharves were entirely swept away, and "the eastern river bank washed away 40 feet . . . almost every tree was blown down." Dead cattle from two miles around Parris Island were thrown in the river. Many of the survivors were crowded into the Quarantine Hospital.

The only physician on St. Helena Island was Dr. W. Peters. His labors were heroic. Immediately after the storm, Dr. Peters alone treated 70 surgical injuries. He also treated 100 cases of malaria and reported 100 cases of diarrhea and a case of dysentery caused by foul drinking water. Babcock reported the organization of the Sea Island Relief Committee in Beaufort and the assignment of subcommittee chairmen "at various disbursing depots." In Beaufort, 75 to 100 men were busy cleaning debris and burning it. Babcock instructed the Relief Committee to distribute the supplies "judiciously . . . none but those willing to work and deserving of assistance should receive it."[5]

Immediately following the storm, many people on the sea islands were too stunned to imagine recovering from such a calamity. As Dr. Babcock noted on September 4, "The Negroes will need assistance. As yet they have been too much demoralized by their misfortune to rebuild. The people are homeless, hungry, and in immediate need." Adding to the horror of the aftermath was the resurfacing of the bodies of drowning victims from the rivers and creeks. When a person drowned in salt water, his corpse sank to the bottom. As decomposition occurred, gases built up in the body, and in a day or two the bloated corpse bobbed to the surface wherever the tidal current has carried it. In the sea islands, ubiquitous blue crabs had a day or two to feast on corpses on the river bottoms. They usually attacked the extremities first, so that when a corpse resurfaced, it often lacked ears, fingers, and toes. In the week following the Storm of 1893, hundreds of these horribly disfigured bodies were recovered. Many were buried in mass graves without religious ceremony. On Coosaw Island "42 people were buried in two parallel trenches . . . 91 feet by 130 feet long . . . just above high water." According to Gullah tradition, which included a belief in a "water underworld," people who died by drowning were not to be buried in a sanctified graveyard. As Dr. Babcock put it, "The superstitious negroes have denied to the drowned the right of burial in the graveyards." Thus, hasty burials and mass graves such as those at Hazel Farm on Lady's Island and on Coosaw Island reflected a horror and sense of doom unique to the sea island Gullah.

White residents, too, were stunned and demoralized. Robert E. Jenkins, quarantine officer on Hilton Head Island and a descendant of sea island planters, wrote to Governor Tillman that he had "suffered severely in the storm" and was "anxious to leave Hilton Head." He requested transfer to Grahamville on the mainland. Likewise, C. E. Foye requested help from the state in leaving Hilton Head Island: "The storm which swept our coast on August 27 ruined me and I am obliged to leave Hilton Head Island." Foye asked to be appointed trial judge in Grahamville.

Next to burying the dead, the most urgent problem following the storm was to prevent the spread of disease and avert contagious infection. A *Boston Herald* headline on September 9, 1893, read, "Now it is Pestilence; Disease Follows Disaster at Beaufort, South Carolina." As Babcock reported to Governor Tillman, "The Negroes are suffering from malarial fever caused by exposure and dysentery from bad water." He recorded that every high-water hurricane in the sea islands during the nineteenth century was followed by an outbreak of malaria. This was true in 1817, 1854, and 1871. After the 1817 hurricane, some islands were abandoned altogether and could not be replanted because the slaves refused to return.

On St. Helena Island, Dr. Peters worked tirelessly for two weeks without help and without remuneration. He had treated nearly 700 people, mostly for malarial fever and dysentery. He asked Dr. Babcock whether the state could replenish his supplies and medicine, which were exhausted. Babcock recommended that Dr. Peters be at least partially compensated for his heroic labor. Dr. Peters promised not to abandon the island people. "I feel very deeply for the colored people," he told Babcock. Dr. Peters had been the only physician on St. Helena Island for the previous ten years. Like most St. Helena Island residents, he had lost everything in the storm and expected nothing from the destitute sea islanders, but made it clear that he could not continue without some help.[6]

On September 2, 1893, the editor of the *Charleston News and Courier* made his way to Beaufort to survey the damage and interview the survivors. His article, "The Brave Men of Beaufort," included interviews with some of Beaufort's leading merchants and politicians. All had suffered severe personal and financial setbacks. All expressed a determination to rebuild and start over. F.W. Scheper, "one of the largest grocery merchants and financiers in the town," returned from his mountain resort to calculate his loss. "It took me about fifteen years to make what I have lost but I am better off in experience and in ten years, I will make it again," he said. George Waterhouse rushed back from New York to find most of his assets at the bottom of the Beaufort River. Without hesitation he set about to salvage what he could and rebuild. His partner, C. E. Danner, who had witnessed the storm, began energetically clearing the wreckage, wearing a constant "smile of encouragement to the weak-hearted." Niels Christensen, Beaufort's "most extensive and enterprising hardware merchant," not only suffered costly damage to his hardware and lumber business but also to his cash flow.

Christensen had built many of the small cottages inhabited by the sea island farmers. He had offered them generous terms. The storm had swept away most of those modest homes, and Christensen did not expect even the small payments they had regularly made before the storm: "He has thousands of dollars out hardly any of which can ever be recovered." Christensen was, nonetheless, undeterred: "His courage and expressions are sublime, even in his modest, unassuming way. He thinks that in a few years all the scars will be obliterated and after an interval we will resume our wonted prosperity. He is undaunted and will help by his enterprise and means to restore the waste places." State Senator William J. Verdier could never recover what he had lost. The storm had demolished his home and office and devastated his library and law book collection, which included irreplaceable two-hundred-year-old volumes. "He was found early the next morning after the storm after being up all night working in the water, sometimes wading, sometimes swimming," the *News and Courier* editor reported. "He was full of cheer and encouragement to all who approached him. He had saved his favorite yacht Nellie and the lives of his large family of children, and expressed himself grateful." Dr. Hal Middleton Stuart, despite the loss of his drugstore, went straight to work for the good of the community: "The old gentleman was out on Monday and every day since, in rain and mud, in the active direction and suggestion for the cause of sanitary affairs in town." These few interviews were "from the heaviest and most extensive losers and coming from such sources are vastly encouraging."

Despite the brave face of Beaufort's leading men, the situation was desperate. Thousands of people were homeless, starving, and sick. An epidemic was a real threat. On September 5 the Sea Island Relief Committee published an appeal for assistance in the Charleston and Savannah newspapers, hoping it would be circulated "to the American people" by the national newspapers. They noted the "utter desolation . . . on the sea islands of Beaufort County . . . the loss of more than 800 human lives . . . and fully six thousand . . . dependent on charity for an existence." The committee described the sea islands before the storm as "dotted with neat cottages and outbuildings, the result of many years of hard toil and occupied by happy and contented families." These were "now devastated with not an indication of their former habitation except the dead bodies of the families . . . left there by the receding waves as a grim memorial." The survivors were homeless and starving, the flood having totally destroyed the cotton, corn, sweet potato, and vegetable crops. Although the sea islanders "bear their misfortune with fortitude and resignation," the amount of assistance they needed just to survive far exceeded local resources. The committee asked for help for their starving neighbors from "the generous hearted of the land." They asked for contributions of money to be sent to the Bank of Beaufort and food and clothing to be sent to the mayor of Beaufort. Governor Tillman published an appeal to the nation within a few days of receiving Dr. Babcock's report. On September 9 former congressman William Elliott was dispatched to Washington to seek assistance. He visited the supervising surgeon of the Marine Hospital Service to see about getting a hospital ship for Port Royal Sound and conferred with President Grover Cleveland, who promised a revenue cutter and officers for Port Royal.[7]

Help soon poured in from across South Carolina and from out of state. Abbie Holmes Christensen sent ten barrels of clothes gathered in Boston for the Sea Island Relief Committee. George Waterhouse ordered "good grits" worth $500 to be sent from Savannah on his account and distributed free to the needy. The *Baptist Examiner* of New York City distributed Governor Tillman's personal appeal throughout Baptist congregations in the North. The Citizens Permanent Relief Committee of Philadelphia sent $5,000. The New York Maritime Exchange established a Southern Relief Fund and had soon collected $2,434, clothes, and furniture. The Clyde Line of steamships offered to ship and distribute these donations free of charge through its Charleston agent James G. Egerton. When news of the destruction of the sea islands spread across the nation, descendants of the antebellum planters, who had rebuilt their fortunes in other parts of the country, remembered their ancestral homeland with generous cash contributions. Alexander R. Chisholm of 61 Broadway, New York City, a wealthy and successful financier, sent $50 with a note that said, "I was born in that city fifty-eight years ago and am much aggrieved to learn of the disaster which has befallen it." The Chisolm family plantation on Bull River, which he had sold decades before, was the headquarters of the Coosaw Mining Company and the Pacific Guano Company. Twenty-six people had died at Chisholm's Landing during the storm. From Florida, William Hazzard Wigg sent $100. He was descended from one of the pioneer families of the sea islands and was then attorney for Florida's Fifth Judicial Circuit. He identified himself simply as "a former citizen of South Carolina." Hundreds of donations arrived from across the state and nation. The D. E. Converse Company of Clifton, South Carolina, sent "one bale of sheeting: to repair roofs." The citizens of Union, South Carolina, sent $100. The children of St. Peter's Catholic Church of Columbia, South Carolina, sent $5 and the John Wesley Methodist Church of Greenville, South Carolina, sent $20. Dr. John M. Wagner of Charlotte, North Carolina, a "licensed pharmacist of eleven years," offered to travel to Beaufort at the expense of the *Charlotte Observer* and donate his services to the relief committee. George W. Arps and Company, cotton merchants of Norfolk, Virginia, sent $10 "for the hurricane sufferers." The G. F. Harvey Company, manufacturing chemists of Saratoga Springs, New York, sent a box of drugs "for gratuitous use of the sick and suffering."[8]

The most lasting and effective help for the beleaguered sea islands came from the American Red Cross. By September 20 a Red Cross mission had arrived in Beaufort. They spread out among the islands of Beaufort County to assess the need and report to Red Cross headquarters. The advance mission was led by George H. Pullman, who made his first report on September 27. Pullman estimated that thirty thousand people in Beaufort County were in need of food, clothing, shelter, or medical attention. The Red Cross established the Sea Island Relief Fund and solicited contributions from its nationwide network of supporters. George L. Dale was made treasurer of the Relief Fund. Within a few weeks, the fund had collected $11,109.76 and contributions were steadily building. By the end of September, Governor

Tillman had delegated all relief efforts in Beaufort County to the Red Cross. The Red Cross officially took over on October 2, 1893. Clara Barton, the famous Civil War nurse and founder of the American Red Cross, arrived in Beaufort in September and stayed for the next four months. Barton confessed doubt that the Red Cross could succeed in the face of such an immense calamity. Not only were the thirty thousand sea islanders in immediate need; within weeks, petitions reached Red Cross headquarters in Beaufort for aid to thirty to thirty-five thousand more needy people on the mainland. Barton realized that this was the largest effort the Red Cross had ever undertaken.

By January 1894 Barton reported that the Sea Island Relief Fund has received $23,837 in contributions and expended $15,516.03 in the relief effort. It distributed grits ($6,182.50), pork ($3,685.90), and tools, lumber, freight, and hauling ($5,688.97). Barton estimated that the Red Cross was spending $290 per day in Beaufort County. In January she named 345 individual, corporate, and community contributors of assistance. The largest single contribution was $3,003 from the Charleston Relief Committee. The largest private donation was $2,000 from Mrs. M. C. Whitman of Boston. Hundreds of churches, community organizations, civic and business associations, companies, and individuals from New England to Florida contributed to the relief effort. Barton was quick to thank the telegraph, steamship, railroad, and shipping companies that provided months of service free of charge. She described the Western Union Telegraph Company, with its busy local office in the Sea Island Hotel, as "that swift attending angel that has hovered over us for years." The Charleston and Western Carolina Railroad and all connecting lines were filled with goods marked "free for the sufferers and the Red Cross!" Steamship companies, especially the Clyde Line and the New York and Savannah Steamship Company, had cleared their decks for relief supplies for the Red Cross. Barton singled out the Red Cross Chapter No. 1 of Philadelphia for its immediate, generous contribution of tools for rebuilding and planting, the merchants of Boston for their large supply of nails and hardware, and the whole state of Florida which "astonished us by her unfailing generosity." She extended the thanks of the Red Cross to the officers and crewmen of the U.S. revenue cutters *Morrill* and *Boutwell,* dispatched by President Grover Cleveland and Treasury Secretary John G. Carlisle. She also singled out Abbie Holmes Christensen in Brookline, Massachusetts, for large and regular shipments of clothes she had gathered in the Boston area.

Amid the outpouring of national generosity, Clara Barton mentioned one major disappointment. She had specifically requested the aid of the South Carolina General Assembly for the Red Cross effort. Barton's memorial reached the legislature when it convened in November 1893. The memorial was accompanied by a special message from Governor Tillman requesting "relief for the stricken citizens of this proud old state." But the legislature adjourned in December "without having made the slightest provision for these sufferers . . . except the fact that it extended the time of payment of their taxes." The General Assembly's failure to support the relief effort prevented the Red Cross from requesting aid, in good faith, from any other state government. Private charity was the sole support of the Red Cross effort.

By January 1894 signs of recovery began to appear in the sea islands. Early in September 1893, the U.S. Department of Agriculture sent generous supplies of seeds for vegetable planting as soon as the "sea washed ground" was ready. "Turnips, cabbages and lettuce not only cover the islands, but the markets of Beaufort also show their result," the *News and Courier* reported.[9]

The Storm of 1893 received considerable attention from the national press for months after the hurricane struck. *Harper's Weekly* of September 16, 1893, gave lengthy coverage to the disaster, and *Scribner's* magazine published a widely read article entitled "Sea Island Hurricane" by Joel Chandler Harris, the famous author of the "Uncle Remus" stories. Not all the local storm survivors appreciated this national press coverage. S. H. Rodgers, editor of the *Palmetto Post,* wrote an editorial highly critical of Harris's article. The article was, he wrote, "in every way weak . . . unsatisfactory to those of us who were here and saw and felt the storm. . . . Mr. Harris seems to have lost sight of the fact that any white people ever lived here . . . or that white people ever suffered from the hurricane." Controversy over the relief effort and an overtone of racial politics was explicitly revealed in a letter from the Bluffton Township Relief Committee in May 1894: "Many small white farmers are now starving and swallowing pride to appeal for charity . . . the vast contributions made to the Red Cross Association . . . have gone entirely to the colored race . . . some of them are far better off today than they ever were before and among others are to be found a heritage of beggary that will take scores of years to wipe out."[10]

The town of Beaufort did not recover quickly from the Storm of 1893, and the lingering effects were readily apparent to Frederick Christensen when he returned to Beaufort a year after the hurricane: "The town looked old and dilapidated. Not a house (except perhaps D. C. Wilson's) but needed a coat of paint. In fact, the Beaufort I remember looks no more like the present one than 'A' looks like 'Z'. Many of the fine old trees are gone. But I will stay here . . . until Beaufort is back where she should be."[11]

Next to the loss of human life, the most serious lingering effect of the hurricane was the nearly fatal damage to the prized phosphate mining industry. Much of the companies' large capital investment had been floating on the rivers and bays when the hurricane struck. It was nearly a total loss. In fact, the largest industry in Beaufort's five-hundred-year history never fully recovered from the effects of the Great Storm.

The hurricane of 1893 could not have struck at a more inopportune time for Beaufort County's phosphate industry. The August 1892–August 1893 period had been the industry's most productive year, and Beaufort County was the center of that enterprise. The phosphate production of 1893 was particularly notable because the national economy was in the depths of the worst depression in American history. The Panic of 1893 had begun two months after the inauguration of Democratic president Grover Cleveland, and it sunk the national economy into a deep depression. Many who lived through the depression of 1893–96 claimed it was worse than the Great Depression of the 1930s. Despite national hard times, Beaufort County's phosphate industry was expanding, and the wages of thousands of sea islanders was the backbone of prosperity.

In 1892 five major companies were in operation: Coosaw Mining Company, the Sea Island Chemical Company, the Oak Point Phosphate Company, the Pacific Guano Company, and the Farmers Mining Company. On January 1, 1893, the Sea Island Chemical Company and the Oak Point Mining Company consolidated with the Coosaw Mining Company to form the largest phosphate mining company in the United States. The state Phosphate Commission described the industry in Beaufort County before the storm: "Coosaw River was a busy scene on Saturday, August 25th. It was alive with huge dredging machines, washboats, and numbers of lighters and small craft. The numerous tugboats flitting to and from, the shrill scream of whistles, the clank of chains as the huge dippers were lowered to the bottom and raised the load of phosphate rock, the sullen roar of the John Kennedy as the mighty endless chain revolved with thirty-six ponderous dippers weighing more than a ton each . . . the whole scene presenting a picture of active industry never to be forgotten."

After the night of August 27, the scene entirely changed: "On Sunday night . . . our coast was swept by a hurricane the fury of which is indescribable, leaving in its wake ruin and desolation. . . . Looking down the Coosaw River from the mouth of Brickyard Creek not a living object could be seen, not a craft of any description seen afloat . . . blackened cranes, the barnacle covered bottom of a sunken dredge or washboat . . . The mining fleet, the pride and support of the people of this part of the state, lay wrecked and ruined in the marshes and woods and along the shores . . . from Parrott Creek to the Whale Branch trestle." Wrecked or sunk in the Storm of 1893 were 12 dredges, 11 washboats, 10 tugs, 106 lighters, and 95 tonging flats worth approximately $750,000. This was more than half the total capital assets of all the mining companies in Beaufort County.[12]

Years later the storm was still claiming victims. The strain of rebuilding lives and fortunes, the trauma of death and loss, and weakened constitutions due to the lingering affects of malaria and dysentery all caused many premature deaths. Two prominent examples were George Waterhouse and John J. Dale. Waterhouse had lost a fortune in the storm. His cotton-ginning, brokerage, real estate, and mercantile businesses were substantial enough in 1892 to attract the president of the New York Stock Exchange to Beaufort with an eye to purchase the Waterhouse Corporation. That transaction never occurred, and when the hurricane struck, Waterhouse's assets were destroyed. He set about to rebuild his wrecked businesses to support his large family and educate his five growing children. Waterhouse was a quiet New Englander who stoically bore his many responsibilities. He had been generous with his time and money toward civic projects and his beloved Baptist Church of Beaufort. Now, in the greatest crisis since the Civil War, they needed him even more. But in 1894 his health failed, and he died of a heart attack on a trip to Saluda, North Carolina. Waterhouse was only fifty-six years old, and his family always asserted that the hurricane was the proximate cause of his early demise. His funeral at the Baptist Church of Beaufort in August 1894 was one of the largest in the town's history. His coffin was carried from Fairfax, South Carolina, on a special funeral car of the Charleston and Western Carolina (C&WC) Railroad. At the funeral Beaufort's entire commercial establishment was joined by nearly five hundred sea island blacks who knew George Waterhouse as a kind and generous friend and employer. He is buried in the graveyard of the Baptist Church.

John J. Dale's health, too, was broken by the destruction of his agricultural enterprises in the hurricane. He retired to his northern home in Townsend, Vermont, and never returned to Beaufort. He died in Vermont in 1896. Dale had come to Beaufort as "a gallant soldier of the Federal Army" and stayed to manage the cotton brokerage business of John G. Nicols. When Nicols moved to Florida, the business became J. J. Dale and Company. Dale bought cotton land all over Beaufort County. He became the largest planter on the sea islands and owned country stores at Frogmore on St. Helena Island, on Lady's Island, on Port Royal Island, and at Yemassee. One of his stores was at a crossroads on Kean's Neck near the phosphate works of the Coosaw Mines, the Pacific Guano Company, and the Oak Point Mines. Today the community and post office is called Dale, South Carolina. When J. J. Dale died in 1896, his death also was blamed on the hurricane. As his obituary noted, "The firm lost heavily by the great storm of 1893 and only by superhuman effort was it able to ride through. Of course this depressed Mr. Dale, and since then his health has grown more and more feeble." Dale and Company was important to Beaufort County, not only because Dale was an enterprising agronomist, but also because he brought in J. Ross MacDonald from Pennsylvania, George Wilkins from Vermont, and William Keyserling from Lithuania, each of whom had a large impact on twentieth-century Beaufort.[13]

The Great Storm of 1893 was not the only hurricane to strike Beaufort County during the 1890s. On October 2, 1896, another hurricane visited the coast. In 1896 the wind "blew as hard as 1893, but only for two hours." There was a very high tide but no deadly tidal wave as in 1893. The cotton crop for 1896 was destroyed, several boats were sunk, and the roof was blown off of the Rhett House. But there was no loss of life. Once again, the phosphate fleet was heavily damaged.

In 1898 two hurricanes struck Beaufort County. On August 30, 1898, a storm struck that did little damage to the town but considerable damage at sea. The pilot boat *Scheper* dragged three anchors and went ashore near "the site of Gage's old mill." The *Bessie May* was high and dry against the bluff, and the old tug *Stono* was wrecked. The ferry house and dock were swept away, and the fill dirt around Scheper's Wharf was washed out.

Offshore the damage was severe. Five vessels were lost with all hands off Bay Point, Hilton Head, and Hunting Island. A large, full rigged, steel-hulled ship was driven ashore on Parris Island. The coasting schooner *Mary O'Neill* was wrecked on Pritchard's Island. Niels Christensen bought the wreck for $116 to salvage the hardware from it. Another schooner, the *Caroline V. Pose,* was beached on Bay Point. It was carrying a cargo of coal for C. E. Danner. Captain William Murphy, the schooner's master, spent the winter of 1898–99 in Beaufort repairing his vessel and salvaging its cargo. He became so enamored of the old town that he made it his regular winter resort for ten years. He loved the balmy sea island climate and especially the winter hunting. Murphy was a native of Maine who had run away to sea at the age of fourteen and spent the next fifty-four years sailing the world's oceans. He became a notable character in Beaufort and regaled a generation of local boys with tales of exotic ports and life on the high seas.

One of the greatest losses in 1898 was the death of Captain Henry Von Harten, the most experienced pilot on the Port Royal bar. His pilot boat had been wrecked on Hilton Head in the storm. On September 12 he and one crewman took the catboat *Fritz* out to Hilton Head to salvage the wreck. The *Fritz* was struck by a squall, capsized, and sank. Henry Von Harten and his crewman were drowned.

On September 28, 1898, another hurricane was reported in the West Indies. By October 1, it was pounding the sea islands. It wrecked the Christensens' yacht *Nomantura* and floated a barge over the seawall into town. Torrents of rain flooded the fields, and what was left of the sea island cotton and the rice crop after the first storm was destroyed by the second. Frederick Christensen commented, "The poor will have a bad time of it this year."

The next year, a report on August 9, 1899, alerted Beaufort that a "West India hurricane" was headed its way. The storm did great damage in the Caribbean but vacillated off the Florida coast. All the naval vessels in Port

Royal Sound moved upriver to seek shelter, and the pilot boats and tug boats laid out all their anchors. Everyone in town took precautions. The hurricane of 1899 produced only a few hours of high winds and no high water. Little damage and no loss of life was caused by the last hurricane of the nineteenth century, but after the deadly experiences of 1893 and 1898, no one in Beaufort County took any chances.[14]

The last decade of the nineteenth century was the most violent and most costly period of tropical storm activity in Beaufort County's long history. Every community on the southeastern Atlantic Seaboard is vulnerable to dangerous West Indian hurricanes, but only the 1900 storm that struck Galveston, Texas, has exceeded the catastrophe that Beaufort County experienced on August 27, 1893. Such uncontrolled, profoundly costly natural disasters can change the course of a community's history. A generation of Beaufortonians marked the passages of their lives by the events of the Great Storm of 1893. The local newspaper published retrospectives on the 1893 hurricane on its fortieth and fiftieth anniversaries.[15] For Beaufort County, the Storm of 1893 and its aftermath marked a turning point in the fortunes of the region. An era of prosperity was ending, and the hurricane was a portent.

Chapter 2

Beaufort County Economy at the Turn of the Century

THE DECLINE OF PHOSPHATES

The sea island hurricane of 1893 signaled the end of a grand era of economic prosperity. During the 1890s, several other economic, political, and natural changes occurred that collectively altered the fortunes of the county. Phosphate was most responsible for the economic prosperity of the 1870s and 1880s. At its peak in the 1880s, the industry employed more than three thousand workers in high-paying jobs and pumped hundreds of thousands of dollars into the local economy. In 1892, the year before the great hurricane, the phosphate companies were operating at full capacity. The year 1891–92 fell 33 percent short of the peak year of 1888–89 but was, nevertheless, very profitable; estimates were that the 1892–93 year would produce a record 260,000 tons.[1]

The Great Storm of 1893 demolished the phosphate fleet and seriously damaged most of the shoreside facilities. The capital expense of replacing the fleet and repairing the processing factories, or "works," could not be justified in the depressed economic circumstances of the 1890s. For twenty years South Carolina had monopolized the United States domestic production and the majority of South Carolina phosphates came from Beaufort County. But in the late 1880s, new deposits of richer phosphates were discovered in Florida. Before the Carolina phosphate companies could rebuild from the ruinous Storm of 1893, their dominance of the industry was lost.

In 1891 South Carolina exported 50,189 tons of processed phosphate, while the new mines in Florida exported 35,203 tons. The next year the state exported 55,315 tons while Florida exported 77,234 tons. The hurricane demolished the local phosphate industry. By the time its owners could rebuild and resume production, Florida had surged far ahead. Throughout the 1890s, the old Carolina mining companies continued to decline. By 1903 Beaufort County's phosphate production was declining at a rate of 50 percent per year. The *Beaufort Gazette* described the economic reality: "The phosphate found in Florida is of superior grade . . . yet lower cost to mine." By 1907 Florida was producing 62 percent of domestic phosphate. New deposits in Tennessee accounted for 26 percent of domestic production. The once proud South Carolina mining industry supplied a paltry 10 percent of U.S. production. As the twentieth century opened, new phosphate deposits were being discovered in Utah, Idaho, and Wyoming and near Nashville, Tennessee. It was the end of an era for Beaufort County.

The decline of the phosphate industry in Beaufort County was hastened by political interference from the state. The mining business had begun during the Reconstruction era as the Republicans encouraged industrial development across the state. When the richest phosphate deposits were discovered in 1870, the state licensed phosphate companies to extract the rock from state waters and pay the state a royalty of fifty cents per ton of rock excavated. In its peak year, 1889, this royalty produced nearly $300,000 in revenue for the state treasury. In fact, between 1880 and 1896, the Coosaw Mining Company alone paid $600,998 in phosphate royalties to the state, one half of all royalties collected in the peak years of production.[2]

Most of the company owners were northerners, however, and that fact created a political bias in much of the state. The industry also benefited Beaufort County, whose commercial establishment was largely nonnatives and whose fusion politics perpetuated the last black Republican stronghold in the state. When Benjamin R. "Pitchfork Ben" Tillman launched his populist campaign for governor in 1890, he specifically campaigned against the lowcountry phosphate companies. He promised to double the state royalty to one dollar per ton of excavated river rock. Angry upcountry cotton farmers elected Tillman in a landslide, and in 1891 the General Assembly doubled the phosphate royalty. The timing was disastrous. The phosphate companies were already operating on razor-thin margins, and the increased production from Florida was lowering prices each year. In some years in the 1890s, the cost of producing a ton of phosphate was greater than the price it could secure.

In addition to the ruinous state royalty, state bureaucrats increased their supervision of the industry. When the industry began in 1872, the Reconstruction government established an Office of Inspector of Fertilizer and Guanos to oversee the industry. This office was abolished in 1878 and the Comptroller General was named phosphate inspector and charged with collecting the royalty. In 1879 the General Assembly created the Board of Agricultural Commissioners, which assumed oversight authority and appointed the phosphate inspector. After Tillman was elected, the General Assembly created a new Board of Phosphate Commissioners. One appointee to the board was the attorney general, John A. McLaurin.[3]

In addition to collecting the punitive state royalty, the attorney general and the phosphate commissioners began legal proceedings against the Coosaw Mining Company, Beaufort County's biggest industry. The essence of the case was that the 1870 state grant to the company of an exclusive right to mine the Coosaw River rock was only intended to last twenty-one years. Thus, the Coosaw Mining Company monopoly expired in 1891. The company argued that the original 1870 grant had given them a perpetual monopoly. As the deadline loomed, the state went to court. The case finally reached the United States Supreme Court in April 1892. South Carolina's most famous lawyers argued the case in Washington. General Edward McCrady and Augustine Smythe of Charleston represented the Coosaw Mining Company. Attorney General McLaurin of Columbia and Henry Augustus Middleton Smith of Charleston presented the state's case. Justice Louis Harlan's opinion for the court's majority concluded that the company's claim to exclusivity was correct but upheld the state's argument that the contract was for only twenty-one years.

The 1892 case was another blow to Beaufort County's biggest company. As news of the decision reached Beaufort, the Coosaw Mining Company's smaller competitors swarmed over the rich deposits in the Coosaw River. In April 1892 the huge dredge *Oglethorpe,* belonging to the Beaufort Mining Company, moved to the Coosaw River.

In November 1892 Governor Tillman came to Beaufort with Attorney General McLaurin, Phosphate Inspector Jones, and two members of the state phosphate board to see for himself the famous mining enterprises. Tillman was venturing into enemy territory. The governor's party stayed at the Beaufort House Hotel. Several local citizens interviewed "Pitchfork Ben" Tillman and to their surprise "found him exceedingly entertaining and pleasant." Colonel D. C. Wilson and M. E. Lopez, superintendent of the Coosaw Mines, escorted the governor's party around the phosphate works. Jacob Paulsen, superintendent of the Beaufort Phosphate Company, showed off their factory on Spanish Point. W. H. C. Delano of the Carolina Mining Company on Battery Creek entertained the governor's party with a large dinner on the banks of the creek. At every event, phosphate managers and commercial leaders lobbied the governor to lower the phosphate royalty. Throughout the day "there was talk of excessive royalty as compared with the present value of the rock."[4] But the General Assembly took no action.

During the 1890s the Democratic regime continued to hamper the phosphate companies, while Beaufort's commercial leaders lobbied for legislation to save the industry. In 1897 W. H. Lockwood and S. H. Rodgers, two Democrats, went to Columbia to appear before the phosphate commission. For several years the Coosaw Mining Company had stockpiled phosphate rock that it could not sell because it could not afford to pay the state royalty. Lockwood and Rodgers requested special dispensation for the Coosaw Company to sell the accumulated rock without paying the royalty. The commission refused their request. The men returned to Beaufort empty-handed, reporting that "there is much feeling in Columbia against the Coosaw Company." In 1903 the Coosaw Mining Company closed its last operating factory in Beaufort County. The state collected only fifteen thousand dollars in phosphate royalties in 1903. Fifteen years earlier, the state had collected nearly three hundred thousand dollars.[5]

Some of the smaller phosphate companies with lower overhead outlasted the Coosaw Mining Company. The Central Mining Company had bought out the Farmer's Mines on Lucy Creek in 1896. In 1904 the Central Mining Company petitioned the Phosphate Commission to reduce by 60 percent the eight-thousand-dollar royalty, contending that it would shut down otherwise. The petition stated that the company added seventy thousand dollars a year into the local economy in wages and purchases. The *Beaufort Gazette* backed the Central Mining Company's petition and noted, "Some years ago, a committee of local citizens went to the Governor to reduce the royalties and save the . . . Coosaw Mining Company. The state refused and the Coosaw Mining Company shut down." The county's anger was expressed in the newspaper's editorial: "Beaufort County has felt the heavy hand of legislation hostile to our phosphate interest for many years. One by one the great mining companies have been forced to the wall. . . . we hope this last one will not be crushed for a matter of $4,800 per year!"[6]

Throughout the 1890s the phosphate companies laid off workers, merged with their competitors, and halted operations in desperate attempts to stay afloat. In 1895 the Brotherhood Mine on Battery Creek shut down for nearly a year. When the price of Carolina river rock rose to fifty cents per ton in 1896, the Brotherhood Mine resumed partial operations. The Farmers Mine on Lucy Creek, which had been operating with a skeleton crew, rehired seventy-five men to pick river rock. By 1896 the Oak Point Mines had closed, while the Pacific Guano Company on Chisolm Island employed only a hundred men. In the company's heyday of the 1880s, it had employed nearly two thousand men. Frederick Christensen observed in 1897 that "the phosphate mines are virtually dead. Those that are still open are only doing so in the forlorn hope that the royalty will be reduced by the legislature."[7]

The decline of the phosphate companies caused many of Beaufort's leading men to leave the county for better opportunities elsewhere. In 1898 J. M. Lawton, superintendent of the Central Mining Company (formerly Farmer's Mines), left Beaufort for Charleston. In 1899, when the Baldwin Fertilizer Company moved its headquarters on the Beaufort River to Charleston, the three local managers all lost their jobs. In 1903 William Waterhouse, George Waterhouse's oldest son and publisher of the *Beaufort Gazette,* sold the newspaper to Niels Christensen and moved to East Orange, New Jersey. Even the Christensen brothers considered leaving Beaufort. The mine closings had reduced the Christensen hardware business to the point that it could no longer support Captain Niels Christensen's large family, who thought it might be necessary to send Niels Christensen Jr. to Boston "so he can work year-round."[8]

The loss of thousands of wage-earning jobs in the phosphate industry was one of the principal causes of the exodus of sea island blacks to greater opportunities in Savannah, Charleston, New York, and other urban centers. For two decades thousands of sea islanders had found ready wages and steady employment on the river lighters and barges and in the phosphate cuts. Local sea islanders called it working "on the rock." Families were proud when their sons were promoted to "dredge han's." During the 1890s these jobs disappeared. Black outmigration from the sea islands, which began in the 1890s, continued for half a century and had a profound effect on twentieth-century Beaufort County.[9]

The collapse of the phosphate companies at the turn of the century shattered the local economy. First to feel the effect was the maritime activity in St. Helena Sound and Port Royal harbor. Between 1894 and 1901, maritime exports from Beaufort County declined 96 percent. The following table shows the diminishing monetary value of exports.

Year	*Value of Export*
1894	$4,939,417
1895	$4,155,619
1896	$4,316,259
1897	$2,605,896
1899	$358,886
1900	$132,561
1901	$166,189

The report that included this table concluded, "The great falling-off since 1894 and particularly since 1896 has been due mainly to the decline of the local phosphate business."[10]

Early in 1904 the Central Mining Company announced that it would close its factory on Lucy Creek. It was the last of the local phosphate companies. By 1904 French capitalists owned it, and the local vice president, Emile Van Espen, admitted that they had not declared a dividend since they bought out the Farmer's Mines in 1896. By the end of 1904, phosphate company properties were being sold at auction. In December auctioneer James M. Crofut sold the remaining assets of the defunct Beaufort Phosphate Company on Spanish Point. H. F. Scheper bought for five hundred dollars real estate that had cost fifteen thousand dollars twenty-five years before.

Local merchants bought the docks. Jerry Potter bought the sunken dredge for fifteen dollars; it had "originally cost many thousands." He purchased the washer tubes, shed, tower, and water tank for scrap.

The *Charleston News and Courier* summed up the decline of Carolina phosphates: "It is a really sad story that the phosphate industry presents in the state today. The companies have made little if any money in years and one by one have gone out of business." When the Central Mining Company shut down in 1904, Frederick Christensen described the effect on the local economy: "This will be another severe blow to Beaufort. When the Naval Station closes down that will be the last blow to our commercial life. Then we will reach rock bottom because there will be nothing left but our farming interest to lose."[11]

The phosphate industry gave one last gasp in 1906 when a conglomerate of southern fertilizer manufacturers combined to form the Virginia-Carolina Chemical Company. The company bought the abandoned assets of the old Coosaw Mining Company on Summerhouse Point and the four-thousand-acre tract of the Pacific Guano Company on adjacent Chisolm Island. It sent Ben Rivers to supervise the operation. The Virginia-Carolina Company made substantial investments on the site, reconstructing the railroad across Chisolm Island to Summerhouse Point, rebuilding the old drying shed, washer, and wharf and extending the loading pier into the Bull River to a channel depth of twenty-two feet. The new drying shed was five hundred feet long, sixty feet wide, and fifty feet high. The washing tower was eighty feet high. At the Pacific Guano site, the company refurbished the offices, outbuildings, and "fine old homes built in the halcyon days of the phosphate industry."

Rumors of a return of the phosphate industry caused momentary land speculation on Spanish Point. In 1907 Governor Martin F. Ansel brought the Phosphate Commission to Beaufort to visit the new industrial site. Among the dignitaries were Attorney General Lyon, Comptroller General Jones, and reporters from the *News and Courier* and the *State.* They stayed at the Sea Island Hotel and were entertained at dinner by Beaufort mayor C. C. Townsend, lawyer W. J. Thomas, and County Auditor Hal Pollitzer. The next day the governor's party went fishing with J. M. Legnick, Frederick and Niels Christensen, and J. M. Rhett.[12]

It was a hopeful moment that did not last. From 1904 to 1908, the Virginia-Carolina Chemical Company battled a price-fixing lawsuit brought by the United States Interstate Commerce Commission. The company could not compete against the larger, New York–based American Agricultural Chemical Corporation, and its local operations were a ghost of what the industry had once been. When fertilizer production was disrupted in 1914 and 1915 by the outbreak of World War I, it was the end of South

Carolina's phosphate industry.[13] Only the "cuts" on Chisholm Island and the oyster-covered piles of refuse rock at Spanish Point, Lucy Creek, and Bull River remind us today of the largest industry Beaufort County ever had.

THE RISE AND FALL OF THE PORT ROYAL NAVAL STATION, 1890–1907

The second pillar of the Beaufort County economy in the 1890s was the United States Naval Station at Port Royal. Naval vessels had used Port Royal Sound as an anchorage and rendezvous point since the Civil War. In 1877 the secretary of the navy established Port Royal as a fourth-class naval station. The warship USS *New Hampshire* was dismasted and permanently anchored in Port Royal Sound as a supply vessel and machine shop. In 1882 a naval coaling dock was built at the foot of the railroad, and in the same year the navy began purchasing land on Parris Island for shoreside facilities. As the last decade of the nineteenth century commenced, discussions in Washington and South Carolina centered on building a full-fledged naval shipyard on Parris Island.

The Beaufort business establishment knew that a United States naval shipyard would be a great boon to employment, commercial growth, and economic development. Beaufort's commercial elite and the state congressional delegation went into high gear to capture this prize. In March 1890 five of Beaufort's leading businessmen were dispatched to Washington to lobby the naval commandant, Admiral David Porter, the U.S. Navy Bureau of Yards and Docks, and the Congress on behalf of the Port Royal Naval Station. The delegation was led by Colonel Duncan C. Wilson and included Bay Street merchants George Waterhouse and J. J. Cummings, banker W. H. Lockwood, and old-time Beaufortonian Dr. Henry Middleton Stuart. The group stayed at the fashionable Elliott House on Pennsylvania Avenue, whose proprietor, C. C. Willard, later renamed the hotel the Willard. Waterhouse wrote to his daughter Mary that the party met with Secretary of the Navy Stephen B. Elkins and the Senate Naval Appropriations Committee and briefly with President Benjamin Harrison. D. C. Wilson was their spokesman. "He has done admirably and presented a strong case for Port Royal," Waterhouse noted.[14]

What the Beaufort delegation was seeking in 1890 was a congressional appropriation to build the largest, most expensive, and most essential facility for a naval shipyard, a permanent dry dock. During the 1880s the navy was building larger, heavier, and deeper-draft battleships to match the naval armament of the great European powers. The new dreadnoughts were outgrowing the older dry docks in Portsmouth, Boston, Brooklyn, and Philadelphia. In addition, United States foreign policy during the 1890s was directed to Latin American and Caribbean affairs.

One week after the Beaufort delegation returned home, Admiral Porter wrote to Senator Matthew C. Butler of South Carolina and Congressman Elliott of Beaufort stating that "you might search the whole coast of the United States and not find a place so well adapted for the purpose of a naval station as the harbor at Port Royal." In April, Beaufort sent a second delegation of citizens to Washington to appear before the Congressional Committee on Naval Affairs. Colonel Wilson was accompanied by Captain Niels Christensen and Judge Thomas Grimke White.[15]

The efforts paid off with a naval appropriation in excess of five hundred thousand dollars. In June 1891 construction commenced. The dry dock on Parris Island was designed to be the largest such facility in the United States. It was to be 500 feet in length and 120 feet in width, "the largest on the Atlantic coast and twenty-feet wider than any in the United States." The dry dock required six thousand pilings and consumed two million board feet of lumber. The pumps could discharge seventy-five thousand gallons of water per minute. The whole dry dock could be filled in one hour. A ceremony was held on June 28, 1891, "Carolina Day," to mark the groundbreaking. Congressman Elliott was the keynote speaker. He recounted the legendary past of Port Royal Sound, recalled the dreams of Jean Ribaut and Pedro Menendez for the great harbor, and predicted that the U.S. Navy would finally allow Port Royal Sound to realize its maritime potential. "I firmly believe," Elliott said, "that the work we are now inaugurating is but the first in a series of events that will someday . . . erect an imperial city on these beautiful waters."[16]

In 1892 the pace of naval activity quickened. Captain L. A. Beardslee was given command of the Port Royal Naval Station, and Congressman Elliott introduced legislation to purchase more lands adjoining the Parris Island station and to build a hospital. An inspection of the site by Commodore Farquhar, chief of the Bureau of Yards and Docks, concluded that the construction progress was satisfactory and predicted that when it was finished, "South Carolina will have one of the finest dry-docks in the world."[17]

In January 1893 five of the navy's largest and most advanced warships spent three weeks in Port Royal Sound practicing gunnery, fleet maneuvers, and general drill. On station in January 1893 were the USS *Kearsarge,* the USS *Philadelphia,* and the USS *Vesuvius.* The *Vesuvius,* launched in 1886, carried the most advanced technology of the day. It was a 246-foot, 950-ton, twin-screw cruiser. Officially designated a "pneumatic gunboat," the *Vesuvius* was popularly known in the fleet as "the dynamite cruiser." In addition to 3-pounder, rapid-fire cannons, it had fifty-five-foot pneumatic tubes fixed in its hull to launch self-propelled torpedoes. This was remarkably advanced weaponry when one considers that the Battle of Port Royal Sound, only thirty years earlier, had been fought with muzzle-loading cannons. During fleet maneuvers and gunnery practice, spectators lined the shores of St. Helena, Parris, and Hilton Head Islands, and excursion boats dotted the edges of Port Royal Sound. Expectations for the Port Royal Naval Station were running high in 1893.[18] That was before the sea island hurricane.

The storm of August 1893 did major damage to the naval station and set back construction on the dry dock for many months. The timber docks were swept away, many buildings were blown down, and most of the expensive machinery was inundated and rusting. Forty feet of shoreline were washed away and much of the channel dredging had to be redone. Damage to the dry dock alone was estimated at $37,170.[19] Perhaps the greatest damage, was to the reputation of Port Royal Sound. Before the storm Port Royal was considered the safest harbor on the southern coast. After the storm questions about the safety of the harbor continually cropped up, and enthusiasm for the Port Royal Naval Station naturally diminished.

Nevertheless, the navy pressed ahead. In 1895 the great timber dry dock was completed. It was 448 feet long, 66 feet wide on the floor, and could hold ships of 25-feet, 6-inches draft. On March 11, 1896, the largest vessel in the U.S. Navy, the battleship USS *Indiana,* entered Port Royal Sound for maintenance at the new dry dock. The commanding officer of the *Indiana* was Captain Robley D. "Fighting Bob" Evans, one of the most famous naval officers of the era. In 1898 he commanded the USS *Iowa* at the Battle of Santiago de Cuba. In 1907 Admiral Evans commanded the "Great White Fleet" that circumnavigated the globe. Frederick Christensen remarked, "The dry-dock at Parris Island is the only one in this country large enough to hold the great ship . . . the nearest other being in Halifax, Nova Scotia." The arrival of the *Indiana* was another moment of great celebration. On March 13 Governor John Gary Evans of South Carolina invited Governor William Y. Atkinson of Georgia to Port Royal to mark the occasion. Political speeches, the usual round of congratulatory toasts, and the salute of the naval guns filled the day. The refreshments included hard liquor. Many got tight and some got drunk. Frederick Christensen remarked wryly that the two governors "can each drink a good deal of liquor before they have to be carried home, so they must be gentlemen of the highest stamp." Despite disapproving of the behavior of some southern politicians, Christensen concluded, "This day will probably be a landmark in the history of the port." Local optimism was bolstered when the navy used the occasion to announce a sixty-thousand-dollar appropriation for the machine shop adjacent to the dry dock.[20]

In October 1896 the USS *Newark* and USS *Raleigh* were at the Port Royal Naval Station. In March 1897 the giant battleships USS *Texas* and USS *Maine* steamed into the sound. Several excursionists from Beaufort traveled downriver aboard the *Pilot Boy* to see the gathering of naval might in Port Royal Sound. The *Texas* and *Maine* by themselves mounted more firepower than the entire Union fleet that entered Port Royal Sound on November 7, 1861.[21]

No one knew at the time how famous the USS *Maine* would become. The *Maine* and the *Texas,* both launched in 1886, symbolized the growth of United States naval power and a new era of imperialism in American foreign policy. The USS *Indiana,* launched in 1890, was the first of a new class of super battleships that included the USS *Massachusetts* and USS *Oregon.* These vessels matched in size, speed, and firepower anything in the European battle fleets. These battleships were the beginning of the so-called Great White Fleet that toured the world in 1907 and signaled the entrance of the United States as a great power on the world stage. Beaufort County was proud to play an important role in this new era, and local business was good.

The Caribbean Sea was a focal point of American strategic interest in the 1890s, and the hot spot was the Spanish-owned island of Cuba. Cuba was the largest remaining European colony in America. Throughout the nineteenth century, Cuban dissidents had unsuccessfully sought independence, something the other Spanish colonies in Central and South America had won by 1830. Cuba was a hemispheric anachronism, and the majority of Americans were as anxious to rid the region of this vestige of empire as the Cuban dissidents. Beaufort had antebellum connections to Cuban politics. Cuban freedom fighter General Ambrosio Gonzales married William Elliott III's youngest daughter, Harriett, and they had produced the influential Gonzales family of South Carolina. The brothers Narciso Gener Gonzales and Ambrose Elliott Gonzales founded the *State* newspaper in Columbia in 1891. The *State* was attentive to Cuban politics and an ardent supporter of Cuban independence and American intervention. Ambrose Elliott Gonzales was appointed ambassador to Cuba by President Woodrow Wilson. In addition to the Gonzales brothers, M. E. Lopez, the longtime superintendent of the dominant Coosaw Mining Company, was a Cuban émigré. Lopez and his family were fixtures of Beaufort's business elite for a generation.

In March 1893 the USS *Atlanta* was dispatched from the Port Royal Naval Station to Key West to prevent the secret shipment of arms and artillery bound for Cuba from Baltimore or Philadelphia. The USS *Kearsarge* remained at the Port Royal Naval Station and patrolled the South Carolina coast. In 1895 the Cuban revolution flared up again, and the Spanish government sent fifty thousand troops under General Valeriano "Butcher" Weyler to suppress the rebellion. He rounded up thousands of Cuban farmers and held them in concentration camps, giving American "yellow" journalists ample human interest stories with which to inflame U.S. citizens. These developments encouraged congressional war hawks. Frederick Christensen remarked that Senators Henry Cabot Lodge, John Sherman, William E. Chandler, and John Tyler Morgan "and the other Jingos in congress have been doing their best to get us into a war with Spain." In April 1896 the U.S. House of Representatives passed a resolution recognizing the Cuban rebels as legitimate belligerents. Only twenty-four congressmen voted against the resolution. Of the nine Democratic opponents, one was Colonel William Elliott of Beaufort, a cousin of the Gonzales brothers.[22] Elliott knew the history of the sea islands, of which his ancestors had been such a big part. Should war break out and the Spanish navy take the offensive, one of their likely targets would be Port Royal Sound, as it had been a target of the Union navy in 1861 and of a Spanish fleet from Cuba in 1742. Elliott's ancestors had been forced to evacuate on both occasions.

But American popular sentiment was high for intervention. There was great confidence in the nation's new fleet of dreadnoughts. When rioting in Havana intensified in January 1898, the USS *Maine* was dispatched from Port Royal Naval Station to Havana Harbor to protect American citizens. As the great ship entered the harbor on February 15, 1898, a gigantic explosion ripped through the hull and sank the ship in minutes. Two hundred sixty-two U.S. sailors perished. American journalists asserted Spanish complicity, and war fever swept the nation. The popular cry was heard, "Remember the *Maine;* to hell with Spain."

In Beaufort the loss was felt personally. In October 1897 the USS *Maine* was detached from the North Atlantic Squadron and stationed at Port Royal "near enough to Cuba to be available there within a day or so if necessary." Beaufortonians had been guests aboard the ship, and the officers and crew were personal acquaintances of local merchants and naval station employees. The local newspaper the *Palmetto Post* agreed that "the consensus of opinion is that the Battleship Maine was destroyed by a torpedo or a submarine mine maliciously placed for the purpose of destruction." But it added the interesting personal intelligence from Captain Charles D. Sigsbee of the *Maine* that a week before the explosion, someone from a hostile crowd in Havana had given him a pamphlet that read, "Death to America; Death to Autonomy! Long live Spain; long live Weyler!" In the margin of the pamphlet was the cryptic, handwritten note, "Look out for your ship."

War talk spread across the community, and the pace of activity at the naval station quickened. Many expected Port Royal to be a major support base for any naval actions against Cuba: "We hear a good deal about this place . . . being used as a center from which to distribute munitions of war." But there was also concern about the unprotected entrance to Port Royal Sound. The *Palmetto Post* summed it up this way: "In case of war, what protection has this harbor? Nil!"

Beaufortonians had real reason to fear a Spanish attack. Reports appeared in the city that Admiral Pascual Cervera, in command of a Spanish fleet that crossed the Atlantic to challenge the American blockade of Cuba, planned to raid South Carolina after defeating the American fleet off Cuba. Will Elliott, son of the congressman, along with local boys Victor Blue and William Townsend Jr., were put on twenty-four-hour watch duty. Twice during 1898, strange vessels appeared at night off Port Royal Sound. Local artillery batteries were manned and prepared to fire. The first vessel was a government tug on its way to Key West. The second was a tramp steamer with a Portuguese pilot who did not recognize the signals to halt his vessel. The steamer was nearly fired on before it was identified.

The navy also recognized the vulnerability of Port Royal Sound. On March 24, 1898, four old, slow, heavily armed monitors arrived at the Port Royal Naval Station. The USS *Puritan,* USS *Terror,* USS *Maintonomah,* and USS *Amphritrite* were to be employed as floating batteries between Bay Point and Hilton Head. In April the powerful battleship USS *Iowa* was cleaned and painted at the Parris Island dry dock on its way to the Caribbean. Shortly afterward, the armed tugs *Algonquin* and *Nezinscott* took on coal and water at Port Royal on their way to Key West. Beaufort merchant D.W. Crocker reported that "things are very lively at the Naval Station." This reassured local skeptics, who noted that "we have a formidable fleet in these waters should the Spaniards make an attack at this important point."[23]

On April 11, 1898, President McKinley asked Congress for authority to order military intervention. Two weeks later Congress authorized the use of troops against Spain and passed a resolution recognizing Cuban independence. The navy established a blockade of Cuba and enforced it with superior naval firepower. In May 1898 the USS *Marblehead,* USS *Nashville,* and USS *Windom* engaged the Spanish forts guarding Havana and two Spanish warships, the cruiser *Aphonso XII* and the gunboat *Legazpi,* in a sharp artillery duel. The Spanish ships were forced back into the harbor and four hundred men of the Spanish garrison were killed by U.S. naval gunfire. The U.S. fleet suffered only eight casualties. At the same time, a U.S. Navy "flying squadron" was patrolling between Charleston and Port Royal, and the monitors USS *Passaic* and USS *Nantucket* were serviced at the Parris Island dry dock.

Captain C. H. Rockwell was the commandant of the Port Royal Naval Station during the Spanish-American War, and many local men served at the station. Lieutenant George MacKay was the head of the engineering department; Dr. C. G. Richardson was in charge of the hospital ward; Lieutenant Sam McGowan was paymaster; and Lieutenant Lawrence Sanders was deputy paymaster. On April 2 the Beaufort Volunteer Artillery received orders to stand by for signal duty on the coast. On May 4, 1898, the Beaufort Volunteer Artillery was called up for active duty. In 1892 the state militia had established three companies of naval militia to be used for maritime activities and coastal defense. These special naval militia units were naturally drawn from

Georgetown, Charleston, and Beaufort. The Beaufort Volunteer Artillery was redesignated the Third Division, South Carolina Naval Militia.

Local men were assigned to United States Navy units where their special skills were needed. J. H. Haynesworth became a mate on the ocean tug USS *Hercules,* and Micah Jenkins became a mate on the USS *Massasoit.* Lieutenant Lawrence Sanders became paymaster aboard the USS *Kearsarge.* Jonathan O'Brien and W. H. VonHarten were transferred to the Brooklyn Navy Yard. Other men were assigned to harbor tugs in Port Royal Sound and to shore batteries and signal stations on Hilton Head and Land's End. Captain H. D. Elliott was assigned as master of tugs for Port Royal Sound. Harbor pilots John Murray, Micah Jenkins, and P. L. Lea were commissioned as master's mates to command the Navy tugs *Bristol, Hercules,* and *Confidence.* Many Beaufort boys formed the tug crews.[24]

In June the scout boat *Peoria* stopped to refuel at Port Royal while delivering dispatches to Key West, and the tug USS *Hercules* towed the monitor USS *Passaic* to Key West. Word reached Beaufort that twenty-seven thousand troops had left Tampa Bay bound for Cuba. At Santiago Bay the old collier *Merriana* was run into the harbor and sunk to block the channel. This ship, formerly the SS *Rita,* had often visited Port Royal. On July 1 and 2, the U.S. fleet decisively defeated a Spanish fleet sent to lift the blockade at the Battle of Santiago de Cuba. This battle sealed the fate of colonial Cuba. The USS *Vesuvius,* "the only dynamite cruiser in the U.S. Navy," particularly distinguished herself in action. The *Vesuvius* had been a regular visitor at Port Royal. On June 12, 1898, word reached Beaufort that a force of Marines and bluejackets had been landed at the harbor of Guantanamo.[25]

Within a few weeks, the blockade and superior U.S. ground troops forced the Spanish government to sue for peace. On August 25, 1898, the "Beaufort Volunteer Artillery boys who belong to the Naval Militia were mustered out and returned to Beaufort." Most of the officers of the Beaufort Volunteer Artillery retained their commissions and their pay for several more weeks. As soon as the "splendid little war" was over, political trouble began for the Port Royal Naval Station and shipyard. The ships that had served in the blockade of Cuba were sent to dry docks in Portsmouth, New York, and Brooklyn. The larger dry dock on Parris Island was ignored. The navy explained its decisions by saying that the local station was "too far from men and supplies."[26]

The Spanish-American War was the high-water mark of the Port Royal Naval Station. Thereafter, naval activity at Parris Island began to diminish, and political support for the shipyard began to wane. The biggest blow to the naval station came when the City of Charleston and its aggressive mayor, J. Adger Smythe, set their sights on capturing the shipyard. Mayor Smythe's principal ally was the former governor and now U.S. senator Benjamin "Pitchfork Ben" Tillman. He was a member of the Naval Affairs Committee and had little interest in supporting Beaufort County. He saw Beaufort County as a troublesome nest of Yankee do-gooders, carpetbaggers, and ex-slaves led by the "King of Beaufort County," Robert Smalls. He disparaged the county as "the niggerdom of Beaufort." In addition to his dislike of Beaufort County, Tillman wanted to secure the votes of Charleston, the state's largest city. Tillman, a hero to upcountry farmers, had never gotten many votes from conservative, old, "bourbon" Charleston. He wished to guarantee their support for his repeated terms in the U.S. Senate. Thus, the rabblerousing, populist senator formed an unholy alliance with Charleston's blueblood mayor to move the Port Royal Naval Shipyard on Parris Island to a large old plantation site called Chicora Park on the Cooper River north of Charleston.

Another opportunity for the Charleston boosters came when it was discovered that teredo worms had taken a terrible toll on the wooden dry dock on Parris Island. The worms had consumed large sections of the timber dry dock in a matter of months and were gradually consuming all the wooden dry docks on the East Coast. The navy decided to rebuild all its dry docks of cement at huge expense. Plans had called for three concrete dry docks on Parris Island even larger than the timber one. This was a huge investment at a naval station that had lost its luster in some navy circles. The Charleston forces leaped into the political fray over naval appropriations in Washington.

The long-range goal of the Charleston maritime and commercial interests was to get the U.S. Army Corps of Engineers to dredge the entrance channel into Charleston Harbor. The harbor entrance could only carry ships of fifteen feet of draft at low tide. The new screw-propelled steam vessels could only enter the harbor at high water, placing Charleston at a considerable disadvantage to other harbors on the coast, especially Port Royal Sound. If the navy selected Charleston as the site for its southern shipyard, then the Corps of Engineers would have to dredge the channel to accommodate their largest battleships. This action would also permit the port to accommodate the largest merchant vessels in the Atlantic trade.

In 1899 Mayor Smythe and Senator Tillman met with Admiral Mordecai T. Endicott, chief of the Bureau of Yards and Docks. In 1900 the navy appointed a commission to study the case for Charleston and the case for Port Royal. It recommended abandoning the shipyard and dry dock at Parris Island and relocating the facility to the Cooper River. It was obvious that Senator Tillman had considerable, if indirect, influence on this commission. As a member of the Committee on Naval Affairs, he was in a powerful position to affect naval appropriations. And the navy had far more at stake than its investment on Parris Island.

Once the commission made its report, Senator Tillman effected a political maneuver that hit Beaufort like a thunderbolt. On May 8, 1900, Will Elliott, a young lawyer and son of Congressman William Elliott, received a telegram from his father stating that "Tillman got the Senate Naval Committee to amend the Port Royal Naval appropriation leaving it to the Secretary of the Navy to decide whether to spend the money at Port Royal or at Charleston." Lawrence Sanders, a naval veteran of the Spanish-American War and railroad agent for the Charleston and Western Carolina Railroad, hustled the news to his friends Niels and Frederick Christensen. A mass meeting of Beaufort citizens was hastily arranged. They agreed to send a committee to Washington to lobby Navy Secretary John D. Long, Senator Tillman, and any others who would hear them. W. H. Lockwood was chosen chairman; Niels Christensen Jr. was secretary. The committee included Mayor William Townsend, chosen because he was a Republican; State Senator Thomas Talbird, chosen because he was a friend of Tillman's; Tom Martin, who reportedly had "influence with Tillman"; and Charles E. Danner, who represented the Bay Street merchants. The committee was given $130 for its expenses.[27]

The news from Washington was not good. The Beaufort committee encountered a more powerful committee from Charleston, which had set up camp in the capital to snatch the naval shipyard away from Beaufort County. In a few days, Charles Danner came home alone "thoroughly discouraged and down hearted." The Beaufort committee had received no public assurances, and naval officials seemed prejudiced against the Port Royal Station. Senator Tillman was openly working for Charleston, and Congressman Elliott had "reached the end of his rope." The Charleston committee seemed to enjoy "smooth sailing."

Back in Beaufort, Niels Christensen Jr. tried to rally the citizens to action. A new "Committee of Twelve" was formed to exert political pressure wherever it could. This committee represented all segments of the community and all points of the political compass. William H. Lockwood was chairman. Former state senator William J. Verdier and rising politician Niels Christensen Jr. were influential members. William Waterhouse, eldest son George Waterhouse, was the secretary. William Waterhouse had recently purchased the *Beaufort Gazette,* founded in 1898 by William Elliott. Most important, the Committee of Twelve included Robert Smalls. Smalls had retired from politics after his congressional defeat in 1886. He nevertheless remained the godfather of Beaufort County's black political establishment and an icon in the National Republican Party. His membership on this important committee was a testament to his continuing political influence. It was also an example of the operation of fusion politics in Beaufort County while Jim Crow politics stifled the rest of the state.

The committee traveled to Savannah to seek support from that city's commercial community, which also benefitted from the Port Royal Naval Station. Smalls offered to mobilize the Georgia delegation to the Republican National Convention. The whole committee sought out Georgia congressmen to press the case for Port Royal.

Beaufort leaders also played the Yankee card. Niels Christensen Jr. wrote an article for the *Nation*. Niels Christensen Sr. wrote a letter attacking Tillman. State Senator Thomas Talbird, a Tillman ally, opposed sending the letter, but the committee voted five to four to send it. This was the beginning of a long political rivalry between Tillman and Christensen.

All this activity met with some success. The Savannah Pilots Associations supported the Beaufort County effort, and the chief Savannah pilot, Paulsen, personally escorted Niels Christensen Jr. and S. H. Rodgers of the *Palmetto Post* back to Beaufort aboard his tugboat. Most important, Robert Smalls returned from Washington with the news that Navy Secretary Long had appointed Smalls to a commission to study moving the naval station from Port Royal.

In August 1900 the *Savannah Morning News* weighed in on behalf of Port Royal: "In determining the question whether the naval station should be removed from Port Royal, the interests of the whole South Atlantic coast should be taken into consideration.... The interests of Charleston and the wishes of the Navy Department ... are not the only ones. Savannah being the most important commercial port on the South Atlantic coast, the port having by far the largest commerce, her interests should have great weight with the commission"[28]

Despite Georgia's support and successful placement of allies in key positions, the tide was running against Beaufort County. In February 1901 the U.S. Senate Committee on Naval Affairs held hearings on "the proposed transfer of the naval station from Port Royal, South Carolina to Charleston, South Carolina." Many experts testified to the clear superiority of the harbor at Port Royal to the relatively shallow channels into Charleston. Chief among these men was Professor Lewis M. Haupt, one of the foremost ocean scientists of the day. He reported that the natural channel into Port Royal Sound had remained over twenty-two feet since it was surveyed by the British Army in 1779, while the Charleston bar had silted in during the same period. Haupt pointed out the futility, or impermanence, of dredging and building jetties at dynamic tidal inlets. He used the example of Manasquan, New Jersey, where "the jetties were completely buried under the accumulated sand bank which they created until ... the channel returned to its original position." To counter this testimony, Senator Tillman called Colonel Peter Hains of the Army Corps of Engineers, who presented the corps' plan to dredge Charleston to a depth of twenty-six feet, enough to float the navy's largest battleships.

Both sides were given an ample hearing and the testimony even included some sharp exchanges between Hilary A. Herbert, a former secretary of the navy who favored Port Royal, and Senator Tillman. History recorded few instances when "Pitchfork Ben" Tillman was ever bested in verbal exchanges, and Secretary Herbert was simply no match. In any case, the political deck of cards was stacked against Port Royal, and the committee voted to spend most of the money on a new facility at Chicora Park on the Cooper River. For all intents and purposes, that decision was the end of the Port Royal Naval Station.[29]

It was also the beginning of the Charleston Navy Yard and the modern Port of Charleston, which could not exist without the Army Corps of Engineers' dredging project. By 1902 construction of the Charleston Navy Yard had begun. The first large dry dock on the Cooper River was in operation in 1909. Within eight years the Charleston Navy Yard had seventeen hundred employees.

The influence of the Charleston Navy Yard on twentieth-century South Carolina cannot be overestimated. The whole South Carolina Public Service Authority (also known as Santee Cooper) and the Lake Marion and Lake Moultrie public works projects, the largest public works projects in the state's history, were begun to provide electrical power for the Charleston Naval Shipyard. By the time it closed in 1994, the Charleston Naval Shipyard had spent more than half a century as the state's largest single employer.[30] One has to wonder what might have been the modern history of Beaufort County had all of this activity taken place on Parris Island.

Despite the end of major appropriations and the shift of its activity to Charleston, the navy did not immediately abandon Port Royal Sound. Navy warships continued to visit. In May 1901 the USS *Hartford,* USS *Lancaster,* and USS *Amphitrite* were in Port Royal Sound for artillery practice. The training ship USS *Topeka* was permanently stationed at Parris Island. Talk circulated in town about making Port Royal Sound the principal East Coast site for torpedo boat practice and of turning Parris Island into a naval training station. In November 1903 the USS *Chicago* visited the Port Royal Naval Station. In November 1905 the USS *Texas* spent several weeks in Port Royal Sound practicing maneuvers with a flotilla of torpedo boats. In December 1905 the USS *Nevada* and USS *Florida* refueled at the Port Royal coal dock.[31]

By 1906 it was expected that the navy would close its recruit training facility in Norfolk and move it to Parris Island. The naval appropriations bill included ninety-four thousand dollars for that purpose, and the good news buoyed the Beaufort community. In April 1907 the U.S. Navy's Atlantic

Torpedo Flotilla was at Port Royal replenishing with coal and practicing maneuvers. Throughout 1907 a small crew of skilled workers was employed at the Parris Island machine shop fabricating specialized wood and metal products. Also in 1907 Congressman James O'Hanlon Patterson visited Beaufort to explain that he had rounded up enough votes in the U.S. House of Representatives to fund the naval training station on Parris Island but that Speaker of the House Joe Cannon, a Republican, had killed it.[32]

Throughout this period, the naval station was the regular training facility for the Third Division, South Carolina Naval Militia (the old Beaufort Volunteer Artillery). The naval militia was provided with several armed launches to train with in Port Royal Sound. These launches were thirty-foot, three-ton vessels powered with four-cylinder, twelve-horsepower, gasoline-powered (naphtha) engines. Each launch had a signal mast, an air whistle, a "watermelon hood" over the officer's seats, and a Hotchkiss gun, a small rapid-fire cannon. Lieutenant H. E. Scheper was in command of Beaufort's Third Division. Beaufort lawyer W. J. Thomas was the paymaster. Lieutenant commander Laurence T. Dubose of Charleston was in command of all three divisions of the South Carolina Naval Militia. The principal supply station for the naval militia was the old customs house wharf on Parris Island. In 1906 the three divisions were in Port Royal Sound practicing gunnery and flotilla maneuvers and preparing for a joint summer cruise.

In June 1906 the Chicora and Lafayette Companies from Georgetown and Charleston were invited to Beaufort to celebrate the 130th anniversary of the Beaufort Volunteer Artillery. The arsenal was the headquarters for the occasion. A marksmanship contest and a banquet at the courthouse were the principal events. Governor Duncan Clinch Heyward and Adjutant General Frost of the state militia were the guests of honor. The whole town entertained the guests in the "good old Beaufort manner."[33] All of this was, of course, a mere shadow of what the naval station had been during its 1890s heyday.

In 1903 the navy sent two companies of marines to Parris Island under the command of U.S. Marine Corps first lieutenant Benjamin Bernard Woog. Their purpose was to protect and maintain the expensive facilities the navy had left behind on Parris Island. The men built a tent encampment while the marine barracks was being renovated. Captain Woog established a laundry at the station and kept the men busy practicing landings with three old steam launches left at the naval station. In August 1903 Captain Woog visited Savannah to seek men interested in volunteering to serve in the rugged, elite corps. To his surprise, forty Georgia men signed up. Captain Woog returned to Parris Island with these recruits and began drilling them in basic training.[34] This modest beginning was the birth of the U.S. Marine Corps Recruit

Depot, Parris Island, the most important institution in twentieth-century Beaufort history.

FORT FREMONT

Another consequence of the military buildup at Port Royal Sound during the Spanish-American War was the construction of Fort Fremont at Land's End on St. Helena Island. Imminent hostilities with Spain prompted the War Department to upgrade its antiquated harbor defenses on the East, West, and Gulf Coasts. Port Royal Sound was one of the most vulnerable harbors on the Atlantic shore. The federal Coastal Defense Act of 1898 included funds for Fort Fremont. The fort was named in honor of General John Charles Fremont, a native of Savannah, famous western explorer, and a pioneer of California. During 1898 the fort was rushed to completion. Huge reinforced-concrete bunkers protected two monstrous 10-inch disappearing cannons, which were elevated into firing position by steam-powered hydraulic lifts and then lowered behind the bunker for cleaning and reloading. These 10-inch guns could overawe Port Royal Sound and hit targets well out to sea. Fort Fremont was first manned by the U.S. Army's 16th Coast Artillery. The first garrison commander was Charleston native Captain Johnson Hagood. About 1905 the 127th U.S. Army Coast Artillery garrisoned Fort Fremont. In 1911 the army decided to abandon Fort Fremont because its military technology had become obsolete. The 127th Coast Artillery remained at Fort Fremont until 1914, when it transferred to Fort Crockett on the Mexican border to protect the United States against Pancho Villa and his raiders.

At the turn of the century, the army garrison at Fort Fremont was an integral part of the Beaufort community. The officers were regularly invited to town social events, and the enlisted men socialized in Beaufort and Port Royal and on St. Helena Island. The garrison fielded a baseball team that competed with two town teams in Beaufort and a Marine Corps team from Parris Island. The fort and quarantine hospital were provisioned by the navy tug *Colonel Elder*. Beaufort boys made up the crew of the government tug. Some veterans of the Fort Fremont garrison settled in Beaufort when their army duty was complete. One settler was a nineteen-year-old Greek immigrant named John Demosthenes, who was assigned to Fort Fremont in 1908. When the fort was decommissioned, Demosthenes was discharged from the army but remained to take over the tailor shop on Parris Island. He and his descendants ran the tailor shop on Parris Island for more than fifty years and became the vanguard of several influential Greek families who made Beaufort their homes.

Not all the socializing with the garrison was friendly. At the turn of the century, South Carolina strictly controlled the distribution of alcoholic beverages through the state "dispensary" system. Illegal, private bootleggers were called "blind tigers." The Fort Fremont garrison offered a ready market for blind tigers on isolated St. Helena Island. Drunken brawls between the garrison soldiers and sea island blacks were a regular occurrence, particularly after payday. In 1910 one of these fights escalated into a full-scale riot between a group of soldiers and sea islanders. Six soldiers were shot in the mêlée and one later died from his wounds.

Periodically the Fort Fremont garrison fired the big guns, much to the delight and entertainment of local residents. In July 1903 Captain Knowlton put the 16th Coast Artillery through its paces. A crowd of locals gathered at the shore on St. Helena and Parris Islands. Local excursion boats dotted Port Royal Sound. William Waterhouse described the spectacle for the *Beaufort Gazette.* First, he wrote, the "blue gray muzzles appeared ominously above the grass covered embankment. Then a deafening boom shook heaven and earth. Out of the cloud of smoke, a giant projectile carried two miles across the sound. It could be followed by the naked eye. When it splashed down it sent a geyser hundreds of feet into the air. When the smoke cleared from the grassy embankment, the gun had disappeared into its protective bunker." The sound of the great guns was easily heard in downtown Beaufort, recalling for many old-timers the day of the "Big Gun Shoot" in 1861.[35]

THE RISE OF TRUCK FARMING AND THE TRANSITION OF SEA ISLAND AGRICULTURE

The third pillar of the Beaufort County economy at the end of the nineteenth century, after phosphate mining and shipping, was agriculture. The end of the century saw the beginning of a gradual shift in local farming away from the traditional coastal crops of cotton, corn, sweet potatoes, and rice toward a variety of vegetables or "truck" crops. The transition from cotton to truck farming was hastened by the decline in cotton prices beginning in the 1880s and the completion of railroad networks between the sea islands and the large urban markets of the Northeast. The decline and eventual demise of sea island cotton between 1890 and 1920 was another economic revolution for Beaufort County. It had a profound social, cultural, and demographic impact.

The collapse of cotton prices in the 1880s prompted several local planters to begin experimenting with a variety of truck crops after the Civil War. By 1912 truck crops—such as tomatoes, cabbages, and carrots—had surpassed cotton as the principal agricultural cash crop of Beaufort County and within a decade had entirely supplanted the once-famous sea island cotton.

In 1868, according to local newspaper accounts, a Mr. Maloney came to Beaufort from Philadelphia representing a Pennsylvania "seed commission house," the crop lending companies of the day. S. D. Gilbert from Salem, Massachusetts, planted several acres of vegetables on Port Royal Island in 1869. Two old local residents, Dr. Joseph Johnson and Mrs. Caroline Givens, planted cucumbers on "two vacant lots in the back of town." The crops flourished, but Maloney never returned to pay for them. The next year Dr. R. R. Sams and Jerry Potter grew good crops of radishes, snap beans, green onions, and Irish potatoes on Dataw Island. With no reliable transportation to get the vegetables to market, however, they gave up after two years. In 1875 James Crofut planted a sizeable crop of Irish potatoes on Port Royal Island "in Spanish moss in trenches."[36] Crofut, a native of Connecticut, was probably aware of the vast market for Irish potatoes in the New York area. These early experiments with truck crops proved that the sea islands were ideal for vegetable farming. In 1877 E. W. Doane leased Cat Island and planned to "devote all his energies to truck farming." On adjoining Cane Island, C. G. Kendall abandoned cotton and planted only vegetables. He was confident in his prospects, "having secured some thirty reliable German laborers." The truck crop in the spring of 1877 was a financial success. Irish potatoes grown in Beaufort County that year reached the New York market in May and June, long before garden crops from Virginia, New Jersey, or New England were ready for harvest. Beaufort potatoes fetched $6.50 per barrel. That same spring W. B. Davis and Son shipped 122 crates of peas "by steamer from Port Royal" and was harvesting eleven acres of string beans as the first shipment left. The ability of sea island farmers to deliver fresh vegetables to the New York market before many northern farms had even begun to plant ensured a high price and profitable return. The farmers' ability to produce two and even three crops per season provided added security. The local paper concluded that truck crops were "much more safe and profitable . . . than anything that could be planted on the islands, our soil and climate being admirably adapted to truck farming."[37]

The year 1877 proved to be a turning point in the agricultural history of Beaufort County. By the fall of that year, it was obvious that the sea island cotton crop was not going to meet expectations. Heavy spring rains and a serious infestation of the "cotton caterpillar" had destroyed fifty percent of the crop before it was harvested. In addition, black small farmers could not afford or did not know how to apply the newly developed and useful insecticide "Paris Green," which could have saved much of the crop. One black farmer on Parris Island had nine acres planted in sea island cotton. Had he spent $4.50 on the new insecticide, he would have produced three bags of cotton (approximately fifteen hundred pounds). As it was, he would be lucky to get one bag (five hundred pounds) to market. In 1877, with sea island cotton selling for twenty cents per pound, that was the difference between an annual income of $300 and an annual income of $100. In addition, a severe drought in 1876 had ruined the upland (short-staple) cotton crop in Hampton County and caused widespread destitution. Two bad years in a row made many local farmers look seriously at alternatives to cotton. The local newspaper summed it up this way: "Sea island cotton prices make it impossible for white planters to pay labor and make money.... They must turn to more profitable truck crops."[38]

In November 1877 the principal partners of J. J. Dale and Company from St. Helena Island came to Beaufort to investigate the possibility of truck farming. The partners were John J. Dale, J. R. Macdonald and J. H. Macdonald. Dale was a former Union soldier from Vermont, and the Macdonald brothers were farmers from Pennsylvania. They stayed at the Sea Island Hotel. At the time J. J. Dale and Company was the largest cotton-planting firm on the sea islands. Over the next decade, the partners diversified their planting operations and expanded to the mainland. During the 1880s they took on a new partner, George Wilkins from Vermont. In 1888 the company hired a young immigrant from Lithuania, William Keyserling, to operate and maintain their four active cotton gins in Beaufort County. Eventually Keyserling rose to become general manager and, in 1907, a partner of the company. With the death of John Dale in Vermont in 1896, the company became the Macdonald-Wilkins Company, and it would be the largest agricultural enterprise in Beaufort County in the early twentieth century.[39] Its successor, Seaside Farms, is still in operation today, managed by Ross Macdonald Sanders and his sons. They are truck farmers who have not planted cotton for three generations.

The diversification of agriculture had a positive effect on the whole county economy. When agricultural production was profitable, the old and often abused barter economy of exchanging crop futures for credits at the country stores was no longer necessary. In 1879 a correspondent from the market town of Varnville reported, "Business is brisk.... The merchants here pay cash for produce of all kinds and let parties buy goods where they please. It is pleasant to see so much hard money in circulation." In addition, new and enterprising farmers moved to Beaufort County specifically to engage in the new truck-farming business. Most notable of these was W. H. McLeod, who had moved from Springfield, Georgia, in 1884. He began buying promising vegetable planting land on Port Royal Island along the line of the Port Royal and Augusta Railroad. McLeod built a country store at the whistle stop of Seabrook, and the store soon became the post office of a busy farming community. By the turn of the century, W. H. McLeod's son, C. E. McLeod, was the largest vegetable farmer in Beaufort County.[40]

The introduction of truck farming hastened the end of one of the oldest agricultural traditions of the lowcountry, the open range for livestock. Since early colonial times, livestock had been allowed to roam freely on uninhabited land. On the sea islands, whole islands were set aside simply for stock raising, giving rise to many islands being named "Hog," "Horse," "Goat," or "Bull," among others. Where several families occupied an island, gardens were fenced in, livestock were marked, and neighbors looked out for each other's stock. This was easy to do and caused few disputes when growing cotton, which the livestock were not interested in eating. But when cotton fields were converted to vegetables, free-roaming livestock became a problem and led to disputes among neighbors.

By 1877 fence disputes reached government councils at the local and state level. Those who managed livestock asserted that it was the responsibility of the planters to fence in their own fields to protect their crops—what was called "fence law." Farmers claimed that it was the responsibility of the stockmen to fence in their pastures to control the range of their stock—or "stock law." This might seem like a minor issue today, but throughout rural America in the nineteenth century, the imposition of stock laws marked the formal end of the American frontier. It was nothing short of the end of a venerated American way of life. In some southern and many western states, fence and stock laws led to bloody feuds and range wars. In the American West, cowboys lamented, "Don't fence me in!"

In Beaufort County the fence law–stock law controversy pitted the traditional rural way of life against the commercial realities of a profitable new agricultural system. The Beaufort newspaper, ever progressive and on the side of commerce, editorialized that a stock law was necessary "to keep livestock out of the fields . . . unless a law is passed it will put an end . . . to the new truck-farming industry in this vicinity." It noted that the stock law was good for the sea island planters but "very controversial" on the large, untilled mainland section of Beaufort County (now mostly Jasper County). The General Assembly did not enact a state stock law until 1902, and that law exempted large tracts of mainland Beaufort County.

In Hampton County, where an open-range tradition went back to the region's colonial settlement, the "stock law" was so unpopular that the entire county was exempted from the 1902 state law, if the county voters so voted in a local referendum. In addition, Hampton County was allowed to impose a two-mill tax in 1902 to build a public fence of "three strand wire" along the northern border of the county from the Salkehatchie Swamp to the Savannah River and on the county's southern border along the Charleston and Savannah Railroad (Charleston and Western Carolina Railroad in 1902). In essence, this fenced in the whole county. Within this vast enclosure was an open range for cattle, sheep, and horses but not hogs. Hampton County was only required to erect "suitable gates for public roads" through their public fence.[41] Hampton County tried to fence out the modern world for as long as they could. Along the Savannah River, where vast tracts of forest were owned by private hunt clubs or timber companies, the open range for livestock remained a tradition until the 1920s. In the South Carolina lowcountry, traditional ways were relinquished slowly and reluctantly.

During the 1890s Beaufortonians expended much energy to preserve and protect the declining sea island cotton industry. In January 1892 the Southern Cotton Convention was held in Augusta, Georgia. George Waterhouse represented the sea island cotton interests at the convention. A ginner and broker of cotton for twenty-seven years, Waterhouse was a fastidious and studious New Englander who knew the cotton business inside and out. On January 26 he rode the "uptrain" from Beaufort to Augusta, where his speech to the Cotton Convention caused a bit of a controversy. He wanted the convention to lobby the U.S. Congress to impose a tariff on imported cotton. What an irony this was. Sixty years earlier, South Carolinians had challenged the federal government's right to impose a tariff and begun the march to secession and civil war over that issue. Sea island cotton planters from Beaufort had been among the first to object to federal tariff policy in 1819. They wanted the federal government to keep its hands off their business. By 1892 a Beaufort cotton broker was asking the federal government to save the same industry. Waterhouse pointed out that "U.S. cotton planters . . . purchase supplies from protected manufacturers . . . but compete in open markets against crops from far cheaper labor markets . . . where production costs are lower." Egyptian cotton sold to U.S. manufacturers for three cents less per pound than domestic sea island cotton. Waterhouse observed that the 1891 sea island cotton crop in the United States was sixty-eight thousand bags (34 million pounds). American manufacturers bought twenty-six thousand bags of United States long-staple cotton but also bought sixty thousand bags of Egyptian cotton for three cents less per pound. Waterhouse wanted the Cotton Convention to lobby for "parity" for sea island cotton. However, the vast majority of cotton grown in the South was upland (short-staple) cotton, and upland cotton planters were traditional free traders. The convention rejected Waterhouse's resolution.

In 1892 the *Palmetto Post* published a series of editorials entitled "The Cotton Question." Agreeing with Waterhouse's position, the paper saw one of the traditional pillars of the local economy disappearing and used its public influence to save it. The paper noted that "the price of sea island cotton is one-fourth of what it was twenty years ago . . . not that the cotton is worth so much less but that the market price is driven down by an inferior foreign product." One editorial contended that to switch to another crop would be very disruptive to the local economy because of the "years of experience in growing cotton." S. H. Rodgers, *Palmetto Post* editor and community leader, pointed out that domestic and international manufacturers were consuming more cotton each year and textile mills were springing up all over the South.

He concluded, as Waterhouse had, that "the home producer of cotton should be protected."[42]

The political approach did not work, so in 1896 the Beaufort business community launched a scheme to build a local cotton mill to bypass both the domestic and foreign manufacturers. With the national economy emerging from a sharp depression begun in 1893, the price of cotton had dropped to a ruinous three cents per pound. Local businessmen were desperate to save this industry. In January 1896 Mr. Bailey from Charleston came to Beaufort and offered to put up fifty thousand dollars if the community would match that amount. The one hundred thousand dollars in capital was sufficient to build a small textile mill. The opportunity prompted Captain Niels Christensen to call a community meeting to introduce the plan and to seek subscriptions to raise the money. A committee was formed to raise the funds: it comprised W. R. Bristol, a jeweler; Charles Danner, clothing merchant; William Waterhouse, eldest son of George Waterhouse; E. A. Scheper, grocery merchant; and S. H. Rodgers, editor and publisher of the *Palmetto Post*. Then a paper corporation was created with Mr. Averill and Mr. Rathborne of Charleston, W. H. Lockwood, S. H. Rodgers, and E. A. Scheper named to the board. In April Niels Christensen Jr. led a Beaufort delegation to a textile convention in Spartanburg. There they visited some of the state's most modern mills.

The idea of a Beaufort cotton mill came to naught. The local community could only raise thirty-seven thousand dollars even though E. A. Scheper and George Holmes doubled their subscriptions. The committee that visited Spartanburg learned that small cotton mills were a thing of the past. Christensen cautioned that a small mill was likely to be inefficient, noncompetitive, and unprofitable. The Beaufort cotton mill fizzled, and it was just as well. Sea island cotton was on its way out, and attempts to save it were futile. In 1897 many local farmers switched to short-staple cotton. It was easier to raise and produced greater yields, and the price of long-staple seed cotton had dropped below three cents per pound.[43]

Beaufort County planters raised cotton for another generation, although total production declined as common short-staple cotton displaced sea island cotton. Between 1901 and 1906, Beaufort County averaged only 6,180 bales of short-staple cotton (3,090,000 pounds) and barely 2,000 bales of long-staple cotton (1,000,000 pounds) per year. In those years Beaufort was the lowest volume producer of cotton in the state except for rice-growing Georgetown County. Some years, however, were better than other years when the rain, caterpillars and price cooperated. One good year kept local planters hoping for another one. For example, in 1905 Beaufort County produced 8,159 bales (4,079,500 pounds) of short-staple cotton worth $407,950 at 10 cents per pound and 2,469 bales (1,234,500 pounds) of sea island cotton worth $177,768 at 14.5 cents per pound. In 1905 the county's cotton growers sent hopeful delegations to the state conventions. Captain R. G. W. Bryan of Levy (now in Jasper County) represented Beaufort County at the South Carolina Cotton Growers Convention in Columbia in March, "even though there is only one county in the state that grows less cotton than Beaufort County." Later that year William P. Waterhouse of the Waterhouse Company in Beaufort and William Keyserling and M. D. Batchelder of the Macdonald-Wilkins Company on St. Helena Island represented Beaufort at the Sea Island Cotton Growers Association meeting in Charleston. The delegates agreed not to sell seed outside of South Carolina as a means to limit competition from Georgia, Florida, and the West Indies and to raise sagging prices.[44] This was a double irony because the Bahamas, Florida, and Georgia had been the sources of the long-staple cotton seed introduced to the South Carolina sea islands in 1790. But Waterhouse, Batchelder, and Keyserling could be forgiven for not noticing the irony. After all, Waterhouse's father was from Maine, Batchelder was from Vermont, and Keyserling was from Lithuania.

The 1905 crop was unusual, the best in fifteen years. Generally, 1903 to 1917 were "particularly bad crop years." The World War I years (1917–18) saw a momentary spike in the price of American cotton, but the boll weevil struck the sea islands in 1917 and destroyed the entire crop on Daufuskie Island. That catastrophe was the end of sea island cotton in Beaufort County.[45]

As cotton was declining on the sea islands, rice was also declining on the blackwater rivers of the mainland. On the Combahee River, Beaufort and Colleton County planters struggled to succeed, but competition from Arkansas, Texas, and Louisiana put them out of business by World War I. South Carolina rice fields had to be planted and harvested by hand as the soft river mud would not support machinery. The hard clay of Arkansas supported machinery, and the domestic rice business was gradually mechanized. That competitive disadvantage helped put the Carolina planters out of business. Frederick Christensen toured the rice district of Beaufort County in 1902 and left a description: "The roads up there are very pretty. Every little way I came upon the ruins of old palatial plantation residences. None of these antebellum homes are left. Nothing left but decaying Negro quarters and grand old oak avenues. But on the Combahee River, wealthy white planters still find it pays to raise the famous Carolina rice." The last of the Combahee River rice planters was former governor Duncan Clinch Heyward, who abandoned the business in 1914 and sold his plantations to northern capitalists. The Heyward family had been planting rice in Beaufort County for 173 years, since 1741, when Colonel Daniel Heyward had landed his piragua on the banks of Euhaw Creek and carved Old House Plantation from the "Indian Land" frontier. Governor Heyward was the last of one of South Carolina's most historic lines. But this was not the last rice planting in Beaufort County. On the Savannah River, where vast fortunes had been made before the Civil War, John Heyward Lynah continued to plant rice on Fife and Rice Hope Plantations until his death in Savannah in 1935. Every year for seventy-four years, Lynah placed a sheaf of rice on the wall of his plantation house and replaced it the following year. When he died at the age of eighty-seven, he was buried with that sheaf of rice on his coffin. The once world-famous Beaufort County rice industry died with him.[46]

As cotton and rice declined, truck farming increased. Between 1900 and 1906, the acreage devoted to truck farming increased 52 percent, and the total value of the product increased 246 percent. Farmers hoped that truck farming would make up for the decline in cotton in the coastal counties. At the turn of the century, most of the new farms were adjacent to or near the tracks of the old Port Royal and Augusta Railroad. Before automobiles and highway bridges, the railroad was the only reliable way to transport bulk crops from the sea islands. Hence, most of the early farms were on Port Royal Island or in the mainland Yemassee district. The vegetable crops in 1904, listed in the table below, were typical of the industry.

Vegetable	*Total Packed*	*Total Value*
Asparagus	1249 crates	$6,869
Beans	4078 crates	$5,095
Cabbage	?	$1,691
Cucumbers	9786 crates	$8807
Lettuce	1484 crates	$1,488
Peas	16,611 crates	$16,611
Potatoes (Irish)	19,860 crates	$79.440
Squash	820 crates	$615
Total		$120,730

By 1906, the production and sale of vegetables from the same area nearly doubled to $236,569. A state farm publication of 1907 noted, "The growth of the truck business of the Beaufort section has been phenomenal. . . . Men have started with nothing and made fortunes in a few years." The Agriculture Department highlighted the Whipple brothers from Rhode Island. They made five crops on thirty acres in a single year (1906) and netted ten thousand dollars. It would have taken six hundred acres of cotton to net the same amount in 1906. The *Beaufort Gazette* crowed, "Fortunes are being made by truck farmers in Beaufort today. . . . We need more truck farmers to move to Beaufort County.[47]

Several enterprising farming families moved to Beaufort County to take advantage of the new truck-farming business. One of these men was John W. "Jack" Gray Sr. (1869–1942). Gray was the oldest of eight children from an old planting family near Barton in Barnwell (now Allendale) County.

Gray and his wife Telie Shuman had six children. The agricultural economy around Allendale, like most of South Carolina, was ailing. In 1905 and 1906, three of the Grays' six children died of disease. In 1906 Gray rode the "down train" to start over. He rented two hundred acres of Myrtle Bush Plantation on Port Royal Island and moved his family into the overseer's house. In 1911 he bought the farm and added acreage over the years. In 1926 the *News and Courier* used him as an example of the success that could come to an intelligent and persevering truck farmer: "No man made better lettuce, or better potatoes, or more of either." In 1926 Gray harvested and shipped 7,534 barrels of Irish potatoes from seventy-two acres of well-prepared ground. That was more than 100 barrels of potatoes per acre, an "absolute record" for Beaufort County. During the 1920s he built a large home on the farm, bought a townhouse on "the Point" in Beaufort, and sent his son to the University of Georgia. Jack Gray's story was an example of the success possible on the new farms in Beaufort County.[48]

The success of truck farming caused a momentary real estate boom in Beaufort County. In 1901 D. C. Wilson put his Port Royal Island vegetable farm up for sale. William Keyserling managed the sale. Wilson claimed he had spent $2,300 since 1898 improving and preparing the fields and in 1900 had received $4,200 from the potato crop alone. Claude E. McLeod, whose property adjoined Wilson's, "did much more." Eventually Captain Niels Christensen and Abbie Holmes Christensen bought the Wilson farm for the Port Royal Agricultural School operated by Dr. Joseph Shanklin.

In 1907 several property transactions garnered notice across the state. One man bought 400 acres on Port Royal Island in 1905 for $4,500 and sold 220 acres of the same land in 1906 for $5,000. West Point Plantation on Port Royal Island was bought in 1905 for $2,500 and sold in 1907 for $10,000. Palmetto Island was sold in 1906 for $1,000 and six months later for $2,000. The new owner intended to plant vegetables and asserted that the island was worth five times what he paid. Perhaps he was right: in 1905 Gustave Sanders reassembled several parcels of Dataw Island for $1,800; in 1907 he sold the island for $10,000. Also in 1907, a Yonge's Island planter paid $1,000 for Admiral Beardslee's 300-acre farm on St. Helena Island opposite the naval station. The same farmer took an option on all of Cat Island (approximately 400 acres) for $14,000. These were enormous sums in 1907, prompting the *Beaufort Gazette* to predict that "Beaufort is destined to become the trucking center of the coast."[49]

Some of this real estate boom was caused by technological improvements in transportation. Gasoline launches had been introduced to the sea islands shortly after the turn of the century. These swift, efficient, and cheap little vessels navigated the isolated sea islands and reliably transported perishable vegetables to market despite strong tides and inclement weather. Individual planters could afford these vessels, and any reasonable mechanic could maintain the simple, lightweight engines. Inexpensive, compact naphtha engines also propelled farm engines and machinery. This was not only the beginning of the end of paddle-wheel freight boats among the sea islands but also the beginning of the end of working livestock. Within a generation the harnessed oxen or mule, the sine qua non of nineteenth-century agriculture, was replaced by the gasoline-fueled tractor.

In 1905 Mr. Ziegler, manager of the Armour Refrigerator Car Company, visited Beaufort during the truck season. He stayed at the Sea Island Hotel and witnessed the first vegetables being harvested in May.[50] Soon refrigerated railroad cars led to an explosion in the production and transportation of perishable vegetables in Beaufort County. The technology of refrigerated railroad cars was also the beginning of "air conditioning," which fifty years later had such a profound effect on life in the Carolina lowcountry.

In 1907 Beaufort County farmers, led by E. B. Legare of Charleston, organized the Beaufort Trucker's Exchange to "cooperate in claims against commission agents and the railroads." Beaufort attorney W. J. Thomas was elected president and Edna Lawton secretary. D. W. Meyer, M. G. Elliott, and E. M. Bostic formed the board of managers. Other organizers were C. L. Paul, Sam Paul, J. W. Varn, and H. R. Sams.[51]

One of the first things the Trucker's Exchange requested of the railroad was a special "truck train" during the height of the vegetable-harvesting season "so as not to hold up passengers or mail waiting for large loads of vegetables." Not only did the Charleston and Western Carolina Line begin to run a "truck train" on the old Port Royal and Augusta railroad, but they also considered a new railroad to serve the truck-farming district. Several routes were considered, and the Virginia-Carolina Chemical Company offered a right-of-way across Williman Island through the Dale crossroads on Kean's Neck and down to Bluffton and Savannah. By 1917 this new railroad was completed by the Seaboard Air Line Railroad Company. Its roadbed passed through Hollywood in Charleston County and Wiggins in Colleton County and crossed long causeways and trestles over the Combahee River into Beaufort County. In Beaufort County the new railroad went through Dale and Hall's Island, across the upper Broad River on a long causeway and trestle, and then through Okatie and Pritchardville into Savannah.[52] In 1917 the Long-Bellamy Company built a new warehouse and vegetable trans-shipment facility where the railroad crossed the highway near the Whale Branch ferry. This facility became a busy agricultural community, named Lobeco for the company that developed it.

The truck-farming boom at the turn of the century even attracted some European immigrants to Beaufort County. In 1907 William H. Niver, Beaufort County's state representative, brought three Belgian immigrants to his farm on Parris Island. Henry Vanderkeelen, F. Vanderkeelen, and F. Stoltz, were experienced farmers. They had come from Europe directly to Port Royal aboard the German steamship SS *Wittekind*. They quickly found work with W. H. Niver and others who owned suitable vegetable lands. The *Beaufort Gazette* reported, "All their employers were pleased with them."[53] The Belgians said they hoped to save their wages and buy their own farms. Despite attempts to attract European farmers to the state, the rise of truck farming did not induce any significant immigration from abroad. Most of the farmers who moved to Beaufort to capitalize on the truck-farming boom were from upcountry counties or neighboring states. By 1905 many small black farmers were abandoning cotton and switching to vegetable crops. Within a few years several enterprising African American farmers had joined the bonanza. The local paper noted, "For four years black farmers did nothing, until this year [1905]. . . . now the prospects for success are astonishing." Seed commission agents provided the seed for a variety of marketable vegetables among sea island African American farmers. When the crops were harvested, the commission agents brokered the vegetables to wholesale buyers. Both parties profited from this system when yields were good and prices were high.[54]

Despite the opportunity truck farming offered, most small African American farmers clung stubbornly to cotton for two more decades, especially on St. Helena Island. Cotton, corn, and sweet potatoes had been the traditional crops on St. Helena for so many generations that some black families attached spiritual significance to them. Since slavery days African American farmers had fertilized their small fields with compost made of marsh grass, mud, and barnyard manure. This compost fertilizer was insufficient for good vegetable yields, and as the soil became exhausted from cotton planting, it was no longer sufficient to regenerate the sea island soil. Cotton yields declined, and sea island cotton was gradually abandoned in favor of heartier short-staple cotton. Agricultural demonstration agents promoted heavier applications of new fertilizers and insecticides to improve crop yields. But African American farmers, through lack of cash or attachment to traditional ways, resisted the new techniques. By the 1920s cotton yields on St. Helena Island had dropped to an average of less than a quarter bale (125 pounds) per acre. When the boll weevil struck in 1917, it was a disaster for the county's small farmers. When asked what measures he used to control the boll weevil, one old African American farmer on St. Helena Island answered, "What, me fight dat bug? De Lord sent him here and I can't do nothin' about it."[55]

Chapter 3

Economic Decline and Adjustment

THE PORT ROYAL AND AUGUSTA RAILROAD

In 1900 the Port Royal and Augusta Railroad was one of the most important economic institutions in Beaufort County. It was the primary method of transportation for people and products to and from the county and was the only certain link between the sea islands and the mainland. While the tide governed daily life on the outer islands, for those living on Port Royal Island—most of Beaufort County in 1900—the clatter, clank, and whistle of the old steam locomotives of the Port Royal and Augusta were certainties of daily life for residents of the southeastern border of the state.

The railroad began with high expectations but struggled throughout its history to become a profitable and viable business. Shortly after it opened on March 7, 1873, the international Panic of 1873 collapsed American financial markets and bankrupted eighty-nine railroads. The Port Royal Railroad was forced into receivership and reorganization. Colonel D. C. Wilson was first the receiver and then the president during its lengthy reorganization. He kept the trains running, though not always on time. In 1878 the principal stockholders agreed to transfer their stock to a new corporation, the Port Royal and Augusta Railroad. Chartered on June 29, 1878, the eight directors were Daniel F. Appleton, D. C. Wilson, H. H. Broody, H. A. Robbins, C. L. Rubsamen, A. Marcus, Walter Luttgen, and R. H. Thayer. The corporate attorney was F. R. Appleton. By 1878 the largest stockholder in the railroad was the Georgia Railroad and Banking Company. During the 1880s the Georgia Railroad interests increased their share of the Port Royal and Augusta Railroad, and in 1886 it merged with the other Georgia railroads under a holding company controlled by Georgia stockholders.

In 1887 the Port Royal and Augusta Railroad merged with the Greenwood, Laurens and Spartanburg Railroad Company, the Greenville and Laurens Railroad Company, and the Augusta and Knoxville Railroad Company to form the Port Royal and Western Carolina Railway Company. Of thirteen directors of the new Port Royal and Western Carolina Railway Company, six were from Georgia. The only Beaufort director was Colonel Wilson. These railroad companies rarely showed a profit and seldom, if ever, paid dividends to their stockholders. By 1891 the Port Royal and Augusta line was leased to the amalgamated Central of Georgia Railroad to operate under a South Carolina charter. Several times during these various reorganizations, Colonel Wilson was called in to be interim president and keep the "up" and "down" trains rolling.[1]

Control of the Port Royal and Augusta Railroad by the Central of Georgia Railroad was the source of loud and continuous local complaints in the 1890s. It became a contentious political issue at the state government level. The Beaufort business community's concern was that the controlling Georgia railroad interests were operating the old Port Royal and Augusta line to the detriment of the South Carolina communities that depended on it. The Central of Georgia Railroad also controlled a competing line from Augusta to the rival port of Savannah. The Beaufort business community suspected that the Central of Georgia Railroad was funneling freight and passengers to the Georgia railroad and port and denying traffic to the Port Royal and Augusta Railroad. The Central of Georgia's control of the local railroad coincided with the sharp decline of business resulting from the collapse of phosphates, the decline of cotton, and diminished naval activity at Port Royal. It gave local commentators a large, out-of-state corporate conglomerate to blame for their troubles. In December 1891 Beaufort County state senator W. J. Verdier, introduced a joint resolution in the General Assembly calling on the attorney general of South Carolina to investigate the management of the Port Royal and Augusta Railroad.

The *Palmetto Post* ran several editorials on the controversy. It noted that the railroad "is controlled by a foreign corporation and contrary to the provisions of the charter and in a manner detrimental to the section of the state intended to be benefited." By 1892 the railroad's workshops and headquarters in Port Royal had been abandoned, and the Mallory Line steamers had canceled their stop there because the railroad failed to deliver coal. The local paper claimed that the year before the Central of Georgia got hold of the Port Royal and Augusta Railroad "the harbor teemed with foreign steamers and sailing craft taking cotton and other cargoes to foreign ports, and with coasting vessels transporting coast wise freight." Since the Central of Georgia takeover, "the great port is . . . throttled by the giant corporations of a neighboring state . . . a circumstance pernicious to the future of the whole commonwealth." The Port Royal and Augusta Railroad was "a strangled road."[2]

The Central of Georgia was not entirely to blame. The decline of cotton and general business downturn had forced half the railroads in South Carolina into receivership in 1892. By July1, 487 miles of South Carolina's total of 2,358 miles of railroad were being reorganized under bankruptcy laws.

But the political attack had its effect. In November 1892 President Comer of the Central of Georgia met in Beaufort with South Carolina attorney general John L. McLaurin. The meeting was more like an ambush. Senator Verdier had assembled several witnesses and many documents to prove "that the Central of Georgia controls the Port Royal and Augusta Railway . . . for the purpose of preventing competition and bottling up Port Royal in the interest of Savannah." The *Savannah Morning News* responded to these charges by asserting "it is not the Central Railroad's mission to build a town there." The *Palmetto Post* responded confidently, "When Port Royal is a great city with millions invested here, and her vast expanse of dockage is filled with vessels of all nations, Uncle Sam will still be paying men to scoop out the freshet mud from the bottom of the Savannah River so as not to obstruct the free passage of the terrapin and the oyster bateau!"[3]

The Central of Georgia management protested the characterizations of their operation of the Port Royal and Augusta Railroad. President Comer stated, "The Central has not done anything to injure Port Royal. It would rather be glad if Port Royal furnished a little more business to the Port Royal Railroad." The protests of the Central of Georgia did little good. Local petitions, legislative resolutions, and McLaurin's investigation reached the ears of South Carolina's formidable governor, "Pitchfork Ben" Tillman. Tillman liked nothing better than a fight, especially one that was popular with his South Carolina constituents. The governor sent a sharply worded message to the General Assembly in November 1892. In it he sketched the history of the Port Royal Railroad from its original state charter in 1857. He noted that after its reorganization as the Port Royal and Augusta Railroad in 1878, it had an "active and prosperous career . . . large and commodious docks were built at Port Royal, one of the largest cotton compresses in the South was built, a grain elevator was erected, the workshops of the company were located there. Energy permeated the organization; lines of steamships called regularly at the port. . . . large numbers of vessels used its deep waters. Business steadily increased. . . . everything promised the speedy development of this magnificent harbor as the deepwater outlet of the great grain and meat trade of the West." But, he declared, Port Royal's success attracted the attention of Georgia Railroad investors who acquired controlling interest in the Port Royal and Augusta Railroad: "The officers of the Port Royal and Augusta Railroad were retired and Central of Georgia officers were substituted." The latter officers, Tillman contended, operated the railroad "wholly in the interest of the Central of Georgia Railroad. The result was disastrous to the Port Royal Railroad and to Port Royal harbor."

Tillman contrasted conditions in 1892 with those of a few years before: "The port facilities are neglected, the cotton compress pulled down . . . the grain elevator dismantled, the wharves allowed to rot . . . the machine and car shops removed to some point on the Central of Georgia. . . . the air of desolation around the port strikes even the casual observer." The governor recommended authorizing the attorney general to begin proceedings to revoke the charter of the Port Royal and Augusta Railroad.[4]

The South Carolina state government forced the Central of Georgia Railroad to divest its interest and management of the Port Royal and Augusta Railroad in 1893. For three years the railroad operated in receivership while lawyers and stockholders wrangled. Finally, in 1896 the companies in the lower portion of the state were combined in a new company. The major addition to the conglomerate was the old Charleston and Savannah Railroad, the original line through Beaufort County. On October 3, 1896, all these small, struggling railroads combined to form the Charleston and Western Carolina Line, which became the principal mode of transportation through the region for thirty years. For the generations of Beaufortonians who came of age in the years before World War II, the old "C&WC," with its aging steam locomotives, its coal cars, steam whistles, "truck trains," and antique passenger cars, transported passengers and freight in and out of Beaufort County.

When the Charleston and Western Carolina Line was organized in 1896, D. C. Wilson finally resigned from the railroad board of directors. He had served on the board of the Port Royal and Augusta Railroad for twenty-two years and was the oldest director by a decade. Twice Wilson had been appointed receiver by the bankruptcy courts, and for six years he served as president of the railroad. When he retired in 1896, he was the last Beaufortonian with direct influence over the management of the railroad. It was another sign of the decline of Beaufort's business and commercial community in the 1890s.

As the Port Royal and Augusta Railroad was being reorganized out of existence, Wilson visited the Boston home of his friends Niels and Abbie Holmes Christensen. When the subject of the railroad came up at dinner, Wilson offered the opinion that the change would be good for Beaufort's business. But he was always a promoter and always an optimist. Whenever Wilson's name came up at the Beaufort Club, the local gentleman's hangout, someone would invariably imitate Wilson by hooking his thumbs in his vest, thrusting out his chest, and declaiming, "Gentlemen, we are on the eve of a great change."[5]

No sooner had the Charleston and Western Carolina Railroad Company been formed than it was sold to the Guaranty Trust Company of New York for an "income mortgage." Colonel J. H. Averill of Charleston was appointed receiver by the bankruptcy courts in 1898. Increased maritime activity at the Port Royal Naval Station as a consequence of the Spanish-American War revived local optimism. The new owners, Thomas and Ryan, purchased the railroad and invested money to lay new track and buy new locomotives and cars. Locally, however, the business community knew that it was only being fixed it up to sell "this time to the Atlantic Coast Line Railroad." This, they believed, would result in the "same old treatment as when the Central of Georgia owned it . . . cut off the finest harbor on the South Atlantic coast."[6]

In 1898 Beaufort businessmen opened talks about a new railroad to serve Port Royal. The Black Diamond Railroad of Chicago was proposing to build a line from the Midwest to "some South Atlantic port." This opportunity revived the expectations of twenty years before, and the Beaufort business community leaped into action. Niels Christensen Sr. met with a delegation of mysterious businessmen from Chicago and took them to see Port Royal Harbor. A local committee was hastily formed to survey the line through Beaufort County and secure terminal rights at Port Royal. Mayor Townsend, W. H. Lockwood, E. A. Scheper, William Waterhouse, William Bristol, and State Senator W. J. Verdier formed the committee. They raised eleven thousand dollars for the cause. But the Black Diamond Railroad never came to Beaufort County, and the hopes for a revival of shipping at Port Royal dimmed.[7]

In 1897 the Seaboard Airline Railroad of Virginia was licensed to operate in South Carolina. The company began to construct a new line from Hollywood in Charleston County, across lower Colleton County, to the country crossroads of Dale and Lobeco. The notion surfaced in 1907, and Israel Keyserling, storekeeper at Dale's crossroad, was "very enthusiastic about the prospect of his section should the railroad be put through to the old Pacific Mines." The Seaboard Airline completed this line in 1917 to serve the region's new truck-farming industry. They then attached passenger cars to their regular freight and vegetable trains. This became the shortest route to Charleston in the early twentieth century. The passenger train was called the "Boll Weevil," and it soon became the first stage of the journeys of thousands of sea islanders on their way north. Eventually, the Charleston and Western Carolina Line absorbed the old Seaboard Airline route. The last passenger train from Lobeco to Charleston ran in 1936.

By 1905 the C&WC was running only one train daily from Port Royal to Augusta, except on Sunday. Train No. 12 left Port Royal at 7:25 A.M., stopped at the old depot outside Beaufort at 7:40 A.M., and traveled to Augusta with intermediate stops at Yemassee, Hampton, Fairfax, and Allendale. It arrived at Augusta at 12:20 P.M. From Augusta it traveled back across the Savannah River to Greenwood, Anderson, Laurens, and Spartanburg in the South Carolina upcountry.[8] This passenger rail service continued until after World War II.

BEAUFORT COMMERCE IN AN ERA OF DECLINE (1890–1913)

The decline of cotton, phosphates, and shipping took its toll on the commerce of downtown Beaufort and nearby Port Royal. Signs of decline were visible even before the great calamity of 1893. In March 1892 Reuben G. Holmes, a chief lumber merchant of the 1870s, sold seven thousand acres of timber and farmland in Hampton County to the Boston, Beaufort and Almeda Lumber Company, taking company stock for payment. That sale was the last vestige of a once-busy lumber enterprise. When he went to Devonshire Street in Boston to collect his dividend, the officers and directors had disappeared, and the company had been evicted from their building for nonpayment of rent. In May 1892 the Port Royal Company, which had been formed to develop and utilize the "famous harbor," went bankrupt.[9]

In 1893 not only did the sea island hurricane demolish the town and its commerce, but the Panic of 1893 had also inundated banks, railroads, and the stock market. The three years of depression that followed were the worst the nation had yet experienced. Capital investment disappeared and the buoyant, hopeful attitude of Beaufort's business community disappeared with it. By 1896 Frederick Christensen reported business at Christensen's Hardware, a bellwether of Bay Street commerce, was "very dull . . . seldom taken in more than $20 per day . . . and most of that on credit."

Danner's store on Bay Street carried some of its inventory "consisting of chamber suits, lounges, sofas, chairs, tables, bedstands, bureaus, sideboards, crockery, glassware and lamps" for almost a decade. D. C. Wilson's Port Royal Sawmill on Pidgeon Point, the first big postwar business in Beaufort, had long since grown over with weeds. When the Garrett and Hastings Lumber Company tried to revive the site in 1897, it failed. J. J. Burns and Patrick Calhoun, grandson of John C. Calhoun, took local investors' money to start the Port Royal Land Company in 1896, and it also failed. Mrs. Lawton, a widow and descendant of the planters of St. Peters Parish, "got none of her money back." When Burns and Calhoun left town, they left broken fortunes and broken hearts. Frederick Christensen noted "that Marie Onthank made herself sick for love of Burns." In 1897 the Christensen Lumberyard burned down. The Christensens rebuilt it in six months, but then in 1899 their Port Royal store burned to the ground. They did not rebuild it. By 1901 Frederick Christensen noted in his ledger book numerous foreclosures on the small houses that Captain Niels Christensen had financed on generous terms after the hurricane of 1893. Business had nearly disappeared at the hardware store: "Business is very dull; last month (June 1901) being one of the poorest on record." The following month Christensen lamented, "Business could not be much worse without stopping altogether!"[10]

In the spring of 1903, the Christensen Lumberyard had a hard time securing upcountry timber to saw into lumber. Mainland mills in Cummings (Hampton County) and Ritter (Colleton County) had also nearly shut down. The cotton crop of 1903 failed along with much of that year's food crops. By the late summer, Niels Christensen had to foreclose on small sea island farms, many of which had been acquired by freedmen during the Civil War. In late July 1903, Christensen foreclosed on seven acres that Monday Stuart had bought from the U.S. Direct Tax Commissioners in 1865. In August the same fate befell eight acres on St. Helena Island similarly purchased by Thomas Holmes. The effects of the failed cotton crop rippled through the local economy. The summer of 1903 saw the loss of twenty-two town lots at the "Town Tax Sale." Almost all were black property owners, some of whom had owned the lots since the Civil War. The declining local economy also affected the lifestyle of the commercial elite. Captain Niels Christensen was forced to borrow money to pay for his younger children's education. "He is drawing heavily to get Arthur and Winnie started in college and boarding school," Frederick Christensen reported, also noting that he himself was "hard put to get any money together here. Cash has run so low I have had to stop discounting bills."[11]

As a sign of the times, the *Beaufort Gazette* announced in 1904 that it could no longer afford to publish a weekly edition and would henceforward publish only a monthly edition. In 1907 the *Gazette* summarized the attitude of the Bay Street merchants: "For several years it has been usual here to refer to the good old days of the phosphate industry and the naval station. Some seem to think the future holds nothing of promise."[12]

The business decline led to the departures of the second generation of Beaufort's commercial elite. In 1892 Ben O'Dell, son of James and Alice O'Dell, longtime proprietors of the Sea Island Hotel, left Beaufort for Colorado to prospect for gold. When he struck a profitable gold claim near Pike's Peak, two more Beaufort men joined him there. In 1897 two of Christensen's trusted employees left Beaufort for better jobs. "Mr. Ringbeck left . . . for a job in an electric factory in Indiana. Mr. Tyson left to take a job in Alabama," a local newspaper reported. When William Waterhouse, eldest son of George Waterhouse moved to East Orange, New Jersey, in 1905, Frederick Christensen commented, "Will Waterhouse and family have gone North. Will has gotten a position. . . . thus one more of Beaufort's white families have pulled up and left." When Colonel William Elliott left Beaufort for Columbia, it was a major blow. Elliott left his legal clients in the hands of William J. Thomas and took a position as president and general manager of the Columbia Electric Railroad Company. His son, Will Elliott, who was raised in Beaufort, became a prominent Columbia textile attorney in the 1920s and

1930s. Colonel Elliott's departure "caused much regret in the community as he was a distinguished lawyer and veteran," and prompted him to offer an explanation in the *Beaufort Gazette,* the newspaper he had founded in 1898. Elliott expressed the "unshaken conviction that abundant good fortune will yet be Beaufort's portion ... that substantial agricultural resources ... will contribute to the restoration of the flourishing prosperity of former days."[13] But prosperity did not return to Beaufort, and neither did the Elliotts.

Bay Street commercial leaders battled vigorously to arrest the decline. In 1892 they formed the Beaufort Board of Trade, predecessor of the chamber of commerce, with Colonel Wilson as president, A. P. Prioleau as first vice president, Captain Niels Christensen as second vice president, and Mayor C. C. Townsend as secretary-treasurer. At their first meeting in June 1892, they discussed the "Florida phosphate business ... in relation to our own great industry at home." They noted the completion of the "shell road between Beaufort and Port Royal ... a great gain to both places."

Every year local stores tried to make the most of the holiday season. In 1892 the *Palmetto Post* commented, "As usual, the enterprising and reliable firm of Waterhouse and Danner have all that one could wish in the way of holiday goods. The ladies are always satisfied when Charlie Danner or any of the gentlemanly clerks wait upon them." And the leading merchants continued to invest in their properties, hoping for a business turnaround. In 1893 D. C. Wilson rehabilitated and repainted all three of his commercial properties on Bay Street, and in 1894 George Waterhouse "erected a new cotton gin on the site of the old one destroyed by the storm." One hopeful sign was a visit by James Mitchell, Esq., the chairman of the New York Stock Exchange. Mitchell was the guest of Colonel Wilson and came to inspect the assets of the Waterhouse Company with an eye to purchase. But Mitchell returned to New York and made no investment in Beaufort. Another tantalizing sign occurred in 1895 when Dr. Higham, "a gentleman from New York," engaged Captain Niels Christensen to build a hotel on Bay Point. During 1896 Niels Christensen Jr., fresh out of high school in Brookline, Massachusetts, drew up plans for the hotel, but Dr. Higham withdrew from the investment. The hotel was never built, although hopes for a large resort hotel at Bay Point or Land's End persisted for the next forty years.[14]

In 1898 a group of local investors built a pipe factory in Beaufort. Captain Niels Christensen Sr. constructed the factory for a cost of $4,500. One thousand dollars was spent on machinery. One year later the factory had produced only $700 in income. "Many pipes were sold but not paid for." At the end of the first year, the pipe factory was sitting on "500 gross of pipes in inventory" and had lost $550. The discouraged investors closed the factory. In 1902 another venture fell through. Local investors agreed to purchase $12,000 worth of stock to build a hotel on the bluff in Beaufort "next to Mrs.

Mather's," the site of the current Beaufort Memorial Hospital. The largest investors were C. E. McLeod, Beaufort's most successful vegetable farmer, at $5,000, and Senator Simon Cameron of Pennsylvania, the owner of Coffin Point plantation, at $3,000. The other local investors, however, could not commit the money, and the project fell through. The Christensens, who had spearheaded the project, were "very much discouraged."[15]

In 1904 the Commercial Box Company was formed in Beaufort by C. H. Danner, C. C. Townsend, C. M. Griffen, R. R. Legare, and George Holmes. They produced crates for vegetable farmers and packing sheds. At the same time, Niels Christensen Sr. began manufacturing barrels. However, barrels were no longer preferred for shipping vegetables, especially by rail, and the barrel making soon halted.[16]

Despite the decline and disappointments, Bay Street commercial life struggled on. While a few new merchants appeared on Bay Street at the turn of the century, mostly it was the same businesses that had been in Beaufort for years. Hal Stuart Jr. ran the pharmacy at 127 Bay Street that his father had begun in 1867. C. E. Danner operated the furniture and dry goods store he had started with George Waterhouse thirty years before. William P. Waterhouse collected rent on the property he inherited from his father and managed the Waterhouse Company from his real estate office. He built a new home at 212 New Street in 1897. Dr. J. Allen Patterson was the town dentist but had moved his offices from the Sea Island Hotel to Bay Street. The Sea Island Hotel continued as Beaufort's premier hostelry, operated by James and Alice O'Dell as it had been for thirty years. Rooms were two to three dollars per day in 1903. P.M. Epstin kept his dry goods store at 113–115 Bay Street, where he had been in business since 1868. And, of course, Christensen and Sons Hardware occupied the corner of Bay and Carteret Streets, where they had been since 1877. New men managed some old businesses. James Riley was the new town undertaker at 209 Craven Street, and Charles Cohen was the new agent for the steamboats *Clifton* and *Clayton* that linked Beaufort to Savannah.

A few African American merchants persisted despite the business downturn. Lymas Deveaux was the town butcher and proprietor of the "White Stall" at the Beaufort market. The enterprising H. G. Fisher owned the West Street Palace Café at 39 West Street. He also operated the dray, livery, and hack service next door to the café. Some new businesses did arrive in Beaufort at the turn of the century. Beaufort's first Chinese laundry was operated by immigrant Laem Sing on Bay Street. Known as "Charlie Chin," Sing called his enterprise the Beaufort Laundry. Greek immigrant Nick Paniotti operated the fruit stand next to the old customs house, where a generation of Beaufort's children gathered to enjoy "Dear old friend Nick's" liberal disbursements of candy. Italian immigrant Frank Bondy was the Bay Street shoemaker for fifteen years.

Advancing industrial technology offered new business opportunities in Beaufort. A. L. Gage, son of George and grandson of the famous abolitionist, Fanny Gage, opened Beaufort's first bicycle shop on Bay Street. The rise of indoor plumbing and installation of a city sewer system created business for Robert Thurston, Beaufort's first plumber. Thurston carried his tools in a case, and picked up his work orders at Gage's bicycle shop.[17]

A new business began in 1898 that survives today as one of Beaufort's historic institutions. In March 1897 Mr. George Prentiss from Columbia met with Colonel Elliott about "starting a paper here." The men formed a partnership, and the *Beaufort Gazette* began in 1898. They took their name from Beaufort's first newspaper, which was published during the Nullification Crisis (1828–1833) by William J. Grayson and John A. Stuart. Colonel Elliott was editor for a year and then sold the paper to William P. Waterhouse, who was editor and proprietor until 1902, when he sold it to Niels Christensen Jr. While the *Gazette* was getting started in Beaufort, the *Palmetto Post* continued to publish from Port Royal. In about 1880 the *Post* merged with the *Beaufort Tribune,* begun by William J. Whipper. The paper changed its name to the *Crescent* in 1881, and Samuel H. Rodgers became its editor. The *Crescent* published irregularly during the 1880s but in 1888 commenced regular weekly publication as the *Palmetto Post.* Both newspapers struggled to survive during Beaufort's commercial decline. In 1906 Niels Christensen Jr. and S. H. Rodgers formed a partnership to merge the two papers. Rodgers put up six hundred dollars in capital, and Niels Christensen Jr. became editor and publisher. They retained the name of Beaufort's original newspaper, the *Beaufort Gazette.* The *Beaufort Gazette* has been Beaufort County's newspaper of record throughout the twentieth century.[18]

In 1903 another business that became an important institution in twentieth-century Beaufort began. F.W. Scheper organized the People's Bank across Bay Street from Christensen's Hardware. The directors were F.W. Scheper, H. E. Scheper, and George Holmes. The head cashier and chief operating officer was W. F. Marscher. In 1903 the People's Bank accumulated loans, deposits, and other assets totaling $88,245.33. By 1906 the bank's assets had grown to $123,365.41. In 1907 the directors built a new building on the site of F.W. Scheper and E. A. Scheper's ship chandlery and dry goods store, which had burned in the fire of 1907. The new bank building was made of brick and steel and trimmed with stone. Next to the People's Bank building was the town clock, usefully placed for islanders disembarking from the Lady's Island ferry to calibrate their appointments in town.[19] Many Beaufortonians of the early twentieth century called the People's Bank "the Scheper's Bank" as it was controlled and managed by three generations of F.W. Schepers.

Despite the lean economy, several technological innovations were introduced to Beaufort that altered the life and commerce of the old town in the twentieth century. Since completion of the Port Royal and Augusta Railroad in 1873, telegraph wires extended along the right-of-way to provide instant communications to the sea islands. The Western Union Telegraph office was on the ground floor of the Sea Island Hotel for forty years. During the 1890s Lizzie Poulain and Mrs. R. K. Harley were the town telegraphers. In 1892 the first telephones were installed in Beaufort. In 1904 Frederick Christensen mentioned his first personal telephone conversation, one with Lulu Scheper. In 1906 Beaufort's communications system was consolidated by the formation of the People's Telephone and Telegraph Company. The company was owned by George Holmes and located in the Lafayette House, now the John Mark Verdier House Museum.

In 1903 another technological innovation transformed life and commerce of the community. On July 31, 1903, local photographer Ed Wilson transported the first automobile ever seen in Beaufort; it came from Savannah aboard the steamship *Clifton*. Frederick Christensen described the commotion Wilson's automobile caused in the old town: "Everyone turned out to watch it go by. Great excitement! When it ran over Charlie Steven's dog, the excitement was intense. Then it frightened away the Marshall's horse which smashed up its buggy!" Four months later, two prominent businessmen bought a car in Philadelphia and brought it to Beaufort. George Holmes was a long-time businessman and property owner, and R. A. Long owned Beaufort's first ice plant. Holmes and Long had purchased a Philadelphia-made 1903 Autocar, whose two-cylinder gasoline engine could propel it twenty-five miles per hour on a good road. The autocar had a "tonneau," or barrel-shaped rear seat, to accommodate four or more passengers. The *Beaufort Gazette* was sure that more automobiles would follow because the "excellent shelled roads around Beaufort make automobiling a pleasure."

R. A. Long's 1905 ice plant was another technological innovation. The new plant at the railroad station could make twenty-seven tons of ice per day. This was one of the few businesses to prosper, mostly because of the growing truck-farming industry. With the profits from the ice plant, Long accumulated considerable property in Beaufort. Before the ice plant, ice had been delivered via coasting schooners from Maine. The ice was sawed in blocks out of the fresh water lakes in winter. At Beaufort it was packed in hay bales and stored in a heavily insulated locker building next to Waterhouse's wharf. The ice blocks lasted most of the summer. R. A. Long's plant guaranteed that Beaufort would never run out of ice.

In 1905 another enterprise that would become a fixture in most southern towns for the next three generations arrived. On May 4, 1905, W. P.

Felder and P. R. Felder opened the Felder Bottling Works at 212 Bay Street. The new machinery could produce thirty-five crates per day and offered "soda, ginger ale, sasparilla . . . and the new refreshing beverage Coca-Cola!" The Felder brothers bottling works was the first Coca-Cola bottling plant in Beaufort.

In November 1905 Bay Street merchants sponsored the town's first commercial festival. The Grand Free Street Fair of 1905 was the forerunner of the famous Beaufort Water Festival. The 1905 festival featured such attractions as the "Streets of Cairo," with native costumes; "Old Plantation Minstrels," with song and dance; "Professor Scott," a slack-wire juggler; "Esau, the Master of Reptiles"; and "Doleta," the smallest woman in the world. The Grand Free Street Fair also introduced some technological marvels to old Beaufort. A mechanical Ferris wheel, famous at the Chicago World's Fair as a rival to Paris's Eiffel Tower, was erected on Bay Street. An "Electric Theatre," offering a "moving picture train robbery," introduced the first motion picture to Beaufort County.[20]

The early twentieth century also saw the passing of the great merchants, nearly all of them northerners or immigrants, who had rebuilt Beaufort's economy and established their own fortunes in the 1870s and 1880s. George Waterhouse died in 1894, and John J. Dale died in Vermont in 1896. In 1892 William Kressel died penniless in Charleston. During the 1870s Kressel had been one of the largest merchants on Bay Street—"the one time merchant prince of Beaufort." Kressel, like Moritz Pollitzer, was a native of Bohemia who came to Beaufort during the Union occupation. Although he died a pauper, Kressel left many friends in Beaufort "who esteemed him for his better qualities of mind and heart." In 1899 Moritz Pollitzer celebrated his eightieth birthday. A delegation of Beaufort's leading citizens visited him at his home, the old Verdier mansion on Port Republic Street. Colonel Wilson, John Conant, George Gage, J. B. Kinghorn, Charles Cohen, Charles Danner, William P. Waterhouse, W. H. Bristol, W. H. Lockwood, and S. H. Rodgers presented Pollitzer with a gold-headed walking stick. When Pollitzer died two years later, all the flags in town flew at half-mast.[21]

In 1903 Colonel Wilson died at his Bay Street home. As the *Beaufort Gazette* noted in its lead editorial on his passing, Wilson had been "for many years the principal figure in the larger affairs of this region." Wilson had come with the federal occupation to construct the government facilities. He maintained a lifelong friendship with his mentor, Brigadier General Rufus Saxton, and named his youngest son for the Civil War hero. Wilson stayed on after the war to rebuild Beaufort. He was a pioneer of the lumber and phosphate businesses and inspired construction of the railroad and the naval station. His death occasioned long obituaries in the *State* and the *News and*

Courier. The *Gazette* noted his "cheerful view of life," his charity to the community, and his unceasing intellectual curiosity. Wilson was a constant traveler in the Atlantic world and often visited Europe with his numerous children and grandchildren. These travels brought him in contact with international financiers, some of whose capital found its way to Beaufort County. The 1890s took their toll on Wilson's business empire, but despite "business reverses and disastrous cyclones," he remained hopeful to the end about Beaufort's future. Although Wilson left numerous descendants, none of his children remained in Beaufort.[22]

In 1909 Captain Niels Christensen died. He was buried in the Baptist Church graveyard. His businesses, too, had suffered from the economic decline, but most of his descendants remained in Beaufort to lead the next generation. In 1913 F.W. Scheper died and was buried in the St. Helena Episcopal Church graveyard. Despite business reversals, Scheper left a fortune at his death. His attorney, Will Elliott, estimated that his estate was worth more than two hundred thousand dollars. Scheper was among the last of the great postwar merchants. His death marked the end of an era of great enterprise.[23]

THE DECLINE OF BEAUFORT COUNTY'S MARITIME INDUSTRIES

In 1892, a year before the great hurricane, the port of Port Royal was booming. Phosphate was still profitably mined; sea island and upland cotton remained a good export; much lumber was shipped north; and the railroad still delivered coal to the harbor. With the shipyard construction on Parris Island well underway, expectations for Port Royal's maritime future were high. In March 1892 an article in the *Baltimore Manufacturer's Record* lauded the prospects of Port Royal Sound for the larger, deeper-draft steam vessels of the Atlantic maritime trade. The author, Thomas Grasty, pointed out that Port Royal Sound was the only southern port that could accept the new transatlantic steam packets such the SS *Majestic* and SS *City of Paris.* Port Royal was also more accessible to the Atlantic trade than Mobile, New Orleans, or Key West.[24]

In June 1892 one of these massive steam vessels, the SS *Cottingham,* visited Port Royal to refuel with coal and be loaded with thirty-two hundred tons of phosphate at the docks. When it crossed the bar bound for Britain, it drew twenty-two feet and had plenty of room to spare. Most of the crew of the SS *Cottingham* were Chinese "coolies," whose exotic appearance and even more exotic speech were a constant amusement to the black and white children in the town of Port Royal. In July the *Palmetto Post* noted, "There has been a steady coming and going of steamships for the past two weeks." Port Royal had become a truly international port of the Atlantic world.[25]

The fall was usually the port's busiest season, and October 1892 lived up to expectations. Eight large lumber schooners, listed in the following table, arrived and departed for northeastern ports during the month.

Ship	*Type*	*Cargo*	*Destination*
J. L. Dubignon	Schooner	Lumber	New York
Alma Cummings	Schooner	Lumber	Boston
Clara Donnell	Schooner	Lumber	Boston
L. F. Schmidt	Schooner	Lumber	Baltimore
W. F. Green	Schooner	Lumber	Boston
Jason Haskep	Schooner	Lumber	Boston
Florence Randall	Schooner	Lumber	New York
Florence Shay	Schooner	Lumber	New York

These schooners were towed into the harbor by the steam tug *Juno.* In addition to the busy lumber trade, the Italian bark *Clampa Emelia* arrived from South America, was loaded with phosphates, and departed for the Mediterranean. The largest vessel that month was the British SS *Britannic,* which refueled with coal, was loaded with cotton and phosphates, and returned to England. The *Britannic* also drew more than twenty feet of water when it departed.[26]

In October 1892 a delegation of European investors arrived at Port Royal via the railroad from Augusta. The party was led by D. Steinmann-Haghe of Antwerp, Belgium, and Ernest Bigland of London. They were treated to a harbor excursion aboard Captain Washington Jenkins's *Juno.* Senator W. J. Verdier, Captain T. W. Willett of the naval station, and F. W. Scheper of Beaufort were their hosts. The Europeans represented a consortium of British and Belgian shipping companies with the intention "of establishing a line of steamers from Port Royal to Antwerp and Liverpool." The *Augusta Chronicle* noted that "it is difficult to overestimate the benefit of direct trade between Port Royal and Europe. . . . cotton and fertilizer would find a direct outlet."[27]

As if to give credence to the optimism at Port Royal, on February 1, 1893, the largest steamship to arrive in Port Royal up to that time put in at the Port Royal Shipping Company docks. The SS *British Crown* was "a huge craft": 325 feet long, drawing 25 feet of water and weighing 2,370 tons. It was loaded with 4,600 tons of cargo for the return voyage to Britain and was the ninth large steamship to put in at Port Royal since October 1892. During the fall of 1892 and winter of 1893, 57,425 bales of cotton, or approximately 14,356 tons, were shipped out of Port Royal. In 1894 Port Royal transported the "first direct shipment of flour from a port south of Norfolk": 5,850 barrels of flour, produced by the Noel Mills Company of St. Louis, Missouri, were delivered on twenty-three railroad cars via Chattanooga and Augusta. The flour was loaded aboard the SS *Mexican* and shipped to Liverpool, England. In December 1893 the *St. Louis Republic* newspaper recommended shipping Midwest grain through Port Royal rather than New Orleans. The *New Orleans Picayune* took note and complained of competition.[28]

On April 5, 1894, Colonel A. H. Averill, receiver of the Port Royal and Augusta Railroad, and Englishman Harry Carr of the West India and Pacific Mail Steamship Company arrived at Port Royal to announce that the company would commence regular passenger and freight voyages from Port Royal to Liverpool in that very month. The vessels assigned to the Port Royal–Liverpool run were the SS *Mexican* and the SS *Cuban*. The *Mexican* and *Cuban* were principally to carry cotton, phosphates, and Midwest grain to Britain. In addition, both ships had first-class passenger accommodations. The *Palmetto Post* exulted that this was "the first attempt from any south Atlantic port for first class passengers direct to Europe." A first-class ticket to Liverpool on the West India and Pacific Mail Company steamships cost fifty-five dollars. Within the week, the SS *Mexican* had arrived in Port Royal. It was described as a "magnificent steamer," and the "genial" Captain Norton Alexander was suitably proud of it. The SS *Mexican* was also a "fast steamer," able to make the Atlantic crossing in fourteen days.

The arrival of the *Mexican* was another cause for celebration. Crowds came to the docks to see it, and the captain and crew conducted tours of the ship's "many berths" for first-class passengers. While the ship was in port, Captain Alexander and a company agent took the "up train" to Augusta to stir up more business. When the SS *Mexican* departed, it took not only a cargo of Midwest flour and local cotton and phosphates but also fourteen passengers. Booked for Liverpool were Mr. and Mrs. Quirk and their daughter from Memphis, Tennessee; Mrs. Agipito D'Zabaijuaregui and four children from Port Royal; B. H. Rawson-Walker, the British consul in Charleston, and his two daughters; George R. Howe, the British consul in Pensacola, Florida; Mr. Tallassee of Augusta; and Miss E. W. Mills of Port Royal.[29]

The eight months from October 1893 to May 1894 were some of the busiest months of steamship activity in Beaufort County's history. Fourteen steamships cleared the port for Liverpool. In April 1894 alone, six steamships left Beaufort County harbors for various European ports. On April 15 the SS *Aureth* cleared Port Royal for Liverpool; on April 12 the SS *Castlefield* cleared the Bull River for Ipswich, England; and on April 14 the SS *Resolute* cleared the Coosaw River for Sunderland, England. The SS *Mexican* departed on April 17 for Liverpool, and on April 19, the SS *Glenfield* departed the Farmer's Phosphate Works on Lucy Creek bound for Great Britain. On April 26 the SS *Menkseaton* cleared Port Royal for Liverpool with 17,000 sacks of flour, 6,000 bales of cotton, and 100 cases of meat.

The same month saw ten lumber schooners embark for New York, Boston, Providence, and Rockland, Maine. One schooner, the *Redwing,* arrived from New York with a load of cement. These cargo schooners were towed in and out of the harbor by the steam tugs *Juno, Reliance,* and *Bachelor.* In addition, on April 12 the luxurious steam yacht *Nechan* passed through on its way from St. Augustine to New York. All this bustling port activity prompted Captain Washington Jenkins to start an excursion business aboard his "neat little steamboat, *Lorena,* taking visitors around the harbor." State export statistics confirmed that the year ending June 30, 1895, was the busiest year of maritime activity in Beaufort County history. The value of exports from Port Royal and St. Helena Sounds totaled $5,777,745. In contrast, exports from Georgetown, South Carolina, amounted only to $14,985.[30]

The early 1890s were also the busiest period for harbor pilots. From the 1870s the harbor pilots had been prominent members of the local community. In 1871 the Reconstruction government established a Board of Pilot Commissioners in the coastal counties of Beaufort, Charleston, and Georgetown. Because the harbor pilots had to secure state commissions, the profession was always subject to minor political influences first by Republicans and then by Democrats. As maritime traffic increased, there were at first too few qualified pilots and then too many when the trade became lucrative.

On February 21, 1891, the local pilots formed the Beaufort Pilot's Association and laid down rules for the profession. Because state law required that no pilot's license could be granted to "anyone who owns a boat in the pilotage business," many of Beaufort's longtime pilots were in violation of the law. To remedy this situation, the Beaufort Pilots Association agreed to purchase a minimum of three vessels to serve both Port Royal and St. Helena Sounds. Each licensed pilot would own a share of all the pilot boats. This new arrangement was forced upon the pilots when Thomas F. Welch, secretary of the Beaufort Pilots Association, complained to Governor Ben Tillman that several pilots owned their own boats and used them for other commercial purposes in violation of state law. Assistant Attorney General C. C. Townsend, former law partner of Congressman William Elliott and a longtime resident of Beaufort, examined the issue and advised Governor Tillman not to prosecute but to warn the pilots to obey the laws or face prosecution. In retaliation, the Pilot's Association removed Thomas F. Walsh as its secretary and gave the job to John E. Kessler Jr. In response to Walsh's removal, Governor Tillman struck back in December 1892, removing Kessler and H. F. Von Harten from the commission and replaced them with nonpilots Francis Brotherhood, the superintendent of the Carolina Mining Company Phosphate Works on Battery Creek, and Captain J. K. Peck of the tugboat *Reliance.*[31] For the rest of the decade, the pilots performed their duties through their association and in accordance with state law.

The pilots who served Beaufort County's harbors in the 1890s were William H. Von Harten, H. H. Von Harten Jr., John E. Kessler, Peter Lea, A. J. Walsh, John Murray, John O'Brien, Joseph A. DuPong, James Wigg, and William Schwartz. Some of these pilots had been active for more than twenty years by the 1890s, and some died on the job. In June 1892 James Wigg, the last African American pilot in Beaufort County, died aboard the pilot boat on station in St. Helena Sound. Captain Wigg was "much esteemed among the pilots," and his death occasioned a large funeral at the prestigious old Tabernacle Baptist Church. In September 1898 Captain Henry Von Harten drowned while trying to salvage one of the pilot boats that had been beached on Hilton Head Island during a hurricane. Von Harten was considered "one of the most skillful pilots of this bar."[32]

Captain Joseph A. DuPong died in December 1892. He was the county's most experienced pilot, having worked the Port Royal bar since 1867. His funeral brought out the town's leading citizens. Harbor pilots Peter Lea, John O'Brien, John Kessler, William Schwartz, John Murray, and A. J. Walsh served as pallbearers. The "senior pallbearers" were Captain Henry Von Harten; Captain T. W. Willett of the Port Royal Naval Station; Niels Christensen Sr.; Senator William J. Verdier; Judge T. G. White; F. D. Philips; and publisher S. H. Rodgers. The Beaufort Volunteer Artillery turned out in full dress, led by Captain Thomas Talbird.[33] The early 1890s were the heyday for Beaufort County's pilotage profession. As maritime traffic declined, the professional pilots abandoned the trade or left Beaufort for busier ports.

Beaufort County's busy harbors were marked by numerous navigational aids. Range markers on Hilton Head Island and Parris Island assisted entering vessels, and buoys marked the several ship channels. The major beacon of the Hunting Island lighthouse still warned passing vessels away from dangerous St. Helena shoals, and a smaller beacon on Daufuskie Island aided ships entering Tybee Roads. The principal beacon marking Port Royal Sound was aboard the Martin's Industry Lightship. The lightship had been put on station in the 1880s at the height of the phosphate boom. The original lightship, Light Vessel No. 34, was replaced by a newer model in December 1892. The new lightship, Light Vessel No. 1, was anchored approximately ten miles off Hilton Head Island in fifty-two feet of water near Martin's Industry shoal, which marked the east side of the seaward approach to the Port Royal Channel. The Martin's Industry lightship was a steel-hulled ship painted red with a white deckhouse, black smoke stack, and two forty-four-foot black masts with fixed white lights atop each. The masthead lights were visible for twelve miles. Light Vessel No. 1 was also equipped with a bronze bell, a foghorn, and a twelve-inch steam whistle. For many years Captain John Masson was master of the Martin's Industry lightship. Each year he was given one month ashore. He spent the whole month at the Sea Island Hotel, treated himself to many good meals in the O'Dell's dining room, and, according to Will Elliott, stayed half-drunk for a month. Captain Masson had many friends in town, and when he was forced to retire without a pension, Congressman Elliott secured him a place in the Sailor's Snug Harbor, a seamen's retirement home in Massachusetts. The town took up a collection and sent him off in elegant style in a "slam door" coach, cheering his passage to the steamboat dock as "the Captain bowed like a president going to his inauguration."[34]

Despite the installation of helpful navigation and safety aids, Beaufort County reaped a harvest of shipwrecks at the turn of the century. Many of these accidents resulted in fatalities. No family suffered more than that of Peter Hays. During the Christmas holiday in 1891, Tommy Hays, son of Peter Hays, and George Nichols, son of Dr. E. G. Nichols, went on a hunting trip down Station Creek. When the boys failed to return, a search party was sent after them. Tommy Hays's body washed up on Bay Point, and George Nichols was never found. This was the last in a series of maritime tragedies for the Hays family. Shortly after the Civil War, Hays's oldest son accidentally drowned in the Beaufort River, as did the boy who tried to save him. Hays's older daughter and her infant child were lost at sea in the sinking of the SS *City of Columbus.* And Hays's brother-in-law, harbor pilot Casey, was lost at sea in the hurricane of 1873.[35]

Many wrecks and fatalities occurred offshore. In March 1894 the Russian bark *Riga* wrecked off St. Helena Sound. The crew was rescued by "the gallant work of Captain Washington Jenkins and his brave crew." During the hurricane of August 1898, five large sailing ships were driven onto sandbanks. All the hands on all five ships drowned, nearly one hundred sailors in all. In 1904 the large steamship SS *Deventry* ran aground off of Hunting Island. Two tugs from Charleston and three from Savannah could not free the ship. When Captain George A. Crofut and the large phosphate tug *May McWilliams* arrived from Beaufort, all six tugs then pulled the steamship into deep water. In June 1906 the schooner *Estell,* carrying six hundred tons of coal for the Central Phosphate Mines on Lucy Creek, ran aground in St. Helena Sound. Once again Captain Crofut and the *May McWilliams* towed the sinking vessel to safety in the Coosaw River. On September 9, 1906, the three-masted schooner *Oliver S. Barrett* capsized in a squall. Only one man survived the wreck by floating on a wooden plank for four days. In April 1907 the lumber schooner *Louise Bassett* wrecked at sea after leaving St. Helena sound with a load of lumber from Wiggins' Sawmill on the Combahee River. Nine crewmen were saved from the surf, but Captain Fletcher, who had many friends in Beaufort, drowned. Even the protected inland waters were occasionally dangerous. On October 25, 1906, the Lady's Island ferryboat capsized in "heavy rains and gusty winds." Of nine passengers, three women drowned.

They were Jane Green, Peggy Entice, and Lucy Bryan, "each the mother of several children."[36]

The turn of the century was the denouement of steamboats on Beaufort County's inland waterways. Since 1816 steamboats had been the principal mode of transportation on the Savannah River and among the sea islands of Beaufort County. Even after the completion of the Port Royal and Augusta Railroad in 1873, steamboats remained regular methods of passenger and freight transportation. The inland waterway connection to Charleston was greatly improved by the 1889 dredging of Brickyard Creek. Congressman William Elliott was given much credit for securing the federal funds to dredge the Beaufort River.[37]

Ten steamboats served Beaufort County with regular schedules at the turn of the century: SS *Pilot Boy,* SS *Clifton,* SS *Clayton,* SS *Marion,* SS *Alpha,* SS *Atlantic City,* SS *Star,* SS *Governor Stafford,* SS *F. J. Thistlewood,* and SS *Planter.* The *Pilot Boy, Marion, Star, Clayton,* and *Planter* generally operated on the Beaufort, Edisto, and Charleston run, while the *Clifton, Alpha,* and *Governor Stafford* traveled the Beaufort, Hilton Head Island, Bluffton, and Savannah route. John Foster, captain of the *Clayton,* and Captain F. D. Phillips of the *Pilot Boy* lived in Beaufort.

Captain H. A. Strobhar of the SS *Alpha,* a descendant of a colonial Purrysburg Swiss family, lived in Bluffton for several years. For years the *Pilot Boy* left Charleston every Thursday and arrived in Beaufort on Friday with intermediate stops. Captain Phillips and the vessel remained in Beaufort over the weekend and left for Charleston on Monday morning. The SS *Alpha* made regular runs between Beaufort and Savannah. It left Beaufort every Wednesday and Friday at 8:00 A.M. and sailed from Savannah every Tuesday and Thursday at 11:00 A.M. Intermediate stops were at Port Royal, Hilton Head Island, and Daufuskie Island.

After the turn of the century, several older riverboats were replaced by newer, faster models. In July 1907 the SS *Atlantic City* replaced the SS *Clayton,* which had been a fixture in Beaufort waterways for twenty-five years. In August 1907 the old riverboat *Pilot Boy* was replaced by a new steamer, the *F. J. Thistlewood.* The *Thistlewood* was larger, faster, and more seaworthy than the *Pilot Boy.* It was described as a "remarkable craft" for South Carolina waters. It displaced 500 tons, could make 12.5 knots with a 220-horsepower, triple-expansion, reciprocating steam engine, and drew only two feet of water fully loaded. The *Thistlewood* had been built in Milford, Pennsylvania, specifically for inland river navigation.

The retirement of the *Pilot Boy* in 1912 was a nostalgic moment. The *Pilot Boy* had sailed among the sea islands for more than forty years and had been "one of Beaufort's institutions before the railroad." Its stout hull had survived the Great Storm of 1893 despite being hurled against the bluff at the west end of the bay by one-hundred-mile-per-hour winds. Every boy, it was said, "knew its whistle as it approached the town around the Point." The passing of the *Pilot Boy* reminded Beaufortonians of "picnics, excursions, moonlight sails of long ago when they were barefoot boys and prim little girls." The vessel was sent to Florida to run up the St. John's River from Jacksonville to Crescent City. George Crofut was captain of the *Pilot Boy* during the winter months.[38]

After 1895 traffic from the port of Port Royal declined precipitously. In fact, between 1895 and 1900 exports declined by 96.7 percent. The following table illustrates the decline.

Value of Exports and Imports of Beaufort (Port Royal) for Years Ending June 30

Year	*Exports*	*Imports*
1890	$1,140,656	$24,354
1895	$5,777,745	$77,781
1900	$189,908	$81,042
1901	$129,639	$192,135
1902	$183,234	$132,340
1903	$181,794	$116,510
1904	$131,991	$142,836
1905	$53,650	$3[39]

The principal cause of this decline was the collapse of the phosphate mining industry. A longer-range cause was the decline of the cotton industry both in the sea islands and in the upcountry of South Carolina and Georgia. Contributing to the maritime decline was the loss of the U.S. Naval Station in Port Royal in 1901.

When Frederick Christensen returned to Beaufort by railroad in October 1900, he rode his horse down to Port Royal to see what activity there was on the waterfront. He lamented to his diary, "In our grand harbor there is not a single trading vessel. . . . the Port Royal wharves are empty. . . . Washington officials are opposed to Port Royal. . . . all assumed the naval station would move."[40] Christensen was right. When the naval station moved to Charleston the following year, it was the largest blow to the once-famous Port of Port Royal.

In 1904 a final attempt was made to revive the maritime trade in Port Royal Sound. W. H. Niver published a well-developed proposal for a new ocean terminal on the southwest shore of Parris Island, known as Elliott

Beach. Niver owned the land and most of the surrounding property. He and his brother, Christian W. Niver, had come to Beaufort County in 1865 from Columbia County, New York. They were entranced by the commercial potential of Port Royal Sound, as were many northerners at the time. Over many years, the Niver brothers purchased numerous small parcels of land on Parris Island, eventually owning as much as a third of the historic island. After Christian Niver died, William H. Niver continued their dream of developing their land into an international seaport.

The key to Niver's plan was to extend the railroad to the south end of Parris Island. His proposal was to build a spur of the Port Royal and Augusta Railroad at Burton. The spur would parallel old Jericho Road, pass through Shell Point, and cross Archer's Creek to Parris Island. At the end of the track, seven long piers would extend into deep water. Each pier was to carry standard-gauge rail lines so railroad cars could be loaded directly onto the ships. Niver improved his opportunities somewhat by winning a seat in the General Assembly in 1906. He represented Beaufort County for two terms from 1907 to 1910. But Niver's capital was too little and his plan too late. The railroad never reached Parris Island, and the port terminal was never built. Niver's real estate was sold to the U.S. government during World War I and integrated into the U.S. Marine Corps Recruit Depot on Parris Island.[41]

By 1907 all the steamship companies that had seen such promise in Port Royal Harbor had moved away or collapsed. Gone were the Clyde Line and Mallory Line steamers to New York and Boston. Gone was the West India and Pacific Mail Steamship Line to Liverpool. Long gone was the famous Dominion Line that had inaugurated steamship traffic between Port Royal and Europe in the 1870s. In 1907 the state economic report commented laconically, "Notwithstanding, its natural superiority as a port, Port Royal is at present without any regular coastwise or foreign service of any description."[42] Beaufort County's maritime golden age had passed.

THE BEGINNING OF BEAUFORT COUNTY'S COMMERCIAL SEAFOOD INDUSTRY

The turn of the century saw the establishment of one of Beaufort County's enduring industries. From the earliest days of European exploration, the amount of estuarine seafood available in the salt marshes, creeks, bays, and sounds of Beaufort County was remarkable to all. Native Americans of the lowcountry had obtained a large portion of their protein diet for thousands of years from the oysters, crabs, and fish of the sea islands. Colonial frontiersmen supported their early trading posts and plantations, at least partially, with Beaufort's bounty of seafood. Among the most ubiquitous items listed on the colonial planters' estate inventories were seine nets, casting nets, and fishing tackle used to harvest that bounty. During antebellum days, nearly every sea island plantation had slave boatmen and fishermen whose special tasks were to provide seafood for the master's table and the slave quarters. Before the Civil War, sea island planters became America's first saltwater sport fishermen.[43]

It was not until after the Civil War, however, that the seafood produce of the sea islands was exploited for commercial purposes. Freedmen, who as slaves had regularly gathered oysters for their plantations, continued the practice for money. Minor disputes over territory led the Reconstruction government to pass a law in 1872 regulating the use and exploitation of local oyster beds. Beaufort County had more of these oyster beds than did any other county. That law protected private oyster beds or fisheries and prohibited the use of dredges, or nets, in private oyster beds. But the law also clearly established the right "of every person to collect and carry off oysters . . . and shells below the high-water mark." The law was also careful to reiterate the right of the public to the use of the state's waters for food or recreation: "Nothing shall prevent . . . persons from catching fish, swimming, etc., over oyster beds." The mention of dredges in the 1872 law recognized the recent introduction of mechanical devises for the commercial harvesting of oysters.[44]

The other fishery, common in antebellum days, that was commercially exploited after the Civil War was the "drum fish run." Every spring black and white sea islanders headed out into Port Royal and St. Helena Sounds to fish for giant sea bass, or black drum, which gathered in the deep holes known as "drops." These fish were named for the deep croak they emitted which could be heard on the surface of the water. The croak sounded like the beat of a large bass drum, thus the common name. These fish weigh from thirty to one hundred pounds apiece and have a high percentage of delicious flesh. The meat is customarily cut into thick, double-sided steaks and, in plantation days, was often roasted over an open fire. The drum fish run usually occurred in April and was always an annual occasion for a feast. Some of these fish were so large that they could not be landed in an open boat and thus were dragged to a nearby beach to be cut up. By 1877 there was a regular seasonal market for drum fish steaks in downtown Beaufort, and many sea islanders supplemented both their diets and their incomes by this local product. As the local newspaper commented, "When a man can buy a 60 pound drum fish for 25 cents, he can live cheap enough."[45]

Drum fishing continued throughout the 1880s. Will Elliott remembered trips aboard his father's boat, the *Dolly Dimple,* to "Hole-in-the-Wall" off Bay Point. As many as twenty boats often gathered over a single drop during the drum fish run. By the 1890s groups of sportsmen came to Beaufort to participate in the sport. The *Palmetto Post* noted in April 1892 that a large party had arrived from Charleston to go drum fishing in Port Royal Sound.

Numerous drum fish were brought to the Bay Street market and sold for fifty cents apiece. That same weekend, Beaufortonians J. A. Emmons, George Eustis, George A. Crofut, P. M. Whitman, and D. E. Fullerton went aboard the yacht *Louise* to the drum fish drop at Bay Point. Every April during the 1890s, Frederick Christensen recorded his excitement over the drum fish run. In 1896 he went drum fishing at "the black buoy" and encountered seventy other boats. By 1905 the *Beaufort Gazette* noted that the "Drum fishing season . . . was ushered in with a myriad of sand flies, both harbingers of spring." That year drum fish were selling for two dollars to three and a half dollars apiece.[46]

The product that really launched Beaufort County's commercial seafood industry, however, was oysters. What made the industry possible was the new process of vacuum canning. In 1892 the American Oyster Company of Maryland built an oyster-canning factory in Beaufort. It was the first large seafood business in Beaufort County. The next year L. P. Maggioni of Savannah built an oyster factory on Daufuskie Island. For many years Maggioni and Company was operated by Austrian immigrant Emil Cetchovich. The company survived until 1942. In 1904 Maggioni and Company built another oyster factory at Port Royal, which soon became their principal operation in Beaufort County. Also in 1904 R. K. Harley built a factory on Lady's Island opposite Beaufort. This business gave Factory Creek its name.[47]

The production of these early oyster factories was substantial. In its first year of operation, 1904–1905, the Maggioni factory at Port Royal processed three hundred thousand tubs of oysters. Nearly all the labor was by hand. The factory was a long shed built at a river or creek landing, with benches or stalls on both sides of a long, sloped work table. The "shuckers" sat on both sides of the workbench and opened the oysters by hand using a "cracker" to break the lip of the shell and a flat, iron oyster knife to open the oyster. The oyster meat was then steamed in a cooker, canned in vacuum-sealed cans, and boxed for shipment. Empty shells were tossed out onto the river bank. Huge banks of bleached shells are the most obvious remnant of these early factories. Almost all the shuckers were African American women, and many hands were needed during the oyster season from October through April.

Gathering oysters provided additional employment. This was almost exclusively the work of African American men, who worked in the creeks and rivers of the sea islands using wide, flat-bottomed boats called bateaux. The oystermen propelled their bateaux with oars and sails. Bateaux were "cat-rigged" with a single gaff-rigged sail on a mast stepped in the bow of the boat. The oystermen used the oars, sails, and tides to navigate the rivers and creeks. When they were on an oyster bank, they removed the live oysters with a heavy iron "oyster rake." Sometimes the oysters were loaded directly into the bateau; sometimes they were gathered in iron baskets. The shuckers and oystermen of the sea islands formed a large portion of Beaufort County's labor force in the early twentieth century as cotton declined and the phosphate industry died. Almost all the payment in the oyster industry was for piecework, and many oyster workers remembered important lessons of the phosphate mining business: in 1907 the workers at the large factory at Dulamo, on St. Helena Island, organized themselves into a union to better negotiate for wages.[48]

Nearly as soon as this new industry was introduced, the state government began to regulate it. When Beaufort County's first oyster factory opened in Beaufort in 1892, the so-called reform legislature of Ben Tillman's populist regime passed a law prohibiting out-of-staters from gathering South Carolina oysters and shipping them to out-of-state markets. Maryland's American Oyster Company was forced to suspend operations, much to the dismay of the Beaufort commercial establishment. The *Palmetto Post* commented that the American Oyster Company had "laid out considerable capital for buildings and labor. . . . we hope an accommodation can be found."

In November 1892 a U.S. government survey of Beaufort County oyster beds revealed the potential for a lively seafood industry, a fact that commercial oystermen from Maryland and Georgia had already verified.[49] By 1902 the state required a license to gather oysters from South Carolina waters. The license cost ten dollars for each oyster bateau of less than one ton, which included the vast majority of the boats in Beaufort County. Boats that exceeded one ton paid five dollars for each additional ton. A state Oyster Commission oversaw this new coastal industry. In 1903 the Oyster Commission proposed to the General Assembly that a license plan be established for all the state's commercial fisheries. A ten-dollar license was required for oysters, clams, terrapin, shad, sturgeon, and game fowl. In addition, each boat employed in commercial fishing was to pay a five-dollar license fee and display its license number "in large plain numbers visible on the hull." County treasurers were to collect these license fees.

The official justification for the regulation of commercial fishing was to prevent South Carolina resources from being exploited by out-of-state entrepreneurs. The effect, however, was to force independent oystermen to go to work for the large seafood processing companies just to get their license fees paid. Ten dollars was a large sum of money in 1903. Niels Christensen Jr. weighed in on this issue as editor of the *Beaufort Gazette*. State regulation of Beaufort County's fisheries was "but an opening gun in another attack by the up-country upon this section. . . . not content to destroy our phosphate industry, they now seek control of commercial fishing!"[50]

As soon as he was elected to the state senate, Niels Christensen got himself appointed to the South Carolina Oyster and Fish Commission, and in 1905 he was elected chairman. That year the commission members were

Senator Christensen, Representative J. Walter Doar of Georgetown, and Senator Thomas G. McCleod of Lee County. The commissioners toured all the South Carolina coastal counties to survey the commercial fisheries. In 1906 Senator Christensen introduced legislation to replace the Oyster Commission or Fish and Oyster Commission with a state Board of Fisheries. This Board of Fisheries obtained expanded powers and jurisdiction over all of South Carolina's seafood and freshwater commercial products. Governor Duncan Clinch Heyward signed the law, but Niels Christensen was left off the new board, which consisted of Judge James Rhett of Charleston as chairman, Leonidas M. Gasque of Marion County, and Francis H. Weston of Columbia.[51] For the rest of his long public career, Niels Christensen Jr. was an ardent champion of Beaufort's commercial fishing industry. As the twentieth century wore on and the old cotton economy declined, commercial fishing and truck farming became mainstays of Beaufort County's economy.

Charleston Packet Steamer *Pilot Boy,* along with phosphate tugs *Juno* and *Ivanhoe* on the Bay Street Bluff after the 1893 hurricane. (Courtesy of Parris Island Museum.)

Bay Street, looking west from Carteret Street destruction after the 1893 storm. (Courtesy of Parris Island Museum.)

Phosphate tug *Weymouth* high and dry on the Bay Street Bluff after the 1893 hurricane. (Courtesy of Parris Island Museum.)

A Home (?) After the Storm

St. Helena Island homestead flattened by the 1893 hurricane. (Lawrence S. Rowland Collection.)

The Same Home After the Relief Work

Same homestead rebuilt by relief workers. (Lawrence S. Rowland Collection.)

Thomas E. Miller, Beaufort County delegate to the 1895 constitutional convention. (Lawrence S. Rowland Collection.)

Robert Smalls, Beaufort County delegate to the 1895 constitutional convention. (Lawrence S. Rowland Collection.).

William J. Whipper, Beaufort County delegate to the 1895 constitutional convention. (Lawrence S. Rowland Collection.)

James Wigg, Beaufort County delegate to the 1895 constitutional convention. (Lawrence S. Rowland Collection.)

Isaiah R. Reed, Beaufort County delegate to the 1895 constitutional convention. (Lawrence S. Rowland Collection.)

Memorial Day parade of black veterans of the Grand Army of Republic on Carteret Street in Beaufort. (Courtesy of Parris Island Museum.)

First African Baptist Church, circa 1916. The church held its first service on May 13, 1866. (Courtesy of Parris Island Museum.)

The "down train" of the Charleston and Western Carolina Railroad at the Beaufort depot, circa 1900. (Courtesy of Parris Island Museum.)

L. P. Maggioni's oyster-canning company in Port Royal with oyster smacks and bateaux. (Courtesy of Parris Island Museum.)

Port Royal docks with four-masted schooner, coal tramway, and piles of coal on dock, circa 1910. (Courtesy of Parris Island Museum.)

Parris Island steam launch at Parris Island dock, with a four-masted lumber schooner in the background. (Courtesy of Parris Island Museum.)

Junction of Craven and Carteret Streets, looking south toward the ferry landing on the day after the fire of January 19, 1907. (Lawrence S. Rowland Collection.)

Lady's Island ferry landing at the foot of Carteret Street, circa 1910. The two houses left and center (owned by J. M. Wallace and W. J. Thomas) were built after the 1907 fire. The George Waterhouse home is on the right. (Lawrence S. Rowland Collection.)

The Beaufort Volunteer Artillery (now part of the Third Division, South Carolina Naval Militia) mustered at the Beaufort railroad station, 1906. (Lawrence S. Rowland Collection.)

The *Attaquin,* which served as the Bluffton-to-Savannah boat, from 1890 to 1920. (Courtesy of South Carolina Historical Society.)

Dr. York Bailey near the end of his career practicing medicine for fifty years on St. Helena Island. (Lawrence S. Rowland Collection.)

Bay Street, circa 1915. (Courtesy of Parris Island Museum.)

Sea Island Hotel, circa 1910. (Courtesy of Parris Island Museum.)

The Christensen family at Bay Point, circa 1910. Senator Niels Christensen Jr. is third from left, next to Abbie Holmes Christensen and, in hat, Captain Niels Christensen Sr. (Lawrence S. Rowland Collection.)

Chapter 4

Politics at the Turn of the Century

By 1900 Beaufort County had become, in many ways, a settled society. The many tragedies and triumphs of the Civil War were fading memories and the tumult of Reconstruction was a generation past. The children of the merchants and entrepreneurs, who had rebuilt Beaufort after the war and prospered during the "decades of enterprise," had come of age. Beaufort's white society had all the trappings and expectations of second-generation wealth. Beaufort's black elite had also prospered during the decades of enterprise and had developed settled habits and expectations. The great political compromise called fusion politics, or the People's Ticket, proved acceptable to both the black and white leadership and promoted a degree of racial harmony. But as the decade of the 1890s wore on, Beaufort's economy collapsed, and local politics hardened to exclude African Americans. Beaufort began to resemble the rest of Jim Crow South Carolina. With economic opportunity gone and a hostile whites-only culture emerging in Beaufort County, tens of thousands of black citizens joined the great southern exodus to northern cities.

THE CONSTITUTION OF 1895

The crowning achievement of "Pitchfork Ben" Tillman's populist revolution in South Carolina was the Constitution of 1895. Throughout the "conservative" Democratic regime begun by Wade Hampton (1876–1890), the ruling party had operated under the radical Republican Constitution of 1868. The conservative Hamptonites had considered an attempt to revise the constitution politically controversial and too dangerous. But controversy and danger were the lifeblood of the Tillmanite populists, and a new state constitution was one of their political goals. When the Tillmanites seized control of the Democratic Party in 1890, they were determined to rewrite the constitution and expunge the last vestiges of the Reconstruction regime in the state. This goal was advanced in 1894 when a referendum narrowly approved a call for a constitutional convention to be held in 1895. The convention met in Columbia from September 10 to December 4, 1895. The statewide election of delegates was held in the iron grip of the Tillmanite electoral machine. Beaufort County was the only exception. Of 160 delegates selected, 112 were Tillmanite Democrats, 42 were conservative Democrats, and only 6 were Republicans. All of the Republicans were African Americans, and five were from Beaufort County. The entire Beaufort County delegation was black and Republican: Robert Smalls, William J. Whipper, Thomas E. Miller, James Wigg, and Isaiah R. Reed. Smalls and Whipper were the only two delegates at the 1895 convention who had also attended the 1868 constitutional convention. The performance of the Beaufort delegation in the face of overwhelming, hostile, unified opposition was heroic.[1]

As preparations for the convention were underway in the spring of 1895, Beaufort's black community was stirred to action by the city's last surviving black newspaper, the *New South,* which was published intermittently and owned and edited by Samuel J. Bampfield. Bampfield was a conservative Republican who, as clerk of court, had been a chief beneficiary of the fusion compromise. However, the Tillmanite convention was an affront to all blacks and all Republicans. Bampfield revived his newspaper to oppose the convention. The *New South* noted, "The sole idea of the Democratic politicians of South Carolina concerning the Constitutional Convention is the perpetuation of the Democratic Party." But the Republican Party, rent by factionalism, was slow to respond: "There seems to be a dispute among the politicians of Beaufort County as to who is the leader of the Republican Party. We think it would be far more practical to inquire as to the whereabouts of the party first." The *New South* sounded the alarm to the black majority regarding the desperate stakes involved in the constitutional fight of 1895: "If no action is taken by the Negro majority, the Democrats . . . will succeed in fastening on this people an oligarchy of fraud that will keep the people of this state under their heels for the next half century!" Bampfield's prediction of the state's political character proved accurate, but little prescience was needed to see into that future.

Eventually the Republican Party organized a statewide voter-registration drive to counter the Tillmanite onslaught. But the Democrats used the feeble Republican response to energize their own base of voters. The *New South* noted the "howl of the white Democratic politicians to the tune of Negro domination. . . . the cry is the hollowest mockery ever perpetrated on an innocent people. It reminds one of the funeral March with an old tin pan tied to a mad dog's tail." The newspaper commented powerfully on the boldness of the Tillmanites: "Whites are no longer circumspect . . . no longer afraid of the irresistible current of popular sentiment at the North in favor of honest elections. . . . When it is announced that the Negro is to be wholly eliminated from politics by constitutional enactment and that in the same breath the delegates pledge not to disfranchise a single white man except for crimes . . .

a system of fraud is inaugurated blacker in infamy than that which the new order is intended to replace." Challenging the constitutionality of the Tillmanites' plan, the *New South* declared that "the white supremacy howlers seem to act on the theory that the Negro forms no part of the body politic," an opinion clearly "against the national constitution." And the paper pointed out the hypocrisy of the Tillmanite spoilsmen: "The mockery and falsity of the pretense that honest government is the only aim of these greedy politicians is apparent to all." Finally, the editorial concluded by repeating the real intention of the constitutional convention: "South Carolina Democrats want to establish a species of political serfdom for our people that will prove much more galling than the yoke of bondage recently thrown off." S. J. Bampfield's solution to this crisis was a typically fusionist one. Blacks should join with the "best whites" to overturn the "tyrannical oligarchy" of the Tillmanites.[2]

While the *New South* reflected the opinion of Beaufort's African Americans, Frederick Christensen probably reflected the views of Beaufort's progressive, white commercial elite. As he wrote in his diary, "Senator and Ex-Governor Tillman and Governor Evans of South Carolina and some others of their kind have got up a convention to disfranchise the Negro without disfranchising the whites."[3]

When the convention assembled in Columbia in September, its purpose and outcome were a forgone conclusion. Despite the overwhelming odds and occasional open hostility against them, Beaufort's Republican warhorses made one last, heroic charge. The convention work was divided among several standing committees, and the Republicans were relegated to minor committees. Smalls was assigned to the Committee on Militia and Whipper to the Committee on Amendments. Thomas E. Miller sat on the Committee on Engrossed Resolutions and Ordinances. James Wigg was assigned to the Committee on Miscellaneous Matters, and Isaiah Reed was assigned to the Committee on Eminent Domain. Everyone at the convention knew that the only committee that mattered was the Committee on Rights of Suffrage, chaired by ex-governor Ben Tillman himself.[4]

Smalls, Whipper, Miller, and Wigg made speeches to the general convention opposing the suffrage provisions proposed by Tillman's committee. The most impressive convention speech was that of Thomas E. Miller, who opened with words from Lincoln's Second Inaugural Address: "with malice toward none." He catalogued the contributions of African Americans to the founding of the republic and their loyal service in all of America's wars. Miller noted that "although we have purchased this land of our birth by our past deeds, you . . . say that we must not vote because we are an alien race." He admitted the corruption of the Reconstruction regime but defended the progressive measures of the Constitution of 1868, which were about to be erased. The most influential measure had been the establishment of universal public education for all races, championed by Robert Smalls. "Greatest of all," Miller noted, "[was] the establishment of the public school system." Miller's speech included a biting criticism of the adherents of the Confederate Lost Cause: "The majority of you blame the poor Negro for the humility inflicted upon you during that conflict, but he had nothing to do with it. It was your love of power and your extreme arrogance that brought it upon yourselves. You are too feeble to settle up with the government for that grudge. This hatred has been centered on the Negro and he is the innocent sufferer of your spleen."

Miller concluded his speech with a ringing indictment:

> Oh countrymen, there is no good to come to this State out of this proposed act. Let us kill it and return to the constitutional provisions we now have. . . . I would that you could see the future as I see it. I would that our statesmen would use their energies . . . in a better cause. . . . Labor to bring immigrants into . . . the dear Old State. Strive to induce capital to come in our midst. . . . Labor, let us all, to banish from our State caste prejudice and hatred of one man for another. Let us cease to legislate in favor of one or against any class of people. Let us tell our people that this is the common heritage of whites and blacks. . . . Let us labor to prove that we are part of this nation.[5]

James Wigg followed Miller. Three years earlier, the *Palmetto Post* had dubbed him a "very un-influential yellow man," but the paper was wrong. James Wigg was a substantial farmer and landowner on St. Helena Island, the place with the largest number of independent landowning black farmers in the state. Wigg's route to education and status was an interesting one. Born a slave, he was a Beaufort County native. A youngster during the wartime occupation, he was employed as a waiter by Union officers on Hilton Head. General David Hunter took a liking to him. After the war, Hunter brought Wigg to Washington and enrolled him in the Whalen Institute. There he became an earnest and successful student of theology. He returned to Beaufort, acquired land and wealth during the boom times of the 1870s and 1880s, and rose to prominence by his election as school commissioner on the People's Ticket of 1888.

Although he had fallen out with the fusionists by 1892, he returned to prominence as a delegate to the constitutional convention. Wigg directly challenged the doctrine of white supremacy and dared the convention to adopt a literacy test for voting, applying the same standard to black and white citizens: "You charge that the Negro is too ignorant to be entrusted with the suffrage. I answer that you have not, nor dare you, make a purely educational test of the right to vote." A landowner and taxpayer, Wigg challenged the white Democrat presumption that blacks paid no property taxes: "You say that he (the Negro) is a figurehead and an encumbrance to the State, that he pays little or no taxes. I answer that you have not and you dare not make a purely property test of the right to vote."

The next day Smalls and Whipper defied the whole convention. Smalls charged that only the "crackers" were duped by the fraudulent nature of the new constitution and asserted that a straight literacy test would produce a white majority of only fourteen thousand votes. Smalls warned that if the economic and political climate turned more hostile, blacks would abandon the state. This prediction was perhaps the most accurate, prescient assessment of South Carolina's future at that famous convention. From his Beaufort County perspective, Smalls clearly foresaw one of the most important stories of twentieth-century South Carolina. The 1893 hurricane and the rapid decline of the phosphate industry had already begun to fuel the great black exodus.

William J. Whipper challenged the white Democrats' assertion that the Reconstruction regime had imposed a black tyranny on South Carolina. In Beaufort County, for two decades following the 1876 Democratic capture of power in the state government, a black majority of twenty to one had nonetheless shown a willingness to support a mixed local government. This fact was in truth a compliment to Robert Smalls from the man who most bitterly opposed the fusion compromise in 1888. Whipper charged the Tillmanites with inciting the crime of lynching and mocked the white supremacists for "trying to show their superiority by defrauding old slaves."[6]

Though hopelessly outnumbered, these forensic battles by the Republican minority were widely reported in newspapers and took their toll on the Democratic majority. Ben Tillman himself found it necessary to rise and answer these challenges. His line of defense was to catalog the crimes of the Reconstruction regime twenty years in the past. He charged that a spiteful U.S. Congress had imposed its will on South Carolina over the objections of President Andrew Johnson and employed an army of occupation to engineer the radical Constitution of 1868 and to fix "the rule of the Negro over the Anglo-Saxon." Rampant corruption, confiscatory taxation, and ruination of the state's credit followed. During his litany of Reconstruction crimes, Tillman highlighted a particularly corrupt state senator from Barnwell named Charles Leslie. "C. P. Leslie was, I believe, a Negro," Tillman asserted. At that point James Wigg rose to his feet and interrupted Tillman to state that C. P. Leslie was, in fact, a white man. Wigg pointed out that "all of those you are reading about are white men." Ben Tillman shot back, "I will find you plenty of 'Nigs' after a while Mr. Wigg," which prompted the general laughter of the convention.[7] Tillman was not shy about his racial bias, nor was the convention.

Tillman singled out Robert Smalls for special obloquy. He rightly identified Smalls as the spiritual leader of the African American delegation and the icon of the diehard Republicans. He recited the fraud charges against Smalls from 1877 to diminish his character and to undermine the high moral ground claimed by Beaufort's African American delegates. Smalls rose to defend his reputation. He produced documents supporting his case and justifying Governor Simpson's pardon of 1879. Smalls then made one of the most eloquent orations at the 1895 convention:

> Mr. President, I am through with this matter. It should not have been brought up here. All the thieves are gone; they are scattered over the nation, but I have remained here. My race has honored me with a seat on this floor, and I shall serve them to the best of my ability. My race needs no special defense, for the past history of them in this country proves them to be the equal of any people anywhere. All they need is an equal chance in the battle of life. I am proud of them and by their acts toward me I know they are not ashamed of me, for they have at all times honored me with their votes.
>
> I stand here the equal of any man. I started out in the war with the Confederates; they threatened to punish me and I left them. I went to the Union Army. I fought in seventeen battles to make glorious and perpetuate the flag that some of you trampled under your feet. Innocent of every charge attempted to be made here today against me, no act or word of yours can in anyway blur the record that I have made at home or abroad.[8]

Overlooked amid all the uproar over suffrage at the constitutional convention of 1895 were the profound changes made to the structure and power of local government. One of the most important changes of the radical Constitution of 1868 was the establishment of elected county commissioners and the devolution to them of considerable local taxing authority. This was the beginning of "home rule" in South Carolina and a revolutionary change from the antebellum constitution, which recognized hardly any local authority. These county governments soon became little engines of overtaxation and corruption during the Reconstruction era. The Democrats wished to curtail local authority, particularly regarding taxes, and by 1890 they had amended the Reconstruction constitution to restrict the taxing and spending authority of the counties. The Tillmanites wanted to do more. They wished to concentrate as much power as possible at the state level and emasculate county governments. They were responding to the unpopularity of local government among rural landowners who shouldered a disproportionate share of the local property tax burden. They were also responding to what legal scholar James L. Underwood called "the disdain with which local governments were held by many citizens who viewed local officials, especially county councils, school commissions and local tax authorities, as the undisciplined fountainheads of excessive spending, taxing and borrowing."[9]

Tillman led the fight to reverse the "home rule" provisions of the 1868 constitution. Tillman and his "farmers' movement" saw local government as nothing more than "urban boosters laying tax and debt on rural farmers." They sought to create new, smaller counties as a way to enhance the political control of the rural farmers' movement in the state. All these goals were accomplished at the convention of 1895. Provisions in Articles VI, IX, and X of the Constitution of 1895 required that all local property assessments be approved by the General Assembly, that county-bonded indebtedness be limited to 8 percent of the assessed value of property in the county, and that county taxes could only be used for purposes specified by the General Assembly. The approved purposes for county government expenditures by Article X, section 6, of the Constitution of 1895 were education; public roads, bridges, and buildings; prisoners; payment of jurors; payment of county officers; litigation; quarantine; courts; support of paupers; and paying off existing debt.[10]

In addition to restricting the fiscal authority of county governments, the 1895 constitution liberalized the conditions for forming new counties or local secession from one county to join another. The effect of these provisions was the creation of nine new counties over the next quarter century. Two of those new counties were formed from parts of what had once been Beaufort County. The new counties were Saluda (1895), Bamberg (1897), Cherokee (1897), Lee (1902), Calhoun (1908), Dillon (1910), Jasper (1912), McCormick (1916), and Allendale (1919). The two formed from old Beaufort County were Jasper County, which incorporated much of the mainland section of Beaufort County, and Allendale County, which included a piece of Hampton County that had earlier been the northwest corner of Beaufort County. These new counties all included new county seats, new courthouses, and numerous new county officials, all of whom became part of the South Carolina Democratic machine. Most important, each new county included its own legislative delegation.[11]

After 1895 local power shifted dramatically from elected county commissioners and school commissioners with their own taxing authority to each county's legislative delegation. The new county delegations consisted of one senator and a number of state representatives based on population. Each county also had an elected supervisor and two or more commissioners appointed by the governor on the recommendation of the county legislative delegation. Other local boards and commissions could be formed through special legislation. The General Assembly and governor almost always deferred to the county legislative delegations in local matters. Most important, virtually all funding for local government came from an annual "supply bill," a collection of local needs and initiatives submitted by the county delegations and passed by the General Assembly. The constitution mandated local election of several county officials, called constitutional officers. These were the sheriff, treasurer, auditor, clerk of court, and probate judge. But their independence was limited by the fact that their budgets were controlled by the county legislative delegation through the supply bill.

The influence of each county delegation in the state house of representatives varied with a county's population. But each county's influence in the senate was equal. Thus, while the large Charleston County delegation was predominant in the house, the rural counties dominated the senate. The reality of power was that each county's senator held an iron grip over his constituents, particularly through the annual supply bill. This condition persisted until ratification of the Home Rule Amendments in 1973 shifted fiscal authority back to elected county councils. The political culture created by the 1895 constitution—especially the great power of state senators over county affairs—was the origin of the state's notorious "good old boy" system of local politics. Beaufort County was governed under these conditions through most of the twentieth century.[12]

The Constitution of 1895 contained specific Jim Crow provisions to control and racially segregate public life in South Carolina. Beaufort County's African American delegates protested in vain as the Tillmanite majority did pretty much as it wished. On one provision, however, Robert Smalls exercised his famous sense of humor to embarrass the convention and amuse the state. The convention was debating a provision prohibiting interracial marriage. Robert Smalls rose to speak. Rather than object to the provisions, he stunned the convention by offering to strengthen it. Smalls wanted to outlaw interracial cohabitation as well as interracial marriage. Smalls proposed an amendment that would disqualify for public office or emolument any white man who cohabited with "a Negro, mulatto or person who has one-eighth Negro blood." Smalls's amendment further stipulated that any offspring of such cohabitation should "be entitled to inherit and acquire property the same as if they were legitimate." James Wigg observed that if the amendment passed, there would be many freedmen who could qualify for public office. In debate Smalls commented that in present-day South Carolina, a Negro who "improperly approached" a white woman would "be hanging from the nearest tree . . . before daylight—and perhaps properly so." On the other hand, if any white man "who insulted or debauched a Negro were treated likewise, this convention would have to be adjourned sine die for lack of a quorum."

Smalls's comment created an outburst of laughter. His amendment was defeated 103 to 22, but his tactic was considered a moral triumph in sympathetic northern newspapers. The debate was reported in the *State* in

Columbia and the *Charleston News and Courier,* much to the amusement of the South Carolina electorate.[13]

The Constitution of 1895 was passed by the convention on December 4, 1895. It was never submitted to South Carolina voters for approval by referendum. Thomas E. Miller had offered an amendment to ratify the constitution by popular referendum, but the convention defeated it. In one last act of protest, the entire Beaufort County delegation refused to ratify the constitution. The journal of the convention recorded, "The President announced that the Constitution was now ready for the delegates to attach their signatures thereto. The call was by counties and the various delegates affixed their signatures. When Beaufort County was called Mr. Smalls, on behalf of the colored delegates, asked and obtained permission to be excused from signing the Constitution."[14]

This was the funeral of political Reconstruction in South Carolina. For the next half century, state and local government was held in the iron grip of the white Democratic Party. The period of fusion cooperation between the races had almost ended. For Beaufort County's black majority, it was another harsh blow in a decade of troubles.

BEAUFORT COUNTY'S LINGERING FUSION POLITICS

The literacy test for voter registration imposed by the Constitution of 1895 was the principal instrument employed by the white Democratic Party in South Carolina to disfranchise African American citizens. But the determination of whether a citizen could "understand the constitution" was left to the local election boards. In Beaufort County, African American voting power persisted, particularly in Beaufort municipal elections, for nearly twenty years after 1895. If Beaufort County's economy had held up, there was a real likelihood that black political participation would have lasted even longer. But the decline of phosphates, shipping, and cotton drove African American citizens and Yankee capital away from Beaufort County and diminished their influence.

In 1900 Beaufort County found itself once again geographically and politically divided. The populous and heavily black sea islands dominated the sparsely settled mainland neighborhoods around Ridgeland, Grahamville, Hardeeville, Bluffton, and Barrell Landing. On the mainland, as had been the case twenty years before with Hampton County, the old southern families had not been displaced by the war and had not lost their land to tax foreclosures. Thus the white southern families returned to those communities after the Civil War. They were strongly Democratic and many were Tillmanites. They all resented black Republican political control over their county, but some supported the fusion compromise as the best their minority position could expect.

The new constitution gave the mainland group an expectation that the Democratic Party might seize control of Beaufort County. In 1896 the party held a mass meeting in Bluffton to elect a "clean, white Democratic ticket." This was the first political "camp meeting" in the county since the Civil War, and it recalled the politics of antebellum days. Within a few years the Democrats managed to elect an all-white county government but not the one that the Bluffton Democrats had anticipated. The fusionists put up candidates to oppose the "straight-out" Democrats in the Democratic primary. As Frederick Christensen recorded it in 1898, "the real fight is in the Democratic primary, all nominated there are sure of election. The election is only a form." Many of the white fusionists who became Democrats were sons or grandsons of northern and foreign immigrants who had been Republicans in the 1870s and fusionists in the 1890s. The Democratic primary of 1898 was a case in point. In that year Frank Hardee of Bluffton was forced into a run-off for superintendent of education with Harry Dopson, a Beaufort merchant. Samuel H. Rodgers, the fusionist editor of the *Palmetto Post,* was narrowly defeated for county treasurer by B. H. Adams of Grahamville, and Hal C. Pollitzer, son of Moritz Pollitzer, defeated Smith Johnson of Ridgeland for county auditor. Hal Pollitzer remained auditor for the next twenty-five years. His election was aided by the fact that his wife was Mary Guerard from a very old lowcountry family with property near Bluffton. Local elections at the turn of the century regularly pitted Beaufort men against mainlanders from Bluffton, Hardeeville, Grahamville, and Ridgeland.

These political rivalries often turned personal and conjured up memories of the bitter, violent struggles of the Reconstruction era. When Niels Christensen Jr. was elected to the board of education in 1899, the Democratic superintendent of education, Frank Hardee, tried to have him removed. Hardee circulated a petition claiming that Christensen was "a Republican and obnoxious to the people." Niels Christensen Sr. had been a prominent Republican in the 1870s and 1880s, but his son was secretary of the Beaufort Democratic Club and had always voted Democrat. Christensen successfully defended himself in local newspapers.[15] That election was the beginning of Niels Christensen Jr.'s long political career. He was the last of Beaufort's fusionist politicians, and for forty years he was dogged by accusations that he was descended from a Union soldier and was too friendly to Beaufort's black citizens. The accusations were well founded, but voters persistently elected Christensen to local and state offices despite or, more accurately, because of his reputation.

The lingering Republican influence in Beaufort was reflected in Frederick Christensen's personal diary. He was a keen political observer. He observed in 1896 that many Democrats had voted for Republican William McKinley for president instead of populist Democrat William Jennings

Bryan: "Even state Senator Verdier says he did not vote for Bryan. What next?" In 1900 Frederick Christensen, Neil's business partner and younger brother, refrained from signing an oath to support Democratic nominees because of a rumor that the Republicans might make up a slate of candidates. Frederick Christensen agreed only to participate in local races and to support only fusion candidates.

In June 1900, during the Democratic primary, all the statewide candidates stumped the Beaufort County courthouse. Half the crowd was black. The candidates, Christensen observed, were "as a whole a mighty poor lot of politicians . . . men of very little education or culture who had been unable to make a living at anything else." Only Governor Miles McSweeney of Hampton appeared to be "an astute politician." Christensen noted with interest a rumor that U.S. Senator John McLaurin had broken with Tillman and was floating the idea of forming "a white mans Republican Party in South Carolina." In the 1890s McLaurin was one of the few politicians to advocate high tariffs and the industrial development of the South. These "New South" attitudes made him attractive to Beaufort's commercial elite. Niels Christensen Jr. met with McLaurin on several political matters but came away unimpressed. Frederick thought that he was an "up-country cracker." McLaurin had been Tillman's attorney general and had harassed the phosphate companies at his boss's bidding. Beaufort's commercial community had no reason to regard him highly. However, any professed enemy of Ben Tillman found friends in Beaufort.[16]

McLaurin's feud with Tillman was very public and made scandalous national news. Tillman accused McLaurin of taking a bribe to vote for the treaty ending the Spanish-American War. McLaurin called Tillman a liar. The feud erupted into a fistfight on the U.S. Senate floor in February 1902, which occasioned the suspension of both men from the body. President Theodore Roosevelt withdrew an invitation for Tillman to attend a White House dinner. When Tillman, "like the ass he is" (in Frederick Christensen's opinion), refused to let the matter drop, his nephew, Lieutenant Governor James H. Tillman, retaliated by withdrawing an invitation to the president to attend the 1902 South Carolina and West Indian Exposition in Charleston.

What emerged in Beaufort County politics after the 1895 revolution was a perennial contest between "straight out," or Tillmanite, Democrats, whose voting power was among the mainland white farmers, and the moderate Democrats—even some crypto-Republicans—of Beaufort and the sea islands. These political contests were fairly evenly matched with local offices divided nearly equally. In 1896 Beaufort County senator William J. Verdier was defeated for reelection by Thomas Talbird. It was a significant election and the most important victory of the Tillmanites. State senators were uniquely influential in county politics after the constitutional changes of 1895, and Verdier had been a chief architect of the fusion compromise of 1888. He also had always been an outspoken anti-Tillmanite. The 1896 primary was the end of Verdier's political career. When Verdier died in 1902, Frederick Christensen characterized the man: "He was respected, liked or feared by all. . . . had ability and force . . . he had an overbearing way that won him many enemies and estranged friends. . . . he had no fear of man and little of God. . . . would not go to a hospital and wasted away in the prime of life." His nemesis, Thomas Talbird, was Beaufort's leading Tillman man. He was an active member of the Democratic machine, secretary of the party executive committee in 1890, and vice president of the state conventions of 1894 and 1898. Like Verdier, Talbird was a descendant of one of Beaufort's old, established, antebellum families. His political alliance with the white farmers on the mainland was natural, even familial. After 1895 Talbird rode the Tillmanite groundswell into the senate, where he served for eight years.

Senator Talbird became famous in history when, on January 15, 1903, he accompanied Lieutenant Governor James H. Tillman and two other friends on a stroll down Gervais Street in Columbia. At 1:45 P.M. the four men encountered Narciso Gener Gonzales, the editor of the *State* newspaper of Columbia. Gonzales was the grandson of William Elliott III of Beaufort and the founder, with his brother Ambrose Elliott Gonzales, of the *State*. N. G. Gonzales was probably the most prominent and most persistent anti-Tillmanite in South Carolina. He and his newspaper had failed to stop the Tillman revolt in the 1890s. However, when James Tillman, Ben's nephew, ran for governor in 1902, Gonzales and the *State* were relentless in their political and personal attacks on him. Tillman was defeated in the primary and blamed Gonzales and the *State* for his political demise. When Tillman and Gonzales encountered one another on the corner of Main and Gervais Streets across from the state capital, Tillman pulled out a pistol and shot Gonzales through the body. The newspaperman died four days later. Gonzales's murder was a national sensation and a metaphor for South Carolina politics in the Tillman era. One of the prosecutors in the trial was Will Elliott, formerly of Beaufort, and a kinsman of Gonzales. Talbird was one of the defense witnesses at the Lexington County trial. Although Gonzales was unarmed, the jury ruled the killing to be self-defense. Thomas Talbird was an eyewitness to one of the most famous murders in South Carolina history.[17]

THE FORMATION OF JASPER COUNTY

The division of Beaufort County politics between the mainlanders and the sea islanders offered insufficient power to the straight-out Democrats. Their desire for complete control of the "courthouse gang" was the political motive for the formation of another mainland county south of Broad River. In 1901 the Beaufort County treasurer, B. H. Adams of Grahamville, "started on a scheme to divide the county at the Broad River." The object was to create a new county out of the mainland south and west of the Broad River and to establish the new county seat at Ridgeland on the Charleston and Savannah Railroad. The proposed name of the new county was "Heyward, after one of the signers of the Declaration of Independence." Adams's plan was well organized and widely circulated on the mainland but not much further. It struck the Beaufortonians "like a thunderbolt."

Niels Christensen Jr. and George Waterhouse Jr., whose brother, William Waterhouse, then owned the *Beaufort Gazette,* led the opposition to the new county movement. Christensen attended a meeting at Barrell Landing, and Waterhouse prepared a flyer to combat B. H. Adams's pamphlet touting the new county. Beaufort's principal objection was that partition would, once again, increase the black majority in the remainder of Beaufort County. As Frederick Christensen put it, "the principal reason why Beaufort opposes the scheme is that it would make this a black county again."[18] The Beaufortonians staved off this initial attempt in 1901. However, the issue remained alive on the mainland and often resurfaced over the next eleven years.

In 1906 Senator Niels Christensen Jr. proposed securing federal money to improve Screven's Ferry on the Savannah River, which connected lower Beaufort County with the city of Savannah. In 1907 Colonel Dan Kingman of the U.S. Army Corps of Engineers offered specific recommendations on how to improve the crossing. Christensen's *Beaufort Gazette* proposed a bridge to Hutchinson Island that would bring the road to the Savannah River Bank opposite the city. In Georgia the Chatham County Commission offered to help pay for these improvements. The *Savannah Morning News* promoted the project as an important link in the ambitious "motor road from Maine to Florida." In October 1907 a joint meeting of the Beaufort County and Chatham County Commissions discussed cooperation in road improvement and bridge construction. Niels Christensen Jr. promoted these developments. He proposed to pave the road from Savannah to Beaufort so "the great highway once traveled by stage coach . . . will once more throb with life as the use of the automobile becomes more general." But when the Beaufort County Commission was asked to provide ten thousand dollars toward the plan, they objected "because so little business comes to Beaufort from that section of the county."[19] This self-serving insularity by the Beaufort County Commission was the last straw for the mainlanders. Mainland voters and property owners petitioned the legislature over the next three years. In October 1910 the movement for a new county convinced Governor Martin Ansel to appoint a commission to study and report on the new county boundaries. The commission was composed of four men, two from Beaufort County and two from the proposed new county. If the commission reported favorably, Governor Ansel was obligated to call for a referendum among the citizens of the region. The referendum required a two-thirds majority to pass.

During the fall of 1910, Richard Manning Jefferies, principal of the Ridgeland grade school, emerged as the leading spokesman for the new county. In November 1910 he and several Ridgeland businessmen incorporated the Ridgeland Publishing Company to publish the *Jasper Herald,* the first newspaper in Ridgeland since the Civil War. R. M. Jefferies, a twenty-two-year-old graduate of the University of South Carolina, was the editor. Born in Union County and raised in Gaffney, he had moved to Ridgeland to take his first job as a schoolteacher. Jefferies later moved to Walterboro, opened a law practice, and was elected to the state senate in 1927. He served in the General Assembly for thirty-one years and was one of the most influential men in the state. He was a leading advocate for rural electrification and helped pass the South Carolina Public Service Authority legislation in 1934 to create the Santee-Cooper hydroelectric project. As president pro tempore of the senate, he succeeded to the governorship on the death of Governor Joseph E. Harley in 1942. He held that post from March 1942 to January 1943.

Jefferies and the Ridgeland boosters trumpeted the cause of the new county to the mainland neighborhoods. In 1910 they began calling the new political subdivision Jasper County. Jefferies addressed a rally of eight hundred people in Ridgeland in November. He argued that the new county made sense because all mainland residents would be within twenty miles of the new county seat at Ridgeland. At the time some mainlanders had to travel seventy miles to reach the Beaufort courthouse. Jefferies repeated the common complaint that roads on the mainland received little benefit from the old county.

Opposition to Jasper County arose in Beaufort, but it was too little and too late. J. S. Claghorn, Beaufort County supervisor, summarized the principal concern of the Beaufortonians: "Such a split would leave us of the . . . island section in the black belt. While the Negroes are lethargic in politics now, they would not be so for long . . . if put in a majority." Claghorn, Edward D. Raney, Gus Sanders, and C. E. Bellinger formed a committee to petition the legislature to "avert this calamity." Eventually, the new county lines were drawn to leave Bluffton and Hardeeville in Beaufort County to preserve a white voting majority for Beaufort County. Hardeeville remained part of Beaufort County for the next forty years, a curious gerrymander that was not corrected until 1951, long after the state's modern highway system had linked Hardeeville and Ridgeland on the Ocean Highway. Hampton County lost 30 percent of its land area to the new county but perceived no disadvantage. Hence, the county did not oppose Jasper County's formation.[20]

When the referendum was held on July 18, 1911, the vote overwhelmingly favored the new county: 283 to 21. The vote in the mainland neighborhoods was revealing:

	Yes	*No*
Gillisonville	49	8
Grahamville	58	8
Grays	14	1
Ridgeland	77	0
Tillman	85	4

It was reported that when the referendum results were announced, the "13,000 people of Jasper County went wild with glee." Considering that the total population of the new Jasper County was less than ten thousand, the glee must have spilled over to Beaufort and Hampton Counties.

The referendum of 1911 was only advisory. Ultimately, the General Assembly had to pass a law to create the new county. Despite the opposition of Beaufort County legislators and a tepid petition from the Beaufort Board of Trade, the act creating Jasper County was signed into law on January 30, 1912. A delegation of Ridgeland boosters went to Columbia to celebrate the event. They were the leaders of Jasper County: R. M. Jefferies, J. P. Wise, W. S. Cooler, Charles E. Perry, J. M. Langford, and W. J. Ellis. On March 12, 1912, Jasper County held its first primary election for local county offices. The results were as follows:

County Commissioners	W. D. Floyd
	V. Kirby Smith
	Theodore Malphrus
County Supervisor	W. H. Woods
Sheriff	H. H. Porter
Superintendent of Education	R. M. Jefferies
Coroner	W. J. Nettles
Treasurer	J. S. Berg
Auditor	W. A. Vaigneur
Probate Judge	W. A. Sauls

In 1912 Jasper County sent James C. Richardson, a storekeeper from Garnett, formerly part of Hampton County, to Columbia as its first state senator and Lucius Hutson of Grahamville as its first state representative. Jasper County achieved its own statehouse delegation and its own courthouse gang. A courthouse was erected in Ridgeland in 1915.[21]

Chapter 5

Political Eccentricities on the Sea Islands

Town Politics, 1892–1913

The formation of Jasper County in 1912 pushed Beaufort County and the sea islands further outside the state's political mainstream. Beaufort preserved its uniqueness for several more years. Most notably, the City of Beaufort retained a racially mixed town council until 1913. The city government was composed of an intendant (mayor) and six wardens, who each represented distinct, single-member city wards. The First, Second, and Third Wards encompassed the Bay Street commercial district and white residential districts on the eastern and southern parts of the town. The Fourth, Fifth, and Sixth Wards contained large black majorities in the northern and western areas. Throughout the 1890s, George Holmes was intendant. Holmes was a wartime dry goods merchant from Bedford, New York. He wed Julia Hazel, daughter of a Lady's Island planter named Joseph Hazel. He was one of the many northern entrepreneurs who remained in Beaufort and amassed a considerable fortune during the decades of enterprise. Holmes's politics were notably middle of the road. He was known for his generosity to the returning southern families after the war but generally supported the Republican Reconstruction regime. He survived a profiteering scandal in the 1870s and was elected intendant in 1892 as a fusionist and civic reformer. Holmes was known as a parsimonious Yankee in both his public and private life. In 1893 the *Palmetto Post* complimented Holmes by noting that "Holmes and his council not only reduced debt but kept down expenses." George Holmes was typical of Beaufort leaders at the turn of the century. He had gained the trust and respect of black sea islanders and white southerners alike. Nevertheless, the straight-out Democrats ran Harry Calhoun against Holmes for intendant in 1896. Frederick Christensen commented that "Holmes will get the support of the good citizens." Many blacks voted, and Holmes swamped Calhoun in the election.[1]

Blacks and whites served as wardens, and city jobs were divided between blacks and whites as well. The longtime town marshal (or police chief) was B. H. Houston, a black man. George Gage, a white man, handled the town's money. Gage was a Gideonite whose mother, Frances Gage, had been one of the most prominent abolitionists in America. He had made considerable money in the lumber business in the 1870s and 1880s. During the 1890s, in semiretirement, Gage agreed to audit the town's accounts and stayed on for many years as treasurer. He had the reputation as Beaufort's last white Republican. Until he died, Gage voted with the blacks and defiantly voted for any Republican who would run. Despite that idiosyncrasy, everyone in Beaufort trusted him with their money.

The straight-out Democrats tried for years to unseat the fusionist and racially mixed city government. In 1898 Frederick Christensen observed that "Mr. Holmes has done nothing as mayor to gain opposition yet many are dissatisfied. He has paid part of the town debt, built the market and shelled Craven, Port Republic and other streets." Still the Democrats ran the Bourbon Smith Johnson against him in 1898. Christensen noted that "Mr. Johnson . . . is popular among the Negroes and the drinking class of whites. He will be able to put up a good fight against Mr. Holmes." But Holmes won again. Finally, in 1902, when Holmes was seventy years old, he stepped aside for C. C. Townsend. Originally from Canandaigua, New York, Townsend was the former law partner of William Elliott, Beaufort's most prominent attorney. The Christensen brothers thought he was "rather extravagant." Townsend served for years as mayor with a mixed town council. From 1902 to 1904 two of the six wardens were Bourbon Democrats: H. T. Danner and R. R. Legare. Two more were white men with strong Republican associations: George Holmes and J. B. Kinghorn, a recent Scottish immigrant and Bay Street merchant. And two wardens were African American: G. Mitchell and B. Simmons.[2]

Despite the fusion system, racial tension was always close to the surface in city politics, and individuals on both sides were willing to stir up trouble. In 1904 racial tension threatened to break out into riot and upset the delicate balance of fusion politics in the city. The center of the controversy was Marshal B. H. Houston. In March 1904 a series of robberies and break-ins alarmed the merchants and property owners. Mr. Rountree's shop, Bush's Barber Shop, and Rahal's and Horkovitz's stores were reportedly "all robbed in rapid succession." When Hull left Beaufort for a vacation, his home on Carteret Street was ransacked. These robberies were not aggressively investigated. In addition, a recent fire in town was too slowly extinguished. The African American Steam Fire Engine Company and town police were blamed for the mishap. Houston was the chief of both organizations. Beaufort property owners called a meeting of white citizens and formed a committee consisting of F. W. Scheper Jr., H. T. Danner, Niels Christensen Jr., Tom Elliott, George Waterhouse Jr., M. Cohen, and William Marscher to demand action.

This movement alarmed the black citizens, who packed the council chambers. The white citizens' group hired W. S. Tillinghast and Thomas Talbird to represent them, and the black citizens enlisted William J. Whipper and Julius I. Washington to defend their marshal. The lines could not have been more clearly drawn: black versus white, Republican versus Democrat, Whipper and Washington versus Tillinghast and Talbird. Rumors and threats circulated throughout the community. The town council was in the middle. Commentary at public meetings was brutally candid. Houston was accused of incompetence and cowardice. Niels Christensen Jr. of the "citizens commission" called Houston "the obnoxious colored marshal" and accused him of doing nothing to stop the robberies. Whipper became "much worked up" in his defense of Houston, and the black crowd became unruly. A full-scale race riot was imminent. Faced with pressure and threats of violence, the town council split three to three on whether to dismiss Houston. Mayor Townsend cast the deciding vote to retain Houston as town marshal but to remove him as chief of the Steam Fire Engine Company. This decision mostly satisfied the black crowd and may have averted a riot. But the straight-out Democrats seethed with anger and worked hard to capture control of town council in the next election.

In the 1906 election, H.T. Danner, T. Brooks, and B. C. Adams represented the white wards while Edward Wallace and Joe Robinson represented the black wards. In the Fourth Ward, the Democrats ran E. F. Ricker against George Holmes, who had been the swing vote in the 1904 crisis. Once again Holmes prevailed with the support of the black community. Ricker lost the election because word circulated in the black wards that he wished to replace black policemen with white policemen. Ricker denied the story but lost the election anyway. The delicate political balance on the town council survived for several more years.[3]

The collapsing economy and the declining black population progressively weakened the influence of Beaufort's black community. By 1913 the white voters finally elected a "straight Democratic ticket." The white Democrat intendant in 1913 was C. C. Townsend, and the town wardens were Sam Paul, Charles Cohen, T. H. Harms, George L. Tucker, A. L. Gage, and E. D. Raney. Two blacks, Edward Wallace and W. H. Washington, stood for election but were defeated. This was the end of the last mixed-race elected government in South Carolina and another requiem for Reconstruction.[4]

THE SOUTH CAROLINA DISPENSARY AND THE RISE OF SENATOR NIELS CHRISTENSEN JR.

One of the most controversial policy changes of the Tillman administration was the creation of the South Carolina Dispensary. The Dispensary Act was passed on December 24, 1892, and hurriedly signed into law by Governor Tillman. The dispensary was a major step, or misstep, on the state's long road to banning alcoholic beverages in 1915—that is, Prohibition.

The evils of alcoholic abuse had been long observed in South Carolina. Beginning in the seventeenth century, colonial authorities had attempted to control the sale of liquor to the Indians. In 1740, the Commons House of Assembly prohibited the sale of liquor to slaves without authorization. By the 1820s religious and civic groups had begun to emulate northern temperance societies. The first temperance society in South Carolina was organized in 1829. Thereafter, South Carolina always had an organized group promoting the statutory Prohibition of strong drink.

The first Beaufort County temperance society was created on March 1, 1877. While the chief organizers were northerners, it was noteworthy that the leadership of the "Temperance Union" was biracial. The black mayor of Beaufort in 1877, Alfred Williams, was president. George Gage and J. A. Whitman, the Bay Street jeweler, formed the executive committee along with Samuel J. Bampfield, Robert Smalls's son-in-law. They met at the Methodist church and soon had 130 members. The Beaufort Temperance Union sponsored outlying societies. A society formed on Lady's Island with forty-four members and another at Atlantic Sawmill on Spanish Point with thirty-nine members. Even the "wicked city of Port Royal 'signed a pledge' to refrain from drinking before noon," as the local paper put it.[5] The temperance movement grew in size and influence in the 1880s.

The highlight of Beaufort's temperance movement was the visit of Clara Barton on March 20, 1894, to celebrate the ninetieth anniversary of the birth of Neal Dow, the founder of the temperance movement in America. The local Women's Christian Temperance Union chapter organized a reception at George Waterhouse's home. Mary Hamilton was president of Beaufort's WCTU, and Martha Reed was president of the "Band of Hope." Fifty children assembled to greet Clara Barton. They sang "Onward Christian Soldiers" and "Temperance Boys and Girls Are We." After the songs Clara Barton delivered an inspirational address. In 1882 the General Assembly passed a local option law, and by 1891 sixty towns and several counties in South Carolina had prohibited liquor. Beaufort County, however, was never one of them. Despite the commitment of several prominent families to the temperance movement and the power of Beaufort Baptist Church, the county never got in step with the rest of the state's drive toward Prohibition. In 1891 a statewide referendum on Prohibition showed a 56 percent majority in favor of outlawing alcohol. In fact, all but eight of South Carolina's thirty-five counties returned strong majorities favoring Prohibition. The eight holdouts were Charleston, Richland, Georgetown, Marion, Chesterfield, Williamsburg, and, of course, Beaufort. Five of the dissenters were in the lowcountry.[6]

Governor Tillman believed that total Prohibition was impractical. Hence, when the General Assembly sent him a Prohibition bill in 1892, he substituted his own bill outlawing the private sale of liquor and founding the South Carolina Dispensary as the only legal purveyor of alcoholic beverages in the state. The law also established a special police force of "dispensary constables" to enforce the new law. Illegal private purveyors of liquor—bootleggers—were known as "blind tigers," the most famous of whom was Charleston city councilman Vincent Chicco, who openly flouted the state laws. Attempts to enforce the dispensary laws led to violent confrontations. The Darlington "Dispensary War" was the most famous of many confrontations across the state.[7] In 1894 a gunfight between several armed citizens and several dispensary constables broke out at the Darlington railroad station. When the smoke cleared, two local citizens and one constable lay dead.

A Board of Control sat in Columbia, and each county had a local dispensary board. The state board negotiated bulk sales from liquor manufacturers and supervised the statewide distribution of liquor in glass bottles embossed with the palmetto seal. The liquor was stored in a huge warehouse in Columbia and issued to local outlets that were controlled by county dispensary boards. The Board of Control and local dispensary boards soon became tools of political patronage and were soon thoroughly corrupted by the large amount of money flowing through the system. Resistance to the system was widespread and corruption scandals were equally widespread.

Dispensary outlets were established in Beaufort, Port Royal, Bluffton, Yemassee, and Ridgeland (in Beaufort County until 1912). But in Beaufort County it proved particularly difficult to enforce the dispensary laws. The system was never popular, so local cooperation was half-hearted. The *Palmetto Post* weakly noted in 1894, "we may not like the law but we must obey it." In addition, many blind tigers operated on sea islands only accessible by boat. When the dispensary constables broke up a "blind tiger" operation, Beaufort County juries refused to convict them. As the *Beaufort Gazette* remarked in 1903, "Beaufort County juries for years refused to convict the 'blind tigers.' Beaufort juries will not uphold the Dispensary Law."[8]

The first Beaufort County dispensary trial occurred in January 1894. Dispensary Constable T.W. Holloway arrested Captain E. F. Daniels of the SS *Alpha,* one of Beaufort's steam packets, on December 28, 1892, five days after the law took effect. Captain Daniels not only resisted arrest but also assaulted the eager, impudent constable. When the case finally came to trial before Judge T. G. White, W.A. Barber of Columbia was sent as prosecutor. Captain Daniels hired State Senator William J. Verdier as his defense attorney. The trial ended in a hung jury and a mistrial.[9] Captain Daniels was well known in Beaufort and commanded considerable sympathy from the public. The dispensary laws met the same kind of resistance for the next fifteen years.

Sometimes local law enforcement was complicit in the "blind tiger" trade. In the late 1890s, a former deputy sheriff called "Mick" was the best known "blind tiger" in Beaufort. "Mick" was Tom Walsh, a Catholic Irishman and popular character in town. Walsh raised a large family of boys in Beaufort at the turn of the century, and his eldest son, Emmett Walsh, later became the Roman Catholic bishop of Charleston. Not only was Tom Walsh the best-known bootlegger, but he also ran his business out of a building owned by his fellow Catholic, Senator Thomas Talbird. The busiest blind tigers were at Parris Island. This was not surprising. The U.S. Naval Station on Parris Island provided ready cash and a ready market for liquor among the sailors. The international seaport town of Port Royal across Battery Creek provided another ready market. In July 1903 state dispensary constables apprehended the principal "blind tiger" on Parris Island, R. D. Dansler. Constables T. J. Harmon and J. R. McAdams seized 173 bottles of beer and one gallon of whiskey. Emulating the militant temperance advocate Carrie Nation—but for totally different reasons—Dansler smashed another fifteen gallons to prevent confiscation.[10]

Within a month of this incident, Niels Christensen Jr. began a campaign to reform the state dispensary system. Niels Christensen Jr. was raised by a New England mother in a teetotaling household so this issue was a natural one for him. He had just purchased the *Beaufort Gazette,* and his editorials entitled "Dispensary Under Fire" established him as one of the state's progressive reformers. He wrote that a "storm is brewing across the state. . . . the Dispensary System is the irritating cause. . . . there is widespread suspicion that it is rotten." Christensen kept up his attack on the dispensary for months. He recounted the wholesale defiance of the law in Charleston, where the "notorious Chicco" remained one of the city's most popular characters. He also noted the inability of state prosecutors to convict any blind tigers in Beaufort County.[11] Christensen's attack on the dispensary not only established him as a sworn enemy of Senator Ben Tillman but also launched his own long, influential political career.

The following year, 1904, was a general election year. Christensen decided to challenge Thomas Talbird, the county's leading Tillmanite, for the state senate. Christensen was only twenty-eight years old. Talbird had been Beaufort's state senator for eight years. Christensen wished to make dispensary corruption his springboard to election, but the contest revealed other, deeper divisions in Beaufort County. The outcome of the 1904 election also revealed a further nuance in Beaufort County's fusion politics.

When the primary campaign began in August 1904, Tom Walker, the county Democratic Party boss and state dispenser, pulled out all the stops to support Talbird. Walker made the Bay Street dispensary party headquarters and chartered the paddle wheeler SS *Louise* to bring a crowd of Tillmanites from Bluffton, Barrell Landing, and Okatie. Frederick Christensen described this crowd from south of the Broad River as "crackers."

Some of the "crackers" repeated the story that Niels Christensen's sister Winnie was seen "kissing a Negro girl on the street." The story was untrue but, like many such political rumors, it conjured up images that had the ring of truth. To many locals, the Christensens, especially Niels's mother, Abbie Holmes Christensen, a wartime Gideonite, were thought to be too friendly with blacks. In addition, Winnie never married and was thought eccentric and "mannish." Niels Christensen, however, did not let the insult pass. He went to lawyer W. J. Thomas, who revealed that the source of the rumor was Mickey Cohen. Thomas advised Niels to be armed when he encountered Mickey Cohen since the latter was known to carry a pistol. Christensen caught up with Cohen at the lumberyard and beat him until he retracted the story. No gunplay ensued. News of the fight spread quickly through Beaufort, and according to Frederick Christensen, "everyone seemed delighted."

This was not the end of rumors. The *State* covered a political meeting in Newberry County where Hub Evans, a prominent Tillmanite and Board of Control member, charged that Christensen's father had been "a Yankee officer of Negro troops during the Civil War." This charge was, of course, absolutely correct. It prompted a defensive letter from Captain Niels Christensen Sr. himself, written from a summer resort in Townsend, Vermont. In addition, almost all the members of the Henry Middleton Stuart Camp of the United Confederate Veterans in Beaufort signed a letter defending Niels Christensen Sr. as a "good citizen of Beaufort for thirty-five years . . . a man of industry and fair dealing and one of the largest taxpayers in the county." The letter was signed by the camp commander, Lt. Colonel Joseph O'Hear Sanders, as well as a number of Confederate veterans, including Judge Thomas Grimke White, S. H. Rodgers, B. C. Adams, S. M. Key, and R. R. Sams, among others. Old Dr. Henry Middleton Stuart refused to endorse the letter because Captain Niels Christensen "was conspicuous in Reconstruction times with [James M.] Crofut as a Negro leader."[12] Niels Christensen Jr.'s senate campaign conjured up all the old memories of Civil War and Reconstruction. The rumors were calculated to end Christensen's political career, but in Beaufort County, most of its citizens, even its prominent white citizens, were Union veterans, not former Confederates.

The Democratic primary campaign of 1904 was a whirlwind affair. It lasted less than three weeks and was over by the end of August. Young Niels Christensen was a dervish of activity. He stayed on the road visiting every community on the mainland. He traveled by rail, steamboat, and horseback. Every rural community had several clients of the N. Christensen and Sons lumber and hardware businesses. Christensen pressed his customers into political service and developed his own countywide patronage network. When he attacked the corruption of the Tillmanite political machine in general, and specifically the dispensary system, he hit a popular chord with Beaufort County voters. By 1904 the Tillman machine in Beaufort County was suffering under the weight of more than a decade of accumulated grievances. Nearly every family had personal stories or resentments to which Christensen's reform campaign appealed.

While Christensen stayed on the campaign trail, his younger brother Frederick kept supporters in Beaufort up to date on all campaign activities. Christensen's hardware store was their campaign headquarters. Frederick recorded that his job was to "keep in touch with his workers in town, mail out circulars" and promote his brother's candidacy at home.

Niels Christensen Jr.'s final campaign stop was a speech at the county courthouse in Beaufort on August 28, the day before the primary election. A large crowd attended, and some of Thomas Talbird's supporters got "tanked up" and tried to interrupt the proceedings. Frederick confessed to his diary that he did not expect his brother to win: "The other side seems confident, they allow us only 60–70 votes in town . . . [W. J.] Thomas thinks the town is split and Niels has the edge in the county."

Indeed, the town was split. The old southern families supported Talbird, while the commercial elite was divided. In Beaufort there were still a number of African American professionals and businessmen who could not be denied the right to vote based on any fair literacy or property test. They were all behind Christensen. Some white Beaufortonians such as William Keyserling and Henry Scheper, Christensen's natural allies, were supporting Thomas Talbird.

When the vote was tallied, W. J. Thomas's assessment proved accurate. Christensen won the primary election by ninety to one hundred votes across the county. Talbird won by five votes in Beaufort but Christensen outpolled him by twenty votes in Grahamville and Tomotley, twelve votes in Hardeeville, and just as narrowly in Bluffton and Port Royal. It was a watershed election for Beaufort County because it broke the back of Tillman's local "dispensary ring. " In addition to Niels Christensen's victory, James Rhett (county treasurer), Hal Pollitzer (county auditor), and S. H. Rodgers (school commissioner) all won salaried county positions, "thus beating all of the 'ring' candidates."

This was the election also that made Jim Eddie McTeer sheriff of Beaufort County for the first time. J. E. McTeer Sr. served three terms before his death in 1926, when his son replaced him. When J. E. McTeer Jr. became sheriff, he was twenty-two years old, the youngest county sheriff in the United States. He remained Beaufort County sheriff for the next thirty-seven years. The McTeers, father and son, were sheriffs of Beaufort County for nearly fifty years. Their legends abound to this day.

When the tally was announced, Christensen supporters formed a parade. According to one account, "As soon as the vote was taken the boys hired a band . . . they formed at the Gazette, marched up Bay Street to the Commercial Club and played 'Picked Poor Robin Clean.'" The group assembled at the Sea Island Hotel to celebrate. Some of Talbird's supporters formed a counterdemonstration and "yelled for Talbird."[13]

Because of the unique power given to state senators by the Constitution of 1895, Christensen's election was the most important local election of 1904. A commercial entrepreneur and owner of the *Beaufort Gazette,* Christensen held office for twenty years. Early in his career he was close to the African American leadership of Beaufort County and a regular visitor to the Prince Street home of Robert Smalls. Even in the age of Jim Crow, Senator Christensen saw himself as the white patron of Beaufort's declining black citizenship. His mother would have tolerated nothing less. Niels Christensen was a child of Reconstruction and a descendant of Beaufort County's great social revolution. Many of his most influential constituents shared the same heritage.

While he was an eccentric public figure in the state, he was quite traditional for Beaufort County. He cobbled together an alliance of blacks and whites, northerners and southerners, rural and urban interests, and made it work for two decades. He was Beaufort County's last fusionist politician. Later in his career, he followed the white Democratic Party line.

When Christensen entered the senate he found allies in the progressive wing of the Democratic Party, which was emerging as a powerful force in the state. For the next seventy years, South Carolina politics divided between populist Democrats led by Ben Tillman, Coleman Blease, and "Cotton Ed" Smith and progressive Democrats led by Governors Duncan Clinch Heyward, Martin Ansel, Laurence I. Manning, and, of course, the incomparable James F. Byrnes, whose first congressional seat in 1910 included Beaufort County. Like all good New South politicians, Christensen struggled to promote economic development in an age of decline. He brought home many local improvements, mostly bridges and highways, of historic importance to twentieth-century Beaufort County.

Once elected, Niels Christensen made good on his promise to reform the state dispensary system. In Columbia he found many other progressives whose constituents were fed up with dispensary corruption. Governor Duncan Clinch Heyward of Colleton County, the last of the legendary Combahee River rice planters, called for dispensary reform in his 1905 annual message to the General Assembly. The legislature passed a joint resolution that established an investigating committee with broad power to examine all aspects of the state dispensary. Senator Christensen was chosen for this powerful and high-profile committee. The senior senator, James Thornwell

Hay of Kershaw County, was made chairman. The committee divided into three subcommittees to investigate the dispensary leadership, as well as the accounting, inventory, and operations of the county dispensaries. Christensen was assigned to the subcommittee to investigate the county dispensaries. His partner was young Representative J. Fraser Lyon of Abbeville, later attorney general of South Carolina. Both men became well known statewide because of their committee work. The results of this investigation were submitted to the General Assembly in July 1905 and widely covered by the South Carolina press. The *Beaufort Gazette* published the committee's complete report. The corruption that everyone suspected was revealed. The *Gazette* also published Senator Tillman's lengthy defense of the system. Despite Tillman's last-ditch appeal, the 1906 election returned Senator Christensen to office and a thoroughly anti-dispensary legislature. Beaufort's house members—William H. Niver of Parris Island, Joseph C. Bailey of Okatie, and R. R. Legare of Beaufort—unanimously opposed the dispensary. The Hampton County delegation—Senator W. Sidney Smith and Representatives Julius P. Youmans and Grafton Geddes Dowling—also opposed the dispensary. When the General Assembly convened in 1907, the state dispensary was doomed. The Carey-Cothran Bill, one of the General Assembly's first tasks, was signed into law on February 16, 1907. It closed the state dispensary and allowed each county to choose whether it wished to continue a county dispensary or to go "dry." By 1909 only six counties retained their dispensaries for the legal sale of alcohol: Charleston, Richland, Aiken, Florence, Georgetown, and, of course, Beaufort.[14] The rest of the state had gone dry.

Beaufort County operated its local dispensary from 1907 to 1916. The local "non-political" dispensary board comprised Dr. M. G. Elliott of Beaufort, merchant and truck farmer H. G. Burckmeyer of Port Royal, and J. S. Graves of Bluffton. Later, Hal Pollitzer was longtime chairman of the board. All were friends of Senator Niels Christensen. Dispensary offices were located in Beaufort, Port Royal, Yemassee, Ridgeland, and Bluffton. To make the county dispensary system work, local law enforcement had to conduct a "special sweep" in 1907 to close down all the blind tiger operations. Between April and July 1907, L. S. Densler of Port Royal, Tom Eaton on Parris Island, E. B. Boyd at Hardeeville, R. F. Fraser at Pocotaligo, S. J. Hazel on St. Helena Island, and W. I. Allen, George Williams and D. A. Stradley in Beaufort were arrested for bootlegging. Christensen supported strict enforcement of the county dispensary laws even though that position was unpopular. Some thought his strict values would cost him the 1908 election, but he won again.

The most famous dispensary case during these years involved a man named Jim Solomons, a "liquor drummer" from Columbia who peddled liquor to the county dispensaries. While in Beaufort County in 1907, he was arrested for taking a bribe, thus violating a clause of the antigraft provision of the Carey-Cothran Act. Solomons was well known in the state, and Attorney General J. Fraser Lyon wanted him locked up. He stood trial in Beaufort before Judge Thomas Grimke White. Solomons was defended by former state senator Thomas Talbird, adding a political flavor to the trial. Judge White ruled against the opinion of Attorney General Lyons and let Solomons go, stating that "what he did, did not constitute a bribe." Thus county dispensary laws proved as difficult to enforce as the state laws had been. In fact, late in 1907 St. Helena Island petitioned to be a separate municipal corporation "solely for the purpose of establishing a dispensary on St. Helena Island." The petition asked that the town center be established at the oyster factory on Edings Creek. Opponents wanted to move the town center to the Frogmore Post Office near the Brick Church and Penn School. The municipality was never formed, but blind tigers flourished on St. Helena Island and liquor was readily available. From 1907 to 1916, the county dispensary netted about $16,000 per year in public revenue. After paying W. E. Campbell, clerk for the board his annual salary of $1,100, the salaries of three special constables ($943 per year for each), and $1,346 in travel expenses, the remainder was locally distributed as listed below.

Beaufort County	$3,824
Beaufort County Schools	$3,824
Town of Beaufort	$2,056
Town of Port Royal	$452
Town of Yemassee	$500
Town of Ridgeland	$464
Town of Bluffton	$228[15]

Georgia adopted complete Prohibition in 1907, and that was big news in Beaufort. In 1914 a Prohibition committee formed to promote a statewide referendum on the issue in South Carolina. J. Fraser Lyon was executive director. In 1915 South Carolina held a referendum on Prohibition, and its proponents won in a landslide. Even Beaufort County finally returned a majority in favor of Prohibition. On January 1, 1916, the whole state went dry. Two years later, South Carolina became the fourth state in the nation to ratify the Eighteenth Amendment.[16]

"THE LITTLE BREACH IN BEAUFORT": RACE POLITICS, 1908–1916

The years before World War I saw race politics reach its peak as the Democratic Party worked tirelessly to enforce the voting restrictions of the Constitution of 1895. In 1908 Senator Tillman recommended that the General Assembly repeal the Fifteenth Amendment, one of the constitutional bedrocks of the Reconstruction era. In 1913 Representative Frederick Williams of Pickens offered a concurrent resolution asking the U.S. Congress to repeal the Fifteenth Amendment on the grounds that "the Negro . . . has given the United States only anxiety, strife, bloodshed and hookworm." The resolution passed the house 70 to 46. Perhaps some black South Carolinians took comfort to learn that Frederick Williams committed suicide on July 20, 1913.[17]

In April 1908 the Beaufort County Republican Party held its convention in Beaufort. Fifty-five delegates attended. They chose George A. Reed as chairman, former state senator Samuel Green as convention chairman, and the venerable Robert Smalls as permanent, honorary party chairman. Smalls, Reed, and Isaac Myers were elected delegates to the state convention, if one were to be called. Beaufort Republicans demonstrated their awareness of national civil rights issues when Beaufort attorney Julius I. Washington offered a resolution of thanks to Senator Joseph B. Foraker, Republican of Ohio, for his lone, courageous support of the black army regiment that had been court-marshaled en masse for the infamous 1906 riot in Brownsville, Texas.

Beaufort's black Republicans exerted their influence with the town council to get Caesar Brown elected marshal in 1908. Brown was the last in a long line of African American police chiefs stretching back to 1878. The following year Brown was replaced as town marshal by L. B. Simpson, the first white town marshal in thirty years. Simpson was a U.S. Army sergeant recently discharged from the garrison at Fort Fremont. The town council justified the change to the black community by asserting that the four hundred marines on nearby Parris Island necessitated a white town marshal. The town council reportedly encountered "no opposition to the change from the colored citizens who acquiesced in it."[18]

Factionalism and rivalry among local white Democrats allowed black Republicans to use their swing votes to influence municipal politics for a few more years. That factionalism divided Democrats into supporters and opponents of Senator Christensen. The senator had steadily gained influence since his election in 1904. He served on the Senate Finance Committee for seventeen years (1905–1922) and was its chairman from 1914 to 1922. Under South Carolina's constitution, that post made Christensen second only to the governor in his personal power. This made him many friends across the state. But in Beaufort the Christensens were always a bit controversial. Christensen's mother, Abbie Holmes Christensen, was an old abolitionist who never abandoned her reformist impulses. The family had been Republican until Niels Christensen Jr. became politically active as a Democrat. His lineage made Christensen permanently suspect to the populist wing of the Democratic Party.

The factions in Beaufort were complicated and fluid, but the opposition generally centered on Thomas Talbird, former senator and Tillmanite leader. Political rivalries were also fueled by business competition. The Christensens were closely associated with the new Beaufort Bank founded by Walter E. Richardson in 1908. The bank built a new building in front of the Waterhouse cotton gin at the west end of Bay Street in 1910. George Waterhouse Jr. was the bank chairman for several years. Richardson's bank was the rival of the older People's Bank founded by F.W. Scheper in 1903, of which the Scheper brothers and George Holmes were the principal stockholders. William F. Marscher was cashier and chief operating officer. These influential Beaufortonians usually aligned with the anti-Christensen faction, even though they, like the Christensens and Waterhouses, descended from northern or immigrant roots. Also, many of the old southern families such as J. M. Rhett, R. R. Legare and W. J. Thomas were Christensen allies even though they had strong southern family connections.[19]

In 1910 these factions split the city's Democratic Party machine. At the April meeting of the Beaufort Democratic Club, George Beckett, a young lawyer from Savannah, introduced a motion limiting the Democratic primary for municipal elections only to those who voted the straight Democratic ticket in all elections: municipal, county, state, and national contests. This motion was specifically aimed at Frederick Christensen and other former Republicans who often split their votes between local and national elections. The motion was defeated by the entrenched Christensen faction. In response, the minority bolted the party organization and formed a rival club called Beaufort Democratic Club No. 2. The leaders of this rival faction were George Beckett, Thomas Talbird, County Supervisor J. S. Claghorn, and Beaufort mayor W. F. Sanders. Other members were Gus Sanders, E. W. Bailey, S. C. Cunningham, J. M. Baker, and W. H. Steinmeyer. This opposition faction even started its own newspaper, the *Beaufort Democrat,* to rival the *Beaufort Gazette.* The principal financial backers of the new newspaper were H. E. Scheper and F.W. Scheper. H. E. Scheper said that he hoped "it would only be a short time before we succeed in putting the Gazette out of business."

The leaders of Beaufort Democratic Club No. 1 were Niels Christensen Jr., Hal Pollitzer, S. H. Rodgers, J. M. Rhett, R. R. Legare, W. R. Eve, and Dave Mittle. What energized this split among the Beaufort white establishment was the upcoming off-year municipal election in January 1911. Mayor W. F. Sanders had defeated R. R. Legare in 1909 by getting all the black Republican votes and a minority of the white Democratic votes. The irony of this factionalism was that the group that employed the African American vote to swing the election in their favor was the more populist and hard-right Democratic faction. As the *Beaufort Gazette* editorialized, "This is perhaps the only town in the state in which Republicans hold the balance of power."

The solution to this state of affairs, according to Beaufort Democratic Club No. 1, was to establish an all-white Democratic primary for municipal elections just as those for state and county elections. The all-white Democratic primary, along with control of all the county election boards, was the principal device by which white Democrats controlled state politics. However, the city of Beaufort had never established a primary system. Hence, according to the *Gazette,* the result was that "for years there have been no primaries. White candidates for Intendant . . . have fought each other in the election and . . . the one who controlled the Negro vote won. . . . whites versus whites and the Negro [was] the deciding factor." The answer was to establish a municipal primary and force all the Democrats to support the winners. But as long as the Democrats were split, no primary would be organized.[20]

As the election approached in January 1911, the black Republicans hastily organized a convention to unify their votes. The 1911 municipal election pitted Intendant W. F. Sanders against the Democratic establishment candidate R. R. Legare, who was backed by Niels Christensen Jr. James Riley was chairman of the Republican convention held on January 4, 1911. Thirty-one African American delegates attended. As expected, they nearly unanimously nominated W. F. Sanders for reelection as mayor. Their reasons for supporting a white Democrat were that Sanders led the party faction that opposed the municipal primary and had bolted from the party establishment. According to the Republican convention, W. F. Sanders "had declared himself to favor leaving the ballot with the Negro voter and nipping in the bud a scheme to foist white primaries on the town; the Negro voters should give him their hearty support next Monday."

The nomination was formally made by delegate George Lawton and seconded by former town marshal Ben Houston. In Houston's seconding speech, he said he had been voting since 1876 and that "we have the privilege of coming to this hall because Mr. Sanders . . . formed Club #2. He took an obligation to give us the ballot. Mr. Sanders is willing to do what is right . . . he should have our support." Convention secretary W. B. Rivers said, "A certain class of men have tried to take our vote away from us and Mr. Sanders . . . jumped in and saved our vote for us. We ought to work for him and vote for him." Delegate H. G. Fisher stated that "he had tried to break away from Mr. Sanders but couldn't stand the other man. When the most important thing we possess, the ballot, is about to be taken away from us and we know Mr. Sanders has taken a stand to preserve our ballots . . . I stand for his endorsement."

When the convention voted, it supported W. F. Sanders for reelection by a vote of 27–4. One of the four votes against the nomination was that of Town Warden Edward Wallace who represented Ward 5. In spite of his opposition to the convention majority, the convention endorsed Wallace to return to the town council. After the convention, however, they placed C. A. Andrews on the ballot. The Republican convention also endorsed M. W.

Hare, a white man, for Ward 3; John H. Stevenson, a white man, for Ward 4; and J. H. Dixon, a black man, for Ward 6.

The united black Republicans scored a partial victory. W. F. Sanders defeated R. R. Legare 155–104. The 86 black votes cast clearly decided the election for Sanders. In addition, John Stevenson won in Ward 4, and C. A. Andrews, the only black warden on the town council, won in Ward 5. In Ward 6, a predominantly black district, E. D. Raney, a white Democrat outpolled black Republican J. H. Dixon 14 votes to 11. Raney was the first white man to represent Ward 6 in thirty years. Nevertheless, all but two of the candidates endorsed by the Republican convention won their races.

The election of 1911 was a disappointment for the Christensen faction. Not only had they lost most of their races but Frederick Christensen was also defeated for reelection as warden from Ward 1 by W. M. Steinmeyer. Niels Christensen's response was immediate. On the editorial page of the *Beaufort Gazette,* he declared his support for an all-white local Democratic primary. He pointed out that Beaufort had 204 registered white voters and only 96 registered black voters, and yet divisions among the white Democrats had allowed the Republican minority to control municipal elections for two consecutive election cycles. Christensen contended that Beaufort's reputation was harmed by the lingering influence of the black vote. Strangers would ask, he claimed, "Why, I understand you folks down there are dominated by the Negro Republican." The answer, in Christensen's view, was to institute a white primary: "Give us Democratic primaries in the town of Beaufort and you will never have cause to be ashamed of having a truthful report of a municipal election wired to the daily papers."[21]

Indeed, the statewide Democratic power structure was watching city politics in Beaufort. The town was the only government that still had blacks in office. A national election was approaching in 1912, and southern Democrats felt they had a good chance of unseating President William Howard Taft, a Republican. The last thing they wanted was a resurgence of the black Republican Party in South Carolina. During the political excitement in the fall of 1912, the two Democratic factions in Beaufort united not only to back the presidential candidacy of Woodrow Wilson but also to establish an all-white primary for the municipal elections scheduled for January 1913. On October 10, 1912, Beaufort Democratic Clubs Nos. 1 and 2 met to bury the hatchet and plan their all-white primary. During the next week the two clubs canvassed all the Democratic voters in Beaufort and determined that 80 percent of them favored a municipal primary.

On Monday, October 28, 1912, the clubs held a joint meeting at the arsenal. They merged their leadership and formed a single Beaufort Democratic Club. The president and secretary of the new club were from the Christensen faction, or Club No. 1, while the two vice presidents were from the opposition Club No. 2. All members agreed to have a municipal primary in December and pledged to abide by the result. The officers of the new Beaufort Democratic Club were W. J. Thomas, president; W. H. Steinmeyer, first vice president; Gus Sanders, second vice president; and George Waterhouse Jr., secretary.

When the primary was held in December 1912, the Democratic nominees for municipal offices were former mayor C. C. Townsend for mayor, R. A. Long for commissioner of public works, Sam Paul for Ward 1, Charles Cohen for Ward 2, T. H. Harms for Ward 3, George Tucker for Ward 4, A. L. Gage for Ward 5, and E. D. Raney for Ward 6. The black Republicans offered opposition only in Wards 5 and 6.

The municipal election was held on Monday, January 13, 1913. The Democrats swept the ticket. C. C. Townsend was elected mayor and Sam Paul, Charles Cohen, T. H. Harms, George Tucker, E. D. Raney, and A. L. Gage were elected wardens. In Ward 5, A. L. Gage defeated Ed Wallace twenty-one votes to nine, and in Ward 6, E. D. Raney defeated W. H. Washington sixteen votes to ten. The *Beaufort Gazette* crowed, "For the first time in many years the town council will be composed of all white men."[22]

The city election of 1913 was a milestone in the political history of the state. It was the end of the last mixed-race government in South Carolina. The white Democratic Party had finally purged the state of the last vestige of Reconstruction. Black Republicans had controlled the state from 1868 to 1877. They had ruled Beaufort County from 1868 to 1888. And through fusion compromises and shifting alliances, they had managed to elect black Republican officials to state, county, and municipal offices from 1888 to 1913. Perhaps it was fitting that the last Republican stronghold in the state had been Beaufort, where the party had begun fifty years earlier.

While the municipal election was playing itself out, the nation, too, was enacting its own political revolution. Nineteen twelve was the year Woodrow Wilson was first elected president of the United States. Except for Grover Cleveland, Wilson was the first Democrat in the White House since the Civil War. The Democrats also won majorities in both houses of Congress. It was the first time since 1860 that Democrats controlled both the executive and legislative branches of the national government. Nearly a half century of Republican ascendancy concluded, and the Progressive Era in national politics had begun. The effects of the election of 1912 resounded all the way to the local level.

When the 1912 campaign opened in Beaufort County, the black Republicans were initially enthusiastic. They convened what was called the "Beaufort County Regular Republican Convention" on October 22 in "the Hall on Greene Street." Sixty-three delegates attended and James Riley was again elected party chairman. The *Beaufort Gazette* remarked, "It was the most representative gathering of Republicans held here for many years. Many young men attended for the first time." The convention nominated a "full county ticket" as follows:

State Senator:	B. H. Houston
State Representatives:	F. F. Jones
	A. Williams
Clerk of Court:	A. C. Reynolds
Sheriff:	C. H. Heyward
County Supervisor:	James Riley
Superintendent of Education:	W. S. Dudley
Coroner:	W. I. Allen

Finally, the Beaufort County Republicans endorsed William Howard Taft for reelection. At first it appeared there might actually be a contest in Beaufort County. Niels Christensen reminded all Democrats of their duty to vote. He pointed out that the 1908 election had returned a mere fifty-four-vote majority in the national election. Unless every Democrat voted, he said, "there is always the danger that Republicans will elect." But the 1912 election was a crushing and demoralizing defeat for Republicans. Not one of their local candidates was elected. William Howard Taft won only two states, Vermont and Utah, and garnered a mere four electoral votes.

The ballots were barely counted before the seismic shift in federal government patronage reached the local level. Throughout the long Republican ascendancy, black Republicans in South Carolina had maintained a semblance of authority by clinging to federal patronage jobs. In Beaufort in 1912, the most prominent of those were Customs Collector Robert Smalls, Deputy Collector Julius I. Washington, and Postmaster George Reed. Before the end of November, Beaufort's congressman, Jimmy Byrnes, was maneuvering to shift these federal patronage jobs to his Democratic supporters. Byrnes wanted W. F. Colcock to replace Smalls as collector. He also wanted Edward D. Raney to replace Postmaster Reed. By early December 1912, Beaufortonians learned that those seeking offices with the customs or postal service should apply to Congressman Byrnes. Those seeking appointment as U.S. attorney or U.S. marshal should apply to Senator Tillman. These were high-paying jobs for Beaufort. The collector received eighty dollars per month, and his assistant, who did most of the work, was paid ninety dollars per month. By 1912 there was barely enough maritime traffic in Beaufort or Port Royal to cover the expenses of the office. But with Beaufort's economy in decline, there was no dearth of applicants. The postmaster's job was the real plumb. It paid eighteen hundred dollars per year.

In the waning days of the Taft administration, the president issued an executive order placing all local postmaster jobs under the U.S. Civil Service, thus fixing in place all Republican political appointees. The South Carolina congressional delegation lobbied President-elect Wilson to rescind Taft's lame-duck order and open up those numerous small-town appointments to loyal Democrats. They urged Wilson to swift action "for the reason that in the South this opens wide the door to Negroes and they believe this order was issued for the purpose of perpetuating Republicans in office." Wilson complied with their wishes. Smalls, Washington, and Reed lost their jobs.

Robert Smalls had held the collectorship for twenty years. When he finally gave up the post, he wrote a letter of thanks to Booker T. Washington, the renowned black leader and educator, who had intervened on Small's behalf in the waning days of the Taft administration. Smalls wrote in part:

> I . . . feel gratified to know that I have . . . so conducted my office with the assistance of my competent deputy, for all these years and have not had a single complaint. . . . During the twenty odd years I have held the position of Collector, I have succeeded to so manage affairs that when I leave it, I will do so with credit to myself, my family and the Race. . . . When we go out of office, we go clean. So when the excellent history of . . . the Negro shall be written, the Customs House at Beaufort, while conducted by colored men, can be easily attached . . . for whatever inspiration it may be to the race.[23]

It was ironic that these last blows against the old Republican ascendancy were delivered by two of the state's best-known progressives. Niels Christensen Jr. was a leader of the progressive Democrats for twenty years; yet he engineered the all-white municipal primary that ended the last mixed-race government in South Carolina. Congressman Jimmy Byrnes, who as U.S senator, Supreme Court justice, and President Harry Truman's secretary of state, became a famous New Dealer and, consequently, the most influential South Carolinian of the twentieth century. However, in 1913 he struck the final blow against the last African American officeholders in Beaufort County.

Beaufort's progressives had one last task to accomplish to ensure that black Republicans would never have influence again. Their plan nearly backfired. In 1915 the progressive Democrats wanted to replace the old town charter, with its single-member wards, with the more modern and efficient "council-manager" form of municipal government. The voters would elect a mayor (no longer the old intendant) and two town councilmen. All these positions would be elected at-large, thus disbanding the old wards. At-large elections would also eliminate any possibility that black voters could elect their own neighborhood representatives. The mayor and council would hire a professional manager to direct the police, fire department, and public works department and oversee the daily operations of the municipality. To alter the town charter, the voters had to approve the change in a referendum scheduled for April 14, 1915.

Not everyone in Beaufort favored the change. Such a plan limited the day-to-day authority of the mayor and eliminated municipal fiefdoms such as public works. By this time the City of Beaufort had a municipal water system with an elevated tank on Prince Street and a municipal electric system with a steam-generating plant at the railroad depot. Both provided revenue to the town government. The opposition was led by former mayor W. R. Bristol, a Bay Street jeweler, and by Public Works Commissioner R. A. Long. The council-manager form of government was also demonstrably less democratic. Beaufort's black voters almost unanimously opposed it.

The referendum question was first put before the all-white Democratic primary, where it won a strong majority, encouraged by Senator Niels Christensen Jr. The Democrats pledged to abide by the results of the primary, but a fair number of them bolted the party and voted with the black Republicans. In 1915 the city of Beaufort had 298 "qualified voters." Of these, 231 were white Democrats, and 67 were black Republicans. Eighty-two percent of "qualified voters" voted, but the new town charter to create the commission government barely won. Only 102 voters favored the new charter while 89 voters opposed it. Only 46 black voters participated and all voted against the commission government plan. They were joined by 43 white Democratic bolters. If all the eligible black voters had participated, they would have won the election 110 to 102. The results and their implications alarmed the white Democrats and briefly revitalized Beaufort's black Republicans.

When the municipal commission government began during the summer of 1915, Charles E. Danner was elected mayor. Walter Richardson of the Beaufort Bank and W. F. Marsher of the People's Bank were chosen councilmen. They hired R. C. Horne, a well-qualified professional from the upcountry, as the first town manager. In reviewing the town's finances, Horne discovered that several prominent citizens and major town businesses had not been paying their fair share of municipal taxes for several years. According to his calculations, they owed the city considerable sums in back taxes. Horne aggressively pursued these tax evaders. The most prominent was the People's Bank, whose chief operating officer was Councilman Marscher. When Horne and Police Chief Dan Mann went to the bank to present the town's bill, Marscher locked the door in their face. Another prominent tax deadbeat was George Holmes, who lived in the George Parsons Elliott House. He sued the city for defamation and hired Thomas Talbird to represent him.

This donnybrook was widely covered by the *Beaufort Gazette,* and many citizens demanded full restitution from the wealthy and privileged tax evaders. A hasty meeting of the new town council was called and their response to the affair was to fire R. C. Horne. Mayor Danner sided with Marscher to let Horne go. Walter Richardson voted to keep him. It appeared that the old factions of Beaufort's establishment were still at work.

By this time, the whole town was outraged and demanded a recall election of the mayor and town council. The election was set for September 28, 1915, and Town Clerk R. R. Legare, a Christensen ally, led the opposition to Danner and the council. Once again, the white Democrats of Beaufort were dividing against themselves.

Mayor Danner and Councilman Marscher made an unabashed appeal to black voters and outraged the whole Democratic establishment. On September 22, 1915, the Colored Progressive Club met in the "largest Negro society hall in the city." A large crowd turned out to hear the leaders of Beaufort's black community urge them to vote to retain Mayor Danner and Councilman W. F. Marscher in the recall election the following week. George Reed, Reverend Daniel Bythewood, Julius I. Washington, B. H. Houston, Dr. N. J. Kennedy, and Reverend BenChavis gave speeches supporting the incumbents. One speaker was forced to deny publicly a rumor that he was being paid five hundred dollars to work against the recall. Another rumor circulated in the black community "that whites from the upcountry would come down on election-day and prevent them from voting."

The night before the election, a second "enthusiastic meeting of colored voters" was held to "impress on every member the importance of voting for Messrs. Danner and Marscher on the next day," according to the *Beaufort Gazette.* The Colored Progressive Club, the president of which was Julius I. Washington, also organized this meeting. The *Gazette* had accused Washington of currying favor with Danner and Marscher "with a view of getting offices." He vehemently denied the accusation. The Colored Progressive Club forcefully asserted that they were acting on the most basic political principle. Several speakers "urged that this was an opportunity that may never come again and the Negroes should stand together and vote for those who want their vote and against those who do not want them." On Tuesday, September 28, 1915, they stood together. With the help of a solid black vote, Danner and Marscher survived the recall election.[24]

This election attracted considerable attention and even elicited a comment from Governor Richard I. Manning. The *Charleston News and Courier* editorialized on September 11 that the open appeal to black voters was a threat to white rule: "The report that in the recall election which has been ordered in the town of Beaufort, one of the political factions is seeking to break down the Democratic primary, will excite grave apprehension throughout South Carolina among all those who recollect conditions as they were before the Negro vote was eliminated as a political factor in the state." Beaufort County was still overwhelmingly black, and divisions among white voters would permit blacks to control the balance of power. "But the Democrats of South Carolina have a right to expect that white men in Beaufort calling themselves Democrats shall respect the machinery which the party has established for the express purpose of maintaining white supremacy in South Carolina," the newspaper declared.

More candid commentary regarding Beaufort's black voters appeared in Columbia's *State* newspaper: "The primary in South Carolina is a white primary. Its purpose is to place the election of public officers exclusively in the hands of white voters. It strips Negroes of political power effectually, so long as it is maintained and qualified Negro electors are in a minority, it lawfully renders the 'war amendments' enfranchising the Negroes practically null and void. It enables the white men of South Carolina to snap their fingers at the amendments." The *State* described the "little breach in Beaufort" as a threat to the "whole line of white men's political defenses" in every possible election.

After Beaufort's black voters swung the recall election in their favor, the *News and Courier* weighed in with a warning against "the very mistaken idea that the Negro has permanently laid aside political ambitions. The only reason the Negro is out of power is because the white people of the South by their absolute concert of action have made it unprofitable and futile for him to be in politics. There are thousands of Negroes in South Carolina who are eager for the opportunity to get into politics." Former governor John Gary Evans of Spartanburg, chairman of the state Democratic Party, wrote a letter to Niels Christensen Jr. that was printed in bold type on the front page of the *Beaufort Gazette.* The letter was intended to exert party discipline over Beaufort's wayward Democrats: "White men, who are confronted at the polls with Negro domination, as you are in Beaufort, should certainly pull together and never divide on any question that will give the Negro the balance of power. . . . White supremacy in this state can only be maintained by the strong determination on the part of white citizens to stand by and maintain the white primaries."

Even Governor Richard I. Manning, the most progressive Democrat of his generation, felt it necessary to comment on the "little breach" and to reinforce his commitment to ironclad white supremacy: "I believe in the rule of the white people. I do not feel it is proper for the governor to meddle in local politics as a rule, but in this particular the situation presents a very grave and serious question. The Democratic Party stands for white supremacy and to use the Negro vote in the election among Democrats is setting a very dangerous precedent for all future time. Personally, under no circumstances, would I accept a nomination or election to any office at the hands of the Negro."[25]

While the Democratic Party was extinguishing the last vestiges of black rule in the state, Beaufort's Bay Street businessmen understood the necessity for cordial race relations at home. When the new chamber of commerce established its permanent working committees, one of the most important was the committee on "Race Co-operation." Some of Beaufort's most important citizens agreed to serve on this committee. W. J. Thomas was chairman. C. R. Paul, W. G. Morrall, R. V. Bray, and Sam Levin were members. They expressed their sincere interest in promoting racial harmony in Beaufort by inviting a leading black merchant, George Watson, to serve with them. Despite such expressions of "race co-operation," the city of Beaufort imposed an all-white police force in 1916. The *Beaufort Gazette* trumpeted the news: "All white police force . . . for the first time since the war, the regular police force of Beaufort is made up entirely of white citizens." The chief of police was Dan Mann and the patrolmen were J. B. Evans and W. H. Lubkin. By 1916 there was only one mixed-race institution in the city of Beaufort, the fire department, which was composed of three volunteer companies, one white and two black. The fire chief was Dave Mittle, and the assistant chief was William G. Kinghorn. The white company was the Washington Fire Company, and their foreman was Harry Danner. The black companies were the Pioneer Fire Company and the Hook and Ladder Company, the foremen of which were, respectively, George Morrison and Peter Gantt.[26] With that much-reduced exception, Beaufort County's government and politics were lily white.

Chapter 6

Social Institutions in the Victorian Age

Beaufort's white society reached a certain peak of wealth and culture as the nineteenth century came to a close. Several civic and cultural institutions, some of which have survived more than a century later, represented the intellectual aspirations and social expectations of the second generation after the war. These institutions helped overcome the political and personal animosities that the Civil War and Reconstruction had spawned. But even in the second generation, every Beaufortonian knew who was descended from Yankees and who was descended from "secesh." Beaufort's northern and southern white families cooperated, socialized, and even intermarried, but occasionally old biases surfaced among the children of the veterans.

One enduring institution was the Clover Club. The Clover Club was founded in December 1891 by Mary Waterhouse, eldest daughter of George Waterhouse. The club's purpose was intellectual stimulation for young ladies "similar to some of the college clubs of the North." They met once a week for "singing, reading, piano playing and other exercises." Thirteen young women made up the original membership. They were Miss Mary Waterhouse, Miss Reed, Miss Saunders, Miss Wilson, Miss Givens, Miss Scheper, Miss Hay, Miss Fuller, Miss Richmond, Miss Mitchell, Mrs. George Gage, Mrs. Charles Danner, and Mrs. W. R. Bristol. Mrs. W. R. Bristol was elected the first president of the Clover Club and retained that position for the first quarter century of the club's existence. The clover was chosen as their symbol because it represented "unity, harmony and simplicity." The original membership contained a mix of descendants of northern and southern families, and the local paper noted that "three states are represented in the club, Miss Richmond from New Jersey, Miss Mitchell from Pennsylvania and Miss Saunders from New York." Throughout the 1890s, the Clover Club remained the arbiter of Beaufort's white female society. By 1903 they were meeting monthly. By then Mrs. J. R. Macdonald, Mrs. R. K. Harley, Mrs. E. E. Legnick, Orrie Dale, Mabel Burn, Winnie Christensen, and Bessie Kinghorn had been added to the club. In December 1903 the monthly meeting was held at the east Bay Street home of Mary and Jane Waterhouse. Mrs. R. K. Harley and Miss Mary Waterhouse presented two papers on German history. Agnes and Marie Scheper performed a piano duet, and a social hour followed with cake, chocolate, and confectionary.[1]

The Clover Club sponsored civic activities that bore fruit in the new century. By 1903 the club had collected books for a circulating library in donated space above Scheper's store and staffed a reading room for several hours a week.[2] This "Clover Club Circulating Library" was the beginning of the Beaufort County Public Library system, and by the end of the twentieth century, it had become a multimillion dollar public enterprise. In 1906 the club met on the first Monday of every month. In December 1906 Elizabeth Crofut, later Mrs. George Waterhouse Jr., presented a piano recital. Crofut was just back from music school in Savannah. For the next fifty years, she and her sister, Marguerite "Rita" Crofut, would teach piano and violin lessons to generations of Beaufort youngsters in the home of their father, Captain George A. Crofut, on Laurens Street.[3]

In 1903 Mary Waterhouse extended her civic activities across the state. She was elected chairman of the Committee on Civics of the South Carolina Confederation of Women's Clubs. From that position she promoted Arbor Day celebrations in public schools statewide. The poem chosen to be read by the state's school children was "The Palmetto Tree" by Julia Baker of Beaufort, a literary mentor to many of Beaufort's young women. Baker, descendant of an antebellum family, was described by the *State* newspaper as "a frail, quiet little woman living her simple life in a remote corner of the state." Her poem was published and read throughout South Carolina for many years on Arbor Day:

> The pine may rise majestic
> Flame bright the maple be
> But I praise the lone palmetto
> that stands beside the sea.
> Its green fans nodding plume-like
> In every passing gale
> It stands an ancient warrior
> All in its coat of mail.[4]

In 1892 several women resurrected the Female Benevolent Society. This organization had been chartered in 1815 by the leading women of antebellum Beaufort to aid destitute, abandoned, and sick women. When it was reorganized in 1892, women of "all religious denominations" were invited to join to establish "a shelter for worthy, aged and poor women, regardless of religious belief."[5] This ancient society remained active throughout the twentieth century.

The Ladies Civic League of Beaufort began at the turn of the century to undertake public projects for the betterment of the community. In 1905 the group asked the county sheriff to prosecute "those who cut down shade trees alongside the roads in violation of the law." They published Section 457 of the 1902 Criminal Code for South Carolina, which prohibited cutting "any tree within ten-feet of a public road . . . trees should be left standing as convenient shade for travelers." Violators were to be fined two dollars. In 1907 the Civic League put on a flower show for the community, planted trees and shrubs around the Baptist Church, planted flowers around the railroad station at the end of Depot Road, and landscaped a small park on the southeast corner of Craven and Carteret Streets.[6]

The chief men's club of the era was the Ribaut Club, begun in September 1891. While the women's organizations pursued intellectual and civic activities, the Ribault Club was entirely social. Edward Burn, W. H. Lockwood, and J. M. Legnick were the first officers of the club, and within six months they enlisted forty-five members. The group commandeered a large room over Dr. H. M. Stuart's Apothecary at the corner of West and Bay Streets that became known as Ribault Hall. This place was the center of Beaufort's white social life for nearly two decades.

On February 5, 1892, the Ribault Club put on a dramatic performance of "Our Boys" at the arsenal. Tickets were thirty-five cents each. In March the club had its first supper in its new hall, and it was deemed a great success, with "many songs and much good humor." In January 1894 the Ribault Club entertained the Clover Club with an "exchange of courtesies." The Ribault Club provided the entertainment, and the Clover Club provided the refreshments.

For many years the Clover Club and the Ribault Club jointly hosted community events. In March 1898, with the Spanish-American War looming and the Port Royal Naval Station on alert, the clubs jointly arranged a dinner at Ribault Hall for Captain C. H. Rockwell, commandant of the naval station. Mrs. Mabel Ellis Danner and Jane Waterhouse sang, accompanied by Bessie Crofut on the piano, Marguerite Crofut on the violin, and their father, George Crofut, on the cornet. The centerpiece of the occasion was Captain Rockwell's speech on the navy's plans for Port Royal Sound.[7]

Frederick Christensen was president of the Ribault Club in 1903 and 1904. The year was filled with "dances, picnics, excursions to Bay Point aboard the paddle wheelers Pilot Boy and Summer Girl, and musical entertainment." In August 1903, the Ribault Club hosted a large Monday dance with music by the Beaufort Cornet Band. Ladies in attendance were Flora

Adams, Ruth Batchelder, Marie Brown, Amy Elliott, Edna Lawton, Carrie Pollitzer, Ella Sayre, and Kate, Lucy, and Marion Emmons. Young men were Charles Bellows, W. S. Bernard, C. A. Chaplin, F. H. Christensen, J. A. Emmons, A. L. Gage, W. G. Hill, W. M. Sanders, H. E. Scheper, E. C. VanNeas, and W. E. Wood. On September 10, 1903, the Ribault Club held its twelfth anniversary card party. Bessie Kinghorn, Mrs. W. H. Hull, Elizabeth and Rita Crofut, Legare Sanders, and O'Hear Sanders, as well as Frederick Christensen, all attended.[8] These young women and men were the children and grandchildren of the merchants, financiers, and professional men who had rebuilt Beaufort after the war. They were nearly evenly divided between northern and southern families. By 1900 they were all thoroughly Beaufortonians.

Occasionally Beaufort's prosperous, insular little social world was jarred into reality by "outside" unpleasantness. One such event occurred on January 16, 1900, involving Mrs. Middleton Stuart Elliott of Charleston, the wife of the surgeon at the naval station on Parris Island. Her husband was a descendant of the Rhetts, Stuarts, and Elliotts of Beaufort and eventually became admiral and chief of the Naval Medical Corps. When the Ribault Club announced a winter dance and invited the naval officers to attend, Mrs. Elliott arranged a competing dance at the naval station. She refused to invite Beaufort's ladies and gentlemen, stating, "There are no gentlemen in the Ribault Club." According to Frederick Christensen, "The boys at the club were much exercised." They authorized their president to refuse any invitation to a naval station dance. Sam McGowan said that "if the club invites another naval station lady to a Ribault function, he'll resign!" The only Beaufort men invited to the naval station dance were Lawrence Sanders and Will Elliott. Their inclusion on this occasion was significant. Will Elliott, son of Congressman William Elliott, was Dr. Middleton Stuart Elliott's first cousin, and Lawrence Sanders was the eldest son of Colonel Joseph O'Hear Sanders, adjutant of Beaufort's Henry Middleton Stuart Camp of the United Confederate Veterans. The purpose of this social snub was to exclude the sons and daughters of Beaufort's "Yankee" merchants.[9]

The Ribault Club pressed on, and the city's unique southern society continued its happy ways. Dr. and Mrs. Middleton Stuart Elliott were soon gone, and so was the naval station. Within two years Will Elliott and his father had moved to Columbia. Congressman Elliott's failure to preserve the naval station and shipyard on Parris Island probably cost him his seat in Congress as much as congressional redistricting. On Christmas Day 1900, Lawrence Sanders married George Waterhouse's second daughter, Adelaide, uniting two of Beaufort's southern and northern families. They moved to New York, where he became an accountant and eventually vice president of the D. Appleton Century Publishing Company. The Appleton family had been the original financiers of the Port Royal and Augusta Railroad, where young Lawrence Sanders found his first job as a ticket agent. Thus, Beaufort's northern business connections continued to provide opportunities to the city's aspiring young men. Unfortunately, fewer and fewer of those opportunities were in Beaufort.

Beaufort had other significant "mixed" marriages. Perhaps the most important North-South wedding of the era was the 1880 union of Henry C. Pollitzer, son of Beaufort's merchant king Moritz Pollitzer, and Mary Elliott Guerard of Oak Forest Plantation near Bluffton. Mary Elliott Guerard was a descendant of the Huguenot immigrant Jacques Guerard and thus a member of one of South Carolina's most distinguished lowcountry families. Mary Elliott Guerard was a direct descendant of Governor Benjamin Guerard, the state's first post-Revolution governor. The Guerards had amassed great wealth before the war (328 slaves and sixteen thousand acres in 1830) but, like much of the lowcountry aristocracy, wound up with much land and no money after the war. This was a classic union of new money with old aristocracy. The wedding was held at William Porcher's Calhoun Plantation near Bluffton, and the young couple lived in "Squire" William Pope's house in Bluffton. Later they moved to 314 Charles Street. Twenty years later Hal and Mary Pollitzer's beautiful daughter Etta met Huntington Hartford, heir to the A&P grocery fortune, on a steamer sailing from New York. They married in Bluffton on June 1901. As Frederick Christensen noted, "they met on a steamer headed south [and] fell in love. . . . he is said to be very wealthy." This was Beaufort's most famous society marriage of the era, but it was not the only one.

In 1892 Annie Cornelia White of Beaufort married George Lawrence of New York at the Knickerbocker Club in New York City. Annie Cornelia White was the daughter of Beaufort's cantankerous municipal judge and proud Confederate veteran Colonel Thomas Grimke White. Groomsmen at the wedding included Lewis Morris, Gouverneur Morris, and William LeGendre. Wedding guests included Roosevelts, Stuyvesants, Winthrops, Biddles, and Lippincotts, a fair representation of New York's turn-of-the-century aristocracy.

Beaufort's social life continued its brisk pace despite the business decline. Thanksgiving Day 1906, was an exhausting example. After a midday Thanksgiving dinner, the Commerce Club organized an afternoon Ladies Day at the Pigeon Point golf links, the first golf course in the county. At 9:00 P.M. the Ribault Club hosted a Thanksgiving dance. Nearly all the members of the Ribault Club, the Clover Club, the Civic League, and Commerce Club attended. A full orchestra from Savannah provided the music, and refreshments were served at midnight. The music and dancing went on until 2:00 A.M. The popular dance of the day was a "German," consisting of intricate figures improvised and intermingled with waltzes.

By Christmas 1906 everyone had recovered sufficiently to plan an even larger holiday ball. The *Beaufort Gazette* reported that: "the hall of the Ribault Club never looked better. . . . Smilax festooned the walls, Christmas trees lined the corners of the hall." The occasion was enhanced by family reunions and college students home for the holidays. A "German" was led by Frederick Christensen and Rita Crofut. Refreshments were served at midnight. Ladies at the Christmas Ball were Marie Brown, Elizabeth and Marguerite Crofut, Orrie Dale, Carrie Duckworth, Edith Kinghorn, Edna Lawton, Marjorie McKenzie, Annie Paul, Lu Prioleau, Mary and Hammie Sanders, Nella and Omie Sanders, Julia Walker, and Annie White. Men attending were Frederick and Niels Christensen, George DeTreville, J. A. Kinghorn, William Kinghorn, William Lockwood, James O'Dell Jr., Sam Paul, Allen Paul, O'Hear Sanders, Legare Sanders, Niel Sanders, H. E. Scheper, C. Van Ness, and J. B. Walker. Even this happy occasion furnished signs of Beaufort's business decline. The day after Christmas, young George DeTreville, son of one of Beaufort's most famous antebellum families, left for Hopkinsville, Kentucky, where he had accepted a new job.[10]

Many of Beaufort's youth learned to dance from Maude O'Dell, perhaps Beaufort's most famous export at the turn of the century. Maude O'Dell was the daughter of James and Alice O'Dell, proprietors of the Sea Island Hotel. Tall, beautiful, and talented at song and dance, she was educated at Miss Kelly's Seminary in Charleston and Boston's New England Conservatory of Music. As "Tillie" O'Dell, she parlayed her talent and striking stage presence into a prominent Broadway career and a fortunate New York marriage.

Tillie O'Dell's career began in Beaufort "with pink teas and church socials." In 1892 she conducted a dancing class in Beaufort. The class met on Monday night for the two weeks before Lent. The classes were accompanied by Massey's String Band. For a few years, O'Dell had a regular dancing school in Port Royal. She would commute from Beaufort to Port Royal by horseback along the Old Shell Road. She saved three hundred dollars from her work in Beaufort and Port Royal, and by 1894 she moved to New York, where she entered the American Academy of Dramatic Arts. An introduction to Broadway producer Daniel Frohman launched her stage career. She acted in the Broadway productions of *Blue Jeans, Amazon,* and *Tobacco Road.* Tillie O'Dell married into the wealthy Doremus family of New York and moved to an estate on Long Island Sound. She moved back to Manhattan when she discovered that the steam packet from Boston woke her up every night with its whistle. She often returned to Beaufort, occasionally accompanied by her good friend Billie Burke, another Broadway star.[11]

Another institution active in the economic and civic life of Beaufort was the Commerce Club, which in 1913 became the chamber of commerce. All the Bay Street merchants were members. They were heavily involved in economic and political matters affecting the community and were always enlisted to promote schemes for local economic development. Occasionally they also sponsored community social activities. In January 1904 the Commerce Club sponsored a "Winter Masquerade Ball." The whole town turned out for the occasion, which was held at the courthouse on Bay Street. The Schepers, Pollitzers, Dales, Christensens, O'Dells, and Samses sponsored the event. Among the guests were the army officers from Fort Fremont. These men filled the social gap created by the removal of the naval station from Parris Island. These exchanges with the army garrison bore fruit when the commanding officer of Fort Fremont, Captain John Knowlton of the 16th Coast Artillery, married Julia Danner, the daughter of Bay Street merchant Charles E. Danner.

One of the grandest events of the era occurred in April 1905, when Beaufort hosted the annual state convention of the Knights of Pythias, the honorary society of the Episcopal Church. Three hundred "knights" from across the state gathered at the courthouse on Bay Street. Governor Duncan Clinch Heyward of Walterboro attended and delivered the welcoming address. Governor Heyward was introduced by J. Albert Kinghorn, chancellor and commander of Beaufort's Lodge No. 27. All of Bay Street was decorated for the occasion. The knights were entertained by the Allen Brass Band, which held an open-air concert at the Sea Island Hotel. Afterward they boarded the paddle wheeler SS *Clifton* for an excursion to Fort Fremont. There they were treated to a seventeen-gun salute for the governor and a fish supper hosted by the army garrison. In the estimation of the *Beaufort Gazette,* it was "one of the most interesting events in the history of Beaufort."[12]

Excursions like that aboard the *Clifton* were standard social features of the age. Summer excursions were almost always by boat. Sea islands and sea breezes made the summer tolerable on the water. Sometimes the excursions were by private yacht, such as the August 1903 voyage of the launch *Blanche,* a vessel belonging to William Keyserling, general manager of the Macdonald-Wilkins farm enterprises on St. Helena Island. The *Blanche* was powered by one of the new, swift, and efficient naphtha engines. The vessel was regularly used to carry passengers and cargo from Frogmore to Beaufort. William Keyserling invited a large party of Beaufortonians to "a delightful launch party" that circumnavigated Port Royal Island, visiting Benton's plantation on the Broad River, Whale Island in the Whalebranch River, Sam's Point on Lady's Island, and Old Coosaw on the Coosaw River. Women passengers aboard the *Blanche* were Hermine Scheper, Edith Calhoun, Ruth Batchelder, and Helen and Blanche Wilkins, as well as Cora Townsend, Etta Cohen, and Bessie Purse of Savannah. The men of the crew were George Wilkins Jr., Leo Calder, James O'Dell Jr., William Kinghorn, Mark Batchelder, and William Keyserling.

Larger crowds could be accommodated by chartering one of the many commercial steamboats that served the sea islands. In August 1905 the Ladies Parsonage Society of the Baptist Church of Beaufort sponsored a "moonlight excursion" aboard the SS *Summer Girl,* a steamboat owned by Charles Danner, which made regular runs between Beaufort, Port Royal, Parris Island, and Fort Fremont. The Parsonage Society's excursion went from Beaufort to Bay Point and back in time to catch the sunset and moonrise over Port Royal Sound. It cost twenty-five cents and was widely attended by "a happy crowd."[13]

During winter months, when the waters were cold and uncertain, excursions were usually carriage rides to country destinations. In 1907 George Waterhouse Jr. took a group of guests on a carriage ride from Beaufort to S. M. Benton's plantation on a bluff overlooking the Broad River. The carriage party included Elizabeth and Rita Crofut, May Elliott, Orrie Dale, Jane Waterhouse, Adelaide Waterhouse Sanders, Edward Dale, E. C. VanNess, and Frederick Christensen. Dr. and Mrs. W. R. Eve drove their carriage from their neighboring plantation to enjoy the "usual courteous hospitality" of the Benton's. The central feature of the excursion was a sea island oyster roast amid the "beautiful grove of live oaks" on the Broad River bluff.[14]

As always, the churches remained the mainstay of Beaufort's culture and society. The old Episcopal and Baptist churches recovered after the Civil War and prospered during the decades of enterprise. St. Helena Episcopal Church became the central cultural institution for antebellum families who returned to Beaufort after the war, particularly during the tenure of Reverend Joseph R. Walker, who was rector for fifty-three years. Reverend Walker's service as rector (1824–1878) spanned the antebellum, Civil War, and Reconstruction eras. For the old southern families, his return after the war was one of the few reassuring aspects of Reconstruction Beaufort. The church got a new roof in 1874 thanks to the generosity of St. Peter's Parish of Perth Amboy, New Jersey. The altar still in use at St. Helena's was carved by sailors of the USS *New Hampshire.* In 1876 St. Helena installed a new organ with the help of sailors from the Port Royal naval station, and in 1877 further repairs were donated by the legacy of Mr. B.T. Moore of Plainfield, New Jersey. When Reverend Walker died in 1878, the oldest church in Beaufort was nearly back to its prewar glory. The church got a bigger organ in 1885 and went through substantial structural repairs after the hurricanes of 1893 and 1896. In 1897 the Sea Island Hotel hosted a fund-raising event to defray the cost of hurricane repairs. Alice O'Dell contributed the dining room at the hotel, while Mrs. Dale, Captain Crofut, and E. E. Elliott provided the music. Within the month, the repairs were completed under the supervision of Arthur Marscher, and the old church was restored. The whole town contributed to preserve the oldest structure in Beaufort.[15]

New England merchants in Beaufort after the war contributed to the revival of Richard Fuller's Baptist Church. In the year immediately after the war, white and black Baptists worshipped together. Within a few years, however, the black Baptists formed their own congregations at the Tabernacle Church on Craven Street and the First African Baptist Church on New Street. The Baptist Church of Beaufort became the white congregation. This was theologically the closest southern denomination to the Congregational churches of New England. George Waterhouse's regular and substantial generosity was rewarded after his death in 1894 by a plaque inside the church and by the erection of Waterhouse Memorial Park, across Charles Street from the Baptist Church, a donation of Mayor C. C. Townsend and the city wardens in 1905.[16] At the turn of the century, the Baptist Church of Beaufort was the largest white congregation in the county. The Methodist congregation in Beaufort turned their antebellum church on Scott and Prince Streets over to the African American Methodist congregation. After the war the *Palmetto Post* reported that "Methodism lay dormant for many years," but by 1892 the white Methodist congregation had revived under the direction of Reverend E. L. Meynardie of Charleston and Reverend H. M. Mood. In 1884 Abbie Holmes Christensen used part of her sizable Holmes family inheritance to build a modern sanctuary on Carteret Street. Her intention was to have a Union Chapel shared by several denominations, but within a few years it became the regular home of the white United Methodist congregation of Beaufort. In 1892 the Carteret Street Methodist Church hosted the conference of the Methodist Episcopal Church, South, in Beaufort. In 1892 the pastor was Reverend A. J. Cauthen, and the congregation numbered 104 members.[17]

One of the most influential institutions in twentieth-century Beaufort was begun in 1906. In that year the congregation of Beth Israel built the first Jewish synagogue in Beaufort on a lot on Scott Street behind the old arsenal. Beaufort already had a long Jewish history before the establishment of Beth Israel synagogue. One of Beaufort's most prominent colonial merchants was Peter Lavien, a Danish Jew from the West Indian Island of St. Croix and the half brother of Alexander Hamilton, the famous patriot and first U.S. secretary of the treasury. By the antebellum era, several Jewish families from Savannah had expanded their businesses across the river into the Beaufort District. The most prominent and most permanent of these families were the descendants of John Solomon of St. Peter's Parish. On the eve of the Civil War, the most famous Jew of the Confederacy, Secretary of War Judah P. Benjamin, owned a house in Beaufort where his wife and mother lived for several years. Civil War occupation and then Reconstruction brought several Jewish businessmen who contributed significantly to the decades of enterprise. Among these 1870s merchants were Moritz Pollitzer, Jacob Apple,

P. M. Epstin, and William Kressel. In 1888 William Keyserling arrived from Lithuania and soon brought his four brothers, Joseph, Mark, Michael, and Israel, to Beaufort. These and several other Jewish families founded the congregation of Beth Israel in 1906. On November 8, 1906, the congregation elected its first slate of officers and trustees: M. S. Epstein, president; J. B. Keyserling, vice president; David Mittle, secretary; Morris Levin, treasurer; and M. Cohen, H. Kramer, and E. M. "Max" Lipsitz, trustees.[18]

Several institutions and events in Beaufort at the turn of the century were organized specifically to honor Civil War memory. Most, but not all, celebrated the Lost Cause. In Beaufort, perhaps unique in the state, there were as many prominent white Union veterans as there were Confederate veterans. In July 1892 Beaufort's most prominent merchants and businessmen gathered to honor the fiftieth wedding anniversary of Mr. and Mrs. John Conant. Conant was a Union Army veteran who settled in Reconstruction Beaufort and became a successful dairy farmer. His Magnolia Farm occupied much of the land south of Beaufort along what is now Ribaut Road. Not only were almost all of the guests northerners, but many were also Union army or navy veterans. Many who were not veterans were missionaries of the Port Royal Experiment. Those present included Moritz and Anna Pollitzer, George and Harriett Waterhouse, Colonel and Mrs. D. C. Wilson, Mr. and Mrs. George Gage, Mr. and Mrs. E. C. McLeod, Mr. and Mrs. James M. Crofut, Mrs. Alice O'Dell and Miss Maude O'Dell, Mrs. H. C. Judd, Mayor (Intendant) Joseph W. Collins, Mr. and Mrs. J. W. Lockwood, Mr. and Mrs. J. A. Kinghorn, Mr. Silas Wallace, Mr. J. C. Mayo, Captain and Mrs. George A. Crofut, Miss Ohlandt, Miss Onthank, Mrs. Frederick Eustis, and others. Colonel D. C. Wilson toasted John Conant as "Captain Conant, Civil War veteran who lost a son in the war . . . a sacrifice that made the United States the greatest and most progressive nation in the world." George Waterhouse toasted John Conant as a brave Union veteran and catalogued the remarkable technological changes that had occurred during the course of their fifty-year marriage: "improvements in steam, electricity and, of course, the great Civil War." This was not only the celebration of a long marriage but also a celebration of the Union victory by many of its veterans and much of Beaufort's commercial elite.[19]

The most noteworthy Confederate institution at the turn of the century was the venerable Beaufort Volunteer Artillery, which had begun as the local militia company in 1758 with the construction of Fort Lyttelton on Spanish Point. By 1776 the unit had adopted the name it was known by through four wars and 142 years, providing regular military service in the Revolutionary War, the War of 1812, the Civil War, and the Spanish-American War. During the Civil War it served as an active part of the Confederate army in battles from Port Royal Sound (1861) to Bentonville, North Carolina (1865).

During Reconstruction the Beaufort Volunteer Artillery was revived as a social organization by Dr. Henry Middleton Stuart, a veteran of the unit. After Governor Wade Hampton's election in 1876, it was a regular unit of the Volunteer Troops, State of South Carolina. In 1892 the Beaufort Volunteer Artillery was redesignated the Third Division, Naval Militia of South Carolina. Despite the reorganization, the Beaufort Volunteer Artillery continued to meet as a social, ceremonial, and Confederate memorial organization. By the turn of the century, it had its own band with Neil Sanders on cornet, Alex Levin on violin, James O'Dell Jr. on piano, Samuel Townsend on base cornet, and William Hutchings as drummer.

The Beaufort Volunteer Artillery took the lead in reviving Carolina Day on June 28. Carolina Day, or Palmetto Day, had been celebrated before the Civil War to commemorate South Carolina's contribution to American independence. On June 28, 1776, Colonel William Moultrie and a handful of artillery crews from the 2nd South Carolina Regiment at Fort Sullivan defeated a British attack upon Charleston Harbor. The unlikely victory made Sergeant William Jasper of Beaufort District a national hero and gave rise to the palmetto flag as the ensign of the state. After the Civil War, Carolina Day became the white counterpart to the black Fourth of July celebrations. In 1892 the Beaufort Volunteer Artillery celebrated Carolina Day with an excursion to Bluffton, and in 1900 it hosted the Savannah Blues, another southern honorary military unit. Beaufort's Bert Jenkins won a marksmanship contest, and a baseball game went to the Savannah Blues, 18–17. In the evening, one hundred guests were served dinner around an anchor-shaped table set up at the courthouse. In 1903 the Beaufort Volunteer Artillery was invited to the Saint Louis World Fair as a representative of "several very old military organizations in the United States."[20]

Beaufort also had a "camp" of United Confederate Veterans. The Henry Middleton Stuart Camp was part of the state organization. Dr. Stuart was the perennial camp commander. Lieutenant Colonel Joseph O'Hear Sanders was adjutant for many years. The major annual event for the Stuart Camp was to conduct ceremonies on Confederate Memorial Day, May 10, the day Stonewall Jackson died. Each year the organization assembled at the United States National Cemetery, where several Confederate soldiers are honorably buried among thousands of Union dead. Confederate Memorial Day was the white counterpart to the traditional black holiday on Memorial Day, May 31. As many of the Confederate veterans began to pass away, Beaufort organized a camp of the Sons of Confederate Veterans in 1897. Several veterans were asked to address the new organization. General James Washington Moore of Hampton's Legion, Dr. Hal Stuart of the Beaufort Volunteer Artillery, the Honorable W. J. Verdier of Hart's Battery, and Judge Thomas Grimke White of White's Battalion exhorted the next generation. Organizers of the

Beaufort Camp of the Sons of Confederate Veterans were H. M. Stuart Jr., Dr. A. P. Prioleau, John M. Baker, Will Elliott Jr., T. O. Hutson, Senator Thomas Talbird, and J.V. Dowling.[21]

The turn of the century saw the passing of many of the old guard of both the Union and Confederate causes. In 1903 Colonel Duncan Campbell Wilson died at his home on Bay Street. Since the Civil War occupation, he had been the leader of the northern merchant community and a tireless promoter of business and industry. As much as any single Beaufortonian, D. C. Wilson had been responsible for Beaufort's prosperity during the decades of enterprise. He was a lifelong personal friend of General Rufus Saxton and the closest personal link to the military occupation that changed Beaufort County forever. His passing was mourned by all Beaufortonoians regardless of color or politics. In 1904 another Union stalwart died with the passing of George Gage. Like D. C. Wilson, Gage had been an integral part of the Reconstruction era. He was born in McConnellsville, Ohio, the son of the famous abolitionist Francis Gage. He came to Beaufort with his mother as a missionary of the Port Royal Experiment. After organizing freedmen's schools on Parris Island, Francis Gage left Beaufort after only a few months. George Gage remained for the next forty-six years. In the late 1860s he surveyed the line of the Port Royal Railroad with Stephen C. Millett. In 1870 he was the chief engineer of the railroad. From 1870 to 1877, during the Grant administration, Gage was the collector of customs for Port Royal Harbor during the heyday of its maritime commerce. In 1877 Gage built a sawmill at the site of the Beaufort Memorial Hospital, and Gage's Mill was a prominent industrial feature of Beaufort for twenty years. In retirement Gage served as town treasurer after, in the words of the *Beaufort Gazette,* "the colored town treasurer absconded with the money" in 1890. All his life George Gage was a staunch abolitionist, an outspoken Unionist, and an ardent Republican. Until the day he died, he always voted with Beaufort's black citizens. But Beaufortonians on both sides of such divisive issues admired and trusted the old abolitionist. When he died, all the stores in Beaufort closed, and business was suspended. His pallbearers were a mix of northerners (George Holmes and George A. Crofut), southerners (R. R. Legare and Harry Danner), and immigrants (Niels Christensen Sr. and J. B. Kinghorn), perfectly representative of Beaufort's postwar commercial community.[22]

Turn-of-the-century Beaufort witnessed the passing of many prominent Confederate veterans and many scions of the antebellum "old guard." In January 1904 Alice Gadsden Lynah died in Charleston. She was the granddaughter of Dr. John Guerard of Bluffton, one of the grandees of antebellum St. Luke's Parish. She spent much of her youth in the old Beaufort District and married Paul Lynah of the Savannah River rice planting family. She is buried with her husband in Bonaventure Cemetery in Savannah. In June

1904 Julius E. Chaplin died at Tar Bluff on the Combahee River. He was the last of eight Chaplin brothers to serve in the Beaufort Volunteer Artillery during the Civil War. Two were killed. They were cousins of Thomas B. Chaplin of St. Helena Island, the plantation diarist. Julius E. Chaplin was buried in St. Helena Churchyard.

In May 1905 Major John Gibbes Barnwell died in Stateburg, Sumter County, South Carolina, at the home of his son, Reverend William H. Barnwell. He was eighty-nine years old and, according to the *Charleston News and Courier,* "a gentleman of the most lovable disposition and highest character." Before the war he had commanded the Beaufort Volunteer Artillery and was a scion of "Tuscarora Jack" Barnwell, Beaufort's founder. He did not return to Beaufort after the war but like many of the refugee planters, he returned home to be buried at old St. Helena's. In July 1905 Ann Reeve Stuart died in Beaufort at the age of seventy-eight. She never married and was "born and lived her whole life in Beaufort, one of the last of the planter class. She was a quiet, unassuming, gentlewoman of the past . . . beloved by all and treasured by her few intimate friends." The *Beaufort Gazette* highlighted the ending of an era by noting, "Only six or seven of those who attended St. Helena when she first worshipped there are now here."[23]

In January 1906 three of Beaufort's antebellum old guard died in different parts of the country. Reverend John Habersham Elliott died in Washington, D.C., at the age of seventy-four. Born and raised in antebellum Beaufort, he was educated at the Beaufort College and was valedictorian of the 1851 class at the South Carolina College. He first read the law with Edmund Rhett and later went into the Episcopal ministry. Elliott ended his career as rector of the Church of the Ascension in Washington, D.C. Reverend John Habersham Elliott was the brother of Congressman William Elliott. After years of exile, he was also brought home for burial at St. Helena Church. The *Beaufort Gazette* noted that there was "a small crowd but a profusion of flowers at St. Helena for his funeral. He was one of the finest examples of a South Carolina gentleman of the generation that saw the Civil War. . . . he was a great example of brave and faithful attachment to the ideals of old Beaufort."

A few weeks later, Reverend Lucius Cuthbert died in Aiken at the age of seventy-three. Born, raised, and educated in Beaufort, Cuthbert moved to Aiken as the Civil War approached. He was the long-time minister of the First Baptist Church of Charleston and the Second Baptist Church of Aiken. He is best known as the biographer of his cousin and mentor, Reverend Richard Fuller. In April 1906 Dr. Paul Pritchard died in Bluffton. Like many of the old planters in the Bluffton area who had not lost their land during the Civil War foreclosures, Paul Pritchard returned to his ancestral home to help rebuild Beaufort County after the war. He was the first man of the old guard to accept a public office during Reconstruction, when he served on a mixed-race county commission during the 1870s. Despite his good-faith public service, he was always a staunch "secesh" and defender of the Confederacy. He had been a classmate of Ulysses S. Grant at West Point, served on General Drayton's staff at the Battle of Port Royal Sound, and later became a major in the Confederate cavalry. He was a "much esteemed gentleman of the old school." But, as the *Beaufort Gazette* noted, "His enthusiasm as a Confederate ended only with his death."[24]

In May 1906 John E. Fripp died at Okatie at the age of seventy-five. He was born and raised on St. Helena Island as the son of William "Good Billy" Fripp. According to the local paper, he was "an old regime planter whose family was among the most ancient and well-known families along our coast." In December 1906 Elizabeth Sams died at the age of seventy-five. She was one of the last surviving children of Dr. Berners Barnwell Sams, the lord of the manor on Datha Island before the war, and she had lived her entire life in Beaufort except during the Civil War occupation. Her many siblings had scattered from Florida to Maryland to Texas. Only her brother, Dr. R. R. Sams, a dentist, remained in Beaufort. In August 1907 J. D. Neal died at his farm at Red Dam. He had served four years with the Confederate army and had a bullet extracted from his battlefield wound. It was "one of the family's prized possessions." He was buried in the Bull Hill Cemetery. In July 1907 N. E. H. Dopson, "a gallant veteran of the lost cause," died in Beaufort. He had enlisted in the Confederate army from Colleton County at the age of seventeen and saw much combat in the 17th South Carolina Cavalry. He married Elizabeth Cummings of Colleton and engaged in Beaufort's busy lumber trade after the war.

The significance of the passing of all these Confederate veterans was not lost on the surviving members of the SCV and the UCV Stuart Camp. At Dopson's funeral, Adjutant Joseph O'Hear Sanders summed it up with Stonewall Jackson's last words: "Another link has been broken. . . . it cannot be long before all who now survive will join the increasing forces across the river in the shade of the trees!"[25] Two years later, Joseph O'Hear Sanders died. He had been a sharpshooter with the Stono Scouts during the siege of Charleston and later was General W. C. Hardee's bodyguard. In May 1907 the *Beaufort Gazette* published a list of Beaufort County residents who were collecting pensions as Confederate veterans or widows of veterans:

Name	*Residence*
R. O. Reynolds	Bluffton
C. W. Beverly	Bluffton
J. A. Buck	Hardeeville
G. M. Blake	Hardeeville

(continued)

Name	*Residence*
W. H. Crosby	Bluffton
A. D. Cooler	Okatie
Joseph Cooler	Heyward
Washington Cooler	Ridgeland
J. S. Coburn	Hardeeville
J. D. Cooler	Bluffton
L. E. Davis	Bluffton
J. H. Hardee	Hardeeville
Francis Humbrot	Ridgeland
F. H. Johnson	Okatie
A. V. Patterson	Bluffton
W. B. Pope	Okatie
A. B. Stone	Beaufort
Samuel Walls	Hardeeville
H. White	Bluffton
A. E. Walker	Bluffton
Charles Wall	Hardeeville
O. T. Zealy	Beaufort

Widows of Confederate Veterans

Name	*Residence*
Marceline Chaplin	Beaufort
Mrs. Coe	Bluffton
Elvira Drawdy	Dale
Rose Farr	Grahamville
Jane Hodge	Beaufort
E. M. Hailford	Bluffton
Elizabeth Holman	Hardeeville
Elizabeth Kirk	Grahamville
Amanda Johnson	Beaufort
Jane Law	Ridgeland
Martha Tuten	Okatie
E. M. Pritchard	St. Helena
Mary Evans Verdier	Port Royal
Martha Wiggins	Bluffton
Elizabeth Williams	St. Helena
Rose Ann White	Beaufort[26]

It was noteworthy that in 1907 only three Confederate veterans lived in Beaufort while the overwhelming majority lived in the mainland communities of Bluffton, Grahamville, Ridgeland, and Hardeeville. This preponderance of Confederate veterans and their descendants on the mainland had a large influence on the postwar geopolitics of Beaufort County and also on the formation of Jasper County in 1912.

EDUCATION IN THE VICTORIAN AGE

A common aspiration of any society that has achieved two generations of wealth and prosperity is the education of the next generation. So it was with postbellum Beaufort. One of the lasting, laudable results of the Reconstruction social revolution was the creation of a statewide system of free public schooling for all citizens, a social commitment that survived the conservative regime of the Hamptonites and the Jim Crow years. But public education was indifferently funded and infrequently regulated and remained very rudimentary in South Carolina. At best, it was never intended to provide much more than elementary literacy, and it did not do very well at that. In 1890, 45 percent of South Carolina's adult population was illiterate. That was insufficient for Beaufort's white families at the turn of the century.

Beaufort had a distinguished history of education before the war, and many of the white families who returned during Reconstruction tried to resurrect the old institutions. Mary Hamilton, daughter of Colonel Paul Hamilton of the Oaks, educated most of Beaufort's white children for more than forty years, first as a private tutor, later as the teacher of the Beaufort Female Seminary, and finally as an employee of the white semipublic school. When she retired and moved to Baltimore in 1909, her students dedicated a stone plaque in her honor.

The trustees of the Beaufort College (chartered 1795), under the leadership of Dr. Henry Middleton Stuart, reconstituted themselves in 1868. With the help of lawyer William Elliott, they regained title to the neoclassical Beaufort College Building (c. 1852) and leased it to the Freedmen's Bureau until 1873. In 1874 Robert R. Fuller, descendant of one of Beaufort's best-educated antebellum families, opened a private school for boys in the college building. The school ran from August 3 to October 16. The fee for boys over ten years of age was ten dollars for the term, and for boys under ten years of age, it was eight dollars.[27] Fuller's school for white boys was the genesis of the Beaufort College Graded School, which was the principal white school in Beaufort during the 1880s and 1890s.

The Beaufort College Graded School was formed in the early 1880s when the boy's school merged with Mary Hamilton's Beaufort Female

Seminary. The Beaufort College Graded School was a cooperative enterprise between the private Beaufort College Trustees, who owned the building, and the trustees of what was called Beaufort School District No. 1, which managed the meager state funds for public education. Despite the idealism of the wartime Gideonites, schools in Reconstruction and post-Reconstruction Beaufort were never integrated. As Judge Jonathan J. Wright explained during a 1873 school commission meeting in Columbia, "while he claimed for his race perfect equality and equal privileges with the white race . . . yet he did not desire social equality or the mixing of races in the common schools of this country." Judge Wright was a black Beaufort County delegate to the South Carolina constitutional convention of 1868 and the first black justice of the South Carolina Supreme Court. His influential opinion was shared by the majority of state school commissioners even at the height of black Reconstruction in 1873.[28]

In 1880s Beaufort, the white Beaufort College Graded School coexisted with the black Public School No. 1 building on the adjoining block of Carteret Street. The black public school was housed in a large frame building constructed shortly after the establishment of the school by Robert Smalls, Richard Howell Gleaves, and others in 1868. Public School No. 1 was neither required by state law nor funded to teach beyond the sixth grade. The Beaufort College Graded School, on the other hand, provided a full curriculum through the ninth grade. These were the principal schools in town and the largest schools in the county at the end of the nineteenth century.

In June 1892 the Beaufort College Graded School held its commencement exercises on the school grounds. This was one of the stellar years in the Beaufort College Graded School's history. It was the year before the Sea Island hurricane of 1893 and the business decline that soon followed. The school enrolled 125 pupils in grades one through nine. Principal D.T. Wilson pronounced the year "successful" and announced the names of all the students who had been promoted to the next grade, handing each successful scholar a "promotion card." The other two teachers at the Beaufort College Graded School were Carrie Givens and Mary Hamilton. The latter had already been teaching Beaufort children for twenty-five years by 1892. Finally, the ninth-grade class was presented its graduation diplomas. The "venerable" Colonel Paul Hamilton, one of the stalwarts of Beaufort College, gave the commencement address and presented the diplomas. This was the first year that the school offered diplomas to its graduates. The 1892 graduates were Charlie Bartless (the only male graduate), Anna Eliza Calhoun, Katie Emmons, May Mitchell, Estelle Richardson, Hammie Sanders, Madie VanNess, Sallie Verdier, and Jane Waterhouse. Earlier in the year the school had published its entire honor roll in the *Palmetto Post*. So many of Beaufort's future business, civic, and social leaders attended Beaufort College Graded School, that the 1892 honor roll offered a glimpse into the town's future:

First Grade: Marie Bonneau, Bertha Cummings, Earl Jones, Willie Kinghorn, Minnie Ohlandt, Willie Verdier, Leo Walsh.
Second Grade: George Bellows, Nina Harrison, Willie Pollitzer, Gregg Richardson.
Third Grade: (None made the honor roll).
Fourth Grade: Charles Bellows, Marie Burckhardt, Alma Cummings, James Irons, Bessie Kinghorn, Nellie Nielson, Lucy Emmons, Addie Scheper, Henry Walsh.
Fifth Grade: Katie Honeman, Walter Richardson, John Robinson, Linwood Rountree, Aggie Scheper, Ida Verdier.
Sixth Grade: Charlie Barnwell, Willie Casey, Carrie Hilton, Bessie Jones, Bertie Kinghorn, Etta Pollitzer, Mary Richardson, Teddy VanNess, George Waterhouse, Rachel Weatherford.
Seventh Grade: Lillie Brasson, Helen Burkhardt, Eddie Dale, Orrie Dale, Lillie Emmons, Annie Hilton, Wellman Latta, Josie McBride, Erma Rountree, Julia Scheper, Lula Scheper, Marie Scheper.
Eighth Grade: Irving Emmons, Grace Tonking.[29]

While the Beaufort College Graded School was a far cry from the lofty ambitions of the antebellum founders, it nevertheless offered a much better education than was available in most South Carolina towns. The only high schools in the state in the 1890s were Charleston High School, Columbia High School, and the Greenville Seminary, all of which were city institutions supported by municipal taxes. Not until the twentieth century did the state government fund high schools across the state. Many graduates of the Beaufort College Graded School went on to boarding schools and colleges across the United States, attesting to the high level of instruction at the school and the high expectations of Beaufort's white families.

Beaufort's northern families tended to return north for higher education while the southern families stayed closer to home. Abbie Holmes Christensen, a graduate of Mount Holyoke School (it was not a "college" when she attended in the 1870s), returned to Massachusetts to educate her sons. The family had a home in Brookline, where the older boys, Frederick and Niels, graduated from high school in the 1890s. During his high school years, Frederick Christensen began the remarkable daily journal that he maintained for more than forty years (1893–1936). The youngest son, Arthur, graduated from Harvard in 1905, where he distinguished himself in athletics. Known to Beaufortonians as "A.O.," Christensen was the "Harvard Champion Strongman" in 1904 and the quarterback of the Crimson football team. He trained by swimming three miles a day in Squam Lake, New Hampshire, a tradition he began as a boy in the Beaufort River. Harvard's Dr. Dudley Sargent described Christensen as "the best proportioned all around athlete he had ever examined." A. O. Christensen maintained Beaufort's antebellum tradition of distinction at Harvard. Both Robert W. Barnwell (1821) and Julius Stuart (1849) had been valedictorians of their Harvard classes.[30] After completing their formal educations, the three Christensen boys returned to Beaufort to manage the family enterprises.

The three Waterhouse girls—Mary, Adelaide, and Jane—returned to the North for their higher education. Their mother, Harriett Parmelee Waterhouse, was the daughter of Reverend Anson Hall Parmelee of the First Presbyterian Church of Livonia, New York. She had come to Beaufort as a Gideonite schoolteacher in 1865. She sent her daughters back to upstate New York to finish their education. All three girls attended Elmira College, the oldest women's college in the United States, during the 1890s. Their younger brother, George Waterhouse Jr., attended Colgate Academy in upstate New York and then graduated from Brown University, the oldest Baptist college in America. He was a close friend and roommate of Harry Emerson Fosdick, one of the twentieth century's most famous evangelists and pastor of the Riverside Church in New York City.[31]

The Citadel in Charleston was popular with Beaufort's young men. Publisher Samuel H. Rodgers sent his sons to that school. The oldest son, Motte Legare Rodgers, was a Citadel graduate and a promising journalist for the *News and Courier* and the *Columbia Register* when he died suddenly in 1892 at the age of twenty-two. Colonel Joseph O'Hear Sanders of Varnville and Beaufort, a Citadel alumnus, sent two of his sons, O'Hear and Legare Sanders, to his alma mater. O'Hear Sanders graduated in 1899.[32]

Some of Beaufort's youth ventured farther afield. Will Elliott, son of the congressman and a living link to antebellum Beaufort, continued his education at Episcopal High School in Alexandria, Virginia, and then graduated from the University of Virginia. He was a young lawyer in Beaufort in the 1890s and became a prominent textile attorney in Columbia. Several Beaufort girls finished their education in Catonsville, Maryland. Therèse and Christine Talbird graduated from Mount de Sales Academy, a distinguished Catholic girl's school. They were daughters of Beaufort's most prominent Catholic family. Their father was Senator Thomas Talbird and their mother, who perished in the 1893 hurricane, was a native of Nice, France. Mary Eliza and Julia Read of Beaufort and McPhersonville finished their education at Hannah More Academy, an Episcopal boarding school in Catonsville. Hannah More Academy was a mecca for southern girls. Two widows of prominent Virginia families had founded it after the Civil War.

The school survived until the 1950s when it merged with St. Timothy's School in Stevenson, Maryland.[33] These well-educated Beaufortonians were products of Beaufort College Graded School.

By the beginning of the twentieth century, the enrollment at the Beaufort College Graded School had outgrown the old college facility. By 1903 the Beaufort School District No. 1 trustees decided to erect an additional building on the Beaufort College grounds. This, of course, required the acquiescence of the Beaufort College trustees, who owned the land. The trustees cooperated and the first structure built with public money on the college grounds was a one-story frame building. When the school resumed in 1904 with the additional classrooms, it had five teachers, with Lucco Gunter as principal. At the 1904 commencement, the community found the operation of the school under Gunter's leadership to be "pleasing." The *Beaufort Gazette* commented that the "colored public school was also . . . an active healthy and efficient institute." When commencement was held in 1905, the cooperative organization of the Beaufort College Graded School was highlighted.[34]

In the early twentieth century, Beaufort County had nine different school districts, each with their own board of trustees. Beaufort School District No. 1 managed both the black public school and the white Beaufort College Graded School in town. Funds for the nine school districts were apportioned by the Beaufort County Board of Trustees. County trustees and trustees of the nine districts were all appointed positions. The county trustees were appointed by the state superintendent of education on the recommendation of the county legislative delegation. The county board of trustees appointed the nine district board members. Only the school commissioner was elected. That position was a full-time paid position equivalent to a superintendent today. Until 1909 all funds for Beaufort County schools were derived from state appropriations. The only local funds for education came from the proceeds of the county liquor dispensary. As Prohibition approached in South Carolina, those funds, like the liquor that provided them, began to dry up. From 1906 to 1907 dispensary profits available for local school funding declined by 32 percent, from $1,400 to $956.[35]

As the twentieth century dawned, a group of Democratic politicians began to challenge the supremacy of the Tillmanites for control of the state government. Historians have called them progressives. They sought to improve the state's economic, civic, and cultural life through government action. Senator Niels Christensen was a charter member of the progressive movement. A major plank in the progressive platform was the improvement of public education. Despite the opposition's rhetoric, the Tillmanites had made major commitments to education during the 1890s, including the establishment of Clemson College in 1895 and the South Carolina State College in 1896. The first president of South Carolina State College was the longtime Beaufort Republican leader Thomas E. Miller. Despite these efforts, public schools across the state remained substandard, and a large portion of adult South Carolinians remained illiterate. The progressives covered the state with educational reform plans and bond issues for new school construction. The consolidation of substandard rural ("one room") schools was popular. The business community embraced education reform as good for the economic development.[36]

The intellectual leader of school reform was Dr. William H. Hand of Columbia. Hand was professor of secondary education at the University of South Carolina and state high school inspector. From 1918 to 1928, he was superintendent of Columbia city schools. In January 1907 Hand came to Beaufort at the request of Senator Niels Christensen. He addressed the whole community, which packed the courthouse. The speech was promoted as a "rare opportunity" and a catalyst for public school reform. Niels Christensen's *Beaufort Gazette* spurred on the local school reform movement. In April 1907 Mrs. Hal M. Stuart offered a retrospective history of Beaufort College, lauding the town's long tradition of educational excellence and urging a community commitment to reform. For the next five months, Niels Christensen published editorials nearly every week promoting educational reform and outlining the steps to achieve it.

Christensen called for raising local revenue for school improvement. He noted that Beaufort County was at the bottom of the list in local funding for schools and that bond issues for school construction had been passed across the state. Summerton had passed a $15,000 bond issue to build an eight-room, brick schoolhouse. Greenwood ($15,000), Florence ($35,000), Lake City ($10,000), and Simpsonville ($45,000) had followed suit. Even rural Hampton and Colleton counties had "seven funded school districts each." In Beaufort, by contrast, the "colored school [was] using a wooden building built with funds contributed by northern friends approached by Robert Smalls." South of the Broad River, there was said to be a "crying need for a two-story building with three recitation rooms" to replace the outmoded schoolhouse at Barrel Landing.[37] This was the beginning of education in Bluffton.

In August 1907 George Waterhouse Jr. was appointed chairman of the Beaufort County Board of Education at the urging of Senator Christensen. Shortly thereafter, movement began in earnest to build a new, two-story brick schoolhouse. The community wanted to integrate the new building with the old Beaufort College because it was reportedly "so well located and of such pleasing architecture." The white school population had grown by

20 percent, and the faculty needed to be increased from five to seven teachers. Also needed was the cooperation of the Beaufort College trustees who owned the property, and some suggested using the Beaufort College Trust Fund for construction. They hoped to attract students from rural Hampton and Barnwell counties as Beaufort schools had done before the war. They also expected to solicit the help of wealthy northern plantation owners who were winter residents of the area. The Clyde, Cameron, Lorillard, and Havermeyer families were specifically mentioned. These families were the vanguard of a wave of wealthy northerners who had begun to purchase declining lowcountry plantation lands as resorts and hunting lands.

In 1908 the trustees of Beaufort College transferred their deed to the college building and property to Beaufort School District No. 1. The contract has a reversionary clause providing for the deed to return to the trustees if the building and grounds ceased to be used for educational purposes. In 1908 funds were raised through a bond issue and a state appropriation secured by Senator Christensen. In 1909 the two-story, masonry addition to the Beaufort College Building was completed. It was an impressive structure, complementing the monumental, neoclassical architecture of the Beaufort College building. The new school contained fourteen classrooms, a library, an auditorium, teachers' offices, and indoor bathrooms for teachers and students, a feature that most homes in Beaufort did not have in 1909.[38] This building was the site of the formative education of all of Beaufort's white children for three generations.

Mary Hamilton retired and moved away the year the new school was finished. The stone plaque honoring her selfless dedication to Beaufort's children was placed in a prominent position at the public entrance of the new school.

BASEBALL

One of the most entertaining community activities was baseball. Beaufortonians, black and white, embraced "America's pastime" with gusto. The U.S. Army occupation introduced baseball to Beaufort County during the Civil War. The game increased in popularity during Reconstruction, and by 1873 Beaufort had an organized, traveling baseball team. On September 4, 1873, the Beaufort Cosmopolitans played host to the Charleston Carolinas. As the *Beaufort Republican* reported, the "Cosmopolitans sported handsome new uniforms" and "seats were provided for visitors" at the Pidgeon Point ball field behind the National Cemetery. Beaufort's loss to the Charleston club did not diminish the home team's hospitality: it hosted a dinner at the Sea Island Hotel for the victors. A few weeks later, the Cosmopolitans traveled to Charleston for a rematch on the Citadel green. Charleston won that game 21–14. Players on Beaufort's first organized baseball team in 1873 were

J. P. Boyce (captain), J. H. Harrison, W. Wilson, W. Kressel, H. C. Pollitzer, J. Plume, J. Meredith, J. N. Wallace, and W. H. Lockwood.[39]

By 1877 Beaufort County supported three ball clubs. Beaufort had the Dauntless Baseball Club while Port Royal was home to the rival Olympics. In addition to the two white teams, the first black baseball team in Beaufort was the Hampton Nine. Ironically, this club was named to "honor the new governor's statesmanship." In May 1877 the Olympics played the Dauntless on Pidgeon Point and lost the game. In August the Dauntless team traveled to Savannah to take on the Chatham Baseball Club. The Chatham Club won 16–5. The custom of exchanging hospitalities was continued.[40]

Baseball grew in popularity during the 1880s and reached its peak at the turn of the century. By 1892 Beaufort had three white teams: the Beaufort Baseball Club, called the Beaufort Nine; the Earthquake Baseball Club, named for the 1886 earthquake; and the Rough and Ready Baseball Club. In July 1892 the Earthquake defeated the Rough and Ready Club 36–17 at Pidgeon Point. The workers at the Coosaw Mining Company formed the Ivanhoe Baseball Club, named for the largest steam tugboat in the phosphate fleet. Local African Americans formed a team called the Spartans of Beaufort, which traveled to Charleston and Savannah for matches. In June the Spartans hosted the black Mutual Baseball Club of Savannah. Although the Spartans lost to the Mutuals 6–0, the *Palmetto Post* deemed it "a very good game." Spectators of both races maintained a lively interest in all the teams and mingled freely at the ballpark.

On July 4, 1892, the Beaufort Nine hosted the Ivanhoe Club of Coosaw Mines. This was as much a social event and Independence Day celebration as it was a baseball game. The Beaufort Baseball Club sported new uniforms for the occasion—"white with blue stockings and blue and white caps." The Ivanhoe Club beat the Beaufort Nine 15–3, but that did not dampen the festivities. Speeches were delivered by Julian Lopez, superintendent of the Coosaw Mines, State Senator W. J. Verdier, Major W. H. Lockwood of the Beaufort Volunteer Artillery, and Lieutenant McKee of the Coast Guard revenue cutter *Boutwell.* The Coosaw Mining Company provided the musical entertainment with "Listen to My Tale of Woe" sung by Captain George Crofut of the *Ivanhoe* and "an Italian song" sung by Mr. Jacob Hessenbuttel, first baseman for the Coosaw Mines team. Dinner at the arsenal was provided by the Beaufort Nine. Two rows of tables reportedly "groaned under the weight of the good cheer." The roster of the Beaufort Nine in 1892 included M. White, pitcher and second base; L. Sanders, catcher; J. McGrath, second base and pitcher; W. C. Bellows, left field and first base; J. Kessler, third base and centerfield; A. Albina, right field and first base; M. Collins, shortstop; George Elliott, catcher, first base, and third base; and W. Schwartz, first base and left field.[41]

Local players often organized impromptu teams for informal scrimmages. In 1894 a number of young men divided themselves into the "Fats" and the "Leans." The roster of the teams was as follows:

"Fats"	Position	"Leans"
W. H. Lockwood	First base	E. R. Elliott
D. Mabie	Second base	W. H. Tyson
D. Mann	Third base	W. R. Bristol
J. N. Wallace	Pitcher	G. A. McLeod
J. E. Kessler	Catcher	E. I. Burn
W. O. Prentiss	Shortstop	P. O. Bellamy
S. M. Key	Right field	P. M. Epstin
J. B. Walker	Left field	G. C. Sherer
B. S. Brown	Center field	R. R. Legare

In 1899 a team organized by Will Elliott defeated a team captained by Lawrence Sanders 10–6. As was the tradition in Beaufort, "after the game they all had a big drunk at the Arsenal." All this activity at the Pidgeon Point ballpark prompted the town council to "build a fence enclosing the ball ground near the cemetery" in 1899.[42]

In 1904 youth league baseball began in Beaufort with the formation of two juvenile teams: the Uptown Team and the Downtown Team. At the same time, a heated rivalry developed between the Marine Corps team from Parris Island and the army team from Fort Fremont. Several close games reportedly brought the rivalry to a "fever heat." In September 1904 both teams traveled to Beaufort's Baseball Park for the entertainment of the community. The marines won. In 1905 the Marines Corps team defeated the Beaufort Nine 4–0 when Captain Lymon of the marines hit a grand slam home run in the ninth inning. A month later, the Beaufort Nine lost to the Hampton Baseball Team 11–4.

By 1907 a regular season of games had developed among the Beaufort Nine and clubs from Port Royal, Hampton, Walterboro, and Early Branch, as well as the marines and the army. In 1907 the Beaufort Nine consisted of S. Bond, pitcher; L. Bond, catcher; B. Rodgers, first base; E. Bero, second base; C. G. Luther, third base; W. Morrison, center field; W. D. Vincent, right field; R. Merrill, left field; and N. Sanders, shortstop.

The Beaufort Nine played many memorable games that year, including a 3–3 tie with the Marine Corps that went twelve innings and was only suspended by darkness. In September they beat the marines 6–2 in a rematch. In fact, the Beaufort Nine only lost one game in 1907, a 4–0 shutout by the Walterboro Club. In August they beat Early Branch 6–2, Fort Fremont 9–5, and Port Royal 24–4. The most memorable game of the 1907 season was a 0–0 July marathon with the Hampton Baseball Club that was also suspended by darkness. The Hampton team, like the Beaufort Nine, was composed of young local men from established families. The Hampton roster in 1907 was H. Goethe, pitcher; Hugh Vincent, third base; C. Dowling, first base; N. Chauvais, second base; R. McDaniel, shortstop; L. Hiers, right field; E. McSweeney, left field; and M. McSweeney, center field.

Because of the close ties of families and friends between the two teams, the social event following the game was as memorable as the match itself. A fair portion of the young men and women from Beaufort and Hampton assembled at the Sea Island Hotel for an evening dance. Festivities continued until 2:00 A.M. In the morning the weary Hampton youth took the "up train" home.[43] Baseball was the first organized team sport in Beaufort County.

WATER SPORTS, 1892–1907

One recreational activity that Beaufort became famous for was boating. Boats had been used for transportation among the sea islands for millennia. Native Americans fashioned boats from rot-resistant cypress logs with stone tools, reaching a level of refinement after a thousand years that impressed even the European explorers. Spanish and British colonists split these log canoes, added a wide board for a keel and built up the sides with lap-strake planks to create interisland cargo vessels propelled by oars or sails. These vessels were called by their Spanish name, periaguas. They carried large mounds of deerskins, barrels of golden rice, and casks of Carolina blue indigo to market. Many periaguas survived to the steamboat era. In the late colonial era, the sea islands around Beaufort became centers for wooden shipbuilding. Shipwrights used the lowcountry live oak, one of the densest woods in North America, for the frame of the vessel and often planked the sides with cypress. This produced some of the strongest and most durable ships built in eighteenth-century America, including the USS *Constitution,* "Old Ironsides," which was built in Boston of live oak from Cumberland Island, Georgia.

Sails gave way to steam, and wood gave way to iron hulls. For more than a century beginning in 1817, most of the produce of the sea islands was transported aboard paddle-wheel riverboats. But recreational boating and personal transportation remained the domain of finely crafted plantation longboats propelled by oars or sails. By the 1840s many of the best of these vessels were constructed in Beaufort by skilled Irish boat builder Michael O'Conner, the founder of St. Peter's Catholic Church (1846). Pleasure sailing in 1790s Beaufort was first mentioned by William J. Grayson.[44] Leisure boating grew into a sport with frequent, informal rowing and sailing races between plantation "gigs." After the Civil War, the commercial elite replaced the planters as recreational boaters. Moritz Pollitzer introduced yachting to Beaufort in 1872 with his handsome thirty-two-foot sloop *Anna,* used exclusively for recreation and entertainment. By the end of the century, most of Beaufort's leading families had recreational rowing or sailing boats. Competition among them was inevitable.

On July 4, 1892, Beaufort held a large sailing regatta. A crowd of spectators boarded the *Pilot Boy* to view the races. When the wind died, the boats were becalmed and the spectators diverted the *Pilot Boy* to Bay Point for an evening excursion. The regatta was delayed until August 1892, when eleven local boats entered the race. They were the *Prescott, Willie, Hunkidori, Guy Curtis, Alpha, Mittie, Alma, Big John, Green, Flirt,* and *Lavender.* The course ran from Battery Creek to a buoy off Bay Point, back up to the Sea Island Chemical plant on Spanish Point, and then back to the starting line at the mouth of Battery Creek. *Prescott* proved superior, and observers said it "sailed like a bird." *Alpha* finished second. The sailboat races continued throughout the 1890s, and a friendly competition developed between the Beaufort and Port Royal boats. Frederick Christensen recalled that the two fastest boats in the area were the *Raymond* from Port Royal and the *Julia* from Beaufort. When the regatta was held in 1900, these two swift craft gave all the other boats a head start, like modern handicapping. When the wind freshened, the unballasted *Julia* had to reduce sail while the *Raymond* sailed through the fleet and beat J. Doane's *Alice* and William Von Harten's *Bertha* by seconds at the finish.[45]

About this time, a technological revolution in boating reached Beaufort. One of the nineteenth century's most useful inventions was the compact and powerful internal combustion engine. This little miracle was perfected by a German engineer, Gottlieb Daimler, in the 1860s. His first application of the engine was on watercraft, but its most famous application, of course, was to propel "horseless carriages." Although the new automobiles were revolutionizing the countryside in the 1890s, they were not very useful on the sea islands until the 1920s. But the gasoline engines proved extremely useful on Beaufort's numerous working launches, interisland craft, and pleasure boats. By 1900 most of Beaufort's affluent families had motorboats. Most of these early vessels doubled as delivery craft and pleasure craft, but to race them was a natural progression.

In 1905 the town of Port Royal established the Port Royal Motor Boat Association and held an annual boat race on Christmas Day. The next year the Army Cycle Manufacturing Company of Charleston was advertising the "Mianus Marine Engine" in the *Beaufort Gazette.* In 1906 Beaufort organized a Motor Boat Club and sponsored a powerboat regatta.[46]

The first of these regattas was held in the Beaufort River on Thanksgiving Day 1906. The whole town turned out for the exciting event. Spectators lined the bluff of the bay and crowded onto excursion boats in the river. The *Beaufort Gazette* correspondent reported that "the waterfront was lined with spectators. It was one of those bright breezy days of early winter when to be outdoors was exhilarating." Fourteen boats of widely varying size and horsepower were entered in the race. The judges on the race committee were Captain George Crofut, Captain Niels Christensen, and Dr. R. A. Riggs of the U.S. Navy Medical Corps. They divided the fleet into three classes according to size and horsepower. The 1906 entries with their owners were:

Boat	*Length*	*Power*	*Owner*
		1ST CLASS	
Imogene	52 ft.	25 hp.	W. Keyserling
Blanche	32 ft.	18 hp.	W. Keyserling
S. Springs	42 ft.	18 hp.	F. Blucher
Mystic	35 ft.	18 hp.	B. B. Chadwick
South Carolina	42 ft.	18 hp.	3rd Division, South Carolina Naval Militia
St. Helena	30 ft.	14 hp.	B. Patz
		2ND CLASS	
Varuna		7 hp.	W. Von Harten
Kiarens		5 hp.	W. P. Roberts
Lotus	24 ft.	5 hp.	H. C. Pollitzer
(No Name)		7 hp.	C. E. McLeod
Pauliah		6 hp.	W. J. Thompson
		3RD CLASS	
Qui Vive	18 ft.	5 hp.	F. W. Scheper
Niobe		5 hp.	R. Drake
(No Name)		5 hp.	R. K. Harley

The race started in front of town according to class. The course took them down the river and around Spanish Point to a buoy in Port Royal Sound between Parris Island and Land's End. The vessels rounded the buoy and raced back to Beaufort, covering about fourteen miles in little more than an hour. The first-class winner was William Keyserling's *Blanche.* The second-class winner was William VonHarten's *Varuna,* and the third-class winner was F. W. Scheper's *Qui Vive.* Keyserling won a fifteen-foot pennant for his victory in the first-class division—a pennant the *Blanche* could proudly sport for the rest of the year. William VonHarten won a twelve-foot pennant, and F. W. Scheper won a new U.S. Ensign for the *Qui Vive.* When the race was held in 1907, the thirty-foot U.S. Naval Reserve launch from Parris Island bested the whole fleet and won the first-class pennant.[47]

These new marine engines were not without their hazards. Within a few months of the 1906 regatta, C. E. McLeod's mahogany boat, one of the fastest in the fleet, burned to the waterline when its overheated engine ignited the combustible naphtha fumes. The fire also burned a boathouse on the Beaufort River bank.[48]

All this boating activity prompted the formation of the Beaufort Yacht Club, chartered in 1907. Within a few years, the yacht club built a clubhouse on a dock overlooking the Beaufort River. The yacht club is still active in the twenty-first century, and the clubhouse stands where it was built, much altered in appearance and surrounded by the Henry C. Chambers Waterfront Park.[49] Motorboat races continued for several years, but the advancing technology soon outpaced the ability of even Beaufort's wealthiest families to pay for it. By the 1920s the regular races were discontinued, but they were forerunners of the Beaufort Water Festival, which began in 1955.

SUMMER MIGRATIONS

On September 5, 1907, the Port Royal correspondent of the *Beaufort Gazette* commented dejectedly, "We think it is time for our Summer wanderers to return home now." The observation highlighted the large number of Beaufort County families who regularly abandoned the hot, humid lowcountry during July, August, and September when the "great heat" was most intense. The summer migrations of lowcountry families had been a tradition reaching back to colonial times. As early as the eighteenth century, Rutledges, Middletons, and other Charleston families were among the first people to make Newport, Rhode Island, a resort for the rich. In the 1830s, the Elliotts of Beaufort took their racehorses to Saratoga, New York, beginning a tradition that survives today. By the 1840s southern planters no longer felt comfortable in the North with their customary retinue of slaves, so they established resorts in the southern mountain towns of Flat Rock, High Hampton, Brevard, and many others in North Carolina.

The tradition of summer migrations continued after the war and, like everything else in Beaufort after the war, bore a unique local twist. In Beaufort transplanted northern families migrated to communities in Massachusetts, Maine, and Vermont, where family and friends remained. Native southern families maintained generations of tradition by sojourns to the Great Smoky and Blue Ridge Mountains of North Carolina and Tennessee.

For example, in 1892 George Waterhouse and George Holmes "summered" in Maine. D. C. Wilson, W. H. Delano, and James M. Crofut escaped to upstate New York. The Dales and Danners returned to Vermont, and Miles Howe, a Beaufort resident for many years, returned to Quebec, Canada, for the summer. H. G. Judd, it was reported, simply went on "a long visit North."

The southerners went to the mountains. Congressman William Elliott had a cottage in Flat Rock, North Carolina, where he and his family customarily spent the month of August. Mrs. W. N. Heyward of Bluffton, migrated to Johnson City, Tennessee, and the Colcocks of Grahamville, retreated to their family place in Brevard. More recent immigrant families also migrated to the mountains. Henry C. "Hal" Pollitzer had a summer place in Saluda, North Carolina, and the Scheper brothers had a retreat in Hendersonville. The Von Harten family also had a summer place near Saluda.[50]

Abbie Holmes Christensen had a family home in Brookline, Massachusetts, to which she and her children retreated for more than twenty summers. Captain Niels Christensen, with few roots in America and many interests in Beaufort, rarely visited New England for more than a few days at a time. However, his son Frederick assiduously recorded his youthful migrations in the 1890s. In May 1897 he traveled directly from Savannah to Boston on the SS *Chattahootchee.* The passage took three days. On the voyage Christensen encountered John Nichols of DeLand, Florida. Nichols had settled in Beaufort after service in the Union Army, established a successful cotton-growing and -ginning business near Beaufort before selling his company and land to J. J. Dale in the late 1870s. Nichols moved to Florida, where he developed vast groves of citrus trees and helped found the town of DeLand.[51]

John J. Dale was from Townsend, Vermont, and he and his large family returned there every summer. In fact, the Dales and their extended family of cousins, including the Danners, Johnsons, and Knowltons, "resorted" to Townsend, Vermont, for three generations. Several other prominent Beaufort families with Vermont origins returned there annually to escape the summer heat. George Wilkins, a partner of Dale's in the McDonald-Wilkins Company, was also from Townsend. When the company reorganized after John J. Dale's death in 1896, a third partner came from Vermont. Mark Batchelder joined William Keyserling, Ross McDonald, and George Wilkins in the McDonald-Wilkins Company. The Batchelder family came from Peru, Vermont, and returned there each summer. The Wilsons, Christensens, Danners, Cuthberts, Dales, and Wilkinses all summered in Townsend, Vermont, in 1906, and the Keyserlings spent much of the summer of 1907 in Townsend. So many Beaufort families "resorted" to Townsend, Vermont, that the nearby *Brattleboro Phoenix* called it the "Beaufort Summer Colony."[52]

NORTHERN VISITORS

Just as many Beaufort families migrated northward to escape the heat of summer, so, many wealthy northern families went to the Carolina lowcountry to escape the winter cold. Many of these northerners bought up impoverished plantation lands, converted them to hunting, fishing, and recreational retreats, and began a movement that reached its peak in the 1920s and 1930s. The first prominent northern investor in Beaufort County was U.S. Senator Donald Cameron of Pennsylvania. Cameron was the son of Senator Simon Cameron, who had been Abraham Lincoln's first secretary of war and later ambassador to Russia. Senator Donald Cameron bought Coffin Point Plantation in 1889. He had previously served as secretary of war in the Ulysses S. Grant administration. Cameron refurbished the old plantation house built by Massachusetts sea captain Ebenezer Coffin in 1800. He became a regular winter sojourner to Beaufort County during the 1880s and 1890s.

Senator Donald Cameron was, among other accomplishments, an organizer of the Pennsylvania Railroad Company. When he arrived in Beaufort, he came on his luxuriously appointed private railroad car, Pennsylvania Railroad Car No. 120. Donald Cameron was often accompanied by wealthy, prominent northerners who were entertained at Coffin Point for the winter months. They renamed the old plantation St. Helena-by-the-Sea. Cameron's wife was Elizabeth Sherman, niece of General William Tecumseh Sherman, and they always brought their four daughters. One of their great friends was Henry Adams of Massachusetts, grandson and great-grandson of American presidents, muckraking journalist, and well-known man of letters. Adams often described his visits to Coffin Point in his journals.

The arrival and departure of the Cameron party was always noted in the local newspaper. While visiting Coffin Point, the Camerons left their private railroad car on a siding at the Beaufort depot. Usually they spent the night at the Sea Island Hotel. The next day they chartered a phosphate tug to carry their party to their landing on Coffin Creek. No doubt, the Camerons influenced other wealthy northerners to visit and invest in Beaufort County.

Henry Adams was not the only national literary figure to visit Beaufort at that time. In 1905 Owen Wister of Philadelphia, author of *The Virginian,* a popular novel of the era, came as a guest of the Calhoun family. He went riding to Laurel Bay with Niels Christensen. Wister was a direct descendant of Major Pierce Butler and Colonel Thomas Middleton of eighteenth-century Beaufort.[53]

Another prominent northerner who was a frequent winter visitor was William K. Vanderbilt. While voyaging south on his beautiful steam yacht *Alva,* he often stopped to replenish his fuel bunkers at the coal dock of the Port Royal and Augusta Railroad. His visits were always accompanied by local speculation that he was scouting the sea islands as a site for a southern retreat. Instead, Vanderbilt decided to purchase land near Asheville, North Carolina, where his son George built Biltmore Castle, the largest private residence in the United States.[54]

One friend of the Vanderbilts did buy land in Beaufort County and remained part of the winter community until his death in 1938. Harry Hollins was a New York financier, a partner of J. Pierpont Morgan's, and a friend of the Vanderbilts. The Vanderbilts and Hollinses traveled through Europe together in 1886. In 1890 Harry Hollins purchased Good Hope Plantation on mainland Beaufort County near Pocotaligo. In 1904 his son, Harry Hollins Jr., purchased a neighboring plantation called Broadmarsh. Both Hollinses were avid hunters and outdoorsmen, and their winter visits continued for nearly sixty years. Harry Hollins Sr.'s son Jack married Beaufort's postmistress, Sallie Mae Kitchins, and made Beaufort his permanent home. Harry Hollins Sr. had to sell Good Hope Plantation during the financial Panic of 1907, but his family owned Broadmarsh until 1949.[55]

Another prominent Gilded Age figure visited Beaufort in 1907. Howard Gould, son of the famous "robber baron" Jay Gould, arrived aboard his palatial steam yacht *Niagara IV* in April 1907. The Gould party replenished coal at Port Royal and anchored for several days off the U.S. Naval Station. While there, Gould spent several days exploring the creeks and islands surrounding Port Royal Sound. William VonHarten was the harbor pilot who brought the *Niagara IV* across the Port Royal bar. The Gould's yacht was 270 feet long, displaced 1,500 tons, and drew 18 feet of water, as large as many of the passenger steamers of the 1870s. VonHarten stayed with the party to guide their explorations aboard the *Niagara IV*'s tender, a 100-foot, 29-knot "racing machine." Gould commented that Beaufort and the sea islands "surpassed anything he had seen on the southern coast." VonHarten took the Goulds to the beach on Hilton Head for a picnic. That spot most impressed the New Yorkers. However, Gould did not invest in Beaufort County.

When L. E. Emerson bought a plantation near Georgetown and H. W. Havermeyer bought one near Beaufort in 1907, the *Charleston News and Courier* commented, "It is gratifying that South Carolina is attracting immigrants of this class. They will bring money to the state and hasten the development of South Carolina. Land bought for hunting now can be planted and developed later prompting rising land values."[56]

The area of Beaufort County most influenced by this movement was the sparsely settled area south of the Broad River. Much of Hilton Head Island had fallen into disuse by 1900. Most of the black population was moving to Savannah, Atlanta, or northern cities where jobs were available. Many of the freedmen's homesteads were abandoned, and Mitchelville, a Civil War–era town, was deserted. In the 1890s large tracts of Hilton Head Island were bought very cheaply and set aside for hunting and recreation. Several plantation properties on Hilton Head changed hands in 1894. Some of these investors were southerners buying back old family properties, and others were northern capitalists looking for winter retreats. In 1894 Montpelier plantation sold to Sara Guerard, a southerner, for $4,500. Bull Island, between Hilton Head and Bluffton, sold to Barbara Walker, a northerner, for $5.50 per acre. Nearby Beef Island sold to Joseph Baynard, a southerner, for $600. Spanish Wells and Braddock's Point Place on Hilton Head Island sold to William P. Clyde, the New York shipping magnate, for $3 per acre.[57]

While few blacks continued to live on Hilton Head in the era of decline, even fewer whites did. One white survivor from the Civil War days who remained on Hilton Head until his death was Dr. F. E. Wilder, who had come to Hilton Head late in the war as part of the military and missionary establishment. He remained to serve the freedmen after the army departed. Dr. Wilder was quite prominent during Reconstruction. He had been a delegate to the 1868 constitutional convention and often represented Hilton Head Island on local boards and commissions. He was always a Republican, so his political status diminished after the elections of 1876 and 1890. By 1900 Wilder had acquired a fair amount of property on Hilton Head and was comfortably ensconced in Otter Hole Plantation. He became the unofficial host for the parade of hunters, fishermen, and northern travelers who visited Hilton Head. His home at Otter Hole was described as a "delightful cottage." There he entertained parties from Savannah, Beaufort, and northern cities. Other than the lighthouse keeper Paul Schwartzer and an occasional detachment of army artillerymen from Fort Fremont, Dr. Wilder was the only white man on Hilton Head Island. In 1903 a large party of local people stayed at Otter Hole for a week of summer fishing, crabbing, and swimming. The party included Charles Pollitzer, Tom Martin, James Martin, and R. Hudson. They motored from Bluffton in the Martins' "handsome launch."[58]

During winter months the visitors to Hilton Head were wealthy northerners. At Christmas in 1906, a large party of them spent the holidays cavorting on the Hilton Head beaches and hunting in the forests. The principal hosts were Mr. and Mrs. William P. Clyde and Mr. and Mrs. J. Sergeant Cram of Philadelphia. The Crams had spent their honeymoon in 1905 at the Clydes' Braddock's Point Retreat. They were entranced by the sea islands and eventually bought property near Bluffton, including Foot Point. Among the northern socialites on Hilton Head in 1906 were Mr. and Mrs. Edward Lawrence of New York; Charles Myers of Atlantic City, New Jersey; Miss Viola McCarthy of Philadelphia; and Miss Annie Craven, Mrs. W. D. Brown, and Mr. and Mrs. E. W. Duflock, all of New York. In addition, the Conners, Cruthers, and Buck families of Philadelphia were on Hilton Head as guests of the Clydes. Among the local entertainments was an oyster roast on the banks of Skull Creek hosted by Mr. and Mrs. J. R. Hudson of Bluffton, assisted by their daughters Mary and Nettie. Local families who joined the party were Mr. and Mrs. Tracey Hudson, Pinckney Reynolds, Barry Graves, and Howard and Matthew Bailey. On Christmas Day, Mrs. Cram and Mrs. Lawrence decorated the Honey Horn Chapel with "a wealth of evergreens" and arranged for a visit by a red-costumed Santa Claus. It was a happy holiday retreat for the "smart set" of the Northeast. The local correspondent for the *Beaufort Gazette* wrote, "Not since before the war has our island been the scene of such gaiety and pleasure among the whites at Christmas."[59]

The most significant property acquisition of this era was the 1902 purchase of Palmetto Bluff Plantation across the May River from Bluffton. This 18,600-acre tract had been assembled in the 1880s and 1890s from eighteen separate antebellum plantations by Savannah publisher and entrepreneur Colonel John Holbrook Estill. Colonel Estill had many interests, but his principal business was publishing the *Savannah Morning News* and the *Macon Telegraph*. He had managed to assemble this huge tract for little more than the price of the timber after cotton had become unprofitable. In 1902 Estill sold the entire tract to Colonel Richard Thornwell Wilson of New York City. Wilson and his family were among the social elite of New York. He had made his early fortune reorganizing southern railroads after the Civil War. He was once president of the East Tennessee, Virginia, and Georgia Railway but later moved to New York and expanded his fortune through banking and finance. The Wilsons lived at 511 Fifth Avenue, the former home of William Marcy "Boss" Tweed.

The Wilsons were sufficiently prominent in New York society that Richard Wilson's son Marshall married Caroline Astor, and his daughter Grace married Cornelius Vanderbilt III. These were only two of the fortunate unions that gave the family the nickname "the marrying Wilsons." In 1912 the Wilson family built an immense mansion at Palmetto Bluff overlooking the May River. The house was three and a half stories tall and thirteen bays wide; it contained forty rooms. It had a ballroom and a giant portico supported by four thirty-foot-tall Ionic columns. The mansion was the center of much high-toned winter social activity for many years. The palatial home, enclosing twenty-eight thousand square feet and the largest private residence ever built in Beaufort County, burned to the ground in 1926.[60]

Recreation was not the only reason northern investors bought up Beaufort County lands. Many purchased large tracts of inexpensive land solely for the timber they contained. In 1906, in an article entitled "Our Vanishing Timber," the *Beaufort Gazette* reported that "a number of men from New York and Norfolk . . . are buying up all the available timberland in the vicinity of Grahamville, Ridgeland and Hardeeville." Loblolly pine, once considered worthless, was fetching handsome prices for pulp and timber. Part of the reason for the rising value of formerly inferior timber was the disappearance of the long-leaf yellow pine that had earlier fed the lumber mills on the Port Royal Railroad. The disappearance of the pine forests in Hampton County closed the lumber mills in Beaufort and shifted the industry to the south end of the county. Some of these land purchases by men from New York were added to the holdings of the Okatee Hunt Club, founded in 1894. Eventually the club owned fifty thousand acres in Beaufort and Jasper Counties.

Some of the 1906 land purchases were the origin of the Argent Lumber Company, which was formed in 1916 by Horace W. Phillips of Suffolk, Virginia, and Ross and William McNeal of Burgaw, North Carolina. The firm built a large sawmill in Hardeeville and ran narrow-gauge railway lines through the forests and swamps of southern Beaufort County. For many years, the Argent Lumber Company harvested the vast timber resources of Okatee Hunt Club. In 1926 the Club refused to sell timber to the Argent Company unless it also bought the land. Thus the company acquired thousands of acres of Beaufort and Jasper County. In 1957 the Argent Lumber Company's assets, including forty-three thousand acres of Beaufort and Jasper County land, were acquired by the Union Camp Corporation.[61]

HUNTING, FISHING, MAROONING

Hunting was the winter activity that attracted most of the northern visitors to the lowcountry. Winter duck hunting was frequent on the mainland swamps and marshes at places like the Hollinses' Good Hope and Broadmoor Plantations. Fields on high ground were cleared, planted, and tended to attract quail, and the pine, oak, and hickory forests teemed with white-tailed deer. Often the uninhabited barrier islands were bought as exclusive hunting preserves for northern visitors, just as they had been for antebellum planters. This tradition was so old in Beaufort County that the barrier islands between St. Helena Sound and Port Royal Sound have been known as the Hunting Islands since the eighteenth century.

In 1903 James McLaughlin of the McLaughlin Brothers Publishing Company in New York bought Fripp and Story Islands as a "hunting preserve." McLaughlin arrived with a large hunting party in December 1903. Among his guests were his two sons and W. F. Britain of New York and Augusta, Georgia. The group arrived aboard the *Trionex,* James McLaughlin's "handsome steam yacht." Their host and guide during the hunting excursion was John N. Wallace, described as "one of Beaufort's crack sportsmen." Wallace employed M. O' D. White and his famous hunting dogs. Many other local men were hired to assist this expedition and McLaughlin, a convivial man, was "a favorite with all who met him."[62]

These winter hunting expeditions became a minor local business around the turn of the century. In December 1904 a large party of prominent and wealthy Brooklynites arrived in Beaufort for a winter hunt on Edings Island (now St. Philips) Island.[63] The party consisted of H. L. Kenyon and a Mr. Grout of New York and Messrs. Fairchild, Lutz, and Danbury of Trenton, New Jersey. Their guide and host was M. O' D. White, who, according to the *Palmetto Post,* was "well-known for his sporting skill, his drivers and his fine pack of dogs." The men packed their tents and gear aboard White's large launch *Mystic* and set out for a week on Edings Island. Several hunters' wives accompanied the party.[64]

Winter hunting grew so faddish that legal steps were taken to conserve local game. In 1893 the General Assembly passed an act "for the protection of partridge, quail, woodcock, pheasant, deer or wild turkey in Beaufort County." The new law made it illegal to sell this game for meat in Beaufort County or to export it from the county to sell. The law carried a penalty of a ten-dollar fine or ten days in jail.

Sport fishing also attracted visitors to Beaufort County but, as in the days of William Elliott III, the locals enjoyed it most often. Whenever the weather was good and the fish were biting, Beaufortonians, black and white, stopped working and went fishing. And Beaufort County's vast salt marshes produced an extraordinary bounty. From Captain Jean Ribault's surprise in 1562 that "two draughts of the ships net was sufficient to feed the whole company of our two ships for a week" to the present day, Beaufort County's saltwater has teemed with fish. So it was at the turn of the century. On October 25, 1895, Frederick Christensen and Gus Chaplin left work and went fishing in Chaplin's boat. They caught twenty-nine whiting and thought it nothing special. For sport fishermen in other parts of America, that might be their total catch for a season. In Beaufort the fishing season lasted all year long, but the locals did not fish much in January, February, or March. The fish were there, but it just was not much fun on the water.

Around 1900, when small marine engines became more reliable, Beaufort's fishermen began to venture out to sea. In June 1907 a party of local men enjoyed a day of deep-sea fishing at the wreck of the *William Lawrence,* located four miles off Bay Point. It was soon discovered that the many shipwrecks off the South Carolina coast made wonderful fishing reefs. The 1907 party had included C. G. Luther, Lon Brooks, W. P. Jay, W. D. Gaunt, J. H. Haynesworth, Dave Mittle, W. G. Kinghorn, E. D. Raney, Dr. M. G. Elliott, and Will Elliott, who returned from Columbia often to hunt and fish.[65]

Another outdoor activity held over from antebellum days was "marooning." Marooning was a camping excursion to one of the uninhabited barrier islands. Marooning was much more elaborate than ordinary camping. First of all, marooning lasted several days, often several weeks. It usually involved large parties and, as often as not, included many women. Boatloads of food, tents, extra clothes, and tanks of water had to be transported to the beach. Many Beaufort families spent their summer vacations "marooning" at regular spots on the beach, and generations of local children were raised with the tradition.

The favorite marooning spot was Bay Point. With wide beaches, nearly constant ocean breezes, and a small creek to harbor sailboats and launches, it was ideal. Before the Civil War, planter families visited Bay Point so regularly that many families built small cottages to camp in. Most of these cottages were destroyed or commandeered by Union lookouts during the war. Shortly after the war, the tradition was revived. "Marooning" was mostly, but not exclusively, a summer activity. In June 1877 the following description appeared in the local newspaper: "The time is approaching when many of our citizens begin to think of Bay Point, and tents and sails are overhauled preparatory to a trip to that spot where the sea breeze is never failing and the fisherman never complains of his luck."[66]

Marooning reached its peak around the turn of the century. In July 1892 Bay Point was a constant convention of "marooners." First a party of young Beaufortonians arrived. As the *Palmetto Post* noted, "Masters Willie Wiggins, Gordon Rodgers and others have been having an outing at Bay Point." They were soon followed by C. E. and H.T. Danner, who "went to Bay Point Monday to spend several days." These parties of local men were soon followed by "several families from Hampton County who spent two weeks on Bay Point." Marooning on Bay Point did not slow down until nearly Christmas, when the weather became too cold. In November, the *Post* later reported, "Messrs Allan Stuart, J. N. Wallace, H. F. Von Harten, and A. F. Felder killed a buck on Edings Island adjoining Bay Point."[67]

Bay Point marooning had become so pervasive a tradition that it was transformed into a commercial activity. Charlie Danner's steamer *Summer Girl* often took excursionists and picnickers to Bay Point. In August 1903 the *Summer Girl* was making regular trips to Bay Point from 12:00 noon to 4:00 P.M. with the promise of returning the passengers to Beaufort in time for a ball game. The cost for adults was fifty cents and for children twenty-five cents. All the excursion activity at Bay Point pushed the true marooners to more distant islands. In August 1903 Frank Ricker, William White, and Albert Kinghorn of Beaufort and J. C. Richardson of Garnett ventured to Pritchard's Island for "a week's maroon."[68]

Summer cottages also returned to Bay Point as marooning grew more elaborate and more formal. These cottages were little more than wooden floors with permanent palmetto or shingle roofs, where gear was stored out of the sun and rain. In July 1905 a marooning party went to Bay Point to occupy the Barnwell cottage for several weeks. It included Mr. and Mrs. Charles E. Danner, Edith and Bessie Kinghorn, Margaret Purse of Savannah, Jennie Bishop, Mabel Burn, Annie White, William White, Irving Kinghorn, J.A. Kinghorn, and William Kinghorn. On the Fourth of July, the marooners were joined by an even larger party of Beaufortonians who reportedly spent the national holiday at the beach "fishing, surf bathing and hunting for turtle eggs to eat." This party included Dr. and Mrs. M. G. Elliott, Elizabeth and Rita Crofut, Hermine Scheper, Jane Waterhouse, H. Mazyck, Frederick

Christensen, W. W. Elliott, W. H. Hull, and George Waterhouse Jr. They were delivered on R. K. Harley's "handsome launch." The roster of visitors revealed that a fair portion of Beaufort's white society spent the Fourth of July 1905 on Bay Point.[69]

Often the men would maroon for several days in advance of the ladies to set up camp, catch fish, and gather turtle eggs to feed a larger party. In July 1907 Harold Scheper, Charles E. Danner Jr., and Allen Paul went marooning on Bay Point for a week. "They left Tuesday morning with a large tent and a supply of eatables," noted the *Beaufort Gazette.* By the weekend they were joined by Misses C. O. Barnwell, Hattie Barnwell, Ruth Rhett, Dorothy Batchelder, and Sarah Barnwell. The women were delivered by the steamer *Summer Girl* and stayed at Charlie Barnwell's cottage.[70]

Chapter 7

The Great Fire and Violent Crime

"RED SATURDAY:" THE GREAT FIRE OF 1907

Next to the Sea Island hurricane of 1893, the greatest disaster in Beaufort County history was the Great Fire of January 19, 1907, which consumed much of downtown Beaufort. It was, like the 1893 storm, one of those unforgettable events by which people marked passages in their lives. To a generation of Beaufortonians, the fire was known as "Red Saturday."

Saturday morning, January 19, 1907, was a clear winter day. The weather was distinguished only by an exceptionally strong south wind that blew straight up the river and into Bay Street, snatching the hats off the men and billowing the skirts of the ladies on the boardwalk. Though the morning was uneventful, much of the town was out for a stroll, and the stores and businesses on Bay Street and Port Republic Street were busy. As the town bustled through its Saturday routine, the Lady's Island ferry docked several times at the foot of Scheper's wharf. Small crowds of sea islanders disembarked each time and ambled through Bay Street to the black-owned businesses on West Street and black churches a few blocks beyond. The oarsmen on the ferryboat had to strain against the increasing wind to force the barge back to White Hall Landing on Lady's Island. By noon the wind had increased to thirty knots and was approaching gale force. Small boats left the river, and the ferry remained lodged at White Hall Landing, waiting for the wind to subside. Because it was an otherwise clear day, the strong wind did not elicit the ominous memories of 1893.

In an empty, unused portion of F.W. Scheper's large warehouse on the waterfront, a small group of teenage boys huddled around a little fire for warmth. Some said they were smoking forbidden cigarettes. Others said they were gambling with grownups. At about 1:00 P.M. a howling wind slipped through the clapboard siding of the warehouse and whipped the embers of the fire across the lint-covered floor. In a moment, the flames burst out, and the wind pressed them against the resinous heart pine that framed the building. The People's Bank behind the wharf was closed on Saturday, but employees in Scheper's store saw the smoke from the warehouse. Many strollers on Bay Street saw the smoke and smelled it as well. The odor of a heart pine fire is a familiar smell to lowcountry residents. Sometimes it meant warmth and food. Other times it meant trouble. The boys fled the warehouse in panic.

At 1:30 P.M. the alarm went off, and the Washington and Union No. 1 Fire Companies responded as quickly as their volunteers could gather. But by the time the first firemen arrived, the warehouse was already consumed, and Scheper's three-story grocery store on Bay Street was in flames. The store was "crowded with goods" and many tried to remove the merchandise. They were routed by the flames, which were driven by the gale winds. In the confines of the rooms and halls, the fire resembled a blowtorch. The building was soon destroyed. During Reconstruction, this had been the famous Stevens House, named for Major General Isaac Stevens, a heroic martyr of the Union cause. The Stevens House was the birthplace of the South Carolina Republican Party and of Robert Small's political career. On the second floor, above Scheper's store, was the Clover Club's meeting room and circulating library. Many of its books and appurtenances were consumed. The Clover Club Library had borrowed space in this building in the meeting room of Harmony Lodge of Ancient Freemasons. The Harmony Lodge, founded in 1756, was one of the oldest in the South. All of its regalia and records were lost to the conflagration.

The People's Bank, built of brick and stone the year before, was gutted. Ohlant's store, Ah Li's Chinese laundry, and, most important, the Dispensary Building were all burned to the ground. The fire crews were powerless to control the blaze. Driven by winds in excess of thirty miles per hour, the flames crossed Bay Street and ignited the large hardware and building supply store of N. Christensen and Sons. Frederick Christensen was able to save the books and papers from his office and twelve to thirteen hundred dollars in cash from the safe at the hardware store, but the rest of the inventory was a total loss. The building supply inventory only provided more fuel for the raging fire. James M. Crofut's next-door crockery store burned "from cellar to roof," a total loss. It was from the second-floor balcony of Crofut's store that Robert Smalls's little daughter Elizabeth had read the Declaration of Independence to an ebullient crowd of freedmen on July 4, 1872, symbolizing the joy and hope of Beaufort's newest citizens. That landmark was also lost within minutes. Next to Crofut's store was the house of George Holmes, which in 1907 was rented to Mrs. Mabel Corey. This building, though damaged, prevented the fire from spreading westward. As the *Beaufort Gazette* recorded, "This was a brick and tabby house and it was largely due to this fact that the fire did not spread further west." The fire companies saved the store of John Levin and the adjacent Hutchings Building occupied by Charlie Chin Sang.

While the fire was blocked from moving westward, nothing could stop it from raging northward up Carteret Street. Driven by the southerly gale, the fire hurtled northward consuming building after building. The pitiful volume of water that the frantic fire crews could deliver was no match for the roaring flames. At one point, the fire even burned through a water hose stretched across Carteret Street. The fire leaped from Christensen Hardware to two adjacent homes. Mrs. Rachel Haynes, a black woman, lived in one. Though her house was destroyed, a gang of men, black and white, working furiously together, saved her furniture. She was effusive in her praise of the men who fearlessly and repeatedly entered her burning house to retrieve her possessions. Across Carteret Street, a solitary young girl pulled down all the wooden fences and removed the boards and posts to keep back the fire. The *Beaufort Gazette* called her "a heroine."

The fire easily crossed Port Republic Street. It burned the office and several buildings of the former state senator Thomas Talbird. Lost in the fire were family records of Beaufort's oldest builders. Talbird's grandfather had built the arsenal in 1798 from bricks left over from the Beaufort District's 1769 courthouse. He also built the first Beaufort College Building on Bay Street in 1803. Talbird's father rebuilt the arsenal in 1851 and built the new Beaufort College Building on Carteret Street in 1852. The records of many of Beaufort's antebellum monuments were casualties of the fire of 1907.

No one even tried to save the city market adjacent to Talbird's. It was an open wooden shed that was almost instantly engulfed. Also destroyed, ironically, was the firehouse of the Washington Fire Company. As the fire leaped across Craven Street it consumed the old Town Hall, scene of much of Beaufort's colorful Reconstruction history. The fire crews were able to save the arsenal principally because it was constructed of brick and tabby. But Mrs. Alice O'Dell's house next to Town Hall burned to the ground. The new Methodist church, built on land donated by Abbie Holmes Christensen and largely with her money, was saved because the roof was covered with tin. At this point the inferno was so intense that resin was drawn out of the pine clapboards covering the buildings on the east side of Carteret Street.

Many roofs of the buildings that burned were made of cedar shingles. The building frames, constructed mostly from southern yellow pine, practically exploded when they caught fire. As they did, the burning shingles were hurled into the air and carried halfway across town by the south wind. As the *Beaufort Gazette* described it, "Huge pieces of fire were carried northward and eastward." Many shingle roofs caught fire, and several houses blocks away from the fire were burned down. Thomas Talbird's and W. F. Sanders' houses on the Point were both destroyed.

During the afternoon of the fire, the whole town pulled together to halt the inferno. The Washington Fire Company was a white organization, while the Union No. 1 Fire Company was a black organization. For many years they had a friendly competition to see which company could produce the "first squirt" when a fire in town needed extinguishing. On "Red Saturday," both labored heroically to halt the progress of the flames. All competition and all racial boundaries were set aside. As the *Beaufort Gazette* reported it, "Many men did noble work. Many whites saved colored homes. Many colored saved white homes."

The flames from Scheper's store and warehouse ignited the old Fuller House on the corner of Bay and Carteret Streets. Colonial merchant John Gordon had built that old house, one of the most prominent in Beaufort, in about 1760. It was later sold to Colonel Thomas Middleton, whose Fuller descendants had lived in it for several generations. In 1907 it was the home of J. N. Wallace. The fire in that house ignited the Stephen Elliott House next door. This was the house where many generations of Beaufort's antebellum leaders were reared, including Brigadier General Stephen Elliott, a martyr of the Confederate cause. In 1907 it was the home of Beaufort lawyer W. J. Thomas.

As the flames leaped from the Elliott-Thomas house to the neighboring home of Mrs. Harriett Parmalee Waterhouse, a crowd of black women appeared to form a bucket brigade from the river to the Waterhouse home. These women were all employees of the Waterhouse Cotton Gin at the west end of Bay Street. Their alert and heroic effort saved not only the Waterhouse home but also two houses behind it, one of which is the oldest house in Beaufort. This remarkable act was the reward of loyalty to Harriett Waterhouse's husband, George Waterhouse, who had been one of the largest and fairest employers in Beaufort for thirty years. Although he had died thirteen years before, Beaufortonians black and white did not forget their old friends or their old obligations.

Despite the extraordinary effort of the firemen who were "fighting the fire with all the power they could" and despite countless individual acts of heroism and generosity, when the smoke cleared, forty buildings were destroyed. The fire of 1907 gutted the commercial center of Beaufort, and invaluable artifacts of its history lay in charred ruins. Property loss was estimated at $175,000 and the *Beaufort Gazette* correctly labeled it the "most serious conflagration that ever visited the old town." In fact, the property loss in the town of Beaufort was greater than in the hurricane of 1893. Of the property lost, only $20,000 worth was insured. Frederick Christensen said that F. W. Scheper had $11,000 in insurance, and W. J. Thomas had $3,000 in insurance. Few others had any insurance. Frederick Christenson estimated their losses at $25,000 to $35,000. But, thankfully, no lives had been lost.[1]

During the afternoon, dozens of cases of liquor that had been extracted from the South Carolina Dispensary Building were stacked in Bay Street.

As the fire burned itself out late in the day, many firefighters and volunteers availed themselves of the state's liquor. As Frederick Christensen recalled, "By 9 P.M. or 10 P.M. most of the firefighters were drunk." Many of the townsmen were also pretty well besotted. To prevent looting, Mayor Townsend ordered the Third Division, South Carolina Naval Militia (Beaufort Volunteer Artillery), to duty to protect the streets. As the *Beaufort Gazette* described it, "Most of the young men, who were firemen, donned their military clothing and went on guard to protect the ruined district from looting and pilfering." In addition, a squad of soldiers from Fort Fremont was dispatched with firefighting equipment. They stayed on to assist in guard duty. Mayor Townsend, fearing trouble, had sent for assistance from the U.S. Army garrison at Fort Screven on Tybee Island. About dusk, the government tug *Gibbon* arrived from Savannah with forty-five heavily armed troopers under the command of Captain Joe Wheeler, son of the famous Confederate cavalry commander "Fighting Joe" Wheeler.

The presence of armed troops in downtown Beaufort angered many of townspeople. The black community that had provided so much of the manpower to fight the fire took it as a sign of bad faith. Some complained of the use of the military and were "loud in their murmurs." But the *Beaufort Gazette* thought the mayor's precautions only prudent and suggested that "only the malefactors could complain about the troops."

Mayor Townsend had placed a curfew on the ruined downtown, and the troops on guard were to enforce it. This led to the only personal tragedy of the day. After dark, and after the curfew, a black man named William Bennett ventured onto Bay Street. He had fought the fire all day and may have been intoxicated by night. The *Beaufort Gazette* reported that he had been warned by a white friend not to venture downtown at night.

Frederick Christensen speculated that Bennett might have been "drunk and sassy." Whatever the cause, one of the armed guards, W.T. Wiggins of the Third Division, shot and killed Bennett at 1:30 A.M. Bennett was a prominent and popular character in Beaufort. He was a cornet player in the Allen Brass Band and thus a well-known figure on most public occasions. The death of Bennett occasioned a very large funeral attended by many regretful white people. This tragedy shattered the racial cooperation that had characterized "Red Saturday." The *Savannah Morning News* reported that the troops from Tybee Island had been sent to "quell a Negro riot over the killing of Bennett," but Frederick Christensen flatly denied the alarmist story. No riot occurred. In fact, Mayor Townsend and Captain Wheeler called for a meeting of black and white citizens to explain the circumstances and offer regrets over the incident. The black community wanted justice and demanded the prosecution of W.T. Wiggins. A month later, Deputy Sheriff

M. O. D. White arrested Wiggins and lodged him in the Beaufort jail. Wiggins made bail at five hundred dollars and awaited his trial. Wiggins was represented by lawyer W. J. Thomas, who demanded a jury trial. Wiggins claimed he had acted only "in the discharge of his duties." He was acquitted two months later.[2]

No national outpouring of charity followed the Great Fire of 1907. Except for the life of William Bennett, only property had been lost. But the Beaufort community rallied together to assist the sufferers from the fire. A local committee was formed, led by George Holmes. George Waterhouse Jr., H.T. Danner, W. J. Thomas, and Dr. C. M. Guffin made up the committee. The committee collected $1,244 locally. The largest contributors were C. E. Danner, Waterhouse and Company, McDonald-Wilkins Company, William Keyserling, George Holmes, Thomas Lee, and Miss Dexter. More than half of the committee's distributions went to black people. Two months after the fire, George Waterhouse Jr. took out a full-page advertisement in the *Gazette* promoting fire insurance from the Continental Insurance Company of New York, the Hartford Insurance Company of Connecticut, and the Phoenix Insurance Company of Hartford, Connecticut. "These companies," Waterhouse assured the readers, "paid their San Francisco losses." On April 4, 1907, the South Carolina dispensary reopened in the Armstrong Store on Bay Street, one block west of the black hole left by the fire. Beaufort began to return to normal.[3]

In the fourteen years between the hurricane of 1893 and the fire of 1907, Beaufort County had gone through a profound change. The rising tide of progress and prosperity, which had characterized the previous twenty-five years, had begun to ebb. The county suffered a series of natural disasters, economic losses, and political disappointments that set the tone for the next half century. Those at the top of the economic ladder were partially insulated from the economic decline. Many managed to cling tenaciously to the business status and social expectations they had inherited. Those who first feel the pinch of poverty during times of economic decline are always the poor, and the poor of turn-of-the-century Beaufort County were almost all African Americans. They were the first to recognize the ebb tide of fortune and were the first to leave.

"LAW AIN'T NO GOOD:" LOCAL VIOLENCE

While the children of Beaufort's commercial elite generally lived the Victorian version of the good life, not everything was idyllic. One social problem that Beaufort County shared with the rest of South Carolina was a high level of crime and violence. And the public response to crime was not always reassuring.

In 1904 the *Beaufort Gazette* catalogued the murders in South Carolina for the previous fifteen years:

Year	*Number of Homicides*
1888	102
1889	111
1890	120
1891	143
1892	105
1893	131
1894	141
1895	210
1896	202
1897	225
1898	247
1899	213
1900	222
1901	102
1902	190
1903	222[4]

In 1900 South Carolina's population was 1,340,316. The murder rate that year was roughly one murder for every 6,000 citizens. And murder was only the worst of the crimes. Stabbings, shootings, robberies, and break-ins were common occurrences. According to the temperance societies, the state suffered a pandemic of drunkenness, which led to much random violence. Other reformers blamed the vice of gambling. A large number of South Carolinians were very poor; some were even desperate. A certain amount of government-tolerated political violence set a bad example to the lawless. Finally, in the 1890s it was common for South Carolina men, black and white, to openly carry sidearms. South Carolina was a biracial society, and simmering resentments and open hostility led to violent confrontations. In many communities, meager law enforcement resources and uncooperative neighborhoods led to vigilante justice, which often accelerated the cycle of violence.

In 1894 the *Palmetto Post* expressed alarm that five recent murders in Beaufort County remained unsolved. A year before, Robert Ford had shot and killed Dan Henderson over a gambling debt. Both men were black. Ford was never apprehended. In January 1894 two sailors from the naval station were shot near Brotherhood Mine, reportedly "by a colored man who escaped." One of the sailors later died in a Charleston hospital. Shortly afterward, Samuel Jenkins "split open the head of a small colored boy with a hatchet." Jenkins escaped. In February 1894 James McTee, a white man, was shot to death in front of a downtown store. The murderer, Eddie Washington, a black man, escaped as well. In March 1894 Caesar Johnson was murdered by Charlie Williams in Port Royal and escaped into the woods. Both men were black. The newspaper commented that the latest murder was "one more in a large list of murders in recent years, followed by the escape of the murderer." The *Post* blamed the violence on out-of-town troublemakers, guns, and gambling: "Nearly every one of the up-country and Georgia Negroes who come here are armed to the teeth with the latest and most improved revolvers." No one dreamed of limiting firearms for either race, so local reformers suggested cracking down on gambling. As one newspaper put it, "The fact is . . . all good citizens should combine to put down the evil gambling . . . one source from which murder is likely to occur." In 1911 one citizen suggested requiring a state license to sell ammunition to control the incidences of shooting.[5] There is little evidence that government at any level did much to eliminate gambling or the sale of ammunition.

When Frederick Christensen returned to Beaufort in 1895 after several years of education in Brookline, Massachusetts, the level of violence that was casually tolerated shocked him. Christensen witnessed a scuffle on Bay Street between a white town constable and a black man. The constable drew his pistol and fired point blank at his assailant, but the gun misfired. The black man ran around the corner of Christensen and Sons Hardware and fled up Carteret Street. The constable fired three more times and missed all three times. Except for the constable's poor marksmanship, the town merchants found the incident unremarkable. Frederick Christensen confided to his diary: "It is funny how the people here take the shooting. I mean the white people. In a civilized country everyone would be stirred up but here no one seems to have anything to say against the constable." Christensen shared his opinion with young Teddy VanNess, who was a stock boy in the hardware store. VanNess, wrote Christensen, "echoes what he hears at home . . . says he thinks it would be a good thing to kill a half dozen Niggers." The following year Christensen was horrified by a lynching in neighboring Colleton County: "Half a dozen white men took a young colored man, his wife and old mother in Colleton County near Broxton Bridge one night last December and beat the man and old woman to death with straps. The young woman escaped alive. This was done because one or all of them were accused of stealing a Bible from a church. Four of the lynchers were tried and acquitted in Colleton County. The evidence was overwhelming but the jury didn't care."

These incidents prompted Christensen to comment on the state of race relations in Beaufort County in 1896. He was, of course, the eldest son of a Union officer and a Gideonite missionary. He was raised in Beaufort with many children of northern and southern background, and he received his highest education in Massachusetts. His opinion was not isolated in Beaufort, where many of the merchants were of northern or immigrant extraction and most of the money was in the hands of such citizens as well. "Oh!" Frederick Christensen lamented. "What a fine country this is where eleven-twelfths of the people are regarded by the influential twelfth as no better than apes. (I've heard this several times since I've been here) and where every other man carries a pistol and all celebrate Christ's birthday by getting drunk. Mr. Johnson promises to show me an unarguable article to prove that Niggers have no soul."[6]

The most horrific murder of the era left a lasting impression on both Frederick Christensen and Will Elliott. During the summer of 1897, a rivalry arose—"Some dispute over a woman," as Will Elliott put it—between two black men. One of the men was small and worked on a phosphate dredge. The other man was huge and menacing. As Will Elliott described him thirty years afterward, "I never in my life saw such powerful shoulders and neck on a man as on this Negro." The large man commandeered a bateau, rowed out to the phosphate dredge and confronted the smaller man. He seized the small man, held him over the water by his feet and cut his throat from ear to ear. He held his victim upside down until he bled to death. Horrified witnesses testified at the trial, and the murderer was sentenced to hang. On the day of the execution, October 15, 1897, a large crowd gathered at the jailhouse. The sheriff, W. O. Prentiss, became alarmed at the size of the crowd. As Frederick Christensen put it, "A murderer was hung today. . . . A great many people came in from the country and the islands to see the operation . . . done in the jail-yard but the high scaffold could be seen from the street . . . noose broke, they hung him twice." Will Elliott elaborated on the incident of the hanging: "When the trap was sprung at the execution, he broke the rope in his fall and in a few minutes regained consciousness. The Negroes gathered around cried out that he must go free. It is a kind of superstition among them that if a condemned man is not hung on the first try, he must go free." When the crowd became restive, Sheriff Prentice hesitated to repeat the execution. Will Elliott was then the attorney for the sheriff, and he advised that the sentence of the court must be carried out, superstition or not. The sheriff and his deputy, Tommy Mann, got a one-inch hawser from the waterfront and repeated the hanging. The rope was so thick that it failed to snap the murderer's neck, and he hung there for several minutes until he strangled to death. The crowd dispersed, murmuring. Frederick Christensen said simply of the murderer, "He showed courage."[7]

In 1898 Beaufort witnessed a double hanging in the jail yard—"something we have not seen for many a long day," said the *Palmetto Post.* The condemned were Jeff Habersham and William Johnson. Both men were black and were convicted of murder. This was the last double execution in the history of Beaufort County and one of the last hangings.[8]

Despite the harsh public nature of the punishments, much crime and violence went unprosecuted, and this led to incidents of vigilante justice. In May 1901 two mechanics at the U.S. Naval Station were suspected of lending government tools to private contractors. This minor corruption was compounded by the fact that the men, Burlingame and Smith, had taken up residence in Beaufort with several "women of ill-fame." Mayor C. C. Townsend went to the house to arrest the men and was rudely treated by the boisterous occupants. Townsend claimed that the denizens of the house insulted his daughter. The incident was inflamed by the fact that the mechanics were white and the women were black. This incited the "excitables" in Beaufort, and a crowd of young white men led by O'Hear Sanders and T. R. Heyward ransacked the house looking for the malefactors. Unsuccessful, they proceeded by boat to Parris Island, located the men, "threatened their landlord, fired their pistols and went home." This mob action angered Niels Christensen Sr., who owned the house that had been ransacked. He sponsored a resolution supported by the Commerce Club condemning the extralegal violence and criticizing Mayor Townsend for encouraging it. Townsend claimed Christensen "did it for spite," while Christensen called the mayor "a hypocrite." The episode interestingly revealed lingering political and social fissures among Beaufort's white elite.

A few months later a black man was arrested for "trespass with felonious intent" and lodged in the Port Royal jail. A group of white men wearing masks broke him out of jail, severely beat him, and ran him out of Port Royal. The group said he was last seen "on his way to Savannah," but Frederick Christensen and "a good many others thought he had been lynched."

These incidents greatly exacerbated race relations in Beaufort County, and in April 1903 a serious race riot nearly broke out. The incident that nearly touched off the riot was the arrest of two black men from Hampton County who were wanted for bad debts in Hampton. They were due to be transported back to Hampton County to face justice, but Beaufort blacks were convinced that the "prisoners were to be taken to Hampton to be lynched." A hostile crowd gathered at the jail determined to save the men from summary justice in Hampton County. Excited rumors circulated in town, and Governor Duncan Clinch Heyward called out the Beaufort Volunteer Artillery to help suppress a riot if necessary. The militiamen quietly assembled at Ribault Hall, where Commander O'Hear Sanders distributed new Metford rifles with which the men had never practiced. Sanders had to load each of the five-shot magazines himself. The following day Sheriff Prentice and two deputies from Hampton, along with some armed city constables, "escorted the two terrified Negroes to the railroad depot." The threatened riot did not occur. As Frederick Christensen noted, "No where was there any looting, threatening or anything else." Within a few days, the town quieted down. This incident highlights the attitude among Beaufort blacks that while Hampton County had become white man's country, blacks, by their overwhelming numbers, could still influence events in Beaufort County[9]

Whenever possible, violence in Beaufort was blamed on "upcountry troublemakers." In August 1903 some white "upcountry visitors" quarreled with a black man on Bay Street. "They seemed to be the aggressors" in Frederick Christensen's opinion, and they proceeded to cut up the Beaufort man. When halted by one of the black town constables, "they refused to be arrested by a nigger policeman." Again, crowds gathered on Bay Street, and a race riot was brewing when Mayor Townsend took the offenders into custody and calmed down the crowd. Fortunately, the local man was not seriously hurt.[10]

A great deal of the random violence in Beaufort County was black-on-black crime. In 1892 Dr. F. E. Wilder had to treat several black men who had slashed each other up in a "free fight" at G.W. Winders's turpentine farm on Hilton Head. George Brown was nearly fatally stabbed but recovered. In July 1903, at a black picnic on Port Royal Island, several men started shooting at each other in jest. When deputies arrived, one of the picnickers explained, "Dey was jus a shooten at one anudder in fun, same as like deers." Unfortunately, Ezekiel Simmons was shot in the leg. His father explained that the shooter "fixed things up by paying the doctor bill." No charges were brought. The next month, an excursion of Beaufort and Savannah blacks aboard the SS *Clifton* broke out into a general brawl in which several men were injured. Edward Frazier cut Jim Newton, while Jim Alexander struck F.W. Green in the face, severely injuring him. The combatants were arrested and fined. In 1906 on Hilton Head Island, in what was described as a quarrel "over a girl," James Butler struck Charles Brown's wife and was confronted by Brown and James Ferguson. "Knives and clubs were employed," and when the mêlée ended, Butler was dead. Brown and Ferguson were arrested and jailed in Beaufort.

Many crimes, even murders, went unpunished or were lightly punished. In 1904 the killer of John Majors on Lady's Island was freed from jail. The victim's neighbor was an old washerwoman who had lived in Beaufort County all her life. Her anger at the failure of the local judicial establishment to maintain a safe and peaceful community probably reflected the opinion of a very large number of black sea islanders: "Law ain't no good! Dey turn'um right loose. If I been them, I kill 'em right thar. Kill for kill." She concluded that if black Beaufortonians wanted justice, they must "take the law into their own hands, like the dominant race!"[11]

Violence and gunplay were certainly not the monopoly of the black community. On August 5, 1903, John Levin shot Charlie Chin Sang "as he stood in front of his door on Bay Street." Both men were well known in Beaufort. Levin was a member of the growing Jewish mercantile community, and Charlie Chin Sang, who operated a popular grocery store in Beaufort, was the town's leading Chinese-American citizen. The shooting was "sensational" in Beaufort because of the prominence of the two men. It resulted from "some trifling misunderstanding between the men for years." Levin claimed Chin Sang had cheated him over a bag of salt. Chin Sang sued Levin for slander, demanding five thousand dollars. Levin became enraged and shot Chin Sang without causing serious injury. The matter was resolved with a fine. Charlie Chin Sang later moved to Charleston.[12]

In 1906 another "sensational" murder occurred on Lady's Island. Old Mr. Harvey, a white man and longtime resident of Lady's Island, became provoked with William Bennett, a black man, over a small debt owed to Harvey. Bennett was armed, drunk, and angry when he shot Harvey to death on Harvey's front porch. Bennett was arrested, tried, convicted, and was hanged on November 1, 1906. William Bennett was despondent until "he was baptized by a pastor of his own race." Afterwards, he made a full confession and repentance from the gallows, calmly unlaced his shoes and "stood without flinching while he was bound and the noose adjusted." At 11:20 A.M. the trap was sprung and Bennett dropped to his death. Only twenty witnesses were allowed into the jail yard, although, as the *Beaufort Gazette* reported, "many Negroes came from the country and stood around outside." Bennett told the jailers he had owed Harvey forty cents.[13]

This was the first hanging in Beaufort County in six years and the first conducted by Beaufort County's new sheriff, Jim Eddie McTeer. It was also one of Beaufort's last hangings. Within a few years, state law prohibited execution by hanging and specified the modern, "humane" method of execution in the electric chair. South Carolina's first use of the electric chair at the Central Correctional Institution in Columbia was on August 12, 1912.

Crime and violence continued in Beaufort County despite attempts at reform. In March 1907 Mr. Davis was murdered in his country store and post office at Grays Hill. The store was robbed and burned to the ground by Lee Fields and James Capen, both black, who were arrested by Sheriff McTeer and Deputy M. O'D. White. Both men confessed and said that Josh Patterson had paid them three dollars to murder Davis, who was described as a "well-liked, hard working farmer."[14]

During the summer of 1907, the town of Beaufort suffered a crime wave. First, there was an attempted robbery of the Beaufort House. Next, three black men tried to break into Gus Sanders's house. Then, a black man entered the bedroom of Sophy Phillips "but fled when she woke." In September the office of Scheper's General Wharf was broken into, and $228 was stolen. None of these crimes were solved because, as the town marshal explained it, "the thieves [were] so wary" and the neighborhood was reluctant to inform on miscreants.[15]

A spate of robberies and killings spread from Beaufort to all corners of the county during the fall of 1907. In October the store of H. H. Porter in Ridgeland was broken into, and one hundred dollars was taken. A week later, William Thompson shot and killed Buddy White in a gunfight at Kean's Neck near Dale. Both men were black and described as "tough characters." White was a Beaufort County native who had returned from six months in Florida. He was a fugitive from the law and was armed with "a heavy Mauser pistol capable of killing at 1,000 yards." Near Coosawhatchie, Ben Bollen cut and seriously injured George Riley. Bollen fled to Hampton County, where he was arrested and jailed. In Port Royal, Ben Givins shot Edward Chisholm in the leg. Both were black men were from Bluffton, and both were oystermen who unloaded oyster bateaux at the Maggioni Cannery in Port Royal. Givens was jailed while Chisholm recovered. On Bay Street in Beaufort, Charlie Chin Sing's grocery store and C. E. Danner's clothing store were both broken into on the same night.

On St. Helena Island, on November 21, a fight broke out between island blacks attending a wedding and soldiers from Fort Fremont, who were drinking nearby. During the brawl, a soldier shot Tony Freeman in the head. The soldier was lodged in the army stockade. This crime spree prompted Niels Christensen Jr. to editorialize in the *Beaufort Gazette* on the need for more police in the city and county. Despite these incidents of crime and violence, Beaufort County prided itself on its peaceful and law-abiding nature. Responding to the perceived need for law and order, in 1909 Beaufort's leading citizens formed a "Law and Order League," a common practice in southern cities of the time. However, at their first meeting the committee had second thoughts about the name and changed it to the Citizens League. This title was less threatening to the black community and more in keeping with Beaufort's polite, peaceful image. The organizers of the Citizens League were all the leading men of the town, including three former or future mayors and several town councilmen. The league's officers were C. E. Danner, president; J. M. Rhett, first vice president; R. R. Legare, second vice president; and J. A. Kinghorn, secretary/treasurer. The executive council comprised W. F. Marscher, C. C. Townsend, David Mittle, W. J. Thomas, and George Waterhouse.

The group's statement regarding law and order reflected its perceptions of peace and racial harmony: "It is probable that there are few counties in the state where deeds of violence are so uncommon as this. Our courts have little to do and our communities are peaceful as a rule."[16]

One crime that did not occur in Beaufort County was lynching. The early decades of the twentieth century were the high point of lynching in America, and most, but not all, lynchings occurred in the southern states. Most, but not all, lynchings were also exacerbated by racial fear and discord, with white mobs more often than not exercising vigilante violence upon black criminals or accused criminals. In Beaufort County public officials went to extraordinary lengths to prevent lynching, and political leaders made very public comments condemning the practice. This position ran against the popular current of the day, as when Governor Coleman Blease (1911–1915) openly endorsed lynching as "necessary and good."

Three episodes in the lowcountry in the early twentieth century illustrate Beaufort County's attitude toward lynching and the way it contrasted with neighboring counties. These three incidents all occurred within a three-month span in 1913 in Beaufort and Hampton Counties. On Saturday night, March 29, 1913, a special dispensary constable, J. Rollin Cooler, was ambushed and murdered on the road just outside Frogmore on St. Helena Island. The crime was a sensation in many regards. Black islanders pointed out that it was the first murder on St. Helena Island in forty years. It was also a race crime, with a white victim and black perpetrators. Cooler was a lawman, but because he was a dispensary constable, many Beaufortonians of both races had little regard for his authority. Nevertheless, Cooler was doing his job apprehending bootleggers, and St. Helena Island was a haven for blind tigers. They paid little heed to the state dispensary system from 1894 to 1907 and little more to the county dispensary from 1907 to 1916. In fact, in 1907 St. Helena Island had petitioned to become a municipality solely for the purpose of controlling its own dispensary. When J. Rollin Cooler and his black deputy, Josh Deas, broke up several stills on St. Helena on Saturday, March 29, 1913, they interrupted several regular weekend festivities and angered a large portion of the island. Dave Reynolds and Jasper Green decided to take revenge. Hiding in a ditch beside the road, they ambushed Cooler and Deas at night. They recognized Cooler because the glow from his ubiquitous cigar lit his face. That was their target. Their shotgun blasts hit him full in the face and killed him instantly. Josh Deas was injured by the same blast.

Dr. York Bailey and a black nurse from Penn School rushed to the aid of the lawmen but could not save Cooler. Before the night was over, Sheriff M. O'D. White had arrested Reynolds and Green and three accomplices and lodged them in the Beaufort jail. The black leaders of St. Helena Island called a mass meeting of island citizens, who reportedly "expressed their indignation at the crime and offered their assistance in running down the guilty party." A. C. Reynolds, former black state representative from St. Helena (1888–1889), wrote a letter on behalf of the community deploring the crime and offering assistance in prosecuting the guilty parties "to the full penalty of the law." Reynolds's letter was sent to each of the island churches, informing their congregations of the mass meeting at Penn School. Reynolds declared, "The good name and reputation for law and order of the Negroes of the island is at stake and must be vindicated."

Meanwhile, feelings in the white community were running high, and rumors of a lynching were circulating. Cooler had a father and five brothers and a large extended family on the mainland to avenge his death. The threat of a lynching aroused Beaufort's black community, which communicated its resolve through the venerable old warrior Robert Smalls. Smalls informed Sheriff White that if a lynching occurred in Beaufort, armed blacks were prepared to burn the homes of white citizens. The Cooler family supported Sheriff White and the legal process despite their anger, and the sheriff took decisive action to avert vigilante justice. The governor called out the Beaufort Volunteer Artillery to guard the jail. When ten to fifteen heavily armed men from Jasper County boarded the train for Beaufort intent on lynching, Sheriff White dispatched several deputies to the railroad depot and forced the men to disarm and return home. In the meantime, the sheriff slipped the prisoners out of jail, placed them quietly aboard a steamboat, and escorted them to Savannah, where they were lodged in the Chatham County jail. Frederick Christensen played a part in the J. Rollin Cooler episode. He armed himself and assisted the guards who escorted the prisoners to the Savannah steamboat. Although this activity caused much excitement, no lynching was permitted. Sheriff White was highly praised by the *Charleston Evening Post* as a "rare example of responsibility and legal obligation." One more mob murder in South Carolina was avoided, and Sheriff White was held up as "an example and a new precedent in South Carolina."

On April 16, 1913, the St. Helena Island community held its mass meeting in Frogmore. They selected a committee to draft a resolution expressing the sentiments of the community. It consisted of Dr. York W. Bailey, D. L. Freeman, W. H. Gregory, Reverend F. Washington, and L. E. Hall as chairman. Their resolution publicly expressed their "regret and disapproval of the atrocious murder committed in our midst." They offered to help in the prosecution of the blind tigers and announced the formation of crime-watch committees "secretly appointed on each plantation to apprehend criminals, locate blind tigers and report to authorities."

The heightened racial feeling surrounding the Cooler murder prompted a remarkable public letter from the wealthiest and most prominent white man on St. Helena Island: J. Ross Macdonald. Originally from Pennsylvania, Macdonald was the founder of the Macdonald-Wilkins Company, the successor to John J. Dale, and the largest cotton planter and landowner on St. Helena Island. He had married Clare Ward, daughter of a Union army officer and a

Gideonite missionary. They had lived on St. Helena Island since the 1870s. He declared, "I have lived on this island for forty years and I believe I know the colored people here as no other white man does. . . . I do not believe a more peace loving or law abiding people can be found in this or any other state. The proof of this is that a handful of white people, never more than 75 . . . have lived on this island in peace and safety among 6,000 Negroes for the past forty years." In Macdonald's opinion, recent trouble was caused by whiskey, and the consequence was "a blow to the fair name of St. Helena."

Dave Reynolds and Jasper Green were brought to trial in July 1913, and though the first trial ended in a hung jury, they were eventually convicted of murder and sentenced to death. Their three accomplices—Ezekiel Sherman, Oscar Middleton, and Robert Middleton—all received directed verdicts of "not guilty" by the judge in the first trial. The black defendants were represented by a black attorney, H. A. McBeth of Savannah, who impressed everyone with his "skill and good judgment." McBeth voiced the sentiments of the "respectable Negro element of Beaufort County" when he condemned the crime, cautioned against accepting circumstantial evidence, and declared that "equal justice applied to the truly guilty parties . . . would once more create the good feeling that heretofore existed between the white and colored people in Beaufort County."

At the end of August 1913, Sheriff White and Deputy Dan Mann escorted Reynolds and Green to Columbia. At the Central Correctional Institution on September 4, 1913, they were both electrocuted. They were the first Beaufort County citizens to suffer that fate. Their bodies were returned to St. Helena Island for burial.[17]

In June 1913 a lynching was averted in Bluffton. The wife of "a prominent citizen" reported being molested in her home by a black man who escaped into the village. A state detective happened to be in Bluffton investigating blind tigers at the request of Hal Pollitzer, chairman of the county dispensary board. Detective Hammond and his black deputy accosted a suspicious black man named William Jackson, who promptly fled and was shot dead on the spot by detective Hammond. A crowd of black people quickly gathered, confronted detective Hammond at a village store, and demanded to know why Jackson had been shot. Hammond's explanation of events satisfied the black crowd, some of whom acknowledged that Jackson was "an ill-behaved half-wit."

Meanwhile, a crowd of white men from Bluffton was joined by four or five armed men from Jasper County who set out to apprehend the fugitive. Spurred on by liquor, the mob wrongly identified Hammond's own deputy, a black man not known in Bluffton, as the perpetrator. Detective Hammond and Mr. Graves hid the deputy on the third floor of Graves's home. The mob forced their way into Graves's home, overpowered detective Hammond, and broke into the upper floor of the house. The black constable leaped from the attic and ran before the wildly firing mob.

Sheriff White, hearing of the trouble in Bluffton, got permission of the governor to mobilize the naval militia and dispatch them to Bluffton to restore order and prevent a lynching. By nightfall, calm had been restored in Bluffton. The violence and mob action were said to be not normal for "the usually orderly town of Bluffton." Several days later the deputy dispensary constable emerged unharmed from the woods across the May River at Palmetto Bluff. He returned to Beaufort to resume his duties.[18]

The epidemic of lynching that plagued the southern states prompted a bold editorial by Beaufort County's most powerful politician, Senator Niels Christensen Jr., who was always, in his long political career, a progressive reformer. He began his life in politics as an eager and effective crusader against the state dispensary, a position that gained him the lasting enmity of "Pitchfork Ben" Tillman. Christensen's 1912 attack on lynching was a direct challenge to South Carolina's populist governor, Colman Blease. Christensen owned the *Beaufort Gazette* and often used its editorial page to promote his political causes. Christensen's 1912 editorial boldly asserted that Beaufort County was free of two crimes, "Negro assaults on women and mob lynching of Negroes." One was a crime against "womanhood," he wrote, and "the other is a crime against society."

Christensen explained why Beaufort County was free of lynching. Law and order prevailed in Beaufort County "largely due to the relations that exist between the races." In Beaufort County "race prejudice is as strong as anywhere, but it is reasonable and just; it insists absolutely on race separation but it does not countenance brutality and mob murder." In Beaufort County white women were safe not because of fear but "largely because [blacks] regard whites as their friends and protectors." In other southern (and some northern) communities, he contended, the "feeling between the races is one of mutual hatred and distrust . . . where rape and murder, lynching and arson stalk abroad . . . and the people sleep with uneasy fear. Such a condition is a mutual pestilence." Christensen concluded that no one was safe when anarchy reigned; only the reign of law, he said, "civilizes society."[19]

In contrast to Beaufort County's antilynching point of view was the attitude in neighboring Hampton County. One of the most sensational, deadly, and gruesome incidents of vigilante justice in South Carolina history occurred in Hampton County in May 1913. The incident began on May 7, 1913, when a black man named Richard Austin allegedly attempted to assault the wife of a prominent Hampton County farmer in her home near Luray. The woman, brandishing a shotgun, chased Austin from her house and raised the alarm. A neighbor, J. G. Folk, shot at Austin as he fled but missed. Austin was heavily armed with a shotgun and a large-caliber pistol. Some local blacks hitched their mules to Austin's wagon to help him escape. George Hanna, a prominent Hampton County white man, gave chase and pursued Austin into a bay swamp on the Hampton County–Barnwell County line. There Austin felled logs and brush to form a makeshift fortress in the swamp. Hanna pursued Austin into the swamp but was wounded by Austin's shotgun. As Hanna lay on the ground, Dr. S. C. Moore went into the swamp to help him and had his arm shot nearly off by Austin's blast. Dr. Moore was taken by train to Columbia but died a few days later. A third man, J. Frank Bowers, entered the swamp to assist Hanna and Moore, but he was killed when two full loads of Austin's buckshot blew off the top of his head.

After the initial gunfight at the swamp, a posse from Hampton and Barnwell Counties converged on Austin's hiding place and surrounded the landlocked "bay swamp," or "bay pond," as they are known in the lowcountry. The first law enforcement official on the scene was Hampton County Magistrate William Edenfield. He put out a call for volunteers. Policeman Harter, Dr. Tison, John Dunbar, and Mr. Hiers from Allendale all responded. They were joined by "two travelers from Fairfax." With these reinforcements, Edenfield approached within twenty feet of Austin's log barricade when he was hit in the chest and stomach with buckshot. Before he died, Edenfield cried out, "Get him boys, for he's got me!"

At this point, Allendale policeman Harter riddled the logs with his sixteen-shot Winchester, but Austin remained unharmed. Austin hung his overcoat on the limb of a tree, and it, too, was riddled with buckshot. The coat was later used to provide the scent of Richard Austin for the "penitentiary bloodhounds" that were sent down from Columbia to help track the fugitive. By this time, night was falling and a large posse had arrived. It was clear that Richard Austin was a skilled and dangerous gunfighter. He had already killed two men on the spot and wounded two more, one of whom later died. And these were some of the leading white men in Hampton County. George Hanna, Frank Bowers, and Dr. Moore were all from old, established, landowning families in Hampton County. Because the killings occurred on the Hampton-Barnwell county line, both Sheriff J. H. Lightsey of Hampton and Sheriff J. B. Morris of Barnwell joined in the chase.

During the night a large posse surrounded the bay swamp, and bonfires were lit to illuminate any escape route. But Richard Austin was not just a lethal gunfighter; he was also bold and resourceful. During the night he walked calmly out of the swamp. When challenged by one of the posse, he explained that he was one of the black men enlisted to haul wood for the fires. Austin added that "he hoped they'd get the Negro who killed two of the best white men in the county." Then he disappeared into the night.

The posse realized too late that Austin had tricked them. They gave chase and sent eight deputies to patrol the old Augusta stage road along the

Savannah River swamp to prevent Austin from escaping to Georgia. These deputies claimed to have spotted Austin crossing the road several hundred yards away. They fired fifty shots in his direction but were prevented from giving chase because, at the time, they were repairing a flat tire on their automobile.

By this time, the Hampton-Barnwell posse had swollen to nearly one thousand men chasing a lone desperado. Governor Cole Blease offered a twenty-five-hundred-dollar reward for the capture of Austin, alive or dead "as long as there's enough to recognize." Clearly the blood lust was aroused in Hampton County, and the *Beaufort Gazette* remarked, "From the temper of the crowd . . . we expect fire will play a part," meaning that Richard Austin might be burned, dead or alive, if caught.

Catching Richard Austin, however, was not at all assured. The "penitentiary bloodhounds" lost his trail on a public road. By the second day of the chase, Austin had disappeared into the Black Creek Swamp, presumably intent on crossing the Savannah River to Georgia. This aroused the Chatham County, Georgia, militia, which sent a posse to surround the swamps near Clyo. The Georgia posse exchanged fire with Austin, and one of them was mortally wounded. The fugitive made his way back through the almost impenetrable Savannah River swamp to South Carolina.

Austin traveled overland and hid for several days in the Coosawhatchie Swamp. While searching for him, the Hampton County posse came across "a Negro hot supper in progress" in the woods. They asked the black people for assistance in the chase, but they "steadfastly refused." The *Beaufort Gazette* commented, "This adds fuel to the fire and what may occur is not known." The lack of cooperation of the Hampton County blacks in the pursuit of Richard Austin was significant. They knew it would end in a lynching, and they were not about to lift a finger to help. The "mutual hatred and distrust" referred to by Niels Christensen in 1912, "where rape and murder, lynching and arson stalk abroad . . . and the people sleep with uneasy fear," had arrived in Hampton County in 1913.

For two more weeks Richard Austin remained at large, and the people of Hampton County remained on alert and on edge. By that time all of South Carolina was watching the lowcountry drama. On May 21 Chief W. C. Cathcart of the Columbia city police received a letter from Chief W. Jackson of Toledo, Ohio, that Austin was there in police custody. The letter was forwarded to Sheriff J. B. Morris in Barnwell, but no one in Hampton or Barnwell believed it was the same Richard Austin. Sheriff Morris correctly assumed that Austin would attempt to return to Georgia and, if successful, would try to contact people he knew in Newington. Morris and Hampton County Commissioner D. T. Padgett traveled to Newington to interview people who knew Austin. On the night of May 29, Morris and Padgett were at the home of Marvin Jarrell, a farmer for whom Austin had once worked. Jarrell lived seven miles north of Newington. While Padgett and Morris were in the front room, Richard Austin appeared at the back door asking for food. Jarrell's daughter delayed Austin at the back door by preparing some food, while Sheriff Morris and Newington police officer Stavinger circled around the house. When Morris and Austin encountered each other, both raised their guns at the same time but Sheriff Morris fired first, felling Austin with a shot to the stomach. Austin rolled over and aimed at Officer Stavinger, who "shot his arm nearly off with a .44 caliber Winchester." Austin collapsed again, crying, "Don't shoot anymore, I surrender."

The gunfight at Newington was the end of the chase but not the end of the drama. Richard Austin was transported to Savannah by wagon for medical treatment. He was treated and lodged in the police barracks in Savannah for several days. While in custody, Austin told his side of the story to his jailers. He said he had moved to Hampton County because he "had got a piece of land and he wanted to settle as a farmer." Austin admitted to killing Bowers but said the other men were killed by accident by the posse. He admitted taking Magistrate Edenfield's gun after he was shot but said he had only done so because the South Carolina men had taken his coat. Austin never got the chance to tell his story to a jury.

On June 4 Richard Austin, escorted by Sheriff Morris, was placed aboard the Bluffton steamer SS *Attaquin.* As Captain George Crofut steered his vessel up the May River to Bluffton, a group of Hampton County deputies led by Sheriff J. H. Lightsey waited at the landing. It was generally acknowledged that if Austin had lived to reach Hampton County, he would have been lynched. A large crowd had gathered at the Hampton County courthouse. As the *Beaufort Gazette* reported, "From the nature of the threats heard on every side, it appeared certain that the crowd would make short work of the desperado if he arrived alive." But Richard Austin "cheated the law" by dying at 4:00 P.M. aboard the SS *Attaquin.*

Although Sheriff Morris and Sheriff Lightsey could only deliver a corpse, that did not end the blood lust of the mob. As Morris and Lightsey drove back to Hampton County the next day with the body of Richard Austin in their car, they stopped for breakfast in Estill. While concentrating on their hominy, bacon, and black coffee, a party of Hampton men stole Austin's body from the sheriff's car and delivered it to the Hampton County courthouse. Two hundred people had gathered there to welcome the captors and wreak vengeance upon Austin's corpse.

Richard Austin's body was put on display for all to see. According to the *Gazette,* "First the toes and fingers were cut off as mementoes, then the head was severed from the body, the right arm was taken off and the body was placed on a fire, singed and burnt. Next ropes were fastened to the body, and it was suspended from the limb of an oak tree. All night long people came, viewed the body of the desperado and then quietly went to their homes. The men were unusually quiet and orderly."

The nearly ritual mutilation of Richard Austin's corpse was as gruesome an episode of mob justice as South Carolina ever witnessed. The two sheriffs probably understood that the blood lust of the populace would not have subsided without some form of public violence. Hampton County had seen the murder of three of its leading citizens by a single gunman. Anger was justifiable, but the mob was soon out of control and both sheriffs knew it. Perhaps that is why they concentrated on their breakfast and allowed the mob to have its revenge. The body swinging from the limb of a large oak tree was, in the words of the *Gazette,* "a symbol of the spirit of revenge in the human breast of the white man when crimes such as those . . . are committed in this country." As gruesome as that episode was, it ended once and for all the drama of the pursuit of Richard Austin. And at least, in the end, the mob was no longer cheering but was quiet, sober, pensive, and perhaps somewhat ashamed of its actions.[20]

Chapter 8

Beaufort's African American Community

AT THE TURN OF THE CENTURY

Beaufort County has always been a biracial community. When the region's African American slaves gained freedom in 1863, they began to form their own society and their own institutions separate and distinct from those of their white former masters. By and large this separation was voluntary. Churches, schools, social clubs, and fraternal organizations divided along racial lines. In many cases antebellum institutions were simply split into two parts, black and white. The most prominent example of this separation was Beaufort's large Baptist congregation. Before the Civil War, the Baptist Church of Beaufort was a mixed congregation of black and white, slave and free people who often worshipped separately. In 1852 the church had 190 white members and 2,645 black members. The congregation built the Tabernacle on Craven Street principally as a praise house, social hall, and Sunday school for black Baptists. During Reconstruction, the Tabernacle separated from the Baptist Church of Beaufort and became the all-black Tabernacle Baptist Church. In 1874 the members bought the church and lot on Craven Street from the Baptist Church of Beaufort for seven hundred dollars. It remains today one of the most historic and important institutions in Beaufort. In 1868 the First African Baptist Church on New Street was formed mostly from the same congregants. They, too, bought their property from the Baptist Church of Beaufort. On St. Helena Island, the Episcopal Chapel of Ease, built in 1749, remained a white church while the Brick Baptist Church, built by Reverend Richard Fuller in 1851, became a black congregation after the war and the mother church of many Baptist congregations on that island. The Wesley Chapel on Scott Street in Beaufort was built before the Civil War as a white Methodist mission. After the war it was briefly a biracial congregation but soon became the all-black Wesley Methodist Church. The white United Methodist congregation took over the Union Chapel on Carteret Street in 1892. St. Helena's Episcopal Church in Beaufort saw many of its black communicants also separate during Reconstruction to form the Grace African

Methodist Episcopal Church on Charles Street, which bought its property from St. Helena's Church in 1872.[1] With freedom, Beaufort blacks simply wanted to own, manage, and craft their own institutions or their own versions of traditional antebellum ones.

Civic, fraternal, and veterans' organizations followed the lead of the churches. Public holidays were evenly divided between black and white. Most of Beaufort's social life voluntarily segregated long before legal segregation became the norm in the 1890s. Beaufort had black and white holidays, black and white schools, black and white fire-engine companies, and even black and white militia organizations. Just as white society reached a peak at the end of the nineteenth century, Beaufort's black society prospered and matured during the decades of enterprise.

Eighteen ninety-two was a watershed year for Beaufort County in many ways. It was the last great year for phosphate mining. Cotton prices were still profitable. It was the peak year for fusion politics in local government. It was the year before the financial Panic of 1893 and the subsequent national depression. And, most important of all, it was the year before the 1893 hurricane.

In 1892 Beaufort County was in a buoyant mood. Industry and commerce were thriving. Black and white merchants and professionals were prospering. Cotton was hanging on, though declining as a profitable crop, securing the small farms that dotted the sea islands. New, more profitable truck crops were introducing progressive alternatives for small farmers. The phosphate industry and the expanding Port Royal Naval Shipyard offered thousands of good-paying jobs to local labor. In politics the "People's Ticket" brought black and white political leaders together for the general progress of the community. While politics in the rest of South Carolina was clearly turning away from the black community, in Beaufort County fusion politics seemed to offer the promise of stability and mutual progress. Eighteen ninety-two was the year of fusion politics' greatest victory in Beaufort County.

At the end of the nineteenth century, the great, black national holiday was Memorial Day, May 30. White southerners celebrated Confederate Memorial Day on May 10 and generally ignored the national Memorial Day. In the South, that was a black holiday. Beaufort's celebration in 1892 was probably the greatest Memorial Day Beaufort ever witnessed. As many as ten thousand people filled the streets on Monday, May 30, 1892.

By the end of the nineteenth century, Memorial Day had outstripped the other two black patriotic holidays: Emancipation Day, January 1, and Independence Day, July 4. Emancipation Day was very much a local Beaufort County event. In almost no other place in America were slaves actually freed on January 1, 1863, so that day was not the "Jubilee" for the rest of black America that it was for the sea islands. And Independence Day only freed white colonists from British rule, not black slaves from bondage. So the day that memorialized America's great Civil War, the most important consequence of which was black emancipation and the Thirteenth Amendment, became the most important African American national holiday in the United States. At the end of the nineteenth century, the increasing grip of Jim Crow laws was stifling Memorial Day celebrations in most southern cities but not in Beaufort. The city became a regional mecca for blacks wishing to celebrate freedom and citizenship on Memorial Day. May 30, 1892, may have been its most spectacular example.

As the *Palmetto Post* reported, "The visitors began coming in on Sunday." On Monday, May 30, "twenty-eight carloads of people came from Augusta and along the railroad line." Six carloads came by railroad from Charleston. In addition, the steamer *Planter* arrived from Charleston "with an immense crowd." Later on Monday, the SS *Alpha* with four hundred aboard and the SS *Bellvue* with five hundred aboard arrived from Savannah. In addition to the out-of-towners, "thousands came from the adjacent islands and countryside." Both the Lady's Island Ferry and the Port Royal Ferry at Whale Branch shuttled back and forth all day long. By afternoon, more than ten thousand people crowded the streets of Beaufort. The women were dressed in "bright holiday attire." Many of the men were dressed in military uniforms. Members of Beaufort's David Hunter Post, Grand Army of the Republic, organized the parade from Bay Street to the U.S. National Cemetery. Along the route and on most of the side streets, booths were set up selling "ample provisions." Red lemonade, ice cream, and "stronger beverages" were all in abundance. The crowd was having such a good time that "many forgot to go to the National Cemetery."

At the cemetery the GAR members had erected a "handsomely decorated stand." The principal orator was A. P. Carter of Atlanta, a national leader of the Grand Army of the Republic. T. F. Gleason, deputy commander of the David Hunter Post, gave a patriotic speech highlighting Beaufort's many Union veterans. Several members of Beaufort's black clergy pitched in with prayers of thanksgiving for emancipation, freedom, and citizenship. The Women's Relief Corps, a GAR auxiliary, decorated the graves of the Union dead and wreathed the speakers' stand in a garland of flowers. A children's choir sang "My Country 'Tis of Thee" and an honor guard of Hunter Post members fired a salute to the soldiers interred in the National Cemetery.

The *Palmetto Post* reported the whole day's celebration: "All had fun and all were well behaved." The opinion of the *Post* was revealing because it was, from its founding in 1881 as the *Crescent,* a staunchly white, Democratic newspaper. Its editor, Samuel H. Rodgers, was a Confederate veteran and a charter member of Beaufort's Henry Middleton Stuart Camp, United Confederate Veterans. Rodgers was also one of Beaufort's most influential fusionists and regularly put the power of his newspaper behind the People's Ticket. His assessment of the Great Memorial Day Celebration in 1892 was significant. The events and speeches were "thoroughly proper for the occasion from a Federal standpoint, and from almost any standpoint."[2]

The success of Memorial Day 1892 encouraged more celebrations, and the hospitality of Beaufort's black community to out-of-town visitors became legendary. In January 1894 the Hunter Post put on a street parade, and the old veterans were escorted by the "two crack colored military companies—the Beaufort Light Infantry and the Sumner Rifle Guards." The military formation was a "sunset parade" followed by speeches and a reception at the courthouse. The success of the GAR in Beaufort encouraged its growth in other parts of the state. In 1892 Robert Smalls, R. F. Greaves, and G.W. Ford, all veterans and members of the Hunter Post, traveled to Hilton Head to round up veterans to "organize a post there."[3]

Other civic and social organizations followed suit. One of the most active black civic organizations was the International Order of Odd Fellows. The Odd Fellows had a very active chapter in Beaufort; its most prominent member was Robert Smalls. In July 1892 the Odd Fellows chartered the *Pilot Boy* for an excursion to Savannah. They were accompanied by a "large party" of guests.[4]

The first black Masonic order in Beaufort was Beaufort Lodge No. 2211, G.O.U. of Freemasons. Lieutenant Governor Richard Howell Gleaves was a prominent founder. It was established during Reconstruction and discontinued in the early twentieth century. During the 1890s the mantel of Freemasonry passed to a newer lodge. On December 8, 1896, a second black Masonic lodge was formed in the city. They were called the Sons of Beaufort Lodge No. 36. The charter leaders were Proctor Glover, first worshipful master; James Riley, first senior warden; and J. O. Singleton, first junior warden. Later worshipful masters were James Riley, Julius I. Washington, Ben Dorman, A.A. Dingle, Theodore Bythewood, James Richardson, and Clarence Washington. All were prominent, influential community leaders. In 1937 the Sons of Beaufort Lodge No. 36 purchased their own Temple at 607 West Street.[5]

By the 1890s Beaufort's African American community was dotted with social and charitable organizations. Some of these societies were the Workers of Charity, the Shekinah Society, the Sons and Daughters of Zion, the Rising Sons and Daughters of Zion, the Rising Sons and Daughters of Benevolence, the Rising Sons and Daughters of Charity, the Mary and Martha Society, the Olive Branch, and the Sisters of Zion. These organizations numbered more than one thousand members. Altogether they owned eleven city lots and twelve thousand dollars' worth of real estate. By 1913 the *Beaufort Gazette* listed eight active lodges and fraternal organizations in the town of Beaufort.[6]

On St. Helena Island thirty separate benevolent and charitable societies were formed between 1870 and 1930. One of the oldest and most prominent of these was the Knights of the Wise Men. The Knights of the Wise Men, Pilgrim Lodge No. 1, at Frogmore corner on St. Helena Island was organized in 1870. The group purchased the property in Frogmore in 1889. The purpose of the Lodge was to insure that its members and their families had proper burials. Sometimes this had to do with providing a proper ceremony; sometimes it had to do with providing funds for the funeral. The Knights of the Wise Men performed numerous other acts of charity, such as tending to a widow's home or farm or calling on the sick. In the twentieth century, the most prominent member of Pilgrim Lodge No. 1, Knights of the Wise Men, was Dr. York W. Bailey, the first black doctor on St. Helena Island and for fifty years, its only doctor. The Knights' ultimate purpose, and that of hundreds like it across America, was the proper burial of the dead. Prominent scholars of African American history and culture have often asserted that this emphasis on burials is a clear retention of African spiritualism and cultural tradition. All these societies collected regular dues from their members and some societies amassed fortunes over the years. In some urban areas, these societies used their funds to found black-owned insurance companies, banks, and other businesses. In 1908 a group formed the Beaufort Colored Insurance Company. Reverend P. J. Chavis was the president; Reverend D. W. Bythewood of Tabernacle Baptist Church was general manager; and Dr. N. J. Kennedy, Beaufort's African American physician, was treasurer. An audit by the South Carolina insurance commissioner, F. H. McMaster, declared the company entirely solvent and "entitled to the confidence of the Negro race."[7]

The funerals of prominent members of Beaufort County's African American community illustrated the function of these civic and charitable organizations. Three funerals in 1903 exemplified the passing of the Reconstruction generation. In July 1903 Ben DeVeaux died in Beaufort. For many years he had been the proprietor of one of Beaufort's most prosperous restaurants. A native of Beaufort, he had been born into slavery. He was a prominent member of the First African Baptist Church and a dedicated Odd Fellow. His funeral at the First African Baptist Church was packed with relatives and friends, black and white. The Odd Fellows managed the ceremony of his burial.

A few days later Laurence Palmer died in a Charleston hospital. He was buried in his native Barnwell. In Palmer's case, the Masonic lodges of Beaufort and Barnwell attended to the burial ceremony. Palmer was a highly skilled carpenter who had migrated to Beaufort County decades before to find employment in the phosphate industry. He was "employed for many years by the Coosaw Company. . . . of late he worked in and around Beaufort." Palmer was well-known and respected in Beaufort's black and white community and had "a reputation for industry and skill."

On July 28, 1903, William Folger died at Port Royal Ferry, now known as Lobeco. Like Palmer, Folger had moved down from Barnwell in 1886 to work in the phosphate industry. He bought a farm and settled at Dale on Kean's Neck. He was a leader of the AME church at Dale and of the Kean's Neck Lodge of Odd Fellows. Folger was noted as a "model farmer" who raised a large family at Dale. His funeral was attended by a "host of friends." William Folger had a reputation as a "good Christian, a charitable, useful citizen and a hearty Odd Fellow." He was one of the founders of the Dale community.

All of these societies held banquets, receptions, and fundraisers. Larger events always involved several societies. A popular form of entertainment was an "excursion," a group tour for merrymaking and recreation. In Beaufort these numerous excursions were most often by chartered steamboat. Occasionally, excursions were by railroad, but that was generally more expensive. Beaufort became such a popular destination for excursions that the *Palmetto Post* noted in 1892, "Excursion mania has seized upon the masses." In fact, by 1892 some in the white community began to complain about "too many colored excursions. . . . the damage done to this town and Port Royal by picnics, excursions, etc., is great . . . and no benefit to those who contribute to such schemes."[8] But excursions to Beaufort remained very popular. They must have been profitable enterprises because they continued for many years.

One of the most popular organizations at all of these events was the Allen Brass Band. Macon Allen, a prominent leader in Beaufort and Charleston and law partner of William J. Whipper and Robert Brown Elliott, formed the band during the early days of Reconstruction. The band first became famous in the lowcountry as the constant herald for Robert Smalls on his boisterous political campaigns. By the 1890s they were by far the most famous band in Beaufort County. They were present at almost all important public events, black and white, for more than forty years. After Macon Allen moved to Charleston, Professor P. A. Roper led the band. During the 1892 political campaign, the Allen Brass Band was particularly active. After playing at a rally for an unsuccessful congressional candidate, General Edwin Marion Moise, the band was lauded by the *Palmetto Post:* "The Allen Brass Band excelled itself by its varied and fine selections. . . . There are few finer bands in the state and the members comprising it are a highly respectable and well-trained body of colored men with Roper at its head." Around 1900 the Allen Brass Band was invited to Washington, D.C., to play in a concert. Among the distinguished members of the audience in Washington was none other than John Phillip Souza. After the concert, Souza, America's greatest band master, made his way to the bandstand to compliment Professor Roper and the Allen Brass Band for their rendition of Souza's composition "Washington Post March." One of the young trumpeters on that occasion was William Bradford Frazier, who became bandleader upon Professor Roper's death.[9]

All this activity and the buoyant mood of 1892 prompted the startup of another newspaper for Beaufort's black community. The *Sea Island Journal* was begun by M. F. Campbell, described by the *Palmetto Post* as "one of our most intelligent colored men." The *Journal* was another in a long line of black-owned Republican newspapers in Beaufort County that had included the *Free South,* the *New South,* and the *Beaufort Tribune.* All these earlier papers had ceased regular publication by 1892. The last black newspaper begun in Beaufort County until modern times, the *Sea Island Journal* declared that it was dedicated to "loyalty and truth."[10] Like much of Beaufort's economy, the new paper did not survive the hurricane of 1893.

Another casualty of the hurricane was the Tabernacle Baptist Church building. The original structure on Craven Street had been built during the 1830s. It was, apparently, a large frame building. When the Great Storm and flood of 1893 struck, the old building collapsed. Almost immediately, church leaders began raising donations to rebuild. In less than eight months they had raised seven thousand dollars, a huge sum of money in 1893. On March 21, 1894, they laid the cornerstone for the new church on the same spot as the old one. As the *Palmetto Post* put it, the "new building is being built on the site of the old one wrecked by the great storm of last August." Almost all the black civic and charitable societies played a role. The Beaufort Lodge No. 2211, G.U.O., of Freemasons laid the cornerstone. George H. Lawton and George Ford were masters of ceremonies. Reverend Darlam of Fort Church in Savannah delivered the keynote address. The whole event was another "big day with the colored population of Beaufort." At the time, the Tabernacle Baptist Church, with nearly two thousand members, was the largest congregation in Beaufort County.[11]

The other very large congregation in Beaufort was the First African Baptist Church on New Street, which was built in 1868 and survived the hurricane. The longtime minister of First African Baptist was Reverend Paul Watson, who in 1907 decided to leave the Beaufort to take over the Calvary Baptist Church in Columbia. By 1907 the congregation of First African Baptist was shrinking, as were many black congregations in Beaufort County. On the other hand, Calvary Baptist was one of the largest congregations in Columbia. His departure was a major event for a large portion of Beaufort's black population, marked by an elaborate ceremony involving much of Beaufort's black leadership. The large church on New Street was reportedly "filled to capacity." Deacon Edward Wallace read the resolutions of gratitude and regret at Reverend Watson's departure. Dr. N. J. Kennedy and lawyer Julius I. Washington, both members of the congregation, gave speeches. All the ceremonial and social arrangements were managed by the deacons: Proctor Glover, Larry Aiken, Isaac Moultrie, and S. J. Harrington.[12] The two events of Beaufort's two largest congregations between 1894 and

1907 were exemplary. In 1894 the mood was still hopeful and progressive. By 1907 the event was another sign of the decline of Beaufort County's economy and the beginning of the decline of its black population.

The declining economy caused the heads of several prominent black families to give up their business enterprises and seek government employment. Such was the case with one of Beaufort's longtime, popular barbers, Nathaniel "Sandy" Frazier. In 1892 he closed his barbershop on West Street to "devote fulltime to his job as Assistant Post Master."[13] This modest but regular income allowed Frazier to remain in Beaufort and produce a large and influential family in the twentieth century. His son, William Bradford Frazier, became the bandmaster of the Allen Brass Band and band director at South Carolina State College in Orangeburg. His granddaughter Rozalie Frazier Pazant founded Beaufort's famous Gullah Festival.

Throughout the era, Memorial Day continued to be the biggest ceremony of the year. Frederick Christensen chronicled each year's events. In 1898 he wrote, "Beaufort was crowded all day by a jolly, good natured crowd . . . interesting, amusing . . . but beyond my ability to describe. Liquor was plentiful and we sold a good many pistol cartridges but nothing to mar the day except an overloaded boat sunk at the wharf . . . everybody fished out." The next year, Christensen noted, "Decoration Day . . . the sidewalks of Bay Street were so crowded they spilled into the street. . . . every boy and young man seemed to have a pistol . . . but no police present. Great deal of liquor sold . . . saw no quarrels, no angry words." In 1899 the Chaplin Cornet Band from Warsaw Island set up right outside N. Christensen and Sons Hardware. They played "Frogmore Time," and a large, impromptu dance took place on Bay Street. "Young men jigged, girls danced and old ladies 'shouted,'" Christensen recorded.

By 1900 some of the white residents of Beaufort had begun to complain about the large, noisy crowds on Memorial Day. Rather than "Decoration Day," the whites called it "Desecration Day" or "Depredation Day." As befit the tenor of the times, the ceremonies became more subdued, more controlled as the twentieth century dawned. On July 4, 1903, Christensen noted, "A quiet day. No fireworks or crackers. No celebration at all here, unless I accept the march of the colored company out some distance beyond saltwater bridge and back." By 1907 the great Memorial Day was even more subdued: "Decoration Day was quietly observed by several thousand Negroes who came from neighboring islands and Savannah and Charleston by the steamers, Pilot Boy, Clifton, Clayton, and Planter. The Summer Girl brought a full load as did the ferries and motor boat fleet. No travelers on the railroad, so the numbers in town were smaller than usual." The comment on railroad travel was revealing. In 1898 the state had enacted Jim Crow legislation segregating railroad cars in South Carolina and reversing Robert Smalls's

1868 legislation forbidding racial discrimination in public accommodations. Segregation did not help the railroad. The Charleston and Western Carolina Railroad was having enough trouble paying its bills without alienating its largest class of customers. In 1907 traditional Memorial Day exercises were held at the U.S. National Cemetery. They were, as always, "dignified and in keeping with the spirit of the day," wrote Christensen, who also noted that "rowdies, young men from the cities did not mar the day." The presence of "extra police and special dispensary constables in town" dampened the enthusiasm of the crowd and signaled the changing nature of public authority in Beaufort County.

The highlight of the 1908 Memorial Day celebration was the keynote speech at the National Cemetery by Booker T. Washington, described as "the leading Negro of the country and an orator who has made a reputation as such wherever he has spoken." In 1910 Memorial Day was marred by a gunfight on Bay Street between Charlie Seymour of Savannah and Beaufort policeman Henry Wallace. Both men were African American. Wallace was shot at four times but was uninjured. Charlie Seymour was shot in the head and died on the street. Dr. R. R. Sams's coroner's jury ruled it justifiable homicide. In 1910 the crowd was estimated at five to six thousand "out of town Negroes." In 1912 only about three thousand people attended Beaufort's Memorial Day. A minstrel troupe, numerous eating stands serving red lemonade, and an evening baseball game provided more wholesome entertainment. By 1913 only twenty-one hundred visitors attended the festivities, but "as usual . . . the town was turned over . . . to the colored population and their visitors." By 1915 the number of visitors further diminished and the celebration was more subdued. As the *Beaufort Gazette* reported, "Decoration Day quietly observed . . . on Monday by the colored population. There was a noticeable decrease in the number that usually come from the nearby cities and surrounding country."[14]

Until the turn of the century, the black National Guard continued to drill and maintain its military organization just as it had during the heyday of Reconstruction. While state authorities rarely called on the black National Guard for more than ceremonial duties, they had been called up by the federal authorities during the Spanish-American War. Beaufort was one of the few places in the state where the black National Guard felt welcome to muster and drill. During July and August 1903, the 2nd Battalion, South Carolina National Guard, made an encampment in Beaufort. Companies A and C were from Charleston. Company B was from Beaufort. Approximately one hundred men made up each company. The commander of the 2nd Battalion was Major George A. Reed, formerly the fusionist sheriff of Beaufort County. The commander of Company B was Captain B. H. Houston, the town constable. The staffs of the 2nd Battalion were G. W. Deas, adjutant;

Charles C. Johnson, quartermaster; Jackson Green, judge advocate; Dr. N. J. Kennedy, surgeon; C. M. English, paymaster; Reverend R. Carroll, chaplain; George H. Lawton, sergeant-major; and William Bennett, music director. Dr. Kennedy, George H. Lawton, and William Bennett, in addition to Major Reed and Captain Houston, were all prominent Beaufortonians.

The Charleston companies arrived in Beaufort on Sunday, July 21, aboard the *Pilot Boy.* They set up their encampment on "the Green" near the National Cemetery and at Hundred Pines where some Civil War artillery embankments still remained. On Sunday they attended the Tabernacle Baptist Church and heard a sermon by Battalion Chaplain Carroll. On Monday they drilled on the Green in the morning, took a cruise on the *Summer Girl* in the afternoon, and held a dance at their armory in the evening. The 2nd Battalion remained in Beaufort for several weeks. This was one of the last musters of South Carolina's famous black National Guard. In 1905 the state disbanded the few remaining companies.[15]

Other black societies found Beaufort hospitable. In August 1903 the Rose of Sharon Beneficial Society held its annual meeting at the New Light Hall. Three hundred people attended. Their meeting was highlighted by an afternoon baseball game between teams from Beaufort and Brunson. The Beaufort team won 21–11. A few days later, the Savannah Lodge of the International Order of Odd Fellows traveled to Beaufort "accompanied by a good band" and was hosted by the Beaufort Lodge. Twelve hundred Odd Fellows and their guests arrived aboard the SS *Clifton* and SS *Clayton.*

In August 1903 six hundred members of the Brown Social Aid Society of Savannah took an excursion to Beaufort aboard the SS *Clifton.* During the day the group "paraded through the streets headed by the Allen Brass Band." They wore "neat uniforms" of white caps, black coats, and white pants. According to the *Beaufort Gazette,* they "made a fine appearance, marching with precision." That evening several Beaufort societies hosted a ball at the Armory Hall.[16]

Beaufort was not the only destination in the county for black excursionists. St. Helena Island was another popular place. In September 1904 Frogmore hosted an immense Labor Day festival. Four hundred excursionists came from Savannah aboard the SS *Clayton.* They disembarked at the Macdonald-Wilkins landing and "marched to the picnic ground in a procession headed by the Warsaw Cornet Band." Twelve hundred locals joined them from surrounding islands. The St. Helena baseball team played a game against the Forrest City Carpenters' Union of Savannah. St. Helena won a close match. Then the whole crowd moved to Paradise Grove on the Penn School Campus. One reason for this occasion was to celebrate the completion of "the College" building on the Penn School campus. This structure was built by the Forrest City Carpenter's Union, and the Labor Day festival was a way of honoring their contributions to the St. Helena Island community. When the picnic in Paradise Grove was over, the Savannah guests were escorted back to the Macdonald-Wilkins landing for the return to Savannah. It was a festive occasion for the sea island community and, according to old residents, "one of the grandest times eyes have witnessed on St. Helena Island."[17]

While Penn School was the oldest and most distinguished of the private African American schools in Beaufort County, it was not the only one. Mather School, a girls' boarding school founded by Rachel Crane Mather of Boston in 1868, was still operating near Beaufort. The Port Royal Agricultural School, founded in 1901 by Niels and Abbie Holmes Christensen, was thriving under the direction of Dr. Joseph S. Shanklin. All three of these schools offered practical education and vocational training beyond the basic literacy instruction of the state-supported public schools. Public school money provided partial support for all three of these private institutions. Mather School specialized in domestic arts and particularly in sewing, which offered the girls a ready source of occasional income for the rest of their lives. When Mather School opened its fall 1903 term, the teachers were S. E. Owen and L. K. Kinsman.[18]

The Port Royal Agricultural School taught modern agronomy to blacks from a broad region. As at Penn School and Mather School, some of the students were boarders. The school was directed by Dr. Joseph S. Shanklin, a graduate of Tuskegee Institute. The curriculum of the Port Royal Agricultural School was entirely practical. As the *Beaufort Gazette* noted, "Students stay the year round and must make a good crop. . . . students are up early, strict discipline is expected. . . . the principal is a practical man." In 1907 there were seven boarding students and one hired hand in addition to local day students to do all the planting. Nine girls did all the cooking. In 1906 the variety and volume of the Port Royal Agricultural School were remarkable, as the following tables indicate.

Spring Crops

Product	*Volume*
White Potatoes	260 bushels
Green Peas	290 bushels
Snap Beans	75 bushels
Squash	45 bushels
Tomatoes	25 bushels
Onions	30 bushels
Oats	20 bushels
Cabbage, Kale, Okra	Samples

Summer Crops

Product	*Volume*
Cotton	4–12 bales
Corn	150 bushels
Peanuts	15 bushels
Sweet Potatoes	100 bushels
Cow Peas	50 bushels
Pecan Nuts	2 bushels
Hay	15 bales
Fodder	800 pounds
Sugar Cane	20 gallons
Watermelons	600
Rice, Pumpkin, Beets, Musk Melon	Samples

In 1907 the students produced 12 bales of cotton, 200 bales of hay, 25 acres of corn, plus sugar cane, sweet potatoes, and garden crops of remarkable variety.[19] This was probably the heyday of the Port Royal Agricultural School. Dr. Shanklin, a protégé of George Washington Carver, the wizard of Tuskegee, was exceptionally well trained, very practical, and obviously effective. The agricultural base of Beaufort County, however, soon suffered a sharp decline, as did the African American population of the sea islands.

The oldest, largest, and most famous of the black schools was the Penn School at Frogmore Corner on St. Helena Island. Penn School went through a major transformation in 1901. That year Laura Towne died. She had devoted her life to the school for nearly forty years. Long after all the other Gideonite missionaries had returned to the North or ceased teaching to marry and raise families in Beaufort, Laura Towne persisted in her dedication to the children of St. Helena Island. She and her friend Ellen Murray labored through three generations of sea islanders. As long as Towne and Murray were alive, the curriculum of Penn School remained fairly classical. The primary grades taught basic reading, writing, and arithmetic, as well as behavior: "Obedience, quietness and school manners are made an especial point." The Grammar Department taught fractions, descriptive writing, and colonial and revolutionary American history. The Senior Department taught algebra and geometry, diagramming sentences, and recent U.S. and Asian history. All three levels taught Bible studies. In 1897 Penn School enrolled 297 students in all three levels.

At the turn of the century, progressive educators in America were promoting vocational and "industrial" education beyond the basic literacy programs of the public schools. In 1890 Penn School changed its name to Penn Normal, Industrial, and Agricultural School. The "industrial education" curricula promoted by Hampton Institute in Virginia and Tuskegee Institute in

Alabama were spreading across the South. Hollis Burke Frissell, principal of the Hampton Institute, visited Penn School in 1900 to recommend this new direction. After the death of Laura Towne in 1901, the Penn School Board of Trustees, consisting mostly of northern philanthropists, began to move the school toward progressive and vocational education. In 1901 the trustees hired P.W. Dawkins from North Carolina, a graduate of Hampton Institute, as superintendent of industries. Dawkins was principally responsible for starting the Penn School Farm, which taught modern scientific farming to the sea islanders. In 1904 the school hired Rossa Cooley, a teacher at the Hampton Institute, as the eventual replacement for Ellen Murray. When Murray died in 1908, it was the end of an era for Penn. Rossa Cooley was soon followed by another Hampton teacher, Grace House. These two women led Penn Normal, Industrial, and Agricultural School into modern times.

The predecessors of today's colleges of education, normal schools at the turn of the century trained teachers. Many normal schools became junior colleges, offering a two-year curriculum; others evolved into state teachers' colleges. While Penn Normal, Industrial and Agricultural School never became a teachers' college, it nevertheless produced graduates who filled a desperate need in the state for literate, black, primary school teachers. Many Penn-trained teachers remained in Beaufort County to help build the growing public school system in the twentieth century. One of Penn School's most distinguished and useful alumni was Dr. York W. Bailey, who went from Penn to Howard University. After receiving his medical degree, he returned to St. Helena Island to practice medicine for fifty years.[20]

On May 26, 1907, Penn held its annual commencement exercises. More than three hundred students were attending the school at that time. The school's closing exercises were among the largest annual events on St. Helena Island. The ceremony in 1907 began at 11:00 A.M., with the students marching into what the *Beaufort Gazette* described as "the beautiful grove." It was customary for the girls to wear pressed white dresses and the boys to wear white shirts and black pants. They formed a triple circle around the flag, saluted, and sang the national anthem. They then marched to Darrah Hall, where the program opened with scripture reading and the singing of spirituals. Rossa Cooley read the honor roll and awarded red ribbons to the successful scholars. The students then adjourned to their respective classes, where recitations were read and artwork and projects were on display. At the agricultural building, vegetables, basketry, and sewing samples were featured. Carpentry work and "excellent blankets" made by the students during the year particularly impressed the guests. A photographic display by Leigh Richmond Miner of the Hampton Institute showing the work of Penn School attracted a large crowd. At 1:00 P.M. lunch was served to the many relatives and guests. In the afternoon students sang spirituals, and Miss Cooley presented a review of the school year. The day was concluded by a student recitation of the "Wreck of the Hesperus" and a student dance called "Frolic of the Seasons."[21]

Another tradition of the Penn Normal, Industrial, and Agricultural School in these years was the Colored Farmer's Conference, an annual harvest event begun in 1905 by P.W. Dawkins, the director of the Penn School Farm. The third annual Colored Farmer's Conference was held on the Penn School campus on October 31 and November 1, 1907. By 1907 P.W. Dawkins had returned to Kitrell College in North Carolina, and J. E. Blanton had replaced him as director of the school farm. Some of the leading participants at the 1907 conference were S. J. Powell of Hilton Head Island; T. B. Williams, agent of the Beaufort County General Education Board; Major R. R. Moton, commandant of the Hampton Institute; and Dr. Joseph Shanklin, principal of the Port Royal Agricultural School. J. Ross Macdonald of the Macdonald-Wilkins Company, the largest employer on St. Helena Island, gave the introduction to the conference. Macdonald's company was the largest farming operation in Beaufort County, and he took special interest in the progress of Penn School Farm. Macdonald was described on this occasion as "one of the great leaders of his race." He was the only local white man to serve on the Penn Normal, Industrial, and Agricultural School Board of Trustees during the heyday of the school.

The 1907 Colored Farmer's Conference featured exhibits of sewing, basketry, cooking, and "fancy work." Farm and garden products were everywhere on display. A "children's corner" highlighted the early work of the school. The central feature of the conference was a roundtable talk by the experts in attendance. The subject in 1907 was a clear indication of the tenor of the times and a harbinger of Beaufort County's future for the next half century: "What do we do to keep the young people away from the cities?"[22]

By 1907 the "Great Exodus" of blacks from Beaufort County was underway, and the community leaders at Penn School that fall could easily predict the depressing effect on their communities if the migration continued. The panelists presented some gloomy facts. Between 1902 and 1907, 141 young men left St. Helena Island for nearby and distant cities. The lure was apparent. Common laborers in Savannah could earn eighteen dollars per month, far more than could be earned on St. Helena Island even if jobs were available. The panelists worried that "Old People cannot work their farms alone [and] will lose land to taxes" if the young people all left. The Colored Farmer's Conference highlighted the disadvantages and dangers of urban living: "The young go to the cities . . . make $18 per month but spend $20!" About a third who left died or came home "to die . . . due to the difficult conditions of city life." The 1907 conference earnestly presented the moral and physical advantages of rural life over city life.[23] The conferees were whistling in the wind. The lure of city lights was too great for the young men of Beaufort County and across the rural South. The Great Exodus that began at the turn of the century did not reverse itself for fifty years. Its effect on Beaufort County was profound.

The years before World War I, which witnessed the beginning of the Great Exodus from the sea islands, also witnessed the passing of the Civil War and Reconstruction generation of African American veterans and political leaders. William J. Whipper, the acknowledged leader of Beaufort County's African American bar during Reconstruction, died in 1907. His burial plot, probably at Wesley Methodist Church on Scott Street, is unmarked and unknown. In November 1907 Richard Howell Gleaves, mentor of Robert Smalls and the highest-ranking African American politician in South Carolina history, died in Washington, D.C., where he had moved after resigning the lieutenant governorship in 1877. On February 23, 1915, Beaufort County's African American community suffered another sad milestone when Robert Smalls died at his home on Prince Street. He had lived, raised two families, and held court from Prince Street for more than fifty years.

Robert Smalls was seventy-six years old and had been in declining health for several years. His funeral on February 26, 1915, was said to be the "largest ever held in the city." His body was displayed at the First African Baptist Church on New Street. The funeral was conducted at the church with all the prominent local clergy contributing eulogies. A funeral procession led by the Allen Brass Band walked across town to the graveyard of the Tabernacle Baptist Church on Craven Street. Smalls's coffin was carried by the Masonic Lodge, Sons of Beaufort No. 36, of which he was a founder, and escorted by the Beaufort chapter of the International Order of Odd Fellows, of which he was also a founder. Robert Smalls was laid to rest with his first wife, Hannah, and his second wife, Annie, in the same family plot. Today a bust of Smalls and a state historical marker on Craven Street attract the attention of tourists to Smalls's grave site.[24]

Robert Smalls was one of Beaufort County's greatest heroes. His life, from slave to war hero to Reconstruction political leader to United States congressman, is one of the most inspiring stories in all of American history. But there was bittersweet irony in the timing of his death. Smalls lived long enough to see much of the Reconstruction political revolution reversed by the advent of the white supremacist politics of the Jim Crow years. He lived long enough to see Beaufort County's black majority disfranchised. He witnessed the pivotal election of 1912 and the eclipse of the national Republican Party. He lived long enough to watch his old fusionist allies in the local Democratic Party alter the Beaufort city charter in 1915 to eliminate the single-member city wards and disrupt the last mixed-race government in South Carolina. And he lived long enough to see the beginning of the Great Exodus from the sea islands, among whom were some of his children.

THE GREAT EXODUS

Contemporary commentators generally agree that the principal causes of the great African American exodus from Beaufort County were economic.[25] The disappearance of the phosphate industry, removal of the naval station in 1901, and decline of maritime traffic removed the main sources of jobs for sea islanders. The decline of cotton as a profitable crop and the collapse of the industry because of the boll weevil infestation in 1917 and 1918 jeopardized the small freedmen's farms that had been the legacy of Reconstruction.

Some of the first migrants from the sea islands, however, pointed to an earlier, more direct cause of their migration—the 1893 hurricane, which wrecked the phosphate industry, ruined the cotton crop, and washed away much of the thin topsoil that had been so carefully tended by the "one bale" farmers. Beyond the physical damage, the storm created a sense of dread among a generation of sea islanders living so close to the sea. Five hurricanes between 1896 and 1911 enhanced that feeling of dread. Some simply moved away to safer, more prosperous places. In the 1920s Clyde Vernon Kiser interviewed many of the migrants in New York City while preparing his book *Sea Island to City: Study of St. Helena Islanders in Harlem and Other Urban Centers* (1930). Essie Roberts and Viola Ware told of how the Storm of 1893 led to their departures.

Essie Roberts survived the 1893 storm, but her story exemplified its lingering effect on thousands of sea islanders. During the height of the hurricane, Roberts's husband was trying to protect his family by leaning his weight against a wall of their house. When the house collapsed, a heavy door sill Roberts's struck husband in the head. The family escaped the house and saved themselves by clinging to a fig tree in the backyard. Because of his head injury, Essie Roberts's husband was never able to work after 1893. He remained in precarious health and died in 1901, a belated casualty of the storm. A few months after her husband's death, Essie Roberts moved to Brookline, Massachusetts, to serve as a maid in the Christensen summer household. She never returned. As she explained years later, "I was frightened by storms for a long time after that."

Viola Ware of St. Helena Island was more direct in her explanation for leaving the sea islands: "The situation on the island that caused me to leave more than anything else was the 1893 storm." Ware's parents were typical sea island small farmers, growing corn and raising poultry to eat and producing a little cotton for cash. The hurricane washed away years of work and crushed her parents' hope for the future. "Then after the storm," she recalled, "my father begin complainin' more than ever about his asthma. He couldn't work. Just got discouraged." In 1897 Viola Ware dropped out of her little plantation school to help her parents. In 1899 she went to New York for a visit and never returned.

Essie Roberts and Viola Ware represented thousands of sea island migrants who were frightened and discouraged by the Great Storm of 1893. This circumstance was well known to the operators and supporters of Penn School. As Elizabeth Jacoway described it in her history of Penn School, "then in 1893 the islands had fallen beneath an immense tidal wave driven forward by a devastating hurricane and followed by torrential rains and flooding. All had been lost, and many left in preference to rebuilding their shattered lives on the island."[26] Supporters tried to reverse this trend by introducing a more practical curriculum at the school and encouraging agricultural diversification. They were unsuccessful. The trickle of outmigration that had begun after the 1893 storm became a flood in the twentieth century.

The first economic cause of this African American exodus from the sea islands was the decline of the Beaufort County phosphate industry, which was well advanced by 1900. Competition from richer phosphate deposits near Tampa, Florida, the 1893 devastation, and ruinous state taxes were triple blows from which the industry never recovered. At its peak in the 1880s, as many as three thousand sea islanders were regularly employed on "the rock," as the locals called the phosphate mines. By 1900 only a few hundred of those high-paying industrial jobs remained in Beaufort County. The last of the original mining companies, the Central Mine on Lucy Creek, shut down in 1906. A new conglomerate, the Virginia-Carolina Chemical Company, tried to revive the industry on Chisholm Island in 1907 but was soon in bankruptcy. The Virginia-Carolina Chemical Company shut down its phosphate works on Summerhouse Point in 1914.

The decline of the phosphate industry, removal of the naval station, and the decline of the local lumber industry also struck hard Beaufort's maritime commerce. The last lumber schooner left Port Royal Sound in 1925. This removed another source of regular employment. In the early twentieth century, half of all the families on St. Helena Island depended on the wages of outside employment for their cash income. When those local jobs disappeared, they had to move.[27]

The same years that saw the end of the phosphate industry and the decline of maritime traffic also witnessed the decline of cotton prices. World supplies of cotton regularly exceeded demand in the two decades before World War I, and this kept cotton prices depressed for a generation. Mark Batchelder, a partner in the Macdonald-Wilkins Company, the largest local cotton grower, recalled that the years from 1903 to 1917 were particularly bad. Beaufort's largest ginner, George Waterhouse Jr., calculated that the break-even price for cotton in those years was twelve and a half cents per pound. At any price below that, the cotton farmer was losing money. For only two years between 1903 and 1917—1905 and 1910—did cotton prices exceed twelve and a half cents per pound.

On Hilton Head Island, a dwindling number of independent African American farmers were still planting a few acres of cotton. The island's largest landowner, New York shipping magnate William P. Clyde, recognized their plight, and in 1908 he invited the whole population of Hilton Head Island to attend a conference and educational meeting at his Honey Horn Plantation hunting lodge. Two hundred fifty islanders attended. Clyde contacted Dr. Booker T. Washington at Tuskegee Institute, who sent Professor S. C. Powell to talk about diversifying crops and improving methods of agriculture. Dr. Ernest Howe lectured about the unhealthiness of Hilton Head's numerous shallow, open wells and explained the salubrious effect of the "deep wells" drilled in the Panama Canal Zone. J. G. Peters of the U.S. Forest Service explained the economics of preserving and nurturing the island's loblolly pine forests. Eventually, the timber value of the trees would exceed the real estate value of the land.

Miss Clayton, a graduate of Hampton Institute, came to teach at the Seabrook School on Hilton Head, and William P. Clyde sponsored a manual training program there. Taking their lead from the Penn Normal, Industrial, and Agricultural School on St. Helena Island, these were generous—even visionary—attempts to improve the sea island economy and arrest outmigration. But they did not succeed. Cotton continued to decline, and the islanders left Hilton Head as fast as they could catch the steamboat to Savannah.[28]

In 1910 cotton prices hit fifteen cents per pound. It was the highest price for cotton in the years before World War I. Even at that price, the "one mule, one bale" farmers of the sea islands could expect to make only seventy-five dollars per year in cash from cotton. Whatever profits the small sea island cotton farmers made in 1910 were swallowed up by the hurricane of 1911.

That hurricane, which struck Beaufort County on August 30, 1911, did more damage on St. Helena Island than had any hurricane since 1893. A petition from St. Helena Island asserted that 130 homes were destroyed and $175,000 in damage was incurred. The cotton crop was a total loss. Freshman congressman James F. Byrnes, "supposing the Negroes were in dire want," proposed seeking federal assistance. Local authorities disagreed. Beaufort County Supervisor J. S. Claghorn visited the islands shortly after the storm. Red Bridge across Chowan Creek was washed out, but according to Claghorn, damage and crop loss reports were exaggerated. A local controversy arose over whether Red Cross assistance would be helpful. The county board of trade, predecessor to the chamber of commerce, dispatched a three-man study committee to St. Helena Island. The three white men, Mr. Dale, Mr. Ford, and Mr. Fripp, all property owners on St. Helena Island, concluded that "Red Cross help was not necessary." A *Beaufort Gazette* editorial entitled "Do We Need the Red Cross?" (presumably written by Senator Niels Christensen Jr.) agreed with the board of trade: "Some think that

National Red Cross assistance is necessary while others say that its injection into this territory would be a community calamity. Heated crimination and recrimination has been indulged in. . . . there seems to be some suffering and a few cases of abject want on the adjacent islands. But is the distress of so great a magnitude to warrant outside assistance? We think not."[29] It must have discouraged sea islanders to realize that the white establishment of Beaufort County, and even their former allies among the progressive Democrats, were unwilling to seek help for their community in a time of great distress.

The emergency of 1911 caused Rossa Cooley, director of Penn School, to cut short her fundraising sojourn in the North and return immediately to organize a relief effort on St. Helena Island. Cooley established a relief fund at Penn School and quickly raised three thousand dollars from northern benefactors. She convinced local farmers to trade their large, round millstones for lumber and materials to rebuild their houses. These stones, left over from plantation days, were not native to the sea islands, where few such minerals exist. They had been used to grind corn on the old sea island plantations. Most of the millstones disappeared from St. Helena Island after 1911, but a few remain as stepping stones on the Penn School campus, reminders of "the struggle of the people in securing the necessities of life."

The 1911 disaster also led to the first cooperative banking plan to provide credit for sea island farmers. This idea fit well with the then-current philosophy of independence and self-reliance in the African American community taught at Tuskegee and Hampton Institutes. In 1912 nine St. Helena Island men formed the St. Helena Co-operative Society, and Penn School trustees financed the new institution with a two-thousand-dollar loan. This locally run African American loan association used its financial leverage to encourage borrowers to practice modern agronomy, plant provision crops sufficient to support their families and livestock, and diversify their crops by planting vegetables as white truck farmers were doing. For the next five years, hundreds of sea island farmers were members of the St. Helena Co-operative Society.

Initially, white store owners opposed the bank initiative. They were accustomed to advancing credit to the sea islanders and found that part of their business dwindling. The largest store on St. Helena was the Macdonald-Wilkins store at Frogmore run by company president William Keyserling. Rossa Cooley convinced Keyserling of the value of the co-op to the whole economy of the island, and for several years the St. Helena Co-operative Society was a local source of independence and pride. However, despite the best efforts of Penn School and the co-op, the hurricane of 1911, like the one of 1893, drove more African Americans to leave the sea islands.[30]

Weather and the worldwide economy further conspired to crush the hopes of the sea island farmers. In 1914 very low prices for cotton made the sea island crop nearly worthless, and in 1915 incessant rains and poor drainage drowned out the cotton. Those two years were the worst years for cotton before World War I. They left the few remaining farmers "practically bankrupt."[31]

The voracious demands for cotton of the European nations at war during World War I caused a sharp rise in the price of the crop. By 1919 the price of cotton in South Carolina soared to thirty-six cents per pound, the highest price in forty years. But that brief bonanza had little effect on the luckless sea island cotton farmers. Between 1917 and 1919, their crops were consumed by the Mexican boll weevil. The boll weevil plague crushed the last hope of the independent black cotton farmers of the sea islands and hastened the exodus from Beaufort County. Sociologist Thomas J. Woofter recorded that the number of commercially viable (twenty acres or more) black-owned farms on St. Helena Island had declined 45 percent between 1920 and 1925—from 366 such farms in 1920 to 202 in 1925.[32]

In addition to the collapse of the cotton economy, after World War I the U.S. government established stringent restrictions that ended forty years of massive, nearly unrestricted emigration from Europe. Consequently, more employment opportunities for African Americans—albeit in low-wage jobs—opened up in the North.[33]

During the 1920s some black farmers began, by sheer necessity, to switch from planting cotton to growing vegetables for market, especially Irish potatoes. As T. J. Woofter noted, "After the boll weevil came, considerable attention was devoted to the Irish potato crop." Potato yield on St. Helena Island doubled between 1919 and 1924. But in 1924, 1925, 1926, and 1928, overproduction of vegetables on the Eastern Seaboard caused a drastic market decline, "reducing the price to a point where it hardly paid to dig potatoes."[34] The small African American farmers of the sea islands suffered the same fate as the large white truck farmers. Many went broke and many moved away.

One segment of the sea island economy that enhanced self-sufficiency was the presence of much livestock. Cattle, hogs, and poultry were found in abundance on the small sea island farms from Reconstruction forward. When hard times arrived in the twentieth century, and particularly after the boll weevil infestation, this basic form of subsistence also began to disappear. One hundred sixty horses and three hundred cattle were sold or eaten on St. Helena Island between 1920 and 1925. The average number of hogs per farm declined from 4.4 in 1920 to 1.3 in 1925. The same was true of poultry. The average number of chickens per farm dropped from 24 in 1920 to 10 in 1925.[35]

Consequently, during the 1920s Beaufort County lost more than a thousand farms. While a few of those farms were owned by white property owners who had "surrendered their farms to the government banks or other creditors or sold them to northern folk for game preserves," the vast majority of losses were those of African American farmers. In a rare editorial comment on the Great Exodus, the *Beaufort Gazette*'s E. O. Wilson noted in 1931 that "the great decrease in farms is due to the Negro migration north." Wilson blamed the exodus primarily on the decline of cotton:

> Prior to 1920, cotton held sway on the islands of the coast. This is an agricultural product that can be planted to advantage by the Negro. Since 1920, conditions have so changed that our people have been forced to abandon the cotton crop almost entirely. . . . . We are no longer considered cotton people. We are truck producers. There is a greater gamble in the trucking game. It is such that the small Negro planter cannot try it to advantage. Thus the old Negro cotton planter is working on the truck farms, in the oyster plants, or he has gone north. His small farm is abandoned, his old shanty fast decaying, weeds and bushes taking the place.

Two years later, in response to an Associated Press report subtitled "St. Helena Island Negroes flocking to Harlem and the island almost deserted," editor Wilson sought the opinion of Benjamin Barnwell, the island's agricultural demonstration agent for many years. Barnwell's opinion was valuable because he was a native of Beaufort County, had witnessed the Great Exodus firsthand, and was also one of the chief resources in the 1920s for Thomas J. Woofter's *Black Yeomanry* (1930). Barnwell, of course, defended the St. Helena Island agricultural community and complimented the efforts of Penn School in preserving the island society. He repeated statistics from Woofter's book on outmigration:

St. Helena Island	*Total population*	*Decrease*
1900	8,819	
1910	6,487	−2232 (25%)
1920	5,157	−1330 (20%)
1928	4,785	−372 (7.7%)

Barnwell ascribed the exodus from St. Helena Island to three primary causes. First was the decline of the phosphate industry in the 1890s that had employed, by his recollection "1,000 Negroes . . . from St. Helena and Ladies Islands." Second was the removal of the shipyard on Parris Island in 1901 and its "huge dry dock . . . where many island Negroes were employed." Third, the boll weevil infestation of 1917–18 ended the sea island cotton industry: "The boll weevil arrived in devastating numbers in 1918. The population had been shrinking before that date and more rapidly than it has since."[36]

The demographic statistics from Beaufort County in the early twentieth century illustrated the economic decline. The total population of Beaufort

County declined 38 percent from 1900 to 1940, all of it attributable to the Great Exodus of the sea island African American population. The white population actually increased in those years, doubling from 3,349 in 1900 to 7,124 in 1940. Beaufort County's African American population, however, declined 54 percent from 1900 to 1940. These numbers were complicated by the formation of Jasper County in 1912. But even if one adds back the African American population of Jasper County in 1920, the decline was still 32 percent. By the time of the 2000 census, despite six decades of population growth in Beaufort County since World War II, the African American population of the county (29,005) was still 9.7 percent below that of 1900. The following tables provide the details.

Beaufort County, Total Population, 1900–1940

1900	*1910*	*1920*	*1930*	*1940*
35,495	30,355	22,269	21,221	22,037[37]

Beaufort County, African American Population, 1900–1940

1900	*1910*	*1920*	*1930*	*1940*
32,137	26,376	17,454	15,571	14,781

In 1940 the U.S. Census Bureau further catalogued the outmigration by individual neighborhood in Beaufort County.

Beaufort County Population by Township, 1920–1940

Township	*1920*	*1930*	*1940*
Beaufort Township (Port Royal and Parris Island)	7,636	8,680	9,748
(Beaufort City)	(2,831)	(2,776)	(3,185)
(Port Royal Town)	(333)	(353)	(342)
Bluffton Township	2,151	2,304	1,835
(Bluffton Town)	(480)	(570)	(459)
Hilton Head Township	2,198	1,474	1,406
St. Helena Township (St. Helena Lady's Island)	5,157	4,620	4,266
Sheldon Township (Mainland)	3,521	3,129	3,208
(Yemassee Town. Half in Hampton County)	(323)	(589)	(684)
Hardeeville Township (Beaufort Co. to 1951)	413	728	1,361[38]

The exodus of African Americans from Beaufort County did not just involve poor tenant farmers (Beaufort County had the lowest percentage of black farm tenancy in the state) or small landowners. The African American professional and mercantile class, which had prospered during the decades of enterprise, was among the first to leave. From nearly a dozen African American lawyers practicing in Beaufort at the height of Reconstruction, only one, Julius I. Washington, was still practicing in Beaufort by 1930. Most of the children of Beaufort's black middle class left for greater opportunities in urban America. Every one of Robert Smalls's children and grandchildren had left Beaufort by 1920. Many entrepreneurs moved to bigger cities with more business. For example, in 1925 J. S. Blocker, owner of the Little Gem Barber Shop, closed his shop and moved to Miami, Florida. This was a loss to the whole community. The Little Gem Barber Shop had been a fixture of Bay Street commerce, and Blocker was "well-liked. . . . his friends wish him well."[39]

To migrate north, sea islanders had to save money for transportation. In the early years of the exodus, travel was by steamboat from Charleston or Savannah to New York. There is a reason that the first line of one of the most famous songs in DuBose Heyward and George Gershwin's opera *Porgy and Bess* is "There's a boat that's leavin' now for New York." That was a common scene before World War I. The first stage was by steamboat to Charleston or Savannah. From those ports, regular steam packet ships made the run to New York, Boston, or Philadelphia almost daily. As the twentieth century wore on, the more common mode of travel was by railroad. In 1917 the Seaboard Airline Railroad opened the "short route" from Charleston to Savannah through Dale and Lobeco in Beaufort County. The train that traveled that road was dubbed the "Boll Weevil" because it opened the year the insect struck Beaufort County. For a generation of sea islanders, the Boll Weevil was the first leg of the exodus. But lowcountry African Americans soon came to call this train the "chicken bone special." The nickname derived from the fact that typical lowcountry migrants had to pack food in shoeboxes because they could not get served in the segregated railroad restaurants of the 1920s and 1930s. By the time they reached New York City, all that was left in the boxes were chicken bones.[40]

While the Great Exodus was a calamity at home, more often than not it worked out well for those who left. Opportunities in urban America usually improved the migrants' lives in the North. In the 1920s Clyde Vernon Kiser, a sociologist at Columbia University, interviewed some of the first generation of migrants from St. Helena Island to New York City. The stories of Martin Washington and John B. Coleman were exemplary.

Martin Washington was born on St. Helena Island in 1878, the son of Benjamin and Ellen Washington. Both his parents had been born into slavery, and his father was a Union army veteran who had been awarded a medal for valor in combat. Benjamin Washington was a private in Company E, 34th Regiment, U.S. Colored Troops, from 1863 to 1866. He engaged in brutal combat on Morris Island and at Honey Hill. After the war he collected a small pension until his death in 1923. Martin Washington was one of eleven children. His father was an uneducated cotton farmer. His mother had a primary education, could read and write, and encouraged education among her children. Washington attended St. Helena Island public schools, where he acquired basic literacy. But St. Helena Island's underfunded primary schools operated only four months a year. In his spare time, when not helping on his father's farm, he hunted, fished, and played on a baseball team. In 1891, at age thirteen, he was admitted to Penn School and had Alice Lathrope and Ellen Murray as his teachers. Washington considered his attendance at Penn School a great privilege and distinction, it being "the oldest and best school of its kind throughout the South for Negroes." He was promoted to the Normal School, and in 1897, at age nineteen, he was hired to operate the school's manually operated printing press. He had several odd jobs on St. Helena Island but, as he recalled, "Business was not good . . . and wages low; therefore, my financial outlook was not encouraging."

In 1901 Martin Washington left St. Helena Island. Four days later he arrived in New York City. As he explained years later, "St. Helena was a beautiful island with pleasant, hospitable and religious people, but it did not offer as many opportunities for a livelihood, for education, and for enjoyment as New York—hence the appeal."

He was encouraged to go to New York by an older brother who had preceded him and who regularly sent home five or ten dollars per month to help support his mother. Martin Washington spent three weeks in New York "experiencing a little hardship" before finding his first job. In 1902 he found a better job with "quite a little responsibility attached to it," fair wages, and four days off per month. Washington continued to improve his employment and his standard of living. In 1908 he took the civil service exam and was appointed a subclerk in the U.S. Postal Service with a salary of six hundred dollars per year. With secure, regular employment, he married Mamie Jones of Savannah in 1909. Within five years he had been promoted and earned twelve hundred dollars per year. By 1923 Washington was a special clerk with the Postal Service and was earning an annual salary of twenty-three hundred dollars. That salary was more than a great majority of whites earned in Beaufort in the 1920s. By local standards, he was a wealthy man.

Martin Washington returned to St. Helena Island only twice, when his mother died in 1904 and when his father died in 1923. But Washington never forgot his sea island homeland. In 1925 he founded the Penn School

Club in New York City, which united some of the scattered alumni. The club raised funds and provided scholarships for two students to attend the school.[41]

John B. Coleman's story was similar. He was born on St. Helena Island in 1888, the first of nine children of Simon and Isabella Coleman. He grew up working in his father's fields: "If it wasn't thinning the cotton or corn . . . it was picking cotton or peas." John Coleman's father was one of the biggest African American planters on St. Helena Island. He owned three farms, the largest of fifty-eight acres at Mulberry Hill. The Coleman home was on Hope Plantation near Club Bridge Creek. Coleman enrolled at Penn School in 1895 and graduated from the tenth grade in 1906. As a teenager, he went to Savannah to work for a government contractor at Fort Screven. However, he was not strong enough for heavy construction work and was soon fired. After several odd jobs on the Savannah waterfront, he was happy to return home to St. Helena Island. His old teacher, Ellen Murray, hired him to teach at Frogmore Plantation Public School near his parent's home. His wages were four dollars per month.

When Ellen Murray died in 1908, Coleman decided to go to New York. To earn passage money, he picked oysters at George Lowden's oyster factory on Club Bridge Creek. In 1909 he attended the Summer Normal School and passed the Beaufort County teacher's examination. Licensed to teach, Coleman was assistant teacher at Frogmore School with a salary of twenty dollars per month. That year he saved enough money to book passage to New York.

In June 1910 Coleman traveled from Charleston to New York City aboard the Clyde Line steamer SS *Mohawk.* He landed at Pier 37, lived with his cousin Walter Days at 126th Street near Amsterdam Avenue, and worked as a longshoreman on the Clyde Line and Mallory Line docks. He returned to St. Helena and used his savings to open a grocery store in 1911. From 1911 to 1916, he "engaged in farming, teaching, storekeeping" and operated a small gristmill, which he purchased from the Sears-Roebuck Company. In 1914 and 1915 his business on St. Helena Island "suffered a severe blow." Because of the poor cotton years, Coleman said, he "could not collect much money from the people."

John Coleman married his first wife, Josephine, in 1916 and left for New York the next day. The newlyweds worked in New York City during the summer and returned to St. Helena each winter to teach school and keep their store. Although his store burned in December 1916 and his first wife died in 1919, Coleman kept up his annual migration from St. Helena Island to New York City for the next four years. In 1922 he married Etta Parker of Wilson, North Carolina. Personal misfortune, fires, and the boll weevil had wrecked his businesses on St. Helena Island, so Coleman decided to "stay up here for awhile." He worked as a longshoreman during the day and as a substitute clerk at the U.S. Post Office at night. In 1923 he secured a position as a regular postal clerk at an annual salary of fourteen hundred dollars. Thereafter, he remained in New York. By 1927 his salary had risen to twenty-one hundred dollars per year, more than he could have hoped to make on St. Helena Island. In 1929 John Coleman, Martin Washington, Helen Polite, James Green, and Lymas Chisholm formed the St. Helena League to assist migrants to New York. This organization was so successful that by the late 1930s it was able to pay sick benefits, unemployment, and death benefits. Their annual dance was the largest party of the year for transplanted Beaufortonians. It united sea islanders throughout the Northeast and netted thousands of dollars a year for the league.

John Coleman retained his affection for St. Helena Island. As he stated in 1928, "I love the island as usual, for I still have most of my folks down there. . . . But conditions there include the elimination of cotton from the farm as a major crop . . . the reduction of the population on St. Helena Island of nearly two thousand people within the last fifteen years," and other circumstances not conducive to prosperity. So he stayed in New York and only returned to bury his relatives. John Brown Coleman died in New York City in 1948.[42]

There was a postscript to Coleman's story. In 1930 his youngest sibling, Isabella Coleman, left St. Helena Island for New York City. Born in 1906, she attended Frogmore School, where her brother was her first teacher. Isabella Colemanthen went to Penn School and graduated in 1923. She worked for several years in the household of Clare (Mrs. J. Ross) Macdonald at Frogmore Plantation and by 1930 had saved enough money to buy a one-way train ticket to New York City for $29.46. On her first trip, she was barred from the first train at Yemassee because the only seats available were on the segregated "whites only" railroad car. She had to wait, alone, late into the night for the next train north. "That was my first bitter experience with segregation," she recalled. When she arrived, she was met by her brother and sister and stayed with her on St. Felix Street in Brooklyn. She held a number of domestic jobs on Long Island and in upstate New York before returning to St. Helena Island in 1933. For several years she kept up the migratory pattern her brother had followed, teaching school on St. Helena Island during the fall and winter and returning to New York or Philadelphia in the summer for more lucrative employment.

While in New York, Isabella Coleman kept up a busy schedule of self-education through lectures at the Urban League, readings at the Brooklyn Public Library, and regular attendance at the Penn Club. She formed her own women's club, the "Thrifty Workers," and joined the Bridgeport Baptist Church. In 1937 she joined the St. Helena League. Isabella Coleman revealed that one reason for the success of the St. Helena League in the late 1930s was that "St. Helena native Harry Chisholm was a numbers runner. He always had money. . . . After the meeting you didn't have to wonder where you were going. Harry would give $40 or $50 towards the entertainment."

In 1938 Isabella Coleman's mother died on St. Helena Island. She used her inheritance to have a small store built at the corner of Seaside and Folly Roads on St. Helena Island, hoping that the rent would support her retirement. Eventually, the Folly Road Grocery became one of the foremost black-owned businesses on the island. Isabella owned the grocery for thirty years. She sold the business to Luther Warren in 1968.

Eventually, she returned to South Carolina and in the 1960s was the first woman appointed to the Federal Housing Administration in South Carolina. She married twice and had one son, Dr. Jonathan Coleman Glen of Savannah. In 1980 Isabella Coleman Glen published her memoirs, *Life on St. Helena Island*. She died in Savannah in 1992 at eighty-six years of age.[43]

The Great Exodus did not cause Beaufort County's economic decline. Instead, it was a symptom of the decline. But like a snowball that gathers size and speed as it rolls downhill, the outmigration caused the gradual economic slide to become a deep, profound depression by the 1930s. By 1935 Beaufort County was one of the poorest places in the United States, partly because so much of its productive human capital had moved away.

Chapter 9

World War I, Parris Island, and the Progressive Era

WORLD WAR I AND PARRIS ISLAND

The only bright spot in Beaufort County's declining economy of the early twentieth century was the arrival of the United States Marines. The buildup for World War I was the proximate reason that the Marine Corps Recruit Depot was established on Parris Island in 1915. However, the arrival of the Marines was preceded by a decade of false starts and political maneuvering.

U.S. Marines had occupied the old naval station since the navy departed in 1901. In 1903 Captain B. B. Woog of the corps began training forty Georgia recruits on Parris Island on his own initiative. From 1904 to 1933, the navy maintained its Atlantic fleet disciplinary barracks on Parris Island and refurbished some of the old buildings as jails. The marines, in the navy tradition, were the jailers.

When in 1908 the navy threatened to move the disciplinary barracks to Norfolk, Virginia, Beaufortonians united to prevent the loss of even that small detachment. Congressman J. O. Patterson introduced an appropriation for fifty thousand dollars in 1908 to convert the naval station into a Marine Corps training base, but the Republican Speaker of the House, Joe Cannon of Illinois, struck the money from the bill. The William Howard Taft administration and the Republican-controlled House of Representatives had no interest in providing funds for Democratic-controlled South Carolina.[1]

In October 1908 the fortunes of Parris Island began to turn when the Navy Department decided to move the Marine Corps officer candidate school, the U.S. Marine School of Application, from overcrowded Annapolis, Maryland, to the underused facilities on Parris Island. The move, however, was only temporary as the Navy Department and congressional leaders preferred New London, Connecticut, or Philadelphia for the permanent site of the school. Marine Corps Lieutenant Colonel Eli Cole took command of the temporary school at Parris Island. Major general George F. Elliott, commandant of the corps, arrived at Parris Island in November 1908, in advance of fifty candidates and a battalion of marines. The local reaction to the marines' arrival and the commandant's visit was buoyant and hopeful. The *Beaufort Gazette* crowed that the city was "glad to see the arrival of General Elliott and his Marines. . . . no arrival for sometime has been so welcome as his. . . . people here will do all they can to make his school a success."[2] It was the beginning of a century of cordial relations and enthusiastic local support for the U.S. Marine Corps.

As the naval station was being refitted, local businesses got many of the contracts. Furniture and plumbing fixtures were purchased locally, and local contractors did much of the installation. Charles E. Danner's SS *Summer Girl* got the navy contract to make daily supply and passenger runs between Beaufort, Port Royal, and Parris Island. The *Gazette* knew the importance of this experiment and urged the merchants and citizens to put their best foot forward: "Success of the proposed expeditionary base for Marines at Port Royal depends in some measure on the cooperation of the citizens of Beaufort and Port Royal. . . . this battalion is to be welcomed. . . . their stay should be made as agreeable as possible.[3]

By January 1909 the barracks had been renovated and furnished. An advance party of 5 officers and 80 marines arrived on January 26, 1909, and 300 followed a week later. The full complement was expected to be 455 officers and men. The effect on Beaufort was immediate. Several officers brought their families and lived in town. In addition to the officer candidates, in April 1909, 318 marines from the Nicaragua expeditionary force arrived from the Panama Canal Zone aboard the USS *Prairie.* Nearly half of this force remained on Parris Island. The local newspaper noted, "The Naval Station is getting busy."[4]

No sooner had the marines arrived than the old specter of competitive politics arose. In June 1909 the *Beaufort Gazette* reported that Charleston politicians were trying to lure the Marine Corps to their city. The paper reminded Beaufortonians of the "bitter experience of 1901" and opined that "Charleston extends no quarter where her interests are involved." In June 1910, while the school on Parris Island was in full swing, the Navy Department announced that the permanent officers' school would be built in Philadelphia or Portsmouth, New Hampshire. Congressman J. O. Patterson seemed to have little influence with the Navy Department, and the *Beaufort Gazette* wearily noted that "the Washington correspondents have for ten years seemed to make opportunities to knock this Port Royal Station. It gets a little tiresome."[5] The Officer's Candidate School was moved to the Norfolk Navy Yard in 1911.

The turning point for Parris Island and Beaufort County was the election of 1910. That was the year that a young lawyer from Aiken, James F. Byrnes, decided to challenge Congressman Patterson for the Second Congressional District seat. Patterson had contracted malaria in the spring of 1910 and was too ill to campaign. Young Jimmy Byrnes was a whirlwind, visiting every courthouse and nearly every neighborhood in the district. After a stump speech at Barrell Landing in August, a correspondent observed that Byrnes's "usual happy strain seemed to take well with the audience." Though Byrnes lost to Patterson in Beaufort County by 177 votes, he narrowly won the Second Congressional District and began a fifteen-year career in the United States House of Representatives. From 1910 to 1925, Congressman Jimmy Byrnes was tireless and effective in delivering federal largesse to Beaufort County. He was well known in Beaufort. His first public job was as a local court stenographer, and he never lost his affection for the "beautiful old town in the tidewater."[6]

The Navy Department had every intention to abandon Parris Island in 1910 and 1911. Before Jimmy Byrnes could build up Parris Island, he first had to save it. His unlikely ally was South Carolina's senior senator, "Pitchfork Ben" Tillman. Tillman had engineered the removal of the naval shipyard from Parris Island to Charleston in 1901. He had no love for Beaufort County, the last stronghold of black Republicans in the state. But Beaufort County's politics had undergone a gradual revolution in the decades since Tillman was governor. Jim Crow legislation and Tillman's 1895 constitution had done their work so well that even in Beaufort County, the black Republicans had been defeated. In 1910 the City of Beaufort was the only government in South Carolina with black elected officials and a mixed-race government. Nevertheless, Senator Tillman promised to save the Port Royal Naval Station. In 1911 he engineered passage of a Senate resolution delaying the navy's plans by calling for a "study" of the naval stations at New Orleans, Pensacola, New London, and Port Royal. The next year, Jimmy Byrnes introduced an amendment to the military appropriations bill in the House of Representatives to keep the navy's disciplinary barracks on Parris Island. That facility stayed there, off and on, until 1933.[7]

Thus, during the waning days of the Republican Taft administration, Senator Tillman and Congressman Byrnes saved Parris Island for future development. The next step was to make use of it. These decades were the beginning of the Progressive Era in national politics, and Jimmy Byrnes was an architect and consummate practitioner of progressivism. The national movement towards a more activist federal government dominated American politics for most of the twentieth century.

The 1912 federal election was a great watershed in American political history and a significant turning point for Beaufort County. Not only was Woodrow Wilson elected president, the second Democratic president since the Civil War, but also both houses of Congress went Democratic for the first time since 1860. The Democratic victory of 1912 ended more than fifty years of Republican federal patronage. Throughout the South, Republican bureaucrats were thrown out in favor of Democratic supporters. In 1913 even Robert Smalls lost his job as port collector to F. H. Colcock, a Democrat and friend of Jimmy Byrnes.

One of Woodrow Wilson's most important appointments was Josephus Daniels as secretary of the navy. Wilson was a reformer and a moralist. Although he was governor of New Jersey when elected president, Wilson's father, a Virginia Presbyterian minister, had raised him in Augusta, Georgia, and Columbia, South Carolina. Southerners thought of Wilson as one of their own, and he took pains to deliver federal largess to the impoverished states of his homeland. A leading Wilson supporter, Josephus Daniels, was the publisher of the *Raleigh Observer* and boss of the North Carolina Democratic Party. When he became secretary of the navy in 1913, he brought Wilson's reformist impulses to the American fleet. Wilson and Daniels were both Prohibition supporters, as were most of their southern constituents. Daniels prohibited liquor aboard U.S. Navy warships. The sailors substituted strong black coffee for liquor and nicknamed a cup of coffee a "cup of Joe" in Daniels's honor.

Secretary Daniels took a particular interest in Parris Island, and only a month after taking office, he made a personal visit to Beaufort County. He was hosted by Mayor W. R. Bristol, Senator Niels Christensen, School Superintendent Dr. William Steinmeyer, lawyer W. J. Thomas, and Postmaster E. D. Raney, a personal friend of Jimmy Byrnes. One of Daniels's old friends with close ties to Beaufort, William Elliott Gonzales of the *State* newspaper, also joined the delegation. Daniels suggested that the old naval station could be used as an educational and training facility. He promised "to pay personal attention to Parris Island" and predicted that "this is just the beginning for Parris Island."[8] In September 1913 Secretary Daniels dispatched an inspection board of the Navy Department to Parris Island to recommend utilization of the old naval station facilities. In 1913 there were 11 officers, 157 enlisted marines, 26 enlisted sailors, and 471 "detentioners" stationed or imprisoned on Parris Island.

As the year 1913 ended, perhaps the most important visit in Parris Island's modern history occurred. On December 29, 1913, Congressman Byrnes hosted a visit by the ambitious new assistant secretary of the navy, Franklin Delano Roosevelt of New York. Their friendship, which began at that time, became important not only for Parris Island but also for the state and nation. Roosevelt was elected governor of New York in 1928, and Byrnes was elected to the United States Senate in 1930. When Roosevelt became president in 1933, he relied on Jimmy Byrnes to usher his revolutionary New Deal legislation through the Senate. The relationship was so close that during the long Roosevelt administrations, Jimmy Byrnes was called the "assistant president." Byrnes was associate justice of the U.S. Supreme Court, director of the War Production Board during World War II, and secretary of state in Roosevelt's last administration. He ended his remarkable public career in 1955 after two terms as governor. Byrnes was the most influential South Carolinian of the twentieth century, but to the people of Beaufort County, he was "our Jimmy."[9]

During 1914, as the war drums increased in Europe, Josephus Daniels and Franklin Roosevelt promoted the idea that Parris Island would be an ideal training facility for the navy or Marine Corps. The outbreak of world war in August 1914 focused the attention of many political and military leaders on preparedness. On December 10, 1914, Senator Tillman and Congressman Byrnes urged Secretary Daniels that Parris Island be used for training naval or marine recruits. At the time Ben Tillman was the chairman of the Senate Naval Affairs Committee, so Secretary Daniels was eager to please him. This meeting was not the last of such communications because within three weeks it was reported that the "Port Royal Station is to be a Marine barracks."[10] Byrnes wrestled with Senator Claude A. Swanson of Virginia, the most senior senator next to Tillman on the Naval Affairs Committee, over the removal of Marine Corps training from Norfolk. But on April 5, 1915, Daniels sent an official letter to Congressman Byrnes informing him of the Navy Department's decision "to establish at Port Royal, S.C., a post which will consist of approximately five hundred officers and men of the Marine Corps."[11]

Large numbers of marines arrived in October 1915. On October 1 Congressman Byrnes announced that 800 marines would transfer from Norfolk to Parris Island "as soon as transports could be obtained." On October 14 Colonel John Lejeune, later Marine Corps commandant, accepted possession of the old Port Royal Naval Station on behalf of the corps. The next week, 750 Marines under the command of Captains Elias R. Beadle, Epaminondas L. Bigler, and Henry N. Manney arrived aboard the USS *Prairie.* On October 28, 1915, Parris Island officially became the United States Marine Corps Recruit Depot, Parris Island, South Carolina. As of 1915 Parris Island was the only recruit depot in the nation and the first military facility ever assigned to the exclusive use of the Marine Corps.[12]

By December 15, 1915, 908 recruits, drill instructors, and officers were permanently stationed on Parris Island. The training command even included field musicians' training.[13] Nineteen fifteen was the beginning of a new era for Parris Island and for Beaufort County.

The Marine Corps Recruit Depot expanded as the war in Europe deteriorated into a bloodbath. In February 1916 Congressman Byrnes proposed recommissioning Fort Fremont to protect Parris Island and the Savannah ship channel. The threat to America's maritime commerce was real and came home to Beaufort in March 1915 when the SS *Carib,* with forty-six hundred bales of Georgia and South Carolina cotton, was sunk by a German mine on its way into Bremen Harbor. The *Carib* had been a Clyde Line packet between Boston and Charleston. The master of the SS *Carib* was Captain Edgar Cole of Savannah. In March 1917 a German submarine sank the SS *Memphis* of the Savannah Line, killing at least one local crewman. In February 1917 a secret U.S. Navy report revealed that the navy had been searching for some time for a possible German U-boat supply base "using a small cove in Port Royal Sound." The navy searched for several days around Port Royal Sound but found nothing. The maritime threat to U.S. shipping was the principal reason for America's entry into World War I on April 6, 1917.[14]

World War I was, of course, an immense stimulant to the development of Parris Island and, consequently, gave a burst of prosperity to Beaufort County. The marine population of Parris Island went from 80 Marines in 1913 to 17,000 Marines in 1918. During World War I, 46,202 recruits trained on Parris Island, more than twice the population of Beaufort County. The federal government spent $4 million building 233 buildings and a cantonment area of 160 acres that is the core of the Recruit Depot to this day. By 1918 Parris Island could accommodate 16,000 men. The facilities included a $2 million electric power plant, three open-air theatres, and a bakery that produced five thousand loaves of bread each day. A Savannah company got the contract to build the power plant. All the roads were crowned and surfaced with oyster shell. Local men performed most of the labor, much of it by sea islanders living on nearby freedmen's homesteads. The economic impact for Beaufort County was, of course, bountiful. As the *Beaufort Gazette* noted early in 1917, "War will mean more to Beaufort than to most other small towns of this state."[15]

Beaufort's response to the nation's entry into World War I was an outpouring of patriotic enthusiasm. In March 1917 hundreds of citizens turned out in front of the courthouse to hear historic and patriotic speeches by city and county officials. Twenty-two of Beaufort's leading citizens, members of the old Beaufort Volunteer Artillery, volunteered on the spot for the U.S. Naval Reserve to patrol the coastal waters for U-boats. Among them were Senator Niels Christensen Jr., Dr. M. G. Elliott, J. W. Varn, Haskell Rhett, R. R. Legare, Leroy Attaway, M. P. Sams, and J. S. Walpole. When President Wilson called for a national draft, 1,406 Beaufort County men immediately registered for the draft. Lawyer W. J. Thomas was appointed chairman of the county Board of Registration, which registered every adult male in Beaufort County. Hal Pollitzer was chairman of the Draft Board, which selected the men for military service. A. R. Sams served as secretary of the Draft Board throughout the war. Beaufort County officials reportedly encountered "no opposition to the draft." W. J. Thomas listed the initial draft registrants by voting precincts. The City of Beaufort's two precincts registered 374 young men, and the next largest numbers came from Tomotley, the railroad stop near Sheldon, with 249 men and the Brick Church on St. Helena Island with 210 men. The Tomotley and St. Helena Island men were overwhelmingly African American. All of Beaufort County's draftees were sent to the new, strictly segregated U.S. Army training facility at Camp Jackson in Columbia.

The response of Beaufort County's black majority was praised in the local and statewide newspapers. As one noted, "The Negroes as a race are earning the commendation of their white neighbors. . . . various draft boards speak well of the Negro conscripts and the South Carolina Preparedness Commission mentioned them favorably in their report." When twenty-eight African American draftees from Beaufort were shipped off to Camp Jackson in October 1917, they "were given an enthusiastic send off by their colored relatives and friends." A band played on Bay Street and led a large parade of citizens to the depot to board the old Charleston and Western Carolina for Columbia.

Beaufortonians enthusiastically supported the marines training on Parris Island. The "pleasant sound" of early morning firing from the rifle range roused Beaufortonians several times a week. When Brigadier General Eli Cole relinquished command of the depot to Brigadier General John T. Myers in August 1918, two hundred Beaufort citizens attended the farewell reception at the Lyceum on Parris Island. Mayor J. A. Kinghorn presented General Cole with a gift of solid silver candlesticks from the citizens.[16] Beaufortonians had not forgotten that Eli Cole had been the first commander of the School of Application in 1909.

America's entry into World War I began a whirlwind of civic activity and community organization on behalf of the war effort. Beaufort's leading women organized a Red Cross chapter, which one hundred citizens paid a dollar each to join on October 19, 1917. Mrs. Marian Lengnick, Miss Ruth Batchelder, Miss Therese Talbird, Miss Lillian Rice, Miss J. S. Walpole, and Mrs. J. L. Paul were the organizers. The headquarters were on Bay Street with branches in Frogmore and Port Royal. When the charter was received, E. E. Lengnick was chairman with Mabel Runnette as vice chair, Therese Talbird as secretary, and F. W. Scheper Jr. as treasurer. Throughout the war, hundreds of Red Cross volunteers collected bandages and supplies, operated canteens at Beaufort and Port Royal, and hosted Red Cross entertainers at the Beaufort High School auditorium on Carteret Street. The Beaufort County chapter also had a "colored auxiliary" that met weekly for knitting meetings.[17]

In the summer of 1917, the old arsenal on Craven Street was converted into a servicemen's club. In September the remodeled building opened as the Sojourners Club. The town put on a banquet there for 150 marines, soldiers from Fort Fremont, and the naval reserves stationed in Beaufort. The remodeled club had a pool table, a Victrola, a piano, easy chairs, library tables, a lunch counter in the old gun room, and a basketball net in the courtyard. Activities at the Sojourners Club were directed by the Beaufort Council on Training Camp Activities. Frederick Christensen was chairman, George Waterhouse Jr., was secretary, and E. D. Raney was treasurer. This effort was so much appreciated by the military command that the week following the arsenal banquet, the corps sponsored a military ball featuring the Marine Corps Band and a smaller jazz band at the county courthouse. All proceeds from the one-dollar admission fee were donated to the Sojourners Club.[18]

The community also formed the Beaufort County Defense Council to promote the sale of Liberty Bonds, Thrift Stamps, and War Savings Stamps. The council also organized food donations through Food Pledge Cards. Again, Beaufort's leading citizens marshaled this effort. George Waterhouse Jr. was chairman of the Defense Council; F. W. Scheper Jr. was treasurer; and R. K. Harley and Dr. William Steinmeyer were food administrators. The Defense Council held "war savings rallies" throughout the county. Each community had area leaders. In July 1918 one such group held a rally in Lobeco. The area leaders were Leroy Attaway for Lobeco and "King" Keyserling for Dale. A large crowd was entertained by "stirring speeches" from George Waterhouse, Reverend G. W. Rockwell of the Beaufort Baptist Church, and Reverend J. J. Stevenson of the Methodist Church. The rally was highlighted by patriotic music from the Marine Corps Band. After the ceremonies, the crowd was treated to "a delicious supper with ice cream at Mr. Attaway's store." The effort paid off. In 1918 Beaufort County had the state's highest per capita sales of Savings Stamps and Thrift Stamps.[19]

The festivities on the Fourth of July 1918 highlighted the wartime partnership between the marines and the Beaufort community. Hundreds of marines attended a field day that included baseball, volleyball, swimming contests, and dozens of private picnics along the bluff. President Wilson's Fourth of July speech was read from the courthouse steps by Major Edwin Denby, USMC, a hero of battles in France. The festivities concluded with a dance at the courthouse led by the Marine Corps Band.[20]

Beaufort County's support efforts were recognized by the federal government in July 1918, when the county was designated a "War Camp Community." This designation entitled the community to receive federal assistance to complement local support. This opportunity was not lost on Congressman Byrnes or his friends in Beaufort. In 1919 Beaufort received twenty-eight thousand dollars in federal money to build a new civic club for servicemen and the community. The Community Club on Carteret Street next to the post office was the center of civic activity for forty years.[21]

Despite Beaufort County's patriotic activities, not everyone supported the war or the Wilson administration. During Reconstruction, Beaufort County had seen an influx of immigrants from Germany. Several Beaufortonians were only one generation removed from their German homeland, and as the *Beaufort Gazette* admitted, "there have been outspoken criticisms by a few of the country's attitude toward the Central Powers."

America's entry into the war was naturally accompanied by a certain amount of wartime paranoia. Congress accompanied its war declarations with several laws controlling antigovernment behavior. In April 1917 J.A. Kempher, a German merchant on Lady's Island, was arrested and jailed for "making incendiary utterances against the U.S. Government." At the same time, an African American man from St. Helena Island was arrested for "sending mail in some suspicious code." A week later Joe Dais of Dale was "heard to make a rash statement against the government." He was arrested, questioned by the sheriff, and released with a warning. The most interesting of these cases was the arrest of N.J. Kennedy, a medical doctor, for violating the federal Espionage Act. Dr. Kennedy was arrested for "making some utterances to a member of the Naval Reserve." He was released on his own recognizance and bound over for trial in federal court in Orangeburg. The war ended before his trial, and the charge was eventually dropped. Dr. Kennedy was one of the most prominent members of Beaufort's African American professional class. He had been politically active since the 1890s and may have expressed resentment of the state's Democratic politics generally or the segregated "progressive" administration of Woodrow Wilson. Whatever his "utterance," Dr. Kennedy was not involved in espionage. The war effort, the universal draft, and war paranoia were also excuses to crack down on idlers and vagrants. In April 1917 Police Chief Dan Mann gave notice that "vagrants must go to work, go to war or go to jail."[22]

When American "doughboys" began to return from the war in France in late 1918, they brought with them a threat far more deadly than German U-boats. The worst pandemic in world history began in the soggy trenches of the western front. Before it ran its course, the Spanish flu epidemic of 1918 killed twenty million people worldwide. In September, President Wilson issued a special message to the nation on how to avoid contracting or spreading the deadly influenza. In September 1918 several cases of Spanish flu were diagnosed on Parris Island. Two marines in critical condition were transferred to a special hospital in Quantico, Virginia. One died. These were the first cases of influenza reported in Beaufort County. By October, Parris Island was quarantined.

Thirteen schoolchildren came down with the flu in October 1918, and all the county schools were closed. During the fall the colleges began to close and send the students home. All the Beaufort boys returned from Clemson in the first week of October, and May Bellamy was sent home from Mary Washington College in Virginia. Beaufort, however, was spared the worst ravages of the epidemic.[23]

When the armistice was signed on November 11, 1918, Beaufort rejoiced with special church services of thanksgiving, a street celebration, and a parade led by the Marine Corps Band. Flags, fireworks, and church bells announced the occasion. At the end of the day, an aged Gullah woman summed up the mood in the expressive wisdom of the sea islands, "Do Jesus 'tank Gawd, I feel so light."[24]

Parris Island played host to many war heroes and Marine Corps luminaries. Colonel John Lejeune, who had received the Parris Island facility in 1915, gained fame as the first Marine Corps officer to command an army regiment in combat. During the 1920s he became commandant of the Marine Corps and a founder of the modern corps. General Lejeune's duties often brought him to Beaufort County in the 1920s.

The largest ceremony General Lejeune attended on Parris Island was the dedication of the monument honoring Charlesfort, Captain Jean Ribaut's French settlement of 1562. The Huguenot Society of South Carolina had lobbied for years to mark the place. Major George Osterhout excavated the site, and on March 27, 1926, General Lejeune, Governor Thomas G. McCleod, and a host of dignitaries dedicated the monument.[25]

General Joseph Pendleton commanded Parris Island in 1918 and 1919. He had led the marine expeditionary forces in Nicaragua in 1912 and Santo Domingo in 1916. When he left Parris Island in September 1919, he was reassigned to his home in Coronado, California, to plan a recruit depot, like Parris Island, to serve the Pacific fleet. Camp Pendleton, California, was later named in his honor. Sergeant Dan Daly made publicity and morale tours of Parris Island after World War I. Next to Sergeant Alvin York of Tennessee, Dan Daly may have been the most famous enlisted man in the United States. He was the only enlisted Marine ever to have earned two Medals of Honor for seaparate actions. He first earned the Medal of Honor in 1900 during the Chinese Boxer Rebellion when a marine expeditionary force broke the rebels' siege of American and European diplomatic missions in Peking and brought them to safety. Daly earned his second Medal of Honor leading a marine assault on Fort Riviere in Haiti in 1915. He capped off his remarkable career by winning the French Croix de Guerre and Medal Militaire as well as the American Distinguished Service Cross for heroism on the western front.[26]

To Beaufort County the most notable hero was Major Edwin Denby, who had a remarkable career in and out of the Marine Corps. He began his military service during the Spanish-American War as a navy gunner's mate aboard the USS *Yosemite* at the Battle of Santiago, Cuba. He was a graduate of the University of Michigan law school and after the Spanish-American War joined the Michigan Bar. He was president of the Detroit Board of Trade and in 1904 was elected to the U.S. Congress. Denby served three terms as a Republican congressman from 1905 to 1911. When the United States entered the war, Denby enlisted in the Marine Corps and was one of the first recruits trained on Parris Island. He soon received an officer's commission, served heroically at the Battle of Belleau Wood, and ended the war a major.

In 1919 Denby was so charmed by Beaufort that he bought the house on Bay Street that had long been the home of George Gage and his children. After Warren G. Harding was elected president in 1920, he named Major Denby secretary of the navy to succeed Josephus Daniels. From 1919 until his death in 1932, Denby was a winter resident and an active participant in the commercial life of the town.

On Memorial Day 1921, Secretary Denby traveled with Congressman Byrnes on an official visit to Beaufort and to his old duty station on Parris Island. Memorial Day 1921 was one of Beaufort's great celebrations. The day and evening were filled with a parade and procession to the National Cemetery, patriotic speeches, and music at the cemetery, supper at the old Sea Island Hotel, a reception at the Community Club on Carteret Street, and finally a dance at the courthouse. Secretary Denby's occasional speech stressed national unity: "I rejoice in the thought that today we meet together to honor both the heroic dead of the North and of the South . . . that this occasion . . . may yet do a little toward destroying the last vestiges of that ancient feud."

Edwin Denby's term as secretary of the navy ended in disgrace. He was in the middle of the Harding administration's infamous Teapot Dome Scandal, one of the worst corruption scandals in American history. In 1924 he was forced to resign, but Beaufortonians knew he was a scapegoat. A *Beaufort Gazette* editorial said, "We are sorry to see Mr. Denby making himself the 'goat' in the oil scandals in Washington. . . . whatever his faults, Mr. Denby is entirely too good to be so used." Despite the collapse of his career in Washington, Denby was always an honored and popular citizen of Beaufort.[27]

On July 25, 1924, the Marine Corps unveiled a monument on Parris Island honoring the men of Parris Island who had given their lives on the battlefields of France. The monument is a bronze statue of a marine in combat gear hurtling over a trench line armed with a 1911 army .45 caliber pistol. Robert Aitken, one of the foremost American sculptors of the time, created the statue. The Parris Island marines dubbed the monument "Iron Mike." It symbolized a heroic era in the history of the U.S. Marine Corps and Parris Island. It also symbolized an important turning point in Beaufort County's history.[28]

World War I was a moment of prosperity for Beaufort County. The Marine Corps Recruit Depot provided virtually full employment for two years. More important for Beaufort County, the marines had come to stay. Parris Island was the first exclusively Marine Corps station in the United

States. Most of the marines who performed so heroically at Chateau-Thierry, Soissons, Belleau Wood, and Saint-Mihiel had trained on Parris Island. World War I established the Marine Corps mystique in the minds of the American public and cemented Parris Island to the heart of the corps. The permanence of the United States Marine Corps facilities in Beaufort County was the most important single factor in the twentieth-century economy of the county.

THE BOLL WEEVIL AND THE END OF COTTON

World War I also saw the end of cotton farming in Beaufort County. The traditional livelihood of sea island farmers had been stagnant for decades, but most small farmers clung to cotton because it was all they knew. Worldwide overproduction and dismal prices had drained the crop's profitability for years, but the Mexican boll weevil finally destroyed the county's once-famous product. Beaufort had the sad distinction of being the first South Carolina county where the pest appeared.

Prior to World War I, cotton prices fluctuated and production followed. In 1910 short-staple cotton sold for fifteen and a half cents per pound or approximately $77.50 per bale. In that year, Beaufort County produced 9,904 bales of short staple cotton and only 1,538 bales of long-staple, sea island cotton. The year 1910 was probably the best for Beaufort cotton in the early twentieth century. In 1910 and most of the decade, Beaufort County was next to last in cotton production in South Carolina. By contrast, Anderson County in the upstate routinely produced ten times the volume of cotton as Beaufort County.[29]

In 1911 the price dropped to ten cents per pound, a price that was not worth the effort of planting, tending, and harvesting. The usual break-even price for cotton was considered twelve and a half cents per pound. The 1911 crop was a 50 percent loss from the hurricane of that year. In 1913 George Waterhouse Jr., owner of the largest working cotton gin in Beaufort, reflected on the short- and long-term prospects for cotton. Prices in 1913 would be approximately ten cents per pound, only half the price of the 1820s and 1850s and barely profitable for the small island farmers, who were mostly African American. The "normal" price of twelve and a half cents per pound was exceeded only once between 1905 and 1915. Waterhouse concluded that "the sea island situation remains unsatisfactory." World overproduction for decades had suppressed the price of cotton. Ironically, in the years before World War I, upstate South Carolina textile mills were importing Egyptian cotton through the port of Charleston, reversing a century of trade.[30]

The small farmers of St. Helena Island supplemented their modest incomes by growing corn, sweet potatoes, and melons. These products fed their families and their livestock, while the surplus could be sold locally. The combination of these crops had provided a stable, subsistence agriculture for several generations. But the farmers still relied on cotton for cash income and were reluctant to change. The boll weevil struck these people with devastating effect.[31]

World War I prompted a momentary spike in world cotton prices. Wartime demand for cotton was enormous and not just for clothing. Modern artillery and rapid-fire weaponry required tons of cotton for their ammunition. It was estimated that a machine gun used a bale of cotton every three minutes. Naval gunnery was the most voracious consumer of cotton. At the Battle of Jutland in 1916, between the British and the German fleets, each warship consumed five thousand pounds of cotton per minute. In addition, twenty thousand bales of cotton were used each year in battlefield medicine. It was estimated that one change of apparel for all the combat troops in World War I required a million bales of cotton. In 1916, for the first time in decades, world consumption of cotton exceeded production by three million bales. This followed three successive years of short crops. In September 1917 W. G. Smith, the South Carolina cotton warehouse commissioner, predicted the price of cotton would reach thirty cents per pound, the highest price in forty years.[32]

The prosperity that was just around the corner for cotton farmers disappeared when the Mexican boll weevil appeared on Daufuskie Island. The march of the boll weevil across southern cotton fields was well documented. It had devastated the crops of Texas, Louisiana, Mississippi, and Alabama by 1916. In the summer of 1916, the weevil had reached central Georgia. A. F. Conradi, a Clemson professor, state entomologist, and a national expert on the bug, had published warnings and recommendations in every local newspaper and through the Clemson extension agents in every county. He recommended planting alternative crops such as tobacco, peanuts, and vegetables before the boll weevil arrived. But few cotton farmers heeded his advice. They could "only see the present high prices" and continued to plant cotton.

On November 2, 1917, boll weevils were reported on Daufuskie Island, the first appearance of the pest in South Carolina. Daufuskie Island is in the southernmost corner of Beaufort County, just across the Savannah River from Georgia. As they did most sea islands, African American farmers populated Daufuskie. There were several ways for Daufuskie Island families to earn money in those years. They grew cotton, and after the harvest the men gathered oysters in the riverbeds, while their wives earned wages as "shuckers" at the L. P. Maggioni Oyster Factory. But in 1917 the boll weevil consumed a large portion of their primary income. Like most black Beaufort County farmers of the era, they were "one horse farmers." The rules of thumb for Beaufort County cotton farmers in 1917 were one bale of cotton per mule, one mule per farmer, and one bale per acre. Professor Conradi reported that infestation normally reached its peak in two or three years, but in 1917 the pest consumed 70 percent of Daufuskie Island's cotton.

Within a few weeks, the boll weevil was detected in Hardeeville and Bluffton. The South Carolina Crop Pest Commission quarantined all Beaufort County cotton. That measure did not succeed. The weevil had invaded Jasper County before the year was out. In 1918 the pest crossed the Broad River and consumed much of the crop on Port Royal, Lady's, and St. Helena Islands. By 1918 the boll weevil had marched up the Savannah River as had General William T. Sherman's army in 1865 and invaded Allendale and Barnwell Counties. In Beaufort the boll weevil was dubbed "the Kaiser's ally." The *Beaufort Gazette* noted the sad irony for Beaufort County's small cotton farmers of "unprecedented wartime prosperity and the worst pest . . . at the same time!"[33]

Everyone offered advice to combat the boll weevil. Professor Conradi and Clemson extension agents advised farmers to plow the crop under and burn the stalks on the first sight of boll weevils. If the farmer insisted on continuing to plant cotton, he should plant as early as possible, fertilize the ground thoroughly (an added expense), increase the distance between rows (reducing production), and apply more weeding and cropping of plants (added labor). J. N. McBride, agricultural agent of the Seaboard Railroad, advised cotton farmers to grow tobacco. In 1918 Blake Crosby, manager of W. R. Pritchard's farm at Pritchardville, gave up cotton entirely and switched to tobacco. C. A. Vincent, county demonstration agent, published a weekly newspaper column. He noted that in 1919 "cotton costs more to produce than the present market price quotation." He advised diversifying crops and even printed a tear-out farmer's pledge form to plant a third less cotton in 1919. In January 1920 the Clemson extension service offered a two-week seminar on boll weevil management at the Community Club. The seminar was also conducted in Bluffton, Ridgeland, and Walterboro. It was noted that neighboring Barnwell County had built a cooperative tobacco warehouse and peanut oil mill to encourage diversification.

In the spring of 1920, the Second Congressional District Banker's Association (encompassing Beaufort, Jasper, Hampton, Barnwell, Colleton, Bamberg, Orangeburg, and Aiken Counties) reported that their entire district was "completely infested with the boll weevil" and asserted, "We do not believe cotton can be grown profitably." They advised their customers to convert to tobacco, sweet potatoes, beans, peanuts, corn, and livestock. They then promulgated a united banking policy: they would no longer lend money to farmers or sharecroppers "where cotton was the only security pledged."[34]

The boll weevil was devastating. By 1918, the second year of the infestation, all of Beaufort County was covered. In 1919 all of Jasper and Hampton

Counties were infested. On Daufuskie Island, where the infestation began, the cotton crop was only 5 percent of what it had been two years earlier. The *Beaufort Gazette* predicted that if the boll weevil continued, "cotton will cease to be a money crop in this county."[35]

From 1918 to 1919, Beaufort County's production plummeted from 4,013 bales to 1,085 bales, a 72.9 percent decline in one year. In 1920, with cotton prices estimated to be forty cents per pound, Beaufort County lost 70 percent of its cotton production, a loss of approximately $420,000 to the local economy. This was an economic disaster for Beaufort County. Some of the county's largest and most established businesses, Waterhouse on Bay Street and McDonald-Wilkins in Frogmore, Dale, and Beaufort, were primarily cotton gins. In fact, George Waterhouse Jr. died of a heart attack on Bay Street in June 1920. He was only forty years old. The strain to his business caused by the cotton collapse likely contributed to his untimely death. The hurricane of 1893 had hastened his father's death, and the boll weevil may have done the same for the son.

Small farmers were struck hardest by the boll weevil. Since Reconstruction, Beaufort County had been a haven for independent, landowning black farmers. Most of them planted cotton. Beaufort County had one of the lowest rates of tenant farmers in South Carolina. Only 29.2 percent of farmers in Beaufort County were tenants in 1920, while the state average was 63 percent. Most of these small farms were twenty acres or less. Nearly half were between three and ten acres. The boll weevil destroyed what meager livelihood they had provided. On St. Helena Island, where the largest concentration of these small cotton farmers resided, production declined by 54 percent between 1920 and 1925.[36] Many of these small farmers followed the path of their parents' generation. When the phosphate industry collapsed in the 1890s and wrecked their sources of cash, they moved away, deepening the economic impact on Beaufort County.

The larger farmers were quick to abandon cotton. At Sheldon, Pat Wall converted his old cotton gin into a tomato paste factory. In 1918 he had harvested 585 bales of cotton, and in 1919 he was down to 120 bales, a 79.4 percent decline. In 1920 he converted his three hundred acres of cotton fields to sweet potatoes and built a potato warehouse on the Charleston and Western Carolina Railroad line. Pat Wall was well known, having worked for many years as a conductor on the C&WC Railroad. In 1924 he succeeded Niels Christensen in the state senate. In 1920 W. P. Hogarth of Burton plowed under his fifty-eight acres of cotton and planted peanuts. His Pear Farm was the only pear orchard in the county. Between the rows of trees, he planted peanuts and lettuce. In April 1920, realizing the shift in agriculture, the Waterhouse Company purchased a peanut oil mill and a Lilliston Peanut Picker that could mechanically dig and pick peanuts.

In December 1920 the *Beaufort Gazette* promoted the new Seacoast Packing Company, a livestock rendering and packing factory under construction on the C&WC line at Hermitage Road. The promoters were Senator Niels Christensen, banker Walter Richardson, and General Manager V. L. Collier. They sought to sell stock in their company and to convince cotton farmers to raise cattle and hogs to provide meat on the hoof for their modern, expensive meat-packing factory. At the end of 1920, they asserted that for Beaufort County "cotton is gone."[37]

In 1922 the *State* newspaper in Columbia published a story on Beaufort County's reluctant agricultural revolution. "Beaufort County no longer fears the boll weevil," it reported. "The pest so completely wiped out the cotton crops the last few years that all the cotton planted this year in the county . . . is not as much as 100 acres."[38] It was the end of a sea island tradition that had begun in 1790.

"BEAUTIFUL BEAUFORT, THE LETTUCE CITY:" HEYDAY OF TRUCK FRAMING, 1908–1928

World War I and the collapse of cotton farming coincided with the heyday of truck farming. In 1908 farmers planted forty-two hundred acres of vegetables in fields mostly along the C&WC line. Proximity to the railroad line was critical to the success of vegetable farming. Truck farming had been expanding into the area of Kean's Neck near the Dale crossroad from 1900 to 1908. In 1908 Seaboard Airline Railroad officials visited Beaufort to examine the route of a short Charleston-to-Savannah line that would tap the area's rich and expanding truck farms. The Seaboard Airline Railroad was completed in 1917.

Truck farming even briefly revived steamboat traffic through the sea islands. In 1911 the Beaufort-Savannah Line added trips for the *Clivedon,* the *Clifton,* and the venerable *Pilot Boy* to "accommodate the potato and cucumber situation" in Beaufort County. They touted their link with the Savannah Ocean Steamship Company, which had four ships leaving each week for New York City and three for Boston. In addition, the Merchant and Miners Transport Company had four steamships leaving Savannah weekly for Baltimore and three for Philadelphia. The companies promised that Beaufort County vegetables could reach New York in sixty-five hours with much cheaper rates than the railroad. Charles Cohen, the company's Beaufort agent, estimated that they would ship fifteen thousand barrels of potatoes to northern markets in 1911.

In 1912 truck farming eclipsed cotton as the county's most valuable agricultural product. Vegetables were valued at more than four hundred thousand dollars, greater than the price of eight thousand bales of cotton and greater than the county's average cotton yield.[39] Small, intensively cultivated fields characterized Beaufort County truck farming in the World War I era. While it was more expensive to plant vegetables than to plant cotton, the yields and profits were far greater when the weather and markets cooperated. The largest vegetable farmer in those years was W. H. McLeod, who had accumulated several thousand acres along the railroad at Seabrook. He had planted truck crops as early as 1884. About 1905 he planted ten acres of experimental lettuce and started an agricultural boom. Ten years later, his son C. E. McLeod was one of the largest landowners and among the wealthiest men in the county.

Two other farms demonstrated the intensive nature of truck farming. Sidney Benton began planting vegetables at Pleasant Farm on the Broad River in the 1880s. By the time of his death in 1908, he had developed one of the state's most productive and profitable farms of any kind. Sidney Benton (1854–1908) was the son of a Union army surgeon who had moved to Beaufort in 1865. In 1884 he married Rosa Ellis of an old South Carolina family. They built a fourteen-room home situated in an oak grove on the shores of the Broad River. Along with W. H. McLeod, Sidney Benton pioneered the lettuce crop for which Beaufort County later became famous. He rarely planted more than one hundred acres. He always considered himself a small farmer. His younger brother, C. U.V. Benton, took over Pleasant Farm at the turn of the century and added the most modern technology to the farm. He was known in Beaufort as "the lettuce king." Benton added a silo, a potato storage shed with climate control, a packing shed on the railroad line, and, most remarkably, an overhead moveable irrigation system for his fields. Two new gasoline engines powered the irrigation system. Benton no longer depended on the weather. In 1913 Benton produced forty thousand dollars' worth of lettuce on twenty-three acres. When the lettuce was harvested, he replanted the ground with cucumbers and made ten thousand dollars more, all in less than five months. Benton's profit on the 1913 crops was from thirty to forty thousand dollars. These were princely sums in 1913. Naturally, many other truck farmers followed his example of progressive, expensive agronomy.

In February 1916 C. U.V. Benton sold Pleasant Farm to his neighbor, W. R. Eve Jr., for nearly sixty thousand dollars. Although it was reportedly "the biggest real estate deal made in this part of the state in sometime," many thought Eve had gotten a bargain. They may have been right. The year 1916 brought some of the highest vegetable prices ever received for Beaufort County produce. Eve made thirty thousand dollars' profit on his 1916 crop of lettuce and celebrated by putting on a barbecue for his two hundred black farm workers. In fact, with his other crops of potatoes, cucumbers, and tomatoes at Pleasant Farm and his adjoining Ocean Bluff plantation, Eve paid for his land purchase in only ninety days.

W. R. Eve Jr. was the son of Dr. W. R. Eve (1852–1915) of Beech Island, South Carolina. Dr. Eve had married Elizabeth Hammond, daughter of the famous James Henry "Cotton Is King" Hammond. Dr. Eve bought Ocean Bluff as a retreat in the 1890s. He traveled often between Ocean Bluff and Beech Island on the old Port Royal and Augusta Railroad. When he gave up the practice of medicine, he retired to Ocean Bluff. His sons, W. R. Eve Jr. and Harford Eve, found the land on Port Royal Island excellent for truck farming. The sons were very successful during World War I. In 1917 the Eves' two truck farms were highlighted as examples of progressive and profitable farming operations at the South Carolina Press Convention. W. R. Eve Jr. became an important figure in Beaufort's economy of the 1920s.[40]

Another example of intensive, profitable truck farming was the operation of Fred and Harry Whipple of Rhode Island. The Whipples came to Beaufort in 1903 to assist the Benton brothers at Pleasant Farm. In 1911 they bought their own small farm near the railroad depot at the end of "North Street extension." The revised 1915 City Charter placed the Whipple brothers' farm within the city limits. In 1911 the Whipples installed an overhead irrigation system. That year they harvested five different crops from a single six-acre field. They grew, in succession, beans, lettuce, peaches, corn, and peas, and earned $4,300 in profit on six acres of ground. In 1912 they harvested vegetables worth an astonishing $32,000 on only eight acres. The Whipple brothers were featured in the U.S. Department of Agriculture's Yearbook for 1912, bringing national attention to Beaufort County's truck-farming business. They continued to set agricultural records. In 1917 they harvested 1,690 barrels of Irish potatoes from a fifteen-acre field and sold them for $10.75 per barrel, earning $18,167.50. In 1922 they sold Whipple Side Farm to the Olivet Brothers Company, produce commission merchants in New York. The local agent for Olivet Brothers was Miles McSweeney, son of a former governor of South Carolina. In eleven years the Whipples made a small fortune truck farming and sold out for a comfortable retirement in Rhode Island. Jack Gray bought Myrtle Bush Farm in Burton in 1911. In 1919, on forty acres, Gray grew lettuce worth $35,000 and Irish potatoes worth $15,500. He harvested nearly one hundred barrels of potatoes per acre in 1919.[41]

The truck-farming boom attracted other enterprising farmers, some of whom remained only for the vegetable bonanza. Others stayed for several generations to make their permanent mark on twentieth-century Beaufort. In 1908 Conrad and Leonard Donner bought Hall's Island between the Broad River and Huspah Creek. There the brothers built a large house and developed a successful asparagus farm. They were successful truck farmers for several years. The Donner brothers were not new to Beaufort. They had emigrated from the Danish city of Altoni in Schleswig-Holstein in 1886 to work in the phosphate industry. When phosphates declined, they took up truck farming. Conrad Donner died in 1916, and his brother sold the farm and moved to Philadelphia. In 1911 James Roe Bellamy bought a small farm near Gray's Hill. His original investment was sixteen hundred dollars. Over the next twelve years, he mastered the truck-farming business and amassed a fortune worth more than a hundred thousand dollars. Bellamy became a leading figure in the commerce and politics of Beaufort County. He served two terms (1919–1920 and 1923–1924) in the South Carolina House of Representatives. One of his investments was a small inn on the corner of Carteret and Boundary Streets in Beaufort, overlooking the Beaufort River. The Bellamy Inn operated until after World War II. Today it houses the chamber of commerce. The location is still known as Bellamy Curve.

In 1908 an enterprising truck farmer from Wilmington, North Carolina, came to Beaufort looking for farmland. By 1912 George W. Trask had purchased Pickpocket Place from E. B. Legare. The farm contained only 125 acres and cost twelve thousand dollars. But it included a large house that G.W. Trask and his family made home. Trask and his wife, Emma, had eleven children. Three of their sons—Neil, the oldest; John, the fourth son; and Harold, the eighth son—remained in Beaufort to add to the family enterprises. Four generations later, the Trask family are still among the largest landowners in Beaufort County.[42]

Some of Beaufort's established commercial families bought and operated vegetable farms just to join the bonanza. Pat Wall developed a truck farm and cannery at Sheldon. H. G. Burckmeyer developed a successful potato and cucumber farm between Beaufort and Port Royal. Meanwhile, Harold Scheper developed an "economically run" truck farm and dairy, Pleasant Point Farm, on the old Cuthbert plantation on Lady's Island.[43]

In 1914 the county truck farmers formed a cooperative called the Beaufort Truck Growers Association. R.A. Long, who, among his many enterprises, owned the ice plant that served farmers along the railroad, was elected president. Hal Pollitzer was secretary. It was expected that the organization would lead to a more stable market and could apply greater leverage for lower freight rates. In 1915 the Beaufort Truck Growers Association sold six hundred shares of stock at five dollars per share. Walter E. Richardson bought two thirds of the stock on behalf of the Beaufort Bank. Richardson was promptly elected cooperative treasurer. R.A. Long remained president and a large part of Beaufort's commercial and agricultural elite were stockholders. The Beaufort Bank loaned funds to the Truck Growers Association to build a packing shed at Burton. In 1919 the Beaufort Truck Growers Association bought the old customs house on Bay Street from the Waterhouse Company for $12,500. The Beaufort Bank also financed that transaction. By 1919 there were five large vegetable-packing sheds along the railroad at Burton, Yemassee, Varnville, Brunson, and Allendale. This was in addition to the private packing sheds on the railroad line owned by the Burkmeyer, Whipple, Eve, McLeod, and Wall farms. The trip down the old C&WC

Railroad from Yemassee to Port Royal was a picture of prosperity, at least for the truck farmers, in 1919.[44]

Although most of the truck farming occurred along the railroad lines, the sea islands were also cultivated for vegetables. In 1912 W. S. Gay and Harry Kessler built a canning factory on Cat Island, opposite Parris Island, and grew large fields of tomatoes and sweet potatoes. In 1912 they produced eleven thousand cases of canned tomatoes on Cat Island. The same year, the Snyder brothers of Bluffton planted twenty acres of tomatoes and okra on Bull Island. They too built a cannery and marketed their product through A. P. Solomon and Company in Savannah. In 1913 they expanded their Bull Island farm to one hundred acres and produced more than one hundred thousand cans of tomatoes and okra.

During the Great War, Charles L. Paul developed a farm on Bermuda Bluff, adjacent to St. Helena Island. In 1920 he planted 160 acres in lettuce, cabbage, potatoes, oats, and peanuts. To get his vegetables to market, Paul employed a thirty-foot, gasoline-powered launch called *Saxon*. In 1918 the Sea Coast Land Company bought eighteen hundred acres of old cotton fields on Daufuskie Island to plant vegetables. This property had once been part of Haig Point and Melrose Plantations. The company expected "to plant extensively" in 1918.

Also during the war, J. W. Bryan developed a large truck farm and vegetable-packing shed on Cane Island. By 1923 Bryan had four hundred acres of fields with two hundred under cultivation each year. He planted spinach, lettuce, potatoes, and tomatoes in the spring, followed by corn and cowpeas. Bryan had two gasoline tractors and two trucks on Cane Island. He also had eight working mules and a herd of twenty cows. He built a packing shed measuring one hundred feet by thirty-six feet and employed twenty-five sea island women for grading and packing his vegetables. This was semiskilled labor for which these women earned a dollar and a half to three dollars per day. Bryan also employed up to sixty-five field hands to pick the vegetables. During the harvest season his payroll was approximately one thousand dollars per week. Like C. L. Paul, Bryan had his own twenty-passenger gasoline launch to ferry workers to Cane Island and haul vegetable crates.[45]

The years during and after World War I were peak years for Beaufort County truck farming. Ironically, those were the same years that the boll weevil was destroying the cotton industry. The principal product in those years was Irish potatoes. In 1917 Beaufort County truck farmers planted approximately twenty-five hundred acres in Irish potatoes. They averaged sixty barrels of potatoes per acre. At $11.50 per barrel, the prevailing price for Irish potatoes on the New York market in 1917, the Beaufort County crop was worth $1,725,000. In 1918 wartime price controls seriously affected the potato market. When federal commissioners tried to fix the price of potatoes at $1.00 per barrel, Beaufort County truck farmers raised a howl. They contacted Congressman Jimmy Byrnes, who arranged a meeting with the food supply commissioner, Herbert Hoover. Pat Wall of Sheldon was sent as a representative of the Trucker's Association. He presented the future president with documentation showing that it cost Beaufort County farmers $149.50 per acre to plant Irish potatoes. At $1.00 per barrel, they would not plant any crops. Hoover relented, but the price was significantly lower in 1918 than in 1917. In 1919 bad weather injured the early Irish potato crop, and the county averaged only thirty barrels per acre.

In 1920, however, with price controls lifted and the weather cooperating, Beaufort County produced the largest Irish potato crop in its history. Truck farmers planted thirty-five hundred acres, averaged sixty barrels per acre, and sold them for $13.50 per barrel. The 1920 crop was worth $2,835,000. In 1921 Beaufort County produced more Irish potatoes than did any other county in the state.[46]

The vegetable bonanza created at least two small industrial operations. The first was R.A. Long's ice manufacturing plant built in 1905 at the Beaufort railroad depot. Long called his business the People's Ice and Fuel Company. Hugh and Pat Wall and W. E. Richardson were investors. By 1911 the truck farmers' demand required him to double the size and capacity of his ice plant from forty-five tons per day to ninety tons per day. Long built a brick cold-storage building that could hold five thousand blocks of ice. As truck farming expanded, a second ice manufacturing company was formed. In 1919 the Burton Ice and Manufacturing Company was formed by William Keyserling, F.W. Scheper, E. L. Allen, and Hal Pollitzer. The Burton plant cost sixty thousand dollars to erect. At the peak of the truck-farming business in 1920, the *Beaufort Gazette* commented, "With the . . . greater demand of the trucking interests, there is no doubt that both the ice factories here will be driven to capacity and more." In 1921 the two companies merged to form the Enterprise Ice and Manufacturing Company with capitalization of two hundred thousand dollars. The Enterprise Ice and Manufacturing Company, with plants in Beaufort, Burton and Allendale, was said to be "probably the largest business corporation founded by local men in the county."[47]

The other local industry that responded to the vegetable boom was the Beaufort Veneer and Package Company, founded in 1909. This company was the creation of Captain Charles Cary Townsend, a native of Canandaigua, New York, who came to Beaufort as a steamboat captain in 1874. He was a longtime warden and mayor of Beaufort. When Captain Townsend died suddenly in 1913, his son Howard Townsend took over the company.

The Townsend veneer plant was a significant local industry. The plant produced barrels and crates mostly for the truck-farming business. The factory was at the Beaufort railroad depot, where it could easily receive shipments of gum and pine lumber from up the railroad line. When it opened in 1909, the plant employed sixty workers for six or seven months per year. All the workers were local African American men. These were good paying jobs. Barrel makers earned $2.00 to $2.50 per day, while crate makers earned $1.00 to $1.75 per day. These were not the wages paid by the phosphate industry in its heyday, but they were significantly more than vegetable pickers earned. In its first year, the Beaufort Veneer and Package Company produced 100,000 barrels for potatoes, 150,000 bushel baskets, 20,000 cantaloupe crates, and 18,000 cabbage crates. Throughout the war years, the veneer plant was a "thriving Beaufort enterprise." When the potato crop reached its pinnacle in 1920, the veneer plant had produced 85,000 barrels by May and was "way behind demand." During the bumper crop of lettuce the following year, the *Beaufort Gazette* noted, "The two ice plants are taxed to their full capacity to supply the demand for icing the cars and the crate factory . . . is scarcely able to meet the demand."[48]

The truck-farming boom encouraged the organization of several agribusiness corporations. In 1917 R. C. Horne of Beaufort and Charlton Ogburn of Savannah formed the Atlantic Agricultural Corporation. The company's initial capitalization was $140,000, and it operated truck farms on the South Carolina and Georgia coast. The corporate offices were in Savannah. During World War I, the Olivet Brothers Company of New York made large investments in Beaufort County. Their South Carolina agent was Miles McSweeney. In 1921 Beaufort realtor H. H. Lake and Sheldon farmer Pat Wall formed the Central Terminal Company to "store, broker, sell and ship farm products from Beaufort County." They planned to "build elevators, wharves, loading docks and warehouses as needed."[49]

At the peak of the boom, farmers began to emulate the antebellum cotton farmers and identify their produce with distinctive names and trademarks emblazoned on their crates and barrels. The Campbell Farm at Sheldon adopted a pyramid and dromedary as their trademark. The E. B. Mitchell Brand of Lobeco was a bell with a cross on it. C. L. Paul on Bermuda Bluff called his produce Rattler Brand and used a coiled snake as a logo. J. L. Butler at Seabrook adopted the trademark Pecan Farm and stamped all his crates and barrels accordingly. J. W. Gray adopted a leafy myrtle bush as his trademark.

Another trademark was the opening magnolia flower of Magnolia Farm. The dairy farm on present-day Ribaut Road was operated after 1904 by F. L. Allison. This dairy on the outskirts of Beaufort had been started shortly after the Civil War by John Conant, a Union army officer who had settled in Beaufort after the occupation. F. L. Allison ran the dairy for John Conant for many years, and after Conant's death, he bought it. Allison was reputedly "the oldest dairyman in the county and the first man in Beaufort to deliver milk in bottles." The Magnolia Farm trademark was thus seen all over

Beaufort every day for a generation. During World War I, Allison made a small fortune himself when he garnered the contract to provide milk, butter, and cheese to the Recruit Depot on Parris Island. In 1926 the city of Beaufort held a contest to adopt a distinctive nickname and logo for the community. The promotional nickname that was adopted was "Beautiful Beaufort, the Lettuce City."[50]

The truck-farming boom had a salutary effect on the Beaufort County economy. It enlarged the deposits of the two local banks, provided thousands of jobs across the county, and encouraged new commercial and industrial enterprises. But it could not fully cushion the shock caused by the decline and fall of the cotton business. Truck farming was, by and large, a rich man's game. To succeed with vegetable planting, a farmer had to have money in the bank or access to capital for the large up-front costs in fertilizer and equipment. Cotton, on the other hand, required only a mule, a plow, and a patch of ground. Truck farming, therefore, was only suitable for a few white farmers. Cotton farming was the domain of small-scale, independent black farmers, and it sank out of sight.

When cotton was destroyed by the boll weevil, the county agricultural agents and the Penn School farm encouraged black farmers to grow vegetables. Benjamin Barnwell, agricultural agent on St. Helena Island in 1922, related the difficulties in transitioning from small cotton farms to small vegetable farms on St. Helena Island. Barnwell called a meeting of eight of the most experienced black farmers on St. Helena Island. Six agreed to try small plots of vegetables, buying seed from Kinghorn Brothers in Beaufort. They immediately encountered problems with free-ranging livestock and soil exhausted by years of cotton growing. Only one farmer, Barry Wroten, continued the experiment. When he asked his neighbors to control their livestock and keep them out of his vegetable field, the neighbors resented his interference with traditional ways. One neighbor pulled up all of Wroten's turnip plants. Another turned out his hogs into his lettuce patch. Despite these obstacles, Wroten persisted and marketed eighty-six baskets of fine lettuce in New York. His up-front costs were $37.75 for seed, fertilizer, and baskets. His transportation and commission charges were $110.63. Wroten was paid an average of $2.31 per basket and retained a profit of approximately $50.00. His largest expense was the $71.38 that the railroad charged for shipment to New York. This type of vegetable farming was too costly and too difficult for most small sea island farmers. However, many converted their cotton fields to Irish potatoes in the early 1920s. The black farmers of St. Helena Island had generations of experience growing sweet potatoes, so putting more land into Irish potatoes was not too difficult. Between 1919 and 1924, the production of Irish potatoes doubled on St. Helena Island. However, just as it looked as though the small farmers were successfully transitioning to a new cash crop, the bottom dropped out of the Irish potato market. In 1925 and again in 1928, overproduction on the East Coast caused prices to crash, wrecking truck farming on St. Helena Island. In 1928 the McDonald-Wilkins Company, the largest planters on St. Helena Island, converted much of their potato acreage to tobacco.[51] It was too much for the small island farmer. The collapse of the potato market in 1925 and 1928 and the Great Depression, which soon followed, forced even more small farmers off the land.

Between 1920 and 1925, South Carolina agriculture was in "rapid decline," according to U.S. Commerce Department statistics. This was mostly because of the collapse of cotton. In those years the average value of an acre of farmland dropped 34 percent, and the total value of all farms in South Carolina dropped 44 percent. While the number of white farmers in the state declined slightly, the number of black farmers declined by 17 percent. In Beaufort County the number of black farmers declined from 2,914 in 1920 to 2,355 in 1925, a drop of 19 percent. At the same time the total value of farms in Beaufort County declined from $6,956,947 in 1920 to $6,009,625 in 1925, a drop of 14 percent. Most of this decline was the work of the boll weevil. Cotton production declined 72 percent between 1920 and 1925. On St. Helena Island, total farmland declined 14 percent, and crop land harvested declined by 63 percent between 1920 and 1925.[52] The boom in truck farming did not compensate for the bust in cotton.

The World War I era saw other agricultural milestones race past. The first was the end of the timber industry in northern Beaufort County. For forty years after the completion of the railroad in 1873, the lumber business in the southeast corner of South Carolina had been a mainstay of the local economy. The business was badly hurt by the depression of 1893–96 that forced many of the smaller, independent sawmills to shut down. In the first decade of the twentieth century, the lumber business began to recover as timber companies consolidated. In 1909 and 1910, Westmoreland Lumber Company absorbed the Combahee Lumber Company, the Charleston Lumber Company, the Hawtree Lumber Company, and the old Atlantic Lumber Company on Spanish Point. The Westmoreland Company built a "magnificent sawmill plant " at Chehaw, Colleton County. The plant had eight steam boilers fueled by the scraps of lumber, large drying kilns, and a wharf capable of loading three schooners at one time. A railroad spur to the Atlantic Coast Line railroad at Green Pond was built. The mill produced 125,000 board feet of lumber per day. The Westmoreland Company controlled tens of thousands of acres in Beaufort, Hampton, and Colleton Counties.

By 1912 most of the assets of the Westmoreland Lumber Company had been acquired by the Hilton-Dodge Lumber Company of Savannah, which controlled vast acres on the South Carolina and Georgia coasts. Hilton-Dodge had ambitious plans to rebuild and expand the old Atlantic sawmill at Sea Island Chemical Company site on Spanish Point. The new mill was to produce 150,000 board feet per day. The Beaufort community had high hopes for a revival of the maritime business at the Port of Beaufort and the addition of new employment. It was reported that "several score of unskilled labor and high priced skilled men will receive employment." In 1913 C. I. Cummings's lumber mill on Pidgeon Point burned to the ground with the loss of six thousand dollars' worth of property and a dozen local jobs. Cummings Mill was the last vestige of D. C. Wilson's old Port Royal Sawmill, begun in 1867 and the origin of Beaufort County's postbellum lumber industry. The mill was never rebuilt.

In 1915 the disruption of World War I pushed the lumber business into sharp decline. Before the Cummings mill or the old Atlantic sawmill could be rebuilt, the Hilton-Dodge Lumber Company went bankrupt. In 1916 the U.S. District Court forced the company to sell off huge tracts of timberland in Beaufort, Jasper, Hampton, and Colleton counties. That was effectively the end of the large-scale lumber industry in northern Beaufort County.[53]

Another milestone was reached in 1920, the end of "free range" for livestock in Beaufort County. The free-range issue, or the "stock law" controversy, had roiled communities across the South for fifty years. In 1902 Hampton County exempted itself from the state stock law, which required each farmer to fence in his livestock on his own property. That part of Beaufort County between the Okatee River and the Broad River remained an open range until 1920, as did a large tract along the Savannah River that is now part of Jasper County. When the General Assembly had enacted a new, tougher stock law in 1908, it exempted that part of Beaufort County bounded by the Okatee, Broad, and May Rivers and the Atlantic Coast Line Railroad track. In 1909 the county built the "Okatee Stock-Fence" of twenty-six-inch hog wire and three strands of barbed wire all the way from T. G. Cooler's land at the Okatee River to the Atlantic Coast Line track at Big Switch, near Switzerland. The county then levied a two-mill tax on all horses, mules, asses, sheep, hogs, goats, and cattle in that part of Bluffton Township to defray the cost of the fence. Small farmers complained about no more "free grass"; truck farmers complained of slack enforcement outside the fence; and everyone complained about the livestock tax. In reality, no one paid attention to the stock law. There were so many disputes and so much acrimony over the issue that in 1919 Senator Niels Christensen called for a stock law referendum in Bluffton Township. It failed by two votes. When the General Assembly passed a new stock law to cover the whole state in 1920, Representative J. C. Bailey of Bluffton led the fight to exempt his township from the stock law while Senator Niels Christensen pressed the fight in the South Carolina Senate to pass the stock law. After it passed, no one in Bluffton obeyed it, and no one in Beaufort County enforced it. Some landowners shot the free-ranging livestock and some cattlemen retaliated with "crop slashing." For promoting the law, W. J. Verdier and his brother were threatened with bodily harm by an anonymous group in Bluffton called the "Free Grass Club." The county sheriff understated the case when he observed that "there is always some difficulty in changing from free range to stock law."[54]

"A VERY UNUSUAL THING HAPPENED:" WOMEN'S SUFFRAGE, 1891–1921

The Great War era witnessed a political milestone for Beaufort County. As Jim Crow and the iron grip of the white Democratic Party excluded African Americans from political participation, another group of citizens entered the political life of the county. Neither Beaufort County nor South Carolina was a leader in the national movement for women's suffrage, but Beaufort County produced some of the state's most progressive women's rights advocates.

Many Beaufort suffragettes were old Gideonites or their descendants. Mrs. W. R. Bristol, Winnie Christensen, Alice Ricker, and Mary Waterhouse were all northern born or descendants of Civil War missionaries. At the center of this group was Abbie Holmes Christensen (1852–1938), whose attachment to progressive causes was a lifelong commitment.

Abbie Holmes Christensen's contacts with Lucy Stone, a suffrage pioneer in Massachusetts, led her to join the National American Women's Suffrage Movement. In 1891 Christensen invited the state's leading suffragist, Virginia Durant Young of Fairfax, to address a group of Beaufort women. From this group Beaufort's equal-suffrage movement grew. It was obviously helpful that Abbie Holmes Christensen's sons, Niels and Frederick, owned the *Beaufort Gazette* from 1903 to 1924, so that national and state news of the equal-suffrage movement was regularly disseminated in Beaufort County. It was also helpful that Abbie's son, Niels Christensen Jr., was a state senator for twenty years.[55]

In 1912, when Kansas, Arizona, Michigan, and Oregon passed constitutional amendments supporting women's suffrage, the events were favorably covered in Beaufort County. In 1913 leading women's civic clubs sent representatives to the fifteenth annual convention of the South Carolina Federation of Women's Clubs. Mrs. W. R. Bristol and Alice Ricker represented the Clover Club. The Civic Club was represented by Mary Waterhouse and Winnie Christensen, and Abbie Holmes Christensen represented the Benevolent Society. Many suffragists pushed their cause at these conventions. The major political issue for South Carolina women in the years before World War I was Prohibition, and much of the organizing force for equal suffrage derived from the nationally powerful Women's Christian Temperance Union. In 1914 the *Spartanburg Herald* noted the progress of women's suffrage in the previous year: "Women in South Carolina have been set to thinking and they are giving serious thought to the question."[56]

In April 1914 Abbie Holmes Christensen held a lawn party at her home on New Street to introduce one of Charleston's leading, progressive suffragettes, Laura Bragg, to Beaufort's club women. After the 1914 South Carolina Federation of Women's Clubs convention, a group of South Carolina club women formed the South Carolina Equal Suffrage Association. Abbie Holmes Christensen and her daughter Andrea were charter members. Two leading progressive women of Charleston were descendants of a prominent Beaufort family. Anita and Mabel Pollitzer were granddaughters of Moritz Pollitzer of Beaufort. In addition, Sarah Barnwell Elliott, a child of antebellum Beaufort and noted novelist, led the suffrage movement in Tennessee and was a national promoter of the Nineteenth Amendment.[57]

In the summer of 1915, an unsigned letter to the *Beaufort Gazette* explained, "Why We Are Suffragettes." The author pointed out the quiet, good works of Beaufort's women's clubs. The Clover Club started the town's first circulating library. The Benevolent Society gave space in their Scott Street building for the books, and the Civic Club was busy planting, landscaping and beautifying every public space in town. The writer thought that "Beaufort owes a large debt of gratitude to the ladies." By their good works, the women of Beaufort had earned the right to participate in politics.

On November 19, 1915, Beaufort women had their first "equal suffrage meeting" at the home of Mrs. J. S. Foster at 509 North Street. A committee of three was appointed, and the "formation of a league was talked about with enthusiasm." This was the beginning of Beaufort County's League of Women Voters. In 1916 the state house of representatives delivered a near majority of fifty-one votes in favor of women's suffrage, and Beaufort women were excited about the larger-than-expected vote. "Next year a majority!" became the activists' rallying cry. In 1917 both North Carolina and South Carolina put equal suffrage amendments on their ballots, and women in both Carolinas vied to see which state would be the first to ratify.[58]

During 1917 and 1918, support for the Nineteenth Amendment to the Constitution was a hotly debated issue, even in conservative South Carolina. In August 1919 Mabel Pollitzer wrote an open letter to South Carolina newspapers explaining the inevitable ratification of the Nineteenth Amendment among two thirds of the state's legislatures and urging the General Assembly to join the majority. The letter was printed on the front page of the *Beaufort Gazette.* "When South Carolina's legislature meets next January" she wrote, "state pride and common justice will dictate prompt action in this forward step toward complete democracy."

Two months later, Senator Niels Christensen, chief of the Democrats' progressive wing, urged the party to drop its opposition to women's suffrage.

Christensen believed that ratification of the Nineteenth Amendment was a forgone conclusion. It was, therefore, "inexpedient for South Carolina Democrats to lose support of women voters by setting themselves against this progressive measure which is inevitable. . . . the Democratic Party is making a serious mistake by holding out against women's suffrage. . . . we are losing the support of women."[59]

Despite Beaufort's best efforts, the General Assembly refused to ratify the Nineteenth Amendment in January 1920. The state house of representatives rejected ratification 93–21, and the state senate declined by a vote of 32–3. Casting one of those three senate votes was the eldest son of Abbie Holmes Christensen. In the end, however, Christensen was correct. The Nineteenth Amendment was ratified by the Tennessee legislature in August 1920, and became the law of the United States.[60] No doubt the loudest Tennessee cheer came from Sarah Barnwell Elliott of Beaufort and Sewanee, Tennessee.

With the ratification of the Nineteenth Amendment, Beaufort's League of Women Voters became active in the county. In 1921 they sponsored a citizenship class at the Community Club. The chairman of the league in 1921 was Mrs. T. L. Kinney; the vice chairman was Mrs. Gilder Horne; the corresponding secretary was Miss Rose Whipple; the treasurer was Mrs. J. Weinberg; and the parliamentarian was Mabel Runnette. Nancy Stratton Christensen was the publicity chairman. Naturally, all league notices were featured prominently in her husband's newspaper. In June 1921 Frederick Christensen noted the first participation of Beaufort's women in local politics: "A very unusual thing happened during the evening." Twenty-five women invaded the meeting of the county commissioners. They announced that they wished to know more about roads and bridges. "The men were somewhat taken aback but welcomed the newcomers." In September 1921 the league entertained County Supervisor W. F. Sanders and Commissioner F. W. Scheper Jr., who explained the "good roads" issue to the women voters. In November 1921 a self-identified "woman voter" offered this assessment of Beaufort's newest political organizers to the *Beaufort Gazette*: "The League of Women Voters is a success so far. Such cooperation, such energy must never fail to bring wonderful results, so women leave the pots and kettles once a week, come join the league and register when the books are open next time."[61]

The work of the League of Women Voters paid off. By January 1922, an election year, the league had fifty-one members, including all the original suffragists and the wives of most of Beaufort's leading businessmen. In 1922 the league declared on the front page of the *Beaufort Gazette* "their intention of using their influence and their votes . . . especially on moral questions like . . . prohibition, carrying concealed weapons and tax reform." During the 1922 Democratic primary, women enrolled for the first time. Of the 1,056 voters enrolled in Democratic clubs in Beaufort County in 1922, 276 were women, or 26 percent of the registered Democrats in the county. Between 1920 and 1922, Beaufort County's voter registration rolls increased by 34 percent, almost all of them new women voters. The number of voters registered in Beaufort County in 1922 broken by precinct down as follows:

Precinct	*No. of Women*	*No. of Men*	*Total*	*% Women*
Beaufort	144	274	418	34%
Port Royal	28	64	92	30%
Burton	37	80	117	31%
Sheldon	21	59	80	26%
St. Helena	7	25	32	22%
Dale	14	31	45	31%
Bluffton	41	124	165	24%
Hardeeville	31	96	127	24%
Barrel Landing	9	51	60	15%
Hilton Head	13	22	35	37%
Total	345	826	1171	29.5%[62]

The influence of the county's new women voters expanded in 1924 when Mrs. Sarah Wall, league president and wife of the new state senator, Patrick Wall, was elected a delegate to the state Democratic Party Convention. In 1929 the lowcountry achieved another milestone in women's political rights when Mary Gordon Ellis of Jasper County became the first woman ever elected to the South Carolina Senate.[63]

While most politically active lowcountry women joined the mainstream Democratic Party, Abbie Holmes Christensen, a life-long progressive, pursued a radically different course. Remaining steadfastly independent, Abbie Holmes Christensen never registered on the Beaufort County Democratic Club rolls. She voted for Republican Calvin Coolidge in 1924 because he was from Massachusetts and Republican Herbert Hoover in 1928 because he favored Prohibition. The old teetotal, abolitionist missionary never reconciled with the Democratic Party even though her son was its local boss for twenty-five years.

Disappointed with the moral direction of both major political parties, in 1932 Abbie Holmes Christensen joined the American Socialist Party. Not only that, but she was also a 1932 South Carolina presidential elector for Socialist candidate Norman Thomas. Abbie Holmes Christensen likely took pride that in 1932 Beaufort County recorded seven votes for Norman Thomas, about the same number of suffragettes in Beaufort County forty years before.[64]

First Beaufort High School at Old Beaufort College campus, 1909–1925. (Courtesy of Parris Island Museum.)

Fort Fremont compound, circa 1910, with fire-control tower on right. (Courtesy of Parris Island Museum.)

View of Bay Street with Anchorage and Elliott Carriage House in background. (Courtesy of Parris Island Museum.)

Walter Richardson's new house on Boundary Street, circa 1910. (Courtesy of South Carolina Historical Society.)

Beaufort Veneer and Package Company at the Beaufort railroad depot, mainstay of the truck-farming industry, circa 1920. (Courtesy of Parris Island Museum.)

Segregated Beaufort railroad depot, circa 1915. (Courtesy of Parris Island Museum.)

Beaufort baseball team, circa 1910. (Courtesy of Parris Island Museum.)

Bay Street looking west, circa 1920. (Courtesy of South Carolina Historical Society.)

Bay Street in the auto age, circa 1920. (Courtesy of Parris Island Museum.)

Rosa Cooley and Grace House at Penn School, circa 1920. (Lawrence S. Rowland Collection.)

Beaufort arsenal, 1910. (Courtesy of Parris Island Museum.)

Robert Smalls High School opened in 1919. This building was constructed in 1925 and burned down in 1931. (Courtesy of Parris Island Museum.)

Beaufort waterfront, 1910. (Courtesy of Parris Island Museum.)

Bay Street, circa 1920. (Courtesy of Parris Island Museum.)

The Community Club on Carteret Street was built in 1919 with War Camp Community money. (Courtesy of South Carolina Historical Society.)

The new Charleston and Western Carolina Railroad depot, built in 1921. (Courtesy of Parris Island Museum.)

Memorial Day, May 31, 1921, in Beaufort. Left to right: Reverend W. M. Seay (Beaufort Baptist Church), unknown, Reverend Maynard Marshall (St. Helena Church), Secretary of the Navy Edwin Denby, Reverend Wells, Mayor R.V. Bray, and unknown naval officer. (Lawrence S. Rowland Collection.)

Beaufort County courthouse, 1930s, with municipal water tower in back. (Courtesy of Parris Island Museum.)

Golden Eagle Tavern with Castle Tower, circa 1930. (Courtesy of Parris Island Museum.)

Edison Marshall and his books at the Golden Eagle Tavern, circa 1933. (Lawrence S. Rowland Collection.)

Beaufort waterfront gasoline launches at the Scheper Dock, circa 1920. (Courtesy of Parris Island Museum.)

Opening of the Lady's Island Bridge, 1927. (Lawrence S. Rowland Collection.)

Savannah steamboat at the Gulf dock at the foot of Scott's Street, 1927. (Courtesy of Parris Island Museum.)

John Mark Verdier House with art studio and fish company, circa 1938. (Lawrence S. Rowland Collection.)

Chapter 10

Economy of the 1920s and the End of the Progressive Era

BRIDGES AND HIGHWAYS

The era of World War I saw another revolution in Beaufort County. In 1903 automobiles first made their appearance on the sea islands, and thereafter the county and the state came under pressure to provide better and more expensive roads for them. In Beaufort County that meant, primarily, building bridges.

The bridges and highways built between 1908 and 1929 determined the patterns of transportation, settlement, and commerce in the county for the next half century. The key figure in this historic development was Beaufort County's longtime state senator, Niels Christensen Jr. Christensen served in the South Carolina Senate from 1905 to 1925. For seventeen years, from 1905 to 1922, Christensen sat on the Senate Finance Committee. For eight of those years (1914–22), he was chairman, the second most powerful position in state government. Each year's annual state budget had to pass through the Senate Finance Committee before being signed by the governor. Thus, in the critical early years of highway building, Christensen was in a key position to help Beaufort County. He was also a progressive, willing to increase the state budget and indebtedness to promote economic development. However, not everyone shared his optimism or his vision of the future. In 1907 the principal mode of personal transportation in Beaufort County was horse and buggy. Few could imagine the future of automobile travel. Niels Christensen could. In a 1907 editorial promoting a paved road from Beaufort to Savannah, he wrote that "the great highway once traveled by stagecoach . . . will once again throb with life as the use of the automobile becomes more general."[1]

The first great project in the county's road-building era was the bridge across the Whale Branch River at the site of the ferry that had been established in 1733. This permanent crossing had been a dream of Beaufortonions since 1794, when William Elliott II obtained a franchise and formed the Port Royal Bridge Company, which built causeways to the edge of the marsh but never spanned the river. For the next 115 years, travel on and off Port Royal

Island was by flatboats connecting the two causeways. The idea of a bridge over the Whale Branch River was revived in the 1850s but interrupted by the Civil War. Not until 1873 and construction of the Port Royal Railroad trestle a mile west of the old ferry was the island permanently connected to the mainland. Automobile transportation revived the hope of a bridge connecting the sea islands to the mainland. In an August 1908 campaign speech in Bluffton, Senator Christensen referred to this history in defending his expensive plan: "One hundred years ago the people of Beaufort wanted a bridge where the Port Royal ferry is. For all these years they have had to use a flatboat. . . . There is more need for a bridge now than ever. Complaints of the ferry are constant. People are inconvenienced waiting for the boats."[2]

In January 1908 Representative Joseph C. Bailey of Bluffton and Senator Christensen introduced bills in the house and senate to authorize a loan to Beaufort County of twenty-four thousand dollars from the state sinking fund to construct a bridge at the Port Royal ferry and to build a road from Bluffton to Pritchardville and Hardeeville to connect with the old Savannah Road. County commissioners were authorized to impose a one-mill property tax to pay off the loan.

Christensen and Bailey had no trouble getting this bill through the General Assembly, and in March 1908 plans for the Whale Branch Bridge were well underway. The bridge was designed by W. F. Brown and Company, engineers of Savannah. The bridge had a 450-foot bed on palmetto pilings with a steel-truss swing bridge of 106 feet on a cylindrical, concrete-center pier encased in steel. The swing bridge spanned a navigable channel that was 15 feet deep. When closed, the span had a vertical clearance of 12.5 feet above high tide. The "double truss, center bearing, swing bridge" was 12 feet wide, sufficient "for two teams to pass."

The contract for the "steel bridge" was awarded to Austin Brothers of Atlanta, Georgia. Their low bid was $24,900. The cost increased, however, when it was decided to replace the wooden approaches with reinforced concrete. Construction continued throughout 1908, and optimism ran high in Beaufort's commercial community that the new bridge "will do much toward developing the town of Beaufort." Merchants, in fact, contributed $35 per month to maintain the ferry operation while construction continued. On February 4, 1909, the Port Royal Ferry Bridge opened for traffic. On April 15, 1909, Beaufort County commissioners formally accepted the bridge. After testing its drawbridge in several weather conditions, the commissioners determined that the "whole structure seemed entirely satisfactory."[3]

The Whale Branch Bridge was a single lane road. This remained the case until the original bridge was finally replaced with a two-lane span in 1930. The 1908 bridge was formally referred to as the Port Royal Ferry Bridge because it crossed where the ferry had crossed for 175 years. Two generations of Beaufortonians, however, called the 1908 edifice "the steel bridge" because it was the first one so constructed in Beaufort County.

The Whale Branch Bridge stimulated business and commerce in northern Beaufort County. Many of the old sea island cart paths were graded and "shelled" with oyster shells, providing a relatively smooth, hard surface. The road from Benton's plantation to the new bridge was graded and shelled, and the road from the Port Royal Ferry Bridge to Pocotaligo was resurfaced with shell. In southern Beaufort County, the road from Bluffton to Pritchardville was also graded and shelled. All this roadwork was the responsibility of the county government. Since colonial times local public roadwork had been performed by requiring several days of labor per year from each farmer and planter in the neighborhood. In antebellum times the planters simply loaned out gangs of slaves. As automobile travel increased, the old system of road maintenance could never keep up. In 1908 the General Assembly passed a new law that permitted local governments to collect a "commutation tax" in lieu of labor from "all able bodied men who were eligible for road duty." The Beaufort County "commutation tax" was $1.50 per man each year. A few years later, in 1913, the General Assembly passed an automobile "license tax" on all vehicle owners. In 1913 the license tax was $5.00 per year. This new revenue source allowed the county commissioners to buy a "traction engine" to replace the three-mule team for road grading. County Supervisor W. F. Sanders claimed the new machine would "do the work of six mules." All this roadwork provided cash wages for local workers.[4]

The arrival of the automobile generated new businesses to provide fuel, repairs, sales, and service for the new machines. R. A. Long opened the first automobile dealership in Beaufort on Bay Street in 1908. He sold the twenty-five-horsepower Northern, known as "the family car." The five-passenger auto came "fully equipped with five lamps, horn and tools." The Northern was advertised as the "quietest operating, smoothest running car in the world." It had "full elliptical springs and three-point motor support to make it wonderfully easy on tires." The only problem with the Northern was that it cost sixteen hundred dollars, more than most Beaufortonians earned in a year. Only the wealthiest Beaufortonians could afford automobiles at that rate. In 1911 Long also started Beaufort's first garage on the southeast corner of Bay and Scott Streets, where the old state Dispensary Building had been. In 1911 R. A. Long and F. W. Scheper ordered for themselves five-passenger Stevens-Duryea automobiles costing four thousand dollars apiece.

W. R. Bristol, the Bay Street jeweler and longtime mayor, became the county's first Ford dealer. The 1911 Ford Model T cost $680, and the Ford touring car cost $780. Eventually, Bristol sold the dealership to R. A. Long, who moved to his garage across the street. Later owned by Hugh Wall and Johnny Horne, the Ford dealership stood on Bay Street for fifty years. In 1913

N. Christensen and Sons became the exclusive dealer for the Buick Motor Company. A few years later, the Christensens also sold Overland automobiles. All this competition drove car prices down to the range where ordinary Beaufortonians could afford them. The first African American automobile owner in Beaufort County was Kit Singleton, proprietor of the livery and hack business on West Street. Singleton purchased a Rambler automobile to augment his business. He advertised the auto as "smooth running and luxurious." Kit Singleton thus became Beaufort's first taxi driver.[5]

The next great bridge project spanned the Savannah River from lower Beaufort County (now Jasper County) to the city of Savannah. Since 1762 the principal crossing from lower Beaufort County to Savannah had been the causeway and ferry from Delta Plantation on the Carolina shore to Walnut Hill Plantation on the Georgia side. From 1762 to 1790, the site was called Rochester Ferry. During the antebellum era, the ferry franchise was owned by Dr. James Proctor Screven, onetime mayor of Savannah, and was known as Screven's Ferry. The long causeway across the rice fields on the Carolina shore was the Union Causeway. This route had served for 152 years but was unsuitable for auto traffic. The causeway was too long and narrow and the ferry was too irregular. In 1907 plans were made to move the road north, build a causeway and bridge from the Carolina shore across Back River to Hutchinson Island opposite Savannah, and operate a modern, motorized ferry directly to downtown Savannah. Senator Christensen promoted this improvement vigorously, believing it would stimulate the commerce of both Beaufort County and Savannah. Any crossing of the Savannah River, however, required the cooperation of both state governments and the expenditure of funds from both Beaufort County and Chatham County, Georgia. In addition, a public road across Hutchinson Island required an easement from the Seaboard Airline Railroad, which owned the property.

All these financial, legal, and political obstacles were overcome, and the new Savannah River Bridge opened on September 5, 1914. The causeway crossed old rice fields to the Back River. A two-lane concrete bridge spanned Back River to Hutchinson Island, Georgia. Then, a 150-ton, double-ended car ferry, with modern terminals on both sides of the Savannah River, crossed the river to downtown Savannah. The ferry across the main channel did not obstruct maritime traffic to the Port of Savannah.

Savannah River rice planter T. S. Heyward, who had lobbied many years for a new crossing, wrote in the *Savannah Morning News* that the bridge and ferry answered "the dream of people on both sides of the river for many years. There is no other good crossing except at Augusta." The motorized ferry took only five minutes to cross the river. "Wagons, buggies, carts, automobiles and passengers can come and go with ease and safety on good schedules at low charges." Heyward observed that the old ferry vessel, the *Lila,* had began operating at Screven's Ferry in 1839.

This was not the end of Savannah River ambitions. People on both sides of the river wanted a bridge across the channel. In 1917 Governor Hugh M. Dorsey of Georgia appointed a five-man commission to confer with Senator Christensen and a delegation representing Beaufort, Jasper, Hampton, and Colleton Counties. By 1919 officials of the new Georgia and South Carolina Highway Departments had chosen the site of Baeck's Ferry at Port Wentworth, well upriver from the Port of Savannah. Senator Christensen and several Beaufort County landowners raised objections, and one Georgia company proposed to build a tunnel from Hutchinson Island to Savannah. But the highway engineers' recommendation was a practical one. Both states, three counties, and the federal government contributed to the cost. Construction of a three-mile causeway over rice fields and across Argyle Island took three years, from 1922 to 1925. The Savannah River was spanned by a two-lane, double-truss swing bridge that allowed riverboat traffic to pass upstream to Augusta. On July 16, 1925, the Port Wentworth Bridge was first opened for traffic, and on October 7, 1925, the bridge was formally dedicated. The new bridge was a milestone for South Carolina and Georgia in 1925. It was the first bridge across the Savannah River south of Augusta.[6]

In the early days of "automobiling," long trips through rural wagon paths were pioneering expeditions. Sometimes official "scout cars" were sent along country roads to ascertain the suitability of those roads for travel. After the Whale Branch Bridge opened, it was possible to drive an automobile from Beaufort to Savannah if one had all day to do so. C. E. McLeod of Seabrook made the first through trip from Beaufort to Savannah by automobile on March 20, 1909. McLeod put his family aboard his brand-new Northern and set out from Seabrook at 9:00 A.M. By 1:00 P.M. he was at Bellinger Hill in Jasper County. It took him one hour to traverse the three-mile causeway to old Screven's Ferry and another three and a half hours to cross the river on the *Lila.* After eight and a half hours, it was almost dark when the McLeods reached Savannah. The next day he put his car on the steamboat and shipped it back to Beaufort.

Three months later, on June 25 and 26, 1909, Will Elliott made the first round-trip from Columbia to Beaufort and back. Elliott's car was a two-cylinder Reo carrying five men, including the Elliotts' butler, James Henry Robinson. On the trip south they were delayed climbing over a "sand mountain" in Lexington County and by a lynch mob in Springfield, South Carolina, that was searching for a murderer. While traversing Hampton County, they had to stop frequently to open gates in private fences that crossed the road. It took two days to drive down from Columbia to Beaufort. The return trip was much swifter, consuming nine hours of running time and averaging seventeen miles per hour. The only delays on the return trip were caused by a punctured tire and by "pulling the machine out of a stream that had submerged the road."[7]

In August 1909 an official Georgia "scout car" drove from Brunswick and Darien to Savannah in ten hours, trying to blaze a coastal auto trail to Florida. The same car drove from Savannah to Columbia in nine and a half hours. Sixteen years later, when the Port Wentworth Bridge opened, a motorcade of sixty cars from the Savannah Automobile Club set out across the new bridge for Columbia. At Ridgeland, the convoy split, with half the cars traveling to Beaufort, then on to Columbia via Walterboro, and the other thirty cars going to Columbia through Barnwell, Aiken, and Edgefield Counties.[8] The first Beaufortonian to motor from New York to Beaufort was Arthur O. Christensen in the summer of 1920. His expedition took six days, and he published a running commentary on the roads along the way.

Many of these early expeditions, "scout cars," and automobile clubs were promoting the "good roads" movement. "Good roads" became a mantra of local politicians and commercial interests throughout the South in the early twentieth century. As John Hammond Moore observed in his history of the South Carolina Highway Department, good roads became part of the "trinity of southern progress—industry, education and good roads." Local politicians eventually made their cases in the halls of the national government. For Beaufort County, the most important advocate was Congressman Jimmy Byrnes. While Senator Niels Christensen promoted good roads in Columbia, Jimmy Byrnes was touting them in Washington. When the progressive Richard I. Manning became governor in 1915, the good roads movement was a South Carolina institution.[9]

A prescient 1911 editorial in the *Beaufort Gazette,* probably written by Niels Christensen Jr., stated, "There are now 34 automobiles in Beaufort. . . . The development of the automobile in the United States makes 'good roads' a necessity. Beaufort County is no exception. . . . we now have only a few superior roads that are adapted to automobiling. . . . the roads will eventually have to be improved. . . . Northern tourists will come in large numbers . . . and will bring their automobiles." The accuracy of Niels Christensen's vision of the future qualified him to rank with Robert W. Barnwell (1801–1882), the antebellum "oracle of Beaufort," as the soothsayer of twentieth-century Beaufort.

In 1913 Jimmy Byrnes tried to secure a twenty-million-dollar federal appropriation for "good roads" across the nation. He failed in 1913 but succeeded in 1916. In 1915 Senator Christensen attached a twenty-thousand-dollar loan to the annual supply bill. The funds were used to repair the "steel bridge" across Whale Branch, replace the Chowan Creek bridge that connected

Lady's and St. Helena island with a reinforced concrete span, and initiate "permanent road building" on Port Royal Island. In 1916 the wooden Chowan Creek span was replaced by a concrete one designed by Shand Engineering of Columbia. However, the upcountry engineers were unfamiliar with lowcountry "pluff mud." The day the new Red Bridge was to open, it settled nine feet into the mud of Chowan Creek. Beaufort County withheld all payment until the bridge was repaired. In justifying the expense of repaying this loan to the county taxpayers, Niels Christensen wrote, "Beaufort needs to wake up to the opportunities that good highways leading to her sister counties would offer. . . . with well developed highway, they would be here by the score, especially in the summertime."[10]

In 1917 the county commission estimated that it would cost $263,000 to create a "comprehensive plan of thoroughfares stretching across the county . . . joining up with links to neighboring counties." At the same time, the state superintendent of road construction stated that no suitable road-building material existed in Beaufort County. "Good roads" would require shipping in "Augusta gravel," a large additional expense. This was the beginning of hard-surface or "macadam" roads in Beaufort County. The ubiquitous oyster shell roads that had characterized the sea islands for nearly two centuries began to disappear, and by the end of the twentieth century, the only shell roads were ornamental private driveways. Sixty-eight miles of roads were planned for permanent hard surfacing in 1917. They were the Beaufort-Yemassee road via Pocotaligo, the road from Garden's Corner to the Combahee Ferry, and the road from Bluffton to Hardeeville. Improvements to the Savannah River causeway and the road from Beaufort to the Port Royal Ferry Bridge added to the cost.

In March 1917 the General Assembly authorized Beaufort County to hold a "good roads" bond referendum on or before November 1, 1917. The county commission opted to hold a referendum for only $150,000 of the required $263,000 on May 15, 1917. At the same time, the members appointed themselves the new highway commissioners of Beaufort County to oversee road-construction expenditures. On May 15, 1917, the county's first highway bond referendum failed miserably. Nearly 90 percent (89.7 percent) of voters opposed the good roads initiative. Only three "yes" votes were recorded from Lady's, St. Helena, Hilton Head, and Daufuskie Islands. Not a single "yes" vote was recorded from Hardeeville, Barrell Landing, or Tomotley. Taxpaying voters obviously saw no need for the so-called good roads that the progressives promoted.[11]

Despite this overwhelming rejection by local voters, Senator Christensen was persistent. In the 1919 state supply bill, he included another good roads bond bill. He also increased the commutation road tax from one day's labor or $1.50 per man per year to six days or $6.00 a year. The 1919 bond bill also included money to fund a separate library building on Carteret Street to meet "the earnest request of our colored citizens for a library facility," and $6,000 to $12,000 to improve Beaufort High School. With help from the federal and state governments, Beaufort County managed to obtain enough money to hard-surface its principal highways. By 1923 the main highway from Beaufort to Yemassee was hard-surfaced.[12] This connected Beaufort to the Ocean Highway, now United States Highway 17A, which went from Charleston through Summerville, Walterboro, Ridgeland, and Port Wentworth. The Ocean Highway was the first paved highway through the lowcountry.

While the county struggled to fund the longer trunk routes to the mainland, the city was improving its streets. In 1916 the city cleared, widened, and improved Depot Road from the end of Bay Street to the train depot. From the opening of the Port Royal Railroad in 1873, to the advent of auto travel, Depot Road was the chief entrance to Beaufort. After automobile travel became more common, the main road into Beaufort shifted to the Port Royal Ferry Road, or "Yemassee Highway" (now U.S. Highway 21), which connected to Boundary Street. In 1917 the city paved Bay Street for the first time, surfacing the street with brick from its east end at New Street to its west end, a block west of the county courthouse. Five years later, in 1922, the city paved Carteret, Craven, and Charles Streets. In 1930 Bladen Street was paved.[13] The other streets remained oyster-shell lanes until after World War II.

One stimulant to the good roads movement in South Carolina was a sizeable infusion of federal aid. In 1916 President Woodrow Wilson signed the Federal Aid Road Act, which authorized $75 million in federal revenue to improve "rural postal roads," many of which were in the South. Jimmy Byrnes had been a chief congressional leader of the good roads movement, and some of this federal money reached the Second Congressional District. This was the beginning of a national network of hard-surface automobile highways. For the lowcountry of South Carolina, the most important of these national highways was the Ocean Highway, now U.S. Highways 17 and 17A.

The idea of an Ocean Highway to connect coastal communities from Virginia to Florida for automobile travel began before 1908. In November 1908 A. H. Heyward of Lucknow Plantation, one of the last Savannah River rice barons, wrote a remarkable letter to Senator Christensen, encouraging him to promote the replacement of "random roads running aimlessly hither and thither through the Atlantic coast states" with "a superb, macadamized highway which could hence forward be known as the Atlantic National Autoway." Such a road would aid the economic development of the rural South. Heyward observed that "it is to the wealthy tourists that we of the South should appeal. . . . They would benefit Beaufort more than Charleston or Savannah, for a spin across your new steel bridge to your charming riverside winter home nestled 'neath the great live oaks would bring a class of tourist whose favorable predilections would leave behind them a train of golden eagles." Heyward's vision complemented Christensen's ambition. The letter and an accompanying editorial was reprinted in the *Charleston News and Courier* and the *Savannah Morning News* with favorable commentary in both cities. The *News and Courier* particularly captured the essence of the automobile revolution in America. The paper declared that a hard-surface highway following the "old King's Road built in colonial days" from Wilmington, North Carolina, to Savannah, Georgia, would open up commercial transport as well as tourist travel. It would be much more efficient than steam railroads, with "each vehicle a separate unit, traveling independently and making its own schedule."[14] The personal freedom and independence of automobile travel expressed in that editorial propelled the automobile revolution of the twentieth century.

Commercial and political interests in all the Atlantic Seaboard states shared the vision of South Carolinians and Georgians. In 1921 the South Atlantic Coastal Highway Association was formed to lobby for federal, state, and local funds to advance the Ocean Highway. The purpose of this promotional organization was "to open up development of tens of thousands of acres now idle." It pointed out that "tourist travel by automobile has more than quadrupled in just two or three years . . . bringing thousands of tourists and millions of dollars" to the lowcountry. The association held annual conventions in the major cities along the route. The 1921 convention was in Savannah, where Senator Niels Christensen represented Beaufort County. When the convention returned to Savannah in 1924, Christensen was a keynote speaker. By then he was near the end of his political career, and his convention speech was a swan song. In it he revealed his understanding of Beaufort County's past and his unfaltering confidence in the future: "We have been an isolated people. Waterways have always and until this very day, presented barriers that have kept us apart. A new epoch has now begun with the bridging of our great rivers."

Construction of the Ocean Highway was fraught with difficulty. Large rivers, wide bays, and trackless swamps had to be crossed. Federal, state, and local politicians had to find public money, and competing local commercial interests had to be balanced. In the lowcountry the biggest controversy was to establish the route from Charleston to Savannah. Citizens of Walterboro, in Colleton County, wanted it to go through their town, while Beaufort Countians wanted it to go through Garden's Corners, bypassing Walterboro. When the original Ocean Highway was constructed, Walterboro won. The first road was the route of U.S. Highway 17A through Walterboro and Yemassee, skirting Beaufort County at Pocotaligo before turning west to Ridgeland,

Hardeeville, and Port Wentworth. The Combahee River was not bridged until 1927, and the road to Jacksonboro was not paved until 1929. In those days it was known as the Combahee Shortcut. Despite all the difficulties, the Atlantic Coastal Highway was completed in 1925. It provided a hard-surface autoway from Calais, Maine, to Key West, Florida. It had cost nearly $50 million. Florida alone spent more than $10 million building the road all the way "overseas" to Key West.[15] For two generations of Beaufortonians, the Ocean Highway was the only auto link to the rest of the United States.

The availability of federal money for highway construction compelled many southern states to organize their highway systems. In fact, it was a requirement of the Federal Aid Road Act of 1916 that each state establish a governing agency to oversee and regularize highway construction before receiving any federal aid. Consequently, in 1917 Governor Richard I. Manning signed legislation creating the South Carolina Highway Commission to manage the brand-new South Carolina Highway Department. Beaufort County established its first Highway Committee in 1920. The committeemen were W. J. Thomas, J. G. Hudson, W. R. Williams, and F. W. Scheper Jr. After 1917 local highway planning and construction were increasingly controlled by the state government.[16]

The last great project of the era was to build the Lady's Island Bridge in 1927. The Whitehall Ferry to Lady's Island was established in 1762 and had been an integral part of Bay Street commerce for 165 years. The plan to link Port Royal and Lady's Islands began almost as soon as Whale Branch Bridge was completed. In 1910 F. H. Cothran of Greenwood, engineer and surveyor, measured the distance from Carteret Street to Lady's Island. Harbor pilot W. H. Von Harten took soundings in the channel. Also, a representative of Austin Brothers Construction Company of Atlanta, contractor for the Whale Branch Bridge, visited the site to estimate the cost. Within two weeks, Austin Brothers submitted an estimate of $68,315 for the bridge. The money was unavailable in 1910, but the idea never died. In 1911 the county commissioners, urged by Senator Christensen and the other legislators, proposed floating a seventy-thousand-dollar "bridge bond" to be repaid with a three-mill property tax increase. This required a referendum of Beaufort Township (Port Royal Island) and St. Helen Township (Lady's Island and St. Helena Island) taxpayers. The referendum was cancelled because of the hurricane of 1911 and not reconsidered until 1913.[17]

By 1913 several obstacles to the bridge had appeared. First, the bridge crossed the Atlantic Intracoastal Waterway, an inland navigation project of the U.S. Army Corps of Engineers, and thus required a federal permit. This obstacle was handily overcome when Congressman Byrnes secured special legislation permitting construction of a bridge over the Intracoastal Waterway.

A second obstacle was the opposition of the black residents of St. Helena Island to building the bridge at all. Rossa Cooley, the principal of Penn School, was the spokesperson for the opposition from St. Helena Island. In a 1913 letter she asked, "Is now the right time for a bridge, the cost of which is so great as to be a heavy burden on the people? . . . The majority of the people on St. Helena Island, it is safe to say, do not want the added burden of taxes. . . . when the petition was signed, many did not understand the merits of the question." She suggested that "a good motor launch with a regular schedule will suffice." However, Beaufort property owners and Bay Street commercial interests wanted the bridge, and a bridge bond referendum was rescheduled for January 1914. When the vote was held, the referendum was approved 213 votes to 103 votes. Every Port Royal Island precinct voted for the bridge (202–36), and every precinct on Lady's and St. Helena islands opposed it (67–11).[18]

While the bond issue was delayed, the legislative delegation established a commission to select a site for the crossing and oversee the contractors' bids. Frederick Christensen, William Keyserling, and Dr. M. B. Cope were appointed to the commission. Almost immediately a controversy arose over the location of the bridge. Three sites were considered. The first was from the New Coosaw Mines on Spanish Point across to Lady's Island. This was the shortest span. The second was from Carteret Street to the White Hall Ferry landing on Lady's Island, the site favored by the Bay Street merchants. The third location was the site of Fisher's Ferry, from the foot of Hancock Street across to the western point of Lady's Island (now Marsh Harbor). Cost estimates were obtained for each location. Ultimately, the second site was chosen. Accusations of special influence were made against Senator Christensen, and the whole project was shelved because of World War I. In the meantime, the county commission recovered control of White Hall Ferry. It purchased a motorized ferry boat, built new landings with floating docks useful at all tides, and established a regular schedule of ferry passages every half hour. Henry Lubkin was the ferry captain.[19]

When the Lady's Island Bridge project revived in 1919, the cost estimate by state highway engineer, H. C. Orr, had risen to $100,000. Finally, in 1923, the bridge commissioners, Frederick Christensen, Dr. M. B. Cope, Charles Luther, George Wilkins, and Harold Scheper authorized the driving of test pilings in the channel at the foot of Carteret Street. In 1924 the U.S. Army Corps of Engineers renewed the permit to cross the Intracoastal Waterway. Construction was set to begin in January 1925. By then the estimated cost had risen to $300,000. Of that amount $120,000 was raised from local bonds, and $180,000 was provided by the new state Highway Commission. The plan called for a two-lane concrete and creosote-timber bridge with a steel-truss swing span across the center of the channel. When the bids were opened on January 29, 1925, the American Bridge Company of Baltimore won the contract with a bid of $295,000.[20]

Construction began in the summer of 1925 and continued for two years. By January 1927, the steel-truss swing portion was delivered by barge and placed on its pedestal. On Good Friday, April 21, 1927, the first car crossed the Lady's Island Bridge. Mayor R.V. Bray of Beaufort, Mayor and Mrs. F.W. Scheper Jr. of Port Royal, Mr. and Mrs. J. A. Benham and Mr. and Mrs. R. K. Harley, president of the People's Bank, made the first trip in F.W. Scheper's new Cadillac sedan. After three months of finishing work, the bridge formally opened on July 7, 1927. With false starts, funding problems, and political squabbles, it had taken seventeen years to bridge the Beaufort River.

The opening of the Lady's Island Bridge was a grand celebration. On Thursday, July 7, 1927, the white citizens held a parade with a float that copied the double-truss swing bridge. A seventeen-year-old local belle, Dolly Elliott, daughter of Dr. M. G. Elliott, was the queen of the day and rode a float across the bridge. Hundreds of cars followed. Politicians made speeches. Lawyer W. J. Thomas was referred to as the "Father of this beautiful bridge." Former senator Niels Christensen, who had garnered most of the state funds, did not address the crowd. His silence reflected the changing politics of the 1920s. The Progressive Era had passed, and a new, more conservative Democratic leadership had taken over Beaufort County politics. Despite that political coloration, the great celebration concluded with a community barbeque on the bluff.

The next day, Friday, July 8, 1927, the African American citizens of Beaufort and St. Helena held their celebration. Even the *Beaufort Gazette* acknowledged that the black celebration had far eclipsed the white one. Two parades, one from Beaufort and one from St. Helena, met on the bridge and marched as one into town. The Beaufort parade was led by the Allen Brass Band. The St. Helena parade was led by the Warsaw Band, an institution that was fifty years old by 1927. The Warsaw bandmaster led the parade with an umbrella, reminiscent of the New Orleans Mardi Gras and "second line" marches, and performed the "Wahoo Dance" all the way across the bridge. H. G. Fischer was overall event chairman, and Benjamin Barnwell chaired the St. Helena delegation and was master of ceremonies for July 8. Prayers and speeches were offered by Reverend D. C. Washington, Dr. M. P. Kennedy, and lawyer Julius I. Washington. The keynote speaker was Dr. Robert A. Wilkinson, president of South Carolina State College. The day concluded with a barbeque for several thousand celebrants at Beaufort High School. By all accounts it "was one of the greatest celebrations the colored people of this section have ever had," harkening back to the great Memorial Day celebrations of Reconstruction days.[21]

In 1929 highway and bridge construction, as well as the whole structure of state government, experienced a profound change when the General Assembly passed, and Governor John G. Richards signed, a $65 million state highway bond bill. The 1929 Highway Bond Act was revolutionary from several perspectives. First, it was the largest bond bill and the greatest amount of debt that the state had ever undertaken. Second, it established "the entire state as a Bond District," a radical departure from historic practice. Third, it immediately made the Highway Department the largest and most powerful state agency. Throughout the Great Depression of the 1930s, the Highway Department became, directly or indirectly, the largest employer in the state. Also, the department with its huge budget became a regular political whipping boy. Ironically, Governor John G. Richards, the conservative Democrat who signed the progressive act, saw his political career come to an end. Olin D. Johnston of Spartanburg, who had vigorously opposed the Highway Bond Bill and lost, went on to be elected governor and had a long career as a progressive United States senator.[22]

After 1929 the Highway Department assumed responsibility for most rural highways in the state. Consequently, the responsibility of county governments for roads and bridges almost disappeared. In fact, the state highway department even took responsibility for many municipal streets in cash-strapped cities and towns. Among these were most of the streets in Beaufort. The great Highway Bond Bill of 1929 was South Carolina's recognition that the visionary "good roads" advocates of the previous thirty years had been correct. Safe, efficient, hard-surface highways were essential to economic development in the automotive age.

PROGRESS IN PUBLIC EDUCATION

Just as the era of World War I was a time of transition in modes of transportation, so was it a time of transition in public education. The progressive politicians of the early twentieth century believed, as holy writ, that the way to build the so-called New South was to promote "industry, education and good roads." The state government devoted large resources toward the improvement of public education in South Carolina. In Beaufort County the whole structure of education was transformed as a consequence.

Throughout the late nineteenth century, the state had provided only rudimentary education for a few months of the year. In most of South Carolina, this rudimentary education was provided in the traditional, rural, one-room school houses by teachers with very minimal training. Students who sought education beyond elementary school had to move to urban centers or seek private educational opportunities. In Beaufort County several excellent, privately supported institutions provided secondary education for a select few students.

In Beaufort the white families supported the Beaufort College Graded School, which was a public-private partnership for many years. Public funds were solicited to pay the teachers, and the private Trustees of Beaufort College provided the facility in the antebellum Beaufort College Building. As educational reform swept the state, Beaufort's white families added grades to the graded school curriculum, eventually providing nine full grades for white students. In 1908 the white community received a state appropriation sufficient to operate a high school. Beaufort High School opened in the fall of 1908 with 160 students in grades one through nine, and only one "teacher of the high school grades," Mary Shotwell of Berea, North Carolina. In 1909, after a petition signed by all the leading white citizens of Beaufort, the Trustees of Beaufort College deeded the old college building over to the public school district to facilitate the construction of a modern school building to house grades one through ten. The new school building, complete with indoor plumbing, was opened in 1909. This was the beginning of Beaufort High School and the beginning of the educational transformation of Beaufort County.

The first graduation from the new Beaufort High School building took place in May 1910 in the new auditorium attached to the rear of the old Beaufort College Building. The assembly room was filled to capacity. The commencement address was delivered by Dr. S. C. Mitchell, president of the University of South Carolina and one of the state's leading voices for educational progress. Graduate Allen Paul read the poem "Looking Forward." Catherine Batchelder read her own prize-winning essay, "Charms of the Sea," and class leader Daisy Weinberg read her essay, "Thinking and Living." The school choir sang popular favorites of the day: "A Laughing Song," "Song of the Armorer," and "Oh Lovely Night." At the conclusion of the ceremony, the *Beaufort Gazette* correspondent linked the past to the present. The last song served to "speed the happy throng out into the moonlight that flooded the tree shaded campus and the massive columns of the classical portico under which many boys of long ago entered Beaufort College School."[23]

African American students also had educational opportunities beyond elementary level at four privately funded institutions in Beaufort County. The oldest and largest was the Penn School, whose transition to the "Penn Normal and Agricultural School" after the death in 1901 of Laura Towne reflected the emphasis on practical training for African Americans promoted by Tuskegee Institute in Alabama and the Hampton Institute in Virginia. The latter college was closely associated with Penn Normal and Agricultural School in the early twentieth century. The second oldest school was the Mather School for girls (founded in 1868) on Port Royal Island, which also emphasized practical training and Bible-based education. Both Penn School and Mather School grew out of the missionary zeal of the Reconstruction era. In 1901 the Christensen family endowed the Port Royal Agricultural School, which provided practical education for African American girls and boys on a residential campus. Penn, Mather, and the Port Royal Agricultural School all served both boarding students and day students. In 1908 shipping magnate William P. Clyde endowed a high school and adult-level training program at the Seabrook School on Hilton Head Island. Within a few years this school took the name of its benefactor. The Clyde School was a high school–level agricultural and domestic training program under the tutelage of the Tuskegee Institute. William Clyde sold his Hilton Head estate in 1916 and died in 1923. The Clyde School closed shortly thereafter. During the early twentieth century, the mission of each of these private schools was absorbed by the growing state-supported public school establishment.

In April 1912 Penn School celebrated its fiftieth anniversary. It was a memorable occasion. Hundreds of islanders attended along with forty white supporters. The activities on Saturday, April 14, and Sunday, April 15, were organized by Rosa Cooley and Grace House, both former teachers at Hampton Institute. On Sunday the activities centered in Darrah Hall and featured an introduction by Dr. H. B. Frissell, president of the Hampton Institute, and a speech by Dr. S. C. Mitchell, president of the University of South Carolina, who promoted the benefits of industrial training. Dr. Mitchell urged that the vocational mission be undertaken by the public schools in Beaufort County as it had been in other South Carolina communities.

In 1912 Penn School remembered its historic roots by inviting remarks from Mrs. William Jenks of Philadelphia, niece of Laura Towne, and Mrs. T. E. Ruggles of Milton, Massachusetts, sister of Ellen Murray. Murray died in 1908 and is buried next to Laura Towne in the graveyard of the Brick Baptist Church. Poems, prayers, and songs interspersed the speeches. One song, the "St. Helena Hymn," was specifically written for Penn School during the Civil War by John Greenleaf Whittier. A newspaper correspondent noted, "The singing by a male quartet was exceptionally good."

One of the features of Penn School's golden anniversary was the dedication of Cope Hall, the new industrial training building. Dr. Frissell spoke for the trustees at the ribbon cutting, and St. Helena farmer Tom Fields spoke for the islanders. The historic highlight of the occasion was the speech at Darrah Hall by Robert Smalls, who recalled "the early days of the school when he went north to solicit funds and there met President Lincoln who endorsed his mission."[24]

Penn School's fiftieth anniversary was a turning point in Beaufort County's history. Robert Smalls was old and ailing by 1912, and this was one of his last public appearances. He died three years later. Penn School itself did not survive the next half century. Both were icons of Beaufort County's unique Reconstruction history.

In March 1918 Mather School likewise celebrated its Golden Jubilee. It too was a grand occasion. F. M. Brist, superintendent of the Beaufort National Cemetery, and Mather School trustee George Waterhouse Jr. presided over the festivities. The activities were highlighted by a speech by Major Edwin Denby, former congressman and U.S. Marine Corps combat hero of World War I. Denby's patriotic address included "generous recognition of our colored troops." The Mather students, all teenaged African American girls, "uniformed in white middies," drilled, sang patriotic songs, and raised a historic flag over the campus. The Mather School's lead teacher, Miss Fischer, read a poem written for the occasion. Successful alumnae gave testimonials to the value of Mather School education. Supporters and dignitaries from all over America attended the golden anniversary of the historic institution. Katherine S. Westfall represented the Women's Board of Chicago. Dr. Brink and Mr. Garabrant arrived by train from New York City to represent the out-of-state trustees. The *Beaufort Gazette* noted, "Singing by the school was a marked feature. . . . in a most impressive manner the students sang 'Swing Low Sweet Chariot,'" one of the traditional hymns of the sea islands.

One of the most important speeches was delivered by Dr. P. P. Watson of Lincoln University titled "She Did What She Could." It was a tribute to the life and work of the school's founder, Rachel Crane Mather, whom Watson had known for many years. P. P. Watson had also been the speaker at Mather School's first high school commencement in 1901. Remarks by Professor Lee of Benedict College in Columbia concluded the celebration.

The Mather School anniversary was a thoroughly integrated affair as the school had many local white supporters and benefactors. Reverend R. P. Ingersoll of the Baptist Church of Beaufort delivered a sermon. Mayor and Mrs. C. E. Danner attended both days' events. Among the most active local supporters were Rose and Callie Whipple, sisters of the Whipple brothers whose farm west of Beaufort was a pioneer in advancing modern agronomy in truck farming. The entire Whipple clan attended the Mather School ceremony.[25]

The year following Mather School's Golden Jubilee, Beaufort County School District received its first state appropriation for a "Beaufort Negro high school." On March 25, 1919, the state high school inspector, J. A. Stoddard, informed the Beaufort school district that their request for funds for an African American high school had been conditionally approved. One of Stoddard's conditions was that the curriculum alter "the over-emphasis now given to advanced mathematics, history and the study of Latin rather than the more useful subjects of English, Arithmetic and practical training." Stoddard's 1919 report also drew attention to "the need for a larger school plant including five or six acres of land, with an adequate building for the accommodation of the pupils enrolled from the first grade through the high school." This was the beginning of Robert Smalls High School, and it came none too soon. In 1919 Beaufort County's rate of illiteracy was more than 25 percent.[26]

The county public school district made another advance in providing high school education for African American students in 1921 when it undertook financial responsibility for the operation of the Port Royal Agricultural School. The school then changed its name to the Beaufort County Training School and became part of the public school establishment. Little else about the school changed for many years. Professor Joseph Shanklin remained its head until World War II, and his wife, India, continued to be the lead teacher and instructor of what was called "Domestic Science." Two hundred twenty boarding and day students were enrolled at the Beaufort County Training School in 1929. The school continued to seek private contributions to supplement the state operating fund. The Christensen family, which had originally endowed the Port Royal Agricultural School in 1901, continued to be the school's principal local support. In 1931 the Beaufort County Training School received a major grant from the Rosenwald Fund to build a new classroom building on the campus. To celebrate the occasion, March 9, 1931, was declared "Rosenwald Day" at the Beaufort County Training School. Students and staff honored the legacy of benefactor Julius Rosenwald with a program that included presentations on "The Life of Julius Rosenwald" by Frederick Washington and "The Rosenwald School Movement" by Mary Lee Donaldson. Rosenwald, president of the Sears-Roebuck Company of Chicago, had dedicated much of his large fortune to building school houses for impoverished rural communities in the American South. Several of the one- and two-room, rural "Rosenwald Schools" were used in Beaufort County in the early twentieth century.

The Beaufort County Training School continued to function throughout the 1920s and 1930s with enrollment regularly exceeding two hundred students. The school was so closely associated with its superintendent, Joseph Shanklin, and his wife, India, that it was known locally as the "Shanklin School." In 1939 India Shanklin died while undergoing surgery in a Savannah hospital. Joseph Shanklin kept the school going for a few more years, but enormous social changes in Beaufort County diminished the need for the school and much of its mission was subsumed by the growing public school establishment. Joseph Shanklin retired in 1944 after forty years of leading the school. The Beaufort County Training School closed a few years later, and its students transferred to the public schools.[27]

The progress of public education took a giant step forward in 1924 when the Beaufort County School Board purchased eleven acres of land at the corner of the Port Royal Road (now Ribaut Road) and Boundary Street from local attorney George W. Beckett. There they planned an entire school campus for African American students from grades one through eleven. This was to be the site of the new Robert Smalls High School for the next forty-seven years. The new high school was named to honor Civil War hero and Reconstruction political icon Robert Smalls, who had done so much to establish public education for African American students in Beaufort County and in South Carolina. The new Robert Smalls High School was opened in 1925, just ten years after the death of its namesake. The original building was of wooden-frame construction built on the "California Plan," meaning all on one floor. It had ten classrooms, a domestic science room, library, teacher's lounge, a five-hundred-seat auditorium, steam heat, sanitary drinking fountains, and indoor bathrooms for boys and girls. The new Robert Smalls High School covered 20,700 square feet. Compared to the school facilities of the past, it was a modern marvel. The high school cost thirty thousand dollars in 1925.

At the same time, the Beaufort County School Board built a new Beaufort High School for white students on Bay Street. The original Beaufort High School on Carteret Street had run out of space for all grades by 1918. In 1924 the school board issued $100,000 in county bonds to build the new white high school. It was also completed in 1925. It was a two-story brick building with eight classrooms, two science laboratories, teacher's rooms, superintendent's office, and a seven-hundred-seat auditorium. The white high school cost three times what the Robert Smalls High School originally cost and served barely half the number of students. This was common for the time. In 1913 annual per pupil expenditures for white students in Beaufort County was $36.89 while annual per pupil expenditures for black students was $8.57.[28]

The first principal of Robert Smalls High School was Reverend D.W. Blythewood. He was raised in Beaufort, graduated from Lincoln University with baccalaureate and seminary degrees, and was principal of an elementary school in Edgefield, South Carolina, before returning to his hometown as pastor of the historic Tabernacle Baptist Church in 1896. He was the church pastor for twenty-two years before being chosen as the first principal of the first public high school for African Americans in Beaufort County. D.W. Blythewood was one of the moving spirits behind the new high school. From 1918 to 1926 he managed the budget, designed the new curriculum, hired the first teachers, and oversaw the construction of the new campus. Only a few months after moving into the new building, Reverend Blythewood died of a heart attack at the ferry wharf on Bay Street.[29]

Reverend J. A. Wilson served as principal of Robert Smalls High School from 1926 through 1931. He was also the pastor of the First African Baptist Church. In 1929 Robert Smalls High School fielded its first football team. Appropriately, they took the name "Generals." A football field was laid out on low ground along the marsh edge of the campus. Green football jerseys were donated by Mrs. Abe Rudowitz. The first lineup of the Robert Smalls High School Generals in 1929 comprised Leroy Holmes, left end; Andrew Simmons, left tackle; Jack Roberts, left guard; Ben Manigo, center; Henry Singleton, right guard; Medicus Washington, right tackle; Lonnie Ferguson, right end; Solomon Bryan, right halfback; Mathew Ferguson, left halfback; Richard Bee, fullback; and Harold Greene, quarterback.

The Generals began their distinguished forty-year gridiron history with a 12–0 victory over Walterboro High School. When Robert Smalls High School started classes the following year it had 328 students and 10 teachers in ten grades. The 1930 faculty comprised Etta Washington, Lurene Frazier, Mabel Williams, Florence Grant, Martha Simmons, Lizzie Mixon, Helen Sheppard, Edna Moultrie, Betty Lawton, and James Wilson, the principal.

All of the Robert Smalls High School teachers in 1930 had college degrees, and many were taking postgraduate courses during the summer. The 1930 school year opened with inspirational talks from Beaufort's longtime African American doctor, N. J. Kennedy, and Robert Smalls High School alumnus Israel Elliott, who was then attending the Howard University School of Medicine.

In 1931 James Wilson left Beaufort to become pastor of the First African Baptist Church in Savannah, and R. W. McGirt was chosen as Robert Smalls High School's third principal. McGirt was a native of Camden, South Carolina, and a 1913 graduate of South Carolina State College. He came to Robert Smalls High School with the recommendation of Dr. R. S. Wilkenson, president of South Carolina State College and longtime supporter of education in Beaufort County. Barely a month after McGirt's arrival, he was faced with a major crisis.

On Sunday night, November 8, 1931, Robert Smalls High School caught fire and burned to its foundation. Only the brick chimney was left standing. Fortunately, the school board had insurance to cover the loss, and within a month a contract was let to W. A. McCrary and Sons of Columbia to construct a new high school building of fireproof brick and concrete. The new Robert Smalls High School was completed in time for the opening of the 1932 fall term. Robert Smalls High School continued to serve the African American community throughout the 1930s, but the declining black population diminished some of the school's activities. In 1935 only eight students, all girls, qualified for high school diplomas. The class valedictorian that year was Mae Dee Esperanza Myers; the salutatorian was Adelle Miley. In 1938 Professor W. Kent Alston replaced R. W. McGirt as principal. One of Alston's first formal ceremonies at the high school was a commemoration of the one hundredth anniversary of the birth of Robert Smalls. It was a large event attended by Beaufort's black and white leadership. Dr. M. F. Whitaker, president of South Carolina State College, offered the keynote address. W. Kent Alston would remain principal of Robert Smalls High School for nearly thirty years and lead the school into the modern era.[30]

The older private schools continued to function throughout the 1920s and 1930s. In 1925 Penn School added its fine new community building, Frissell Hall, named for longtime Penn trustee and president of Hampton Institute H. B. Frissell. The handsome building was designed by the prominent New York architect John Henry House, brother of Penn teacher Grace House. He was the regular architect for all Penn School construction from 1911 until his death in 1936.

In 1928 the Mather School added Coleman Hall to its campus. The large building on the bluff overlooking the Beaufort River was designed as a dormitory for 50 girls and a dining hall accommodating 150 students. The building had an apartment for a resident teacher and a basement with a modern furnace and storage for trunks. Coleman Hall was decorated in the style of the day with tan and cream walls and dark-stained oak woodwork. The architects of Coleman Hall were Lafaye and Lafaye of Columbia, who had designed the imposing Beaufort Bank building on Bay Street in 1910. The building cost forty-four thousand dollars in 1928. Coleman Hall was named for Alice B. Coleman, who was president of the Women's American Baptist Home Missionary Society of New York City. It was the largest building in an ambitious plan to raise five hundred thousand dollars to expand and modernize the old school.

During the 1920s the financial support for the old Reconstruction schools began to wane. The collapse of the local economy in the 1920s and the national economy in the 1930s constrained the generosity of the traditional supporters of both schools. At the same time, more and more of their original educational mission was being absorbed by the growing public school system. Penn School continued its educational program until 1953. It closed the year before the opening of St. Helena High School barely two miles away. Mather School survived until 1968, when its campus was absorbed by the State Department of Technical and Comprehensive Education. Coleman Hall still stands as a monument to the old Mather School in the center of the Technical College of the Lowcountry campus.

Out on St. Helena Island, the old Penn School campus transitioned to an active community and conference center with a national and international reputation. Frissell Hall, Darrah Hall, and all the historic buildings have been preserved and recognized as a National Landmark District in the midst of the beautiful "paradise grove" of live oaks that so entranced Laura Towne in 1862.

In 1970 Robert Smalls High School was closed in order to integrate its students into the consolidated Beaufort High School. All these schools left behind a legacy of social change and progress from the Civil War, Reconstruction, and Progressive Eras. Each school also left behind large groups of proud, productive, and loyal alumni.

BEAUFORT ECONOMY OF THE 1920S AND THE 1926 COLLAPSE OF THE BEAUFORT BANK

From the start of the twentieth century, Beaufort County's economy struggled to achieve sustainable growth. The collapse of the phosphate industry in the 1890s, the removal of the naval station in 1901, and the steady decline of cotton removed the three pillars of the county's late-nineteenth-century prosperity. In a 1915 editorial, the *Beaufort Gazette* commented, "Probably not for thirty years has there been such stagnation in industry and business in this section." Two developments in the early twentieth century slowed the decline. One was the rise of truck farming, which surpassed cotton in economic value in 1912 and reached its peak in 1920. The other was the arrival of the United States Marine Corps and the establishment of the Marine Corps Recruit Depot on Parris Island in 1915. While these developments became the new pillars of Beaufort's economy, they both suffered severe reversals in the 1920s. The local economy was thrown into a deep and lasting depression that, by the mid-1930s, made Beaufort one of the poorest counties in America.

A stroll down Bay Street in the spring of 1920 revealed signs of technological progress and of daily bustle that masked the vulnerability of the local economy. Poles lining Bay Street carried the multiple wires of the telephone company and the municipal electric generating plant. By 1920 cars outnumbered horses in the streets. Many of the families and businesses that were established during Reconstruction still operated on Bay Street. The west end of Bay Street, once called the Waterhouse Block, had long since been sold off. The Waterhouse Cotton Gin was still on the waterfront, but the clatter of the ginning machines was rarely heard by 1920. The boll weevil had silenced them.

Some of the original machinery installed in 1866 fell to George Waterhouse's partner, George F. Ricker, another native of Maine, who managed the business after Waterhouse's death in 1894. After the boll weevil assault, the old gins were stored in a barn behind the house of Frank Ricker, George Ricker's son, on the corner of Port Republic and West Streets. They rusted there for several years. One of those machines survived from Robert Porteus's antebellum Bay Street cotton gin. That particular machine was believed to have dated from the 1815 or earlier, making it one of the oldest surviving cotton-ginning machines in the United States. When Henry Ford founded his Museum of American Industry in Dearborn, Michigan, he heard of this ancient machine and in 1928 sent some representatives to Beaufort to buy the relic from Frank Ricker. Ricker refused to take any money and donated the old cotton gin to Ford's Greenfield Village (a collection of historic buildings adjacent to the Museum of American Industry), where it has held a place of honor since then. One year later, two well-dressed northerners appeared at Frank Ricker's front door and informed the maid that they had delivered Mr. Ricker's car. "But, Mr. Ricker ain't got no car," replied the maid. "He does now," the men replied. A brand-new Ford automobile was Henry Ford's response to Frank Ricker's generosity.

The west end of Waterhouse Block was occupied by the Beaufort Bank, built in 1914. George Waterhouse Jr. was chairman of the bank's board of directors until his sudden death in June 1920. West of the bank was Albert Gage's bicycle shop and the medical offices of Dr. M. G. Elliott. Gage was the grandson of the abolitionist Frances Gage, and Dr. Elliott was the younger son of the U.S. congressman and Confederate hero Colonel William Elliott. East of the bank was the old customs house, which had been sold to the Beaufort Truck Growers Association in 1919. Next up the block was Kinghorn Brothers Grocery. The Freemasons' Harmony Lodge occupied the second floor of Kinghorn's building. Next to that was Luther's Pharmacy, founded by Charles G. Luther in 1906. At the east end was the busy Wallace and Danner clothing and furniture store. Wallace and Danner had been founded in 1874 by John Newell Wallace and William Porter Danner. William P. Danner died in 1904, and John N. Wallace died in 1916, one of the last of the Reconstruction merchants. Wallace had been born in Jackson, Ohio, migrated to Beaufort after the Civil War, and formed a successful partnership with the Danner family. The Danners from Charleston became "old Beaufortonians" by virtue of William P. Danner's 1878 marriage to Eliza Mary Johnson, daughter of the Confederate hero Colonel Benjamin Johnson, who was killed at the first Battle of Bull Run. Hence, the Wallace and Danner store was one of Beaufort's most successful North-South Reconstruction partnerships. It survived until 1970. Next to Wallace and Danner was Bristol and Hall Jewelers, another Bay Street business begun during Reconstruction. William R. Bristol came to Beaufort in 1876 from Connecticut to work in the store of his father-in-law, P. M. Whitman. He later took over the jewelry store and in 1926 passed it on to his business partner, Arthur Hall. Bristol was Beaufort's mayor for twelve years.[31]

Just east of Bristol and Hall, on the river side, was the rambling River View Hotel, managed by Mr. and Mrs. Lorenz Wilder. The River View had superseded the old Sea Island Hotel. After the death of James Odell, his widow, Alice, ran the Sea Island Hotel by herself for several years. By World War I, the old building needed repair and expensive modern upgrades that the business could not afford. In 1916 Alice Odell sold the hotel to the Knights of Columbus as a hospitality house for U.S. Marines. Hence, the

River View Hotel was practically the only guest accommodation in Beaufort in 1920. Lorenz Wilder was the son of Dr. Francis Wilder of Hilton Head's Otter Hole Plantation. Dr. Wilder had come to Hilton Head with the Union occupation and never left, serving the island's dwindling population until World War I. He was a Republican delegate to the constitutional convention of 1868 and a longtime local officeholder. He died in Beaufort in 1924 at the age of eighty-seven and was buried in Shelburne, Massachusetts. When the River View Hotel burned in 1925, the fire nearly ignited all of Bay Street, provoking memories of the Great Fire of 1907. Three brick storefronts replaced the hotel, and later the Art Deco–style Ocean View Café was added to the block.

The stout tabby walls of the old John Cross Tavern had stopped the River View fire of 1925 from doing further damage. The MacDonald-Wilkins grocery store and the Palace Market butcher shop occupied the first floor of the old three-story tabby building constructed by Captain Francis Saltus in about 1800. Across Scott Street from the grocery store, on the river side, was the auto showroom and garage of the Wall Motor Company, Beaufort's Ford dealership. These buildings were built on the site of the old Dispensary Building, destroyed in the 1907 fire. The automobile dealership, begun by R.A. Long in 1908, was sold to Hugh and Patrick Wall in 1918. Next to Wall Motor Company was the handsome brick and masonry building of the People's Bank, which had been gutted by the 1907 fire. Beaufortonians called it simply "the Scheper Bank." The town clock stood in front of the bank. On the riverfront behind the People's Bank was the MacDonald-Wilkins Company warehouse. It had been built as a cotton gin and warehouse in 1909. By 1920, however, the gins were rarely used, and the building was being converted to a feed, seed, and grocery warehouse. During the 1920s company president William Keyserling acquired the remaining assets. For the next generation the old brick warehouse at the foot of the Lady's Island Bridge was called the Keyserling Building.

On the north side of Bay Street, at the far east end, across from the Stephen Elliott Park, were the three imposing homes of Harriett Parmalee Waterhouse, J.W. Thomas, and John N. Wallace. The latter two houses had replaced the older Fuller and Elliott homes that had fallen victim to the fire of 1907. At the corner of Carteret and Bay Streets, the city's most prominent commercial spot, stood the impressive brick storefront of N. Christensen and Sons hardware store. It had been built in 1910 to replace the colonial era building, which burned in 1907. N. Christensen and Sons was the local agent for Overland Automobiles, which were displayed on Carteret Street behind the hardware store. By 1920 the Christensen store had occupied that corner of Bay Street for forty-four years. Westward, next to Christensen Hardware, was the empty lot where James M. Crofut's hardware store had stood before the 1907 fire. The lot was later used by the Ford dealer across the street to display used cars. The next building to the west was Morrall Furniture Company, a new enterprise of John Fripp Morrall, begun in 1917 and destined to be a twentieth-century fixture of Bay Street commerce. Tragically, the building burned to the ground in 1987 along with Johnny Morrall's large collection of Beaufort historical material. Next door was George Holmes's old tabby building, used in 1920 as rental housing. Its stout tabby walls, dating from colonial times, had blocked the Great Fire of 1907.[32]

George Holmes was one of the most interesting and long lived of Beaufort's Reconstruction merchants. Born in Bedford, New York, in 1829, he became a Beaufortonian through his marriage to Julia Hazel, daughter of the planter Joseph Hazel of Lady's Island. Holmes moved to Beaufort before the Civil War to work in the store of his brother-in-law, John S. Filer, a Connecticut merchant who had married Julia Hazel's sister. Both Filer (Fyler) and Holmes remained in Beaufort during the Union occupation and prospered during Reconstruction. Holmes amassed considerable real estate, served as fusionist mayor until 1902, was a founding investor in the People's Bank, and lived in grand style in the George Parsons Elliott house until his death in 1919. He was buried in Bedford, New York. Next door to George Holmes's building was C. K. Batchelder's hardware store. Charles Keyes Batchelder and his brother Mark had moved to Beaufort in the 1880s from Peru, Vermont, to join the thriving business of a fellow Vermonter, John J. Dale. When the company became MacDonald-Wilkins, Mark Batchelder was a partner. As the cotton trade declined, Charles K. Batchelder opened a hardware store in Charlie Chin Sang's old building on the corner of Bay and Scott Streets. He operated the store until 1923, when the business was sold to Schwartz and Webb and renamed Beaufort Hardware.

Across Scott Street, on the north side of Bay Street, stood the ancient John Mark Verdier House, one of Beaufort's premier historical monuments. The building was constructed between 1790 and 1800 as a home and business site of the Beaufort merchant and Swiss Huguenot descendant John Mark Verdier. In 1920 and through much of the twentieth century, it was known as the Lafayette House because it was erroneously believed that in 1825 the Marquis de Lafayette had delivered a speech from its elegant federal-style portico.

By 1920 the Verdier House was a symbol of Beaufort's declining fortunes. The building was one of many owned by George Holmes. It had little paint and was festooned with commercial signs and telephone wires. The third floor, where an elegant ballroom had once opened onto the portico, was occupied by the Home Telephone Company. An unsightly web of overhead wires emanated from the telephone company's switchboard at the Verdier House to all corners of the town. Telephone lines stretched to the railroad depot where they met long-distance wires to the mainland. On the second or main floor were the law offices of Claude Aman, a slightly eccentric attorney who frequently made public accusations against Senator Christensen when he was at the height of his influence. During Prohibition, Claude Aman had a brisk practice defending bootleggers and rumrunners. On the ground floor was Blocker's Little Gem Shaving Parlor.

Across Scott Street, in the middle block of Bay Street, were Sheppard's Barber Shop and Pool Parlor, Weinberg's Dry Goods and Cigar Factory, Breedin's Dime Store, the Brown Furniture Company—its motto was "Marry the girl and see us"—and Lipsitz's Dry Goods and Grocery. Across West Street, Morris Levin's dry goods occupied the old drug store owned by Dr. Henry Middleton Stuart. Goldberg's watch repair, the Busy Bee Café, Schein's Department Store, and Spark's five- and ten-cent store followed. On the corner of Charles Street stood the Old Post Office and the offices of the *Beaufort Gazette.* The post office building dated from antebellum days. It had been the town's post office for nearly one hundred years until it was replaced in 1914 by a modern brick building on Carteret Street.

On February 7, 1924, a fire started in the ceiling of the *Beaufort Gazette* building. Strong west winds fanned the flames and threatened the whole block. The heroic response of the Washington Fire Company, the Pioneer Fire Company, and the Hook and Ladder Fire Company, whose volunteers entered burning buildings to fight the flames, saved all but the Old Post Office and the *Gazette* building. The *Gazette* was then owned by the Christensens, and rumors circulated that the fire had been arson against Senator Christensen. The investigation concluded that the fire was accidental. In 1925 the Christensens sold the *Gazette* to a consortium of local businessmen who operated the company through the Beaufort Chamber of Commerce. No investor was permitted to own more than a 10 percent share of the newspaper. The sale of the *Beaufort Gazette* was a sign of the changing local politics of the 1920s. The burned-out lot became a parking lot and has been one since then.[33]

Off Bay Street were several busy enterprises. Tally's Bakery and Jack Culp's popcorn stand were on opposite corners of Carteret and King Streets. Swain and Covar operated an auto repair shop in what was called the "West Street garage." Kit Singleton still had his livery stable and taxi stand at 115 Scott Street, and James Riley's mortuary was at 209 Craven Street.

Beaufort's commercial establishment launched several schemes in the era of World War I that they hoped would stimulate economic progress. In April 1915 Mr. and Mrs. Hall Waring of Bedford, New York, purchased 550 feet of waterfront property next to Mather School. They bought the property from the Waterhouse Corporation, owners of the old Fuller Hermitage Plantation, which stretched across the neck of land from Battery Creek to the Beaufort

River. Like many who followed in the twentieth century, the Warings hoped to parcel out their section of the bluff in lots to sell to their northern friends. The Warings' home cost five thousand dollars and included a small house for two servants. The impressive twenty-foot bluff on the west side of "the Bay" had centuries earlier been the site of the Royal Navy careening wharf and rope walk of 1748. Mather School had its campus on the bluff from 1868 to 1974. South of Mather School were the remains of George Gage's sawmill. Before the automobile, the bluff was too far from town for real estate development. Gus Sanders was the first to build his Tudor-style house on the bluff in 1907. In 1902 the Christensen brothers launched a scheme to build a resort hotel on the bluff, but they could not secure enough investors and the scheme collapsed. In 1916 a local consortium formed the Beaufort Development Company and bought the Crofut property, which stood, as the *Gazette* described it, "on the bend of Port Royal Road owned for many years by James M. Crofut. . . . it borders on the Beaufort River and is most desirable for home seekers." This was the beginning of the residential neighborhood along Ribaut Road. By the 1930s all the riverfront lots along Ribaut Road were filled except Wilson Park, donated by the Waterhouse Corporation in honor of Colonel Duncan Campbell Wilson.[34]

Beaufort's businessmen also had high hopes for two industrial enterprises. In 1917 the American Shipbuilding Corporation was formed by Walter Richardson and R. C. Horne Jr. of Beaufort and Charlton G. Ogburn of Savannah. They raised $320,000 in capital, built a shipyard, launching slip, and deepwater pier on the end of Spanish Point. They then convinced the C&WC Railroad to revive an old spur line to Spanish Point. The American Shipbuilding Corporation built a large, oceangoing barge of steel-reinforced concrete, a new, faster, and cheaper method of ship construction employed as an emergency measure during World War I. They laid the keels for two more barges before the postwar recession drove them out of business in 1922. The shipyard had employed hundreds of local laborers at its height in 1918 and 1919. For a generation, Spanish Point was known as "the shipyard." It was the last major industry to occupy one of the most heavily industrialized locations in Beaufort County. Spanish Point had been the site of Stuart Town, the ill-fated Scots settlement of 1686, of Fort Lyttelton (1758–1779), and of Fort Marion (1809–1815). In the 1870s D. C. Wilson built the Sea Island Chemical Company plant at the end of Spanish Point. Next to it, on the bluff, was the massive Atlantic Sawmill. In 1892 the Coosaw Mining Company took over the Sea Island Chemical Company, and the site became known as New Coosaw. The American Shipbuilding Corporation was the last gasp of a half century of industrial enterprises on Spanish Point. From the heyday of phosphates to the end of World War I, thousands of Beaufortonians had labored for good wages at the site. Phosphate ships and lumber schooners had been regular visitors to its deepwater wharves. During the 1920s a crate-and-barrel shop briefly occupied the site, and during the 1930s the old buildings were utilized by a seafood-canning company. By mid-century vestiges of once-mighty industries lay rusting and overgrown by vines, brambles, and underbrush.[35]

Another local industry for which Beaufortonians had high hopes was the Seacoast Packing Company, which was incorporated on December 10, 1919. The original incorporators were a "who's who" of local elites, including Niels Christensen, James Roe Bellamy, William Keyserling, F. W. Scheper Jr., and Walter E. Richardson. Richardson and Scheper were presidents of Beaufort's two banks. Christensen was state senator, and Bellamy was state representative. Keyserling was president of the MacDonald-Wilkins Company. Any business those men invested in attracted considerable attention. Their aim was to sell stock in the new company through local subscription, raise $150,000 in capital, and build a modern livestock-rendering and meat-packing factory along the line of the C&WC Railroad. To advance their project they held a "community dinner" in October 1919 at the new "war camp Community Club" on Carteret Street. At the dinner they formed a committee of local business and professional leaders to promote the new venture and solicit subscriptions. The "stock pledge committee" for Beaufort included Niels Christensen, Israel Keyserling, E. E. Lengnick, Albert Gage, R. V. Bray, B. E. Detreville, F. W. Scheper Jr., C. S. Adams, W. H. Hull, and George Waterhouse Jr. The committee to solicit Jasper, Hampton, Allendale, and Colleton Counties consisted of Walter Richardson, W. J. Thomas, William Keyserling, C. G. Luther, W. W. Niver, Peter Lea, R. C. Bramlett, W. P. Jay, and Senator Christensen. Their meeting in Hampton was chaired by Randolph Murdaugh. In Estill it was led by E. M. Peeples and A. R. Youmans. Any enterprise backed by the collective effort and capital resources of these prominent leaders could hardly fail, so the whole business community rallied behind the Seacoast Packing Company stock-subscription drive. A prominent Beaufort County farmer commented that "the time has certainly arrived for a packing plant here as the boll weevil has cleaned out the cotton crop and if the farmers of Beaufort, Jasper and Hampton Counties expect to make a living in the future, they will have to turn their attention to stock raising."

To support the new corporation became a matter of civic pride. Not only would the new packing plant provide jobs and economic development, but it would also help farmers recover from the loss of cotton by providing a modern livestock-processing, sales, and distribution center. By January 1920 nearly two hundred investors had pledged to buy seventy-six thousand dollars' worth of Seacoast Packing Company stock.[36] In May 1920 the stockholders selected the board of directors, and they in turn elected the officers of the company. The board of directors comprised William Keyserling,

F.W. Scheper Jr., Walter E. Richardson, William Copp, Niels Christensen, Harry Danner, J. L. Butler, R. H. Butler from Beaufort County, W. A. Darlington from Allendale County, and W. S. Rentz from Hampton County. The board elected Keyserling as president, Copp as vice president, and Harry Danner as secretary-treasurer. Christensen, Scheper, Richardson, and Butler made up the executive committee.

Most stock subscriptions were in the range of $100 to $500, but four old-line Beaufort enterprises and one out-of-town investor accounted for $23,500 worth of stock, more than 30 percent of the new company. The outside investor was William Copp of Georgia. The four local investors were the MacDonald-Wilkins Company, N. Christensen and Sons, George Waterhouse and Company, and Bellamy Brothers. By July 1920, $110,000 of stock had been subscribed, and the Beaufort Truck Growers Association had become a major investor by pledging to purchase $5,000 in stock. Brooks Engineering of Georgia was selected to construct the new factory on the old Fuller Hermitage property next to the railroad line. The estimated cost of the factory was $85,000.[37]

An additional client for the Seacoast Packing Company plant appeared on the scene. A. H. Ehrenreich was president of Ocean Leather Company of Newark, New Jersey. This company proposed to harvest sharkskin and process it into marketable leather at the Seacoast Packing Company facility. The Ocean Leather Company planned other tanneries in Morehead City, North Carolina, and in the Bahamas. By 1921 a working agreement was reached between the two companies, and Ocean Leather Company sent Mr. Phinney, "a fisherman of long years experience off the coast of Massachusetts," to handle the local business of the company. Local investors expected both companies to generate a payroll of four thousand dollars per month. Like the Seacoast Packing Company, Ehrenreich hoped to raise capital from stock sales to the Beaufort business community.[38]

In fall 1920 the three-story factory was under construction. V. L. Collier was hired as manager of the Seacoast Packing Company, and C. L. Brooks of Brooks Engineering Company of Georgia was the superintendent of construction. But trouble arose just as work began. The postwar recession hit Beaufort hard. Despite their stock pledges, many local investors began to delay their stock purchases. "The matter of collections is becoming difficult and there is great need that everyone who can possibly do so, pay up their subscriptions promptly." By the spring of 1921, the cash flow problem had become an emergency. Frederick Christensen met with the organizers of the Seacoast Packing Company on March 19, 1921. "Richardson, Keyserling, Scheper, Niels and I got together (again!) and discussed packing house affairs," he wrote. "The situation seems pretty bad to . . . plan to fire Collier and put the office in the hands of trustees." In June 1921 the Seacoast Packing

Company agreed to lease its factory to the Southern States Packing and Provision Company for fifteen thousand dollars per year as long as fifteen thousand dollars in credit could be obtained from a local bank. Since the Seacoast directors and investors were also directors and major stockholders in the Beaufort Bank, this was easy to promise.

Despite an extremely generous lease offer and desperate attempts to get local investors to redeem their stock pledges, the Seacoast Packing Company was bankrupt by July 1922. Construction costs had ballooned 47 percent above original projections. The factory never saw a single day of operation. In 1923 bankruptcy Judge E. K. Bryan ordered the sale of the empty factory to R. C. Horne for eighty-five thousand dollars. He was practically the only bidder. Horne was president of the Beaufort Truck Growers Association and a director of the Beaufort Bank, from which he received credit for the purchase. The purchase price was barely sufficient to make partial payment to the Seacoast creditors. The stockholders lost their entire investment.[39]

The Seacoast Packing Company scheme had been promoted by Beaufort's leading businessmen. Its failure was said to be a great blow to the community's "confidence in their business judgment and integrity." But those men had honestly put up their own money and were the biggest losers in the bankruptcy. Niels Christensen and Sons, formerly the largest taxpayer in Beaufort County, struggled to remain solvent. In 1921 Frederick Christensen had to reduce expenses and trim the payroll because of the business depression. Lumber inventory was so large that space to store it had run out, and sales were so slow that the inventory was rotting on the lots. Frederick Christensen commented that the family company was "laboring along with a mass of obligations like a deeply laden freighter in a heavy sea." By 1925 the Christensen's ship went down. N. Christensen and Sons went into receivership in November 1925. In an act of good will, the Beaufort business community united to guarantee fifty thousand dollars of the Christensen's debt and keep the fifty-year-old-company afloat.[40]

The institution at the heart of business was the Beaufort Bank, which had been founded in December 1908 by twelve Bay Street merchants and professional men: P. M. Epstein, Charles E. Danner, J. M. Lengnick, Charles G. Luther, George Waterhouse Jr., R. R. Legare, Wallace and Danner, Inc., F. H. Christensen, P. L. Lea, P. A. Sauls, C. C. Townsend, and W. J. Thomas. They hired the dynamic young Walter E. Richardson as their cashier and chief operating officer. W. J. Thomas was the first president, and George Waterhouse Jr. was vice president. Original capitalization in 1908 was twenty-five thousand dollars, raised by selling 250 shares of stock at one hundred dollars per share. In 1914 the new bank was built on land purchased from the Waterhouse Company. The new building, with furnishings and an eight-by-ten-foot vault, cost twenty-two thousand dollars. Along with the People's

Bank at the other end of Bay Street, it was the most impressive commercial building in Beaufort. The architect was R. L. Lafaye of Columbia.[41]

The Beaufort Bank expanded rapidly under the leadership of Walter E. Richardson. By 1915, its assets exceeded two hundred thousand dollars, and branch banks opened in Yemassee, Varnville, Hampton, Brunson, and Estill. In large measure, the bank assumed the personality of its charismatic young chief operating officer. Walter E. Richardson had grown up in Beaufort, where his father, Dr. C. G. Richardson, practiced dentistry in the 1880s and 1890s. W. E. Richardson was educated at Beaufort College Graded School and was always at the top of his class. He was handsome, popular, and by World War I the fair-haired boy of Beaufort. He came to the bank from an earlier job at the Planters and Merchants Bank of Hampton. In 1915 he moved his young family into what was described as "a handsome new home on Boundary Street."[42]

The Beaufort Bank continued to grow, and by 1920 its assets, at $723,201.35, surpassed the older Peoples Bank. Deposits had risen from $61,301.88 in 1910 to $500,725.13 in 1920. The Beaufort Bank paid stock dividends every year from 1910. By 1921 those dividend payments exceeded $50,000 annually. In 1922 the Beaufort Bank became the first bank in the county to exceed $1 million in total assets. By any measure, the Beaufort Bank was a success. With numerous branches and connections to nearly every major enterprise in the region, the Beaufort Bank was the bellwether of the local economy.[43]

But trouble was brewing for the Beaufort Bank and for the local economy. In the mid-1920s, overproduction of Irish potatoes and other vegetables along the Eastern Seaboard eroded and then shattered the New York vegetable market. The heyday of truck farming was over by 1925. In addition, expenditures for Marine Corps training on Parris Island were sharply reduced after the war, especially during the parsimonious Republican administration of President Calvin Coolidge. In July 1924 the Beaufort Bank reached its pinnacle with assets of $1,391,321.95. Deposits were $822,451. But it would be another twenty years before any Beaufort bank reached that level. Ninety days after July 1924, deposits shrank 13 percent and assets declined 6.5 percent, never to rise again. By 1926 bank assets had declined 14.6 percent from their 1924 high. With loans and discounts making up 86 percent of its assets, and many of those loans uncollectible or questionable by 1926, the bank was in distress. During the weekend of July 10–11, 1926, rumors circulated through the town about the bank's shaky condition. On Sunday, July 11, a "large and representative gathering" of citizens assembled at the Community Club. The bank officers and directors explained that "the late season has delayed truck returns and they have been seriously curtailed by the break in the tomato market. But the Intermediate Credit Bank is giving every assistance."

With reassurances from Beaufort's leading businessmen, the *Beaufort Gazette* reported, the citizens "unanimously voted confidence in the condition and management of the Beaufort Bank." On Monday morning, July 12, 1926, the Beaufort Bank closed its doors for thirty days "to prevent a possible run."[44]

The closure froze the checking and savings accounts of a large portion of Beaufort's families and brought much of Beaufort's commerce to a dead stop. The bank was placed in the hands of the state bank examiner, W. W. Bradley, who made a preliminary examination and appointed W. J. Thomas receiver during the bank's reorganization or liquidation. Thomas appointed F. W. Scheper Jr., E. E. Lengnick, and R. V. Bray appraisers. The branch banks in Brunson, Hampton, and Varnville also closed on July 12, and the state bank examiner made L. B. Tuten, W. Fred Lightsey, and Hugh O. Hanna receivers of the branches. The bank at Yemassee was reorganized and bought out by a group of local investors led by B. M. Mixon. In September a Hampton County grand jury returned indictments against all the officers and directors of the Beaufort Bank and its four branches.[45]

The Beaufort Bank was not alone in its misery. In 1926, 120 South Carolina banks were in the hands of receivers. In October bank examiner Bradley was indicted for malfeasance and conspiracy. Governor Thomas McLeod named Albert S. Fant the new state bank examiner. Fant had a mess to straighten out throughout the state. The Beaufort Bank collapse was one of the largest and most contentious. When the local appraisers submitted their report to the receiver on October 21, 1926, they stated that the bank had liabilities in the form of checking accounts, savings accounts, and certificates of deposit in the amount of $723,990.63. Assets, mostly real estate and furniture, were worth $128,844.78. Depositors were going to recover only a pittance of their money.

The fallout from the Beaufort Bank collapse affected the region for years. Many leading businessmen and stockholders put up personal notes and real estate mortgages for the bank to use as collateral during its reorganization. Bank director and longtime Beaufortonian R. R. Legare managed the attempted bailout. When it became apparent that the bank was beyond reorganization, the bankruptcy judge, T. J. Mauldin, directed receiver W. J. Thomas to return all the notes and mortgages. By the end of 1926, the *Beaufort Gazette* was swamped by legal notices of creditors' suits against the Beaufort Bank.[46]

One aspect of the bank's failure that resonated for a decade was the failure of the bank officers to cancel properly several notes and mortgages that had been paid off by local property owners. This omission exposed the property owners to double liabilities for default. This problem came to light in December 1926, when the Federal Intermediate Credit Bank in Columbia, which had provided credit for the Beaufort Bank, informed R. T. W. Roberts of Jasper County that he owed a large amount of money for a bank mortgage that he had already redeemed. When the bank failed, local mortgagees and note recipients had paid off whatever notes they could to provide cash for the bank's reorganization. Bank officers, in some cases Walter Richardson himself, had told these customers they would receive their cancelled notes and mortgages in the mail. But those notes and mortgages were never cancelled and never mailed. When the Federal Intermediate Credit Bank in Columbia seized the paper assets of the Beaufort Bank, it was assumed that those uncancelled notes and mortgages were accounts receivable. A Columbia bankruptcy judge ruled in 1927 that the Federal Intermediate Credit Bank was entitled to collect on those notes and mortgages. The only recourse of local bank customers caught in this situation was to sue the Intermediate Credit Bank. Five years later, in 1932, the South Carolina Supreme Court decreed in favor of a property owner, John W. Gray of Burton, finally resolving the dispute in favor of landowners and against the Intermediate Credit Bank. During those years, some of Beaufort County's largest landowners and bank stockholders lived with both the threat of federal foreclosure and the bitter knowledge that they had been defrauded by their own bank and their friend Walter Richardson.

Several of Beaufort's wealthiest and most prominent citizens went bankrupt or had to sell off their assets to avoid bankruptcy. In January 1927 Beaufort County senator Patrick Wall was forced into bankruptcy. He lost his truck farms and packing sheds in Port Royal and Sheldon and was sued by a dozen creditors. Acutely embarrassed, he moved to St. Simon's Island, Georgia, declined to run for reelection, and stayed away from Beaufort for five years. Patrick Wall was also director of the Beaufort Truck Growers Association, a leader of the Port Royal Masonic Lodge, and a deacon of the First Presbyterian Church. He died the year he returned from Georgia at age sixty-four. N. Christensen and Sons was dragged into bankruptcy in 1927 due to its heavy involvement in the bank. Most of the notes offered to bailout N. Christensen and Sons in 1925 became worthless when the Beaufort Bank failed in 1926. Their newspaper property was auctioned in March 1927. The Waterhouse Company sold off much of the real estate that George Waterhouse Sr. had acquired during Reconstruction, including the lots along Ribaut Road and at Shell Point Farm. Another big loser in the Beaufort Bank failure was the former navy secretary Edwin Denby. Denby returned only once to Beaufort after the bank failure. He died in Detroit in 1929 at fifty-eight years of age.[47] The failure of the Beaufort Bank was a catastrophic event in Beaufort County's business life. It was the end of the business and commercial legacy of Reconstruction and the local beginning of the Great Depression.

The failure of the Beaufort Bank reached throughout the community. The Beaufort Truck Growers Association was deeply entangled with the bank. R. C. Horne was president of the association and had formed the Truckers Supply Company to supply ice, packing crates, fertilizer, and whatever material the truck farmers needed. The company was owned by the association's leading members and was heavily indebted to the bank. When the bank failed, the Truckers Supply Company also went belly up. The company had purchased several real estate parcels once owned by the phosphate companies, the most prominent of which was Spanish Point. This was the same site acquired by the American Shipbuilding Company in 1917. Horne had been president of that company as well. These properties had been used as collateral for loans from the Beaufort Bank, which provided operating capital for the Truckers Supply Company. In 1926 this financial house of cards collapsed, leaving the investors and partners in the Truckers Supply Company as broke as the stockholders in the Beaufort Bank.

One of Beaufort County's largest and most successful truck farmers, former state representative James Roe Bellamy, was forced into bankruptcy by the collapse of the Truckers Supply Company. Bellamy had used the profits from his successful vegetable farms to invest in Beaufort commercial property between 1916 and 1925. In 1927 the bankruptcy court foreclosed on a dozen of Bellamy's city lots on Bay, Port Republic, West, and Carteret Streets.

In October 1927 four of the most prominent real estate holdings of the Beaufort Bank were sold at auction. The Beaufort Bank building itself was sold to the People's Security Company of Charleston for $16,750. That amount was $8,250 less than the original cost of construction. A sizeable tract along Bay Street was sold to C. L. Baxter for $4,350. The Palace Market building, the old antebellum building built by Francis Saltus, was sold for little more than a $5,000 mortgage attached to the property. This was the only property where the bidding was competitive between Mr. Walsh, a truck farmer from Gray's Hill, and Calhoun Thomas, son of receiver W. J. Thomas. Calhoun Thomas was the successful bidder. Modern practices might question the discretion of allowing the son of the bankruptcy receiver to bid on property that was auctioned by his own father. Calhoun Thomas eventually acquired the old Custom House and industrial property on Spanish Point, previously owned by the Truckers Supply Company. Also sold at auction in October 1927 was a six-acre tract at the intersection of Depot and Ribaut Roads for $1,205. The successful bidder was the Christensen Realty Company, which had avoided bankruptcy when N. Christensen and Sons went under.[48] These property transactions and many others, emanating from the failure of the Beaufort Bank, represented a shift from old owners to new and, in many cases, from old money to new.

In addition to the myriad civil suits that resulted from the bank failure, several high-profile criminal cases were brought against the bank officers and directors. Indictments were filed in the state's Fourteenth Circuit Court. Walter E. Richardson hired young attorney Edgar Brown of Barnwell to defend him. Brown got the case moved from Beaufort to Jasper County, the only county in the Fourteenth Circuit that had no branch of the failed bank. On February 27, 1928, a Ridgeland jury convicted bank president Richardson and W. P. Jay, a cashier, of making false statements to the state bank examiner and sentenced each to one year in state prison or one year "on the public works of Beaufort County." Both had to pay a five-hundred-dollar fine. In the same trial, R. C. Horne was acquitted, in a directed verdict from Judge Milledge Bonham, of conspiracy in lending money to the American Shipbuilding Company.[49]

Far more serious and of higher profile were the indictments brought in Federal District Court in Columbia against W. E. Richardson, R. C. Horne, Beulah Harvey, H. B. Macklin, E. B. Mitchell, Harry Bowers, Patrick Wall, J. L. Butler, W. R. Eve Jr., J. Sims, and N. P. Bryan for defrauding the Federal Intermediate Credit Bank of Columbia of between $800,000 and $1 million. In addition to the huge sums involved, this complicated proceeding became the longest federal trial in state history up to that time. It garnered front-page coverage in the state's two largest newspapers for several weeks, beginning in January 1928. Early in the trial, charges against Mitchell, Wall, Butler, and Sims were dropped, and the trial continued against the rest of the defendants. The specific charges were "conspiracy to violate the federal farm loan act . . . and the making of false statements to obtain advantages of credit and influence from the Federal Farm Loan and Intermediate Credit Bank of Columbia." During the trial, testimony revealed that Walter Richardson had realized the crisis the Beaufort Bank was facing and tried to resolve it by misleading the Intermediate Credit Bank regarding the Beaufort Bank's solvency. Richardson and Horne had formed the South Carolina Agricultural Credit Corporation to provide credit for farmers. The prosecution asserted that this company was a fraudulent enterprise established to deceive federal bankers. Evidence included an admission by Walter Richardson that he had "signed names of other persons to paper for $110,000." One key piece of testimony was provided by young assistant bookkeeper Ed Nelson, who stated that he saw Beulah Harvey, the bank's chief bookkeeper, change one overdraft from the South Carolina Agricultural Credit Corporation from $128,089.11 to $6,131.31. Walter Richardson had signed off on that fraudulent alteration.

After providing this damning testimony, Nelson returned to Beaufort and married Pauline Thomas, daughter of receiver W. J. Thomas and sister of Calhoun Thomas. He was appointed city clerk and treasurer in 1931 and lived a quiet life in Beaufort for the next forty years. F. H. Daniel, manager of the Intermediate Credit Bank, testified that Walter Richardson had assured him that the South Carolina Agricultural Credit Corporation had only $200 in doubtful loans to Beaufort County farmers when the actual amount of uncollectible loans held by the company was closer to $200,000. Ultimately, the prosecution claimed that the Beaufort Bank and its agent, the South Carolina Agricultural Credit Corporation, had conspired to defraud the federal Intermediate Credit Bank of approximately $1 million.[50]

Further drama was added to the trial in Columbia when an unnamed assailant attacked R. C. Horne in the lobby of the Jefferson Hotel on January 23, 1928. Horne was only slightly injured, but presiding judge Ernest F. Cochran ordered special constables to protect the principals. On February 14, 1928, after six weeks of testimony, a federal jury convicted Richardson, R. C. Horne Jr., and Beulah Harvey of bank fraud. The four other defendants, W. R. Eve Jr., Harry Bowers, N. P. Bryan, and H. B. Macklin, were acquitted. A week later, Richardson and Horne were sentenced to one year in federal prison. Beulah Harvey was spared prison on a recommendation of mercy from the jury.[51]

The conclusion of the federal trial in Columbia was, of course, not the end of the case or of its political repercussions. Appeals lingered for more than a year and the political fallout reached to the White House. In March 1928 former governor and now senator Coleman Blease, a member of the Banking Committee, offered a U.S. Senate resolution calling for the Justice Department to investigate the Federal Intermediate Credit Bank in Columbia. Senator Blease also called for hearings before the Senate Banking Committee on the activities of the Intermediate Credit Bank. At the same time, Congressman Butler Hare of the state's Second District introduced a bill in the U.S. House of Representatives to have Beaufort County vegetable farmers "who lost heavily in the bank failure" receive retroactive credit from the federal bank in Columbia, which had been withdrawn at the time of the Beaufort Bank failure. The Hare Bill was never brought to a vote. Senator Blease's resolution failed in the Republican-controlled Senate, and the Justice Department stonewalled his call for an investigation. The Republican chairman of the Senate Banking Committee refused to schedule hearings. Senator Blease resigned from the committee in a huff and publicly blamed the failure to act on Secretary of the Treasury Andrew Mellon, perhaps the most powerful member of President Herbert Hoover's cabinet. With characteristic populist bombast, Blease accused Mellon of "hypocrisy and deceit" in covering up the "corruption" in the Columbia federal bank. This might have been bad politics in Washington, but it briefly made good press in South Carolina. It did little good for Blease, however. Two years later he was defeated for reelection in the Democratic primary by the consummate politician James F. Byrnes.

Rebuffed by Congress, Niels Christensen, a friend of Walter Richardson before and after the bank failure, enlisted the help of Senator Ellison D. "Cotton Ed" Smith and Representative William F. Stevenson to secure an audience with President Herbert Hoover. Congressman Stevenson, though not representing Beaufort County, had been a personal friend and political ally of Niels Christensen since 1907 when, as members of the General Assembly, they had worked together to expose corruption in the state dispensary system. On April 23, 1929, they met President Hoover in the White House. Christensen, Smith, and Stevenson appealed to President Hoover to urge his Justice Department to seek a new trial for Richardson, Horne, and Harvey. The president listened politely and did nothing. Attorney General W. D. Mitchell, refused to seek a new trial. Three weeks later, the legal appeals finally reached the United States Supreme Court. The high court declined to review the bank fraud case. It was the end of the line for Richardson, Horne, and the few supporters they had remaining in Beaufort.[52]

Richardson served his year in the Atlanta Federal Prison and then moved to Columbia, where he lived for thirty years, a bitter and broken man. Occasionally he returned to Beaufort, where he still owned a few small parcels of real estate. While in Beaufort he occupied a small office next to Frederick Christensen above the Christensen Hardware store. R. C. Horne served his sentence as the bookkeeper at the Women's Federal Reformatory in Alderson, West Virginia. Bette Eve, daughter of acquitted codefendant W. R. Eve Jr., married Johnny Horne (no relation to R. C. Horne), who acquired the bankrupt Ford dealership of R. A. Long and Pat Wall on Bay Street. Horne Motor Company was a commercial fixture until the 1960s. The business pioneer R. A. Long, who had built the city's first ice plant, its first electric power plant, the municipal water system, and directed the municipal public works department, was broken by the bank failure. He took his own life in Atlanta in 1935. Finally, in 1930 receiver W. J. Thomas liquidated all the bank assets he could find and distributed the proceeds to the Beaufort Bank depositors, who received approximately nine cents for each dollar they had placed in the bank.[53]

The failure of the Beaufort Bank did immense harm to the local economy and to local families. It created bitterness, distrust, and recrimination for many years and was talked about for generations. While most of the Beaufort community blamed Walter Richardson for the fiasco, a minority persisted in the belief that the bank could have been saved by reorganization. That group thought that its destruction was brought on by receiver W. J. Thomas to benefit his family and friends. The Christensen family, which saw its financial and political fortunes ruined by the bank failure, held to this conspiracy theory. The Waterhouse family, neighbors of the Thomas family at the east end of Bay Street, recalled the tragic death in 1914 of Thomas's little daughter,

Tennessee Thomas, who was kicked in the head by Harriet Waterhouse's horse, tethered in the yard next door. The Thomas family never forgot the tragedy. The Waterhouses, who lost a fortune and were nearly bankrupted by the bank failure, never spoke of it again. The two families lived next door to each other for more than sixty years.

A political turning point was tied to the Beaufort Bank failure as well. Before the bank collapse, Beaufort County politics was still dominated by the Christensen machine and their allies. When Senator Niels Christensen left office in 1924, he influenced the election of his friend, Pat Wall, to succeed him in the state senate. James Roe Bellamy, who served two terms in the state house of representatives,was also a friend and political ally of Niels Christensen. All of these men were major stockholders in the Beaufort Bank. None of them returned to politics after the bank failure.

Pat Wall was succeeded by Beaufort lawyer W. Brantley Harvey Sr., who was state senator for twenty-three years. Harvey served a decade as chairman of the Judiciary Committee, one of the most powerful posts in state government. Like Niels Christensen before him, Brantley Harvey's senate seniority made him one of the most influential politicians in the state. In 1928 Calhoun Thomas was elected to the state house of representatives. He too served for twenty years. For more than thirty years, Thomas was chairman of the local Democratic Party and the acknowledged political "boss" of Beaufort County.[54] Because Harvey and Thomas had come to Beaufort from Hampton County, where they descended from old, established families, they were called by some the "Hampton County gang." The appellation had historical meaning because the 1920s witnessed the end of a political coalition that had emerged from the commercial elite of Reconstruction Beaufort and the return to political dominance of the "old southern" families of Hampton County. In some measure the New South practitioners were replaced by the defenders of the Old South in the 1920s. Descendants of the Hampton County secessionists of 1878 had recaptured their homeland from the Republican carpetbaggers and blacks they had abjured fifty years earlier.

The bitterness and betrayal felt in Beaufort by the Beaufort Bank failure was expressed in a candid editorial in the *Beaufort Gazette* published shortly after the verdicts and sentences were handed down in Columbia. "We can look back now and see where many people in Beaufort County were made the laughing stock of others," the *Gazette* editorialist lamented. "On the night of the failure of the Beaufort Bank, how many true and loyal citizens lingered at the Community Club until almost daybreak ready and willing to do what was in their power to help reopen the bank. How many men and women traveled over the county . . . asking people to sign away their deposits for five years without interest." The people were not told at that time what only a few insiders knew, "that there was not the slightest chance in the world to reopen the bank .... No, instead of that, they went further and got people to give mortgages on their homes and then went out and sold them, getting mad at others who would not sign." Expressing sympathy for the small depositors and contempt for the "insiders" who used the bank's cash for their own benefit, the writer said, "We would like to know what became of the money that belonged to the depositors. . . . some depositors owed more to the bank than they ever had in the bank altogether."

The *Gazette* summarized the nature of the calamity to the Beaufort community: "Old men and women . . . have been left penniless. . . . young couples, happy in the thought that they would someday have a home that they might call their own and old negroes who saved for years what little they could spare from their small earnings were all rendered penniless overnight." The sentences had been too light to do justice to the distress, betrayal, and harm these bank manipulators had caused. Beaufort's economy and society "has been trampled on by some men who were held in the highest esteem by society."[55]

The Beaufort Bank failure was indeed a turning point in Beaufort County's business and political life. It marked the end of the grand plans and confident boosterism that had characterized Beaufort's business life since the Civil War. It discredited the New South ideologues who had dominated Beaufort's business, political, and social life since Reconstruction. It marked the end of one political faction and the rise of another. And behind it was the vague feeling that the children of the Yankee occupiers had finally been displaced by descendants of "secesh." But, more important than the disharmony and settling of old political scores, the Beaufort Bank failure of 1926 rung down the Great Depression upon Beaufort County.

Chapter 11

Low Life in Hard Times

Prohibition, Crime, and the KKK in 1920s

For a small community, Beaufort County had more than its share of crime and violence. Much of the crime and some of the violence were due to the continued activities of bootleggers and rumrunners, for which the area had become famous during state and federal Prohibition. One community response to the rise of crime and violence was the organization of the county's first chapter of the Ku Klux Klan. This, of course, marked the nadir of local race relations.

Beaufort County witnessed several sensational murders during the 1920s. While "sensational" murders in that era were usually interracial, not all of them were. In 1922 B. S. Brown and George Bettison, both well-known white men in Beaufort, engaged in an altercation on Bay Street in which Brown allegedly called Bettison a "vile name" and Bettison struck Brown in response. Brown's son, Ralph Brown, witnessed the fight and was dispatched by his father to Bettison's home to "straighten out the matter." During that visit, Ralph Brown struck Bettison in the head, and Bettison, an elderly man, died from the wound. During the trial in December 1922, Ralph Brown claimed self-defense, and a jury of prominent Beaufort white men acquitted him. The case was considered sensational because of the prominence of the perpetrators. B. S. Brown was the owner of Brown Furniture Company, a prominent Bay Street business. Although Ralph Brown was acquitted in court, the community generally condemned the Brown family for overreacting against the hapless George Bettison.[1]

In 1923 an altercation occurred between Beaufort merchant Abe Rudowitz and a former employee, George Fortin, who had moved to Savannah. When Fortin returned to Beaufort in June 1923, the two men encountered one another at the steamboat dock on Bay Street. An argument ensued. Fortin struck Rudowitz. In response, Rudowitz drew a revolver and shot Fortin four times, killing him on the spot. After a coroner's inquest and an investigation by Solicitor Randolph Murdaugh, no charges were brought against Rudowitz because many witnesses claimed his act was in self-defense.

Fortin's body was shipped to his home in New Bedford, Massachusetts, at the request of his family.[2]

A month later, on July 3, 1923, a fire burned down the store of Mr. and Mrs. W. D. Brown on Hilton Head Island. An investigation uncovered the bodies of the couple in the charred ruins. What at first appeared to be a tragic accident was later revealed to be a cold-blooded murder. The Browns were among only a handful of white people on Hilton Head. While no money was missing from the rural store, the couple's son-in-law, W. E. Campbell of Sheldon, pointed out that two of Brown's firearms, a shotgun and a pistol, had disappeared. Further investigation revealed that the couple had been bludgeoned to death before the store was burned.

Sheriff J. C. Bailey and W. E. Campbell followed the trail of the killers to the Hilton Head ferry landing where a boat and two pairs of oars had been stolen on the night of the murders. Two black men from Beaufort, Julius Garvin and Frank Gaines, were traced to Charleston, reportedly on their way to Philadelphia. When Garvin was discovered in the Charleston jail on larceny charges, officers searched his belongings in the presence of W. E. Campbell and discovered Brown's pistol, watch, and other belongings. Later Frank Gaines was arrested in Port Royal, and a search of his house on Jericho (Shell) Point uncovered more of the Browns' possessions, including the shotgun, which was hidden in an outhouse. Eventually both men admitted to the murders and were sentenced to death. Julius Garvin and Frank Gaines were electrocuted in Columbia on December 21, 1923.[3]

Occasionally, the Recruit Depot on Parris Island was the source of local crime and violence. On Sunday, April 5, 1924, three Parris Island recruits attacked and robbed Kit Singleton, Beaufort's best-known taxi driver. The men had hired Singleton's cab to take them to Yemassee. They were eventually captured by sheriff's deputies and turned over to the provost marshal on Parris Island. Singleton was not seriously hurt, but the incident was notorious because the victim was one of Beaufort's oldest and best-known black entrepreneurs. A more serious incident occurred a few months later when three Parris Island recruits deserted the post by stealing a boat. They rowed to Port Royal and tried to reach Yemassee. Sheriff Bailey apprehended two of the recruits and soon thereafter discovered the headless body of the third on Horse Island near Archer's Creek. It was later disclosed that the two recruit deserters had murdered the third to steal his money and clothes and had cut off his head to conceal his identity.[4] The Marine Corps did not take kindly to lawlessness by its recruits. That incident was the worst one of the 1920s, and very little local crime by Parris Island recruits was reported thereafter.

The most troubling murders of the 1920s, as today, were the killings of law enforcement officers in the line of duty. Two such incidents occurred in Beaufort County. On January 6, 1925, a "rural policeman" named Paul

Carden was shot and killed by brothers Willie and Ben Heyward while delivering a warrant to arrest Willie Heyward. Entering the home of Willie Heyward near Seabrook, Carden was met by the blast of both barrels of a double-barreled shotgun. He died within minutes. Carden's partner, Deputy Hubert Randall, exchanged gunfire with the fleeing suspects. Still under fire, Deputy Randall carried Paul Carden's body to their patrol car. Although the Beaufort County Sheriff's Department and those of neighboring counties were put on high alert, the Heyward brothers made good their escape.

On January 8, 1925, Carden was buried in Magnolia Cemetery on Bladen Street. The funeral was conducted by the chaplain of Ribault Chapter, No. 43, of the South Carolina Knights of the Ku Klux Klan. All the pallbearers were Klansmen in hooded regalia. The funeral was conducted according to established rituals of the Ku Klux Klan, of which Carden had been a member. The newspaper reporter noted that those attending Carden's funeral were "the most serious and determined looking crowd of citizens ever assembled in this community."[5]

The Paul Carden murder was the first case for Beaufort County's newly elected "boy sheriff," James Edward McTeer, then only twenty-two years old. Sheriff Ed McTeer never gave up on the case even though the Heyward brothers were long gone. Willie Heyward remained at large for seven years. In January 1932 he was arrested by police in Philadelphia and extradited to South Carolina. Subsequent investigation by McTeer concluded that Ben Heyward had been the assailant at the Seabrook gunfight. Ben Heyward remained at large for fourteen years until he was finally arrested in Akron, Ohio, in October 1939. Sheriff McTeer, Solicitor Murdaugh, Deputy Randall, and Highway Patrolman F. R. Harper traveled to Cleveland to take custody of the prisoner. Before Ben Heyward returned to South Carolina, however, the circumstances of his case attracted the attention of a prominent black attorney and Ohio state representative, Chester K. Gillespie.

Ben Heyward's extradition from Ohio to South Carolina became a minor skirmish in the early civil rights struggle. Lawyer Gillespie appealed the extradition request and received a delay from a Cleveland municipal judge. In the meantime, Gillespie used the *Cleveland Call and Post,* an African American newspaper, to publicize the case and elicit popular reaction. The story that Ben Heyward and lawyer Gillespie revealed—or concocted, depending on one's point of view—was one of a dramatic epic of fugitives from southern justice. Heyward claimed that in 1925 he and his brother were confronted by a large mob of white men following a dispute over pay with his white employer. The "mobsters," in Gillespie's account, fired into the house and burned the house down. Ben and Willie Heyward fired back in self-defense and killed Paul Carden in the shootout. The Heyward brothers escaped and lived in the swamp for four months before catching a ride on an empty railroad boxcar that finally stopped in Ohio. The brothers parted in Pittsburgh, and Willie Heyward was later arrested in Philadelphia. Ben Heyward had lived quietly in Akron for thirteen years. He was a World War I veteran and in 1938 was entitled to what was called "bonus pay" for his service. His wife in Beaufort threatened to reveal his whereabouts unless he turned over all his bonus pay to her. When he refused, she turned him in.

Lawyer Gillespie asserted that Ben Heyward could not get a fair trial in South Carolina because of "the atmosphere of race hatred and prejudice existing in [the state]." Gillespie called South Carolina "a savage and uncivilized state" and claimed that Heyward stood a good chance of being lynched, citing the 1930 record of South Carolina lynchings compiled by the National Association for the Advancement of Colored People. The case was appealed all the way to Ohio governor John W. Bricker. To counter the argument and the negative publicity, Sheriff McTeer proved to the Ohio courts and to the Ohio governor that there had never been a lynching in Beaufort County. The Ohio governor and Ohio courts agreed with McTeer. Ben Heyward lost his extradition appeal, Gillespie lost his public crusade, and the accused man was returned to South Carolina to face trial.

Ben Heyward was tried in the Beaufort County courthouse by Solicitor Randolph Murdaugh. On March 3, 1940, a Beaufort County jury convicted Heyward of murdering Paul Carden and sentenced him to death. On April 26, 1940, he was electrocuted at the Central Correctional Institute in Columbia. The trial concluded with compliments to "our fine solicitor" Randolph Murdaugh and with particular gratitude to Sheriff Ed McTeer for his "untiring efforts to capture Heyward."[6]

On June 6, 1927, black gunmen murdered another white Beaufort County law officer in the line of duty. Rural policeman E. F. Langford responded to a report of reckless driving on the Yemassee Highway (U.S. 21) by two black men and one woman in a Buick with Georgia license plates. Langford located the car and the Georgia men at a baseball game between a Beaufort team and a Savannah team at Gray's Hill. Attempting to arrest Frank Francis of Savannah, Officer Langford struck him with his pistol, and the man attempted to throw Langford to the ground by his collar. During the altercation, Paul Francis came up behind Langford and shot him twice in the back. W. A. McDaniel, who had accompanied Langford, returned fire with his two-shot derringer but retreated when Paul Francis and three other black men fired at him from different directions. McDaniel then went for help. Deputy Sheriff Gerald McTeer, W. A. Deloach, and Ralph Brown returned to the ball field to find a crowd of white men gathered at the scene. Four black men and one woman were on the run. The men were Frank Francis, Paul Francis, Sam Simmons, and Robert Adams. The woman was Ethel Francis, wife of Frank Francis. Abraham Gadsden was also identified as one of the gunmen. When the body of Officer Langford was retrieved, it was discovered that he had been beaten, kicked, stabbed, and otherwise brutalized while on the ground. The coroner reported that Langford had been shot twice in the back, shot twice in the hand, stabbed two times in the chest, bitten six times on the arm, and that his skull was crushed. A newspaper report concluded, "From the looks of his body, he was butchered up after being helpless on the ground." The sensational and brutal nature of the crime naturally aroused passions in the white community.

The Francis family, Simmons, and Adams were captured in Ridgeland while trying to escape to Georgia. This provided the community with the convenient scapegoat of "out-of-town trouble makers." An editorial in the *Beaufort Gazette* summed up the racial nature of the incident as follows: "The colored citizens in Beaufort, as a class, are law abiding and respectable and they do not approve of the lawlessness that characterizes these Georgia Negroes." The prisoners were sent to jail in Columbia for their own protection. On Monday, June 27, six prisoners were transported from Columbia to stand trial in the Beaufort County courthouse for the murder of Officer Langford. Tensions were so high, and the Beaufort community so rife with rumors of violence, that Governor John G. Richards ordered the 263rd Coast Artillery Battalion to guard the courthouse and sent a "Machine Gun Company" of the state National Guard to Beaufort to escort the prisoners to trial. Governor Richards declared, "There will be no lynching. The National Guardsmen are under orders to shoot to kill if necessary."

In this high-tension atmosphere, the trial proceeded. As the local paper noted, "Never has a trial excited such interest in Beaufort." After nearly a week of testimony and arguments, the trial concluded on Saturday, July 2, 1927. The jury deliberated for seven hours finally handing down three convictions for murder, two convictions for murder with recommendations for mercy, and one conviction for manslaughter. Ethel Francis and Robert Adams were sentenced to life in prison. Sam Simmons was sentenced to ten years in prison for manslaughter. Paul Francis, Frank Francis, and Abraham Gadsden were sentenced to die in the electric chair on August 12, 1927.

The executions were delayed by appeals, which did not reach the South Carolina Supreme Court until January 1929. Finally, Associate Justice Eugene S. Blease (brother of the famous governor and senator, Coleman Blease) upheld the convictions and sent the case back to Beaufort for a new execution date. The execution was then set for September 27, 1929, but three days before they were carried out, Governor Richards commuted the sentences to life in prison. The governor's decision was unpopular with most of Beaufort's white citizens, but Judge J. Frank Johnson, who presided at the trial, agreed with the governor's decision, except with his commutation of Paul Francis, whom Judge Johnson believed to be the real killer. Ultimately, no one was executed for the murder of Officer Langford.

When the *Beaufort Gazette* editorialized on the root cause of crime and violence in Beaufort County, in addition to blaming the convenient scapegoat of "Georgia Negroes" and other out-of-town troublemakers, it pointed the finger at "bootleg liquor." As the editorialist put it, "Bootleg liquor was largely responsible for the condition which brought about this murder and it was the duty of policeman Langford to suppress that traffic. There is something behind this killing more than the arrest he was making and it must be that some bootlegger took part in this killing from motives of his own besides the man who was being arrested."[7]

Indeed, national and state laws prohibiting the manufacture, distribution, sale, or consumption of alcohol during the 1920s instigated most of the crime in Beaufort County. Throughout the 1920s, enforcement of the Prohibition laws was the overwhelming preoccupation of federal, state, and local law enforcement agencies. The political road to Prohibition in Beaufort County had always been uncertain, even reluctant. Senator Niels Christensen always supported Prohibition, raised as he was in a teetotal household dominated by his reformist mother, Abbie Holmes Christensen. She was a leader of the local Women's Christian Temperance Union. Senator Christensen had led the fight to close the corrupt state dispensary in 1907. When Beaufort County chose to keep its local dispensaries open rather than go completely dry, Christensen authored legislation requiring countywide referendums in those counties that still sold liquor. In 1909 Beaufort County voted, narrowly, to continue selling liquor through the county dispensary, which dispensed forty thousand dollars in annual revenue to the county government, county schools, and the towns of Beaufort, Port Royal, Yemassee, Bluffton, and Ridgeland. In the public debate over the county dispensary in 1909, the chief defenders of the liquor trade were southerners, R. R. Legare in Beaufort and W. R. Hubbard in Hardeeville, while the proponents of Prohibition were northern-born Niels Christensen in Beaufort and J. Ross Macdonald on St. Helena Island.

When the local referendum was held in August 1909, the "wets" won a narrow victory with 277 votes for the dispensary and 239 votes against it, countywide. Only five counties remained wet from 1909 to 1915: Beaufort, Charleston, Georgetown, Richland, and Aiken. In those years before statewide Prohibition, Beaufort County officials found it nearly impossible to enforce the local dispensary law and close down the blind tigers. It seemed that nearly every sea island country store sold bootleg liquor and was a "menace to the good order of the community." Nothing highlighted this problem for local law enforcement more than the 1913 murder of Dispensary Constable J. R. Cooler on St. Helena Island.[8]

In the waning days of the liquor dispensary, the Kean's Neck community (Dale crossroads) held a public meeting in 1915 at their schoolhouse to consider incorporating the community. As on St. Helena Island more than a decade before, the promoters of incorporation of Kean's Neck candidly admitted that they aimed to permit a municipal liquor dispensary in the community. The local Baptist elder, Edwin Jackson, opposed incorporation and "fulminated against demon liquor." In a novel defense of the wet position, Henry Ben Barnwell pointed to the progress of the war abroad. The heaviest drinkers, the Germans, were on top, while the Turks, who were teetotalers, were on the bottom. Heyward's analysis of world affairs "got the loudest applause." Kean's Neck was never incorporated.[9]

In 1915 South Carolina held a statewide referendum on Prohibition. The national temperance movement sent a "flying squad" of activists, led by Oliver Stewart of Chicago, to Beaufort County, one of the few counties expected to vote wet. Temperance rallies led by the Women's Christian Temperance Union were held at the Carteret Street Methodist Church. The *Beaufort Gazette,* owned by the Christensens, came out strongly in favor of Prohibition. George Waterhouse Jr., also raised in a teetotal household, spoke at Prohibition meetings in Bluffton and Hardeeville, along with Mayor C. E. Danner of Beaufort. On September 14, 1915, South Carolina voted overwhelmingly for statewide Prohibition: 40,581–16,538. In Beaufort County the drys finally won a narrow popular vote victory, 188–156 votes. Of course, 1915 was deep into the Jim Crow era and few African Americans voted in the Prohibition referendum. In fact, two of only three precincts in Beaufort County to return a majority of wet votes were those controlled by the few black voters left in Beaufort County. Beaufort City Precinct No. 2 voted 34–10 against Prohibition, while St. Helena Island Precinct voted 9–2 against it. Notably, only twenty years earlier there had been more than six hundred registered voters on St. Helena Island. The third precinct to vote against Prohibition was the town of Port Royal, where merchants had succeeded for many years selling bootleg liquor to sailors and marines. Port Royal voted 19–0 against Prohibition.

Beaufort County's belated, divided endorsement of Prohibition barely slowed the liquor trade. South Carolina imposed statewide Prohibition on January 1, 1916. Barely eight months after Prohibition began, State Constable W. R. Pinckney estimated that eight thousand gallons of liquor were shipped into Beaufort County each month, only 25 percent less than had been regularly distributed by the county dispensary before Prohibition. Pinckney admitted that he had intercepted only one fourth of the illegal liquor shipments, and when he made an arrest, county courts often released his prisoners. In October 1916 state constables arrested two black men for transporting liquor to St. Helena Island. When they were arraigned before Judge Thomas Grimké White, he dismissed the case, saying, "White men do the same thing all the time."[10] It was an inauspicious start for Prohibition in Beaufort County.

On January 16, 1919, the Eighteenth Amendment to the Constitution was ratified. It declared the liquor trade illegal throughout the United States as of January 1920. This was backed up by federal legislation in the form of the Volstead Act of 1919. While these federal initiatives did not much change the situation in South Carolina, they added the force of federal law to the antiliquor crusade. They also added a substantial force of federal law enforcement officers and the seaborne power of the United States Coast Guard to the campaign against the illicit liquor trade. While much liquor was smuggled into the county, the majority of liquor sold and consumed was homemade. Isolated, often uninhabited islands were perfect locations for operating illegal stills. In addition, uninhabited woodlands in the southern parts of the county were havens where bootleggers operated undiscovered for years. Between 1920 and 1933, when the Eighteenth Amendment was repealed and Prohibition ended in the United States, more than 160 large, commercial-size liquor stills were discovered and destroyed in Beaufort County. That is one large still each month for thirteen years.[11] This count did not include hundreds of small stills operated for personal or neighborhood use.

When Prohibition began, Beaufort County's longtime sheriff was M. O'D. White, whose father, Judge Thomas Grimké White, had been notoriously lenient on local bootleggers. Sheriff White died in 1920, before national Prohibition took hold, and was succeeded by James Bailey of Bluffton. Bailey secured many liquor arrests between 1920 and 1925. In October 1921 he made fifteen arrests and destroyed nine stills in a single week, a record at the time. In 1923 he discovered the "largest still captured in the vicinity of Beaufort" on Eddings (now St. Philip's) Island run by "a man from Savannah." Prohibition enforcement occupied most of Sheriff Bailey's time and effort. Of twenty-six cases on the court docket for June 1924, seventeen, or 65 percent, were for bootleg liquor. Despite Bailey's efforts some Beaufort citizens were concerned that the liquor trade was flourishing and generating other forms of lawlessness.

In 1922 Mayor J. A. Kinghorn complained of lax enforcement of Prohibition laws and signed a city ordinance rescinding the taxi licenses of drivers convicted of liquor trafficking. And in 1922 concerned county citizens formed a Prohibition Enforcement Committee with A. P. Toomer as chairman. They were to "gather information on bootleggers and pass it on to proper authorities." Despite these efforts, the liquor trade flourished, and in 1924 Bailey lost his reelection bid to J. Edward McTeer, the "boy sheriff."

Citizens' misgivings about Sheriff Bailey were confirmed when in January 1932 he was arrested for bootlegging.[12]

McTeer remained sheriff of Beaufort County for thirty-seven years and became a legend as the "high sheriff of the lowcountry." His early career was consumed by trying to suppress the liquor trade in Beaufort County. As McTeer stated in his published memoir, "Moonshine stills were far from being a rarity in Beaufort County. . . . Quite the contrary, they were more than abundant." But Sheriff McTeer was a skilled outdoorsman intimately familiar with the woods and waters of his homeland. Few places in Beaufort County escaped his notice. Hilton Head was famous for making bootleg liquor. On September 30, 1926, Sheriff McTeer led a raid of county deputies, state constables, and federal agents from Savannah across the island. Four copper stills capable of producing eight hundred gallons of liquor were destroyed. While most of the moonshiners disappeared into the woods, McTeer arrested three of Hilton Head's leading bootleggers, Watson Gooding, Ezekiel Green, and W. M. Riley. A few days later he raided another notorious haunt of bootleggers at Red Bluff, an isolated neck south of the Broad River. There he destroyed four large copper stills capable of producing nine hundred gallons of liquor. While all the moonshiners disappeared, the raids were "the largest . . . made in Beaufort County within less than one week." The following year, Sheriff McTeer organized a sweep of the whole county, netting thirteen stills from Pritchardville to Dale in a single week. The largest seized were two copper stills at Bellinger Hill capable of producing 500 gallons of liquor. Altogether, the thirteen stills destroyed in the 1927 raid could produce 1,250 gallons of liquor, and all but one was operating at the time of the raid. In 1929 Sheriff McTeer destroyed a 225-gallon still on Morgan Island. Dennis Smalls, the alleged operator, of Lady's Island, was released on bond. In 1930, during a sweep of the south end of the county, McTeer discovered the largest single still ever found in Beaufort County during the Prohibition era. It was a copper still capable of producing 450 gallons of liquor. The operators were long gone. The largest capture occurred in March 1931, when eighteen stills capable of producing thousands of gallons of liquor were destroyed.[13]

Fortunately for Sheriff McTeer and his deputies, most bootleggers avoided confrontation with the lawmen. Many of those arrested were fined, given light sentences, and were back in business within the year. But there were occasional gunfights. In October 1928 Sheriff McTeer and rural policeman C. F. Koth led a waterborne raid on Pinckney Island. They destroyed four large stills capable of producing approximately six hundred gallons of liquor. The stills were estimated to be worth twelve hundred dollars, and they were just beginning to operate at full capacity in preparation for "the holiday crush which is only about two months off." Pinckney Island became the most dangerous place in Beaufort County for lawmen. In 1930 sheriff's deputies were forced off Pinckney Island three times by gangs of black men with guns. On January 25, 1931, Deputy W. M. Cooler and another lawman were fired on from the woods and nearly killed on Pinckney Island: The shots from concealment "tore through between the two men and knocked the mud from their coats." After demanding the surrender of the hidden gunmen and receiving no answer, the "two officers made their way to their boat and left." Sheriff McTeer stated that "this is the fourth time officers have been forced off this island. No white people live there and . . . they manufacture liquor and get it out on boats." It took Sheriff McTeer and ten deputies to force their way onto the island to destroy the stills.[14]

As numerous as were the stills, their economic value was modest compared to the smuggling of foreign "bonded," or manufactured, liquor into the United States. Beaufort County was perfect for smuggling. Thousands of miles of navigable rivers and creeks reaching thirty miles inland and spilling out to three large deepwater sounds with easy access from the ocean made Beaufort County irresistible. McTeer recorded that "stills were abundant to be sure, but even greater magnitude was the gigantic import business done by foreign companies. . . . These were the 'rum running days'! An era in which captured cargoes of fine quality contraband liquor were often valued at $100,000 or more."

Rumrunners often landed their cargo on isolated barrier islands and buried the whiskey for later transportation to the mainland. These nighttime landings were not always successful. In January 1922 a "liquor schooner" was driven ashore in a storm a mile south of Fripp Inlet onto Pritchard's Island. Sheriff Bailey had to borrow a boat from a friend to reach the site. The sheriff's party ran aground at Station Creek and spent a cold and stormy night in Port Royal Sound. The lawmen did not reach Fripp Inlet until late the next day. By then the liquor schooner had escaped. In October 1927 a seventy-five-foot "liquor runner," or high-powered speedboat, wrecked on Hilton Head Island. Before Sheriff McTeer could reach the wreck, the crew had escaped after burying most of its cargo. Sheriff McTeer later discovered forty gallons of corn whiskey, twenty-one bottles of bonded whiskey, and a "ten gallon keg of rare wine." This was only a fraction of the cargo that had been unloaded, but the estimated value of this fraction was twenty-eight thousand dollars.[15]

On September 22, 1930, a big boat reportedly operated by "Nassau Negroes" was captured in the Whale Branch River. This was the famous rumrunner *Joan Marie,* which had made several trips from the Bahamas in the 1920s. The captain, Octavus Russell, and the whole crew were all said to be from Nassau Island. They had unloaded most of the cargo when Sheriff McTeer seized the boat. A month later, another large rumrunner was captured on Lemon Island. The vessel was disguised as a "prawn boat" with commercial markings on the hull, a shrimp-trawling rig on deck, and a sixty-five-horsepower gasoline engine. The ice hold, where shrimp should have been stored, was filled with two thousand bottles of bonded liquor. Both of these cargos were destroyed at the dock on Bay Street and the contents poured into the Beaufort River. Only a few bottles were saved for evidence. Hundreds of townspeople gathered at the dock to watch the procedure, including several fishermen in boats, "hoping that the fish would all get drunk."[16]

The largest cache of contraband liquor during Prohibition was discovered in a "swampy lagoon" near Hardeeville, on November 1, 1928. There Sheriff McTeer confiscated and later destroyed eighteen hundred cases of Cuban rum worth $129,000. This load had been delivered by small speedboats, which had offloaded the rum from a freighter in the Savannah River. The smugglers had disappeared. A few months later a "Chicago style" crew unloaded a large rumrunner in a creek near Bluffton. Fifteen trucks, three automobiles, and more than a dozen guards armed with tommy guns were employed. The operation was so large that it attracted the attention of several Bluffton citizens. When C. W. Martin, owner of the local oyster factory, went to investigate, he was kidnapped at gunpoint, driven around the countryside for several hours, and then dropped off in Yemassee, thirty miles away. Several other locals glimpsed the operation and reported it to Sheriff McTeer, but the rumrunners were well on their way north by the time McTeer reached the scene. Two local men, Arthur Graves and Osborn Graham, were later arrested and fined for serving as "lookouts" for the smugglers.[17]

An automobile accident on the highway between Ridgeland and Hardeeville (still part of Beaufort County) in 1928 illustrated the resourcefulness of these "whiskey runners." On October 23, 1928, a Chrysler sedan was hit by a truck and overturned in a ditch. When Sheriff McTeer arrived on the scene, the driver was still there. The car contained 150 quarts and 60 pints of "old Kentucky bottle and bond." The auto had been extensively modified to make it a "special whiskey runner's machine." A false bottom had been built into the frame with the upholstery replaced to disguise the liquor tank. The trunk had a honeycomb to carry quart bottles. The driver had two Georgia license plates and two New York plates in the trunk. He was lodged in the Beaufort County jail but within twenty-four hours had paid his five-hundred-dollar bond with money wired from New York City. Sheriff McTeer estimated the car's contraband to be worth approximately five thousand dollars. He noted that these "liquor runners" had engines modified for speed, beefed-up suspensions to carry heavier loads, and often spiked their fuel with ammonia to create a smoke screen.[18]

The extraordinary effort to halt the liquor trade led to some overzealous law enforcement activities that infringed on civil liberties and occasionally led to tragedy. Federal Prohibition laws had given agents the right to enter and search private property without a judge's warrant. Unwise use of this extraordinary police power in a county where almost every household had firearms was a prescription for calamity. The two most celebrated cases of law officers trying to enforce unpopular laws were the Pittman case of 1925 and the Elliott-VonHarten case of 1928.

On the night of May 21, 1925, a federal Prohibition agent and two state constables boarded Captain L. G. Pittman's small commercial fishing vessel, moored for the night in the Whale Branch River. Pittman was sleeping on-board at the time. When agent Alonzo Seabrook entered the cabin, Pittman awoke, seized his Winchester rifle, and fired one shot before being killed by Agent Seabrook. The officers had been looking for rumrunners on Hall's Island and boarded Pittman's vessel suspecting that it was a smuggler's boat. No liquor was found on Pittman's boat, and landowners who had known Pittman claimed he was a harmless fisherman and trapper from Brunswick, Georgia, who sold his catch to local markets. Several prominent citizens became indignant over the killing of Captain Pittman and accused the agent of murder. Among them were W. A. Campbell of Sheldon and L. J. Williams of Coosaw. These men confronted Seabrook, who threatened to arrest them for "interfering with a federal officer" and boasted that he could not be arrested by any state or local law enforcement officials. Solicitor Randolph Murdaugh considered the coroner's inquest and issued a warrant for Seabrook's arrest on charges of murder. A Beaufort County Grand Jury agreed with Solicitor Murdaugh. Major Lloyd Grandy, the chief federal Prohibition agent in the state, defended Seabrook, claiming he was on duty pursuing a suspected smuggling ring. The case against Alonzo Seabrook and state constable Frank Harrington, charged as an accessory, was moved to the Federal District Court in Charleston. Eventually United States District Judge Ernest F. Cochran issued a directed verdict of "not guilty" for the two officers.

Beaufort citizens were not the only ones outraged by the Pittman murder case. The *State* newspaper called the federal officer's claim of immunity "grotesque." The *Anderson Mail* sympathized with Pittman's natural reaction to protect his floating home: "Aroused at the midnight hour by several men crawling on the deck of his boat, he shot. And he was shot down." The *Greenville News* headline on the Pittman case blared, "A sacrifice for prohibition." And the statewide weekly *South Carolina Gazette* commented that "such action as has been taken in the Pittman case will tend to arouse justifiable resentment and render the Prohibition law even more difficult of enforcement."[19]

The second case of too-zealous enforcement involved two of Beaufort's most prominent citizens. On May 2, 1928, Major Charles P. Elliott, a decorated World War I veteran, and Herman VonHarten were anchored off Bay

Point, fishing, when they were fired upon without warning by Coast Guard Patrol Boat No. 221. Elliott and VonHarten claimed that their boat was hit several times and that one bullet passed within six inches of VonHarten's head and lodged in the wheelhouse of Elliott's boat. The fishermen were so angered by the assault that Elliott lodged a formal complaint with the adjutant general of the army requesting a court-martial inquiry. VonHarten swore out a warrant with Sheriff McTeer against the commander of the Coast Guard patrol boat.

The Coast Guard reported very different circumstances. Chief Boatswain's Mate Sodderberg, commanding Patrol Boat No. 221, claimed that he hailed Elliott's boat, and when it did not stop, he directed six shots across the bow. When Elliott's boat halted and was searched by the Coast Guard crew, they found no illegal liquor and saw no evidence that their shots had struck the boat. When Charleston County sheriff J. M. Poulnot attempted to serve the warrant for Sheriff McTeer, the commandant of the United States Coast Guard base in Charleston, Lieutenant Paul W. Collins, refused to surrender Sodderberg.

Within a few weeks, the Coast Guard sent a board of inquiry from Norfolk, Virginia, to investigate the incident. The board convened at the Community Club, and although a large crowd had gathered to support the local men, the officers insisted on holding their investigation in secret. Eventually, the board of inquiry upheld the Coast Guard's version of the incident. As no one had been harmed in the confrontation, the matter was dropped.

In addition to the Pittman and Elliott cases was the celebrated case of Beaufort mayor Richard Van Bray. On March 12, 1923, Bray won the Democratic primary for mayor of Beaufort. The victory virtually assured him of winning the office in the May election. Before he was installed, however, he got into an altercation with a federal revenue agent on Bay Street. The dispute turned to fisticuffs and was witnessed and likely cheered on by a sizeable crowd. Bray badly beat the federal officer, much to the delight of the locals. The fact that agent Harold Smith was from Massachusetts added fuel to the altercation and made Bray a champion of southern honor. The cause of the altercation was never made clear. Many assumed it had to do with overzealous use of federal law enforcement authority, but family tradition held that the federal agent made an insulting comment about the "Waterhouse women," one of whom, Jane Waterhouse, was R.V. Bray's wife. Whatever the cause, Bray was indicted and convicted in federal court of "interfering with a federal officer in the discharge of his duty." He was sentenced to serve a year in the Atlanta Federal Penitentiary.

In June 1923 Mayor Bray surrendered to federal marshals in Charleston. In a show of solidarity with the popular mayor, a large portion of the county's political and commercial leadership accompanied him. The Beaufort delegation included Trower Craven, chairman of the Beaufort County Democratic Party and the man R.V. Bray bested in the March primary election; Johnny Morrall, representing the chamber of commerce; J. C. Sparks from the city council; F. B. Webb, representing the board of trade; and Senator Christensen. In addition, J. Heyward Jenkins, J. B. Keyserling, Walter Barwick, and Homer Young, personal friends of R.V. Bray's, accompanied the party. Senator Christensen also took a group of local leaders and Bray's family members, including W. J. Thomas, Walter Richardson, Reverend F. G. Helms, Reverend C. B. Burns, Mrs. George Waterhouse Jr., and Mary Waterhouse, to Washington, D.C., to appeal the verdict against Bray. Accompanying the Washington delegation was J. Fraser Lyon of Abbeville, former state attorney general and one of the state's most distinguished lawyers.

Despite these appeals, Mayor R.V. Bray was incarcerated in the Atlanta Federal Penitentiary. While serving his sentence, Bray continued to conduct city business by letter and telephone. The story was picked up by newspapers across the South with the regular headline, "Mayor Was Directing City Affairs From His Jail Cell." Bray served less than half of his one-year sentence. The political campaign on his behalf eventually reached President Calvin Coolidge, who signed an order for his release. Bray was back in Beaufort by November 23, 1923.

As with many political issues of the day, Beaufort's man of influence in Washington was Congressman Jimmy Byrnes. Not only did he get the president to release Mayor Bray, but he also engineered the removal of the obnoxious Agent Smith from South Carolina with the observation that "Smith should be inflicted on the constituents of those congressmen who reside in Boston."[20]

These three cases pitted local authorities against federal authorities and, in the minds of Beaufort County citizens, illustrated the high-handed nature of federal law enforcement. Prohibition laws became increasingly unpopular as the decade of the 1920s rolled on, and eventually a movement to end Prohibition gained momentum. In May 1930 attorney Claude Aman announced that he would be a candidate for South Carolina's Second Congressional District. The principal issue on which Aman intended to campaign was "repeal or modification of the Eighteenth Amendment." Aman had spent much of the previous decade representing bootleggers and rumrunners in the Beaufort County court and knew firsthand how unpopular and unenforceable the Prohibition laws had become. In addition, an outspoken wet candidate for governor, Ashton Williams, campaigned across the state in 1930 advocating a repeal of the Prohibition laws. Although Claude Aman received few votes against the incumbent congressman, Butler Hare, Ashton Williams was the clear Beaufort County winner in the gubernatorial primary. Williams also won in Charleston and Florence Counties. The primary returns prompted the *Beaufort Gazette* to ask, "Is Beaufort County wet?" The local newspaper stated that ending Prohibition would put the bootleggers out of business, get "rotten intoxicants" off the market, and relieve "the crushing burden of taxation." In addition, "It has been apparent during the recent years that it is almost impossible to enforce the liquor laws."

In February 1931 a statewide movement was organized in Columbia dedicated to repeal of the Eighteenth Amendment. Thirty men from around the state formed the group, and Beaufort County representative J. Heyward Jenkins was elected permanent chairman. The public statement the group released said that "the very foundations of our state and national government are being threatened, those rights that South Carolina has always held dear are being trampled, racketeering is becoming rampant. . . . the liquor traffic, though one of the largest businesses in the country is being carried on untaxed. The law has failed."[21]

Repeal was the principal dispute at the 1932 state Democratic Party convention. While the delegates sharply divided over Prohibition, they were united to nominate Governor Franklin Delano Roosevelt of New York for president. At the national convention, South Carolina delegate F. A. DesPortes, a state senator from Winnsboro, was one of four delegates asked to address the convention on the subject of Prohibition. When he demanded that the Eighteenth Amendment be "ripped out of the Constitution and not leave one vestige there," he got the loudest applause from the delegates. DesPortes resigned from the state senate in 1933 to become a prominent New Deal diplomat in Latin America and an architect of Roosevelt's "Good Neighbor Policy" toward Central and South America. He died in Gorgas Hospital in the Panama Canal Zone in 1944.[22]

In 1933 the Beaufort County legislative delegation took the lead in attacking Prohibition. Representative C. W. Martin of Bluffton introduced the "Beer Bill" in the house, calling for state-regulated, state-taxed liquor sales. Calhoun Thomas championed the bill to enactment. In the senate, Beaufort County's W. Brantley Harvey introduced a measure to provide local control of the liquor trade and distribute most of the liquor tax revenue to the wet counties. In November 1933 South Carolina held a referendum on the repeal of the Eighteenth Amendment. While the state voted narrowly against repeal (32,994–31,236), Beaufort County voted overwhelmingly for repeal (287–45). In the Port Royal and Hilton Head precincts, only one voter supported Prohibition in 1933. On St. Helena Island, only two voters remained dry.[23] Franklin D. Roosevelt had campaigned for repeal in the race for president, and on December 5, 1933, the Twenty-first Amendment was ratified to repeal the Eighteenth Amendment. It was one of the first accomplishments of FDR's "New Deal for the American people." It ended Prohibition in America and the rumrunning wars in Beaufort County.

The 1920s also saw the first appearance of the Ku Klux Klan in Beaufort County. When the Klan was founded during Reconstruction and became prominent in some upcountry South Carolina counties, its presence in Beaufort County would have been pointless, even dangerous. The well-armed, politically active black majority would not have permitted it. But as the Jim Crow years deepened and the black majority left the county, the sea islands and vicinity began to look and behave more like the rest of the Deep South. Crime, violence, and the perceived or imagined influence of "outside troublemakers" were the primary justifications for the appearance of the Ku Klux Klan in Beaufort County.

As of September 16, 1921, Beaufort had its first organized chapter of the Knights of the Ku Klux Klan. The local chapter was dubbed Ribault Chapter, No. 43. Beaufort's reaction to the appearance of the KKK may have been unusual for a small southern community. As Frederick Christensen noted in his diary, "The colored people and some whites have been agitated over the forming of a band of the KKK. . . . it has been met with a good deal of opposition so they are very much on the defensive. . . . the whole thing seems to be falling to pieces." But the Ribault Chapter did not collapse. It prospered during the 1920s, garnering several hundred members, sponsoring numerous public events, and exerting considerable political influence. At the time of its formation, the local newspaper was still owned by the Christensens, who published national and local opinion pieces critical of the Klan. In response, local organizers defended the Klan in the *Beaufort Gazette,* which it published in its dedication to free speech and a free press. The result was a lively, revealing debate on one of the most sensitive subjects of southern history.

The leader of Beaufort's Klan chapter was Charles L. Paul. He was a well-known and generally popular character in Beaufort, having served two terms on city council. Charlie Paul was very open in his opinions but immediately found himself on the defensive. The *Beaufort Gazette* published quotes from the *New York World* attacking the KKK and reprinted in full an article from *Leslie's Illustrated Weekly* entitled "A Nightgown Tyranny," that compared KKK tactics to Russian Communists and early Italian Fascists. The *Gazette* criticized the terror tactics of the old Reconstruction-era Klan and asserted that its presence in Beaufort would breed suspicion, anger, and mob violence. The editorialist, doubtless Niels or Frederick Christensen, noted, "here in Beaufort we have a community notable for the good feeling that exists between the races and where there is that religious tolerance that is one of the blessings this government was founded to preserve."[24]

In response to this attack, C. L. Paul forwarded a letter from Elizabeth Tyler of Atlanta, Georgia, who was "grand chief of staff of the women's division of the Klan and head of the propaganda department of the organization." She strenuously denied Klan lawlessness and, regarding the Klan's supposed prejudice against blacks, Jews, and Catholics, she said, "I take exception to the statement that the Ku Klux Klan is anti-Jew and anti-Catholic. On the contrary, it is a Christian, Protestant organization. . . . Any fraternal organization has the unquestioned right to select its membership and this organization is no more anti-Catholic than the Knights of Columbus are anti-Protestant and no more anti-Jew than the Sons of Israel are anti-Gentile."

Local kleagle Charles L. Paul assured the mayor that no parades would be held in Beaufort and that all local members had pledged "to uphold the law and . . . that no methods would be tolerated that are contrary to the law." Even Beaufort's most prominent attorney, W. J. Thomas, when asked by Frederick Christensen, said he believed the local Klan "had some good intent." Such assurances did not convince many Beaufort County citizens. In October 1921 the *Gazette* noted, "Reports continue that suspicions as to the purposes of the Klan, especially among the colored people of the county are creating uneasiness."[25]

In November 1921 a new and locally influential voice entered the debate on behalf of the Klan. Reverend Maynard Marshall of St. Helena's Episcopal Church wrote a long editorial that was placed on the front page of the *Gazette*. Reverend Marshall stated that because he had been criticized, he should offer his opinion. Reverend Marshall said that he had "diligently sought information" regarding the Klan and had concluded "that the KKK is not 'anti' anything . . . that its purposes are honorable and constructive and that its methods are scrupulously law-abiding." Reverend Marshall delivered his opinions of Catholics, Jews, and blacks. He claimed to admire the Roman Catholic Church and then described in detail his theological differences with the Papacy. He professed love for "the Great Hebrew Race" and his pity of them for their rejection of Jesus Christ as the Messiah. While he professed to welcome Jews to the United States, he did "absolutely resent that the name of Jesus Christ should be hesitatingly spoken in legislative halls or on political occasion; or that institutions, holidays, social practices or common phraseology of Christian character should be haltingly used under government auspices out of deference to Jewish sentiment." Regarding African Americans, Reverend Marshall had this to say: "I love the Negro race. I have been in charge of Negro churches and hope to be so again. I desire for the Negroes in America more than justice and free opportunity for self-development. I regard them as our weaker brothers who rightly demand our love and help. But I am of the profoundest conviction that the solution of the 'Race Problem' in America is to undo the grievous error perpetrated by and upon our nation in enfranchising the Negro." He then recommended constitutional repeal of the Fifteenth Amendment. As outrageous as Reverend Marshall's printed opinions may seem in the twenty-first century, they were probably not far from mainstream Protestant thought in 1920s America.

Reverend Marshall's bold defense of the KKK drew swift, eloquent responses from local and national sources. In the next issue of the *Gazette,* Beaufort's most prominent Jewish businessman, William Keyserling, asked a series of questions. Keyserling questioned the "love" Reverend Marshall professed for Catholics, Jews, and blacks. He also challenged Marshall and the KKK to "reconcile a professed, unqualified allegiance to the Constitution . . . with an organized effort to impede the operation of the fundamental guarantees of citizenship to the Negro and freedom of religion to the non-Christians or non-Protestants."

Reverend Marshall also received a learned response from Rabbi Meir Jaffa of New York, who challenged Maynard Marshall's basic "philosophy of history . . . that down to the Great War, God was running history autocratically, but since that event, He seems to be willing to take advice from good people, preferably Anglo-Saxon Protestants." The essence of this revised and modern moral philosophy seemed clear to Rabbi Jaffa—that "the apparently strong should be made stronger and the apparent weak should be made weaker, all in accordance with the teachings of Nietzsche." Some of Beaufort's most prominent women also publicly criticized the Klan. Abbey Holmes Christensen and Clare Macdonald formed a branch of the Committee on Interracial Co-operation. They privately chastised Reverend Marshall. The Macdonalds left St. Helena Church. Mary Waterhouse publicly upbraided the Klan when it tried to take over the Community Club.[26]

Learned philosophical arguments and civil action aside, the most effective weapon against the Ku Klux Klan in Beaufort County was ridicule. Max Lipsitz, one of Bay Street's most prominent Jewish merchants, attended one of Klan's first meetings held at the Carteret Street home of Beaufort attorney George Beckett. One Klan member noticed Lipsitz and declared, "Max, you can't join the Klan, you're a Jew!" To that Lipsitz replied, "Don't worry boys, I'm not here to join. I just came to sell ya'll some sheets." Even the Klansmen broke up in laughter. The joke circulated around town in a matter of hours and has been repeated for seventy-five years. Max Lipsitz's humor has been a metaphor for Beaufort's attitude toward the Ku Klux Klan for most of the twentieth century.

Sheriff J. E. McTeer did not take the Klan very seriously. He pointed out in his memoir, "Beaufort's Klan was a source of enjoyment to all her people. Everyone loves a parade and when Klansmen with their colorful robes would announce they would march, black and white would line the streets to see the preacher on his white horse lead them." Even though the Klansmen wore concealing robes, McTeer noted that Beaufort's black citizens amused themselves by identifying the men in disguise: "Standing with them, I would hear my colored friends identifying them as they passed."

McTeer recalled a single incident of mob action by the Ku Klux Klan in Beaufort during the 1920s, and that turned out to be a good laugh as well. An old fisherman on Albergotti Creek named Brooks had taken up with a black common-law wife. They lived in a shack by the creek and sold oysters. This situation offended the Klan's moral and racist sensibilities, so it organized a mob demonstration, or "night raid." At the time membership was declining, and this raid aimed to reinvigorate the organization. On the appointed night, the Klansmen gathered at Brook's shack. There was little secrecy in the event because everyone in Beaufort had known about it for days. Brooks and his wife were well prepared, "waiting on either side of the door, he with a shotgun and she with a chamber pot." As two night-riders broke into the house, according to a popular account, Brooks fired the shotgun over their heads and his wife "began dealing telling blows with the chamber pot, both yelling like Comanche's." The Klansmen ran through the bushes in full retreat, and "pieces of cloth which hung on the cat claw briers defined the path of the Klan's retreat." Once again the Klan had become an object of ridicule.[27]

Despite its marginal existence, the Ku Klux Klan did exert some political influence, even if peripheral, and contributed to the rightward shift in the local Democratic regime. There were still a few black voters in Beaufort County, and their waning influence was exercised through black civic and fraternal organizations and their churches. An outspoken leader of the African American community was B. H. Houston, former chief of police and a retired officer in the South Carolina National Guard. When the Ku Klux Klan formed in Beaufort, Houston gave voice to the opposition and suspicion of the African American community. Many blacks remembered a time only a few years past when black voters controlled Beaufort's municipal politics. As a consequence of his leadership in opposing the Klan, Houston received a threatening note: "Ben Houston: You are given three weeks to leave the city. You and your club have spoken against the KKK. You are the leader." There was no signature. The anonymous, secret threat of violence was a common Klan tactic, but it caused such uproar in Beaufort's white community that Charlie Paul was forced publicly to disavow any association with the note: "I am in a position to say most positively that no person connected with the Knights of the Ku Klux Klan had any relation to or even any knowledge of this missive." Whether the Klan was guilty or not, community pressure once again forced it to retreat.

In 1923 several prominent Beaufort municipal leaders—Mayor R.V. Bray, Albert Kinghorn, Hal Pollitzer, and Reverend Burns of the Carteret Street Methodist Church—walked out of a Klan meeting, which led to a brief boycott of the Kinghorn and Christensen businesses. A year later, the Klan was more successful in attacking Senator Christensen. On March 14,

1924, the KKK sent an anonymous letter to all members of the state senate asking that Christensen be expelled, threatening personal violence if the request was not heeded. The letter stated, "Christensen has done all in his power to attract their [KKK] attention and will have only himself to blame if he becomes their guest." The letter blamed the Bay Street fire of 1924 on "the oppressive conduct of the Christensen family." While the letter was unsigned, the text referred to Beaufort lawyer George Beckett and old Beaufortonian C. S. Johnson. Both denied authorship. No one admitted sending the letter, but two pamphlets accompanying it were traced back to Beaufort attorney Claude Aman.

While KKK influence may have contributed to Senator Niels Christensen's retirement in 1924, it was unlikely that it played a major role.[28] The larger reason for the decline in influence of the Christensen faction was economic. Niels Christensen was closely associated with several high-profile and costly business failures in the 1920s, including that of N. Christensen and Sons in 1925. These failures and the sharp business decline that hit Beaufort in the 1920s undermined the credibility of the progressive Democratic faction. In addition, the Christensens stated that their patriarch was supporting a wife and four small children with high family expectations. They maintain that he left politics in order to make a living. Nevertheless, the Ku Klux Klan seemed to have had a role in the rightward lurch of Beaufort County's Democratic establishment in the 1920s.

The Ribaut Chapter of the KKK was visible and prominent in Beaufort throughout the decade. For many years the city of Beaufort had an ordinance forbidding "masked parades." When the Klan controversy erupted in 1921, Charlie Paul had given his assurances to Mayor J. A. Kinghorn that the Klan would hold no parades in the city limits. But in 1924, the ordinance was amended to permit such parades upon special request. Thereafter, the Klan openly paraded in Beaufort and held their fiery cross ceremonies on "their own ground on the corner of Boundary and Charles Streets."

The Klan also participated in civic and community events. In 1924 the KKK made a "handsome donation" to the Parent Teacher Association of the new Port Royal Elementary School. The money allowed the association to purchase and install "an electric light plant" for the school. On Christmas Eve 1925, the Ribaut Chapter sponsored "a Santa Claus attended by Klansmen in regalia" in downtown Beaufort. Santa, called Kris Kringle, was to "add to the common cheer of Christmas" for the children of Beaufort. The local Klan was quick to announce, "All children irrespective of race, creed or color, are invited to approach him without fear."[29]

The pinnacle of Klan influence in Beaufort County came on June 14, 1927, when Ribaut Chapter, No. 43, hosted the regional convention, or "Klonverse," of all Klan chapters in lower South Carolina. More than a thousand Klansmen from Aiken to Charleston descended on Beaufort. Special train cars ran from Columbia and Charleston, and hundreds of automobiles clogged the streets. The crowd of delegates was too large for the Community Club so they met in the auditorium of the Beaufort Graded School three blocks away. The state Grand Dragon, Albert Hill of Spartanburg, addressed the delegates, and Klanswomen provided refreshments. A parade in full regalia, with the Grand Dragon as parade marshal, was staged on Carteret and Bay Streets. Because the 1920s Ku Klux Klan considered itself a nativist, patriotic organization, it always held ceremonies on June 14, National Flag Day. In 1927 a huge American flag led the parade through Beaufort, and all the Bay Street merchants displayed the Stars and Stripes. The Klonverse of 1927 was the high point of Klan influence in Beaufort County and a commercial success.[30]

Throughout the 1930s the Ku Klux Klan remained active and politically influential in upstate South Carolina. Their particular targets in the industrial cities of Greenville and Spartanburg were labor organizers and black voter-registration drives organized by the Communist Party of the United States of America. In 1934 a Klan chapter was organized in Bluffton. Fifty men paraded in regalia and conducted a fiery cross ceremony. A local commentator noted that "Bluffton has been notably depopulated since the night of the parade."[31]

During the 1930s the Ku Klux Klan in Beaufort County declined in membership, and their public activities virtually ceased. In 1939 the local Ribaut chapter of the KKK tried to revive the organization by holding a large meeting and parade. The organizers asserted, "The Klan is coming back in leadership as it was in 1928."[32] But the public parade never occurred and the local chapter never regained the public influence it had during the 1920s.

Chapter 12

High Life in Hard Times

PLANTATION SOCIETY OF THE 1920S AND 1930S

As the economy of Beaufort County and the lowcountry collapsed, the value of real estate also declined. The end of commercial rice production in the lowcountry in 1914, the disappearance of commercial cotton due to the ravages of the boll weevil in 1917 and 1918, and the collapse of the vegetable market in 1925 and 1926 meant that there were few profitable uses for the once-rich plantation land of the sea islands and lowcountry. As a consequence, the value of lowcountry real estate fell steadily for two decades. Treasurer Rivers Varn calculated in 1936 that the total value of all taxable property in Beaufort County in 1935 was $3,851,210. That amount was 6 percent lower than it had been eight years before (1927: $4,096,670) and virtually the same as it had been seventeen years before (1918: $3,847,813). The stagnation and decline of lowcountry land values encouraged a new kind of land speculator during the 1920s and 30s.[1]

This was the era when wealthy northern families or hunt club groups bought up vast acres of lowcountry land and set them aside for hunting and outdoor recreation. These large private estates and hunt clubs employed the land for its lowest and least productive possible use. In a historical sense, the land reverted to the same use that precontact Native Americans made of it—hunting wild game that the land naturally produced. Only this time, the hunters did it for sport, not for food. Hundreds of thousands of acres of lowcountry land were thus taken out of production and utilized for the amusement of a privileged few. The economic consequences of this movement were not lost on local politicians.

In 1917 local economic boosters and political leaders from Beaufort, Jasper, Hampton, and Colleton Counties formed the Southern Carolina Association to encourage the economic development of the region. In their minds, one of the largest obstacles to the economic development of the four-county area was what they called the "hunting club evil." At that time nearly half of the land in Jasper County was owned by hunt clubs or by "wealthy residents of other states." The leaders of the Southern Carolina Association were Senators Henry Klugh Purdy of Jasper County, Edward R. Ginn of Hampton County, and Niels Christensen of Beaufort County. These men invited South Carolina attorney general Thomas H. Peeples to meet their association in Beaufort to determine what legal or legislative action they might take to encourage hunt club members and owners of large estates to open up their properties for development. They proposed to regulate South Carolina hunting licenses "in proportion to the acreage controlled." Larger holdings would pay higher fees for hunting licenses. They also proposed to levy a special property tax on very large hunting preserves: two cents per acre for every acre over five thousand acres, four cents per acre for every acre over thirty thousand acres, and five cents per acre for every acre over fifty thousand acres. The hunt clubs hired Charleston and Ridgeland attorneys to represent their interests. Clearly the "special tax" was unconstitutional, but the political threat prompted Senators Christensen and Purdy to meet privately with Landon Thorne of New York, treasurer of the vast Okatee Club. The senators asked the club to develop part of their holdings to "help the local economy." Thorne asserted that the Okatee Club had no desire to sell any of their holdings, but they would be willing to lease some of their property for agriculture to assist financially the Southern Carolina Association and cooperate with the county governments in "drainage, good roads and school improvement." The Okatee Club also agreed not to lobby against the hunt club legislation in the General Assembly. While the special tax was never enacted, the large northern property owners in the lowcountry found it advantageous to cooperate with the local and state political establishment.[2]

But the lowcountry's economic decline was not caused by the "hunt club evil." Rather, the hunt clubs were a symptom of the general agricultural depression that had been underway for decades. And the acquisition of very large tracts of lowcountry land for winter recreation and hunting brought some of America's most prominent business and industrial luminaries to the plantation lands of the Old South. Thus, a new and different plantation society emerged in the early twentieth century, as signaled by the organization of the Carolina Plantation Society on March 23, 1932. Membership in this exclusive club was limited to "bona fide non-resident owners of, and part-time residents upon, a plantation in the coastal section of the State of South Carolina." This exclusive club limited its membership to seventy and permitted only 25 percent of its members to be local residents. In addition, those local memberships were restricted to Charleston residents. As stated in the group's constitution, "The objects of the society shall be to promote the social pleasure of its members, and the assembling and exchange of information." The formation of the Carolina Plantation Society in 1932 was the formal recognition of a historical movement that had been underway since the 1870s.

In Beaufort County this movement was begun by J. Donald Cameron, a Pennsylvania senator and President Ulysses S. Grant's secretary of war, who began regular visits to the old Coffin Point Plantation in 1878. He bought this property in 1889. For thirty years he spent several months each winter at St. Helena-by-the-Sea. A retinue of distinguished northern guests often accompanied Senator Cameron and his wife, General William Tecumseh Sherman's niece. William P. Clyde, the New York shipping magnate and owner of the Clyde Line company, followed the Camerons. During the 1890s Clyde accumulated more than twenty thousand acres of sea island cotton land on Hilton Head Island. He used the island as a private hunting preserve and winter retreat for twenty years. Also, in 1890 Harry B. Hollins, New York investment banker and J. Pierpont Morgan's business partner, bought Good Hope Plantation in Beaufort (now Jasper) County. Hollins's three sons, Harry Jr., Gerald, and Jack, also bought lowcountry estates. Jack Hollins married a local girl, Sallie Mae Kitchings, spent most of his life in Beaufort, and became the local contact for the northern "plantation set." The last Hollins property in the lowcountry, Broadmarsh, was sold in 1949. The most famous of Harry B. Hollins's children was Marion Hollins (1892–1944), one of America's best women golfers in the 1920s, who became a California real estate developer. She then founded the world famous Cypress Point Golf Club at Pebble Beach, California.[3] Another pioneer of this new plantation society was Richard T. Wilson of New York, who purchased the 18,500-acre Palmetto Bluff tract from Colonel J. H. Estill of Savannah in 1902. There he built the largest private residence ever built in Beaufort County and invited members of the most prominent Gilded Age families to join him for winter sojourns. Since Wilson's son married Caroline Astor and his daughter married Cornelius Vanderbilt II, these sojourns were obviously successful.

In addition to these large private estates, northern businessmen pooled their capital to form large, incorporated hunt clubs. The leader in this movement was the vast Okatee Hunt Club organized in 1894. Eventually the Okatee Club encompassed fifty thousand acres of what is now Jasper County. A lavish clubhouse was built to entertain winter members and guests, and a private stop on the Charleston and Savannah Railroad was established for the convenience of the members. By 1909 three more hunt clubs—the Chelsea Club, the Spring Island Barony Club (1902), and the Good Hope Club—had absorbed thousands more acres of the lowcountry.[4]

By the 1920s this recreational use of Carolina plantations. begun by the Camerons, Clydes, Hollinses, Wilsons, and Okatee Hunt Club, had entered its second generation. The collapse of the local economy coincided with the peak of local influence of this new plantation society. The World War I era saw significant changes among these large property holdings. The financial Panic of 1907 wrecked some of these early investors, including Harry B. Hollins. J. P. Morgan helped the Hollins Company through that downturn, but with Morgan's death in 1913, H. B. Hollins and Company was forced into bankruptcy. In 1909 Good Hope Plantation was sold to Herbert Pratt, but Harry Hollins Jr. had purchased Broadmarsh Plantation on the Pocotaligo River in 1904 and that property remained in the family for thirty-five more years. In 1912 the Spring Island Barony Club was sold at auction by a court-appointed liquidator, Henry Buist of Charleston. Colonel William M. Copp of New York purchased Spring Island out of bankruptcy. He owned Spring Island until his death in 1940. In 1916 William P. Clyde sold Honey Horn Plantation and all of his Hilton Head lands to New York investor Roy Rainey. Clyde died in New York City in 1923 at the age of eighty-four. About the same time another wealthy northern family made its first investment in Beaufort County. In April 1909 Mr. and Mrs. J. Sergeant Cram of Philadelphia bought the five-thousand-acre Foot Point Plantation, part of the colonial Devils Elbow Barony on the Colleton River. Nearly a century later, Cram family descendants still own considerable property in Beaufort County.[5]

The early twentieth century was also the era of grand yacht travel. In the Gilded Age, it was fashionable to travel south aboard palatial steam yachts, often flying the burgee of the New York Yacht Club. Many of these large vessels "wintered" in Beaufort. Senator Donald Cameron usually traveled to Coffin Point aboard his yacht *Almeda*. Richard T. Wilson kept the *Alice* at Palmetto Bluff and used it to ferry guests and supplies from Beaufort and Savannah. His son-in-law, Cornelius Vanderbilt II, occasionally brought his 233-foot steam yacht *North Star* to Beaufort County in the early twentieth century. As maritime technology advanced, steam yachts were superseded by smaller, sleeker, and more efficient gasoline-powered yachts. In 1917 Richard T. Wilson Jr. replaced the *Alice* with a "new motor boat cruiser" for Palmetto Bluff. This new vessel was a forty-foot "military type express cruiser of the submarine chaser type." It had two six-cylinder gasoline engines and could cruise at twenty-two knots. During the summer, Wilson took his new yacht north for use with the New York Yacht Club cruise to Newport, Rhode Island.[6]

Another yacht regularly in use in Beaufort County was the *Sabege* of William L. Hurley of Camden, New Jersey. Hurley bought Dr. Francis Wilder's Otter Hole Plantation on Hilton Head Island in 1916. Each winter until his death in 1928, he came south with the *Sabege* and used it to transport guests to Hilton Head and to entertain them with cruises among the sea islands. In January 1921 the *Sabege* took a "jolly crowd" of northern guests from Hilton Head up the Broad River to Sheldon to attend a hog sale at Oak Grove, the plantation of Hurley's friend W. E. Campbell.

During the 1920s large private yachts stopped in Beaufort on their way to and from Florida. In March 1923 six yachts were anchored off Beaufort at the same time. They were the *Thelma,* the *Ambassadress,* the *X.L.,* the *Everglades,* the *Colita,* and a yacht belonging to Felix du Pont. Another grand yacht that regularly visited Beaufort was that of Solomon Guggenheim of New York, who went quail shooting with his old friend Harry B. Hollins Sr. One of the last of the great yachts to visit Beaufort was the presidential yacht *Sequoia,* which stopped in Beaufort on March 3, 1932. The *Sequoia* carried First Lady Lou Henry Hoover, wife of President Herbert Hoover, to Florida. Mrs. Hoover spent the night in Beaufort, where she was generously welcomed by the local Daughters of the American Revolution. Mrs. Hoover also made a courtesy call to Parris Island.[7]

The most regular visitor was Harry Payne Whitney's *Captiva.* Whitney (1872–1930) was one of the most socially prominent of the plantation set. He came from an old New York real estate family and was president of Whitney Realty Company. He was also director of the Guaranty Trust Company and chairman of the Metropolitan Opera Company. Most important, in 1896 he married Gertrude Vanderbilt, daughter of Cornelius Vanderbilt I. Harry Payne Whitney was thus the brother-in-law of Grace Wilson Vanderbilt of Palmetto Bluff. Whitney owned Cypress Plantation on the Combahee River. Almost every winter during the 1920s, Whitney left the *Captiva* moored in the Beaufort River while he hunted at Cypress Plantation. The Captiva was "luxuriously appointed" and had a crew of fifteen. Captain Cole and the *Captiva* crew were well known in Beaufort during the 1920s. Each year, on their departure, the captain and crew treated their local friends to a "farewell dance" at the Community Club.[8]

The 1920s saw a generational shift in the lowcountry plantation society. Richard T. Wilson (1829–1912), J. Donald Cameron (1833–1923), and William P. Clyde (1839–1923) were all gone. Some of their heirs tried to maintain the tradition and others sold out. Some were burned out. On Tuesday, March 2, 1926, the mammoth Wilson mansion at Palmetto Bluff burned to the ground. It was never rebuilt, and later generations of Wilsons, Astors, and Vanderbilts vacated the lowcountry. On July 21, 1927, forty-one thousand acres of the Wilson-Vanderbilt estate in Beaufort and Jasper counties were sold to W. H. Page of Lyons, Georgia, mostly for timber. The sale price was $450,000. With forty rooms and a ballroom, the Wilson mansion at Palmetto Bluff was the largest private residence ever built in Beaufort County. The mansion enclosed 23,550 square feet of floor space. Its destruction in 1926 was an epitaph to the Gilded Age in the Carolina lowcountry.[9]

The Roaring Twenties brought new owners and new money to the impoverished lowcountry. In 1926 Arthur Lyman of Boston bought Bonny Hall on the Combahee River and Felix du Pont bought Nemours just down the river. In 1927 Joseph S. Stevens of New York City bought Myrtle Grove Plantation on the Colleton County side of the Combahee River. In April 1927 Gerald Hollins, son of Harry B. Hollins, twin brother of Jack Hollins, and a member of the New York Stock Exchange, bought Speights Plantation on the Ashepoo River, continuing his family tradition in the lowcountry.

In May 1927 a major new investor made his first purchase in the lowcountry. Charles Lanier Lawrance was a neighbor of Harry B. Hollins in East Islip, Long Island, and had often visited the lowcountry as his guest. Lawrance first purchased Whitehall Plantation in Colleton County and the following year bought Hamilton Ridge Plantation on the Savannah River in Hampton County. The Hamilton Ridge tract contained more than thirteen thousand acres. The agent for both purchases was Jack Hollins. Charles L. Lawrance was an important example of the "new money" of the 1920s. He made his fortune as "one of the pioneers in the field of aviation." Lawrance gained fame and fortune as the designer of the "world renowned Whirlwind Motor." Lawrance's nine-cylinder, 250-horsepower, radial aircraft engine propelled the *Spirit of St. Louis* and Charles A. Lindberg on the first solo flight across the Atlantic Ocean in 1927. When Lindberg became a national icon of American courage and ingenuity, the men who built his aircraft shared in his glory. Charles L. Lawrance's company was bought out by the Wright Aeronautical Company, established by Orville and Wilbur Wright, and Lawrance became the company president. It was noteworthy that the first members of the "plantation set," Donald Cameron and Richard T. Wilson, had made their fortunes building railroads and William P. Clyde by owning steamships. The "new money" that replaced them was acquired building aircraft, the newest form of transportation.[10]

In August 1927 Bayard Dominick of the New York investment-banking firm of Dominick and Dominick bought Gregorie Neck Plantation on the Tullifinny River. Gregorie Neck Plantation contained more than two thousand acres. It was bought from the Garbade family of Ridgeland and George Garbade was retained as caretaker for the Dominicks. In October 1927 C. E. Hutton of New York City, a member of E. F. Hutton and Company, bought four Combahee River rice plantations: Laurel Spring, Rose Hill, March, and Stock Plantations. Together they encompassed more than four thousand acres. The seller was Theodore P. Ravenel of Charleston, who last harvested rice at Laurel Spring and Rose Hill in 1925. Hutton owned country homes in Roslyn, New York, and Palm Beach and was a member of the New York Yacht Club. A few months later, his more famous brother, E. F. Hutton, bought Prospect Hill Plantation on the Edisto River and Cypress Plantation on the Combahee River. Both plantations encompassed more than five thousand acres. The agent for these transactions was Jack Hollins in association with Christensen Realty Company of Beaufort. In 1927 Hollins used his commissions to purchase Paul and Dalton Plantation on the Combahee River. It adjoined the former estate of Harry Payne Whitney, Cypress Plantation, acquired by E. F. Hutton.[11]

Large purchases continued. J. Sergeant Cram purchased Victoria Bluff in March 1928. The site adjoined his Foot Point property acquired twenty years before. The Victoria Bluff site, "one of the best deep water frontages on Port Royal Sound," had long been envisioned as an industrial site for sawmills and shipping wharves. At one time it had been promoted as the Atlantic terminus of the Southern Pacific Railroad. Mr. and Mrs. Cram planned to use the property as part of their hunting preserve. In July 1928 Z. Marshall Crane of Dalton, Massachusetts, bought Hope Plantation on the Edisto River and commissioned Charleston architects Simons and Lapham to build a hunting lodge there. Marshall Crane (1878–1936) was the owner of the Crane Paper Company of Massachusetts, a director of the Boston and Albany Railroad, and son of U.S. Senator Murray Crane of Massachusetts. Both of these transactions were handled by Jack Hollins and the Christensen Realty Company.[12]

In the spring of 1929, Philip A. Carroll bought Federal Hill Plantation on the Pocotaligo River in Beaufort County. Carroll was a New York lawyer with the Sherman and Sterling law firm, a large Maryland property owner, and a direct descendant of John Carroll of Carrollton, signer of the Declaration of Independence. Federal Hill comprised sixteen hundred acres of rice fields and high ground. Carroll was a friend of Harry B. Hollins Jr., and once again, Jack Hollins was the sales agent. The Pocotaligo region was a distinguished neighborhood in the late 1920s. Federal Hill Plantation was surrounded by prominent neighbors. To the north was Robert McCurdy's Tomotley Plantation and the Lorillard Estate, owned by E. E. Lorillard, son of Pierre Lorillard, founder of the giant tobacco company and developer of Tuxedo Park, New York, where several of the plantation set had their permanent residences. E. E. Lorillard was married to Bessie Screven, daughter of Confederate hero Major John Screven, who had once owned Castle Hill Plantation at Pocotaligo. In 1929 Castle Hill was owned by John Stanton Williams of New York. To the south was Harry B. Hollins Jr.'s Broadmarsh. Across the Pocotaligo River in Jasper County was the 6,000-acre Mackay Point Plantation owned by Dr. George Widener of the Philadelphia utilities fortune, and next door to him was the 3,000-acre Gregorie Neck Plantation of Bayard Dominick. Just up the road was the 5,000-acre Buckfield owned by S. H. Kress, founder of the Kress five and dime retail chain. Kress had a private railroad siding off the Atlantic Coast Line that ran through Buckfield Plantation. In 1928 and 1929, 140,000 acres of Beaufort and Jasper County plantation lands changed hands. Most of these plantation sales were managed by Jack Hollins.[13]

Another influential family with large property holdings in the lowcountry was the Pratt family. Frederick Pratt was president of Standard Oil Company and an associate of John D. Rockefeller Sr. and Jr. His brother, Herbert Pratt, acquired Harry B. Hollins's Good Hope Plantation in 1909 and was a fixture of the plantation set in the 1920s. In May 1929 Frederick Pratt concluded "one of the largest real estate sales ever made in this section" when he assembled ten antebellum plantations into the giant Chehaw-Combahee Plantation in Colleton County. The whole tract encompassed nearly all of Colleton Neck from the Chehaw River on the east to the Combahee River on the west. It included the antebellum plantations of Whaley, Magwood, Oak Hill, Middleton, Riverside, Tar Bluff, Woodburn, Brick House, Walnut Hill, and Field's Point. The Chehaw-Combahee Plantation of Frederick Pratt engrossed more than ten thousand acres. The mainline of the Seaboard Air Line Railroad ran through the plantation, and the town of Wiggins was right in the center of the property.

Chehaw-Combahee Plantation included some of the Carolina lowcountry's most historic places. At Tar Bluff in August 1782, Colonel John Laurens was killed in a skirmish with the crew of a British galley on the Combahee River, one of the last battles of the Revolutionary War. And Chehaw Plantation was the location of many hunting tales in William Elliott's 1846 classic *Carolina Sports by Land and Water.* In fact, *Carolina Sports by Land and Water* was kept in print during the 1920s and 1930s by the Abercrombie and Fitch Company of New York, which used the book to help sell fashionable sportswear to the Carolina plantation set. Frederick Pratt's Combahee-Cheeha Plantation is today the heart of the ACE Basin environmental preserve. The Standard Oil connection to the lowcountry was completed when Frederick Ewing, the company vice president, purchased Huspah Plantation in Beaufort County from Elizabeth Crofut Waterhouse in 1936. Huspah had been the last large tract assembled by George Waterhouse Sr. during the prosperous years of Reconstruction.[14]

The crash of the New York Stock Exchange that began on October 23, 1929, had a profound effect on the lowcountry plantation society. Many of these men had made their fortunes in stock speculation, and many others, as bank officers, directors, and stockholders, had financed that speculation. The stock market crash ruined several plantation owners, and the Great Depression that followed hurt most of the rest. The wave of large land purchases that characterized the period from 1927 to 1929 ended abruptly. During the

1930s, as the national and local economies hit bottom, the annual migration of northeastern socialites, financiers, and industrialists grew less frequent and less ostentatious.

Later generations of the plantation set did not always prosper in the lowcountry during the Depression. In 1932 Richard T. Wilson Jr.'s daughter Louisa Turnure, described as a "fashionable divorcee and sportswoman," married Wendell Simmons, the manager of her plantation near Bluffton. They were married in Ridgeland by Jasper County clerk of court Dan Horton. At the time of their marriage, Wendell Simmons was under a twenty-two month sentence for bootlegging. In 1933 tragedy struck the extended family when young William K. Vanderbilt Jr., age twenty-six, was killed in an automobile accident outside Ridgeland. Another sad event occurred in 1934 when young Edith Drexel Cram, wife of Harry Cram of Foot Point Plantation, died suddenly of pneumonia in New York City. She was only twenty-two years old, had spent most of her brief marriage in Beaufort County, and was a popular visitor to Beaufort. Edith Drexel Cram was the daughter of Philadelphia financier Anthony J. Drexel and the granddaughter of the famous "Robber Baron" Jay Gould. Edith Drexel Cram's death was compounded by the death of the infant to whom she had just given birth. The tragedy reportedly "cast a spell of gloom over the Bluffton community."[15]

During the 1930s several large land purchases were made by investors with more than transitory, recreational interest in the lowcountry. Descendants of local families returned as large landowners or replaced the northerners. In 1931 Henry Legare Sanders (1876–1932) returned to Beaufort to join with his brother-in-law James O'Hear Witsell in purchasing three thousand acres of phosphate company land on Chisholm Island. Sanders was a local boy who had made good. He had been raised in Beaufort, second son of Colonel Joseph O'Hear Sanders and Mary Sue Goethe Sanders. During the 1890s he was educated at Beaufort College Graded School, where his father was principal. As an accountant for the Atlantic Coast Line Railroad, he had accepted an accounting position with the Cincinnati Car Company in Ohio, major manufacturers of electric streetcars. By 1910 Sanders was treasurer of the Cincinnati Car Company, the Cincinnati Traction Company, and the Ohio Traction Company. In 1925 he became vice president of the Cincinnati Car Company. From 1929 to 1931 he was president of the Cincinnati Car Company, one of the major industrial enterprises of the Ohio Valley. In 1931 he took early retirement to enjoy the pleasures of his youth—hunting and fishing in the lowcountry. H. Legare Sanders died, unmarried, at the home of Dr. M. G. Elliott in Beaufort in 1932. Chisholm Island passed to his sister and brother-in-law.[16]

In 1933 Arthur Barnwell Jr. (1878–1955) of New York City bought Cuthbert Plantation on Lady's Island and spent many of his later years in

Beaufort. His purchase of the old plantation made Barnwell "one of Beaufort's largest landowners." Arthur Jr. was a success story of the post–Civil War planter diaspora. Arthur Barnwell Sr., fifth son of Edward Barnwell III of Prospect Hill on the Edisto River, was forced by necessity to become a Charleston cotton factor during Reconstruction. Very successful, he amassed a fortune that exceeded four hundred thousand dollars and in 1880 bought the old Buena Vista Cotton Mill in Greenville County. This became the Pelham Mills Company, one of the most successful textile mills in the South. He and his wife, Maria Wilkinson, moved to New York City, where they raised their four surviving children. Arthur Barnwell Jr. was educated at Episcopal High School in Alexandria, Virginia, and Phillips Andover Academy in Massachusetts; he graduated from Yale in 1903. He was a star athlete who was offered a contract to play professional baseball with the Cleveland Indians. Arthur Jr. was equally successful in business. In 1907 he became a member of the New York Stock Exchange and formed his own investment firm, Arthur Barnwell and Company, at 100 Broadway. He lived at 25 Fifth Avenue. In 1935 he retired from active business, saying, "The New Deal has taken all of the fun out of the stock market." Thereafter, he spent much of his time at his Pleasant Point estate. There he built a mansion with an indoor swimming pool and spent the 1930s entertaining a parade of fashionable friends from New York while contributing to the economy and civic life of Beaufort. Arthur Barnwell Jr. died in Charleston in 1955. He had no children.[17]

Occasionally the northern plantation set, beleaguered by the Great Depression, were bought out by local investors, reversing the trend of the previous fifty years. Such was the case in 1936 when Charles L. Lawrance, the aviation pioneer, sold his huge Hamilton Ridge Plantation of 13,378 acres to Hampton County senator George Warren. This return of a great tract to local ownership was "regarded locally as a sign of better times and of better local demand for land." Eventually Senator Warren amassed 25,000 acres of land and became "the largest individual landowner in the lowcountry." Senator Warren was a founder of the South Carolina Wildlife Commission in 1952 and was its first chairman. Much of George Warren's property is now Lake Warren State Park in Hampton County.[18]

Some northern investors preferred to make their imprint on the lowcountry through architecture. Kate Gleason (1865–1933) of Rochester, New York, had the largest impact of the era in the town of Beaufort, and her influence is apparent there eighty years later. Gleason was an heir to the fortune left by her father, William Gleason, the founder of the Gleason Gear Works. That company was and remains one of America's premier machine tool companies, credited with inventing and perfecting the bevel gear, without which modern, high-speed machinery would not work. A precocious, ambitious Cornell graduate, Kate Gleason made major contributions to her father's success. She was secretary-treasurer of the company from 1890 to 1913, the first woman inducted into the American Society of Mechanical Engineers in 1914, and the first female president of a national bank, the First National Bank of East Rochester in 1918. She came by her enterprise and progressive feminism honestly. Her father was a visionary industrialist, and her mother, Ellen McDermott Gleason, was a supporter and benefactor of Susan B. Anthony and the suffragette movement. While serving as the bank receiver and later president, Kate Gleason became interested in architecture and house design, particularly the construction of prestressed concrete houses, of which she built many in East Rochester. She was the only female member of the American Concrete Institute. Real estate development became her passion. After World War I, she rebuilt much of war-torn Septmonts, France, and in 1927, she commenced the first housing development at Sausalito, California.

Kate Gleason came to Beaufort in 1926 at the urging of her young administrative assistant and traveling companion, Elizabeth Sanders. Libby Sanders was the daughter of Lawrence Witsell Sanders and Adelaide Waterhouse and H. Legare Sanders's niece. She was born in New York, raised in Montclair, New Jersey, and graduated from Smith College in 1924. Libby Sanders spent much of her youth in Beaufort at the Bay Street home of her grandmother, Harriett L. Waterhouse. She loved the town and insisted that Kate Gleason come to see it. It was a fortuitous visit. Gleason fell in love with Beaufort and began buying local property at a time when Beaufort badly needed investment. In 1927 Kate Gleason formed a real estate development company called Sea Islands Incorporated to "buy, sell and develop real estate, to build homes for tourists . . . to build apartments and hotels." Gleason bought the De Saussure-Verdier property on Bay Street, Verdier Bluff and Gage's Sawmill on the Beaufort River Bluff, Datha Island, and a large tract on Lady's Island. She had plans to develop all of her property but only realized a few of them before her death in 1933.

On Lady's Island, Kate Gleason built Colony Gardens, a winter resort of cottages and apartments with a swimming pool, river dock, and an eighteen-hole golf course. Colony Gardens was the first commercial golf resort in Beaufort County. It opened in 1933. Kate Gleason's most important contribution to the Beaufort economy was the construction of the Gold Eagle Tavern, which opened on February 7, 1930. The Gold Eagle Tavern was built at the east end of Bay Street. For twenty-five years it was Beaufort's premier hostelry and a famous center for writers and artists. The Gold Eagle brought luster to the city during the impoverished 1930s, but its architecture was uncharacteristic. Gleason had become enamored of French provincial architecture during her trips to Europe and imposed this style on the Gold Eagle Tavern, complete with a three-story, round turret overlooking the Beaufort River. The Gold Eagle was managed by Belle and Lorenz Wilder, former proprietors of the River View Hotel, which had burned in 1925. In 1935 the Wilders bought the hostelry from Gleason's estate. When she died in 1933 without direct heirs, Gleason left much of her estate, estimated to be $1.4 million dollars, to be used for scientific and educational enterprises of benefit to Rochester, New York, and Beaufort. Eventually the trustees donated Kate Gleason's property on Verdier Bluff for a park and the site of Gage's Sawmill for a community hospital. Kate Gleason Memorial Park and Beaufort Memorial Hospital on Ribaut Road are Kate Gleason's most prominent legacies in Beaufort.[19]

In 1930 Frederick H. Barnes of Bay Shore, Long Island, New York, bought Fort Fremont at Land's End, St. Helena Island, from the War Department. The property included concrete artillery bunkers, outbuildings, and 175 acres. The price paid was reportedly "the largest paid for a county estate on the coast to date." Barnes hired a New York architect to design a "Spanish Villa" in a style Addison Mizner had made popular in Florida. Frederick Barnes planned to create a sunken garden in the old artillery emplacements. Barnes had a number of Long Island friends "who are also contemplating acquiring country estates on St. Helena." It was hoped that a winter colony of wealthy northerners would "restore some of the former glory to the island." A large movement of wealthy northerners to St. Helena Island never occurred in Barnes's lifetime. Today Fort Fremont is being redeveloped as a Beaufort County park.

Another wealthy northern investor on St. Helena Island was Dr. A.W. Elting of Albany, New York. Dr. Elting was chief of surgery at Albany Hospital and professor of surgery at Albany Medical College. Dr. Elting bought part of the Tom Fripp Plantation at the north end of St. Helena Island. His new hunting retreat included the site of St. Helenaville, the antebellum planters' summer resort and a Civil War refugee camp on Village Creek. It also included Pine Island, a jewel of the sea islands that thrusts into the Morgan River with unobstructed views of St. Helena Sound and the Atlantic Ocean. In 1931 Dr. Elting built his hunting lodge on Pine Island in the "great camp style" of the Adirondack Mountains. The dark brown shingle exterior with dark green trim was unlike traditional sea island architecture, but the lodge, in the words of the *Beaufort Gazette,* "slipped with effective unobtrusiveness into the brown and green woods which surround it." The bricks for the foundation, the timbers for the frame, the solid mahogany staircase and the "handsome hand carved mantles" had been salvaged from the ruins of Dr. Joseph Jenkins's plantation mansion at Land's End, from whose veranda St. Helena planters had watched the Union navy steam into Port Royal Sound on November 7, 1861.[20]

More typical of the era of the plantation society was the large brick mansion built at Clarendon Plantation on Port Royal Island in 1935. Clarendon

Plantation was a five-thousand-acre estate assembled in 1928 by H.W. Corning, "a capitalist of Cleveland, Ohio." The property included the sites of the earliest English settlements on the sea islands. Corning's mansion overlooked Whale Branch River near the site of John "Tuscarora Jack" Barnwell's 1704 trading camp. The house contained eighteen rooms and cost nearly seventy-five thousand dollars. The new brick structure, reminiscent of the Virginia tidewater, was "given a coat of whitewash, which lends it a mellow air of age." The grounds around the house were covered by "hundreds of azalea and japonica bushes . . . making the Corning estate a veritable fairyland." Clarendon Plantation is one of the few surviving large estates in the rapidly developing sea islands. For many years it has been owned by the family of Ann Cox Chambers, proprietors of the Cox communications empire, which owns the *Atlanta Journal and Constitution.* Ann Cox Chambers's father, James M. Cox, was governor of Ohio, 1920 Democratic presidential nominee (his running mate was young Franklin Delano Roosevelt), and, most important, a pioneer investor in the newest communications technology of the 1920s, broadcast radio.[21]

The most spectacular contribution to the architecture of the lowcountry by the plantation set was the house that C. Leigh Stevens built at Auldbrass Plantation in 1939. Auldbrass was a 4,253-acre estate on the Combahee River assembled by C. Leigh Stevens, a prominent industrial engineer and sometime visiting lecturer at Harvard. It encompassed five antebellum rice plantations, some of them dating to the 1730s: Old Combahee, Mount Pleasant, Mount Alexander, Richfield, and Carlton. The planter families that had owned these plantations were the McPhersons, Hardens, Heywards, Cuthberts, Izards, and Middletons, some of the most distinguished names in Beaufort and South Carolina history.

In 1939 C. Leigh Stevens commissioned Frank Lloyd Wright, the most influential architect America ever produced, to design a house and "plantation complex" that reflected the lowcountry environment and was suitable for the activities of the plantation set. The result was the most remarkable structure built in Beaufort County since Prince William Church in 1751 and one of only two Frank Lloyd Wright–designed houses in South Carolina. The Auldbrass Plantation complex, complete with stables and outbuildings, is an assemblage of low, horizontal structures that complement the low-hanging vegetation of the lowcountry forests. Throughout the main residence are decorative details of Native American design, evocative of the Yemassees and their predecessors, who once ruled those forests.

The most remarkable feature of Frank Lloyd Wright's creation was that there were no right angles anywhere in the main residence. Supposedly inspired by the gnarled and irregular shapes of the ancient live oaks, Wright designed one of the most unusual buildings in the South. Carefully restored and preserved by Hollywood movie producer Joel Silver, Auldbrass Plantation is listed on the U.S. Department of the Interior's National Register of Historic Places as a distinguished example of the twentieth-century "Plantation Society" style.[22]

The 1930s witnessed the passing of some charter members of the Carolina Plantation Society. In 1933 Arthur Lyman died in Waltham, Massachusetts, and in 1935 Bonny Hall Plantation was sold to Nelson Doubleday, the New York publisher. The most important transition was the death of Harry B. Hollins Sr., on March 2, 1938. Hollins was the last of the founders of the lowcountry plantation society. He had spent every winter for nearly half a century in his beloved lowcountry, first on his own estate and later on those of his three sons. He had founded H. B. Hollins and Company in 1878, was an original organizer of the Knickerbocker Trust Company, and vice president of the Central Banking and Trust Company. Three weeks after his death, his wife of fifty-one years, Evelina Knapp Hollins, died at their home at 14 East 60th Street in New York City.[23] Three years later the nation plunged into World War II. The rapid postwar development of Beaufort County gradually eroded and then consumed most of the large estates.

Two transactions among the plantation set had profound effects on the history of Beaufort County. In 1937 the Union Bag and Paper Company purchased 18,600 acres of Palmetto Bluff Plantation from the Varn Turpentine and Cattle Company of Estill, South Carolina. This was the residue of the Wilson-Vanderbilt estate. Eventually the Palmetto Bluff tract became part of 56,000 acres of timber and forestland owned by the Union Bag and Paper Company in Beaufort and Jasper Counties. After 1937 Alexander Calder (1886–1962), chairman, president, and major stockholder of Union Bag and Paper, used the old Vanderbilt mansion at Palmetto Bluff as a hunting lodge to entertain his business associates. After World War II, Union Bag and Paper merged with Camp Lumber Company to become the giant Union-Camp Corporation. In 1957 Union-Camp acquired the land and timber assets of the Argent Lumber Company of Hardeeville to become the largest landowner in the lowcountry. The Union-Camp timberlands in southern Beaufort County are now the site of the Sun City Hilton Head retirement community (established in 1993) and of the University of South Carolina's New River Campus (established in 2004). They have thus become the epicenter of one of the most dynamic real estate booms in Beaufort County history.[24]

Of all the plantation society transactions, the most influential was the sale of Roy Rainey's estate on Hilton Head Island in 1931 to Alfred Loomis and Landon Thorne. Roy Rainey was one of many investors whose fortunes were wiped out in the 1929 stock market crash. In March 1931 he had to sell his Hilton Head Island estate, where he was said to have "enjoyed many seasons of wonderful hunting." The information released to the newspapers in 1931 asserted that Loomis and Thorne had purchased twelve thousand acres for $250,000.[25] Edwin Thorne Jr., however, recalled that they bought "about twenty thousand acres," for which they paid $120,000 cash "because they had cash on the barrelhead in those days."

This purchase was not the Thorne family's first experience on Hilton Head Island. In 1848 Samuel Thorne, progenitor of the family, accompanied his father on a business trip to Charleston and Hilton Head. On Hilton Head, sixteen-year-old Samuel Thorne purchased a sea island "marsh tacky" pony and rode it back to his home in Millbrook, New York. He left a journal of his youthful adventure, which is a prized family possession.[26] The story of Alfred Lee Loomis (1888–1975) and Landon K. Thorne (1888–1964) was the most fascinating and important of all the intriguing stories of the plantation set. Loomis and Thorne were Yale classmates and partners in the 1919 takeover of the New York bond-trading firm of Bonbright and Company. They became brothers-in-law when Thorne wed Loomis's sister Julia in 1911. Loomis and Thorne became fabulously wealthy in the 1920s by creating the system of financing necessary to provide capital for the new, rapidly expanding electric utilities industry. In doing so, they made a valuable contribution to the national welfare. Their financial prowess became legendary on Wall Street when in the spring of 1929 they sensed the danger in the overheated stock market and converted most of their huge stock portfolio into long-term treasury bonds and cash.

They used their cash in 1931 to purchase the Rainey estate on Hilton Head Island. The property included Honey Horn Plantation and a hunting lodge built by William P. Clyde. For nearly twenty years, the Loomis and Thorne families spent a portion of the winter months on Hilton Head. They continued to buy land on the island throughout the 1930s, eventually amassing twenty-two thousand acres that stretched from Braddock Point (Harbor Town) to old Fort Walker (Port Royal Plantation). The Loomis and Thorne sojourns to Hilton Head during the 1930s and 1940s represented the apogee of the lowcountry plantation society.

Betty Loomis Evans, Alfred Loomis's daughter, recalled the island in the 1930s: "There was no one there at all, only a few black families, and they spoke nothing but Gullah. It was the most beautiful place you've ever seen. Julia [Thorne] brought her horses there and fixed up the house with the most beautiful rugs and antiques. They threw huge parties, inviting all their family and friends. Early in the morning, a boy would come and light a fire in the bedroom while we were still asleep. . . . Everybody would get up at the crack of dawn and go hunting. And you never saw such hunting. It had every animal known to man." Paulie Loomis, Alfred Loomis's son, recalled the hunting parties: "It was like a safari. After a morning shoot, they would find a shady spot for a picnic. A black man would come along, all trimmed out in a waiter's uniform, and bring tables, and tablecloths and chairs, and china. You couldn't believe your eyes. . . . they would grill quail and great big oysters in the shells and melt butter. It was a feast."

Alfred Loomis was a successful businessman and a highly respected amateur scientist with many publications in scientific journals. Loomis used his great wealth to build a private research laboratory in the basement of his mansion in Tuxedo Park, New York. There he invited some of the world's most renowned scientists to visit, work, and live in luxury. Some of these scientists later built a workable radar machine at the Massachusetts Institute of Technology and others helped manage the Manhattan Project during World War II. Some were guests on Hilton Head Island. The most famous of these was Ernest Lawrence, the "Cyclotron Man," for whom the Lawrence-Livermore Laboratory in California was named. Other famous guests were the King of Sweden and FDR's secretary of war, Henry L. Stimson, who was Alfred Loomis's elder cousin and mentor.

Between 1949 and 1951, the vast Loomis-Thorne estate on Hilton Head Island was sold to the Hilton Head Company and Honey Horn Plantation, two companies formed by General Joe Fraser and Fred Hack of Hinesville, Georgia, and Olin McIntosh of Savannah.[27] The Loomis and Thorne lands permitted Joe Fraser's son, Charles Fraser, to begin the real estate revolution that transformed Beaufort County over the next fifty years.

BEAUFORT AS A WRITER'S AND ARTIST'S COLONY

The unique beauty of the Carolina lowcountry that attracted the plantation set also attracted writers and artists to Beaufort during the 1920s and 1930s. Some were prominent writers from other places who came to Beaufort to enjoy the mild winter climate and for whom Beaufort evoked the mystery and romance of lost civilizations and faded glory. Others were Beaufortonians who had found success beyond Beaufort and were drawn back by powerful memories. Governor Francis Richard Lubbock of Texas summed up Beaufort's effect when he wrote a memoir in 1900. After six decades of excitement and achievement on the Texas frontier, the nonagenarian Lubbock never forgot his youth in Beaufort. "Through all these years," he wrote, "Beaufort has been one of the pleasures of my memory."[28]

In antebellum times Beaufort's privileged and wealthy planter class had produced a significant number of literary lions of the Old South. This tradition was honored by their descendants, wherever the planters' diaspora took them. Rhett descendants managed and contributed to the *New Orleans Picayune* after the war, and Sarah Barnwell Elliott (1848–1928), the Tennessee suffragette and Sewanee resident, was a successful short story writer and novelist in New York. Elliott's collection of short stories, *Some Data,* recorded her impressions of her childhood in antebellum Beaufort and recounted the heroic and tragic circumstances of her favorite cousin, Confederate general Stephen Elliott. And, of course, the Gonzales brothers, Narcisco Gener Gonzales and Ambrose Elliott Gonzales, grandsons of William Elliott III, Sara Elliott's uncle, founded the *State* newspaper in Columbia, South Carolina's largest newspaper for more than a century.[29]

The missionaries of the Union occupation began a new literary tradition in Beaufort. They became fascinated with the oral literature of the Gullah freedmen preserved in songs and stories. Many missionaries collected and later published these unique yarns and ballads. Lucy McKim and William Francis Allen published Gullah songs in 1867. *The Letters of Laura Towne,* published in 1912, Harriett Ware Pearson's *Letters from Port Royal* published in 1906, and *The Journal of Charlotte Forten,* finally published in 1953, expressed fascination with these sea island songs and stories. Charlotte Forten's letters inspired poet John Greenleaf Whittier to write "Song of the Negro Boatmen at Port Royal."[30]

Abbie Holmes Christensen spent nearly her whole life in Beaufort and was a friend and benefactor of sea island blacks long after the other missionaries had returned to the North. She made an early academic study of the oral literature of the sea islands. In 1875 she published two stories of "Negro Folklore" in the *New York Independent* and in 1892 published a collection of these sea island stories in a book entitled *Afro-American Folk Lore as Told 'Round the Cabin Fires on the Sea Islands of South Carolina.* That work was an early publication of the American Folklore Society. Much of this tradition reached a national audience through the famous "Uncle Remus" stories of Joel Chandler Harris. A Georgia native, Harris began writing "Negro dialect" stories for the *Savannah Morning News* and the *Atlanta Constitution* in the 1870s. Both Christensen and Harris published versions of the famous "Tar Baby" story. Another native Beaufort author, Ambrose Elliott Gonzales, began publishing Gullah dialect stories from the lowcountry in the *State* newspaper in 1892. He collected these stories in a 1922 book entitled *Black Border: Gullah Stories of the Carolina Coast.* Gonzales's book includes "A Gullah Glossary," an early attempt to capture the English creole dialect of the lowcountry. Using these early written accounts and later field work, linguists have recovered African vocabulary, grammar, and syntax that has survived to the present day.

Gonzales asserted that the first recorder of the "Tar Baby" story was Colonel Charles Colcock Jones of Georgia before the Civil War and included Jones's and Harris's versions of the famous tale as the conclusion of his book. Abbie Holmes Christensen's friend, Clare Macdonald of St. Helena Island, contributed to this growing body of local literature with her charming story "Recollections of Juliana: A Sketch in Ebony," published in 1924. In 1932 and 1933, Professor Lorenzo Dow Turner of Fisk University in Nashville,

Tennessee, spent several months studying the Gullah dialect of the sea islanders on St. Helena Island. After years of scholarship, he published *Africanisms in the Gullah Dialect* (1949), which has remained the classic work of Gullah scholarship in America to this day.[31] These early forays into the oral literature of the sea islands have generated a scholarly industry of Gullah studies for linguists, anthropologists, sociologists, and historians in the twentieth and twenty-first century.

A more conventional Beaufort author was Julia Aldrich Baker (1854–1907), who was born and raised in Beaufort in the last days of the antebellum era. Impoverished by the war, she lived in Beaufort with her sister Fanny for forty-two years. Julia Baker was well known locally for her poetry and was a literary mentor to the young women of Beaufort, who established the Clover Club literary society. Her poetry was of the inspirational religious variety, and her best-known poem, "Mizpah," was printed on postcards and sold as a fundraiser by the Ladies Parsonage Society of the Baptist Church of Beaufort. A collection of her poetry entitled *Gleams of Truth* was published in Spartanburg in 1904, a few years before her death. When she died in 1907, she was too poor to afford a gravestone and was buried in an unmarked grave in the Baptist cemetery. In 1912 the Clover Club dedicated a marker for her grave that included two lines from "Mizpah."

Julia Baker's poetry reached a national and international audience after her death. In 1910 some of her poems were published in London under the title *Mizpah—A Calendar for 1911*. In 1913 E. P. Dutton of New York published the calendar as *Mizpah*. And in 1936 Baker's poetry was collected and published in Boston in a book entitled *In Mellow Light*.[32]

The most lasting contribution the Clover Club made to Beaufort's literary life was the establishment of the Beaufort Township Library, now the main branch of the Beaufort County Public Library. The Clover Club started its circulating library in 1901 and staffed it with volunteers. First located in a room of the Harmony Masonic Lodge above Scheper's store, the Clover Club library burned, along with Scheper's store, in the Great Fire of 1907. Remarkably, all but fifty books were saved from the flames. The library moved for a while to a room in the *Beaufort Gazette* building and then settled in the Ladies Benevolent Society building on Scott Street. By 1914 the Clover Club circulating library had grown to over twelve hundred books and was bursting out of its reading room on Scott Street. Since 1912 there were discussions in the Clover Club and town council of applying for a Carnegie Endowment grant to establish a true public library. The 1907 fire had consumed the Town Hall on the corner of Carteret and Craven Streets, and in 1912 the town council gave the Clover Club a ninety-nine-year lease on the empty lot upon which to build a library. The club raised money for several years. In 1915 their project got an enormous boost when Senator

Niels Christensen authored special legislation permitting a one-half-mill tax on Beaufort Township property owners for the library. This revenue allowed the town to obtain a $7,350 grant from the Carnegie Endowment. The Clover Club donated its entire collection, which by 1915 had grown to two thousand books. The town council appointed five township library trustees. Three trustees, W. R. Bristol, H. C. Burkmeyer, and E. E. Lengnick, were appointed by the Clover Club, and the council appointed Hal C. Pollitzer secretary-treasurer. The new Carnegie Library was built on the site of the old town hall in 1915 and 1916. In November 1916 the Clover Club convened its first public meeting in the new Carnegie Library.[33]

Beaufort also produced some luminaries of the national stage and screen in the early twentieth century. Their influence brought the American Feature Film Corporation to Beaufort in 1917. The principal contribution of Beaufort to the national stage was Maude Odell Doremus (1870–1937). Maude Odell was born and raised in Beaufort. She grew up at the Sea Island Hotel, which was owned and operated by her parents, Alice and James Odell, for forty years. She was educated at the Ursuline Convent in Columbia and Miss Kelly's School in Charleston before attending Boston's New England Conservatory of Music. In 1894 Maude Odell entered the American Academy of Dramatic Arts in New York. There she met the New York producer Daniel Frohman, who started her on her stage career. Over the next twenty years, Maude Odell acted with the biggest stars of the New York stage. Her greatest early success was in the role of Antoinette in *The Prisoner of Zenda.* The play was one of the most successful productions of the era and ran for four hundred continuous nights in New York City. Maude Odell reached her peak as a dramatic actress before World War I. She then found a second, successful career in musical comedy when she performed in *Little Boy Blue, The Student Prince,* and *Show Boat,* among other productions. One of Maude Odell's friends and costars was Billie Burke, perhaps the most famous actress of the era.[34]

Maude Odell returned to Beaufort annually for several weeks, usually during the summer, when Broadway was on hiatus. She loved Beaufort, and wherever she went—New York, London, Boston, Washington—she took "delight in sticking up for the attractions of Beaufort." Her mother, Alice Odell, entertained many stars of the New York stage at the Sea Island Hotel. When Alice Odell sold the old hotel in 1918, her daughter bought the Edward Barnwell House at 1405 Bay Street for her mother.

Maude Odell was a great swimmer and built a bathhouse on the river in front of her house. It was said that when she and her friend Billie Burke went swimming in the 1920s, all of Beaufort stopped to watch. During the 1920s Maude Odell twice tried to retire to Beaufort and both times was lured back to the New York stage. She had great stage triumphs as a character actress in the 1930s, when she was over sixty years old. In 1931 she played a blackface Maum Hannah in a stage adaptation of *Scarlet Sister Mary,* a Pulitzer Prize–winning novel by South Carolina author Julia Peterkin, and in 1933 she acted as the show-stopping evangelist Sister Bessie in Erskine Caldwell's *Tobacco Road,* which had a record run of 750 consecutive Broadway performances from 1933 through 1937. Odell probably reached her largest audience not on stage but through the new medium of broadcast radio. She first broadcast a singing concert on WGBS in New York City, on January 10, 1926. The show was an evident success because thereafter she sang to a national audience every Thursday night on the *Maxwell House Coffee Hour.*[35]

Throughout her career, Maude Odell remained loyal to her hometown. When in Beaufort, she often interrupted her vacations to direct or star in theatrical productions at the arsenal and the Bay Street Theater. She proudly introduced the charms of Beaufort to American entertainment moguls. In December 1911 Henry W. Savage, said to be "the largest theatrical producer in the United States," stopped in Beaufort aboard his yacht *Joyeuse* just to spend a few days with Maude Odell. Savage said that "Beaufort's waterfront is one of the prettiest he had ever seen."[36]

These connections bore fruit for Beaufort in 1917 when the American Feature Film Company sent representatives to Beaufort to scout the location for a studio and winter quarters. They were so impressed that they spent the winter of 1917 and 1918 in Beaufort. The company announced plans to use Beaufort as the locale of a movie called *The Rise and Fall of the Confederacy.* They planned to use "scenic and historic backgrounds" and do much of the film shooting "in the antebellum homes." Beaufort was all abuzz with the prospect, and merchants eagerly anticipated "large sums of money turned loose in this section." The American Feature Film Corporation was brought to Beaufort by Maude Odell's uncle, Jack Clancy, a Beaufort entrepreneur and frequent visitor to New York City. However, Beaufort's foray into the new motion picture industry was interrupted by World War I and the film was never made. The town then waited seventy years to be rediscovered by Hollywood.

Sadly, Maude Odell never managed to retire to Beaufort. In 1937 she was found dead of a heart attack in her dressing room just before a performance of *Tobacco Road.* Her death prompted the following tribute from the *Charleston News and Courier:* "She died in costume . . . long was she South Carolina's principal representative on stage. She was one of its queens in the halcyon days of the American theater and she was still prominent in these changed seasons." She is buried in the graveyard of the Roman Catholic Church on Carteret Street.[37]

Despite her remarkable Broadway career, Maude Odell may not have been Beaufort's most famous actress. Esther Dale (1885–1961) was seen by millions of Americans because she became a famous character actress in the new medium of talking motion pictures. She culminated a long career by working in television dramas. Esther Dale was the daughter of Beaufort planter and entrepreneur John J. Dale. She spent her childhood in Beaufort and at the family home at Frogmore on St. Helena Island. Every summer the Dales returned to their hometown of Townsend, Vermont. When Esther Dale was old enough for high school, she stayed in Townsend, where the town supported a distinguished secondary school called the Leland and Gray Seminary. Esther Dale starred in all the school plays and graduated with honors in 1903. She went on to study music and voice in Berlin and pursued an international career as a concert singer. In the 1920s she retired from the stage and became head of the voice department at Smith College.

In the 1930s Dale returned to the stage in the role of temperance crusader Carrie Nation. In 1934 she moved to Hollywood. Esther Dale was not a statuesque beauty like Maude Odell, but she became widely known to national audiences for playing a quintessential American character, the tough, resilient country woman. Esther Dale made more than 112 movies between 1935 and 1960. Some of the best known were *In Old Kentucky* (1935), *Broadway Serenade* (1939), *Back Street* (1941), *The Egg and I* (1947), *Ma and Pa Kettle* (1949), *Monkey Business* (1952), and *North to Alaska* (1960). During the 1950s and 1960s, Esther Dale had regular roles in two popular television series, *Wagon Train* and *Maverick*.[38]

Like Maude Odell, Esther Dale did not forget her old hometown. In 1931 she visited her sister, Mrs. E. H. Evans, on St. Helena Island. While in Beaufort she attended the December meeting of the Clover Club. At the end of a full program, Mary Waterhouse reported Esther Dale's presence and introduced a concert of international folk songs sung by Miss Dale. She was accompanied by Elizabeth Crofut Waterhouse on the piano and Marguerite Crofut on the violin. The program had obviously been rehearsed in secret and presented as a surprise Christmas gift to the members. It was one of the most memorable meetings of the Clover Club and said to be "a great gift to her friends and relatives."[39]

During the 1930s there was another curious, coincidental, and controversial connection between Beaufort, South Carolina, and Townsend, Vermont. In 1932 the *New York Evening Graphic* newspaper announced the organization of a "back-to-nature" commune of New York intellectuals on Cat Island in Beaufort County, South Carolina. The commune and health resort was the brainchild of the author, publisher, and health expert Bernarr McFadden (1868–1955). A genuine American eccentric, McFadden was born in Missouri, orphaned at an early age, and grew up poor and sickly. Determined to improve himself, he embarked on a rigorous schedule of exercise, weight lifting, and vegetarianism. When his regimen worked, McFadden wrote it up in a national bestseller, *The Athlete's Conquest* (1892). Thereafter, McFadden became the multimillionaire publisher of *Physical Culture* and *True Story* magazines and the *New York Evening Graphic* newspaper. One of McFadden's lifelong convictions was that nudity and maximum exposure to fresh air promoted good health.

In 1932 McFadden sent his advertising manager, Gilbert Parks, to Beaufort to purchase five-hundred-acre Cat Island. Once a prosperous truck farm, the McFadden colony on Cat Island proposed to grow its own food in the vegetable fields developed by W. S. Gay and Harry Kessler about 1912. The "back-to-nature" colony promoted itself in the New York press as a "Twentieth-Century Brook Farm," where all property was shared communally and everyone contributed to chores. The group's lack of knowledge regarding the locale was revealed by their plan to pay the men three dollars per day for planting the crops "eight hours per day in winter and ten hours per day in summer." In Beaufort County, even the antebellum slaves had not worked that long in the heat of summer. During the spring of 1932, R. J. Cantrell of Brooklyn, New York, went to Cat Island as manager, and several New Yorkers accompanied him. The colony included an Englishman and a German woman. In 1932 they bought a motorboat, a cow, chickens, pigs, and planting seeds.

McFadden's New York publications promoted the experiment as a "Back to Nature Colony in the Heart of Dixie." They explained their communal philosophy as follows: "The land will be owned by the group as a whole. There will be separate houses for married couples and dormitories for the unmarried men and women.... All things pertaining to the social and economic life of the colony will be co-operative and the property will be owned in common. Freedom is to be the keynote. Every member may do or think what he pleases without interference by governing boards ... so long as he does not disturb the rights of anyone else. There will be no restrictions as to creeds, color, race or economic, political or social philosophy in the selection of the members."[40]

The controversy began when the most conspicuous freedom the group practiced was freedom from clothes. When the local press learned that nude swimming and sunbathing was permitted on Cat Island, the information became fodder for sensational news stories. When reporter Clothilde Martin interviewed the colony's residents for the *Charleston News and Courier,* they were surprised by the news coverage. The German girl exclaimed, "Oh, but dat iz awful!" and the Englishman admitted sheepishly, "Well, er, it was very hot the other day." It was also rumored that the Cat Island colony was a "love cult," an accusation vigorously denied by the residents. Additionally, the Cat Islanders had to reassure the local press that it was "not connected in any way to any communistic or socialistic organization."

The sensational news coverage attracted the attention of Beaufort County Sheriff Ed McTeer, Governor Ibra Blackwood, and the local Ku Klux Klan. As Sheriff McTeer recalled, locals predicted that "the river will be full of naked people!" or "they'll come to town to shop in the nude!" McTeer had no wish to interfere with the colony, but Governor Blackwood sent two state constables to investigate. The sheriff took them out to Cat Island by boat and, sure enough, encountered some naked people. According to McTeer, the constables, who had brought their wives along for the boat ride, fled in terror and never filed a report. It was never clear whether communism or nudism attracted the Ku Klux Klan to the events, but when rumors spread that it might take action against the Cat Island "nudist colony," Klan leader Colonel M. O. Dunning of Savannah asserted, "I know nothing of the conditions on Cat Island, but if they are not approved of by the people of Beaufort County . . . I and the Klan will be in sympathy with the people. We stand for law and order."

Colonel M. O. Dunning was himself an interesting character. He was born and raised in Ridgeland during the 1890s. As a young man, Ed McTeer noted, "he had studied combustion engines and could make them run." In fact, Dunning was an expert auto mechanic when there were very few in the lowcountry. He began his career in Beaufort but traveled over a wide area with his tools in a canvas sack. He made five dollars per day. In 1913 Dunning was in Hampton County when the pursuit of Richard Austin occurred; he was a prominent member of that posse. When World War I began, he enlisted in the U.S. Army Air Service. Dunning became an outstanding pilot and was commissioned an army lieutenant. He became a combat flying ace and returned to Savannah as a hero. Known as "Chief" Dunning, he had political ambitions and attached them to the Ku Klux Klan. He was appointed customs collector of the Port of Savannah and Prohibition administrator for the federal Southern District. His political career disappeared with Prohibition and the KKK's decline in the 1930s, so to denounce the Cat Island colony was an anticlimax. According to Ed McTeer, it was not harassment by the sheriff, the governor, or the Klan that drove the "nature colony" from Cat Island. Instead, it was the "ferocious Beaufort County mosquitoes, red bugs and sand gnats that took their toll on the nudists' tender and exposed skins . . . and accomplished what the strong arm of the law had failed to do. The nudist colony closed up their tents and stole silently away."[41]

Bernarr McFadden established another health spa and created local controversy in Townsend, Vermont. In the 1930s, he purchased Deerbrook Farm in the hills above Townsend. The farm had been converted into a summer camp in 1924. While there was no record that McFadden ever visited Cat Island, he was often at Deerbrook Farm. He flew his own airplane from New

York to a landing strip on the farm, which caused nearly as much sensation in Townsend as the nudists on Cat Island created in Beaufort. McFadden was known to land at Deerbrook Farm and emerge naked from his plane. Perhaps McFadden had learned of the sea islands from Esther Dale or from other residents of Townsend who recalled the "Beaufort summer colony" of years gone by.[42]

During the 1930s the center of Beaufort's literary community was the Gold Eagle Tavern. But even before the hotel opened, Beaufort attracted literary figures of all types. In 1917 and 1918, George Kennan, a noted war correspondent who covered events in Russia, spent the whole winter in Beaufort reportedly "trying to raise money for Siberian exiles of the Czars liberated by the Russian Revolution." Kennan resided at the Anchorage, the old William Elliott House on Bay Street that had been renamed by the Beardsley family, which owned the house for more than thirty years. Kennan went on to become famous as a historian of the Russian Revolution, ambassador to the Soviet Union, and the author of writings that became the basis for the post–World War II diplomatic "containment" policies that challenged Soviet expansionism in the 1950s. In 1919 Elsie Clews Parsons, anthropologist and founder of the American Folklore Society, spent several months on St. Helena Island studying Gullah culture. Nationally known poet Edwin Markham (1852–1940) visited Beaufort in 1924 and gave a public reading at the Community Club. And in 1928 Mrs. William Sydney Porter, the widow of "O. Henry," America's most famous short story writer, visited many historical spots in Beaufort County.[43]

After the Gold Eagle Tavern opened in 1930, it hosted a parade of notable literary figures. Several writers did much of their work while living or visiting in Beaufort. The central figure of the group was Edison Marshall (1894–1967), a prolific author who published fifty-seven books between 1920 and 1964. He also published numerous short stories, one of which, "Heart of Little Shikara," won the O. Henry Award as the best short story of 1921. Marshall's novel *Benjamin Blake* (1941) was the basis of two Hollywood movies, *Son of Fury* (1942) and *Treasure of the Golden Condor* (1952). During the 1930s Marshall lived much of the year in Augusta, Georgia, and often visited Beaufort to stay at the Gold Eagle Tavern. The Marshalls were friends of Kate Gleason, who entertained them aboard her yacht *Eleanor of the Isles* when they were in Beaufort.[44]

Another literary friend of Kate Gleason was Helen Christine Bennett, a feature writer for several popular magazines. Between 1910 and 1940, Helen Bennett published articles in *Pictorial Review, People's Favorite Magazine,* the *Saturday Evening Post, Cosmopolitan,* and the *American Magazine.* In 1928 Bennett wrote a laudatory article entitled "Kate Gleason's Adventures in a

Man's Job" for the *American Magazine.* Her essay highlighted Gleason's role as a female pioneer in the business world. Kate Gleason and Helen Bennett were good friends and often met at the Gold Eagle Tavern.[45]

In 1935 Garr Williams, a famous cartoonist and special features writer for the *Chicago Tribune,* spent part of the winter at the Gold Eagle Tavern. Another author and illustrator with a vacation home in Beaufort was Elmer Inglesby Ransom (1892–1942), who lived in Augusta and owned a "cottage on the river" in Beaufort, where he spent vacations with his wife and two daughters. He wrote fishing and outdoor stories for *This Week* magazine, among others, often illustrating his own work. In 1941 the University of Georgia Press published an anthology of his short stores titled *The Last Trumpeter and Other Stories.* After his death, his sketches were collected and published in *The Woodland Book* (1945).[46]

The Gold Eagle Tavern hosted a busy artists' colony during the 1930s. In June 1935 the painters Mary Hope Cabaniss and Walter W. Thompson held their first classes. The program was called the Beaufort-Brevard Art Colonies. The artists presented exhibits, held receptions, and taught classes for several weeks. They specialized in landscapes and outdoor scenes. The classes were conducted at the Gold Eagle, and much of the studio work was done in the old Lafayette House, now the John Mark Verdier House Museum. Local amateur artists and art teachers from regional schools and colleges enrolled in the Beaufort-Brevard Art Colonies seminars. The programs were repeated in Brevard, North Carolina, later in the summer. The seminar concluded with an exhibition of students' works. The Beaufort-Brevard Arts Colonies program was a small but successful local institution for the rest of the decade. It enhanced Beaufort's reputation as a literary and artistic community.[47]

In 1939 Hollywood icon Clark Gable visited Beaufort. He was traveling with comedian Allan Jenkins and his wife. Gable came and went without fanfare while Jenkins and his wife stayed on for a few days. Another literary notable who visited Beaufort and stayed at the Gold Eagle Tavern was Frances Parkinson Keyes (1885–1970), who was the widow of New Hampshire governor and U.S. Senator Henry W. Keyes. During her long career she wrote more than fifty books of biography, travel, and fiction. Her most famous books, *Dinner at Antoine's* (1948) and *Steamboat Gothic* (1952), were national best sellers.[48]

Beaufort's African American community did not ignore this local literary flowering. In 1940 Zora Neale Hurston (1901–1960) visited Beaufort for a lecture and reading at Robert Smalls High School, Beaufort's black high school. Hurston was one of the most prolific woman writers of New York's Harlem Renaissance. She published seven books of fiction and folklore between 1934 and 1948. Her best-known book was the novel *Their Eyes Were Watching God* (1937). Born in Eatonville, Florida, Hurston attended Morgan

Academy (now State University) in Baltimore and Howard University in Washington, and in 1928 she received a B.A. in anthropology from New York City's Barnard College. Her visit to Beaufort was a major event for the African American community. The faculty and students at Robert Smalls High School turned out for a "special chapel" on May 14, 1940. A student chorus presented a music program, and Hurston was introduced by school principal W. Kent Alston. Her presentation enlightened all age groups in the audience, and it was said that "her charm and graciousness won an everlasting place in the hearts of all who heard her." Hurston died in poverty in Eatonville, Florida, in 1960. She was buried in an unmarked grave until the famous novelist Alice Walker placed a stone over her remains thirteen years later. Walker's 1982 novel, *The Color Purple* (later adapted into a movie and a Broadway musical), was said to have been inspired by Hurston's life and work.[49]

When World War II began in Europe, a number of literary figures from Great Britain and the continent escaped to the United States, some finding refuge in Beaufort. A regular winter resident in the early war years and denizen of the Gold Eagle Tavern was Elizabeth von Arnim, also known as Mary Annette Beauchamp, Countess Russell (1866–1942). She was a regular guest at Tidalholm, Beaufort's new hostelry of the 1930s. The inn was formerly the Edgar Fripp House and had been converted to an inn by Natalie and Adam Haskell. Countess Russell was the sister-in-law of the British philosopher and mathematician Bertrand Russell. As a young woman she had married the German aristocrat Count Henning August von Arnim and lived on a large East Prussian estate. From this experience she wrote her first book, *Elizabeth and Her German Garden* (1898). After von Arnim's death, she returned to England, briefly married Bertrand Russell's brother, and resumed her literary career in Switzerland, London, and the French Riviera. Her best-selling novel *Mr. Skeffington* was published shortly before she fled to America. Countess Russell was known in Beaufort for her morning walks around town with her pet cocker spaniel. She died in a Charleston nursing home in 1942.[50]

The most famous literary refugee was W. Somerset Maugham (1874–1965), who was living in Paris when the Nazi blitzkrieg overwhelmed France in the spring of 1940. He escaped to America and wrote a noteworthy essay about the fall of France. At the time, Maugham was one of the most famous authors in the world. His many books, led by *Of Human Bondage* (1915) and *The Moon and Sixpence* (1919), had been translated into a dozen languages and sold all over the world. He was brought to the United States by his American publisher, Nelson Doubleday, who deposited Maugham at his comfortable guest house at Bonny Hall, Doubleday's Combahee River plantation. There Maugham wrote one of his most popular novels, *The Razor's Edge* (1944). He wrote numerous articles, mostly for *Redbook* magazine, which praised America's war effort and brought favorable attention to Beaufort's efforts to boost the morale of Marine Corps recruits on Parris Island. In 1942 Maugham visited Beaufort's USO Club to research an article on USOs in the Southeast, and he was a frequent diner at the Gold Eagle Tavern.[51]

Another wartime resident was best-selling novelist Erskine Caldwell, the author of classic southern novels such as *Tobacco Road* (1932) and *God's Little Acre* (1933). During 1944 and 1945, Caldwell lived part-time in Beaufort while editor and president of a local newspaper, the *Beaufort Times.* In a sense, Caldwell was a war refugee as well. While on a tour of the Far East with his second wife, the photographer Margaret Bourke-White, he was in the Soviet Union in 1941 when the Germans unleashed their blitzkrieg on Russia. Caldwell fled the war, divorced Bourke-White, and retreated to Beaufort with his third wife. The *Beaufort Times* was published during the war and sold out to the *Beaufort Gazette* in 1946.[52]

The pinnacle of Beaufort's literary fame in the early twentieth century came with the publication of Francis Griswold's novel *A Sea Island Lady* in 1939. Francis Griswold was a native of Albany, New York, and a friend of Kate Gleason. In the 1920s he was captivated by the beauty and history of the Carolina lowcountry. As Griswold put it, "Little justice, it seems to me, has been done to this section of the South . . . full of beauty and pain, full of profound implications for the heart of man." In 1930 he published *Tides of Malvern,* a novel based on the history of Charleston and the lowcountry from its sixteenth-century West Indian origins to the 1930s. Kate Gleason introduced Griswold to Beaufort, and he became a regular guest at the Gold Eagle Tavern. He then began work on his historical novel about Beaufort. Kate Gleason's secretary, Libby Sanders, led Griswold to the many historic sites in Beaufort County and introduced him to the Beaufort residents whose stories provided the basis for *A Sea Island Lady.* As Griswold described his research, "time passed in exploring old houses, ransacking attics, talking with the oldest inhabitants."

It took Griswold seven years to write *A Sea Island Lady,* and when it was published in 1939, the book consumed 962 pages. Unfortunately for Griswold, and perhaps for Beaufort, *A Sea Island Lady* reached the public a few months after that earthquake of a southern novel, *Gone With the Wind. A Sea Island Lady* was widely reviewed and was a financial success for the author and publisher. It went through six printings within two months of its publication. Despite the success of Griswold's book, it was overshadowed by Margaret Mitchell's blockbuster, and for a generation of Americans, the heart of the Old South was thought to be the hills of middle Georgia and not the sea islands of South Carolina.

The major periodicals of the day published reviews of *A Sea Island Lady.* The *New York Times* called the book "an amazing performance. . . . Francis Griswold has something to say which could only be said at such length as this." *Time* magazine said "it is extraordinarily warm, full and actual" and *Commonweal* called it "one of the very best novels of the current year." The review in the *Saturday Review of Literature* was reserved for the magazine's editor and cofounder Stephen Vincent Benét, a Pulitzer Prize–winning poet and novelist. Benét's backhanded compliment was, "In its first four hundred-odd pages, Mr. Griswold has told an admirable and moving story." The book was, of course, twice that long. *A Sea Island Lady* never became a Hollywood movie and never elevated its characters to the icons of the Old South that Scarlett O'Hara and Rhett Butler became, but it told an accurate story of Beaufort's Civil War and Reconstruction history. A careful reader of Griswold's novel can identify important persons of Civil War and Reconstruction Beaufort, and events of Beaufort history are presented with chronological and geographical precision. A reader must conclude that Griswold's sources provided clear, vivid memories and that he was conscientious in presenting them.

Beaufort's Civil War and Reconstruction history was not typical of the Deep South, and Griswold's novel was, like Beaufort's history, unique. The heroine of Griswold's novel was not a displaced plantation mistress but rather a northern missionary teacher, Emily Moffat, who had come to the sea islands as part of the "noble experiment." Married first to a Yankee preacher and then to an ex-Confederate cavalier, Emily represented the political clash and personal reconciliation of North and South that was Beaufort's distinctive Reconstruction experience. Before he finished proofreading *A Sea Island Lady,* Griswold moved to Santa Barbara, California. He never wrote another book, but nearly seventy years later, *A Sea Island Lady* stands as the greatest literary monument to Beaufort County history.[53]

Perhaps the commercial success of *A Sea Island Lady* prompted Charleston writer Josephine Pinckney to make her contribution to Beaufort history. Her novel *Hilton Head* (1941) was based on the life of South Carolina's first English settler, Dr. Henry Woodward. Hollywood never invented a life more adventurous or accomplished than Henry Woodward's, and Pinckney marshaled all available historical information to tell her story of South Carolina's first frontier.[54]

In 1944 another talented daughter of Beaufort made her debut as an author of short stories and novels. Ann Christensen Head was born in Beaufort in 1915, the eldest daughter of Senator Niels Christensen and his wife, Nancy Stratton of Boston. Ann Christensen Head was educated in the Beaufort public schools and, following family tradition, finished her high school education in Massachusetts. She graduated from the Cambridge School in Kindel Green, Massachusetts, and attended Antioch College in Ohio. Her first published story, "Impossible Journey," described the Beaufort and sea island surroundings of her childhood. It appeared in *Cosmopolitan* magazine.

Ann Christensen Head found success as a fiction writer. Her novels included *Fair with Rain* (1957), *Always in August* (1961), and *Everybody Adored Cara* (1963). Her short stories appeared in the *Ladies Home Journal,* the *Saturday Evening Post, McCall's, Redbook, Good Housekeeping,* and *Cosmopolitan.* Ann Christensen Head married and divorced Howard Head, who designed and manufactured Head Skis. She returned to her hometown and married Beaufort physician Stanley Morse. She died in 1968.[55]

Samuel Hopkins Adams (1871–1958) was the literary bridge between old and new Beaufort and led a literary circle after World War II. Adams was born in Dunkirk, New York, raised by a "liberal, even heretical" Presbyterian minister, and educated at Hamilton College, where three generations of Adamses had preceded him. He started writing as a reporter for the *New York Sun* and then moved to *McClure's Magazine.* A protégé and friend of fellow Hamilton College graduate Alexander Woollcott, Adams entered the famed Algonquin Circle of New York literary opinion makers. He wrote more than fifty books between 1905 and 1955, including novels, biographies, and political exposés. Seventeen of his books or short stories were made into movies, including *Flaming Youth* (1931), *It Happened One Night* (1934), and *The Harvey Girls* (1948). His biography of his mentor, *Alexander Woollcott: His Life and His World* (1945), won a National Book Critics Award in 1946. His last book, *Grandfather Stories* (1955), was published in serial form in the *New Yorker.*

In 1935 Adams adopted Beaufort as his winter home. He built a small house on Battery Creek and was a frequent guest at the Gold Eagle Tavern and Tidalholm. After the war Adams's presence attracted a literary circle that included Ellery Sedgwick, publisher of the *Atlantic Monthly,* Charlton Ogburn Sr. (*This Star of England*), Charlton Ogburn Jr. (*Merrill's Marauders, The Mysterious William Shakespeare*), and E. B. White (*Charlotte's Web*). Adams was a generous and convivial man with a wide circle of South Carolina friends and admirers. He wrote often about Beaufort in national magazines. A winter resident of Beaufort for twenty-three years, Adams died in Beaufort in 1958 at the age of eighty-seven.

In 1950 Adams wrote an essay, "My Favorite Town," that described Beaufort's appeal to his writing friends. Of his and his wife's first impression of Beaufort in the spring of 1935, Adams wrote, "The spell was cast as we turned off the main route, pursuing the vague report of an old and quiet city out among the sea islands. . . . The approach to Beaufort threads through broad marshlands and across shining rivers. There are far vistas of wooded islets, unpeopled and unapproachable across the high-waving reeds of the morasses. The effect was strangely other-worldly."

Adams described the old town: "We entered the town proper between a long double row of royal palmettos and rounded a curve to blink amazedly at a floral riot in a private yard. There were camellias enough in that one clump to choke the biggest display window on Fifth Avenue. Overhead a pair of chinaberry trees were festooned with the soft gray Spanish moss and spangled with the golden traceries of the wild jasmine. For background there spread the broad expanse of reed and river with a lordly white yacht on its way to Florida." Adams and his wife also fell in love with Beaufort's "lovely, belvedered mansions, the picturesqueness of the old arsenal and the older slave quarters, the ancient 'tabby' buildings, constructed from a unique amalgam of oyster-shell mortar, the noble architecture of St. Helena's set in the bowered luxuriance of its churchyard, its spreading live oaks and the bewildering profusion and variety of its flowers."

Ultimately, it was neither the flowers nor the buildings that convinced the Adamses to make Beaufort their home, but the birds. Compelled to stop at the post office because the ox cart they were following had stopped there, they heard "across the street a mockingbird improvis[ing] elaborately in the branches of a live oak which might have been two centuries old but was more likely three." They looked at each other and said, "This is it!"[56] Adams and his spouse spoke for a generation of artists and writers and for millions of tourists who followed them.

Port Royal Naval Station on Parris Island, 1900. (Courtesy of Parris Island Museum.)

USS *Indiana* in the dry dock on Parris Island, 1896. (Courtesy of Parris Island Museum.)

Officers' Candidates School, Parris Island, class of 1909. (Courtesy of Parris Island Museum.)

Baseball game on Parris Island, 1910. (Courtesy of Parris Island Museum.)

First plane on Parris Island, 1919. (Courtesy of Parris Island Museum.)

"Iron Mike," memorial to U.S. Marines on Parris Island, erected 1924. (Courtesy of Parris Island Museum.)

Dedication of the Ribaut Monument on Parris Island, 1926. Left to right, front row: Congressman Thomas S. McMillan, Congressman Butler Black Hare, Brigadier General Eli Cole, Major General John A. Lejeune, Senator Ellison D. Smith, Secretary of the Navy Curtis D. Wilbur, Governor Thomas G. McLeod, Jules Henri (first secretary of the French Embassy), and Captain Frederick A. Traut (commandant, Sixth Naval District), and Daniel Ravenel (secretary of Huguenot Society). Second row: Albert Simons (monument designer), Mrs. Harry Lee, Mrs. John A. Lejeune, Lieutenant Colonel Edwin Denby, Mrs. J. W. Wadsworth, Captain W. T. Cluverius, USN (aide to Secretary Wilbur), Mayor Stoney of Charleston, Brigadier General Harry Lee, and State Senator Niels Christensen Jr. Third row: Mr. Bacot (former president, Huguenot Society); Reverend A. S. Thomas (chaplain of Huguenot Society). (Courtesy of Parris Island Museum.)

USAS *Los Angeles* at Parris Island mooring mast, 1934. (Courtesy of Parris Island Museum.)

Yemassee Junction during World War II: a steam lumber train headed west and a passenger train headed north. (Courtesy of Parris Island Museum.)

Graduated Marines on a troop train from Port Royal to Yemassee during World War II. (Courtesy of Parris Island Museum.)

President Franklin Roosevelt visiting Parris Island, April 14, 1943. (Courtesy of Parris Island Museum.)

First Beaufort Memorial Hospital, opened 1944. (Courtesy of Parris Island Museum.)

Ventura PV-1 bombers at the U.S. Naval Air Station Beaufort, 1944. The bombers were used for submarine patrols along the coast. (Courtesy of Parris Island Museum.)

Beaufort waterfront, 1963. (Courtesy of Parris Island Museum.)

Charles Fraser, founder of Sea Pines on Hilton Head Island. (Lawrence S. Rowland Collection.)

Chapter 13

Depression and the New Deal

DEPRESSION YEARS

When the Great Depression began in 1929, Beaufortonians barely noticed. The county's economy had been stagnant or declining since the 1890s. The loss of the phosphate industry in the 1890s, removal of the naval station, and the end of cotton farming were hard blows. The population of Beaufort County followed the economy. Between 1900 and 1930, it declined by 38.5 percent, from 35,495 in 1900 to 21,815 in 1930. Depopulation was the hardest blow of all, and all other economic statistics sank as people left the region.

When the stock market crashed on October 23, 1929, the event was not even mentioned in the *Beaufort Gazette.* For many Beaufortonians, their depression had begun on July 12, 1926, when the Beaufort Bank failed. The checking and savings accounts of many families disappeared. They could not imagine that things could get worse, but they did.

By the mid-1920s Beaufort County had a sole economic asset, truck farming. The complete dependence of the local economy on this industry was the main reason for the bank failure. The locals had put all their cabbages in one basket, and that basket had fallen off the train. The price of Irish potatoes, Beaufort County's chief cash crop, declined by 48 percent from 1929 to 1931. In 1929 five pounds of potatoes sold for twenty-nine cents on the New York market. In 1931 five pounds sold for fifteen cents. Those farmers who were able to do so diversified their crops so that the second largest cash crop, by volume, was cabbage. In May 1931 the cabbage market collapsed entirely. There were simply no buyers for Beaufort County cabbages.[1]

The years that followed were no better. Farmers switched to tomatoes in the early 1930s. They were harder to grow and harvest, but they offered higher profits. Tomatoes that could not be sold fresh could be canned, a fact that prompted the construction of several tomato canneries. In June 1932 the Peninsular Canning Company of Florida leased the empty factory of the defunct Seacoast Packing Company on the Charleston and Western Carolina railroad line. The firm offered to buy all the "surplus tomatoes . . . that cannot be shipped" to can them or make canned tomato juice. The plant expected to produce thirty thousand cans per day and employ "over one hundred women" during the peak of the tomato season. R. C. Hutchinson was the plant manager. The Peninsular Canning Company was brought to Beaufort County by Miles McSweeney, the governor's son and a farm entrepreneur in both Beaufort County and Palmetto, Florida. On Lady's Island the L. P. Maggioni Company converted its factory from oyster canning in the winter to tomato canning in the summer. The Maggioni Company had been in business in Beaufort County for forty years since it began canning oysters on Daufuskie Island in 1893.

In 1932 the tomato canning factories were busy. However, busy canneries were a bad sign for tomato planters. It meant that they could not sell their product on the fresh vegetable market, which offered higher prices and greater profits. In fact, the high cost of planting and harvesting tomatoes meant that farmers often lost money when their only market was the canneries. That was the case in 1932. As if to highlight Beaufort's depression, in 1933 the county's largest and oldest agricultural business, Macdonald-Wilkins Company, declared bankruptcy.[2]

Throughout the 1930s the uncertain market for fresh vegetables held down the local economy. In 1934 the truck farmers' fortunes went from bad to worse. That year not only did the fresh vegetable market collapse but farmers could not even sell their tomatoes to the canning factories. "Heretofore it was possible to can the surplus ripe tomatoes," the *Beaufort Gazette* reported. "This year even this cannot be done very successfully. Too much rain has ruined the fruit. Very little of it is fit for canning." In 1935 truck farmers cut back on their production, reduced their borrowing, and hired fewer workers, thereby compounding the poverty of the poorest in the county. Early that year the *Gazette* observed that "farming is the only major industry in the county. Should the farmers experience failure again this season the future of farming in Beaufort County will be at an end." In 1935 farmers sold barely enough fresh vegetables to plant in 1936, saving Beaufort's last industry for one more year.

The market improved a little in 1936, and the New Deal's government programs were of some help. But the crops failed in 1937 and 1938, and the prospect for 1939 was dismal. "Our people are in the depths," wrote the *Gazette.* "The farmers have lost money during the last two years. They do not know what to do." They had hoped that 1939 would be better, but with a decade of disappointment behind them, they were pessimistic. "Unfortunately," the paper noted, "we are a trucking community and when the farmers have a bad year it hurts the whole community." Beaufort County truck farmers not just had a bad year; they had a bad decade.[3]

John M. Trask, who eventually became the largest vegetable farmer in Beaufort County, began planting independent of his father in 1934. George W. Trask had established his family's farming and real estate interest in Beaufort County in 1908. In 1934 he turned over management of his original farm, Pickpocket Plantation in Burton, to his son, John, who recalled the struggles of truck farmers and farm workers in the Depression years. On one of the largest farms in the county, he earned only twelve hundred dollars in 1934 and only twenty-four hundred in 1935. The only good year Trask had during the 1930s was 1936, when he made twelve thousand dollars after expenses.

While times were hard enough for the planters, they were desperate for the workers. Nearly the only work available in Beaufort County was farm labor. John Trask recalled that standard wages for field workers on the vegetable farms was thirty cents per day. Mule drivers received premium wages at fifty cents per day. It was a far cry from the two to five dollars in daily wages that were common during the halcyon days of the phosphate industry. If a field hand worked all year at the prevailing rate, his annual income would be $90. Mule drivers earned $150 per year. But truck farming was a seasonal enterprise and farm workers did not work year round. If the laborers had not grown their own food or caught fish, they would have starved.[4]

Many in Beaufort County looked to the federal government as their only salvation during the worst years. The principal contribution of the government was the Marine Corps Recruit Depot on Parris Island, and even there appropriations for the corps were sharply cut in the last days of the Hoover administration. In July 1932 one hundred civilian employees at Parris Island were put on indefinite furlough. At the end of 1932, appropriations were reduced by 20 percent, and Marine Corps personnel diminished by 1,780 men. This level of austerity again raised the specter of closing Parris Island. "Should this program be carried through by administration officials," lamented the *Beaufort Gazette,* "it means the possible abandonment of the Marine Training Station now at Parris Island or so curtailing activities at that post as to require only a small squad of caretakers." That was what had happened to Parris Island after the navy abandoned the station in 1901.[5]

The decline of Beaufort County's last industry drove the local economy into grinding poverty. Land values declined during the 1930s, if any buyers could have been found. Retail sales plummeted, and deposits in the last remaining bank in the county reached historic lows in 1936. Although the local newspaper tried to suppress the story, Beaufort County citizens starved to death in the 1930s.

In 1935 an editorial in the *Beaufort Gazette* commented that "increased activity in real estate is the true barometer of improved conditions in the Beaufort section. Truck farming is the principal industry of the community followed by real estate sales." But like truck farming, real estate was in a deep slump. Sales soon slowed after the 1929 market crash. By the mid-1930s sales had nearly ceased. The same 1935 editorial noted that "real estate agents and lawyers have not made any real money from real estate transactions in recent years. The office of clerk of court has not been rushed recording transfers of property." Lack of demand lowered the tax value of county property and thereby lowered public revenue. "A study of the levy sheets for the past six years (1926–1932) will disclose that there has been a radical revision downward in the levy on real property in the county," the paper reported. County Treasurer Rivers Varn reported in 1936 that real property values had declined 6 percent from 1927 to 1935. The total value of taxable property in Beaufort County in 1935 was $3,851,210.[6]

This decline in property values and tax revenues forced local government to tighten their belts. As the *Gazette* commented, "it is necessary to curtail expenditures. This will make it impossible to continue permanent improvements everywhere." In January 1932 the city council reduced the salaries of its employees, mostly police and street maintenance workers, by 20 percent. Between 1927 and 1933 county property tax levies declined by an average of 35 percent. The *Gazette* editorialized, "We doubt if there is any county in the state that can report such a county-wide reduction in the tax levy as Beaufort County." But because of the "firm sound course" of the county commission, "not a single teacher or creditor of the county has suffered a minute." Somehow, Beaufort County met its financial obligations in the teeth of the Depression.[7]

Retail sales also slumped. The U.S. Census Bureau reported that in 1931 Beaufort County had 251 retail stores with retail sales of $2,610,000. The county lagged behind its neighbors, Hampton, Colleton, and Barnwell counties. By 1933 Beaufort County total retail sales were $1,456,000, down 55 percent in two years. In 1936 there were 232 employees in retail stores in Beaufort County, and they earned average wages of $56.75 per month.

In 1938 the annual report of the South Carolina Tax Commission published economic statistics for the state extracted from the Department of Commerce Consumer Market Data Handbook for 1936. The statistics for Beaufort County at the bottom of the Depression were comparable to those of an undeveloped colony.[8]

Beaufort County, Economic Statistics, 1930–1936

1930	Total Population	21,815
	% White	28.7%
1933	Total County Retail Purchases	$1,456,000
1933	Total County Wholesale Purchases	$682,000

(continued)

1933	Per Capita Retail Purchases -	$67.00
1933	Service, Amusement and Hotel Receipts	$82,000
1933	Number of Personal Income Tax Returns	152
1930	Number of Houses Wired for Electricity	446
1936	Number of Residence Telephones	191
1934	Number of Passenger Cars Registered	1,268
1934	Number of Commercial Vehicles	320
1935	Value of Farmlands and Buildings	$3,726,000
1935	Relief Expenditures	$236,000
1935	Average Number of Persons on Relief	3,506
	% of Total County Population	16%

After the Beaufort Bank closed in 1926, the county had one financial institution, the old Peoples Bank, which only survived by the exercise of extraordinary measures. Total assets of Beaufort's banks had peaked in 1923 at $3,777,163. Thereafter, deposits and assets declined steadily for thirteen years. Even after the Beaufort Bank failed, deposits in the Peoples Bank did not increase. The assets of the Peoples Bank hit rock bottom in March 1936 at $369,516.06. The county's financial institutions declined 90 percent in the thirteen years between 1923 and 1936.[9]

By 1932 the People's Bank was on the verge of bankruptcy. To save its last financial institution, Beaufort citizens and merchants met at the Community Club on July 21, 1932. All the bank stockholders agreed to pledge their stock to a new corporation reorganized as the People's Holding Company. In addition, Mayor W. R. Bristol and the city council declared a "five day holiday during which all the business houses including the bank should be closed." The merchants and citizens agreed to this extraordinary business moratorium. In addition, it was said, the depositors, "white and colored," cooperated almost unanimously in this banking and business "holiday."

Beaufortonians expected the People's Bank to receive assistance from the federal government's Reconstruction Finance Corporation. When the People's Holding Company was organized, three directors were chosen by depositors and two directors were chosen by stockholders. Depositors pledged to leave 30 percent of their deposits in the bank for at least two years. These extraordinary, cooperative measures were designed to "give the only remaining financial institution in the county time in which to rehabilitate itself." Despite heroic self-sacrifice, it was apparent by 1932 that the People's Bank was insolvent and would soon be placed in the hands of a receiver. "It was either re-adjustment or receivership," noted the *Beaufort Gazette.* "The bank failure of 1926 had taught the people that bank receiverships were not to be desired." On August 11, 1932, the state issued a new charter to the People's Holding Company. The stockholders met and selected R. K. Harley, F.W. Scheper Jr., H. R. Pollitzer, L.A. Hall, and W. H. Ohlandt as directors. The officers were R. K. Harley, president; H. R. Pollitzer, vice-president; M. Toland Sams, cashier; and F.W. Scheper Jr., chairman of the board. Because the reorganized People's Bank was "a matter of community interest, [the officers] deemed it advisable to create an advisory board." The board consisted of large depositors who would meet monthly, consult with the board of directors, and assist in the institution's operations. Its members were E. E. Lengnick, H. E. Danner, J. R. Bellamy, R. L. Varn, and Jasper Woods.[10]

The People's Bank was reportedly "the first bank in the South to declare a moratorium." The cooperative measures taken by the bank, the merchants, the municipal government, and the depositors attracted attention throughout the region. Beaufort's example was "watched with interest throughout the United States and information was requested from some of the most prominent businessmen in the country." As if following Beaufort's example, for two weeks in March 1933 all the banks in the nation were closed by President Franklin Delano Roosevelt's proclamation. When the "holiday" was lifted on March 18, 1933, the People's Bank of Beaufort was one of only ninety-seven banks in South Carolina that were permitted to reopen.[11] The bank survived the crises of 1932 and 1933, but it did not prosper. In fact, its deposits and total assets declined for three more years, reaching rock bottom on March 18, 1936, when its deposits were $341,024.33 and total assets were $369,516.66.[12]

One of Beaufort County's most enterprising responses to the Depression years was to open an exchange market in a vacant building on Bay Street. The Beaufort Barter Exchange was managed by N. M. Polk and J. K. Nettles. Its purpose was to permit sea islanders to "conduct a co-operative community business without the use of legal tender currency [money] by issuing credit certificates in exchange for goods sold to it and accepting the same in return for goods sold by it." The Beaufort Barter Exchange was not organized for profit but "for the sole benefit and welfare of all who participate in its operations." People with anything to sell brought their items to the barter exchange and either placed them on consignment or accepted "credit certificates" in lieu of cash. According to the *Beaufort Gazette,* these credit certificates could be used at the barter exchange or be spent "outside with those willing to accept this form of money. . . . Already a list of professionals, mechanics and various forms of service has agreed to accept this form of payment. It is expected that soon most stores will accept at least partial payment in it." The Beaufort Barter Exchange was a local adjustment for a community that by 1933 was almost entirely out of money. It remained in operation through the 1930s.[13]

Beaufortonians faced the grim poverty of the Depression years with considerable sardonic humor. Each year for more than twenty years, local citizens enjoyed an "annual Valentine's Ball." Since 1918, the ball had been held at the Community Club. When the organizers met in 1933, they selected the Depression as its theme. The "Depression Ball" was held on Friday, February 10, 1933. All the ladies were asked to wear "evening dresses worn in 1925 and the gentlemen are asked to wear out-of-date suits." For Beaufortonians the year 1925 had been significant. It was the last year of economic normalcy before the Beaufort Bank failure and the start of the Great Depression in Beaufort County.[14]

While Beaufort's commercial establishment used barter to stimulate trade and humor to lighten the mood, the sea island citizens on the lowest rung of the economic ladder experienced the 1930s as matters of life and death. Rumors of hunger, deprivation, and malnutrition had circulated in Beaufort County for years. Local authorities had denied, disparaged, or suppressed those stories. In 1932 one story broke out and attracted attention to hunger in Beaufort County. In 1931 a forty-two-year-old African American woman from Seabrook, Sarah Smalls, died in Nurse Catherine Deveaux's "colored hospital." Catherine Deveaux was the nurse, midwife, and medical practitioner for Beaufort's African American population. She was respected, even revered, for her years of service. The cause of Sarah Smalls's death was listed "malnutrition." Clotilde Martin, Beaufort's correspondent for the *Charleston News and Courier,* reported the story of starvation, and her article was repeated in several daily newspapers. Beaufort County aid workers gave the same cause of death for a ten-year-old African American girl in Sheldon in 1931. Although the facts were much disputed at the time, it seemed clear that at least these two deaths were from lack of food. Defending her article, which was sensationalized in the Charleston newspaper, Clotilde Martin stated, "There are hungry people in Beaufort County. . . . If you don't believe it, go to Catherine Deveaux and let her tell you about the pitiful cases reported to her. . . . Go to Dr. Kennedy . . . if you want to find out whether or not there are people actually hungry . . . in Beaufort County." Martin summed up the circumstances for Beaufort County's poorest citizens in the depths of the Depression: "For too long Beaufort County Negroes have lived off the surplus of their white employer's truck . . . and when lean years come to their employers, the negroes are bound to suffer."[15] By 1935, Beaufort County had become one of the poorest places in the United States.

COMMERCIAL SEAFOOD INDUSTRY

The Depression of the 1920s and 1930s saw the last vestiges of Beaufort County's once proud maritime industries disappear. The end of the phosphate industry and the removal of the naval station knocked the pins from under the maritime businesses that had surrounded Port Royal Sound from 1870 to 1901. The early twentieth century saw the passing of not only many of the symbols of that era but also of the proud mariners.

First the ships disappeared. The last year of recordable maritime traffic in Port Royal Sound was 1912, and it was a far cry from the heyday of the 1880s. Thirteen lumber schooners cleared Port Royal in 1912. Among them was the three-masted schooner *Delight* commanded by Captain Hutchinson, who had sailed vessels into Port Royal Sound since 1876 and remembered the busy commerce at Port Royal. "Captain Hutchinson is an old timer," the *Beaufort Gazette* observed. "He was here thirty-six years ago, in 1876, when Port Royal was more prosperous than it is now." On November 8, 1912, Captain Hutchinson and the *Delight* began their last trip from Port Royal bound for New York with 431,300 board feet of southern yellow pine.[16] That was the end of an era. The year 1912 also saw the last square-rigger in Port Royal Sound. In late October the barkentine *J. B. Rabel* entered Port Royal from Port Reading, New Jersey, with 570 tons of coal for the C&WC Railroad. The ship was "an almost extinct type as are almost all square-riggers. Fewer than a dozen remain in the Atlantic fleet." The end of these elegant ships prompted an old Beaufortonian to sigh, "Alas for departed glory."[17]

Occasionally, lumber schooners from "down east" visited the sea islands, but they came less and less often. When two schooners appeared at the same time in 1922, the visits prompted vain hope for the revival of the maritime trade. The *Rosalie Hull* of Savannah loaded lumber from the Howard White lumber mill in Yemassee and the *Ann G. Ross* of Boston took on lumber from the Argent Timber Company of Hardeeville. Both ships were four-masted schooners of approximately 1,200 tons and bound for New York. But the maritime traffic did not return to Port Royal. In 1925 the *Albert H. Willis,* with 650 tons of yellow pine, left Port Royal Sound for New York City. Seventy cars of the Charleston and Western Carolina Railroad were needed to fill the ship to capacity. The schooner's departure marked the end of commercial sailing on Port Royal Sound.[18]

Steamboats that had been such an important part of island life for more than a century also disappeared. In 1909 the SS *Clifton,* the venerable packet from Beaufort to Charleston, ran aground in a storm off Pigeon Point, caught fire, and burned to the waterline. C. E. Danner sold the *Summer Girl* to John Peck for use on the St. John's River between Jacksonville and Green Cove Spring, Florida. The side-wheeler *Pilot Boy,* the longest-serving packet boat in the islands, was disabled in a 1915 gale off Hilton Head Island on its way to Savannah. Its passengers and crew were rescued by the crew of the navy cruiser USS *Oneida.* The vessel was recovered and repaired but was sold and taken out of packet service. That *Pilot Boy* was the second boat of that name to serve Beaufort. The original *Pilot Boy* began the

Charleston-Beaufort-Savannah run in 1867. The second *Pilot Boy* was built in Charleston in 1885. It was driven high and dry against the Bay Street bluff by the Hurricane of 1893, dragging large sections of the Waterhouse wharf with it. The vessel survived the storm but not the technology of the twentieth century. As the *Beaufort Gazette* noted in 1915, "The advent of gasoline freighters is causing the river steamers to disappear."

In 1923 the SS *Islander,* the "longtime Beaufort-Savannah packet boat" was sold to a Petersburg, Virginia, investor for use as an excursion boat on the James River. By the 1920s the SS *Clivedon* was the last steamboat in operation. In March 1934, W. H. Cory announced that the *Clivedon* would be taken out of service for repairs. The *Clivedon* never returned to regular service. Its retirement ended the steamboat era that had begun in 1816.[19]

In addition to the obvious impact of railroads and automobiles in the decline of maritime and riverboat traffic, the twentieth century witnessed advances in marine engineering and technology that diminished the importance of Port Royal Sound to the Atlantic maritime trade. In the late nineteenth century, slow-turning reciprocating steam engines, fired by coal, gave way to oil-fired steam turbine engines. The change from reciprocating to turbine engines meant that propellers could turn many times faster, producing the same power with much smaller diameter. This reduced the draft necessary for ocean vessels and made Port Royal's deep harbor less necessary. In addition, the shift from coal to oil increased steamships' fuel capacity and thus their range of travel. Port Royal had always been a coal port, but the Atlantic maritime trade and the U.S. Navy no longer needed coaling stations at Port Royal. In 1910 the U.S. Navy launched its first oil burning, steam turbine battleship, the USS *North Dakota.* In 1927 it converted its last coal-fired battleships, the *Wyoming,* the *Utah,* and the *New York,* to oil. That, too, was the end of an era.[20]

As the ships passed into history so did the mariners of Beaufort's "maritime golden age." In 1908 Beaufort's most famous family of harbor pilots left the profession. Captains W. H. VonHarten and C. H. VonHarten, pilots since the 1870s and 1880s, converted their boat, the *Jenny B,* into a freighter with an auxiliary naphtha engine. The *Beaufort Gazette* noted: "both are pilots with much experience who left the bar . . . to engage in towing, hauling and passenger carrying with their power boats." Their older brother, H. H. VonHarten Jr. (1860–1898), was another famous pilot, who had died in 1898 in a storm off Hilton Head. In 1912 Clarence H. VonHarten (1876–1912) collapsed and died on the deck of the *Jenny B.* He was only thirty-six years old, the youngest son of German immigrant H. H. VonHarten Sr. His older brother, William H. VonHarten died at his Beaufort home in 1924 at the age of sixty years. "He always loved the sea and as soon as he was old enough he began the work he considered his calling," the retrospective in the *Beaufort Gazette* recalled. In the hurricane of 1885, he had swum through the breakers off Bay Point to rescue Captain John O'Brien and the crew of the pilot boat *F. W. Scheper.* For his heroism, he received a medal from the U.S. government, "a valued token left to his family." The Harmony Lodge No. 22, Ancient Free Masons, provided the honors at his funeral.[21]

In December 1922 Captain Peter L. Lea (1864–1922) died on his farm in Burton. He had come to Beaufort from Lynchburg, South Carolina, in 1884 and spent twenty years as a pilot. His father had been a steamboat captain on the Lynches and Pee Dee Rivers, and his grandfather had been an officer in the British navy. When maritime commerce declined, Peter Lea bought a farm and country store in Burton and became a successful vegetable farmer. His daughter, Lila Lea, married Beaufort entrepreneur Richard A. Long.

Two years later, Captain George A. Crofut (1859–1924) died at his family home on Laurens Street. He had spent twenty-three years as the "master of tugs" for the phosphate fleet and finished his career as a steamboat captain for the Savannah-Beaufort Line. He was considered "in the front rank of boat captains along this coast" and was president of the Forrest City Association No. 23, Masters, Mates and Pilots, the mariners union of Savannah. Crofut was born in New Haven, Connecticut, the only son of Bay Street merchant James M. Crofut. In 1881 George Crofut married Elizabeth Onthank of Boston, a relative of Reverend A. M. French, the principal Gideonite missionary during the Civil War occupation. George Crofut was a talented and popular musician in Beaufort with his cornet and his voice. His daughters, Elizabeth Crofut Waterhouse and Marguerite Crofut, taught piano and violin to three generations of Beaufortonians at their home on Laurens Street.[22]

In August 1929 Captain John O'Brien (1869–1929), reportedly the "oldest pilot on this coast," died at his home in Beaufort. He was born on Hilton Head Island in 1869 and spent more than twenty years as a Port Royal pilot. He had commanded a U.S. Navy ocean tug during the Spanish-American War.

Captain Harry Burr died in 1936 at the home of his daughter, Helen Burr Christensen, on New Street. He had been born to the sea in Rockland, Maine, in 1865. His father, Captain Benjamin Burr, was a master of clipper ships in the China trade and later U.S. Consul in Santo Domingo. Harry Burr moved with his father to Port Royal in 1876. A retrospective in the *Beaufort Gazette* recalled: "in those days Port Royal was a very busy place. A great deal of shipping was being done from there and many of its optimistic citizens looked confidently . . . to the day when it would be a great port and the metropolis of the South Atlantic." Harry Burr commanded vessels in the phosphate fleet of the Coosaw Mining Company. During the Hurricane of 1893, he rode the giant Coosaw Mining Company dredge on the storm surge until it crashed into the Whale Branch trestle of the Port Royal and Augusta Railroad.

In 1888 Captain Harry Burr married Lilla Collins, daughter of J. W. Collins, a Massachusetts cavalryman stationed at Hilton Head during the Civil War who had settled in Beaufort. Collins was a successful businessman, state senator, and mayor of Beaufort. Like W. H. Von Harten, Harry Burr was honored by the U.S. government for saving a government launch and its crew off Fort Fremont in the Hurricane of 1898. He swam with a lifeline into a ninety-mile-per-hour gale and brought the launch and crew safely to shore. When the phosphate industry declined, Harry Burr retired to Savannah and then to the Beaufort home of his daughter and son-in-law, Helen and Frederick Christensen. Captain Harry Burr was the last of Beaufort's intrepid seamen of the great maritime era.[23]

As Beaufort County's maritime trade declined and disappeared, the U.S. government reduced its expenditures to support local trade and navigation. One by one, the symbols and institutions of federal support disappeared. In 1910 the lighthouse inspector in Charleston ordered the Martin Industry Lightship moved from the entrance of Port Royal Sound to the entrance of the Savannah River. This change had been requested by the Savannah pilots but was "strenuously opposed" by the Port Royal pilots. Despite objections from Senator "Cotton Ed" Smith of South Carolina, the Martin Industry Lightship was gone by the end of the year. The entrance to Port Royal Sound was "left without a marker." In 1933 the Lighthouse Service decommissioned the Hunting Island lighthouse and put the federal property up for sale. Except for the Civil War years, it had been in operation for seventy-four years.

In 1912, during the waning days of the Republican Taft administration, the U.S. government ordered the Port of Beaufort and its customs house closed by July 1, 1914. The Democratic Woodrow Wilson administration, at the urging of Congressman Jimmy Byrnes, reversed that order. In 1913 Robert Smalls was removed as collector, and the job was given to F. H. Colcock, a friend of Jimmy Byrnes. Colcock held office throughout the 1920s and most of that time was also probate judge of Beaufort County. In 1930 T. R. Webb was appointed collector by President Herbert Hoover, but Webb had even less work to do than Colcock. Finally, on April 13, 1934, President Franklin D. Roosevelt ordered the closing of the Port of Beaufort. Almost no one objected, and on May 13, 1934, the collector vacated his office.[24]

Beaufort County's maritime business did not disappear entirely, however. One maritime industry survived, even thrived, during the long years of decline and Depression. The commercial seafood industry began in Beaufort County in 1891, when South Carolina entrepreneurs J. H. Haynesworth and R. K. Harley built Beaufort County's first oyster-canning factory on Lady's Island. To this day, the branch of the Beaufort River that swept past the old oyster factory is called Factory Creek. In 1893 Savannah's immigrant Italian capitalist, L. P. Maggioni, built his first oyster-canning factory in the county on Daufuskie Island. By 1908 there were eight oyster canneries in Beaufort County providing seasonal employment to thousands of sea islanders.[25]

In 1909 J. H. Haynesworth and George Tucker started a commercial fish exporting business, building a refrigerated cold-storage building on Port Republic Street. They also built two gasoline-powered launches that towed two houseboats and six bateaux "down to the seashore where the first of the season's catch will be made." The flagship of this fishing fleet was the *Ellie Mae*. It was thirty-five feet long and nine and a half feet wide and was chartered "for excursions when not fishing." Haynesworth and Tucker hired twelve fishermen, who used seine nets to harvest their catch. One of the launches was equipped with ice boxes to store the fish. The principal products were spotted sea trout, bass, and mullet. Haynesworth and Tucker hoped to sell in Georgia and South Carolina, and the later catch, in colder weather, would be "shipped north." The *Beaufort Gazette* hoped that this experiment might "be the start of an important local industry." But it was unsuccessful and ceased two years later. The experiment did reveal the utility of seine nets and small, gasoline-powered launches in the commercial seafood industry.[26]

Haynesworth and Tucker had the right equipment in 1909, but they had chosen the wrong product. About the same time they were fishing in Beaufort County, Sicilian and Portuguese fishermen were employing the same technology to catch shrimp off of Fernandina Beach, Florida. Georgia fishermen soon followed, and within the decade Florida shrimpers had found an ample supply of the tasty crustaceans in the waters of Beaufort County. The shrimping industry was improved in 1917 by the introduction of the "otter trawl," a net pulled behind a motorized vessel. Shrimping soon became the busiest, most profitable branch of the lowcountry seafood business and one of Beaufort County's signature industries throughout the twentieth century.

The first Florida fisherman to discover a marketable supply of shrimp in Beaufort County waters was I. R. Messick. Captain Messick came to Beaufort in April 1923 to "test the shrimping possibilities of this locality." In the spring of 1923, he netted only small shrimp, but local fishermen assured him that larger shrimp were abundant later in the season.[27] Captain Charles Vecchio of Fernandina, Florida, followed later in the year and has been credited with starting the local shrimping industry.

In 1909 Vecchio formed the Amelia Prawn Company in Fernandina, Florida, and shipped ten barrels of raw shrimp to New York City. At the time shrimp were not desired seafood in New York, and some taverns in the city gave them away free as cocktail favors. Twenty years later, New York City was consuming three thousand barrels daily, and by 1929 a barrel of shrimp was worth twenty-five dollars on the New York market. Captain Charlie Vecchio came to Beaufort County in fall 1923 with three trawlers to explore prospects for shrimping. By 1925 Vecchio had a fleet of five trawlers in

Beaufort County for four months each year and had built an ice house and shrimp dock on the Port Royal waterfront. Vecchio had more than twenty boats there in 1936.[28]

By 1927 Beaufort was said to be "the state's champion fisheries county." It was by far the largest producer of seafood in the state. The county was home to twenty-one of twenty-eight oyster-shucking sheds and ten of sixteen oyster canneries in the state. By 1930 half of South Carolina's shrimp production came from Beaufort County. In 1927, only four years after the shrimping industry began, fifty licensed shrimp trawlers operated in local waters. They produced 1,503,447 pounds of shrimp in 1927. That shrimp catch doubled by 1929. Three canneries produced 860,128 cans of shrimp worth $215,032 in 1927 and "found ready markets for their goods." By 1934 Beaufort County had sixty-six trawlers in its seasonal shrimp fleet but only five were locally owned. The rest were from out of state, mostly Florida shrimpers. Although South Carolina's seafood production lagged behind that of Florida, Georgia, and Louisiana, it was nonetheless a great bonanza for Beaufort County. The chairman of the State Board of Fisheries in 1927 was E. D. Raney of Beaufort.[29]

In 1928 the county's seafood industry brought even more good news. The Davenport-Brooks Corporation of Florida, "one of the largest shrimp canning corporations in the world," took over the abandoned site of the American Shipbuilding Company on Spanish Point. There it built a $100,000 shrimp canning factory and planned to employ two hundred people during the season. It expected its payroll to be $175,000 to $200,000 annually. In 1929 Brooks-Davenport became Brooks-Hirth-Corbett Corporation. It built an all-steel building on Spanish Point that was 250 feet long and 190 feet wide. It was a modern, all-electric plant that produced nine hundred cases of canned shrimp per day. During the shrimp season from July through November, the Brooks-Hirth-Corbett Corporation employed one hundred white workers and two hundred black workers. Its payroll was $7,500 per day. The company owned a fleet of gasoline-powered shrimp trawlers that were twenty-four feet long and operated by a crew of three men. Every three days during the season, the shrimp boats returned to the factory on Spanish Point and unloaded an average of two hundred baskets per trip. During the 1930s, the shrimping industry provided nearly a thousand local jobs. The *Beaufort Gazette* noted, "The coming of the shrimping industry has meant that Beaufort has been fortunate enough to stave off the *bread line*. It has meant that hundreds of local folk were able to remain here and not go elsewhere to seek employment. This has saved the local merchants from being forced to close shop and pull out."[30]

While the new seafood industry helped Beaufort County survive the depths of the Depression, it was not popular with everyone. Traditional fishermen complained to the State Board of Fisheries that trawling in the inshore waters depleted the supply of sea trout, bass, and drum fish. Several meetings were held between shrimpers and fishermen, and the shrimpers agreed to trawl in deeper water. In 1931 the local legislative delegation convinced the General Assembly to pass a law prohibiting trawling inland waters. Violation was punished by a fine of one hundred dollars. Although the fines have increased, this law has generally governed the industry since the 1930s.

In addition to state regulation, the new shrimping industry encountered problems with the local labor force. In 1933 the entire crew of shrimp "pickers" on Bay Street walked off the job, demanding twice the wages that they were being paid. At the time the shrimp pickers were paid five cents per bucket for deheading shrimp. More disturbing than the wage demands was the fact that the striking workers were armed with clubs and prevented replacement workers from entering the site. The threat of violence brought out Sheriff McTeer, who asserted that anyone had the right to strike but no one had the right to prevent others from working or to threaten violence against those who did. His forceful intervention may have prevented a riot or at least a brawl. As the *Beaufort Gazette* noted, "Things looked a little lively until the sheriff took charge." The factory on the Waterhouse dock briefly shut down, and the shrimp were sent to Port Royal for packing and shipping.[31]

Despite government regulation and occasional labor disputes, Beaufort County's seafood industry thrived. A report in 1932 revealed that the Maggioni oyster factory on Lady's Island processed fifteen hundred bushels of raw oysters each day during the fall and winter season. Oysters were delivered by a half-dozen sailing "bateaux," wide beam, shallow-draft work boats that filled Factory Creek nearly every day. These boats were customarily manned by two black oystermen, who remained out in the river for a week at a time and usually returned with two hundred bushels per vessel. The oystermen took the shellfish with long oyster tongs over intertidal oyster beds that the Maggioni Company leased each year from the state. The factories were required to reseed each oyster bed after harvesting. Effluvia from the city sewer system polluted the oyster beds in the Beaufort River. They were declared off limits by the state health department.

Hundreds of African American women worked in the Lady's Island oyster factory shucking, cleaning, and steaming the oysters. For nearly half a century, they were called to work each day by a steam whistle. Fifteen hundred bushels produced four hundred cases of twenty-four cans each or ninety-six hundred cans of oysters each day. Maggioni had a dozen shucking sheds and two steam-canning plants. The company was the largest industrial enterprise in the county. In 1936 Maggioni dismantled one of its original factories at Dulamo and built a larger one at Sams Point on Lady's Island. This business provided thousands of seasonal jobs for sea islanders. A *Beaufort*

Gazette editorialist observed, "Now that the trucking business has about gone on the rocks . . . our leaders should give more attention to other industries. Our people must live. . . . Largely due to the shrimp and oyster business the Negroes of our islands are able to secure sufficient employment as to live. . . . It is our duty to see that such a condition continues."[32]

On September 26, 1935, Gilbert Phillip Maggioni died suddenly at his longtime home at the Hotel Savannah. He was the president of Maggioni and Company and a pioneer in the southern seafood industry. In 1935 the Maggioni Company was considered "the largest business of its kind in the United States." Phillip Maggioni's funeral was held at St. Patrick's Cathedral in Savannah. He had been president of the Southern Fisheries Association in 1926 and of the United State Fisheries Association in 1928. His death was a great loss to the region and was keenly felt in Beaufort County.[33]

In 1936 Beaufort County acquired another element of its commercial seafood industry when W. G. Ruark and Company of Belhaven, North Carolina, opened the county's first crabmeat-canning factory on the Port Royal waterfront. This factory processed fresh crabs by boiling them in a huge boiler and then picking and sorting the meat, which was packed and sealed in one-pound cans. Ruark and Company expected to supply crabmeat for Atlantic and Pacific (A&P) grocery stores in Washington, Baltimore, Philadelphia, and New York. It employed about fifty sea island "crabbers" who ran trotlines of bait from which the crabs were caught in dip nets. They were paid a penny a pound for crabs delivered to the factory. The company employed about one hundred female pickers, who were paid five cents per pound for clean meat. An average picker could easily earn a dollar a day. Nearly all these jobs went to African Americans, and the new business was much appreciated for its ability to "furnish employment to many Negroes of Beaufort and Port Royal . . . a badly needed payroll for these people." The crab season, unlike the oyster and shrimp seasons, ran almost year round, from April through December.

Beaufort County's crab meat industry took a great leap forward in 1939 when the Blue Channel Corporation of Centerville, Maryland, moved its entire business to Port Royal, where it built the county's most advanced seafood factory. The Blue Channel Corporation was led by its president and principal stockholder, Sterling Harris. Harris and Dr. Carl Fellers, professor of chemistry at Massachusetts State College, had spent six years perfecting a process for cleaning and canning the delicate white meat of the American blue crab, for which they and the Blue Channel Corporation received an exclusive patent in 1938. Blue crab meat was discolored by steaming, reducing its market appeal. Harris and Feller's process solved this problem. The company moved to Beaufort County because the blue crab supply in the Chesapeake Bay had been seriously depleted by 1939, and crabs were abundant among the sea islands. Blue Channel was a pillar of the county's economy for forty years.[34]

On the eve of World War II, Beaufort County's commercial seafood industry was the largest in the state, although Charleston's and Georgetown's businesses were expanding rapidly. For thousands of sea islanders during the hardest years of the Great Depression, the commercial seafood business kept just enough food on their tables and just enough income to prevent them all from abandoning the lowcountry.

THE NEW DEAL IN BEAUFORT COUNTY

By 1930 Beaufort County had officially become one of the poorest places in America. With virtually all the county's industrial activity gone or severely limited by 1930 and its principal sources of employment in the vegetable farming and seafood industries paying low seasonal wages, Beaufort County's economic depression was a decade or more in advance of the nation's. By 1930 nearly half the county's citizens had left the impoverished sea islands for greener pastures in urban America. Thus, when Franklin Delano Roosevelt's New Deal became the nation's political and economic policy, it was much welcomed in Beaufort County.

The general election of 1932 was a watershed in American political history. Roosevelt's landslide swept away a dozen years of Republican ascendancy in the executive and legislative branches of the national government. Beaufort County voters contributed little to FDR's victory, but the county's oldest political friends found prominent places in the New Deal that followed.

South Carolina senator James F. Byrnes became FDR's liaison to Congress. Byrnes had accompanied Roosevelt on his last southern campaign tour and was one of the principal architects of FDR's southern strategy. These national political developments were watched with pride and hope in Beaufort County in the months before the inauguration. The *Beaufort Gazette* reflected that pride: "Senator Byrnes occupies a position in national affairs hardly filled by a solon of the state since the War Between the States. . . . Senator Byrnes is better known as 'Jimmy' in Beaufort. He is no stranger here. . . . We are indeed proud of Jimmy." The newspaper recalled that the friendship between Byrnes and Roosevelt had first been formed in Beaufort County in December 1913, when the men toured the abandoned naval station in preparation for the founding of the Marine Corps Recruit Depot in 1915: "He and President Roosevelt are warm personal friends. . . . They formed a friendship for each other during the Wilson administration when the President was serving as assistant secretary of the Navy and Jimmy was making a name for himself in the house." In the spring of 1933, it was generally acknowledged that Jimmy Byrnes was the real Democratic leader of the Senate, while Joseph T. Robinson of Arkansas was only the nominal majority leader. "Byrnes on deck!" was the way the local paper described his new authority.[35]

Beaufort got more good news in May 1933, when it was announced that Beaufort native Leon Keyserling (1908–1987) had been appointed to a key position in the legal division of the U.S. Department of Agriculture. Keyserling was the oldest child of Beaufort entrepreneur William Keyserling. He was a star student in Beaufort's public schools, attended Columbia University, and graduated from Harvard Law School in 1931. When the New Deal began to take shape in 1933, Keyserling was teaching economics at Columbia. His mentor was economist Rexford Tugwell, a member of FDR's famous "brain trust" and a chief architect of the New Deal. When Tugwell became assistant secretary of agriculture under Henry Wallace, Keyserling joined the Department of Agriculture as a lawyer.

Leon Keyserling spent the rest of his life in Washington. He was later an aide to Senator Robert F. Wagner of New York and helped author important New Deal legislation. Eventually, Leon Keyserling rose to become chairman of the Council of Economic Advisors under President Harry Truman. The *Beaufort Gazette* exuded pride in the success of a local boy: "Beaufort should be very proud of Leon and we extend our congratulations to Mr. and Mrs. William Keyserling." With friends in high places, Beaufort County had reason to hope for some dispensation of federal largesse.[36]

The flagship program of the New Deal was the National Recovery Act (NRA). Under its umbrella, scores of federal programs sought to stimulate economic recovery through federal control of industrial and agricultural planning. Rexford Tugwell was a leading advocate of centrally planned economic systems. General Hugh S. Johnson, who had commanded the War Industries Board for Woodrow Wilson during World War I, was put in charge of the NRA. He adopted the "Blue Eagle" symbol for the NRA and promoted cooperation among industry and labor interests throughout the nation. Within six months, Beaufort County had called a citizens meeting, selected a local board and chairman, and secured the endorsement of Beaufort's business establishment for the NRA. The highest-ranking federal official in Beaufort, postmaster Trower Craven, called the meeting. Hal R. Pollitzer chaired the citizens' gathering at the Community Club. Hundreds attended. Allan Paul was chosen NRA chairman for Beaufort County. G.W. Kinghorn, W. H. Ohlandt, F. H. Rhodes, and Dr. W. M. Steinmeyer formed the executive committee. Later Adam Haskell, owner of Tidalholm, became permanent chairman of the NRA compliance board.

The aim of the NRA was to get all the merchants and businesses in America to follow federal guidelines regarding wages, prices, working hours, and hiring practices. Twenty-eight of Beaufort's most prominent commercial establishments endorsed the NRA guidelines and proudly displayed the

Blue Eagle on their doors. In September 1933 the merchants, the chamber of commerce, and NRA enthusiasts promoted a citywide "Paint-Up, Clean-Up Week." They hoped to put many unemployed painters to work and reduce the inventory of unused paint in local hardware stores. Beaufort had a dilapidated "appearance of poverty" they hoped to correct. The organizers recognized that Beaufort's old buildings were a unique asset, contending that "if these old homes aren't taken care of and preserved, they will soon become unattractive and eyesores . . . detracting instead of lending color to the present scenes. We realize that property owners are up against it, but they should take steps to save their property." It may have been Beaufort's first organized community effort for historic preservation.[37]

The first major New Deal statute was the Emergency Relief Act of May 1933. Congress made available $500 million in grants to the states through the Federal Emergency Relief Agency (FERA). The state established the South Carolina Emergency Relief Administration (SCERA) to distribute these grants to the counties. Governor Ibra Blackwood appointed Malcolm Miller of Columbia to manage the state program. Its responsibility was to approve all local programs and projects for funding. Beaufort County's FERA administrator was R. R. Legare and its advisory board was composed of J. G. Black, Reverend F. B. Mayes, R. W. Cohen, R. V. Bray, and W. C. Brant. Money was distributed through the National Re-employment Office managed by Lamar Carson. All Beaufort County residents seeking employment or relief applied to Carson. His was a very busy office. By January 1934 more than 1,800 Beaufortonians were receiving payroll checks for work on federal programs, and another 450 citizens were receiving direct federal relief. This was 10.3 percent of the county's population in 1933 and about 30 percent of its work force.

Local FERA projects accomplished by the Civil Works Administration (CWA) were paving streets, extending the city water and sewer systems, and repairing the arsenal. County projects included sanitary drainage projects and malaria, mosquito, and gnat abatement. Individuals were paid to teach or assist as home economics teachers or farm and home demonstration agents. Many worked in the library, in public nurseries, or in hospitals as nursing assistants. They were employed in school lunchrooms and as playground assistants. Others found work compiling government statistics for farm surveys, mortgage surveys, commodity and retail price surveys, and a census of American business. In 1933 and 1934, these early New Deal programs spent $292,923 in Beaufort County. While the FERA programs provided immediate relief, the money soon dried up, and in March 1934 President Roosevelt began to phase out the program.[38]

One FERA program continued for months after the revenue dried up. The Federal Surplus Relief Corporation (FSRC) was in charge of distributing food, clothing, bedding, medicine, and other emergency supplies to those in need. In 1935 county FERA administrator R. R. Legare reported that in 1934 his agency had distributed 183,973 pounds of meat, 84,259 pounds of flour, butter, and other food products, 47,619 pounds of fresh vegetables, 30,371 cans of food, 480 bottles of medicine, 250 double blankets, and 7 mattresses to citizens on relief. In addition, the Marine Corps Recruit Depot on Parris Island provided 4,774 pairs of shoes to SCERA for distribution throughout the state. Most of the fresh vegetables distributed in the county were grown in local gardens of fifty acres or less under the direction of the ERA garden supervisor, Lillian Rice. Beaufort's ERA operated its own cannery, which contributed 115,513 cans of vegetables to SCERA.[39]

While these emergency measures provided immediate relief in 1933 and 1934, they were never intended to be permanent programs. Some New Deal programs offered more long-term help. Congress established the Federal Home Owner's Loan Corporation in June 1933, to buy up 80 percent of the value of qualified mortgages, convert them to government bonds, offer longer terms and easier payments to distressed homeowners, and in some cases pay overdue property taxes. Home loans under the 1933 act were limited to fourteen thousand dollars or less. On December 7, 1933, Christine Jenkins became the first Beaufort County resident to receive mortgage relief through the Federal Home Owners Loan Corporation. Jennie Bostick was the second. Thereafter, hundreds of Beaufortonians successfully kept their homes with the help of low-cost government mortgages.

A similar New Deal program applied to farms. The 1933 Farm Loan Act offered extended terms and easier payments to alleviate the credit pressure on local farmers. These loans were administered through the Federal Land Bank in Columbia, and the Beaufort County agent was W. Ed Nelson, former bookkeeper of the defunct Beaufort Bank. In November 1933 Bertha Rieger of St. Helena Island was the first Beaufort County farm owner to receive a low-cost government loan. The second farm loan went to Josephine Bryan. Eventually, hundreds of local farmers received government farm loans.

Credit for farming operations was available through the Beaufort County Production Credit Association, a branch of the federal Production Credit Corporation. The local officers of the PCA in December 1933 were J. R. Bellamy, president; Ben Bostick, vice president; and Jasper Woods, secretary-treasurer. Gustave Sanders and E. D. Raney were also members. The PCA office was on the second floor of the Morrall Furniture Company on Bay Street. Jasper Woods asked for patience from his truck-farming friends as preference for these government loans was given to resident farmers over the larger vegetable "planters."[40] These farm and home refinancing programs were a great aid to Beaufort County.

One of the most successful of the New Deal jobs programs was the Civilian Conservation Corps (CCC), which was established in March 1933 to provide useful employment to unemployed young men between the ages of seventeen and twenty-five. Each CCC "camper" received room, board, and thirty dollars per month in wages, twenty-two dollars of which was sent to the camper's family. The first seventeen CCC camps in South Carolina were established in 1933. Each camp was designed to house two hundred young men. One of these seventeen CCC camps was in Beaufort County.

Many hoped that the CCC camp would be placed on Parris Island, where ample facilities existed and some of the payroll would be spent in Beaufort and Port Royal stores. However, the camp was placed near Hardeeville, still part of Beaufort County in 1933, where men worked on forestry, fire protection, and drainage along the Savannah River. Captain B. L. Vogt, USMC, commanded the Hardeeville CCC Camp. In 1934 Beaufort's camp was moved to Givhan's Ferry in Dorchester County. This CCC branch built the state park at Givhan's Ferry and Edisto State Park on Edisto Island.

The Civilian Conservation Corps was one of the most popular New Deal programs in South Carolina. By 1939 it had employed 31,823 men and 4,340 support personnel in thirty camps throughout the state, and the federal government had spent $36.4 million in the state. The most lasting legacy of the CCC was the creation of the South Carolina state park system. Before the CCC, South Carolina had no state parks. By 1939 the state had fourteen brand-new state parks and recreation areas, including Hunting Island State Park in Beaufort County. They are some of the state's greatest assets to this day.[41]

The New Deal program with the most lasting effect was the Public Works Administration (PWA). The PWA was established in June 1933 to breathe new life into the construction and building trades. Secretary of the Interior Harold Ickes was put in charge of the vast national PWA projects. Public buildings, public schools, and highways across America were built or repaired under PWA programs. The Tennessee Valley Authority (TVA) was the PWA's flagship project. In South Carolina the public highways were the greatest beneficiary of this New Deal program. By 1934 forty-three hundred men per month were employed in paving or otherwise improving the state's highways.

The largest PWA project in South Carolina was the Santee Cooper hydroelectric power project to produce electricity for industry, military installations, and local communities in the southeastern section of the state. Santee Cooper grew into the largest New Deal program in the state and the largest single PWA project on the East Coast. Santee Cooper was opposed from the start by elitist conservationists, native South Carolina owners of family plantations, and "wealthy northerners who hunted in the lowcountry." This group resented the federal exercise of eminent domain statutes, the inundation of farmlands by construction of Lakes Moultrie and Marion, and the displacement of white and black communities in the lowcountry. Senator Jimmy Byrnes's consummate political skill overcame all opposition. The General Assembly, led by Senator Richard Manning Jeffries of Colleton County, created the South Carolina Public Service Authority to qualify for PWA grants and loans that eventually totaled $65 million. R. M. Jeffries, later governor of South Carolina, was the young Ridgeland schoolteacher who led the movement to create Jasper County in 1912. The Santee Cooper project that he and Byrnes championed eventually employed 16,300 men during its construction. It created the largest artificial lake on the East Coast and provided rural electrification across the lowcountry. In 1935 only 2 percent of lowcountry farms had electricity. Twenty-five years later, 74 percent of lowcountry farms had electricity, adding immeasurably to the quality of life in the rural lowcountry.[42]

Even before the giant Santee Cooper power project came on line, Beaufort County was experiencing the benefit of the federal and state government's efforts to provide rural electrification. In 1935 the federal government established the Rural Electrification Administration (REA) to provide federal loans to construct rural electricity lines. In February 1935 the General Assembly passed the South Carolina Rural Electrification Act, establishing the state Rural Electrification Authority (SCREA) to survey new power lines, obtain property easements, build power lines that investor-owned companies deemed unprofitable, and purchase power from producers at discounted rates for rural customers. Backed by federal loans, the Rural Electrification Authority was essentially a competitor with private utility companies. While the private companies objected to the situation, SCREA nevertheless sent these private companies scrambling throughout the countryside in search of new customers.

Two municipal power plants in Beaufort and Hardeeville were bought by the investor-owned South Carolina Power Company, which became South Carolina Electric and Gas Corporation. The company became the present-day SCANA Corporation. Beaufort had a power plant that was built in 1909 at the railroad depot and first provided electric power for the town in 1910. That plant eventually provided power for Port Royal. In 1936 the South Carolina Power Company bought the Hardeeville Light and Ice Company and, with the help of REA loans, extended electric lines along State Highway 46 to Pritchardville and Bluffton. In northern Beaufort County, electric power lines were extended in 1936 to twelve customers at Dale, nine at Gray's Hill, five at Garden's Corner, and eighty customers at Lady's Island and St. Helena Island. As meager as this beginning seemed in 1936, it was the start of development in the lowcountry. The *Beaufort Gazette* got it right in 1936: "We see in the extension of these electrical lines throughout the county, the first step in rural development."[43]

The Public Works Administration provided funds for two notable construction projects in Beaufort. In 1936 a gymnasium and classrooms were added to Beaufort High School. The contract brought $56,300 in construction expenditures to Beaufort. Those facilities were used until Beaufort High School moved to a new building in Mossy Oaks in 1959. At the same time, a PWA grant was matched by county funds to repair and remodel the Beaufort County courthouse. At that time the courthouse was altered from its original Victorian architectural design of 1881 to its present art deco design of 1936. The architect for the courthouse remodeling was J. Whitney Cunningham of Sumter. New offices, a new steam-heating system, and a new lobby were added at that time. The remodeling cost $33,120.[44]

After Federal Emergency Relief Administration funds expired in March 1934, the federal government funded a more permanent welfare employment program, the famous Works Progress Administration (WPA), which was created in 1935 to provide employment to those on relief or otherwise unemployed. While the PWA took on larger contract work on public facilities, the WPA undertook smaller projects, usually under twenty-five thousand dollars. Thousands of construction, repair, improvement, beautification, and public welfare projects were sponsored from 1935 to 1943. The WPA expended $109.3 million in wages for thousands of South Carolinians. Throughout the state, public highways and public schools were the greatest beneficiaries of WPA projects. The state WPA director was Lawrence Monck Pinckney of Charleston.

The WPA left a lasting impact on Beaufort County. In 1935 a work crew supervised by S. Paul Schwartz Sr. excavated "the Lake" on the town's Old Point, built the tide gate on Federal Street, and the public park on the corner of East and King Streets. In 1935 and 1936, WPA workers paved Hancock, Pinckney, Prince, and North Streets and extended the city sewer system along New, Scott, West, and Harrington Streets and throughout the neighborhood. At the same time, WPA projects demolished old "negro schools" in Bluffton and Gray's Hill and replaced them with new ones. They built a school building on Coosaw Island and dug numerous drainage ditches on Hilton Head and Daufuskie Islands. All these projects provided useful employment for unemployed citizens of Beaufort County and welcome payrolls for Beaufort County merchants.

The WPA financed the Beaufort Fine Arts Association through its Federal Arts Project. Six thousand dollars per year supported a new Civic Arts Gallery at the Township Library and the Beaufort City Schools Art Program. Walter W. Thompson of the Beaufort-Brevard Arts Colonies was president of the Beaufort Fine Arts Association. Other officers were Mrs. Fred Newell, Mary Waterhouse, Toland Sams, and Elizabeth Parker. The WPA supported a community-wide children's recreation program directed by Lily Mae Cummings in Beaufort, Eva Verdier in Port Royal, Thelma Crosby in Bluffton, and Mary Pinckney in Pritchardville. Rosa Burr and Marion Grayson directed a WPA recreation program for African American children in Port Royal and Beaufort.

In July 1941 Beaufort County Schools applied to the federal Public Works Administration and the Works Progress Administration for funds to construct a new brick elementary school on Carteret Street next to the old Beaufort College building. The estimated cost in 1941 was eighty-eight thousand dollars. This project was approved but never started before America's entry into World War II. The school was not completed until 1948. Today it houses the University of South Carolina Beaufort's Performing Arts Center.[45]

Of all the New Deal projects in Beaufort County, the one with the most lasting effect on the region, by far, was the creation of the Hunting Island State Park. The idea of beachfront development in Beaufort County had been a dream of local entrepreneurs since the 1890s. Beaufortonians had used Bay Point as a picnic and camping ground since before the Civil War. By the 1890s steamboat excursions to Bay Point were weekly events during the summer, and many Beaufort families "marooned" there for weeks at a time. When automobile travel was in its infancy, some visionary Beaufortonians had plans to build a bridge from Land's End on St. Helena Island to Bay Point. As late as 1933, local promoters were still talking about an automobile bridge to Bay Point.

In 1933 the federal government abandoned the Hunting Island lighthouse, along with the closing of the Port of Beaufort. Local politicians and the chamber of commerce sought to obtain the property from the government to be used as a lifesaving station or public beach. Since the 1890s the greater part of the Hunting Island property, along with neighboring Fripp Island and Pritchard's Island, had been part of the hunting preserve of James McLaughlin of New York's McLaughlin Brothers Publishing Company. McLaughlin had bought the barrier islands in 1903 and was a regular part of Beaufort's winter society until his death in 1918. The islands remained part of the McLaughlin estate until 1933. James Cameron of Harrisburg, Pennsylvania, and Dr. A.W. Elting of Albany, New York, bought the remainder of the McLaughlin estate on Hunting Island. Fripp and Pritchard's Islands were sold to William Dorman of Princeton, New Jersey. In 1935 a group of local business and political leaders met with Cameron to discuss the prospect of his donating his Hunting Island lands to the county for use as a public beach. H. E. Danner, John F. Morrall, L.A. Hall, and State Representative

W.W. Elliott made up that delegation. They found a receptive, generous audience. Both James Cameron and Dr. Arthur Elting agreed to donate their Hunting Island property to Beaufort County on condition that a large portion of the island be set aside as a nature preserve, that the beach always be open to the public, and that the whole project be completed within five years.

The county commission appointed a committee to develop the island into a public park managed by the South Carolina Forestry Commission. Hal Pollitzer was made chairman of the Hunting Island Committee. The creation of Hunting Island State Park was a joint effort of state, county, and federal governments. The largest and most expensive obstacle to the development of Hunting Island was the construction of two bridges and causeways to span the Harbor River and Johnson Creek. The Hunting Island committee applied to the Public Works Administration and the Works Progress Administration for highway construction money and to the Civilian Conservation Corps to place a camp on Hunting Island to develop the park and forest preserve.

The South Carolina Highway Department agreed to survey, cut, grade, and pave Highway 285 from Frogmore to the Harbor River. The PWA made a $124,002.94 grant for the construction of the bridges and causeways. The CCC camp was established on Hunting Island in April 1938. Two months later, the PWA made available its grant for the Harbor River Bridge. A federal grant covered 45 percent of the cost of the bridges and causeways to Hunting Island. The remainder fell to Beaufort County taxpayers. In 1936 Beaufort County voters passed a $300,000 bond referendum to complete the bridge to Hunting Island. While that does not seem like much money today, in the midst of the Great Depression that amount was 7.8 percent of the total taxable wealth of Beaufort County. The 1936 bridge bond caused an increase of 4.8 mills to Beaufort County property owners. The county commission reserved the right to place a toll on the Harbor River Bridge to help repay the bond. It was a great leap of faith at one of the lowest moments in Beaufort County's long history. With the support of two New Deal programs, the highway department, and the state forestry commission, Beaufort County taxpayers were confident. A *Beaufort Gazette* editorial promoting the project said, "Mr. Average Citizen, by agreeing to add eighty-five cents to your annual tax for (possibly) twenty years . . . you can release over half a million dollars in payrolls in the county and secure a Natural Resources Park and Beach development, giving pleasure to thousands and eventually becoming an asset financially to the county."[46]

Management of the new state park system in the 1930s was the responsibility of the state Forestry Service. This was the state agency that developed the plan for Hunting Island State Park. The South Carolina Forestry Service completed the plan for Hunting Island State Park in 1939 and unveiled it to the public in November. The plan included racially segregated beaches on the four-mile ocean front with blacks restricted to the northern end and whites occupying the center and southern ends. Picnic, bathing, and sanitary facilities were built at both ends of the beach. Nearly four hundred housing sites were planned for "cottages" to be leased from the state. Much of the island was set aside as a nature conservation area to meet the terms of the gift from the Camerons and Eltings. The plan met with hearty approval in Beaufort. It was generally believed that Hunting Island was "the best beach this side of Florida."[47]

The Tidewater Construction Company of Gloucester Point, Virginia, won the contract for the Harbor River Bridge with a bid of $422,181.60. The causeways were built by the Merritt Dredging Company of Charleston. While the bridges were under construction, a free ferry operated by highway department offered public access to the beach. In 1941 the state highway commission purchased the Harbor River and Johnson Creek Bridges from Beaufort County, relieving local taxpayers of their assessments and eliminating the need for tolls. As the project proceeded, State Parks spokesmen promoted Hunting Island State Park as a tourist destination. They asserted that it was the closest public beach on the Atlantic Ocean to Atlanta and Chattanooga. Finally, in the summer of 1941, the park opened with a great Fourth of July celebration.

The year following the opening of the Hunting Island State Park proved the Beaufort boosters correct, despite the dramatic and historic changes that had befallen America since the December 7, 1941, Japanese attack on Pearl Harbor, Hawaii. On Sunday, July 19, 1942, more than five hundred cars passed through Beaufort on their way to the beach. It was estimated that three thousand bathers were in the surf and that as many as five thousand visitors had enjoyed the park that day.[48] The stream of cars kept the cash registers ringing at the filling stations and country stores along the route. The opening of Hunting Island State Park heralded the start of Beaufort County's next great industry.

The New Deal introduced a new element to the economic and political life of the community, trade unionism. With the establishment of the Marine Corps Recruit Depot on Parris Island in 1915, the number of local civilians employed there increased steadily until the Great Depression struck in 1929. When in 1931 Herbert Hoover's beleaguered administration proposed sharply reducing federal expenses at Parris Island, civilian employees took the lead in opposing the cutbacks. In 1931 Local No. 379 of the National Federation of Federal Employees held their annual oyster roast and dance at the Community Club. Nearly one thousand people attended the event, along with most of the important federal officials in the region. Colonel M. O. Dunning, customs collector of Savannah, Second District congressman

Butler Hare, and Brigadier General Harry Lee, USMC, of Parris Island all attended. The theme of the event was how to prevent the federal government from closing Parris Island. Local politicians, including Mayor W. R. Bristol, Senator W. Brantley Harvey Sr., and Representative Calhoun Thomas presented speeches at the union gathering.

The Local No. 379 president, Clarence Blume, pointed out that the Marine Corps Recruit Depot on Parris Island had contributed $7 to $10 million annually to the local economy, "more than any other 25 manufacturing enterprises in this section of the state." To close Parris Island, the union chief explained, would further impoverish Beaufort County: "When we realize just a few years ago a bank failure in this county practically paralyzed this section of the state—what do you think it would mean if Parris Island were reduced to a minimum?" FDR's election in 1932, the start of the New Deal in 1933, and Senator Jimmy Byrnes saved Parris Island. All those factors came into play, and with them the political status of trade unions was much enhanced in Beaufort County and the nation.[49]

While the textile unions in the upcountry were nearly at war with the state in 1933 and 1934, Local No. 379 was an integral part of the political establishment in Beaufort County. During 1933 and 1934, the union held meetings in city hall. The local Democratic Party boss, Calhoun Thomas, was a frequent speaker at the meetings. The federal employees' union was highly civic-minded in the 1930s, sponsoring a float in the annual Armistice Day parade in Beaufort and hosting Labor Day picnics at the beach on Lady's Island. These picnics regularly attracted the state leadership of the American Federation of Labor (AFL) and were described as among "the largest and most successful gatherings of labor in the state."[50]

Unions became so generally accepted in Beaufort that in 1939 retail clerks on Bay Street met to consider organizing an American of Federation of Labor affiliate. Clarence Blume invited Aloysius Flynn, state president of the AFL, and Jim Barrett, the union's southern regional organizer, to address the group. When their meeting concluded, Marvin Dukes, president of the chamber of commerce, invited the men to attend the chamber's monthly meeting. By the late 1930s, the local union, representing a fair portion of Beaufort County's regularly employed middle class, had become an important part of the county's political and economic life.

The high point of unionism was Saturday, July 1, 1939, when the state Federation of Labor, including the Textile Workers of America from the upstate mills, held their annual convention in Beaufort. Two hundred delegates filled Beaufort's few hotels and restaurants. Dr. W. M. Seay, pastor of the Beaufort Baptist Church, opened the convention with a benediction. All the local politicians attended the convention. County commission chairman F. W. Scheper Jr. and Mayor J. E. Gill offered welcoming addresses. The convention was chaired by AFL state president Al Flynn. C. M. Fox of the Textile Workers of America was another featured speaker. The chamber of commerce and the Beaufort community hosted a picnic on Lady's Island and a dance at the Community Club. The 1939 state AFL convention was reportedly "one of the largest conventions the city has ever entertained" and was judged a success by visitors and hosts alike.[51]

The New Deal stimulated numerous progressive schemes to boost economic development of the impoverished sea islands. Most of them involved highway construction to promote automobile travel and tourism. Although most were too expensive and too visionary for the 1930s, some of them eventually came to fruition. One proposal that was continuously promoted was a "short route" between Charleston and Savannah via Beaufort. Promoters formed the Coastal States Coordinated Committee to push it forward. In July 1935 the Beaufort County clerk of court, E. Burton Rodgers, presented the idea to Charleston businessmen at a Kiwanis Club meeting at the Fort Sumter Hotel. The Charleston Chamber of Commerce and the city's influential mayor, Burnet Rhett Maybank, signed on to the scheme. The proposed route would cut twenty-three miles from the auto route between Charleston and Savannah. The Coastal States Coordinated Committee proposed a toll road and scenic parkway that would leave Charleston via the Ashley River and Wappoo Cut Bridges, cross James, Johns, and Wadmalaw Islands via the present-day Maybank Highway, and then leap the North Edisto River with a large bridge to Edisto Island. The route would then cross the South Edisto River to Fenwick Island, bridge the Ashepoo River "south of the canal" on the Intracoastal Waterway, and then leap the Coosaw River to Morgan Island. From there the highway would cross Parrot Creek to Coosaw Island and Lucy Creek to Lady's Island and then proceed into Beaufort. The next stage was to convert the old Seaboard Air Line Railway trestle into a highway bridge. The old railroad right-of-way could be converted into a highway leading right into Savannah. Mayor Robert M. Hitch of Savannah endorsed the plan and asked Herschel Jenkins, publisher of the *Savannah Morning News,* to represent the city on the committee. Beaufortonians on the Coastal States Coordinated Committee were State Senator W. Brantley Harvey Sr., State Representatives Calhoun Thomas and W.W. Elliott, Mayor J. E. Gill, truck farmer R.W. Mitchell, and former mayor R.V. Bray.

This bold scheme gained high-level support and was much talked about throughout the 1930s. South Carolina highway commissioners Ben Sawyer and W. Fred Lightsey convinced the highway department to prepare a preliminary survey. The proposed route required seven major bridges and connecting causeways. The bridges across the Coosaw and Broad Rivers would be among the longest and most expensive in the state. The original cost was estimated at $4.5 million in 1935 but had increased 33 percent by 1938. The promoters asserted that the new "short route" would convert "240 waterfront miles of now virtually unsettled sea islands into valuable real estate."[52]

This grand sea island scenic parkway scheme never came to pass during the New Deal years, but it generated continual interest in building a bridge across the Broad River to create a true automobile link between northern and southern Beaufort County. Colonel M. O. Dunning of Savannah, who owned Lemon Island, proposed in 1938 that the Savannah and Bluffton route could be shortened by building the highway across his land. As Dunning noted, "We have south of the Broad River some of the finest citizens and the finest possibilities for property development in the South. These citizens are now so isolated that in order to reach their own county seat, it is necessary . . . to travel through the county seat of Jasper!" In 1935 northern Beaufort County paid 60 percent of the county's property taxes and accounted for 80 percent of Beaufort County's business investment. Dunning surmised that bridging the Broad River might equalize the tax base and improve business activity in Beaufort County.

Plans for a Broad River bridge persisted throughout the 1930s. In 1938 the county appointed a Broad River Bridge Commission to promote the project. F.W. Scheper Jr. was chairman. Jack McTeer of Hardeeville, K. M. Johnston and W.W. Niver of Bluffton, and E. Burton Rodgers of Beaufort completed the Broad River Bridge Commission. With a 1938 Public Works Administration grant, the route was surveyed, the river bottom was sounded, and preliminary engineering plans were drawn. The Broad River Bridge project, like most of the late 1930s schemes, was interrupted by the necessities of World War II, but project was revived in 1947. After some initial opposition from Charleston business interests, who feared losing Beaufort County business to Savannah, the bridge was completed in 1957.[53] The Broad River Bridge cut the distance from Beaufort to Savannah by thirty miles. It also accomplished what Colonel M. O. Dunning, F.W. Scheper Jr., and E. B. Rodgers had predicted: it united the northern and southern halves of Beaufort County.

Another stillborn project was the plan to build a bridge to Daufuskie Island. In 1935 Senator W. Brantley Harvey and Representative Calhoun Thomas requested that the highway department consider the project. The planned route left State Highway 33 at Pritchardville and followed "a country road of 4.4 miles to Palmetto Lodge," the former winter home of the Wilson-Vanderbilt estate. The route crossed the timberland of Palmetto Bluff to Tea Kettle Creek. From there four causeways and two bridges would reach Daufuskie Island at Mongin Corner. A fixed bridge over Tea Kettle Creek and a swing bridge over Ram's Horn Creek on the Intracoastal Waterway were necessary. The estimated cost in 1935 was $413,300. At the time, there were more people living on Daufuskie Island than on Hilton Head Island, and L. P. Maggioni's canning factory was one of the largest enterprises in Beaufort County. The project was deemed too expensive for the few people it would benefit and was never funded. Two years later Palmetto Bluff was sold to Alexander Calder and the Union Bag and Paper Company.[54]

As the New Deal decade came to a close, one important bridge project was completed. In 1937 Representative Calhoun Thomas announced that the highway department, with PWA help, would construct a swing bridge across Battery Creek to connect the town of Port Royal with Jericho Point. This project was locally named the Parris Island Bridge because its southern end connected to the causeway and bridge across Archer's Creek that had first linked Parris Island to the mainland in 1928. Completion of the Battery Creek Bridge cut the driving distance from Beaufort to Parris Island from fifteen to six miles. A major impetus for this project was the Marine Corps' insistence that it needed the bridge to justify further development of the Parris Island recruit depot.

Using a carrot-and-stick strategy, Marine Corps officials hinted that a three-million-dollar "big project . . . at the Marine post" depended upon bridge access to Port Royal and Beaufort. According to the county Democratic boss, Calhoun Thomas, "Marine Corps officials in Washington demanded that the bridge be built if Parris Island is to continue as a marine training base." By the 1930s the Marine Corps was by far the largest economic generator in Beaufort County, so local politicians and local governments leaped to the task. The Battery Creek Bridge was constructed from 1936 to 1939. It cost state and county taxpayers $225,000. As it neared completion in 1939, the corps announced Parris Island construction projects worth $1.1 million, the first phase of a big military buildup. The Battery Creek Bridge opened for traffic on February 6, 1939, and was formally dedicated on February 10, 1939.[55]

Despite the immediate relief that the New Deal had provided in 1933 and 1934 and despite the economic stimulus provided by the PWA, WPA, CWA, and CCC, there were many in Beaufort County who philosophically and politically opposed the intrusive big government of the New Deal. As the decade wore on, political support for the New Deal began to falter in South Carolina and in Beaufort County.

As early as September 1933, local voices began to question publicly some of FDR's policies. Before the New Deal was even six months old, Editor E. O. Wilson of the *Beaufort Gazette* wondered in print about the constitutionality of all the activism pouring out of Washington, D.C.: "Are we forgetting the Constitution, the bedrock on which this nation was built? . . . We should stop and think carefully before continuing too far the course we have followed recently." Wilson questioned the wisdom of the emergency-relief programs: "We do not favor the dole system. . . . Don't let our people think that they need not work and save and that a benevolent government is going to always provide for their wants." In December 1933 truck farmers began to complain that the New Deal jobs programs were competing with local planters for farm labor. A month later Beaufort merchants began to complain that despite all the federal money coming into the county, back debts they had carried for many years were not being paid off. The merchants, it was said, "wonder what is becoming of the money received each week as payrolls. . . . nothing is being applied on past indebtedness. . . . credit cannot be stretched forever." Even Benjamin Barnwell, the "colored farm agent" for St. Helena and Lady's Island, criticized the effect of New Deal programs on African American farmers: "To give food and clothing to strong and healthy people is distasteful, encourages laziness and is a challenge to our self-respect."[56]

When the Civil Works Administration jobs program was cut back because of diminishing funds, Beaufortonians began to take notice of CWA administrator Harry Hopkins and not favorably. When many truck farmers learned that they were ineligible for federal crop production loans, they wondered vociferously what good the New Deal was doing. In 1934 Beaufort attorney and World War I veteran George W. Beckett ran for Congress as a Republican in the First District on a boldly anti–New Deal platform. He opposed the "socialistic and communistic New Deal experimentation . . . interference and competition by government with business and industry and . . . making beggars of our boys." Beckett was badly beaten by the incumbent Democratic congressman, Thomas McMillan of Charleston, but some white voters in South Carolina did begin to drift to the Republican Party over opposition to the New Deal. In addition, the 1934 congressional election was the first time that the few remaining African American voters in South Carolina abandoned their historic allegiance to the Republican Party of Lincoln and Robert Smalls and supported the Democratic Party of FDR and the New Deal.[57]

Beaufort County was not alone in its conservative opposition to the New Deal. The *Charleston News and Courier,* and Conway's *Horry Herald* vociferously opposed the New Deal. In 1935 a South Carolina branch of the conservative American Liberty League was established by northern plantation owner Stanley F. Morse. He used his considerable wealth to publish a steady stream of anti–New Deal and anti-Roosevelt political tracts. Stanley Morse was at the center of a small, wealthy, and influential group of anti-Roosevelt northerners who collected in South Carolina. As World War II approached, they were often staunchly isolationist.[58] Stanley F. Morse's son,

Dr. Stanley Morse Jr., moved to Beaufort, became a prominent physician, and married the novelist Ann Christensen Head, the eldest daughter of Senator Niels Christensen.

By 1935 Beaufort merchants were opposed to the National Recovery Act. When some restaurants were ordered to "surrender" their Blue Eagles for failing to conform to regulations, many Beaufort merchants noted that "Blue Eagle has become a mere nuisance." When President Roosevelt asked Congress to renew the NRA in 1935, the Beaufort business community opposed it. The *Beaufort Gazette* suggested that the NRA would just create "more loafers . . . we urge our senators and congressmen to vote against the NRA and let the people go back to work."[59]

Beaufort County truck farmers turned against the New Deal in 1935. In February they petitioned Congress to alter the Agricultural Adjustment Act (AAA). While the price-parity and crop-reduction provisions of the 1933 AAA had increased the price of cotton, it did not authorize enough acres of cotton to be planted to produce a single bale in the county. In any case, only a few small sea island farms were still growing cotton in 1935. The truck farmers' larger complaint was that none of their fresh vegetable products were included in the AAA price-support system. AAA price supports applied only to "basic commodities." By 1935 the free market for truck crops had depressed the price of vegetables for six years and nearly ended Beaufort County's largest industry. The farmers wanted Irish potatoes, once Beaufort County's largest product, to be declared a basic commodity under the AAA and thus eligible for federal price supports. The petition was signed by William Keyserling of MacDonald-Wilkins Company, J. R. Bellamy of Bellamy Farms, and Hal R. Pollitzer of the Enterprise Ice Company. In this same petition, Beaufort County farmers could not resist the opportunity to request yet another investigation of the federal "Intermediate Credit Bank in our district during the years 1924–25–26, in order that blame for disastrous losses in our territory be placed where it belongs . . . to incompetent, intriguing, conniving and collusive officials . . . and interested connected banks."[60] Nine years after the collapse of the Beaufort Bank, local farmers were still broke and embittered. Irish potatoes were never added to the basic commodities list of the AAA.

In May 1935 the United States Supreme Court declared unconstitutional the NRA and its vast federal regulatory and code structure. The implication of this Supreme Court decision was that much of the New Deal's federal activism was contrary to the United States Constitution. Progressive politicians in Washington were sent scrambling to regroup as Beaufort County's political leaders celebrated. E. O. Wilson's *Beaufort Gazette* was positively gleeful: "The Supreme Court has handed back to the people . . . their God-given rights and has restored back to them the Constitution. . . . according to our way of thinking and what we have experienced . . . the codes may have helped some of the big corporations, but it has played havoc with many of the small businesses. It has done more harm than good; we lost money in the long run. . . . We only hope it is dead."[61]

The response of the Roosevelt administration to the Supreme Court reversals of New Deal activism did not reassure South Carolina conservatives. President Roosevelt proposed increasing the number of justices on the Supreme Court to appoint his own pro–New Deal men and shift the majority on the court. This was the infamous "court-packing" scheme of 1937. Conservatives rallied national opposition to that bold political gambit, and ultimately the court-packing scheme was FDR's greatest political defeat. In Beaufort County the leading men of the local bar were vocal in defending the Supreme Court and in their attacks upon the New Deal. In his June 1937 charge to the Beaufort county grand jury, Circuit Judge J. Henry Johnson delivered a blistering attack on FDR's court-packing scheme and a stalwart defense of the Supreme Court. Judge Johnson's speech attracted statewide notice and the compliments of South Carolina's leading populist politicians, former governor Cole Blease and Senator "Cotton Ed" Smith. The dean of the county bar, W. J. Thomas, called for a round of applause from the packed Beaufort County courthouse for what he called "the most wonderful speech ever made in the South" and received a thunderous standing ovation. The *Beaufort Gazette* editorial called the judge's speech "one of the finest and best discourses on the subject of state's rights that we have ever heard." When the state bar association convened in 1937, attorneys offered a resolution condemning Roosevelt's attack on the Supreme Court. Their resolution passed 86–37, and Beaufort County's state representative, William W. Elliott, voted with the conservative majority.[62]

Conservative opposition to the New Deal was centered on a defense of state rights, and the populist opposition rallied upon the time-honored specter of the "Negro Vote." In the minds of South Carolina and Beaufort County's business and political elite, the New Deal was simply "too Northern, too radical and too minority oriented." In Beaufort County the New Deal gave the oppressed black majority a great political boost when it asked all the local farmers to vote in the "Cotton Referendum" of 1938. This was an attempt by the federal Agricultural Adjustment Administration to mobilize the farmers behind its crop reduction program. In Beaufort County African American farmers provided 83 percent of the affirmative votes for the New Deal plan and overwhelmed the local opposition. White politicians began to complain that blacks were "getting restless!"

When Senator "Cotton Ed" Smith walked out of the 1936 Democratic National Convention because an African American pastor offered the convention's opening prayer, he received a telegram of "congratulations and sincere admiration" from the Beaufort City Council. And when

Georgia's populist governor Eugene Talmadge engaged in a public, highly colorful dispute with New Deal administrator Harry Hopkins over control of relief money in Georgia, E. O. Wilson and the *Beaufort Gazette* defended the "cracker chief executive" and recommended that the General Assembly refuse to provide state matching funds to federal projects without first verifying state control of them. In 1939 Beaufort County senator W. Brantley Harvey Sr. asserted that 37 percent of the public welfare budget in South Carolina was consumed by nonproductive costs of "administration."[63]

Opposition to the New Deal grew louder and bolder when accusations surfaced of communist infiltration in the Roosevelt administration. E. O. Wilson gave these stories front-page coverage. When in 1939 the WPA administration obstructed a congressional inquiry into communist connections among WPA workers, the *Beaufort Gazette* suggested that the administrator in charge, Harry Hopkins, "should be kicked out of office and trailed like the snake he is." Harry Hopkins was the target of much anti–New Deal red baiting. As the *Beaufort Gazette* noted in 1939, "Harry Hopkins built up this pro-communist organization. . . . He was then advanced to a cabinet post which indicates how the president feels about these influences at work to undermine the American government." Particularly singled out was the WPA Writer's Project, which employed a number of out-of-work "intellectuals."

The bugaboo of communist infiltration was neatly linked to the specter of the "Negro vote" when the far-left Worker's Defense League and Worker's Alliance of New York came to Greenville, South Carolina, to register African Americans for municipal elections. The *Greenville Free Press* editorialized, "It is deplorable that the Communists in the United States are misleading the southern Negro and trying to use him to further their own cause." This voter-registration campaign prompted a violent reaction from the Ku Klux Klan in Greenville and a weak demonstration by the Klan's moribund Ribault Chapter in Beaufort County.[64]

In July 1939 E. O. Wilson wrote an editorial entitled "Has This Great County of Ours Gone to Hell?" It expressed the disillusionment of Beaufort County's political and business elite with the New Deal. "In our opinion," Wilson wrote, "the WPA, the PWA are the biggest humbug ever put over on the people. Also are Social Welfare and the Social Security, a farce of course." Wilson expressed southern conservative frustration with the progressive FDR Democrats: "Years ago the Democratic Party in the South was . . . an honor to belong to, but now its nothing but a party for a few Yankee Politicians and their Yankee Negro Party."[65]

Despite the carping and general dissatisfaction with the direction of the New Deal, Beaufort County was showing definite signs of economic recovery by the late 1930s. The county's only financial institution, the People's Bank, had reached rock bottom in 1936, but thereafter deposits and assets in the bank grew steadily. In 1937 total assets exceeded $500,000. Deposits and assets fluctuated in 1938 but topped $600,000 in 1939, $700,000 in 1940, and $800,000 in 1941. The total assets of the People's Bank had grown more than 120 percent in five years. In 1937 Beaufort added a second financial institution with the organization of the First Federal Savings and Loan Association of Beaufort. The charter was granted by the Federal Home Loan Bank, a New Deal institution. This was the first new financial institution formed in Beaufort County since 1910. The organizers were Calhoun Thomas, G.W. Kinghorn, Claude E. McLeod, Louis O. Miller, Loring Terry, and W. E. Nelson. By 1938 they had assembled enough subscribers and enough capital to begin offering home mortgages to residents of Beaufort and adjacent counties.[66]

In 1938 the city of Beaufort added its first new real estate subdivision in twenty-two years when the Waterhouse Corporation deeded a strip of land from Ribaut Road to Battery Creek to the city to construct a divided parkway called Hermitage Road. It was named for the old Fuller Plantation that had occupied the ground in antebellum days. H. H. Lake Real Estate Company divided the land into home sites and sold them as agent for the Waterhouse Corporation. In 1940 Mrs. Lois Floyd bought thirty-two acres of land north of Depot Road and subdivided it into house lots. This subdivision was called Floyd Heights. It occupied much of the land that had been the Whipple brothers' truck farm before World War I.[67]

Just as the banks were growing and real estate development was expanding, Bay Street was adding its first new businesses in many years. In 1939 M. A. D. "Mike" Coclin built a new restaurant on Bay Street on the lot left empty by the burning of the Riverview Hotel in 1925. The Ocean View Café soon became the most popular eatery in Beaufort. It was a thoroughly "modern" establishment. Its architecture was modern art deco style, and it had a modern, stainless steel kitchen. But the most modern feature of the Ocean View Café, and the secret to Mike Coclin's success, was air conditioning. The Ocean View Café was the first building in Beaufort County to be air-conditioned.[68] The Ocean View Café pioneered the technology that transformed Beaufort County and the whole South in the twentieth century.

When the *Beaufort Gazette* published its retrospective on 1940, it proclaimed that it was "the most exciting year in the city of Beaufort since 1926." Twenty-five new homes were built in Beaufort in 1940, almost all of them in the new subdivisions "beyond the high school and on the Port Royal Road." Fordham Brothers opened a supermarket, and the telephone company moved into a new building on Port Republic Street. Even the 1940 hurricane, the worst since 1893, had a salutary effect on local business: "New roofs began to appear and face lifting on houses became popular as new paint jobs occurred on over half the homes and buildings."

The greatest boost to the economy of Beaufort County, however, and the principal reason for its recovery, was the military buildup at the Marine Corps Recruit Depot. The *Beaufort Gazette* reported that "Parris Island began to expand with workmen coming in from everywhere and again prosperity hit the town. A $6,000,000 contract was let on Parris Island and everyone that wanted a job went to work. The town was jammed full with people. . . . Bay Street became so crowded it was almost impossible to find a parking place."[69] Beaufort County recovered from its long depression in the year 1940.

Chapter 14

World War II at Home and Abroad

THE HOME FRONT

From the perspective of Beaufort County, World War II began years before the Japanese bombed Pearl Harbor and even before the German Army invaded Poland on September 1, 1939. The military buildup of the Roosevelt administration was underway before hostilities commenced. In few places in America was that preparation more apparent than in Beaufort County. The Recruit Depot was among the first installations to benefit from increasing expenditures for military preparedness.

During the depths of the Great Depression, however, the federal government came perilously close to abandoning Parris Island, again. In fact, in 1932 the Hoover administration had plans to reduce the Marine Corps station to a mere shell. To reduce federal expenditures as the Depression reduced federal revenues, the Hoover administration projected a budget of just $121,500 for the entire year for Parris Island. In 1929 and 1930, average expenditures had been $146,000 per month! This was the specter that had haunted Beaufort County throughout the 1930s. As E. O. Wilson said in the *Beaufort Gazette* in March 1932, "Rumors have gone the rounds regarding Parris Island with such frequency that we hardly know what to believe. . . . What will Beaufort be without the military post?"

It was fortunate for Parris Island and for Beaufort County that Jimmy Byrnes was South Carolina's senator in 1932, and it was doubly fortunate that the Democrat Franklin D. Roosevelt was elected president in November 1932. In June 1932 the area's state legislators, Representative Calhoun Thomas and Senator W. Brantley Harvey, traveled to Washington to lobby on behalf of Parris Island. Senator Byrnes sponsored an amendment to the appropriations bill that would prevent a reduction in Marine Corps manpower, and Congressman Tom McMillan rallied the state congressional delegation, saying they would "fight to the last ditch" to keep Parris Island open.

The proposal of the lame duck Hoover administration virtually to abandon Parris Island remained alive during the spring of 1933 while the national government shifted from Republican to Democratic governance. Representative Thomas made another quick trip to Washington in January 1933, and the Beaufort Chamber of Commerce sent a delegation to Augusta to enlist the aid of their longtime economic partners in Georgia. The *Augusta Herald* leaped to the defense of Parris Island, saying, "In both a business and social way the ties between Augusta and Beaufort have been close indeed. This has been a condition existing for many years. Augusta is proud of that friendship and . . . what affects Beaufort in an adverse way is of concern to our own people." The Georgia congressional delegation joined South Carolinians in voting to retain Parris Island, and in May 1933 the Florida delegation joined Georgia and South Carolina. This lobbying effort was successful. In June 1933 the Beaufort County Chamber of Commerce received notification from the Marine Corps commandant that Parris Island would be retained as the East Coast Marine Corps Recruit Depot and primary recruit training facility.[1]

Parris Island was saved from the budget ax in 1933, but little extra money was spent there in the early 1930s. When Parris Island got its first swimming pool in September 1933, it was front-page news in the *Beaufort Gazette,* and when the Public Works Administration approved $121,990 in construction grants for Parris Island, all the politicians, Senators "Cotton Ed" Smith and Jimmy Byrnes and Congressman Tom McMillan, raced home to be the first man to bring the good news. For the next three years, the budget for Parris Island was relatively stagnant, although each year promises for the future were heard.[2]

The Roosevelt administration was distracted by domestic emergencies during its first term, but by 1937 the military aggression of Japan in Asia and the aggressive intentions of Benito Mussolini and Adolf Hitler in Europe and Africa focused the attention of the national government on foreign affairs. Military preparedness soon followed. In 1937 Congressman McMillan announced a $2 million building program for Parris Island. It was this program that spurred the highway department to build the Battery Creek Bridge in 1938, known for years as the Parris Island Bridge. Congress and the War Department had even bigger plans for Parris Island. On April 24, 1938, most of the members of the House Naval Affairs Committee and the chairman of the Senate Naval Affairs Committee visited Parris Island. Congressman McMillan hosted sixteen congressmen from across the nation, including Senator Bryan J. Duffy of Wisconsin, who was on a personal tour of the Charleston Naval Shipyard and the Recruit Depot. Among that delegation was a young Texas congressman named Lyndon Baines Johnson. Senator W. Brantley Harvey, Representative Calhoun Thomas, Mayor J. E. Gill, and County Commissioner F. W. Scheper Jr. led the tour. Within two months, the War Department announced a $1.1 million building program, and the WPA put 240 laborers to work on Parris Island. In 1939 the news for Beaufort County was even better. McMillan reported a new building program that totaled $3,847,000. The Parris Island buildup dwarfed all other government programs during the 1930s. By 1939 any able-bodied man in Beaufort County who wanted work could find it on Parris Island.[3]

All this construction on Parris Island was in anticipation of a massive increase in the number of U.S. Marines. In May 1940 Senator Byrnes announced that the Marine Corps manpower on Parris Island would be more than doubled, from 1,558 men to 3,373 men. The buildup anticipated training 750 recruits each month. The *Beaufort Gazette* recorded the impact on Beaufort County: "Beaufortonians are delighted. . . . It means increased employment for the citizens of this community. It will also help the merchants of the city."[4]

In September 1940, as the air Battle of Britain was raging, the War Department announced a supplemental appropriation of $3.7 million for Parris Island. While most of this appropriation was to continue construction of permanent facilities, nearly half was allotted to repair the damage to Parris Island caused by the hurricane of August 11, 1940. The "1940 Storm," as it is known locally, did approximately $1.5 million in damage to Parris Island. The storm surge flooded the parade ground, destroyed sections of the causeway, demolished all the wharves and piers, knocked out the power plant and ice plant, and collapsed two aircraft hangers at Page Field. Almost all of Parris Island was under water. All the vehicles were flooded, and the heavy artillery pieces at Camp McDougal on Hilton Head Island were under water. Most of the recruits were sent to Quantico, Virginia, to complete their training. Despite the hurricane, the buildup continued.

In March 1941 a reporter from the *Charleston News and Courier* recorded the influence of the Marine Corps buildup on the local economy: "This South Carolina seacoast town of normally 3,000 residents is experiencing its biggest boom in fifty years as a result of the expansion of the Parris Island Marine base eight miles away. . . . The boom has been going for about a year with the concentration of 1,500 civilian construction workers on Parris Island and the increase in Marine personnel from a normal 1,000 at the post to as high as 7,000 at one time." Housing became scarce in Beaufort. "Nearly every home in Beaufort now holds four or five families," the *Gazette* noted. Calhoun Thomas estimated that at least one hundred new homes costing $300,000 had been built near Beaufort the previous year. The economic boom encouraged new businesses, which reportedly sprang up "everywhere." Bay Street merchants also saw a rapid expansion of business. According to the *Gazette,* "It has been just like a shot in the arm to them."[5]

All this buildup occurred before the United States entered World War II. After the December 7, 1941, Japanese attack on Pearl Harbor, the pace of construction increased. The government built schools, hospitals, libraries, theaters, taverns, sports complexes, hotels, housing complexes, and churches. In fact, between 1937 and 1945, the government built a small city on Parris Island. Throughout World War II, it was the largest city in Beaufort County by far.

To support this city, the government built the most modern infrastructure in Beaufort County. Three deep wells were drilled to provide fresh water. During the peak of World War II, the Parris Island installation consumed three million gallons of water per day. Parris Island's Deep Well No. 2 was reputed to be the deepest fresh water well in the world. It was thirty-six hundred feet deep, and the water at that depth was about two hundred degrees Fahrenheit. When the three wells proved insufficient for the wartime demands, two more were drilled in Burton, and the water was pumped to Parris Island. The Marine Corps operated the largest water system in Beaufort County for the next thirty years.

Parris Island had its own coal-fired power plant. The generating plant consumed eleven hundred tons of coal per week, which were delivered to the Port Royal coal dock by the Charleston and Western Carolina Railroad and transported to Parris Island on a government-owned five-hundred-ton lighter. In 1942 the parade ground was paved, and by 1945 most of the roads on Parris Island were paved and hard-surfaced. The Marine Corps Recruit Depot had its own Western Union telegraph station, telephone exchange, and post office. The post office on Parris Island was the largest in Beaufort County. In December 1943 it employed more than a hundred clerks to process more than sixty-eight thousand first-class letters per day.

During World War II, the federal government built the first true shopping mall in Beaufort County. In 1941 the two-story, brick post exchange, or PX, was built across the street from the post office. The exchange contained a cafeteria, soda fountain, barber shop, cobbler shop, photo shop, bank, and department store. In its peak year, the Parris Island PX outsold all the merchants in Beaufort County combined. Total sales in 1943 were $34 million. The marines consumed 3,785,000 candy bars, 2,788,000 packs of cigarettes, and 1,440,000 pints of milk in 1943. The weekly newspaper, the *Boot,* had a circulation of twenty thousand, exceeding that of any other newspaper in Beaufort County for forty years.[6]

The recruit population nearly doubled in the three weeks after Pearl Harbor. From 3,373 recruits in 1941, the population increased to 5,276 recruits between December 7 and December 30, 1941. Thereafter, the number of recruits grew to 9,206 in January 1942; 13,000 in August 1942; 14,726 in July 1944; and 18,398 in September 1945. In the four years of World War II, 240,509 Marines passed through Parris Island—ten times the total population of Beaufort County in 1940.[7]

World War II also introduced a social revolution to Parris Island. During 1943 the U.S. Marine Corps built women's barracks for enlisted women marines. On November 5, 1943, a delegation of female officers from Camp Lejeune arrived on Parris Island to inspect the new facility. In January 1944 a Women's Reserve Battalion consisting of fifty-five enlisted women and twenty-one officers was established on Parris Island. It was the beginning of another honored tradition there.

Parris Island brought the first national publicity to Beaufort County since the Hurricane of 1893. On May 4, 1942, *Life* magazine, one of the highest-circulation weekly magazines in the world during the 1940s, carried an eight-page article about the sleepy little railroad crossing at Yemassee with photographs by Alfred Eisenstaedt. During the war, Yemassee became one of the busiest military transit points in the South with sailors headed for the shipyard in Charleston, soldiers headed for advanced training at Fort Stewart, Georgia, airmen headed to Hunter Army Air Field in Savannah to create the famous Eighth Air Force, and, of course, trains filled with Marine Corps recruits headed to Parris Island.

Famous Americans passed through Parris Island during the war. Hollywood heartthrob Tyrone Power was a marine aviator who landed at Page Field. Sterling Hayden, another movie star of the 1940s, received his basic training on Parris Island. One of Parris Island's most distinguished war-era graduates was University of Chicago professor Paul H. Douglas, who reported to Parris Island at the age of fifty and was the oldest Marine ever to win full combat classification. Douglas was promoted from staff sergeant to lieutenant colonel and earned two Purple Hearts and a Bronze Star for combat at Peleliu and Okinawa. For eighteen years after the war (1948–1966), he was a Democratic senator from Illinois and one of the most influential men in Congress.

Parris Island also played host to some of the most famous "Big Bands" of the 1940s. Harry James and Kay Kyser's bands both entertained at the Lyceum, and national icon Helen Keller presented an inspirational lecture.[8] The high point was the visit of President Franklin Delano Roosevelt in April 1943. FDR was only the third sitting president to visit Beaufort County up to that time. George Washington had passed through the Beaufort District on his way to Savannah on his Grand Tour of 1791, and James Monroe stayed in Beaufort in 1819 on his way to Florida. FDR's visit in 1943 was preceded by a large delegation of Secret Service men and featured a special ramp at the railroad siding in Port Royal to accommodate the disabled chief executive. The president toured Parris Island with the depot commander, Brigadier General Emil Moses. All the recruits, station personnel, and civilian employees, as well as many townsfolk, lined the streets and crowded the outdoor theater to cheer the commander in chief.[9]

In 1943 the Navy Department greatly expanded its facilities in Beaufort County when it commissioned the United States Naval Air Station. The wartime air station was the culmination of nearly thirty years of civilian and military aviation history. Barnstorming flight demonstrations had appeared in Beaufort before World War I. In 1916 the Third Division, South Carolina Naval Militia, lobbied the General Assembly to organize an "aero-plane squad." Beaufort boys believed that the navy was willing to provide the equipment and the flight training for the "aero squad." Local militia interest had been interrupted by World War I, but one local boy, M. O. Dunning, became an Army Air Service ace in France. Colonel Dunning "had some very thrilling escapes while overseas, his plane having been shot down behind German lines," in the words of the *Beaufort Gazette.* In 1927 Lieutenant Edward Raney, a West Point graduate and son of the prominent Beaufortonian E. D. Raney, was killed in an aircraft accident at Kelly Field in San Antonio, Texas, snuffing out a promising career in military aviation.[10]

U.S. Marine Corps aviation first came to Beaufort in 1919. At the conclusion of World War I, the Marine Corps decided to move its air squadrons from the naval air station in Miami, Florida, to Parris Island. A grass landing field was established at the "old rifle range." This later became Page Field. Four hangars were built for land-based biplanes and seaplanes. A ramp was also built to give the seaplanes access to the Beaufort River.

On June 11, 1919, the first contingent of Squadron B from Miami, commanded by Major W. G. McIlavain, arrived at Parris Island. Its first public demonstration flight on the Fourth of July, 1919, turned out to be more exciting than planned when the biplane piloted by Clyde Bates spun out, fell two thousand feet, and crashed through the aviators' wooden barracks. Neither Bates nor Marine Gunner Clifford Broom was seriously hurt. By November 1919 Squadron B, First Aviation Force, USMC, was firmly established in its new quarters with six land-based aircraft, six seaplanes, 24 officers, and 210 enlisted men.[11]

The arrival of the Marine Corps aviators spurred civilian interest in Beaufort in building a permanent airfield near town. In October 1919 a committee of Beaufort men led by Dr. M. G. Elliott chose a site at what was called the "old fair grounds" behind the National Cemetery. A group of Parris Island airmen approved the site as suitable for landing aircraft in all wind conditions. Work began on the landing field in 1920 but was delayed because of the potato harvest. This was the beginning of the first civilian aircraft landing field in Beaufort County. In 1928 this field was expanded on property made available by Christensen Realty from its Beaufort Shores housing development on Pidgeon Point. Johnny Horne of Horne Motor Company on Bay Street agreed to provide fuel for visiting aircraft. By 1928 there were two runways, both of which were "tractored and rolled" with grass to stabilize the sandy soil. On Sunday, June 16, 1929, the airport on Pidgeon Point opened with great fanfare. Two thousand cars with five thousand people came from Savannah, Charleston, and Columbia to observe Beaufort County's first civilian air show. Many took their first ride in an aircraft, and all saw Marie Woolsey and Eugene Black perform their death-defying wing-walking exhibition. Hundreds of families enjoyed picnics under the live oak trees that bordered the runways. "It was a great day for Beaufort," the *Gazette* noted, "and will be pleasantly remembered for time to come by those who paid a visit."

In 1932 the Beaufort landing field was provided with runway lights and a powerful beacon atop a 51-foot steel tower. These improvements qualified the field for night landings and allowed the facility to be designated an official "United States Emergency Landing Station" by the Civil Aeronautics Board. By 1932 the north-south runway was 2,490 feet long and the east-west runway was 2,230 feet long.[12]

The enterprising Johnny Horne developed a second civilian airfield at Land's End on St. Helena Island in 1931. On Sunday, August 23, 1931, Johnny Horne flew his Curtis Robin from Beaufort to Land's End and was the first to land at his new air field. His passengers were Sallie Mae Kitchings and James Crofut of Beaufort.[13]

In 1925 another form of aviation developed between the world wars entertained Beaufortonians: the appearance over the county of the huge navy dirigible *Los Angeles.* The giant airship was traveling from Puerto Rico to Lakehurst, New Jersey. The *Los Angeles* passed over the county several times in the 1920s. In 1931, after an airship mooring mast was installed at Parris Island, the dirigible regularly stopped on its ponderous voyages to and from Central America. When the *Los Angeles* visited Parris Island in 1931, people came from all over the state to see the flying marvel. A reporter wrote, "The highway was thronged throughout the day Sunday with people coming from every section of the state to get a glimpse of this great ship."[14]

Throughout the 1930s Marine Corps squadrons were temporarily stationed on Parris Island. In 1935 Fighting Squadron No. 9 performed an air show with eighteen aircraft in various formations. In January 1939 a county committee led by Clarence Blume and W. F. Sample petitioned Congress to establish a permanent air station on Parris Island. Within two months, a group of congressmen and high-ranking naval officers visited Charleston, Savannah, and Beaufort in search of a site for an air base on the southeast coast.[15] No action was taken before the war began.

With America's entry into the war, the Navy Department began seriously to examine sites in Beaufort County for a new air station. In 1942 the Marine Corps built an emergency grass landing strip on Hilton Head Island. This landing field, called Camp McDougal, was on the north end of Hilton

Head Island near the site of Confederate Fort Walker. In the 1920s the Marine Corps used Camp McDougal for artillery practice. This grass landing strip was the beginning of the Beaufort County Airport on Hilton Head.

On April 1, 1943, the Navy Department announced that three hundred officers and seventeen hundred enlisted men would be sent to Beaufort for aviation training. While they had at first planned to use the civilian airfield for training, the government had plans for a permanent installation and began to condemn 3,357 acres of farmland on Port Royal Island as a wartime necessity. The government budgeted $10 million to purchase the land and develop the runways and support facilities for the new naval air station. From April 15, 1943, to May 20, 1943, local newspapers were filled with legal notices of land condemnations for the new military facility.[16]

The United States Naval Air Station, Beaufort, South Carolina, was commissioned on June 15, 1943. Commander Grover Turner was the first commanding officer. The missions of the air station were to provide advanced training for naval and marine aviators and to be a base for antisubmarine aircraft patrolling the southeastern seaboard. In 1943 and 1944, NAS Beaufort trained 1,089 aviators. The most numerous aircraft were the Lockheed PV-2 Ventura twin-engine bomber and ASW patrol plane. The two six-thousand-foot runways were completed by August 1943. Throughout World War II the naval air station was training fighter and bomber squadrons. In addition, antisubmarine patrols of the Eastern Sea Frontier used the station for refueling and land support.[17]

Throughout the war the Navy Department continued to spend more money to support construction projects at NAS, Beaufort. By 1943, there were forty-seven buildings at the station. In November 1943 the navy expanded the concrete apron to accommodate more aircraft, and in 1944 it built a permanent operations building to replace a wooden structure from 1943. All this meant more jobs, more economic activity, and more growth for Beaufort County. The increased military aviation activities were not without their hazards. Navy and Marine Corps aviators used Egg Bank in St. Helena Sound for bombing and strafing practice. It was said that the uninhabited sand bank was just about the same size as a large Japanese warship. Local fishermen learned to stay clear of the place during flight operations. The beaches of the county's isolated barrier islands are still littered with .50 caliber shell casings from aerial target practice. And there were aircraft accidents, some of them fatal. In March 1943 a navy bomber crashed on Hilton Head Island, killing the pilot and crewman. In December 1943 a Lockheed PV-1 Ventura patrol plane with nine crewmen and one marine passenger crashed on takeoff from NAS Beaufort, killing six and leaving four survivors badly injured. Marine Sergeant William E. Thompson showed great courage by returning to the burning wreckage to rescue injured crewmen.[18]

While the massive military buildup on Parris Island and the addition of a very busy U.S. Naval Air Station during World War II dwarfed all other activity in Beaufort County, the civilian population rallied around the war effort as best they could. As during World War I, Beaufort County became an active, patriotic "war camp community." On January 1, 1941, the 263rd Coast Artillery, Beaufort's local National Guard unit, was activated and posted to Fort Moultrie to guard Charleston Harbor. Shortly after World War I, the old Third Division, South Carolina Naval Militia, was changed to a coast artillery unit and the National Guard was placed under the command the U.S. Army. The removal of the local Guard unit and general war preparations prompted the organization of a home defense unit at the county courthouse on April 29, 1941. Forty Beaufort white men between the ages of twenty-one and fifty-five volunteered for part-time military training and standby military service. Among these volunteers were prominent public officials and local farmers who were exempt from the national draft. On July 11, 1941, the state adjutant general, James Dozier, mustered this unit into the South Carolina Defense Force as Company I, 4th Regiment. County Treasurer Rivers L. Varn was elected captain. Company I drilled each Monday night at the Beaufort High School athletic field. Once a month, Company I was treated to an oyster stew or fish supper at the arsenal prepared by company cook Marion Bowers, who, it was said, couldn't "be beat when it comes to preparing seafood of any kind."

Company I never reached full strength because so many of its members had joined the regular armed forces. In January 1942 Ensign Stratton Christensen, USN, offered a speech of encouragement to the company before he shipped out for the North Atlantic. Christensen was a recent Harvard graduate and a young South Carolina state representative (1941–42). A few months later he was lost at sea when his patrol vessel was sunk by a German U-boat near Bermuda.

During World War II, Company I occasionally performed "interior guard duty," or law enforcement work. They were also trained in "anti-sabotage work." While looking for the "enemy within" might seem like an exercise in paranoia today, it affected domestic society in the 1940s. When a fire "reportedly of suspicious origin" burned the Seaboard Airline Railroad trestle across the Broad River on May 20, 1942, Jasper County's Home Guard was called out to hunt for saboteurs. The favorite assignment for the local boys of the Home Guard was beach patrol, when detachments were sent to the barrier islands for weeks at a time to ride horses and watch for German U-boats.[19]

Beaufort County also organized a Civilian Defense Corps. Marvin Dukes was chairman of the county's Council For National Defense and spoke to local chapters of the Civilian Defense Corps. Beaufort County also formed a U.S. Citizens Service Corps, whose assignment was to "fight against inefficiency, insecurity and poor health within the community." This organization comprised mostly women. Mrs. Sterling Harris was director of the county's Citizen Service Corps and Mrs. F.W. Scheper Jr. was vice director. Blanche Wilkins chaired the Family Security Service to help families of servicemen. Mrs. Frederick Christensen was chairman of the Child Care Division. Doris Peeples was in charge of nutritional services, and Mary Ellen Eaves managed consumer services, which assisted in wartime rationing. Mabel Runnette was in charge of library services, while Beaufort's only female attorney, Grace White, was director of information services, in charge of all public information for the county Citizens Service Corps. And, of course, the venerable county chapter of the American Red Cross was reactivated and kept busy on the home front. In 1943 Mrs. George Osterhout was chairman of the local Red Cross chapter, and Mrs. S. P. McDaniel was vice chairman. More than a dozen prominent Beaufort women chaired different committees of the Red Cross, and scores of local girls volunteered their services. Almost everyone in Beaufort County lent a hand in some way to the war effort.[20]

One of the busiest Civilian Defense Corps assignments was that of air raid warden. This applied mostly to the city of Beaufort, where potential air raids would do the most damage. The city was divided into air raid districts that corresponded to the city's fire districts. Each district had a senior air raid warden and several junior wardens. The city's chief air raid warden was Robert O. Smith. There were seventy-eight air raid wardens in the city. They were trained in first aid, poison gas defense, and air raid protective measures. They inspected buildings, informed residents of emergency procedures, and identified fire risks in their neighborhoods. Air raid watches were established atop the tallest buildings: the Gold Eagle Tavern, Breeze Theater, Sea Island Hotel, and county courthouse. The wardens conducted several drills during the war. These drills were announced by blasts from the firehouse siren, followed by the ringing of all the town's church bells. During night drills the town was supposed to extinguish all lights. The air raid wardens enforced the blackout in their districts. On June 10, 1942, and June 24, 1942, the city of Beaufort achieved two successive "100 percent blackout" drills.

Another responsibility of air raid wardens was to man the local observation post of the Ground Observer System of the Army Aircraft Warning Service. The Beaufort observation post was located at the civilian air field on Pidgeon Point. Throughout the war scores of Beaufort men and women were trained in aircraft recognition and proper communications procedures. They provided a twenty-four-hour, seven-day-per-week watch at the post for three and a half years.[21]

Another wartime demand was the "coastal dim out." The glow created by the lights of coastal towns and cities on the Atlantic seaboard could be seen far out at sea and were used as navigation aids by enemy submarines.

The glow also silhouetted American vessels, making them easy targets for enemy torpedoes. In 1943 dim-out regulations were extended fifteen miles inland to include Beaufort. Porch lights, automobile headlights, neon signs, and all other illumination that contributed to coastal glow were regulated as a wartime necessity. While the threat of air raids was remote, the naval war in the North Atlantic was not. German U-boats lurked off the Carolina Coast and often found easy targets. In January 1942 shortly after America entered the war, two ships were torpedoed in North Carolina waters. One was the 3,779-ton Latvian steamship, SS *Ciltviara.* Twenty-one survivors were brought to Charleston to tell their harrowing tale. Another reminder of the proximity of the Battle of the Atlantic was the visit of a Canadian submarine chaser to Beaufort in February 1943. It had been damaged by storms while on anti-submarine warfare patrol.

To avoid the danger of German U-boats, the government greatly expanded the commercial traffic on the Atlantic and Gulf Coast Intracoastal Waterways (ICW), particularly for transporting vital petroleum products from Texas oilfields to the Northeast. Oil barges were constructed for the ICW, and oil was piped across Florida from Tampa to the East Coast. The ICW was promoted as submarine-safe waters. While this transportation system was never fully developed during the war, barge traffic through Beaufort County greatly increased. The increased maritime traffic also created hazards for Beaufort County. On Sunday August 15, 1943, an oil barge knocked out six piers of the Lady's Island Bridge and dropped one end of the span several feet. Automobile traffic was halted for several months, and the Coast Guard operated a ferry across the Beaufort River.

Beaufort was briefly considered for a shipbuilding site. Talk circulated in town about reactivating the old shipyard on Spanish Point, but nothing happened. One consequence of coastal defense planning was the establishment of the South Carolina Port Authority in 1942 to "develop South Carolina port facilities with federal assistance." State Representative Calhoun Thomas was a principal organizer of the Ports Authority, motivated by the knowledge that the federal government "will help such seacoast development for the sake of national defense."[22]

The immense wartime buildup in Beaufort County and the influx of thousands of young men for military training, as well as permanent personnel and their families and thousands of civilian workers, overtaxed limited social resources. Housing was the first crisis. Crime and civil order were the next crises. By 1943 housing in Beaufort for military personnel and their families was critically short. Every home had renters, and every hotel was filled with boarders whose temporary occupancy lasted for months, even years. With a critical shortage of housing, rents were driven higher each month, creating hardships for low-paid military families. This prompted the federal government to impose rent controls in communities affected by the military buildup. In Beaufort County wartime rent controls were imposed on March 1, 1943. These controls required that "all landlords, rooming house and hotel proprietors and everyone else renting out space for living quarters must charge no more than the rent they were charging on March 1, 1942." L. B. Attaway of Charleston was the local examiner and inspector enforcing this policy. He set up a housing office in the old Beaufort College Building. This action prevented the gouging of military tenants in the local market but did not encourage the construction of new housing.

One novel solution to Beaufort County's housing shortage was the floating hotel *Amphitrite*. The *Amphitrite* had seventy-five double bedrooms, thirty private bathrooms, a dining room with bandstand, large kitchen, bar, and recreational sundeck. The ship had been used as a hotel by the Marine Hotel Company since it was decommissioned by the navy in 1924. The *Amphitrite* was berthed at Palm Beach and Fort Lauderdale, Florida, Brunswick, Georgia, Hempstead, Long Island, and Elizabeth City, North Carolina, between 1924 and 1944. This was not the *Amphitrite*'s first visit to Beaufort. In fact, by 1940 the vessel had been a Beaufort visitor for seventy-four years.

The USS *Amphitrite* had been built in 1870 as a Monitor-class gunboat. Civil War marine technology was made obsolete by the development of modern steam battleships in the 1880s. The USS *Amphitrite* was stationed at the Port Royal Naval Station during the Spanish-American War and was dry-docked at Parris Island in 1898. The *Amphitrite* was the first ship dry docked at the Parris Island dry dock in 1895. During 1944 and 1945, the *Amphitrite* hotel was tied up at Sinclair dock and was the most visible sign of Beaufort's housing shortage.

In 1944 local businessmen formed the Beaufort Housing Corporation and applied to the National Housing Administration for credit. Initially they built twenty-six five-room houses in the Oaklawn subdivision of Floyd Heights, west of Ribaut Road. Over the next year, scores of houses were built in Beaufort's first suburbs. These small houses, according to the *Beaufort Gazette*, "greatly alleviated the housing situation" just as the war ended.[23]

The influx of thousands of young men from around the country also changed Beaufort County's conservative southern society. Many young marines, when granted liberty, got drunk, became disorderly, and occasionally got into fights. Altercations between servicemen and local residents nearly started riots in 1942 and 1943. These disturbances were more than Beaufort's two-man police force could manage, so in March 1943 civilian authorities and the Marine Corps command virtually declared martial law. Military police from the Parris Island Provost Marshall's command patrolled Beaufort and Port Royal in jeeps and on foot. The cooperation of the MPs was greatly appreciated by the townsfolk.

The influx of northerners threatened to disrupt Beaufort County's rigidly segregated society. Some marines on liberty, particularly those from northern urban cultures, thought nothing of openly dating young African American women. This not only shocked Beaufort's white society, but many in the black community (whom whites labeled the "better class of Negroes") also strongly disapproved of it. Other white men were quietly cohabitating with African American women, a circumstance impossible to hide in a small town like Beaufort. Editor E. O. Wilson of the *Beaufort Gazette* was not shy in reflecting the white community's opinion. In a 1943 front-page editorial, "Too Much Social Equality and Adultery in Beaufort," Wilson suggested that if the civil and military police were unwilling to enforce Beaufort's conservative social norms, then the Ku Klux Klan might: "The Ku Klux Klan is not asleep on the job." But the Klan was silent during the war, and it is doubtful that military authorities would have tolerated KKK actions against servicemen.

One military activity that did not disturb Beaufort society was the arrival of 250 Italian prisoners of war in October 1943. The men were housed in tents on Pidgeon Point Road and guarded by army sentries. Many of these Italian POWs were employed to help harvest the vegetable crops. During World War II, Beaufort County truck farmers experienced critical shortages of local labor because of the wartime draft or competition from government projects that paid higher wages. According to local observers, the Italian POWs did not mind the work and "seem to be happy in their new location on Pigeon Point Road."[24]

Whatever social disruption was caused by the war, it was far outweighed by the enormous growth in the county's economy. No institution in the county reflected the economic recovery better than the old, established People's Bank. From its nadir in 1936, the People's Bank assets grew slowly until 1940, when deposits and assets surged upward. In April 1942 the People's Bank surpassed $1,000,000 in assets ($1,022,818.46) for the first time since 1923. A year later the bank's assets had grown 57.6 percent to $1,611,681.90. This was nearly four and a half times as large as the People's Bank had been at the bottom of the Depression in 1936, only seven years before. Also, the People's Bank was no longer the only bank in the county. In 1939 a group of local businessmen led by Calhoun Thomas, G. W. Kinghorn, and Claude E. McLeod organized the First Federal Savings and Loan Association of Beaufort. The timing was excellent. Starting with $107,892.58 in total assets, the new financial institution more than doubled in one year. By 1945 assets in First Federal Savings and Loan were $358,833.80. It had grown 233 percent in five years.

World War II was a boom time for Beaufort County, but just as events in Beaufort County presaged America's entry into World War II, its citizens also anticipated the war's end. In 1943 the county grand jury presented a list of projects that had been deferred as "after war work" for Beaufort County. The Broad River Bridge, the Coosaw Island Bridge, a causeway to Warsaw Island, the Daufuskie Bridge, and a public ferry to Hilton Head Island topped the list. In 1944 Beaufort business, farm, and labor leaders formed the Beaufort County Development Association to plan for the economic dislocation anticipated by the end of the war. The association sponsored a large, well-attended barbecue at Beaufort High School, where it "held several discussions about post-war plans for Beaufort and Beaufort County." The president of the local American Federation of Labor chapter, W. A. Schaefer, presided over the event. The principal speakers were navy pilot Lieutenant Paul Moore, who promoted the sale of war bonds, and Representative Calhoun Thomas, who "outlined plans for post-war activities in Beaufort County" and complimented "the leadership taken by organized labor in these plans." The local AFL chapter provided the food, and W. Sidney Smith, president of the Beaufort County Farm Bureau, organized the dinner. In October 1944 the Beaufort County Commission formed the Beaufort County Preparedness for Peace Committee at the request of the state government. This was a countywide committee of leading citizens from Bluffton, Hardeeville, and Seabrook, as well as Beaufort. These committees hoped to stave off the worst effects of peacetime economic contraction so that, as the *Gazette* reported, "through careful planning this county can take its rightful place in the postwar activities of the state and nation."[25]

One project of importance was the construction of Beaufort Memorial Hospital. Since Reconstruction the county had often expressed the need for a community hospital. When the naval station had been established on Parris Island in 1877, local citizens resorted to its hospital in emergencies. In addition, there were two quarantine hospitals during the 1880s and 1890s, one on Parris Island and one on Buzzard Island. The army built a hospital on Land's End, St. Helena Island, for the garrison at Fort Fremont. That hospital was used by local doctors in emergencies before it closed in 1916. In 1910 nurse Catherine Deveaux opened a "colored sanatorium" next to her parent's home on North Street, which she and Dr. M. P. Kennedy operated into the 1930s. Around World War I, the Ladies Benevolent Society, Clover Club, and Red Cross operated a small infirmary, or "lying in hospital," on Scott Street for white women. Often local doctors boarded their sickest patients in their homes until they could be transported to Savannah or Charleston.

When Kate Gleason died in 1933, her will left property on the bluff south of Beaufort for use as a school or hospital. During the 1930s local doctors regularly tried to promote the development of a community hospital, but the project was delayed first by the Depression and then by World War II. In 1934 a group of local citizens led by William Keyserling, Dr.

W. A. Black, Dr. M. G. Elliott, Dr. C. G. Luther, and Dr. W. B. Ryan applied to the Civil Works Administration and the Duke Foundation for funds to build a hospital. In 1935 the General Assembly created a board of regents of the Beaufort County Hospital Association to advance the project. In December 1941 Eleanor Gleason and the trustees of Kate Gleason's estate donated nine acres between Ribaut Road and the Beaufort River "for the proposed Beaufort County Hospital." The regents applied for an $80,000 grant from the Federal Works Administration to build a twenty-five-bed facility and in 1942 received $112,000 to build a forty-bed facility. Wartime exigencies delayed construction until approval could be obtained from the War Production Board. On July 27, 1943, the WPB authorized construction of the Beaufort County Hospital. Wartime delays and inflation had raised the cost to $240,000, but the Federal Works Administration increased its grant and construction began.

Dr. Charles G. Luther was chairman of the board of regents, and Dr. W. A. Black was secretary. One of the largest benefactors, Mrs. Harry S. Cram of Bluffton, was also an influential hospital regent. The architect was Heyward Singley of Columbia. Finally, on May 1, 1944, the Beaufort County Hospital had a grand opening ceremony with speeches, photographs, tours, and a reception. The hospital's first surgeon was Dr. William P. Ryan, and its first general practitioner was Dr. W. A. Black. By December 1944 the hospital had an active auxiliary staffed by many "enthusiastic women of Beaufort." The Beaufort Garden Club, led by Mrs. Arthur Sams, offered to "beautify the grounds of the hospital." It was a long-delayed but auspicious beginning for one of the most important institutions in postwar Beaufort County. Just as the hospital was nearing completion, Congressman L. Mendel Rivers and Senator Burnet R. Maybank announced that the county had been selected as the site for a $5.5 million naval hospital to serve Parris Island, NAS Beaufort, and "possibly the injured of the Naval fleets." The naval hospital was completed in 1946.[26]

From the county's perspective, it was obvious by 1944 that the terrible war was going to end and that the allies would be victorious. Although Parris Island was still busy training Marines, by 1944 German U-boats were hardly a threat to the Atlantic Coast, and the possibility of air raids against stateside targets was all but gone. Many of the young men from Beaufort County, who had first gone to war in the months after Pearl Harbor, were returning home or at least to stateside duty stations. Some were wounded. Many of them were decorated. Beaufort County's community leaders were wise to look to the future and plan for a peacetime economy.

Beaufort County, like the rest of the United States, suffered a sharp recession and economic dislocation at the end of the war. The largest contraction to the local economy was the rapid drawdown at the naval air station. By the end of 1945, NAS Beaufort had only a skeleton crew, and on April 1, 1946, the station was decommissioned. In 1946 the navy declared 1,256 acres of the former station to be "surplus land" and turned it over to Beaufort County. This was the most obvious local sign of the war's end.[27] The wartime boomtown tried to return to normal. But, of course, Beaufort County was never the same after 1945.

The greatest effect of the war on Beaufort County was to make Beaufort, for the rest of the twentieth century, a Marine Corps town. And the greatest gift the Marine Corps gave to the county was a working middle class. For most of Beaufort County's previous two centuries, its social structure had consisted of a small minority of relatively wealthy white families and a very large majority of enslaved or nominally emancipated, relatively poor African American families. Since World War II, the Marine Corps has made Beaufort County a middle-class community by broadening the spectrum of employment and of goods and services for purchase and by fostering social structures that are traditionally associated with middle-class culture. Almost all of that economic and social class, certainly in the northern half of the county, has comprised marines, their dependants, military retirees, or the owners and employees of the myriad businesses that serve them. This economic and social transformation has made Beaufort County not only a more prosperous place but also a better place than it had been to raise families and to exercise the rights and obligations of modern citizenship.

"PROUD TO SERVE": BEAUFORT BOYS IN WORLD WAR II

While World War II profoundly affected Beaufort County, local families reciprocated by making contributions and sacrifices to America's victory. In August 1940 President Roosevelt signed the Selective Service Act, repeating the actions of the Wilson administration in May 1917. Wilson however, had signed the national draft after the United States declared war on Germany, while Roosevelt implemented the national draft in anticipation of war. Roosevelt's political enemies and Republican isolationists used this against FDR in his campaign against Wendell Wilkie for an unprecedented third presidential term. However, Beaufort County responded to the president's call with alacrity and efficiency.

In September 1940 Governor Burnet R. Maybank named five men to be the Beaufort County Selective Service Board: Alan Paul, C. E. Blume, William N. Levin, and Dr. H. C. Foster of Beaufort and Henry R. Williams of Hardeeville. Paul and Levin were veterans of World War I and prominent in the Beaufort Post No. 9 of the American Legion. Clarence Blume was head of the Federal Employees Union local on Parris Island and fourth vice president of the state AFL. Henry R. Williams represented Hardeeville for four terms on the Beaufort County Commission. The Beaufort County Selective Service Board well represented the political power structure of Beaufort County in 1940.

Within a month the board had registered 2,757 Beaufort County men between the ages of eighteen and thirty-five. Of these 838 were white and 1,919 were black. That initial registration represented 12.5 percent of the county's total population in 1940. By July 1942, 500 white men from Beaufort County had been drafted into military service but only 109 black men. State Representative Calhoun Thomas explained this discrepancy by noting, "Educational requirements bar some Negroes from service in the armed forces. . . . they bar a smaller number of white men." Thomas may have been evading an unpleasant fact about Beaufort County. Of the first African Americans registered for the draft in Beaufort County in 1941, 50 percent were "disqualified on account of syphilis." This plague had been recognized by public health authorities in 1938 when it was estimated that 80 percent of Beaufort County's African American population was suffering from syphilis. The discovery of penicillin in 1942 and its application in the armed forces generally solved this problem. As the war continued and the need for manpower increased, the racial imbalance in the draft from Beaufort County began to correct itself.[28] By the end of the war, hundreds more Beaufort men and women contributed military service to the nation. Thirty-eight of them made the ultimate sacrifice.

One recruit from Beaufort County had the distinction of being the physically largest soldier from South Carolina during World War II. Dubbed the "Beaufort Behemoth," Leland Grayson was drafted from Hardeeville. "Arnold" Grayson, as he was known to his friends in Hardeeville, was seven feet three inches tall and weighed 310 pounds. The induction officer at Fort Jackson cried, "Ye Gods!" when he first saw the Beaufort Behemoth. Grayson was judged to be "the biggest human being ever to set foot on this Army reservation." He was too big, as it turned out, for conventional military duty. With size-twenty shoes and a size-fourteen hat, nothing in the army would fit him. One crusty army sergeant, a veteran of World War I, regretted Grayson's rejection, musing, "If a Hun or a Jap ever saw something like that coming at 'em, he wouldn't need a gun. They'd die of fright!"[29]

Once the United States entered World War II, Beaufort County did not have to wait long to be included on the casualty list. Two Beaufort brothers were killed during the Japanese attack on Pearl Harbor on December 7, 1941. Samuel Jackson Bush and Leon Wellington Bush were the sons of retired Petty Officer Adam W. Bush of Beaufort. Like their father, they both enlisted in the U.S. Navy. Samuel J. Bush was a petty officer, first class (E6), and Leon Bush was a petty officer, second class (E5). Beaufort's American

Legion Post No. 9 published a resolution expressing its "deepest sympathy to their family on their loss and hope that their glorious sacrifice will be an inspiration to the members of their race who are now serving their country in the armed services."

The Bush brothers' deaths prompted the *Beaufort Gazette,* a conventionally conservative southern paper, to observe that "these two boys were citizens of Beaufort County . . . and will prove to our state and nation that regardless of race, color or creed, we stand united in common purpose to destroy despotism and to free all peoples who now live under its barbarous masters." The African American Legion Post on Boundary Street in Beaufort was named in honor of Samuel J. Bush.[30]

Not long after the news of the Bush brothers' death at Pearl Harbor, Beaufort received word that Ensign Stratton Christensen was lost at sea in the Battle of the Atlantic. Stratton Christensen was one of Beaufort's rising stars. The second son of Senator Christensen, he graduated from Harvard in 1936 and returned to Beaufort. In 1940 he was elected to the state house of representatives, the youngest member of the General Assembly. Following his father's example—Senator Christensen had been a naval officer in World War I—Christensen joined the navy in 1941. He was commissioned and assigned to duty as executive officer aboard the patrol vessel USS *Cythera,* a converted yacht formerly named *Agava* and owned by Mrs. Edith Hale of Harkness, New York. The ship had been built in Scotland in 1907. During 1940 and 1941, when the Battle of the Atlantic was at a critical stage and Great Britain was barely hanging on against the Nazi assault, American supplies and the Atlantic convoys were critical to Britain's survival. The FDR administration leased much of the U.S. destroyer fleet to the Royal Navy for convoy duty. When the United States entered the war, the navy commandeered many large yachts of the Gilded Age and converted them to war ships. The USS *Cythera* was one of these. They were no match for enemy submarines that lurked in the North Atlantic. The *Cythera* was sunk by a German torpedo on May 2, 1942. A few crewmen survived, but Christensen died at sea. These early losses brought the war home to all of Beaufort County.[31]

One public relations effort the War Department employed to boost morale was to recognize families, particularly mothers, who had contributed more than one son to the war effort. Each mother with four or more children in military service was designated a "Four Star Mother" and given a pin to wear and a decal for her home. They were also recognized in the local press. Sometimes the individual services did more. When the U.S. Navy learned in January 1942 that Mrs. Thomas Horton of Yemassee had five sons in the navy, they not only made her a "Four Star Mother" but also brought her to the Charleston Naval Shipyard to christen the navy ocean tug USS *Chippewa.*[32]

Several Beaufort County families had many sons in uniform. Mrs. W. M. Darby of Beaufort was awarded the Honor Pin as a Four Star Mother at a ceremony at the National Cemetery on April 16, 1942. Lieutenant William Darby, Sergeant Joseph Darby, and Private First Class Lee Richard Darby all served in the army. Petty Officer James Darby was in the navy. Sergeant Joe Darby served six months overseas in the field artillery, and Chief Petty Officer James Darby earned a chest full of medals for nearly two years of combat service in the Pacific. All four Darby boys were parishioners of St. Helena's Episcopal Church. In 1942 twenty-one young men from St. Helena Church were in military service.[33]

Mrs. C. H. Rentz of Burton also sent four sons off to war. Sergeant Bernard Rentz joined the South Carolina National Guard on March 13, 1940, and spent nine months overseas with the army field artillery. First Sergeant Clyde Rentz and Staff Sergeant Lee Rentz both enlisted in the U.S. Army on the same day, January 13, 1941. Lee Rentz served thirty-eight months in New Guinea and the Philippines with the field artillery, and Clyde Rentz served with the Occupation Forces in Germany. Sergeant Medicus Rentz enlisted in the U.S. Army on November 13, 1943, and served twelve months in New Guinea and the Philippines. Mayor J. E. Gill of Beaufort presented the Four Star Pin to Mrs. Rentz.[34]

Another of Beaufort's "fightingest families" was that of Mr. and Mrs. E. Burton Rodgers of King Street in Beaufort. E. "Burt" Rodgers was county clerk of court for thirty-two years (1920–1952) and then served four terms in the state senate (1953–1960). His father, Samuel H. Rodgers, had been editor and publisher of the *Palmetto Post* and half owner of the *Beaufort Gazette* until 1907. He, too, had been a longtime clerk of court.

Three Rodgers brothers served in the navy and one served in the army. Samuel H. Rodgers enlisted in the navy on July 28, 1941, and spent most of the war at the naval shipyard at Charleston. Edward M. Rodgers joined the navy on August 12, 1941, and served four years in the Atlantic fleet. Thomas Legare Rodgers was commissioned a second lieutenant in the army on August 28, 1942. He served eleven months in the Philippines and was a captain in the Coast Artillery in 1946. Legare Rodgers served many years as clerk of court like his father and grandfather before him. Walter I. Rodgers served with particular distinction. He enlisted in the navy on August 11, 1941. Walter Rodgers spent three years in the Pacific theater and fought in some of the heaviest naval combat of the war. He was in battles in the Gilbert and Marshall Islands, the Bismarck Archipelago, New Guinea, Leyte Gulf, and Okinawa. He won the Bronze Star for valor and the Purple Heart for battle wounds. He also earned ten Bronze Service Stars. On December 22, 1944, he was awarded the Silver Star for valor as chief of beach reconnaissance aboard the USS *Caperton* prior to the marine landings on the Marshall

Islands. After the war, he switched services, was commissioned in the army, and retired a full colonel.[35]

Three Kinghorn boys, three Aimar boys, three Bazemore boys, and three Eve boys from Beaufort were also in the armed forces during World War II. The Kinghorn brothers were from one of Beaufort's most prominent families. Their father, J. B. Kinghorn, was a Bay Street merchant and had been mayor during World War I. The Kinghorn boys literally covered the globe. The older brothers, James B. "J. B." Kinghorn and James A. "Albert" Kinghorn were twins. They joined the army on November 19 and 21, 1940. Both were commissioned officers. J. B. Kinghorn, who served in the African, Middle Eastern, and European theaters, won the Bronze Star for valor. He was discharged as a captain with the Third Airborne Division in England in September 1945. Albert Kinghorn served two years in the Burma-India campaign under General Joseph "Vinegar Joe" Stillwell, won the Bronze Service Star, and was as a lieutenant colonel in the U.S. Army Corps of Engineers in 1946. A. Mills Kinghorn outdid both of his older brothers. He was commissioned as a second lieutenant on February 11, 1942. He served fourteen months overseas in the New Guinea and Philippine campaigns. He earned three Bronze Service Stars for combat and was released from active duty as a captain commanding Company B of the 127th Airborne Engineering Battalion. In 1945 Mills Kinghorn was awarded the Silver Star for heroism on Luzon, Philippine Islands. Serving with the Eleventh Airborne Division on Luzon, Kinghorn displayed unusual courage under fire. On Luzon the retreating Japanese had buried 500-pound bombs vertically in the road with the detonators pointed up. Mills Kinghorn's engineering company devised a method of extracting the bombs with a motorized crane. In order to attach the crane, someone had to dig around the possibly booby-trapped bomb and attach a cable. Kinghorn did not permit the enlisted men in his command to perform this deadly task but attached the cables himself, occasionally under fire from snipers. The roads were cleared, the American advance continued, and Captain Mills Kinghorn won the Silver Star for lifesaving courage under fire.[36]

Three Aimar brothers also saw military service. William W. Aimar joined the Marine Corps on February 4, 1943, was overseas for twenty-nine months in the Pacific, and was discharged as a staff sergeant in 1946. Toomer Aimar joined the army on April 4, 1945, too late to see combat in World War II. Charles S. Aimar joined the marines on August 7, 1943, and served eighteen months in the Pacific. Charles Aimar fought in the Battle of Iwo Jima, was awarded the Bronze Star for valor and the Purple Heart for combat wounds, and was discharged as a corporal in 1946. All three Aimar boys returned to become prominent citizens in postwar Beaufort.[37]

All three Bazemores from Port Royal joined the seaborne forces during World War II. Frederick E. Bazemore and Joseph H. Bazemore both joined the navy, while Paul R. Bazemore joined the Coast Guard. Fred Bazemore enlisted on October 24, 1941, served nearly two years in the Pacific, and won a chest full of campaign medals. Joe Bazemore joined the navy in July 1944, became an athletic instructor in the training command, and was discharged as a petty officer, second class, in 1946. Paul Bazemore was a Coast Guard radioman in the Atlantic fleet.[38]

The Eves were raised in one of Beaufort County's largest truck-farming families. Harford Eve Jr., the oldest, joined the army on October 17, 1942, served for twenty-three months in Italy, and won the Combat Infantry Badge and four Bronze Service Stars. He won a battlefield commission and was discharged as a first lieutenant in January 1946. Pinckney Eve joined the army on November 18, 1943, served eight months overseas in the Pacific, and was discharged in 1946 as a staff sergeant. Paul Eve enlisted in the marines on January 13, 1943, served sixteen months in the Pacific, and was discharged as a corporal in January 1946.[39]

Two Levin brothers, two Lipsitz brothers, two Koth brothers, two Frame brothers, two Lake brothers, and two Pollitzer brothers from Beaufort County also contributed military service during World War II. John H. Levin and Jules D. Levin were sons of Mr. and Mrs. Samuel Levin of Beaufort. John H. Levin was commissioned in the U.S. Army Air Corps on December 5, 1941, two days before Pearl Harbor. He served nineteen months in the European theater and won campaign medals for service in Normandy, northern France, the Rhineland, and central Europe. Levin was discharged with the rank of major in the 497th Air Service Group in 1946. His brother Jules D. "Junie" Levin was commissioned in the navy on December 7, 1942, one year after Pearl Harbor. Junie Levin saw combat in the Pacific and won six Bronze Service Stars. He was discharged as a lieutenant in the U.S. Navy Civil Engineering Battalion in May 1946.[40]

The two sons of Mr. and Mrs. M. S. "Max" Lipsitz both served in the U.S. Army Medical Corp. Dr. Hyman D. "Hymie" Lipsitz graduated from dental school and was commissioned on July 2, 1942. He served two and a half years with the U.S. Army Air Forces in the Pacific. His brother, Joe Lipsitz, enlisted in the U.S. Army Medical Corps on October 27, 1942, served most of the war in the general hospital in Augusta, Georgia, and was discharged a staff sergeant in November 1945.[41]

Two Koths from Gray's Hill both joined the navy. Jesse M. Koth enlisted in the U.S. Navy on August 15, 1941, served eighteen months in the Pacific, and was discharged on November 8, 1945, as a petty officer, second class. Daniel L. Koth entered the navy on April 20, 1942, served as a motor mechanic, mostly on Staten Island, New York, for three and a half years, and was discharged as a petty officer, first class, on September 24, 1945.[42]

The Frame brothers from Burton both joined the U.S. Army. Howard J. Frame enlisted on November 5, 1941. He served twenty-two months in the Italian campaigns, won four Bronze Service Stars, and was discharged as a private first class on October 20, 1945. His brother, Everette Frame enlisted on August 29, 1945, too late for combat in World War II. He was discharged as an infantry private five months later.[43]

The two sons of Beaufort realtor H. H. Lake also served in uniform, but neither boy went overseas. Henry L. Lake joined the navy as a flight cadet and on August 12, 1942, completed flight training, and was commissioned on January 8, 1944, but did not finish advanced training before the war ended. Henry L. Lake Jr. enlisted in the army on July 28, 1942. He served eighteen months as a military policeman in the United States and was discharged as a tech 5 in December 1943.[44]

No family from Beaufort County contributed more young men to military service than the O'Quinns. Seven O'Quinn cousins—four from Pritchardville, two from Beaufort, and one from Bluffton—all donned military uniforms. James W. O'Quinn of Beaufort joined the state National Guard on January 13, 1941, was posted to Fort Moultrie with the 263rd Coast Artillery, and then spent nineteen months in the Pacific. Aaron O'Quinn from Pritchardville also served in the National Guard Coast Artillery but was not shipped overseas. Esdorn O'Quinn enlisted in the U.S. Army Air Forces on February 12, 1943. He served sixteen months in Europe and earned nine Bronze Service Stars for combat duty. He was discharged with a sergeant's rank on October 25, 1945. James C. O'Quinn of Pritchardville enlisted in the navy on November 18, 1943, served a year in the Pacific fleet, and was discharged as a petty officer, second class, on December 11, 1945. Perry O'Quinn of Beaufort joined the army on December 20, 1943, served fourteen months in Europe, and earned Bronze Service Stars for combat in the Rhineland, Ardennes, and Central Europe campaigns. He was discharged as a tech 5 in the Army Transport Corps on December 4, 1945. Norman O'Quinn of Pritchardville enlisted in the navy on May 25, 1944, and served the last few months of the war in the Pacific. He was discharged as a gunner's mate, third class, on January 28, 1946. Donald O'Quinn of Bluffton enlisted in the Marine Corps on July 26, 1946, too late to see combat in World War II.

In addition to those cited above, six other Beaufort men received the Bronze Star for valor in combat; two received the Silver Star; and three Beaufort boys received the Distinguished Service Cross, the Distinguished Flying Cross, and the Navy Cross, which were presidential citations for heroism in combat second only to the Congressional Medal of Honor.

Richard Van Bray Jr., son of Beaufort's famous mayor in the 1920s, was commissioned in the army on July 10, 1941. After two years service in the Panama Canal Zone, Dick Bray was posted to England and arrived three days before D-Day. He fought through Europe as an antiaircraft artillery officer. Bray received five Bronze Service Stars for combat in the Normandy, Northern France, Rhineland, Ardennes, and Central Europe campaigns. He was awarded the Bronze Star for valor in the Ardennes Forest during the famous Battle of the Bulge.[45] Marion DeVeaux Jones of St. Helena Island enlisted in the U.S. Army on April 23, 1943. He spent fifteen months in the Pacific as an infantryman. He was awarded the Bronze Star for valor and the Purple Heart for wounds during the campaign for Luzon Island, Philippines. Marion Jones was given a battlefield commission and was discharged as first lieutenant.[46] William C. Henderson joined the army on August 26, 1943. He spent eighteen months in Italy, receiving Bronze Service Stars for combat in the Rome-Arno, Apennine, and Po Valley campaigns. Bill Henderson was awarded the Bronze Star for valor and the Purple Heart for wounds suffered in the Po Valley. He was attached to the Fifth Army under the command of General Mark Clark. Henderson's 38th Infantry Division was the first "selective service division," composed fully of draftees, to be sent overseas and the first American division to land in Italy. Bill Henderson was discharged as a highly decorated private first class on February 1, 1946.[47] Claude M. Capplemann of Beaufort was a career marine who joined the corps on February 20, 1938. Captain Capplemann served nearly three years in the Pacific, seeing action at Guadalcanal, Tulagi, Tinian, and Saipan, among others. He was awarded the Bronze Star for valor and the Purple Heart for wounds received on Namur Island in 1943. In 1944 Capplemann received a personal commendation from Major General C. B. Cates, commanding general of the Fourth Marine Division for service during the invasion of Saipan. Capplemann ended World War II with the rank of major and retired from the corps a lieutenant colonel in 1960. For many years, Claude M. "Pecy" Capplemann was a municipal judge. The Bronze Star and Purple Heart were awarded to Manson Connelly, an army private first class who had been trapped alone behind Japanese lines on Bougainville for two days in 1944.[48]

Another highly decorated Beaufort veteran was William A. Campbell Jr. of Sheldon. Campbell enlisted in the army on September 10, 1941. He joined the new airborne forces as a paratrooper. He parachuted behind German lines in North Africa during the American invasion of Morocco. Most of his company was killed or captured by the Germans, and Campbell was declared "missing in action" for three weeks in January 1943. He fought through the North African campaign and the Rome-Arno offensive in Italy. In August 1943 he was given a meritorious promotion to second lieutenant. In 1944

Bill Campbell transferred to the Pacific theater for the final offensives against Japan. He won four Bronze Service Stars for combat in North Africa and Italy and one Bronze Service Star for combat in China. In addition, Campbell was awarded the Air Medal for bravery and the French Legion of Merit. Bill Campbell had fought literally around the world.[49]

In addition to Mills Kinghorn and Walt Rodgers, two other Beaufort men won Silver Stars for bravery in combat. Dr. Ben Herbert Keyserling was the youngest child of William Keyserling, a widower by 1941. Herbert Keyserling was a medical intern in Charleston in 1941 when he accepted a commission as lieutenant junior grade in the Navy Medical Corps. In October 1941 he was assigned to duty with the First Marine Division at Camp Lejeune, North Carolina. He went with the First Division to the western Pacific and was in combat on Guadalcanal and New Guinea. He won three Bronze Service Stars. When the marines landed at Cape Gloucester on New Guinea, Herbert Keyserling was awarded a Silver Star for courage when he advanced to a forward position to treat wounded marines in their foxholes. He displayed courage and professionalism while under fire from Japanese forces and saved the lives of his fellow servicemen. Like many Beaufort boys who saw combat early in World War II, by 1944 Keyserling was back in the states at Fort Jackson in Columbia and on Parris Island. He was discharged from the navy as a lieutenant commander on March 31, 1946. Dr. Herbert Keyserling practiced medicine in his hometown for more than fifty years and was one of the founders of Beaufort's modern medical community. The Keyserling Cancer Center was named in his honor.[50]

Another Beaufort medical corpsman won the Silver Star for bravery and for saving lives on the battlefield. Henry E. Wallace Jr. entered the army on June 23, 1941. He became a medic and took part in the American offensives in New Guinea and the Solomon Islands. "Hal" Wallace won two Bronze Service Stars and the Silver Star for "gallantry in action" on August 4, 1943, on New Georgia, Solomon Islands. Seeing wounded soldiers under fire, Wallace "left his covered position and crawling through heavy enemy fire to a seriously wounded soldier . . . removed him to safety." He was discharged as a corporal from the Army Medical Department on August 27, 1945.[51]

Two sons of Henry R. and Mabel Pollitzer went to war. Richard Guerard Pollitzer was commissioned in the navy in 1940 after attending Clemson College for two years. He served on destroyers protecting the North Atlantic convoys. Dick Pollitzer's closest childhood friend was Stratton Christensen, who died at sea in the Atlantic a few months after standing as best man at Pollitzer's wedding. Dick Pollitzer's older brother, Jack D. Pollitzer, enlisted in the U.S. Army Air Forces and was tail gunner on a B-17 "Flying Fortress" on missions in Sicily, Italy, and Eastern Europe.

Sergeant Jack Pollitzer's exploits as a B-17 tail gunner were some of the most remarkable stories of the war. He served nearly two years in air combat in North Africa and Italy. In June 1943 he was declared "missing in action" when his B-17 failed to return from a mission over Italy. Two weeks later, Jack Pollitzer, his badly damaged plane, and flight crew reported in from a safe field on Malta. On September 7, 1943, he was aboard a B-17 on a bombing run over Foggia, Italy. The formation was attacked by German fighter planes, and one engine of Pollitzer's flying fortress was knocked out, forcing the plane out of its formation. Immediately, the bomber was swarmed by German fighters. During the desperate aerial combat, Staff Sergeant Jack Pollitzer shot down four enemy fighters in twenty-five minutes, drove off the attacking aircraft, and saved his B-17 and its crew. The bomber continued its mission alone, delivered its bombs on target, and limped back to a friendly hospital base. During the battle Pollitzer shot down two ME-109s, one FW-190, and one RE-2001 fighter aircraft. His record of destroying four enemy fighter planes in a single mission was rarely, if ever, duplicated in the war. On December 26, 1944, at Chatham Army Air Field in Savannah, Sergeant Pollitzer was awarded the Distinguished Flying Cross "for extraordinary achievement . . . in aerial flight . . . outstanding skill in gunnery . . . and calm proficiency in Battle." Both Pollitzer brothers returned to Beaufort to engage in business, as had the three generations of Pollitzers before them. Jack Pollitzer founded the Beaufort Realty Company, still in business sixty years later.[52]

Hollywood could not have invented a story with greater drama or more heroism than the story of "Beau Sam" McGowan of St. Helena Island. Samuel McGowan Jr., was born on the island in 1924, the oldest son of a rural mailman, Sam McGowan, and his French wife, Henrietta Vurpillot. Raised with his two brothers in the woods and waters of the isolated sea islands, "Beau Sam" became an expert hunter and fisherman. He had just entered Clemson College when America entered the war. Beau Sam McGowan left Clemson and enlisted in the army on March 5, 1943. Along with Bill Henderson, he was attached to the 351st Regiment of the Thirty-Eighth Infantry Division. They fought through Italy as part of General Mark Clark's Fifth U.S. Army. On September 30, 1944, the 351st Regiment was in close combat with the German army around Mount Cappello in northern Italy. Beau Sam McGowan's company found itself under heavy mortar fire from a fortified farmhouse. As nearly one hundred German soldiers were assembling for a counterattack, "Staff Sergeant McGowan volunteered to lead a platoon against the enemy stronghold." Using the terrain to hide his platoon's movements, he emerged on the enemy's flank "dangerously close to the impact area of supporting fire." Beau Sam McGowan then led his platoon on a "lightening attack . . . with fixed bayonets" against a numerically superior, strongly entrenched enemy position. It was reported that "Staff Sergeant McGowan personally neutralized two machine guns with hand grenades, killing three Germans and capturing six. Forcing one of his prisoners to load an enemy machine gun, Staff Sergeant McGowan manned the hostile weapon. He fired at a group of Germans in a draw to the rear of the house, killing or wounding 12 Germans and forcing the rest to flee." Even though severely wounded in the leg, McGowan "personally led his men in a ferocious assault on the house." Once the stronghold was captured, McGowan refused to be evacuated until his company had consolidated their new defensive position. For this action, Beau Sam McGowan was awarded the Presidential Distinguished Service Cross on the personal recommendation of General Clark. As the citation read, "The prodigious courage displayed by Staff Sergeant McGowan in the face of heavy odds won the admiration and esteem of his entire platoon and his performance is exemplary of the finest traditions of the armed forces of the United States."[53]

Of all the stories of Beaufort heroism, none exceeded the action of Petty Officer William Pinckney aboard the aircraft carrier USS *Enterprise* at the battle of Santa Cruz in 1942. Bill Pinckney was born in Dale, South Carolina, on April 27, 1915. He dropped out of school in the seventh grade. Pinckney volunteered for service, entering the navy on August 13, 1938. As were most African Americans in the navy, Bill Pinckney was assigned cook's duty. He shipped out aboard the USS *Enterprise,* one of the premier warships in the Pacific fleet. The *Enterprise* had been Admiral Raymond Spruance's flagship at the Battle of Midway in June 1942. On October 26, 1942, the *Enterprise* was hotly engaged with Japanese enemy aircraft off the Santa Cruz Islands. On every naval vessel in combat, each crewman, regardless of his regular duty, has a specific responsibility during battle. Bill Pinckney's battle station was in the ammunition-handling room below decks. There Pinckney and five other sailors passed ammunition up to gun crews on deck. The *Enterprise* took many hits during the battle. One Japanese bomb caused an explosion and fire in the ammunition room. Four of Pinckney's shipmates were killed. Only Pinckney and Gunner's Mate James Bagwell survived. The ammunition room was a cauldron. James Bagwell climbed the ladder to escape but was overcome by heat and fell back to the deck, unconscious. Although he was the smaller man, Pinckney threw Bagwell over his shoulder, climbed the red hot ladder, and carried his injured shipmate to a first-aid station on the hangar deck. Then, Bill Pinckney returned to the burning ammunition handling room, with the ammunition ready to explode at any second, to try to save his other shipmates. When he found them all dead, he struggled back to the hangar deck and collapsed. For his selfless act of courage, Petty Officer William Pinckney was awarded a Purple Heart and the presidential citation for heroism at sea, the Navy Cross.

Bill Pinckney "shipped over" for a second hitch in the navy, mostly spent in San Diego. He left the navy as a petty officer, first class, on June 30, 1946. He and his wife, Henrietta, whom he met at Robert Smalls Elementary School, moved to Brooklyn, New York, where Henrietta worked as a telephone operator, and Pinckney joined the U.S. Merchant Marine. He spent twenty-six years in the maritime service and retired to his wife's home in Beaufort. Bill Pinckney died in 1975.

In 2000 the navy named a guided missile destroyer after William Pinckney. When the USS *Pinckney* was launched in Pascagoula, Mississippi, on June 29, 2002, Henrietta Pinckney christened the new vessel. She was assisted by Ray Bagwell, son of the man whose life Pinckney had saved. Bill Pinckney was described by friends as a modest, even shy man. In later years, when friends and family asked him to reflect on his heroism, he often answered that he had been "proud to serve." That phrase is the motto of the USS *Pinckney*.[54]

In addition to those World War II veterans who survived, Beaufort County's World War II roll of honor bears thirty-eight names of men killed in combat; they are listed below.[55]

Name	*Rank*	*Service*	*Hometown*	*Date / Place*
Baldwin, David	Lt.	USA	Beaufort	1944/Normandy
Ballew, Robert	Gunnery Sgt.	USMC	Yemassee	
Beach, James K.	Seaman, 1st Class	USN	Bluffton	
Bethers, James E.	Pvt.	USA	Beaufort	
Brown, Samuel	Steward's Mate	USN	Frogmore	
Bush, Leon	Petty Officer, 2nd Class	USN	Beaufort	1941/Pearl Harbor
Bush, Samuel J.	Petty Officer, 1st Class	USN	Beaufort	1941/Pearl Harbor
Christensen, Stratton	Ens.	USN	Beaufort	1942/N. Atlantic
Collier, Robert	1st Lt.	USA	Beaufort	
Cooler, Ernest	Pvt., 1st Class	USA	Hardeeville	1944/N. France
Dempsey, Malcolm	Tech. Sgt.,	USA	Beaufort Co.	
Dinneen, Joseph M.	Petty Officer, 1st Class	USN	Beaufort	
Fisher, William P,	2nd Lieutenant	USMC	Parris Island	
Fletcher, Ira	Seaman, 1st Class	USCG	Beaufort	
Gecare, Robert	Pvt., 1st Class	USMC	Parris Island	1944/Saipan
Harter, Ralph	Pvt.	USA	Beaufort	1944/Normandy
Hensley, William B.	2nd Lt.	USA	Beaufort Co.	
Hickman, Perroneau	Cpl.	USMC	Port Royal	
Higgins, Robert L.	Pvt., 1st Class	USMC	Beaufort	
Howard, Daniel	Steward, 2nd Class	USN	Beaufort	

(continued)

Name	*Rank*	*Service*	*Hometown*	*Date / Place*
Huckeba, William W.	Warrant Officer	USMC	Beaufort	1944/Peleliu
Jackson, Herman	Steward, 2nd Class	USN	Beaufort	
Lawson, Bishop	Sgt.	USA	Beaufort Co.	
Lees, Vern	Sgt.	USMC	Beaufort	
Lewis, Robert A.	1st Lt.	USA	Beaufort Co.	
Logan, William R.	Petty Officer, 2nd Class	USN	Beaufort	
Macone, Francis V.	Staff Sergeant	USMC	Beaufort	1944/Halmehara Islands
McCaskill, Bruce	Sgt	USA	Beaufort Co.	
McCoy, William B.	Sgt.	USA	Beaufort Co.	
Mixon, Robert Jr.	Staff Sergeant	USA	Beaufort Co.	
Outlaw, James R.	Pvt.	USA	Beaufort Co.	
Rankin, John O. III	Sgt.	USMC	Beaufort	
Rivers, Rufus	Tech 5	USA	Beaufort Co.	
Simmons, Nathaniel	Pvt.	USA	Beaufort Co.	
Singleton, Samuel L.	Cpl.	USA	Beaufort Co.	
Terry, Raphael I.	Pvt., 1st Class	USA	Beaufort Co.	1944/N. France
Tyson, John A.	Pvt., 1st Class	USMC	Hardeeville	
Ulmer, Charles E., III	Pvt.	USA	Beaufort Co.	

Chapter 15

The Postwar Boom in Beaufort County

On Friday, December 20, 2002, most of the state's political and business leaders gathered beneath the spreading live oaks at the eighteenth green of the world-famous Harbor Town Golf Links on Hilton Head Island. They had assembled to honor the life and work of Charles Elbert Fraser, who had been killed in a freak boating accident in the waters of the Turks and Caicos Islands. Charles E. Fraser (1929–2002) was the most influential Beaufortonian of the twentieth century. During the previous half century, his vision, his intellect, and his energy had transformed Hilton Head Island from one of the poorest places in America to a place of recreation and sport for many of the wealthiest people in America. The real estate boom that Charles Fraser started on the southern end of Hilton Head Island has lasted for fifty years. It has enveloped Beaufort County property adjacent to Hilton Head Island and has spread into neighboring Jasper County. This real estate and development phenomenon has, according to the 2000 federal census, made Beaufort County the fastest-growing county in the state and one of the ten fastest-growing counties in the Southeast. The explosive economic growth from 1950 to 2000 has given the county the highest per capita income in the state. It has produced more wealth for more people than any event in Beaufort County's five hundred years of recorded history.

Charles Fraser was born in Hinesville, Georgia, the son of Lieutenant General Joseph Fraser and Pearl Collins Fraser. He attended Presbyterian College in Clinton, South Carolina, but graduated from the University of Georgia in 1950. He was an excellent student and was admitted to Yale Law School. During the summer of 1950, before starting law school, Fraser worked on his father's timberland on Hilton Head Island. That experience changed Fraser's life and the history of Beaufort County.

General Joseph Fraser Sr. was a Georgia landowner and timber man. He had founded the Fraser Lumber Company in Hinesville in 1920 and, despite the long Depression of the 1920s and 1930s, had been a successful grower and broker of southern yellow pine. Along the way, he came to own much land in southern Georgia. Fraser was called back to duty during World War II and by 1945 had achieved the rank of lieutenant general. As the postwar economy began to expand, Fraser and his partners scouted the depopulated coastal plain of South Carolina and Georgia for useful timber resources. In 1949 Fraser and Fred Hack, a neighbor and fellow timber man, came to investigate timber resources on Hilton Head Island. Unable to secure a timber lease agreement from the island's principal landowners, Alfred Loomis and Landon Thorne, Hack approached Fraser about forming a syndicate to buy Hilton Head timberlands. In 1949 Joseph Fraser, Fred Hack, C. C. Stebbins, and Olin McIntosh of Savannah formed the Hilton Head Company. They purchased eight thousand acres of the Loomis-Thorne estate at the southern end of Hilton Head Island for sixty dollars per acre. That tract was the land on which young Charles Fraser spent the summer of 1950. In 1951 the Hilton Head Company purchased the remaining twelve thousand acres of the Loomis-Thorne estate for six hundred thousand dollars. They formed a second company, Honey Horn Plantation Company, named for William P. Clyde's 1890s Honey Horn lodge. That land had been the epicenter of the Loomis-Thorne plantation society of the 1930s and 1940s. Fred Hack and his family set up permanent residence at Honey Horn. In 1956 the partners partitioned their holdings, leaving the Frasers with forty-five hundred acres on the south end of Hilton Head Island. This was to be Sea Pines Plantation.

At Yale Law School, Charles Fraser spent a good deal of his time examining private planned communities and the legal contracts that created them. He took a course entitled "Land Use Planning and Allocation by Private Agreement." The professor was Myres McDougal, described as "a specialist in the use of private covenants to implement comprehensive land use planning." It is easy to imagine that Charles Fraser's winters in New Haven heightened his dream of a sea island paradise, and that his law school education helped him formulate the legal mechanisms necessary to achieve that dream. Fraser made the most of his education and, as a consequence, became a pioneer and expert practitioner of the development of private, planned, environmentally protected communities.

By 1952 the partners in the Hilton Head and Honey Horn Plantation Companies completed their timber harvesting and paid for the land purchases. To capitalize on their real estate holdings, they knew they had to end Hilton Head's isolation. In 1952 there was no bridge to Hilton Head Island and no regular ferry service. Steamboat service to Savannah had ceased in 1934. In 1953 the Hilton Head landowners convinced the state highway department to open a scheduled daily car ferry from Buckingham Landing on the mainland to Hilton Head Island. Their political ally was State Representative J. Wilton Graves, who owned much real estate on the mainland and was a pioneer investor on Hilton Head Island. In 1956 Graves built the

Sea Crest Motel, the first beachfront hotel on Hilton Head Island. Graves served in the General Assembly almost continuously from 1951 to 1970 and then resigned to take a seat on the South Carolina Highway Commission. He was chairman of the commission in 1973 and 1974. His influence in the statehouse and particularly with the highway department was crucial to the early development of Hilton Head Island.[1]

The ferry to Hilton Head Island carried only five cars and made only six trips per day. As soon as Olin McIntosh built a few beachfront cottages at Folly Field, the ferry was immediately insufficient for the traffic. The state replaced the first barge with a new ferryboat called the *Pocahontas.* It carried nine cars but it, too, was quickly overwhelmed. Fraser, Hack, and McIntosh knew that Hilton Head needed an automobile bridge if it was ever to become a beachfront resort.

The history of twentieth-century Beaufort County could be written by studying its bridges. Of all the bridges built linking the sea islands to the mainland, beginning with the 1873 Port Royal Railroad trestle, none had a greater impact than the span that crossed Skull Creek to Hilton Head Island. The company owners could not convince the highway department to build the bridge so they decided to erect it themselves. Olin McIntosh suggested a toll bridge to self-fund the project, with various Hilton Head development companies guaranteeing the bond payments if the toll revenue fell short, as author Michael Danielson noted: "As would happen often in the future, the developers of Hilton Head proposed to do privately what could not be accomplished through the public sector." Representative Graves helped by sponsoring special-purpose legislation to establish the Hilton Head Toll Bridge Authority in 1954. Construction of the bridge began in 1955 and was finished in May 1956, at a cost of $1.5 million. It was an immediate success. Despite a steep toll of $2.50 per car, forty-eight thousand cars crossed the bridge in its first year of operation. In 1957 the tolls were cut in half and traffic doubled. By 1959 the construction bonds were retired, and the toll was eliminated. When the bridge was dedicated in 1956, it was named for South Carolina's twentieth-century icon James F. Byrnes.[2] In 1956 Beaufort's political and commercial establishment had not forgotten how much "our Jimmy" had done for impoverished Beaufort County in the previous half century.

Before the bridge was built, Hilton Head Island had no centrally generated electricity. Electrical power was obviously essential if Hilton Head Island were to become a resort and real estate development. This electricity must be available and cheap to power commercial and in-home air-conditioning equipment. During the 1950s air-conditioning was a rarity in Beaufort County. Only the Ocean View Café, Breeze Theater, and a few rooms at the hospital were air-conditioned. Beginning in the 1950s and 1960s, however, new homes were built with central heating and air-conditioning equipment that replaced all previous methods of heating and cooling a house. This single innovation required great amounts of electric power. This essential utility was provided by Palmetto Electric Cooperative, a small, rural power provider that had begun as a New Deal Rural Electrification Authority program.

Palmetto Electric began setting poles and stringing wires across Skull Creek in 1955. The next year it provided the first public electric power to Hilton Head Island. The service charge for bringing the wires to the small, isolated homesteads of the African American native islanders was less then two dollars per month. With automobile transportation and electrical power available by 1956, many Hilton Head natives entered the twentieth century for the first time.[3]

As public utilities reached across Skull Creek, Charles Fraser was plowing ahead with his unconventional plans for Sea Pines Plantation. His plans were not only unique and untried but also expensive. Instead of bulldozing roads through forests and dividing the property into rigidly spaced and sized lots, Fraser designed the roads, golf courses, and house lots to fit aesthetically into the sea island environment. He left large open spaces to protect the lush, subtropical forest. Amenities, architecture, and landscape design were all planned to capitalize on Hilton Head's natural beauty.

To attract the wealthy residents he was targeting, Charles Fraser also had to provide first-class guest accommodations on isolated, impoverished Hilton Head Island. In 1959 he completed the William Hilton Inn, the first full-service, beachfront resort hotel in Beaufort County. It cost $1 million. Old-time Beaufortonians could not imagine that such a costly venture in such a poor, remote corner of Beaufort County would turn a profit, but Fraser intended the inn to be a sales mechanism for Sea Pines Plantation. Real estate sales were Fraser's game. The hotel business was an auxiliary to his chief design. In the 1950s and 1960s, the William Hilton Inn was the first introduction for millions of American tourists to Hilton Head and the sea islands.

Charles Fraser's problem was money. Sea Pines Plantation was undercapitalized from the beginning, and Fraser had to rely upon all sorts of imaginative financing to keep the project moving forward. Traditional banks were reluctant to hold a mortgage on so unconventional a scheme. Fraser's most reliable source of capital was the Traveller's Insurance Company, which was willing to lend money only up to the value of the marketable pine timber. One of the Sea Pines Plantation's benefactors and early investors was James Self Jr. (1919–1998), chairman of Greenwood Mills in Greenwood, South Carolina. His father, James Cuthbert Self (1876–1955), was one of the state's great textile industrialists and, through the Self Foundation (founded in 1942), one of the chief philanthropists of Greenwood County. James Self Jr. performed the same service for the Hilton Head community in the 1990s.

Charles Fraser's other financial problem was slow sales. In 1958 only 45 lots were sold and only three homes had been built at Sea Pines Plantation. By 1960, 177 lots had been sold but only nineteen homes had been built. Fraser's sea island paradise was off to a slow start. While his company struggled to pay its bills and acquire capital to expand, its owner brought considerable national attention to Hilton Head Island. During the 1960s articles lauding Sea Pines Plantation appeared in *Progressive Architecture, Sports Illustrated,* and *Fortune* magazines.

More important, real estate values began to rise on Hilton Head Island, and those who had invested early were reaping handsome profits. One ocean front lot that sold for $5,350 in 1957 was resold for $34,000 in 1968. One of James Self's investments of $100,000 had been secured in land that by 1980 was worth $1.7 million.[4] These were the stories that turned Charles Fraser's dream into a real estate bonanza. By the 1960s the outlines of Hilton Head's future were visible to discerning investors.

While Hilton Head Island was aborning, 1950s Beaufort was also creating a middle-class economy. After World War II, the economy in northern Beaufort County was almost entirely dependent on its largest industry, the Marine Corps. And the Marine Corps was very busy in the 1950s. No sooner had World War II ended and the U.S. Navy decommissioned its naval air station in 1946 than Soviet expansionism inaugurated the Cold War and led to the Korean Conflict (1950–53). In June 1950 there were 1,836 recruits training on Parris Island, a mere fraction of the number that had trained on Parris Island during the war. But on June 25, 1950, the conflict in Korea erupted into open warfare. Within three months there were 8,185 recruits training on Parris Island. By March 1952 there were 24,424 of them, surpassing even the greatest number at the peak of World War II. This rapid expansion spilled over into the economy of northern Beaufort County. Jobs were again plentiful for construction projects and thousands of steady, middle-class salaries were available through the federal civil service.

To enhance Beaufort's appeal as a tourist destination, Bay Street merchants and city officials inaugurated the first Water Festival in July 1955. The central attraction of the first one was the navy's Blue Angels acrobatic flight team. The festival was a success. It has been held for fifty-one consecutive, uninterrupted years and is one of the largest tourist events in the state.

The reputation of the Recruit Depot, suffered a tragic blow on April 8, 1956, when a drill sergeant, Matthew McKeon, led the recruits of Platoon 71, 3rd Recruit Battalion, on a disciplinary night march into the mud and marshes of Ribbon Creek. Neither McKeon nor most of his recruits were aware that the deep "pluff mud" of the sea islands was mostly impassable and sometimes dangerous. Nor were they aware of the depth of Ribbon Creek or the swiftness of the current at maximum ebb tide. Half of the platoon of seventy-five recruits fell into the creek, became disoriented in the dark, or got caught in the swiftly ebbing tide. Panic ensued, and six recruits, five of whom did not know how to swim, drowned in Ribbon Creek.

The incident at Ribbon Creek attracted national attention and embarrassed the Marine Corps. Unfavorable coverage appeared in the *New York Times,* the *Washington Post, Newsweek,* and *U.S. News and World Report.* Lurid photographs of the creek and of harsh drilling methods appeared in *Life* magazine. Marine Corps commanders, under pressure and unaccustomed to public scrutiny, court-martialed Sergeant McKeon and overhauled recruit training. The Ribbon Creek incident was the most widely publicized event in Beaufort County since World War II and the publicity was generally unfavorable.[5]

While its national reputation was tarnished in 1956, the other news regarding the Marine Corps in Beaufort County was good. In 1952, because of the Korean Conflict, the navy began buying back land at the old naval air station. It cancelled its leases to several local private enterprises on the property and appropriated $3 million to rebuild the World War II–era runways. On January 1, 1955, the airfield was designated a U.S. Marine Auxiliary Landing Field, a satellite of the Marine Corps Air Station at Cherry Point, North Carolina. During 1955 the runways were repaired and lengthened to accommodate the jet aircraft of the 1950s. In June 1956 the facility was commissioned as the U.S. Marine Auxiliary Air Station (MCAAS), Beaufort, South Carolina. By 1958 the navy had expanded the air station to fifty-three hundred acres, larger than it had been in World War II, and expended $34 million to prepare the station for three thousand marine personnel and their families. In 1959 MCAAS, Beaufort, received its first squadron of supersonic fighter jets, the F8-C Crusaders of Fighter-Attack Squadron 333. With their famous shamrock logo, they were known locally as the "TripTre."[6]

To accommodate the great increase in Marine Corps personnel and their families, in 1957 the government built the 2,565-unit Capehart Housing Project at Laurel Bay on Port Royal Island. Laurel Bay was the largest housing development in Beaufort County until the opening of Del Webb's Sun City Hilton Head retirement community in 1993. The first Marine Corps family moved to Laurel Bay in 1959.

The development of Hilton Head Island at the south end and the rapid expansion of the Marine Corps facilities at the north end of Beaufort County revived 1930s dreams to build a bridge across the Broad River and unite the two halves of Beaufort County. Early plans for an automobile bridge dated to 1938 when engineering plans, river surveys, and submarine borings were made between Port Royal and Lemon Islands. This plan was delayed first by the Depression years and later by wartime necessities. A Broad River Bridge was high on the list of "after war work" compiled by local economic and political leaders. In 1947 the highway department adopted the Broad River Bridge project to cut the driving distance from Bluffton to Beaufort from seventy to less than thirty miles. In 1947 the population of Bluffton was five hundred people.

It was ten years before the Broad River Bridge was finished and open for automobile traffic. The two bridges across the Broad River and Chechessee Creek spanned 7,303 feet (1.4 miles) and 1,642 feet (0.31 miles), respectively. The project cost $2.7 million. The Broad River span alone would be the longest bridge in the state. In 1958 the bridge was dedicated and named for Senator Edward Burton "Burt" Rodgers, the longtime county clerk of court and state senator. During the 1930s he had been among the promoters of the bridge plan and was a charter member of the 1938 Broad River Bridge Commission.

A chief incentive in 1957 was that the Marine Corps wanted the bridge. One of the most frequent complaints about Parris Island since World War II was that it was isolated and too distant from large metropolitan areas. The Broad River Bridge cut the driving distance from Parris Island to Savannah by more than half. The only opposition came from the Charleston business community, which anticipated losing trade to its Savannah competitors. In reply to this opposition, Highway Commissioner Claude McMillan told the Charleston Rotary Club, "The big trouble with Charleston is that you have the usual number of people walking backward, not forward into the future."[7] The Broad River Bridge in 1957, like the Whale Branch Bridge in 1908 and the Hilton Head Bridge in 1956, altered the historic transportation patterns of Beaufort County and laid the foundation for its transformation in the late twentieth century.

In 1959 the growth of the Beaufort community and the continuing desire to serve U.S. Marine Corps personnel and their families prompted the county legislative delegation (Senator Burt Rodgers, Representative Brantley Harvey Jr., and Representative T. Reeves Sams) and local civic leaders (G. G. Dowling and Marion DeVeaux Jones) to lobby the University of South Carolina to place a two-year branch campus in Beaufort. The branch campus opened in the fall of 1959 with seventy-one students. The first director of USC Beaufort was Dr. John J. Duffy, professor of history, who was for many years the vice chancellor for all statewide off-campus programs of the University of South Carolina. The branch campus occupied the old Beaufort College Building (1852) and the original Beaufort High School (1909) on Carteret Street, thus reviving a higher education tradition that began with the charter of the Beaufort College in 1795.

Beaufort High School had moved to a new brick building built in 1925 on the corner of Bay Street and Hamar Street. The public school district also built a new high school for African American students in 1925 on the corner of Ribaut Road and Boundary Street. In 1925 the white Beaufort High School cost one hundred thousand dollars while the African American Robert Smalls High School cost thirty thousand dollars. In 1931 Robert Smalls High School, a wooden structure, burned to the ground and was replaced by a brick building that served until the 1970s. During the 1950s, the farmland between Beaufort and Port Royal was developed as the Mossy Oaks subdivision, divided between the town of Port Royal and the city of Beaufort. In 1959 the Beaufort County Board of Education built a brand-new Beaufort High School in the middle of the Mossy Oaks subdivision.[8] The new Beaufort High School was to be the center of the school desegregation experiments and the social revolution of the 1960s.

Beaufort County's progress in the 1950s was interrupted in 1959 when the sea islands were again struck by a major Atlantic hurricane. On September 29, 1959, Hurricane Gracie made landfall in Beaufort County. The eye of the storm passed over Coffin Point at the north end of St. Helena Island. Gracie was a very intense storm with wind speeds up to 146 miles per hour. Beaufort County sustained $4 million in damages and four deaths. The bridges and causeways connecting the sea islands to the mainland were washed out. The storm damaged 2,394 homes in Beaufort County and sank twelve shrimp boats. But the destruction in 1959 was relatively less than in 1893 or 1940 because the wind blew from the west and held the storm surge out at sea.[9]

By 1960 northern Beaufort County had become a middle-class community, thanks to the largesse of the United States Department of Defense, and southern Beaufort County was witnessing the birth of a whole new community. Thoughtful observers in 1960 could have anticipated the results of the Eighteenth Census of the United States for Beaufort County but many may not have appreciated what a historic turning point it was. By 1960 the population of Beaufort County reached 41,062. The county's population had grown 86.3 percent since 1940. It was the first time since the Civil War that Beaufort County's population exceeded what was enumerated in 1860 (40,053). Because of Civil War losses, the divisions of old Beaufort County by Hampton County (1878) and Jasper County (1912), and the Great Exodus of African Americans (1900–1940), Beaufort County took a full century to exceed its peak population of the antebellum years. Perhaps a more important milestone was that for the first time in 230 years, Beaufort County achieved a white majority population. By 1960 nearly 60 percent of Beaufort County residents were white. It was the first time since the end of the Yemassee War (1728) that Beaufort County was not the buckle on the lowcountry Black Belt. The census of 1960 signaled a profound social, political, and economic transformation for Beaufort County. Beaufort County's per capita income still was below the national average in 1960, but incomes and education levels were rising rapidly in the 1950s and 1960s. By the middle of the 1960s, it was clear that boom times had arrived in Beaufort County. Social change had to follow.[10]

As in the rest of America following the landmark U.S. Supreme Court decision *Brown v. Board of Education of Topeka* (1954), the public schools of Beaufort County became the proving ground for the social revolution of the 1960s. During the 1950s Beaufort County was a typical, segregated, Deep South community. Schools, churches, restaurants, and most public facilities were separated between blacks and whites. Separate "Whites Only" and "Colored Only" water fountains and restrooms were common across the county. The old C&WC railroad depot had separate waiting rooms. Beaufort's downtown Breeze Theater, in the old Beaufort Bank Building, had a separate entrance and ticket window for African American moviegoers, who were required to sit in the balcony. Legally required racial segregation was a legacy of the Jim Crow years in South Carolina, but Beaufort County may have been the last area of the state to adopt strict racial segregation. Not until the 1920s was legalized racial segregation a fixture of the Beaufort community. In 1960 Leroy Browne of St. Helena Island was appointed to the Beaufort County Commission. He was the first African American to serve in public office in Beaufort County since the Beaufort city election of 1913. Leroy Browne was a civil rights pioneer. His public service was a turning point for Beaufort County.

The path to social integration in Beaufort County in the 1960s was made much easier by the dominant presence in the community of the U.S. Marine Corps. During World War II, Marine Corps recruit training was strictly segregated, and Parris Island was all white. African American marines went through basic training at Montford Point, North Carolina. But the courage and sacrifices of African American soldiers, sailors, airmen, and marines during World War II made segregation of the U.S. military seem demonstrably unfair and irrational. After the war the military commanders, from top to bottom, ordered the integration of the U.S. armed forces. In 1949 General Clifton Cates, commandant of the Marine Corps, closed the Montfort Point facility and ordered black recruits to be trained at Parris Island. Initially, black recruits formed separate companies but were soon integrated into white companies. African American women were first accepted into the USMC in 1949. During the early 1950s, the service facilities and social clubs on Parris Island were fully integrated. By 1956 African American drill instructors were commanding platoons of white recruits. As Eugene Alvarez, historian of Parris Island, reported, "Parris Island's integration proceeded smoothly, with few problems on the part of whites or blacks."

As early as 1953, black students from Robert Smalls High School and black citizens from Beaufort and Port Royal signed petitions asking for an end to segregation in Beaufort County public schools. A decade after the U.S. Supreme Court decision of 1954, the Beaufort County School Board in 1964 adopted a freedom-of-choice option, permitting African American students to attend either black Robert Smalls High School or white Beaufort High School. During the 1964–65 school year, only one brave African American student chose to attend Beaufort High School. Rowland Washington entered Beaufort High School as a junior in 1964 and graduated in 1966. That same year black students Craig Washington and Janelle Drake enrolled in the all-white Beaufort Elementary School and Mossy Oaks Elementary School. In the years that followed, several African American students and a few teachers followed Rowland Washington to Beaufort High School. The voluntary integration of Beaufort County schools, by and large, progressed without incident. In Beaufort's schools the process was eased by the large number of military dependents attending. Rowland Washington acknowledged this when interviewed in 2002. Most of his friends "were the military kids that were used to going to school with the African-Americans."

In 1968 the U.S. Supreme Court ruled in *Green v. New Kent* that freedom of choice was no longer sufficient and that public schools should be racially unified. Beaufort County's legislative delegation formed the biracial Beaufort County Community Relations Council to ease the transition to complete integration. In 1969 the Beaufort County School Board voted to close the all-black Robert Smalls High School and St. Helena High School and build a new high school in the Burton suburb, where many U.S. Marine families lived, to absorb the increased enrollment. From 1970 to 1974, before Battery Creek High School was finished, Beaufort High School had to accommodate the overload of students with double sessions of classes (7:00 A.M. to 12:30 P.M. for the first session and 1:00 P.M. to 5:00 P.M. for the second session). As longtime English teacher at Beaufort High School, Gene Norris, reflected, it was "hard on the school, hard on the teachers and hard on the kids. . . . There were some incidents there that were not always pleasant, but nothing like what was happening in some other places."[11] Integration proceeded relatively smoothly in Beaufort County largely because of the pervasive presence of the U.S. Marine Corps in the community. The large federal establishment and its servicemen, employees, and dependents made Beaufort County different from typical southern communities of the 1950s and 1960s.

During the social revolution of the 1960s, Beaufort County became a bit of a refuge for civil rights icon Dr. Martin Luther King Jr. He held retreats for his Southern Christian Leadership Conference at Penn Center on St. Helena Island. Penn Center occupies the historic campus of the Penn Normal, Industrial and Agricultural School. The old Penn School was closed in 1953. The growth of the Beaufort County school system and the establishment of St. Helena High School barely two miles away made continuation of the old boarding school impractical. Penn Center, Incorporated, which followed, became a social, cultural, and historical institution for the sea island community. The visits of Martin Luther King Jr. and the SCLC in the 1960s, though very private at the time, added luster to the reputation of Penn Center as one of the seedbeds of the national civil rights movement. King stayed at the Gantt Cottage on the Penn Center campus. The cottage was named for Reconstruction state representative Hastings Gantt, who served from 1870 to 1874 and donated the land to the school in the 1870s. When Martin Luther King Jr. was assassinated in Memphis, Tennessee, in 1968, the biracial Beaufort County Community Relations Council helped ease tensions in the Beaufort community by calling for a school holiday on the day of King's funeral. The biracial Beaufort Ministerial Union, led by Dr. George Jones of the Baptist Church of Beaufort, organized a public memorial service at the new waterfront parking lot on Bay Street, which was dubbed "Freedom Mall." All in all, Beaufort County's response to the civil rights revolution of the 1960s was exemplary and a worthy tribute to its pathbreaking Reconstruction history.[12]

The residue of the grinding poverty of the early twentieth century was still apparent in Beaufort County in the 1960s. Dr. Donald Gatch made national headlines and annoyed many local political leaders in 1968 by reporting on hunger and malnutrition in Beaufort County. An article on hunger in Beaufort County appeared in the *New Republic* and was repeated in several national newspapers. One of Gatch's claims in that article was that if he had not delivered the poor, African American babies in rural Beaufort County, no other doctor would. This was, of course, not true, and it angered the old medical establishment in Beaufort, which had worked throughout the 1920s and 1930s, often for free, to improve the health of native sea islanders. CBS News sent a camera crew to Beaufort County to document and sensationalize the poverty in Beaufort County. They interviewed Dr. Herbert Keyserling, then chief of staff at Beaufort Memorial Hospital. CBS Television completely misrepresented Keyserling's response to questions on this subject, further alienating the local political and medical establishment. South Carolina senator Ernest "Fritz" Hollings made a personal crusade of this issue, toured Beaufort County with CBS News, and published a book entitled *The Case Against Hunger: A Demand for a National Policy* (1969). He championed the national food stamp program through the U.S. Department of Agriculture and found federal money to fund the Beaufort-Jasper Comprehensive Health Services, a pioneer in rural health clinics across the nation.[13]

In contrast to the perceived malnutrition in Beaufort County was the career of Beaufort County native Joseph William "Smokin' Joe" Frazier, who was born in Burton, on Port Royal Island, in 1944. He dropped out of school at the age of fourteen and, following the twentieth-century tradition of the sea islands, moved to New York to live with relatives. He soon abandoned New York for Philadelphia, where he also had relatives. While working at the Cross Brothers meat-packing plant, he began to work out at a neighborhood Police Athletic League gym. The gym manager and a local boxing trainer both recognized Frazier's athletic potential. It was the beginning of a spectacular boxing career. In 1962 he won the Philadelphia Golden Gloves heavyweight championship, and in 1962, 1963 and 1964, he was Middle Atlantic Golden Gloves champion. In 1964 Frazier joined the U.S. Olympic boxing team and won a Gold Medal by defeating Hans Huber of Germany. After the Olympics Frazier turned professional.

From 1967 to 1976, Smokin' Joe Frazier was one of the world's greatest pugilists. In 1968 he won the New York State Athletic Commission's World Heavyweight Championship. In 1969 he won the World Boxing Association Heavyweight Championship, making him officially the world's greatest boxer. At the peak of his career, Frazier fought three historic matches against Muhammad Ali. In 1971 he beat Ali in Madison Square Garden. In 1973 he lost his heavyweight crown to George Foreman. After Ali won the crown from Foreman, Frazier challenged Ali for the title. In 1974 at Madison Square Garden, Ali won the rematch with Frazier to retain the WBA heavyweight title. In 1975 Frazier and Ali fought a third match in the Philippines dubbed the "Thrilla in Manila." After fourteen brutal rounds, in which Frazier broke Ali's jaw, Frazier could no longer see through his swollen eyes, and his trainer threw in the towel. To this day, boxing aficionados claim that the three fights between Smokin' Joe Frazier and Muhammad Ali are three of the greatest boxing matches of all time. In 1976 Frazier retired from professional boxing with a career record of 34–4–1. His thirty-four victories included twenty-seven knockouts. He remains one of the greatest boxers in the history of the sport and the most famous Beaufortonian of the twentieth century.[14]

While Beaufort was becoming a middle-class community in the 1960s, Hilton Head Island was developing the businesses and institutions of a permanent community. New filling stations and country stores appeared in the late 1950s to accommodate the increasing beach traffic. In 1956 Hilton Head Island got its first shopping center. Coligny Plaza opened that year across the street from the Sea Crest Motel. It was little more than a collection of shops then, but it included a Winn Dixie Supermarket and a drug store, the first such business on Hilton Head Island. Coligny Circle at the end of Pope Avenue became the first "town center" on the island. It was named by Charles Fraser for Admiral Gaspar de Coligny, the sixteenth-century commander of the French navy, leader of the Huguenot faction in French politics, and sponsor of Captain Jean Ribault's historic voyage to Port Royal Sound in 1562. Charles Fraser not only appreciated the value of the sea island environment to resort and real estate sales, but he also understood the lure of five centuries of history to American tourists. Charles Fraser was, in fact, a diligent student and avid collector of Beaufort County's early history.[15]

Hilton Head Island also acquired several new churches during the 1960s. Before the James F. Byrnes Bridge opened, many old African American churches dotted the island. Queen Chapel, AME (1865), First African Baptist (1865), St. James Baptist (1886), Mount Calvary Church (1914), and Central Oak Grove Church were the most prominent. A small Presbyterian chapel was built at Honey Horn Plantation to serve white visitors. After the bridge opened, permanent white congregations were established, and new churches were constructed. St. Luke Episcopal Church was built on Pope Avenue in 1964, reviving the colonial parish established in 1767. First Baptist (1965) on South Forest Beach soon followed, and First Presbyterian Church (1965) on William Hilton Parkway replaced the old Honey Horn chapel. These businesses and institutions reflect the growth not only in tourist and resort traffic but also in permanent retired residents and the thousands of service workers necessary to sustain such a community. During the 1960s Beaufort County's permanent population grew by another 24.6 percent to 51,136.

In 1969 Sea Pines Plantation's Harbor Town Golf Links was the site of the first PGA golf tournament in Beaufort County. It was a great public relations coup for Charles Fraser and for Beaufort County. National television coverage was enhanced by the victory of America's most popular professional golfer, Arnold Palmer, at the first Heritage Classic. The Heritage Classic golf tournament has been one of the largest annual events in Beaufort County for thirty-seven years. The success of the Heritage Classic golf tournament encouraged the development of Sea Pines Plantation as a tennis center as well. In 1973 the Sea Pines Racquet Club first hosted the Family Circle Magazine Cup, one of the premier tournaments in women's professional tennis. This event also attracted luminaries of the sports world and national television coverage to Hilton Head Island.

In 1970 another institution of great importance to modern Beaufort County was inaugurated. The *Island Packet* newspaper was begun as a tabloid-size weekly paper of local interest. The men who started it were two real estate executives with the Hilton Head Company, Ralph Hilton and Tom Wamsley. One of their first investors was Lucy Daniels, a recent retiree to Hilton Head Island. The first issues of the *Island Packet* were distributed to 362 subscribers.

Lucy Daniels's husband was the retired editor of the *Raleigh News and Observer* of North Carolina. Jonathan Daniels agreed to write a weekly, front-page column for the *Island Packet* called "Sojourner's Scrapbook." The association of the Daniels family with the fledgling newspaper gave it instant journalistic creditability, and Jonathan Daniels's column gave it intellectual distinction. Daniels had been press secretary to President Franklin Delano Roosevelt during World War II and an aide to President Harry S. Truman. His connection to the *Island Packet* and to Hilton Head Island also had deep historical roots in Beaufort County. His father was Josephus Daniels, owner and publisher of the *News and Observer* at the turn of the twentieth century and Woodrow Wilson's secretary of the navy from 1913 to 1921. He was principally responsible for establishing the U.S. Marine Corps Recruit Depot on Parris Island in 1915. Josephus Daniels's assistant secretary of the navy was Franklin Delano Roosevelt, and one of Josephus Daniels's chief congressional allies during World War I was Congressman James F. Byrnes. These might have been the most influential personal connections Beaufort County had in the twentieth century.

In 1973 the *Island Packet* was sold for nine hundred thousand dollars to the News and Observer Publishing Company of North Carolina, the Daniels's family company, as was the older county paper, the *Beaufort Gazette.* By 1973, the *Island Packet* had 4,621 subscribers. In 1990 both Beaufort County papers were sold to the McClatchy Company of California. The *Island Packet* became a seven-day-per-week newspaper in 1995. Ten years later, the paper has approximately twenty-one thousand subscribers, reflecting what has been called "the dizzying growth on Hilton Head Island and southern Beaufort County."[16]

The growth of Hilton Head Island during the 1960s prompted the construction of new motels and eventually several large resort hotels along the front beach. In 1963 the Adventure Inn was built next to the William Hilton Inn, and in 1964 the Port Royal Inn was built to enhance real estate sales on Port Royal Plantation, a second beachfront development modeled after Sea Pines Plantation. In 1971 the Holiday Inn Ocean Front opened on South Forest Beach Drive at Coligny Circle. It was not only the first national chain hotel on Hilton Head Island, it was also by far the largest at five stories and two hundred rooms. But this was just the beginning for Hilton Head Island.

In 1967 the Palmetto Dunes Corporation started the third real estate and resort development on Hilton Head Island and in 1976 opened the Hyatt oceanfront resort hotel. The Port Royal Inn on Port Royal Plantation burned down in 1973 and was not rebuilt. By 1982 it had been replaced by the Westin resort hotel. Thus, by the 1980s Hilton Head's front beach was lined by high-rise resort hotels and their accompanying condominium developments.

Amid all this "dizzying growth" in the 1970s, Charles Fraser went broke. The intricate financial house of cards he had created fell victim to the OPEC oil embargo of 1973, which halted the tourist trade, and the national recession that followed. Interest rates went from 7.5 percent to 13.5 percent, while revenues for Hilton Head's new resorts and real estate developments declined. Charles Fraser had expanded his real estate empire rapidly in the 1970s, with posh new developments at Amelia Island, Florida, and Palmas de Mar, Puerto Rico. The financial liabilities of Sea Pines Plantation ballooned from $12,603,000 in 1969 to $282,968,000 in 1975. When the national recession and skyrocketing interest rates struck, Charles Fraser and Sea Pines Plantation were crushed under a mountain of debt. Not only did Charles Fraser lose control of Sea Pines Plantation, but Fred Hack also lost control of the Hilton Head Company, which had developed Port Royal Plantation and Palmetto Dunes Resort. With the Frasers and Hacks pushed aside, the era of modern plantation paternalism ended, and large national banks, insurance companies, and out-of-town corporations took control of Hilton Head Island.

Marathon Oil Corporation and then U.S. Steel Company acquired many of Hilton Head Island's real estate assets. In 1984 U.S. Steel Company sold its Hilton Head assets to a local development company, the Ginn Holdings Company, which was the creation of real estate gunslinger Bobby Ginn. It was a highly leveraged transaction financed by some small, undercapitalized Florida savings and loan corporations. Bobby Ginn was a local boy with deep family roots in Hampton County. His grandfather, Edward R. Ginn (1858–1932) had been Hampton County's state senator for eighteen years (1911–1929). Despite his local pedigree, Ginn was unable to repay the enormous debt he had acquired to effect the purchase of the Hilton Head Company. Payroll checks bounced, banks called in their notes, and bumper stickers appeared on Hilton Head Island that said, "Honk if Bobby owes you."

The Hilton Head Holding Company, which Bobby Ginn had created, went into bankruptcy in 1986. Federal Judge Solomon Blatt, a homeowner at Palmetto Dunes, took charge of the case. Judge Blatt appointed John F. Curry, an experienced resort executive, as trustee for the bankruptcy court. Curry hired a former governor, John C. West, as general counsel for the reorganization. West was also a Palmetto Dunes homeowner and a close personal friend of Judge Blatt. He had not only been governor of South Carolina (1971–75) but President Jimmy Carter's ambassador to Saudi Arabia. These three men—Blatt, West, and Curry—saved Hilton Head Island after a decade of mismanagement, neglect, and financial chaos.

When the dust settled on the reorganization, refinancing, and auctioning of a large part of Hilton Head Island in 1986, several different development companies replaced the few that had controlled Hilton Head Island a decade before. The residents of Sea Pines Plantation pooled their capital to form Sea Pines Associates and purchased the remaining assets of Hilton Head's oldest plantation. Outside of Sea Pines Plantation, the largest investors were the Greenwood Development, which owned Palmetto Dunes and Shelter Cove developments, and the Melrose Company, which revived the moribund

Indigo Run property. Greenwood Development Company was owned by the Self family of Greenwood, South Carolina, who had been pioneer investors in Sea Pines Plantation in the 1950s. By 1990 Hilton Head Island had come full circle after a decade and a half of change, uncertainty, and financial confusion. A South Carolina judge, a South Carolina governor, and a South Carolina textile family put Hilton Head Island back together again.[17]

During the years of Hilton Head's financial collapse and reorganization, the residents and property owners on Hilton Head Island and across Beaufort County began to take notice of the rampant, seemingly uncontrolled development that was consuming Hilton Head Island and spilling over to the mainland. The change in Beaufort County from 1960 to 1990 had been profound. To many old-time Beaufortonians and well-to-do retirees, it was alarming. "Growth control" became the rallying cry for wealthy retirees on Hilton Head, who did not want to see their paradise diminished, and for a growing coterie of young environmental conservationists. Inevitably, this movement became political, and the tension between economic development and growth control has dominated Beaufort County politics for twenty years.

The issue that launched this movement more than any other was the BASF controversy of 1969–70. BASF (Badische Anilin und Soda Fabrik), a giant German chemical company, was expanding its European business into the American market. It wanted to build a chemical plant at Victoria Bluff on the Colleton River next to Foot Point Plantation, the old hunting preserve of the Cram family of Philadelphia. The site was important to BASF because it had deep water access to Port Royal Sound for shipments of raw material. Hilton Head homeowners were opposed to a large, unsightly, and polluting industrial facility next to their island paradise. Most state politicians strongly endorsed the BASF project. Governor Robert McNair, Beaufort County's influential state senator, James M. Waddell, and the local state representative, Wilton Graves, were all enthusiastic boosters of industrial development. The plant was to cost $100 million, require six hundred skilled employees and attract satellite industrial development that would create five to seven thousand additional jobs. This was the kind of economic boosterism that the New South had been famous for since the Civil War. But Charles Fraser and Orion Hack, backed by the wealthy and influential residents of Hilton Head Island, raised $600,000 to fight the project, convened environmental scientists from across the country to bolster their case, and eventually had their lawyers seek a federal injunction to stop BASF. Their most dramatic public relations gambit was to enlist the support of the Hilton Head Fishing Cooperative, an African American enterprise led by native islander Tom Barnwell. The group sailed the local shrimp trawler *Captain Dave* from Hilton Head Island to the Potomac River laden with fresh Port Royal Sound shrimp. Interior Secretary Walter Hickle relented to the national publicity and issued a federal injunction delaying the BASF project, which the German company abandoned shortly thereafter. The BASF controversy was the first great victory for the environmental and antigrowth proponents in Beaufort County. Others would follow.[18]

Many Hilton Head property owners objected to the ten-story Hyatt Hotel at Palmetto Dunes, believing that its height and mass were out of character for Hilton Head Island. But the resort was approved by the Beaufort County Planning Department. The equally large Westin and Marriott resort hotels soon followed. As tourist traffic crowded William Hilton Parkway and fast food restaurants, filling stations, and shopping centers began to spring up along the thoroughfare, local residents and homeowners saw their laid-back island paradise disappearing. Hilton Head residents lost confidence in the ability of Beaufort County government to protect their neighborhoods. Talk began of incorporating Hilton Head Island into a municipality to control the future of the community.

The issue that finally infuriated enough island residents to secede from Beaufort County was the approval and construction of the Four Seasons Centre on William Hilton Parkway, next to Singleton Beach, in 1982. The Four Seasons Centre was a dense beachfront condominium development built on a sandy, treeless tract of land. The condominium units were prefabricated units built in a factory in Georgia and transported by truck to the site. There they were lifted into place, one on top of the other, by crane. They were, in essence, manufactured homes stacked on top of each other. On Hilton Head they were nicknamed "stack-a-shacks." To make matters worse, they were erected alongside William Hilton Parkway in full view of passing motorists.

This was too much for Hilton Head residents. In 1982 they formed a Committee on Incorporation cochaired by John Curry and Thomas F. Baker. Other members of the committee were Brian Carmines, a well-known restaurateur; Ben Banks, editor of the *Island Packet;* and Michael Jordan, partner in the island's largest law firm and the legal brains behind the incorporation movement. This group researched, lobbied, and advocated for incorporating Hilton Head Island. They gathered petitions with thousands of signatures requesting a referendum on incorporation. The state government acceded, and the referendum was set for May 10, 1983.

The only serious opposition to incorporating Hilton Head Island came from the African American native islanders. They knew their voting power would be seriously diluted in a town government as they represented only 13.1 percent of the island's population in 1983. They objected to paying additional taxes with no added services. In addition, they suspected that the growth controls of the new town government would restrict their traditional way of life by outlawing trailers, the preferred form of affordable housing for African Americans in Beaufort County, and restricting the livestock that were a common part of native island homesteads. They saw incorporation as racially divisive and referred to the intention of the new town government as "zoning slavery."

Despite the objections of the African American minority, the referendum went ahead and on May 10, 1983, 60 percent of Hilton Head Island's voters agreed to incorporate as the Town of Hilton Head Island. By the time of the incorporation, the island's population of 17,622 already exceeded that of the 272-year-old county seat in Beaufort. Hilton Head Island was instantly the largest municipality in Beaufort County.[19]

By the 1990s Beaufort County was a changed place. In 1973 the real estate bonanza crossed Skull Creek onto the mainland of Beaufort County. The first "off island" development was Moss Creek Plantation at the foot of the Byrnes Bridge and causeway. Moss Creek had previously been a horse farm owned by Pete Bostwick, a famous Long Island polo player and winter resident of Aiken, South Carolina. After Moss Creek came Rose Hill, the antebellum seat of the Kirk Family, and its spectacular Victorian gothic–style plantation house, one of the few in Beaufort County to survive the Civil War. Colleton River, absorbing much of the site intended for the BASF chemical plant, and Belfair Plantation followed. By the end of the century, the old U.S. 278 corridor leading to Hilton Head Island was lined with upscale golfing and retirement communities. Commercial development quickly followed along U.S. 278. Shopping centers, outlet malls, fast-food restaurants, and national-brand hotels sprang up almost weekly during the 1990s. For the thousands who commuted daily or weekly from Beaufort and Ridgeland to work on Hilton Head Island, the pace of change was stunning. Each trip revealed new land being cleared, a new sign announcing the next new commercial or residential development, or a new building "coming out of the ground." By the end of the century, the historic village of Bluffton on the May River was entirely surrounded by new residential and commercial development. In 2001 the old Town of Bluffton annexed much of the surrounding farmland and leaped the May River to annex the thirteen-thousand-acre Palmetto Bluff property, once the haunt of the Wilsons and Vanderbilts, in preparation for a massive, high-end retirement community. At a stroke, Bluffton became one of the geographically largest and demographically most dynamic municipalities in South Carolina.

The catalyst for the roaring development of southern Beaufort County in the 1990s was the opening of Del Webb's Sun City–Hilton Head retirement community in 1994. This is the largest retirement community in Beaufort County and one of the largest in the Southeast. Sun City–Hilton Head absorbed fifteen thousand acres of the old Argent Lumber Company and Union Camp Corporation timberlands at the intersection of State Road 170, connecting Beaufort, Bluffton and Savannah, and U.S. 278. By 2000 Sun City–Hilton Head had added seven thousand new residents to Beaufort County. To accommodate the Sun City development and the millions of tourists that visit Hilton Head each year, the South Carolina Highway Department built a four-lane "connector" from McGarvey's Crossroads through the timberland to Interstate 95 at Hardeeville in Jasper County. The eight-mile stretch between Sun City–Hilton Head and Hardeeville has become the latest residential and commercial real estate frontier. New hotels, shopping centers, gas stations, and the ubiquitous Wal-Mart Super Stores have opened along this new highway since the turn of the twenty-first century. Most impressively, old-line automobile dealerships from Beaufort, Hilton Head, and Savannah have opened huge new car lots and grand showrooms along the new 278 highway, a concentration of car dealerships promoted in the South Carolina lowcountry and the neighboring Savannah market as the "New River Auto-Mall," named after the river and swamp that now forms the boundary between Beaufort and Jasper Counties. Capping this newest phase of development is the construction of a brand-new eighty-acre campus for the University of South Carolina at Beaufort. With a bond issue funded by the Beaufort County government and generous private donations from Hargray Communication Company, the Palmetto Electric Cooperative, and Lieutenant Governor and Mrs. Brantley Harvey of Beaufort, the new campus opened in 2004. The driving force behind this new college is chancellor Jane T. Upshaw. The central Hargray Building was designed with a neoclassical portico copied from the old Beaufort College Building (1852) in downtown Beaufort and linking the glittering new campus to Beaufort County's two centuries of tradition in higher education. All of this development caused the Bluffton area to grow 164 percent from 1990 to 2000—from 7,202 residents in 1990 to 19,044 residents in 2000.

The explosive growth in southern Beaufort County encouraged the development of new, upscale retirement communities in northern Beaufort County. In 1961 Jack Kilgore built a bridge from Hunting Island State Park to uninhabited Fripp Island. There he built a golf course and began selling beachfront lots. It was the first resort development in northern Beaufort County. In 1983 Dataw Island, at Frogmore six miles east of Beaufort, was sold to Alcoa Properties, a national real estate–development subsidiary of Alcoa Aluminum. Alcoa Properties fulfilled the dream of Kate Gleason, who had planned to develop the property in 1926. By the early 1990s, Dataw Island had won several national prizes for planned-unit developments and was often listed among the top retirement communities in America. William F. Cochran, president of Alcoa South Carolina, Inc., was selected "Man of the Decade" by the Greater Beaufort Chamber of Commerce in 1990. Similar in size and condition was Callawassie Island on the Colleton River, just across the Broad River Bridge from Port Royal Island. After a succession of timber interest owners between 1947 and 1981, Callawassie Island was first developed for residential retirement by a group of German investors who sold out in 1988 to a group of Hilton Head developers, some of whom were lured to South Carolina by Charles Fraser in the 1960s. A few years later, they built a causeway and bridge to neighboring Spring Island and began developing that larger property as well. With ample open spaces and large environmental preserves, Spring Island, once the plantation of George Barksdale Edwards, probably the richest sea island cotton planter in the old Beaufort District, is one of the premier residential developments in South Carolina. Other developments in northern Beaufort County, notably Bray's Island and Bull Point in the Sheldon neighborhood (once the hunting grounds of the Yemassee Indians), followed suit.[20]

By the year 2000, the development of Beaufort County, which had begun in the brain of Charles Fraser in 1950, had totally transformed the county. The population had ballooned to 120,936. Beaufort County's population had grown 194 percent since 1960, and the county had reigned for three decades as the fastest-growing county in South Carolina. By the end of the twentieth century, Beaufort County had also achieved the highest per capita income in South Carolina. In 1950 the per capita income in Beaufort County was one half the national average. By 2000 Beaufort County was the only county in South Carolina that exceeded the national average in per capita income. This peaceful revolution from 1950 to 2000 was as thorough and profound as the revolution imposed by the Civil War conquest, occupation, and reconstruction of Beaufort County.

The transformation that engulfed Beaufort County required new public services, new schools, new roads, and new politics. Beginning in 1990, the Beaufort County Board of Education began a series of bond referenda totaling nearly a half-billion dollars, almost all approved by the voters, that led to the construction of four new high schools, six new middle schools, and a dozen new elementary schools. The two-lane country roads that connected old Beaufort and new Hilton Head in the 1950s had to be replaced by four-lane highways. This required replacing the old two-lane bridges spanning Skull Creek, Chechessee River, and Broad River with giant, elevated four-lane spans. Even those are often overcrowded. Traffic jams on the William Hilton Parkway were alleviated by a four-lane toll road that crosses Broad Creek on Hilton Head Island over the Charles E. Fraser Bridge. Traffic congestion between Beaufort and Lady's Island was relieved by the construction of the J. E. McTeer Bridge, named for Beaufort's famous sheriff.

With the growth in government, public services, and taxes came a new political order. In the 1970s, the last of the old Democratic power brokers gave way first to new progressive Democrats and then to a new, dominant Republican majority. In 1975 Beaufort County's old Democratic establishment reached its twentieth-century pinnacle when W. Brantley Harvey Jr. was elected lieutenant governor of South Carolina (1975–78), the highest-ranking Beaufort County politician since Richard Howell Gleaves, a Republican who served as lieutenant governor one hundred years before (1872–77). At the same time, Beaufort County state senator James M. Waddell was the last of the old-line Democratic power brokers from Beaufort County, serving in the South Carolina Senate for thirty-one years (1961–92) and rising to chairman of the Senate Finance Committee, the second most powerful position in state government (1981–92). Waddell was the last of the old Democratic establishment from Beaufort County that began with Senator Niels Christensen (1902–24), who also chaired the Senate Finance Committee for many years.

In 1976 the "good old boys" of the Beaufort County Democratic establishment were invaded by Harriet Keyserling, a progressive Democrat and native New Yorker who settled in Beaufort after her marriage to war hero Dr. Herbert Keyserling in 1944. She was the first woman elected to the Beaufort County Council and later served in the state house of representatives for fourteen years. In Columbia she aligned with several other white progressives and the few African American members to form a liberal bloc known as the "crazy caucus," often at odds with the old Democratic Party. Her son Billy followed with two statehouse terms of his own. But the demographics of Beaufort County and South Carolina were changing in the 1980s, and soon the old Democratic establishment was swept aside by a resurgent Republican majority. When James Waddell left the South Carolina Senate, he was replaced by a conservative Republican woman, Holly Cork of Hilton Head Island. Since then, Beaufort County's state senator has been a Hilton Head Republican. Through the 1990s and early years of the twentieth century, the Beaufort County Council has maintained a consistent, dominant Republican majority, and Beaufort County has been one of the Republican strongholds in South Carolina. Beaufort County's rising influence in the state was highlighted by the election of Beaufort County native Mark Sanford as Republican governor of South Carolina in 2002 and his reelection in 2006.[21]

As the twentieth century came to an end, Hollywood rediscovered historic Beaufort. The natural aesthetics of the sea islands and the historic ambiance of old Beaufort, which had entranced literary luminaries two generations before, worked their magic on dozens of film producers and Hollywood celebrities. The catalyst for Beaufort's late-twentieth-century fame is best-selling novelist and Beaufort native Pat Conroy. Conroy's father was a U.S. Marine Corps colonel and naval aviator who was stationed at MCAS Beaufort in the 1960s. Conroy graduated from Beaufort High School in

1963 and from the Citadel in 1967, where he was a star basketball player. Conroy eschewed a military career, taught at Beaufort High School, and on rural, impoverished Daufuskie Island, the subject of his first, autobiographical novel, *The Water is Wide* (1972). This became the Hollywood movie *Conrack.* His later novels *The Great Santini* (1976), *The Lords of Discipline* (1980), *Prince of Tides* (1986), and *Beach Music* (1995) were all national best sellers and all set in Beaufort or the Carolina lowcountry. Four of his novels became motion pictures and two (*The Great Santini* and *Prince of Tides*) were filmed in Beaufort. Another best-selling author, historical novelist John Jakes, has been a resident of Hilton Head Island for many years. His Civil War trilogy—*North and South, Love and War,* and *Heaven and Hell*—were made into a television drama. An ardent student of lowcountry history, Jake's latest novel, *Charleston,* is a fictional epic of lowcountry history in the eighteenth and nineteenth centuries.

More famous movies followed. *The Big Chill* (1984), a 1960s generational classic, and *Forrest Gump* (1993), winner of the Academy Award for best picture, were both filmed in Beaufort. *The Jungle Book* (1994), *Chasers* (1994), and *Something to Talk About* (1995) were filmed all, or in part, in Beaufort County. Beaufortonians got used to encounters and friendships with Hollywood celebrities. Robert Duvall, Blythe Danner, and Danner's young daughter, Gwyneth Paltrow, lived in Beaufort for six months while filming *The Great Santini.* The ensemble cast of *The Big Chill*—William Hurt, Glenn Close, Tom Berenger, Kevin Kline, and Meg Tilley—were well known in Beaufort. Nick Nolte and Barbra Streisand stayed in Beaufort while filming *The Prince of Tides,* and Tom Hanks interrupted a local wedding at the Carteret Street Methodist Church (much to the delight of the bride and groom) for celebrity shots while filming *Forrest Gump* in Beaufort and Fripp Island. Julia Roberts and Dennis Quaid stayed in Beaufort while filming *Something to Talk About,* as did Sharon Stone while filming *Last Dance.* Some of these Hollywood luminaries bought property in Beaufort County. Tom Berenger married a Beaufort girl and bought a house on the Okatee River. Hollywood producer Joel Silver (*Lethal Weapon* and *Die Hard*) bought and meticulously restored Auldbrass Plantation, the Frank Lloyd Wright lowcountry plantation classic on the Combahee River.[22]

As the twenty-first century dawned, old Beaufort was again transformed. A stroll down Bay Street in 2006 reveals signs of rising prosperity on the same old buildings that showed signs of poverty or decline in 1920. No remnant remains on Bay Street of the noisy cotton gins of the 1870s or the noisy shrimp docks and seafood-processing sheds of the 1930s. The old Beaufort Bank building at the west end of Bay Street is now a tony tourist restaurant with a deck overlooking the Beaufort River. The old customs house, where Robert Smalls ruled the roost for many years, became the Thomas

Law Building and is still owned by the grandchildren of Beaufort attorney W. J. Thomas. It now houses a real estate office, a jeweler, and a waterfront bar. Next door, heading east, the old Waterhouse Building, where Danners and Kinghorns held sway, has been replaced by a new bank building designed by architect Jim Thomas, grandson of W. J. Thomas. It now houses the Regions Bank, with branches in the suburbs. A gift shop and a jewelry store occupy the building of Wallace and Danners clothing store, and another restaurant, Plums, occupies the riverfront. A shoe store owned by Max Lipsitz's grandson occupies the site of the art deco Ocean View Café of the 1930s and 1940s. Next door, a restaurant with a riverfront bar, a real estate office, and a gift shop occupy the site of the old Riverview Hotel, burned in 1925. The old John Cross Tavern to the east houses the new John Cross Tavern and Harry's Restaurant upstairs and the Coldwell Banker real estate office downstairs. It is apparent on Bay Street that Beaufort's biggest business at the turn of the twenty-first century is real estate. Next to the John Cross Tavern stands the Bay Street Trading Company, worthy successor to the Beaufort Book Store that occupied the site in the 1940s and 1950s. Next door to the east is the three-story tabby structure built by Francis Saltus in about 1800 and for many years (the 1940s through the 1960s) the home of the Belk-Simpson department store, a mainstay of Beaufort commerce for thirty years. It has been restored and preserved at great expense by Beaufort investor and benefactor Richard Stewart. It now houses a gift shop, an art gallery, and an upscale restaurant called, appropriately, Saltus, with a riverfront terrace.

Across Scott Street, where the Wall, and later Horne, Motor Company had its showroom and maintenance shop from 1908 to 1968 and where the South Carolina Dispensary Building stood before the fire of 1907, now stand two clothing boutiques and an upscale household accessory store. On the corner of Bay and Carteret Streets, where the People's Bank stood from 1903 to 1979, the only bank in Beaufort County in the 1920s and 1930s, a new national bank, BB&T, also with branches in the suburbs, now transacts business. It is currently scheduled for conversion into expensive condominiums.

Across Carteret Street at the foot of the Lady's Island Bridge, now renamed for Patrolman Richard V. Woods, killed in the line of duty, stand the Sams-Waterhouse home, in recent years a bed-and-breakfast hostelry called the Bay Street Inn; the W. J. Thomas home, built of concrete after the fire of 1907; and the W. L. Wallace home, built of brick after the fire of 1907. The Wallace home was for many years the medical offices of Dr. W. Burns "Foot of the Bridge" Jones. All three overlook the General Stephen Elliott Park ornamented by two 18-pound British naval guns from the HMS *Vigilant,* which was anchored in the Beaufort River in 1779. On the northwest corner of Bay and Carteret Streets stands the monumental brick hardware store built by Niels Christensen in 1910 and owned since 1948 by Angus Fordham and his son, Duncan. Today it houses a mall of small gift and craft vendors. The arrival of Lowe's and the Wal-Mart Super Store at the Cross Creek Shopping Center, on Jack Gray's old potato farm in Burton, have altered the commerce of Bay Street. Next to the Christensen/Fordham hardware building, where James M. Crofut's store stood until 1907, are a specialty wine shop and a loan company. Where Morrall Furniture Company stood from 1917 to 1983 are the law offices of City Councilman George O'Kelley. The ancient tabby walls of that building stopped the fire of 1907. Immediately to the west is another fancy art gallery. Next door, where Beaufort Hardware Company stood from 1918 to 1990, a clothing store, Blackstone's Restaurant, and the new brick building of the A. G. Edwards brokerage office now stand.

Across West Street, where Jimmy Deere's Western Auto Store stood for forty years and the Greyhound Bus Station and twenty-four-hour grill operated in the 1940 and 50s, a parking lot now occupies the empty space. Facing Bay Street is the John Mark Verdier House Museum, a property of the Historic Beaufort Foundation. The eighteenth-century building was owned by George Holmes from the 1860s to the 1920s, when it housed the telephone exchange, law offices, and a barber shop. Later it housed a fish market and a restaurant before the historic preservation movement was begun by Howard Danner in the 1960s.

The old five-and-dime store of the 1920s through the 1950s has been replaced by Rossignol's fine gift store, whose proprietor, Charles Aimar Jr., is a tenth-generation Beaufortonian and descendant of the Sams family of Dataw Island. On the northeast corner of Bay and West Streets stands Lipsitz Department Store, the last of the old Bay Street merchant families. The Lipsitzes are now in their third generation on Bay Street. Across West Street, where Dr. H. M. Stuart's Apothecary dispensed medicine from the 1860s to the 1920s stands the Rhett Gallery, showplace of popular local artists Nancy Ricker Rhett and Billy Rhett, both descended from prominent antebellum and Reconstruction Beaufort families. Above the Rhett Gallery was once the busy and festive hall of the Ribault Club during the Victorian era. Two more whimsical gift and craft shops occupy the storefronts between the Rhett Gallery and the Schein Building. Morris Schein's department store, a prominent Bay Street business for seventy years, has given way to smaller gift-shop tenants and a restaurant in recent years but now stands empty, waiting for the next generation of Bay Street commerce.

To the west of the Schein Building, most of the space was occupied by Edward's five-and-ten-cent store from the 1940s through the 1980s. Now it is a mall of furniture, gift, and ice cream shops with a well-stocked rare book store on the front. Harvey's Barber Shop, one of the more enduring Bay Street businesses, now in its second generation, and First Citizen's Bank occupy the space that once housed the *Beaufort Gazette* before it burned in 1923.

Across Charles Street, the antebellum George Parsons Elliott House, for sixty years the residence of George Holmes, has survived with professional, legal, and medical offices, while the William Henry Trescott house next door was removed to make way for the three-story Bank of Beaufort building, now Wachovia Bank. From the 1890s to the 1950s, the Trescott House was the home and medical office of Dr. M. G. Elliott and then Dr. W. C. Black. The Trescott House now resides on New Street, where it is a private residence, one of the many historic preservation successes of the Historic Beaufort Foundation. Downtown Beaufort now has four banks. In 1935 it had only one, and that was practically insolvent. Next to the Wachovia Bank, where the famous old Sea Island Hotel once stood, the Best Western motel now stands, one of the community's historic-preservation failures. Across the street from the Best Western, by the Freedom Mall parking lot, is the gleaming new Downtown Marina with occasional mega-yachts transiting to Florida. Two busy carriage companies operate from the waterfront, taking tourists on historic tours of Beaufort's National Historic Landmark District and re-creating the sounds and smells of the antebellum era.

Back on Port Republic Street (renamed from Port Royal Street after the Revolutionary War) where Frank Ricker's home and cotton gin stood, a bank building converted into an art gallery now stands. Across West Street, the Historic Beaufort Foundation preserved the antebellum law offices of Edmund Rhett, and the upscale Beaufort Inn and its dependencies occupy almost the whole block. Gone is James Richardson's cobbler shop. Gone are Kit Singleton's livery stable and taxi stand. Gone is the blacksmith shop and funeral parlor. Port Republic Street, once the site of industry, is now the site of commerce and tourism. Bay Street commerce has transitioned from a core commercial district in the 1960s to a collection of restaurants and galleries, gift shops, and real estate agencies. A few professional offices survive, but most of Bay Streets commerce is tourist oriented. That is natural in that Beaufort County today hosts far more tourists than it houses permanent residents. As a sign of Beaufort County's economic resurgence in the late twentieth century, the new homes built in and around the town of Beaufort, after more than a century, are as large, sumptuous, and expensive as the famous antebellum mansions of the sea island cotton planters. It has taken more than a century, but Beaufort has finally recovered from the Civil War.

The centerpiece of Beaufort's downtown attractions, to tourists and residents alike, is the Henry C. Chambers Waterfront Park. It has been the crown jewel of downtown Beaufort since 1979. The park is named for Mayor Henry C. Chambers (1970–90), the most effective city leader of the twentieth century. Henry Chambers is the great-grandson of Reconstruction merchant king Moritz Pollitzer. Promoting Beaufort is part of his heritage. Chambers championed the waterfront park project against much opposition. When the park was complete, it turned the town around, physically and economically. The Henry C. Chambers Park has been the center of Beaufort's community activities, including its famous Water Festival, for thirty-three years. As of the end of 2006, the park is just completing a thorough restoration after three decades of hard use.

Today the tourist and stroller in historic downtown Beaufort naturally ambles past the old Bay Street buildings, through the green and shaded spaces to the sea wall at the great bend of the Beaufort River, known for three hundred years as "the Bay." Here in 1702 Colonel James Moore assembled his little fleet to attack the Spanish stronghold at St. Augustine. Here in 1706 were built the log blockhouse and palisade fort that marked the southern boundary of English North America and around which the colonial town of Beaufort grew. At the river's edge the traveler's eye is drawn southward to historic Parris Island. On clear Sundays, from the west end of the seawall, the giant stars and stripes of the U.S. Marine Corps can be seen beneath the arch of the J. E. McTeer Bridge standing against a freshening ocean breeze. If the ambler listens carefully, he can almost hear the corners of the proud banner snapping "Semper Fi" with every passing breeze. There Spanish sailors Pedro de Salazar in 1514, Francisco Gordillo in 1521, Pedro de Quexos in 1525, and Angel de Villafane in 1560 tried to plant the arms of Castile. There French Captain Jean Ribault founded the first Protestant colony in the New World in 1562. And there in 1566, Pedro Menéndez de Avilés, the conquistador of Florida, established La Ciudad de Santa Elena, the first colonial capital in America. There on Parris Island, a century before the English settled Jamestown, Virginia, or the Pilgrims set foot on Plymouth Rock, the history of Beaufort County began.

Notes

CHAPTER 1: THE GREAT SEA ISLAND HURRICANE OF 1893 AND ITS AFTERMATH

1. *Palmetto Post,* March 20, 1890. Here and throughout the text, when a particular source or group of sources is cited over several paragraphs, the note reference number will appear at the end of the final paragraph.

2. Bailey, Morgan, and Taylor, *Biographical Directory of the South Carolina Senate,* 3: 1645–46.

3. *Charleston News and Courier,* August 28, 1893. These stories are compiled from the manuscript collection at Penn Community Center on St. Helena Island. They are published in Marsher and Marsher, *Great Sea Island Storm,* 41–44. This book, by two authors with deep roots in Beaufort County, is one of the best pieces of current scholarship on the 1893 hurricane.

4. Frederick Christensen Diary, August 30, September 1, September 2, September 3, 1893; *Palmetto Post,* August 31, 1893; McTeer, *Adventure in the Woods and Waters,* 5.

5. "Report of Dr. J. W. Babcock to Governor Benjamin R. Tillman," September 4, 1893, Tillman Papers; *Charleston News and Courier,* September 5, 1893; *Beaufort Gazette,* October 27, 1908.

6. "Report of Dr. J. W. Babcock to Governor Benjamin R. Tillman," September 5, 1893, September 7, 1893; September 9, 1893, Tillman Papers.

7. *Charleston News and Courier,* September 5, 1893; Frederick Christensen Diary, September 9, 1893.

8. Frederick Christensen Diary, September 18, 1893; *Charleston News and Courier,* September 16, 1893; "Report of Dr. J. W. Babcock to Governor Benjamin R. Tillman," September 7, September 8, September 9, September 11, September 12, September 15, 1893, Tillman Papers.

9. *Charleston News and Courier,* January 9, 1894.

10. *Palmetto Post,* February 8, May 3, 1894.

11. Frederick Christensen Diary, October 15, October 16, October 17, 1895.

12. *Reports and Resolutions of the General Assembly,* 5: 333–36.

13. *In Memoriam: George Waterhouse; Palmetto Post,* May 14, 1896.

14. Frederick Christensen Diary, October 3, 1896, August 30, August 31, September 1, September 3, September 12, September 20, September 28, October 2, October 4, 1898, August 9, August 11, August 12, August 14, 1899; *Beaufort Gazette,* September 5, 1907.

15. *Beaufort Gazette,* September 7, 1933, August 26, September 2, 1943.

CHAPTER 2: BEAUFORT ECONOMY AT THE TURN-OF-THE-CENTURY

1. *Palmetto Post,* September 6, 1888, December 29, 1892.

2. *Palmetto Post,* December 29, 1892; *Beaufort Gazette,* December 31, 1903, September 5, 1907.

3. Shick and Doyle, "The South Carolina Phosphate Boom," 19–23.

4. *Palmetto Post,* March 10, April 7, November 2, 1892.

5. Frederick Christensen Diary, May 5, May 7, 1897; *Beaufort Gazette,* December 31, 1903.

6. *Beaufort Gazette,* March 31, 1904.

7. Frederick Christensen Diary, March 29, March 31, 1896, January 4, 1897.

8. Frederick Christensen Diary, September 18, 1896, July 15, 1898, June 17, 1899.

9. Kiser, *Sea Island to City,* 101.

10. "Letter from Secretary of War Transmitting a Letter from the Chief of Engineers."

11. *Beaufort Gazette,* March 31, December 22, 1904; Frederick Christensen Diary, February 19, 1904.

12. *Beaufort Gazette,* January 25, September 20, 1906, May 16, July 11, July 18, 1907.

13. Schick and Doyle, "The South Carolina Phosphate Boom," 28–30.

14. George Waterhouse to Miss Mary Waterhouse, March 31, 1890, correspondence in possession of the authors.

15. *Palmetto Post,* April 10, 1890.

16. Elliott, *Address Delivered at the Commencement, 1891.*

17. *Palmetto Post,* February 18, August 4, September 15, December 22, 1892.

18. *Palmetto Post,* January 12, 1893.

19. *Palmetto Post,* April 5, 1894.

20. Frederick Christensen Diary, March 11, March 13, March 27, 1896.

21. Frederick Christensen Diary, October 15, October 23, 1896, March 20, 1897.

22. Frederick Christensen Diary, March 4, 1893, March 19, April 16, 1896; Nash, *The American People,* 684–85.

23. *Palmetto Post,* February 24, March 3, March 24, April 14, 1898; Will Elliott Memoir, 74–75, SCL; O'Toole, *The Spanish War,* 108. Memoir of Will Elliott, South Caroliniana Library

24. *Palmetto Post,* May 19, June 23, 1898; Wynn, "History of Troop B, 202 Calvary South Carolina Army National Guard"; Frederick Christensen Diary, April 2, 1898.

25. Frederick Christensen Diary, June 5, June 9, June 12, June 17, 1898; *Palmetto Post,* June 23, 1898.

26. *Palmetto Post,* August 18, 1898; Frederick Christensen Diary, August 25, 1898.

27. McNeil, *Charleston Navy Yard,* 33, 38; Frederick Christensen Diary, May 8, 1900.

28. Frederick Christensen Diary, May 9, May 12, May 16, May 18, May 19, May 23, June 2, July 1, 1900; U.S. Senate, "Removal of the Naval Station, Port Royal, South Carolina," 51.

29. U.S. Senate, "Report to the Hearings before the Committee on Naval Affairs," 3, 4, 66, 68.

30. McNeil, *Charleston Navy Yard,* 33.

31. Frederick Christensen Diary, May 11, May 23, May 31, 1901; *Beaufort Gazette,* November 10, 1903, December 7, December 21, 1905.

32. *Beaufort Gazette,* February 22, 1906, January 3, February 21, April 11, 1907.

33. *Beaufort Gazette,* January 18, May 31, June 21, 1906.

34. *Beaufort Gazette,* August 20, 1903.

35. McTeer, *Beaufort, Now and Then,* 95–97; *Beaufort Gazette,* July 23, 1903, March 24, 1904, December 6, 1906.

36. *Beaufort Gazette,* August 22, 1907; *Port Royal Standard and Commercial,* December 16, 1875.

37. *Beaufort Tribune and Port Royal Commercial,* February 1, May 10, May 17, July 19, 1877.

38. *Port Royal Standard and Commercial,* March 23, April 27, 1876; *Beaufort Tribune and Port Royal Commercial,* September 13, September 27, 1877.

39. *Beaufort Tribune and Port Royal Commercial,* November 15, 1877; Keyserling, *Doctor K,* 1, 5–7.

40. *Crescent,* September 11, 1879; interview with C. E. McLeod III, August 3, 2001.

41. *Beaufort Tribune and Port Royal Commercial,* May 10, September 13, 1877; *Code of Laws of South Carolina, 1902,* 1: 566, 578–79.

42. *Palmetto Post,* February 18, 1892.

43. Frederick Christensen Diary, January 13, January 16, January 17, January 18, March 30, April 3, April 13, April 19, October 7, 1896, March 17, 1897.

44. Frederick Christensen Diary, December 7, 1904; *Beaufort Gazette,* September 3, 1903, March 2, 1905; *Handbook of South Carolina,* 299–300.

45. Kiser, *Sea Island to City,* 106–7.

46. Frederick Christensen Diary, November 8, 1902; Heyward, *Seed from Madagascar,* 246–48; *Savannah Morning News,* December 5, 1935. The authors are indebted to Charles Lynah of Tybee Island, Georgia, for sharing Lynah family archival material.

47. *Beaufort Gazette,* June 16, September 28, 1904; *Handbook of South Carolina,* 299–302.

48. *Charleston News and Courier,* 1926. The authors are indebted to Dr. John W. Gray III of Myrtle Bush Farms for sharing family archival material.

49. Frederick Christensen Diary, June 29, 1901; *Beaufort Gazette,* October 10, November 28, 1907.

50. *Beaufort Gazette,* May 4, 1905.

51. *Beaufort Gazette,* March 21, 1907.

52. *Beaufort Gazette,* May 16, 1907.

53. *Beaufort Gazette,* July 11, 1907.

54. *Beaufort Gazette,* April 13, 1905.

55. Woofter, *Black Yeomanry,* 136–43.

CHAPTER 3: ECONOMIC DECLINE AND ADJUSTMENT

1. "Transcripts of records of proceedings at the meeting of bondholders of the Port Royal Railroad Company," held June 21–24, 1878, at the Union Trust Company of New York; "Charter for the Port Royal and Augusta Railroad Company," June 29, 1878; "Joint Agreement by the Directors of the Port Royal and Augusta Railroad Company, the Greenwood, Laurens and Spartanburg Railroad Company, the Greenville and Laurens Railroad Company and the Augusta and Knoxville Railroad Company," March 19, 1887; "Directors of the Port Royal and Augusta Railway Company," March 19, 1887. All of the preceding are from South Carolina Secretary of State Papers; *Palmetto Post,* March 31, 1892.

2. *Palmetto Post,* April 7, April 14, 1892.

3. *Palmetto Post,* July 7, November 2, November 10, 1892; *Savannah Morning News,* November 6, 1892.

4. *Palmetto Post,* December 1, 1892.

5. Frederick Christensen Diary, September 23, October 11, 1896.

6. "Railroad Index" November 21, March 17, 1898, South Carolina Secretary of State Papers; *Palmetto Post,* March 24, 1898; March 31, 1898.

7. Frederick Christensen Diary, October 7, April 22, 1899.

8. *Beaufort Gazette,* November 2, 1905, February 28, 1907.

9. *Palmetto Post,* March 17, May 12, 1892.

10. Frederick Christensen Diary, June 5, July 25, 1893, October 15, 1896; March 25, October 16, 1897, March 9, 1899, July 1, July 15, 1901; *Palmetto Post,* February 4, 1892.

11. Frederick Christensen Diary, May 12, September 26, September 28, October 23, December 8, 1903; *Beaufort Gazette,* July 23, August 6, 1903.

12. *Beaufort Gazette,* March 24, 1904, April 4, 1907.

13. *Palmetto Post,* July 28, 1892; Frederick Christensen Diary, October 17, December 15, 1897, April 26, 1905; *Beaufort Gazette,* October 6, 1904, August 3, 1905.

14. *Palmetto Post,* June 2, December 22, 1892, January 12, 1893, March 22, April 12, 1894; Frederick Christensen Diary, November 11, 1895, January 27, 1896.

15. Frederick Christensen Diary, March 10, 1899, January 13, January 14, January 17, 1902.

16. *Beaufort Gazette,* June 23, 1904.

17. *Beaufort Gazette,* July 16, 1905, December 10, 1903, January 18, December 22, 1904; Li, "History of the Chinese in Charleston," 43–46.

18. *Palmetto Post,* January 25, 1894; Frederick Christensen Diary, March 21, 1897; *Beaufort Gazette,* November 5, July 30, 1903, January 17, 1907.

19. *Beaufort Gazette,* July 16, 1903, December 27, 1906, November 14, 1907.

20. *Palmetto Post,* April 7, 1892, February 1894; Frederick Christensen Diary, July 31, 1903, June 21, 1904; *Beaufort Gazette,* November 12, 1903, May 4, August 3, November 2, 1905, January 4, 1906.

21. *Palmetto Post,* August 22, 1892, March 22, 1894.

22. *Beaufort Gazette,* September 10, 1903. The authors are grateful to Mr. and Mrs. Robert Mc. C. Wilson of Cedar Grove, New Jersey, for providing family manuscripts and information.

23. Will Elliott Memoir.

24. *Palmetto Post,* March 10, 1892.

25. *Palmetto Post,* June 23, July 21, 1892.

26. *Palmetto Post,* October 6, October 13, October 26, November 10, November 17, 1892.

27. Reprinted from *Augusta Chronicle* in *Palmetto Post,* October 26, 1892.

28. Reprinted from *New Orleans Picayune* in *Palmetto Post,* February 1, 1893; reprinted from *St. Louis Republic* in *Palmetto Post,* January 25, 1894; *Palmetto Post,* April 12, 1894.

29. *Palmetto Post,* April 5, April 12, 1894.

30. *Palmetto Post,* April 5, April 12, April 19, April 26, 1894; *Handbook of South Carolina,* 409.

31. *Palmetto Post,* October 6, October 13, October 26, December 22, 1892.

32. *Palmetto Post,* June 30, 1892, January 5, 1893.

33. *Palmetto Post,* December 6, 1892.

34. *Palmetto Post,* April 7, December 22, 1892; Will Elliott Memoir, 62–64.

35. *Palmetto Post,* February 4, 1892.

36. *Palmetto Post,* March 22, 1894; *Beaufort Gazette,* December 22, 1904, June 14, October 18, October 25, 1906, April 11, 1907.

37. *Palmetto Post,* June 23, 1892.

38. *Beaufort Gazette,* September 20, 1906, July 11, August 8, November 14, 1907.

39. *Handbook of South Carolina,* 499.

40. Frederick Christensen Diary, October 15, 1900.

41. "Prospectus for the Development of Port Royal Harbor and Parris Island"; Edgar, Bailey, and Moore, *Biographical Directory of the South Carolina House of Representatives,* 1: 487, 491.

42. *Handbook of South Carolina,* 496.

43. Rowland, Moore, and Rogers, *History of Beaufort County,* 1: 60, 171, 404–5.

44. *Revised Statutes of South Carolina, 1872,* 404–5.

45. *Beaufort Tribune and Port Royal Commercial,* April 5, 1877.

46. *Palmetto Post,* April 7, 1892; Frederick Christensen Diary, April 22, 1896, April 12, April 13, 1897; *Beaufort Gazette,* April 13, 1905; Will Elliott Memoir, 56.

47. *Palmetto Post,* March 10, 1892; *Beaufort Gazette,* April 13, 1905; Burn, *An Island Named Daufuskie,* 430–41; *Beaufort Gazette,* October 13, 1905, October 14, 1907.

48. Burn, *An Island Named Daufuskie,* 435–38; *Beaufort Gazette,* April 13, 1905, October 14, 1907.

49. *Palmetto Post,* March 10, November 10, 1892.

50. *Code of Laws of South Carolina, 1902,* 1: 885–86; *Beaufort Gazette,* October 8, 1903.

51. *Beaufort Gazette,* April 13, May 4, July 6, 1905, February 22, March 1, 1906; *Palmetto Post,* May 2, 1905.

CHAPTER 4: BEAUFORT POLITICS AT THE TURN OF THE CENTURY

1. Tindall, *South Carolina Negroes,* 80–81; *Journal of the Constitutional Convention,* 1–8; Edgar, *South Carolina,* 443–45.

2. *New South,* March 7, 1895.

3. Frederick Christensen Diary, August 9, 1895.

4. *Journal of the Constitutional Convention,* 20–26.

5. Rogers, *Generations of Lawyers,* 113–15; Tindall, *South Carolina Negroes,* 83–84.

6. Tindall, *South Carolina Negroes,* 60–61, 83–84.

7. *Journal of the Constitutional Convention,* 443–48.

8. *Journal of the Constitutional Convention,* 476.

9. Underwood, *Constitution of South Carolina,* 3: 47–50, 66, 77.

10. Underwood, *Constitution of South Carolina,* 3: 75–77.

11. Underwood, *Constitution of South Carolina,* 3: 72–73; Edgar, *South Carolina: A History,* 445–47.

12. Underwood, *Constitution of South Carolina,* 3: 94–105; Edgar, *South Carolina: A History,* 446–551.

13. *Journal of the Constitutional Convention,* 319; Miller, *Gullah Statesman,* 206–7.

14. *Journal of the Constitutional Convention,* 89, 700, 727.

15. *Charleston News and Courier,* December 7, 1941; Frederick Christensen Diary, June 21, September 3, 1898, July 12, 1902.

16. Frederick Christensen Diary, November 4, 1896, June 19, August 28, 1900; Bailey, Morgan, and Taylor, *Biographical Directory of the South Carolina Senate,* 2: 1008–11.

17. Frederick Christensen Diary, July 4, July 5, July 17, 1901.

18. Frederick Christensen Diary, July 4, July 5, July 17, 1901.

19. *Beaufort Gazette,* September 13, 1906, February 7, September 12, September 26, October 10, December 26, 1907; *Savannah Morning News,* December 26, 1907.

20. *Beaufort Gazette,* October 28, November 4, November 25, 1910, January 20, 1911; Bailey, Morgan, and Taylor, *Biographical Directory of the South Carolina Senate,* 2: 805–6.

21. *Beaufort Gazette,* January 19, March 15, 1912; *Code of Laws of South Carolina, 1922,* 3: 277–78; Bailey, Morgan, and Taylor, *Biographical Directory of the South Carolina Senate,* 2: 1363; Edgar, Bailey, and Moore, *Biographical Directory of the South Carolina House,* 1: 501.

CHAPTER 5: POLITICAL ECCENTRICITIES ON THE SEA ISLANDS

1. *Palmetto Post,* January 12, 1893; Frederick Christensen Diary, December 11, 1896, January 11, 1897; Rose, *Rehearsal for Reconstruction,* 396.

2. Frederick Christensen Diary, August 28, 1898; *Beaufort Gazette,* November 19, 1903.

3. *Beaufort Gazette,* March 24, 1904, January 17, 1907; Frederick Christensen Diary, March 7, March 12, 1904.

4. Story recounted by participants in "Beaufort's Recovery from Reconstruction, 37 Years after the Rest of the State," *Charleston News and Courier,* December 7, 1941.

5. *Beaufort Tribune and Port Royal Commercial,* March 1, March 15, 1877.

6. Huggins, *South Carolina Dispensary,* 120.

7. Edgar, *South Carolina: A History,* 441–42; *Palmetto Post,* April 5, 1894.

8. *Palmetto Post,* April 5, 1894; *Beaufort Gazette,* October 8, 1903.

9. *Palmetto Post,* January 25, 1894.

10. Frederick Christensen Diary, November 3, 1901; *Beaufort Gazette,* July 23, 1903.

11. *Beaufort Gazette,* August 27, October 8, November 10, 1903.

12. Frederick Christensen Diary, August 2, August 3, August 22, 1904.

13. Frederick Christensen Diary, August 28, August 30, 1904; McTeer, *Beaufort, Now and Then,* 109–11.

14. Huggins, *South Carolina Dispensary,* 184–92; *Beaufort Gazette,* July 16, 1905, January 4, September 20, 1906, February 10, 1907.

15. *Beaufort Gazette,* February 28, April 4, June 13, July 11, July 18, October 10, 1907.

16. Huggins, *South Carolina Dispensary,* 192–94; *Beaufort Gazette,* August 8, 1907.

17. *Beaufort Gazette,* January 30, 1908, January 31, 1913; Edgar, Bailey, and Moore, *Biographical Directory of the South Carolina House,* 1: 502.

18. *Beaufort Gazette,* April 30, August 6, 1908, August 5, 1909.

19. Bailey, Morgan, and Taylor, *Biographical Directory of the South Carolina Senate,* 1: 306; Tetzlaff, *Cultivating a New South,* 184–8.

20. *Beaufort Gazette,* April 28, June 2, August 4, 1910.

21. *Beaufort Gazette,* January 6, January 13, 1911.

22. *Beaufort Gazette,* October 11, October 25, November 1, 1912; January 17, 1913.

23. *Beaufort Gazette,* October 25, November 12, November 29, December 13, 1912; Miller, *Gullah Statesman,* 243–44.

24. *Beaufort Gazette,* March 2, April 16, September 24, October 1, 1915.

25. Reprinted from *Charleston News and Courier,* September 11, 1915, in *Beaufort Gazette,* September 17, 1915; reprinted from the *State* in *Beaufort Gazette,* October 29,

1915; reprinted from *Charleston News and Courier* in *Beaufort Gazette,* October 1, 1915; reprinted from the *State,* September 28, 1915, in *Beaufort Gazette,* October 1, 1915.

26. *Beaufort Gazette,* July 2, 1915, August 18, 1916.

CHAPTER 6: SOCIAL INSTITUTIONS IN THE VICTORIAN AGE

1. *Palmetto Post,* February 25, 1892, January 25, 1894; *Beaufort Gazette,* December 10, 1905.

2. *Beaufort Gazette,* December 10, 1903, September 8, 1904.

3. *Beaufort Gazette,* December 24, 1904, December 6, 1906.

4. Reprinted from the *State* in *Beaufort Gazette,* November 26, 1903; *Beaufort Gazette,* November 14, 1907.

5. *Palmetto Post,* March 10, 1892.

6. *Beaufort Gazette,* November 2, 1905, February 21, 1907.

7. *Palmetto Post,* February 4, March 17, 1892, January 25, 1894; Frederick Christensen Diary, March 9, 1898.

8. *Beaufort Gazette,* August 27, September 10, 1903; Frederick Christensen Diary, June 21, 1903.

9. Frederick Christensen Diary, January 16, 1900; Barnwell, *Story of An American Family,* 154, 350.

10. *Palmetto Post,* December 15, 1892; *Beaufort Gazette,* December 6, 1906, January 3, 1907; "Beaufort Family: Guerard-Pollitzer"; Frederick Christensen Diary, June 27, June 30, 1901.

11. *Palmetto Post,* February 18, 1892; Spieler, "Maude O'Dell: From Bay Street to Broadway"; McTeer, *Beaufort Now and Then,* 128–29.

12. *Beaufort Gazette,* May 4, 1905.

13. *Beaufort Gazette,* August 27, 1903, August 3, 1905.

14. *Beaufort Gazette,* February 21, 1907.

15. *History of the Parish Church of St. Helena,* 78–79, 159–62; *Palmetto Post,* March 5, 1885, October 6, 1892.

16. *Beaufort Gazette,* April 13, 1905.

17. Tetzlaff, *Cultivating a New South,* 154–55; *Palmetto Post,* June 2, 1892.

18. *Beaufort Gazette,* November 1, November 8, 1906; Keyserling, *Doctor K,* 1–3.

19. *Palmetto Post,* July 28, 1892.

20. *Palmetto Post,* May 26, 1892; Frederick Christensen Diary, June 28, 1900; *Beaufort Gazette,* August 20, 1903, November 1, 1906.

21. *Beaufort Gazette,* April 25, 1907; *Palmetto Post,* September 9, 1897.

22. *Beaufort Gazette,* June 23, 1904.

23. *Beaufort Gazette,* January 7, June 23, 1904; reprinted from *Charleston News and Courier* in *Beaufort Gazette,* May 4, 1905; *Beaufort Gazette,* July 6, 1905; Barnwell, *Story of an American Family,* 73.

24. *Beaufort Gazette,* January 18, April 19, 1906; Barnwell, *Story of an American Family,* 78.

25. *Beaufort Gazette,* May 31, December 6, July 25, August 6, 1907.

26. *Beaufort Gazette,* May 2, 1907.

27. *Port Royal Standard and Commercial,* August 20, 1874.

28. *Port Royal Commercial and Beaufort Republican,* October 30, 1873.

29. *Palmetto Post,* July 7, 1892, March 10, 1892.

30. Frederick Christensen Diary, February 22, March 2, 1893; *Beaufort Gazette,* September 22, 1904, April 25, 1907; Barnwell, *Story of An American Family,* 130.

31. *Palmetto Post,* March 31, July 14, 1892.

32. *Palmetto Post,* June 23, 1892; *Beaufort Gazette,* October 24, 1907.

33. Will Elliott Memoir, 17–19; *Beaufort Gazette,* July 6, 1905, September 12, 1907.

34. *Beaufort Gazette,* September 10, 1903, March 31, June 16, 1904, May 4, 1905.

35. *Beaufort Gazette,* July 18, August 1, August 29, 1907.

36. Edgar, *South Carolina: A History,* 463.

37. Moore, *Columbia and Richland County,* 352–53; *Beaufort Gazette,* January 17, April 4, April 25, July 18, 1907.

38. *Beaufort Gazette,* April 4, August 1, August 29, 1907; Liollio Architecture, *A Historic Structure Report,* 11–12.

39. *Beaufort Republican,* September 4, September 25, October 2, 1873.

40. *Beaufort Tribune and Port Royal Commercial,* May 21, August 9, August 16, October 4, 1877.

41. *Palmetto Post,* June 2, June 9, July 7, July 14, 1892.

42. *Palmetto Post,* May 3, 1894; Frederick Christensen Diary, June 28, July 18, 1899.

43. *Beaufort Gazette,* June 23, September 28, 1904, July 6, August 3, 1905, July 25, August 1, August 29, September 5, 1907.

44. Rowland, Moore, and Rogers, *History of Beaufort County,* 1: 182–85, 292–93, 381.

45. *Palmetto Post,* July 7, August 25, 1892; Frederick Christensen Diary, June 27, 1900.

46. *Beaufort Gazette,* December 21, 1905, May 24, December 6, 1906.

47. *Beaufort Gazette,* November 29, December 6, 1906, August 1, 1907.

48. *Beaufort Gazette,* March 21, 1907.

49. Marvin H. Dukes Jr. interview.

50. *Palmetto Post,* July 14, July 21, August 25, September 1, September 8, October 6, November 2, 1892; *Beaufort Gazette,* July 16, September 5, 1907.

51. Frederick Christensen Diary, October 2, 1896, May 26, 1897, August 4, 1901.

52. *Beaufort Gazette,* July 16, 1902, July 6, November 2, 1905, June 14, October 18, 1906, May 30, July 18, July 25, August 22, 1907; reprinted from *Brattleboro Phoenix* in *Beaufort Gazette,* August 29, 1907; Frederick Christensen Diary, September 26, 1906.

53. *Palmetto Post,* February 18, 1892, January 25, April 5, 1894; Dabbs, *Sea Island Diary,* 197–98; Frederick Christensen Diary, March 12, March 22, 1905.

54. *Palmetto Post,* July 28, 1892.

55. Hollins, "Have You Packed the Purdy?" 9, 13, 17; *Beaufort Gazette,* March 3, 1938. The authors are indebted to Judith Hollins Lamb of Shelter Island, New York, for sharing her research and family history.

56. *Beaufort Gazette,* April 11, 1907.

57. *Palmetto Post,* February 8, 1894.

58. *Beaufort Gazette,* July 23, August 20, 1903.

59. *Beaufort Gazette,* January 3, 1907.

60. Spieler, "Palmetto Bluff Plantation: A Lowcountry Saga"; correspondence of Charles E. Fraser, October 26, 2001. The authors are grateful to Charles E. Fraser of Sea Pines Plantation, Hilton Head Island, for sharing his research on the Wilson family.

61. *Beaufort Gazette,* January 4, 1906; Perry, *Moving Finger of Jasper,* 153–55; Ferrell, *Argent: Last of the Swamp Rats,* 15–25.

62. *Beaufort Gazette,* December 10, December 31, 1903.

63. *Beaufort Gazette,* December 22, 1904.

64. *Palmetto Post,* January 5, 1893.

65. Frederick Christensen Diary, October 25, 1895; *Beaufort Gazette,* June 6, 1907.

66. *Beaufort Tribune and Port Royal Commercial,* June 21, 1877.

67. *Palmetto Post,* June 21, November 2, 1892.

68. *Beaufort Gazette,* August 6, August 13, 1903.

69. *Beaufort Gazette,* July 6, 1905.

70. *Beaufort Gazette,* July 11, 1905

CHAPTER 7: THE GREAT FIRE AND VIOLENT CRIME

1. Full accounts of the fire of 1907 are in the *Beaufort Gazette,* January 24, 1907, and Frederick Christensen Diary, January 19, 1907. The initial account in the *Beaufort Gazette* reported the date of the fire as January 21, 1907. Frederick Christensen's diary recorded the date as January 19, 1907. The newspaper subsequently corrected the error. See *Beaufort Gazette,* April 11, 1907.

2. *Beaufort Gazette,* January 24, February 21, March 21, 1907; Frederick Christensen Diary, January 19, January 21, May 26, 1907.

3. *Beaufort Gazette,* March 21, April 4, April 11, 1907.

4. *Beaufort Gazette,* January 7, 1904.

5. *Palmetto Post,* March 8, 1894; *Beaufort Gazette,* January 13, 1911.

6. Frederick Christensen Diary, December 23, December 24, 1895, January 2, October 30, 1896.

7. Frederick Christensen Diary, October 15, 1897; Will Elliott Memoir, 84–85.

8. *Palmetto Post,* February 24, 1898.

9. Frederick Christensen Diary, May 19, July 28, 1901, April 21, 1903, April 23, 1903.

10. Frederick Christensen Diary, August 21, 1903.

11. *Palmetto Post,* June 23, 1892; *Beaufort Gazette,* July 23, August 6, 1903, January 7, 1904, March 1, 1906.

12. *Beaufort Gazette,* August 6, 1903.

13. *Beaufort Gazette,* November 1, November 8, 1906.

14. *Beaufort Gazette,* April 4, 1907.

15. *Beaufort Gazette,* August 29, September 5, 1907.

16. *Beaufort Gazette,* October 10, November 7, November 14, November 21, 1907, September 2, 1909.

17. Edgar, *South Carolina,* 468; Miller, *Gullah Statesman,* 294; Tetzlaff, *Cultivating A New South,*186–87; *Beaufort Gazette,* April 4, 1913; repinted from *Charleston Evening Post* in *Beaufort Gazette,* April 11, 1913; *Beaufort Gazette,* April 25, August 1, August 15, August 29, September 5, 1913.

18. *Beaufort Gazette,* June 13, June 20, 1913.

19. *Beaufort Gazette,* December 27, 1912.

20. *Beaufort Gazette,* May 9, May 16, May 23, 1916, June 6, 1913.

CHAPTER 8: BEAUFORT'S AFRICAN AMERICAN COMMUNITY AT THE TURN OF THE CENTURY

1. Information on the formation of black churches is from Spieler, "Beaufort County Blacks and History: The Black Role in the History of Beaufort County," 91–94. Specific

information regarding property transactions is from Beaufort County Register of Deeds. See also Simkins and Woody, *South Carolina During Reconstruction,* 384–85.

2. *Palmetto Post,* June 2, 1892.

3. *Palmetto Post,* July 14, 1892, January 25, 1894.

4. *Palmetto Post,* July 21, 1892.

5. Tindall, *South Carolina Negroes,* 285; Spieler, "Black Freemasonry in Beaufort."

6. Tindall, *South Carolina Negroes,* 284; Spieler, "Social Societies Helped Blacks"; *Beaufort Gazette,* September 12, 1913.

7. Hanson, *History of the Knights,* 2–10; *Beaufort Gazette,* October 1, 1908, June 16, 1911. For the importance of burials, see Pollitzer, *Gullah People and Their African Heritage,* 141–43, and Creel, *A Peculiar People,* 313–17. *Beaufort Gazette,* July 23, August 6, 1903.

8. *Palmetto Post,* August 11, 1892.

9. Powers, *Black Charlestonians,* 172; *Palmetto Post,* July 21, 1892; Pazant, *Never Too Late,* 13. William Bradford Frazier was Rosalie Pazant's father.

10. Repinted from *Sea Island Journal* in *Palmetto Post,* August 11, 1892.

11. *Palmetto Post,* March 22, 1892.

12. *Beaufort Gazette,* January 17, 1907.

13. *Palmetto Post,* February 18, 1892.

14. Frederick Christensen Diary, May 30, 1898, May 30, 1900, July 4, 1903; *Beaufort Gazette,* June 6, 1907, May 21, 1908, June 2, 1910, June 7, 1912, June 6, 1913, June 4, 1915; Tindall, *South Carolina Negroes,* 303–4.

15. *Beaufort Gazette,* July 16, August 27, 1903; Tindall, *South Carolina Negroes,* 288. William Bennett was killed after the Great Fire of 1907.

16. *Beaufort Gazette,* August 13, August 27, 1903.

17. *Beaufort Gazette,* September 8, 1904.

18. *Beaufort Gazette,* November 13, 1903.

19. *Beaufort Gazette,* November 29, 1906, September 26, 1907.

20. Hegstrom, *Penn: A History, 1862–1982,* 89, 91, 94–105, 108, 113; Wolf, "Laura Towne and the Free People," 375–405.

21. *Beaufort Gazette,* May 30, 1907.

22. *Beaufort Gazette,* November 14, 1907; Hegstrom, *Penn: A History,* 107.

23. *Beaufort Gazette,* November 14. 1907. For an excellent history of Penn School in this era see Jacoway, *Yankee Missionaries in the South,* 63–81.

24. Bailey, Morgan, and Taylor, *Biographical Directory of the South Carolina Senate,* 1: 574–75; Miller, *Gullah Statesman,* 244–45.

25. Woofter, *Black Yeomanry,* 83–102; Kiser, *Sea Island to City,* 89–94; Jacoway, *Yankee Missionaries in the South,* 71–72, 189; Devlin, "South Carolina and Black Migration," 249.

26. Kiser, *Sea Island to City,* 97–100; Jacoway, *Yankee Missionaries in the South,* 72. See also Devlin "South Carolina and Black Migration," 249, and Johnson, *Social History of the Sea Islands,* 206–7.

27. Woofter, *Black Yeomanry,* 87–88, 116; Jacoway, *Yankee Missionaries in the South,* 185.

28. Kiser, *Sea Island to City,* 107; *Beaufort Gazette,* April 16, 1908, September 5, 1913.

29. *Beaufort Gazette,* September 8, September 15, October 13, October 20, 1911.

30. Jacoway, *Yankee Missionaries in the South,* 82–86; Kiser, *Sea Island to City,* 105.

31. Jacoway, *Yankee Missionaries in the South,* 93.

32. Kiser, *Sea Island to City,* 110; Woofter, *Black Yeomanry,* 138; Jacoway, *Yankee Missionaries in the South,* 139. For South Carolina cotton prices, see Devlin, "South Carolina and Black Migration," 260. For more on the boll weevil in Beaufort County, see chapter 14.

33. Kiser, *Sea Island to City,* 112; Devlin, "South Carolina and Black Migration," 205.

34. Woofter, *Black Yeomanry,* 142.

35. Woofter, *Black Yeomanry,* 144; Jacoway, *Yankee Missionaries in the South,* 185.

36. *Beaufort Gazette,* April 30, 1931, January 5, 1933; Woofter, *Black Yeomanry,* 263.

37. Petty, *Growth and Distribution of Population,* 228–29. U.S. Census figures for 2000 courtesy of Ian Hill, Beaufort County Planning Department.

38. *Beaufort Gazette,* July 10, 1941.

39. *Beaufort Gazette,* January 8, 1925.

40. The story of the "chicken bone special" was told by Theodore Simmons of Dale, South Carolina, at a Dale Community Preservation Area Committee forum held at James J. Davis Elementary School on July 27, 1999.

41. Washington, "Life Story of Martin Washington," 248–53.

42. Coleman, "My True Life Story," 253–74; Glen, *Life on St. Helena Island,* 46–47.

43. Glen, *Life on St. Helena Island,* 7, 21, 23–25, 32–36, 45–47; *Beaufort Gazette,* October 8, 1992.

CHAPTER 9: WORLD WAR I, PARRIS ISLAND AND THE PROGRESSIVE ERA

1. *Beaufort Gazette,* May 14, 1908.

2. *Beaufort Gazette,* October 22, November 19, 1908.

3. *Beaufort Gazette,* December 17, 1908; June 7, 1912. From 1903 to 1923, the *Beaufort Gazette* was owned by the Christensen family. At the same time, Niels Christensen Jr. was Beaufort County's state senator. He often wrote the editorials. Hence, the *Beaufort Gazette* fairly represented the opinions of Beaufort's commercial and political establishment in the years surrounding World War I.

4. *Beaufort Gazette,* January 28, April 14, 1909.

5. *Beaufort Gazette,* June 3, 1909, June 9, 1910.

6. *Beaufort Gazette,* August 11, August 25, September 1, September 15, 1910; Byrnes, *All in One Lifetime,* 12.

7. *County Democrat,* December 23, 1910; *Beaufort Gazette,* January 20, January 27, 1911, May 31, 1912.

8. *Beaufort Gazette,* May 2, May 16, 1913.

9. *Beaufort Gazette,* September 12, December 18, 1913; Byrnes, *All In One Lifetime,* 49; *Biographical Directory of the American Congress,* 643.

10. *Beaufort Gazette,* December 17, December 31, 1914.

11. *Beaufort Gazette,* March 11, April 16, 1915.

12. *Beaufort Gazette,* December 31, 1914, October 1, October 22, October 29, November 5, 1915.

13. *Beaufort Gazette,* October 22, December 10, 1915.

14. *Beaufort Gazette,* March 4, 1915, February 25, October 6, 1916, March 23, 1917.

15. Alvarez, *Parris Island,* 30, 31; *Beaufort Gazette,* March 9, August 31, 1917, October 3, 1919.

16. *Beaufort Gazette,* March 9, March 30, June 8, September 7, September 14, October 12, October 26, 1917, September 6, 1918.

17. *Beaufort Gazette,* July 6, October 19, 1917, August 9, 1918.

18. *Beaufort Gazette,* September 14, September 28, October 5, 1917.

19. *Beaufort Gazette,* October 19, 1917, April 12, July 12, 1918.

20. *Beaufort Gazette,* July 5, 1918.

21. *Beaufort Gazette,* July 26, 1918, May 9, 1919.

22. *Beaufort Gazette,* April 13, April 27, 1917, September 6, 1918.

23. *Beaufort Gazette,* September 27, October 11, October 25, 1918.

24. *Beaufort Gazette,* November 15, November 22, 1918.

25. *Beaufort Gazette,* January 11, May 8, 1924, March 18, March 25, April 1, 1926; Alvarez, *Parris Island,* 46.

26. *Beaufort Gazette,* September 19, September 26, 1919, August 20, 1920.

27. *Beaufort Gazette,* January 10, April 11, 1919, February 25, May 27, June 3, 1921, February 22, April 24, 1924, October 8, 1925, May 12, 1927, November 2, 1933.

28. *Beaufort Gazette,* July 27, 1923, July 10, 1924.

29. *Beaufort Gazette,* December 16, 1910, June 30, 1911, April 26, 1912, April 2, 1914.

30. *Beaufort Gazette.* February 17, 1910, September 5, 1913, October 29, 1915.

31. Woofter, *Black Yeomanry,* 138–45.

32. *Beaufort Gazette,* September 14, December 7, 1917.

33. *Beaufort Gazette,* June 30, 1916, November 2, November 30, 1917, October 4, October 25, 1918.

34. *Beaufort Gazette,* January 5, October 25, 1918, February 28, 1919, January 2, 1920.

35. *Beaufort Gazette,* September 6, 1918, June 20, October 31, 1919.

36. *Beaufort Gazette,* January 2, February 6, 1920; Woofter, *Black Yeomanry,* 138–39.

37. *Beaufort Gazette,* March 5, March 26, April 16, December 17, 1920. The shell of this factory still stands near the old Port Royal Railroad tracks. It has been known for years as the "pickle factory," a later use.

38. Reprinted in the *Beaufort Gazette,* July 14, 1922.

39. *Beaufort Gazette,* March 19, 1908, August 4, 1910, June 2, 1911, March 29, 1912.

40. *Beaufort Gazette,* March 12, 1908, August 4, 1910, January 28, February 4, April 21, May 26, 1916, July 6, 1917.

41. *Beaufort Gazette,* October 25, 1912, August 29, 1913, August 3, 1917, February 27, 1920, September 8, 1922, December 15, 1927.

42. *Beaufort Gazette,* March 5, 1908, March 1, 1912, March 12, 1914, August 18, 1916, March 6, March 13, 1924; Trask, *Carolina Trasks,* 73–75.

43. *Beaufort Gazette,* May 31, 1912, April 16, 1915.

44. *Beaufort Gazette,* October 22, 1914, January 14, 1915, April 25, December 19, 1919.

45. *Beaufort Gazette,* May 31, August 16, 1912, January 25, 1918, March 12, 1920, July 6, 1923.

46. *Beaufort Gazette,* May 4, June 15, August 31, September 7, 1917, June 20, 1919, May 28, 1920, March 18, 1921.

47. *Beaufort Gazette,* October 13, 1911, December 5, October 10, 1919, August 13, August 20, 1920, January 14, 1921.

48. *Beaufort Gazette,* March 25, April 1, September 23, 1909, January 12, 1912, February 21, 1913, July 20, 1917, May 21, 1920, April 1, 1921.

49. *Beaufort Gazette,* July 13, 1917, June 7, 1918, June 10, 1921.

50. *Beaufort Gazette,* January 30, February 13, February 20, 1920, June 24, 1921.

51. *Beaufort Gazette,* May 12, 1922, September 13, 1928; Woofter, *Black Yeomanry,* 142–43.

52. *Beaufort Gazette,* June 25, November 5, 1925; Woofter, *Black Yeomanry,* 271.

53. *Beaufort Gazette,* June 17, 1909, March 17, 1910, December 20, 1912, July 25, October 17, 1913, January 1, 1915, March 3, 1916.

54. *Beaufort Gazette,* January 23, May 21, 1908, January 7, June 24, 1909, June 6, May 30, October 17, 1919, August 13, August 27, 1920, January 28, February 11, March 11, May 6, 1921.

55. Tetzlaff, *Cultivating A New South,* 95–97.

56. *Beaufort Gazette,* November 8, 1912, May 9, 1913; reprinted from *Spartanburg Herald* in *Beaufort Gazette* April 23, 1914; Tetzlaff, *Cultivating a New South,* 111.

57. *Beaufort Gazette,* April 30, 1914; Tetzlaff, *Cultivating A New South,* 197; Barnwell, *Some Data, and Other Southern Stories.*

58. *Beaufort Gazette,* July 9, November 19, 1915, February 4, 1916, January 26, 1917.

59. *Beaufort Gazette,* August 8, October 10, 1919; Tetzlaff, *Cultivating A New South,* 199–200.

60. Edgar, *South Carolina,* 471.

61. *Beaufort Gazette,* July 22, August 5, September 2, 1921; Frederick Christensen Diary, June 6, 1921.

62. *Beaufort Gazette,* April 14, August 18, 1922.

63. *Beaufort Gazette,* June 19, 1924, September 20, 1928; Bailey, Morgan, and Taylor, *Biographical Directory of the South Carolina Senate,* 1: 475–76, 3: 1661.

64. Tetzlaff, *Cultivating a New South,* 218–23.

CHAPTER 10: ECONOMY OF THE 1920S AND THE END OF THE PROGRESSIVE ERA

1. *Beaufort Gazette,* October 10, 1907

2. Bailey, Morgan, and Taylor, *Biographical Directory of the South Carolina Senate,* 1: 470; *Beaufort Gazette,* August 13, 1908.

3. *Beaufort Gazette,* January 23, March 19, April 9, May 7, May 14, October 8, 1908, February 4, April 15, 1909, September 23, 1921, May 1, 1930.

4. *Beaufort Gazette,* April 9, October 8, 1908, March 11, 1909, March 7, 1913; *Code of Laws of South Carolina, 1922,* 2: 203, 3: 870–71.

5. *Beaufort Gazette,* June 11, 1908, March 24, April 7, 1911, February 28, June 6, 1913.

6. *Beaufort Gazette,* September 10, 1914, August 17, December 14, 1917, August 8, 1919, October 7, 1921, July 20, 1923, July 16, September 10, September 17, October 8, 1925.

7. *Beaufort Gazette,* March 25, July 1, 1909; "First Auto Trip to Beaufort," in Will Elliott Memoir.

8. *Beaufort Gazette,* September 2, 1909, September 10, 1925, July 23, 1920.

9. Moore, *South Carolina Highway Department,* 31–43.

10. *Beaufort Gazette,* December 1, 1911, December 25, 1913, February 25, December 10, 1915, March 3, August 11, 1916; Moore, *South Carolina Highway Department,* 45.

11. *Beaufort Gazette,* March 9, March 30, May 18, 1917.

12. *Beaufort Gazette,* November 16, 1917, December 20, 1918, March 7, 1919, March 12, April 9, 1920, June 15, 1923.

13. *Beaufort Gazette,* March 10, 1916, June 1, 1917, July 7, 1922, September 4, 1930.

14. *Beaufort Gazette,* November 8, November 26, 1908. Moore, *South Carolina Highway Department,* 45–46.

15. *Beaufort Gazette,* March 11, March 18, July 22, 1921, April 17, 1924, June 25, 1926, January 7, 1926, April 28, 1927.

16. Moore, *South Carolina Highway Department,* 45–49; *Beaufort Gazette,* March 23, 1917, January 4, 1918, May 28, 1920.

17. *Beaufort Gazette,* March 17, March 31, 1910, April 7, October 6, 1911.

18. *Beaufort Gazette,* August 22, September 19, November 20, 1913, January 8, 1914, February 5, 1914.

19. *Beaufort Gazette,* October 29, 1915, February 22, 1918, March 7, 1919, June 4, 1920, May 20, 1921.

20. *Beaufort Gazette,* May 18, 1923, February 22, 1924, April 10, November 6, December 25, 1924, January 29, 1925.

21. *Beaufort Gazette,* January 13, March 3, April 21, July 7, July 14, 1927.

22. Moore, *South Carolina Highway Department,* 84–97.

23. *Beaufort Gazette,* April 30, September 10, December 10, 1908, June 23, 1910, May 26, 1911.

24. *Beaufort Gazette,* April 19, 1912; Jacoway, *Yankee Missionaries in the South,* 86–87.

25. *Beaufort Gazette,* April 15, 1918.

26. *Beaufort Gazette,* April 11, June 6, 1919; Robinson and Dortch, *Blacks in These Sea Islands,* 36–37.

27. *Beaufort Gazette,* April 5, 1928, January 17, 1929, March 12, 1931, December 14, 1939; Robinson and Dortch, *Blacks in These Sea Islands,* 40–41.

28. *Beaufort Gazette,* October 31, 1913, March 16, April 6, 1923, September 25, 1924, January 28, 1926.

29. *Beaufort Gazette,* March 14, November 21, 1929, September 25, 1930, January 1, September 24, November 12, November 19, December 10, 1931, May 12, 1932, May 30, 1935, April 13, 1939; Robinson and Dortch, *Blacks in These Sea Islands,* 36–38.

30. *Beaufort Gazette,* April 16, 1925, July 19, 1928, May 21, 1936; Jacoway, *Yankee Missionaries in the South,* 154–55, 220, 248–49.

31. *Beaufort Gazette,* April 23, 1914, June 25, 1915, February 4, 1916, June 17, 1937; Bailey, Morgan, and Taylor, *Biographical Directory of the South Carolina Senate,* 2: 825; interview and family papers of the Ricker family courtesy of Beaufort artist Nancy Ricker Rhett, granddaughter of Frank Ricker; Danner family genealogy courtesy of Ruby Ellis Danner Hryharrow, great granddaughter of William Porter Danner.

32. *Beaufort Gazette,* January 2, March 26, 1920, June 4, 1925; Keyserling, *Doctor K,* 132–3.

33. *Beaufort Gazette,* March 7, December 25, 1913, January 17, June 6, 1919, January 2, 1920, March 26, 1920, February 8, February 15, 1924; April 18, 1935; Niels Christensen III interview.

34. *Beaufort Gazette,* April 23, 1915, September 8, 1916.

35. *Beaufort Gazette,* July 20, 1917, December 26, 1929.

36. *Beaufort Gazette,* August 22, October 3, December 12, 1919, January 9, 1920.

37. *Beaufort Gazette,* May 7, May 14, July 9, 1920.

38. *Beaufort Gazette,* September 24, December 17, 1920, January 21, February 18, 1921.

39. Frederick Christensen Diary, March 19, 1921; *Beaufort Gazette,* November 5, December 17, 1920, June 17, July 8, 1921, July 7, 1922, May 4, 1923.

40. *Beaufort Gazette,* July 8, 1921; Frederick Christensen Diary, March 5, March 21, 1921; Tetzlaff, *Cultivating a New South,* 220–1.

41. *Beaufort Gazette,* December 17, December 24, 1908, March 25, 1909, December 10, 1913, April 23, 1914.

42. *Beaufort Gazette,* March 11, December 17, 1915, February 8, 1934; Williams, *Railroads and Sawmills,* 24, 257, 313, 327, 330.

43. *Beaufort Gazette,* November 30, 1917, March 21, 1919, March 12, April 30, 1920, August 26, 1921, January 6, 1922.

44. *Beaufort Gazette,* July 10, October 16, 1924, January 8, April 16, June 9, October 8, 1925, January 7, April 22, July 15, 1926.

45. *Beaufort Gazette,* August 5, August 19, August 26, September 30, 1926.

46. *Beaufort Gazette,* October 7, October 21, November 18, December 30, 1926.

47. *Beaufort Gazette,* December 16, 1926, January 6, January 27, June 2, 1927, March 17, March 31, 1928, February 11, 1929, April 28, 1932; Bailey, Morgan, and Taylor, *Biographical Directory of the South Carolina Senate,* 3: 1661.

48. *Beaufort Gazette,* January 6, January 13, October 6, 1927.

49. *Beaufort Gazette,* October 13, 1927, March 1, 1928; *Charleston News and Courier,* October 11, 1927. Edgar Brown was a state representative during this trial. He later served fifty years in the legislature, including forty-three years in the South Carolina Senate and thirty years as president pro tempore. His seniority and power in South Carolina were legendary.

50. *Beaufort Gazette,* October 13, 1927, January 12, January 19, January 26, 1928, September 3, 1931.

51. *Beaufort Gazette,* January 26, February 16, February 23, March 1, April 12, 1928.

52. *Beaufort Gazette,* March 1, April 5, May 31, 1928, May 2, May 16, 1929; Bailey, Morgan, and Taylor, *Biographical Directory of the South Carolina Senate,* 1: 150–1; Byrnes, *All in One Lifetime,* 55–56; *Biographical Directory of the American Congress,* 1655.

53. *Beaufort Gazette,* May 23, November 14, 1929, February 27, 1930; information from Dick Horne, son of Johnny Horne, via Susan Rushton, Beaufort High School graduates.

54. *Beaufort Gazette,* July 16, 1914; Edgar, Bailey, and Moore, *Biographical Directory of the South Carolina House of Representatives,* 1: 511–69; Bailey, Morgan, and Taylor, *Biographical Directory of the South Carolina Senate,* 1: 690–91.

55. *Beaufort Gazette,* March 1, 1928.

CHAPTER 11: LOW LIFE IN HARD TIMES

1. *Beaufort Gazette,* December 15, 1922.

2. *Beaufort Gazette,* June 8, 1923.

3. *Beaufort Gazette,* July 6, July 20, December 28, 1923.

4. *Beaufort Gazette,* April 10, July 10, 1924.

5. *Beaufort Gazette,* January 8, January 15, January 22, 1925. "Rural policemen" was the designation given to senior sheriff's deputies in the 1920s.

6. *Beaufort Gazette,* February 4, 1932, reprinted from *Cleveland Call and Post* in *Beaufort Gazette* December 7, 1939; *Beaufort Gazette,* March 7, 1940; McTeer, *High Sheriff of the Low Country,* 42.

7. *Beaufort Gazette,* June 9, June 30, 1927, July 7, 1927, January 31, September 5, 1929, October 22, 1931.

8. Tetzlaff, *Cultivating a New South,* 103–4; *Beaufort Gazette,* January 23, 1908, March 4, March 11, July 8, August 19, 1909, February 7, March 14, April 4, 1913.

9. *Beaufort Gazette,* January 21, 1915.

10. *Beaufort Gazette,* July 30, August 20, August 27, September 3, September 10, September 17, October 1, 1915, January 7, October 27, November 3, 1916.

11. The number of liquor stills is compiled from published newspaper reports from 1920 to 1934. It is undoubtedly conservative as not all raids were reported and only the largest stills were mentioned in the newspaper.

12. *Beaufort Gazette,* October 14, November 4, 1921, February 3, 1922, March 16, 1923, June 26, 1924, January 14, 1932.

13. McTeer, *High Sheriff of the Low Country,* 3; *Beaufort Gazette,* October 7, 1926, November 24, 1927, January 17, 1929, March 20, 1930, March 26, 1931.

14. *Beaufort Gazette,* October 25, 1928, January 29, 1931.

15. McTeer, *High Sheriff of the Low Country,* 5; *Beaufort Gazette,* January 13, 1922, October 6, 1927.

16. McTeer, *High Sheriff of the Low Country,* 6–8; *Beaufort Gazette,* September 25, October 30, 1930, July 23, 1931.

17. *Beaufort Gazette,* November 8, 1928, February 28, March 21, 1929.

18. *Beaufort Gazette,* November 1, 1928; McTeer, *High Sheriff of the Low Country,* 11–12.

19. Reprinted from the *State* in *Beaufort Gazette,* May 28, 1925; reprinted from the *Greenville News* and *Anderson Mail* in *Beaufort Gazette* June 11, 1925; reprinted from *South Carolina Gazette* in *Beaufort Gazette,* June 25, 1925.

20. *Beaufort Gazette,* March 16, June 22, July 20, 1923, August 24, 1925, February 24, 1927, May 10, May 17, 1928.

21. *Beaufort Gazette,* May 15, September 11, 1930, February 5, 1931; Edgar, Bailey, and Moore, *Biographical Directory of the South Carolina House of Representatives,* 1: 535; *Biographical Directory of the American Congress, 1774–1961,* 1007.

22. *Beaufort Gazette,* May 26, July 7, 1932; Bailey, Morgan, and Taylor, *Biographical Directory of the South Carolina Senate,* 1: 388–9.

23. *Beaufort Gazette,* April 6, October 26, November 9, November 16, 1933; Edgar, Bailey, and Moore, *Biographical Directory of the South Carolina House of Representatives,* 1: 539; Bailey, Morgan, and Taylor, *Biographical Directory of the South Carolina Senate,* 1: 690–1.

24. Frederick Christensen Diary, October 1, December 6, 1921; *Beaufort Gazette,* September 16, September 23, 1921.

25. *Beaufort Gazette,* September 16, September 23, October 7, 1921; Frederick Christensen Diary, October 1, 1921.

26. *Beaufort Gazette,* November 4, November 11, 1921; Tetzlaff, *Cultivating A New South,* 208–11.

27. Beaufort merchant Joe Lipsitz and older Beaufortonians who knew his father swore by the truth of this story. McTeer, *Beaufort, Now and Then,* 133–34.

28. *Beaufort Gazette,* November 11, 1921, April 3, 1924; Tetzlaff, *Cultivating A New South,* 205–6; Bailey, Morgan, and Taylor, *Biographical Directory of the South Carolina Senate,* 1: 306–7.

29. *Beaufort Gazette,* January 25, 1924, June 11, December 24, 1925, May 15, 1926.

30. *Beaufort Gazette,* May 5, June 9, June 16, June 23, 1927.

31. *Beaufort Gazette,* April 16, August 13, 1931, May 11, 1933, December 13, 1934.

32. *Beaufort Gazette,* February 9, 1939.

CHAPTER 12: HIGH LIFE IN HARD TIMES

1. *Beaufort Gazette,* July 4, 1919, April 2, April 9, 1936.

2. *Beaufort Gazette,* January 19, February 9, 1917; Bailey, Morgan, and Taylor, *Biographical Directory of the South Carolina Senate,* 3: 1941.

3. *Constitution of the Carolina Plantation Society,* 27–30; *Who Was Who in America,* 233; Hollins, "Have You Packed the Purdy?" 13, 17; Outerbridge, *Champion in a Man's World,* 4, 119.

4. *Beaufort Gazette,* April 29, 1909; Perry, *Moving Finger of Jasper,* 153.

5. Hollins, "Have You Packed the Purdy?" 10–13; *Beaufort Gazette,* April 15, 1909, March 29, 1912, October 17, 1919.

6. *Beaufort Gazette,* January 2, 1908, January 14, 1909, January 20, 1911, December 27, 1912, March 2, 1917.

7. *Beaufort Gazette,* January 28, February 11, 1921, March 23, June 1, 1923, February 27, 1930, March 3, 1932.

8. *Beaufort Gazette,* February 3, 1922, December 7, June 22, 1923, January 29, 1925; *Who Was Who in America,* 1: 1340.

9. *Beaufort Gazette,* March 4, 1926, July 21, 1927; Fraser, "Memorandum: Great Stories," October 26, 2001.

10. *Beaufort Gazette,* January 27, April 7, May 26, 1927, January 19, April 5, 1928; Hollins, "Have You Packed the Purdy?" 12.

11. *Beaufort Gazette,* August 4, October 27, November 10, 1927, January 14, 1928; *Who Was Who in America,* 4: 479.

12. *Beaufort Gazette,* March 28, July 12, 1928; *Who Was Who in America,* 1: 273.

13. *Beaufort Gazette,* March 14, April 25, August 22, 1929; *Reflections of People,* 134.

14. *Beaufort Gazette,* May 16, 1929, July 16, 1936; Perry, *Moving Finger of Jasper,* 148–50; Elliott, *Carolina Sports by Land and Water,* 124–38.

15. *Beaufort Gazette,* March 3, 1932, November 23, 1933, November 1, 1934.

16. *Beaufort Gazette,* June 30, 1927, October 17, 1928, July 30, 1931.

17. *Beaufort Gazette,* January 5, February 9, 1933; Barnwell, *Story of An American Family,* 244–325.

18. *Beaufort Gazette,* March 19, 1936; Bailey, Morgan, and Taylor, *Biographical Directory of the South Carolina Senate,* 3: 1683–84.

19. *American National Biography,* 9: 111–12; *Dictionary of American Biography,* supp. 1, 348–49; *Rochester Democrat and Chronicle,* January 10, 1933; *Rochester Times Union,* January 20, 1933; *Beaufort Gazette,* July 14, 1927, January 30, March 27, 1930, July 6, July 20, 1933.

20. *Beaufort Gazette,* December 31, 1931.

21. *Beaufort Gazette,* July 28, 1928, April 4, 1935.

22. Loring, *Auldbrass,* 7, 13, 95, 131.

23. *Beaufort Gazette,* April 13, 1933, January 10, 1935, March 3, March 24, 1938.

24. Spieler, "Palmetto Bluff Plantation: A Lowcountry Saga," September 19, 1985; *Beaufort Gazette,* April 8, 1937; Ferrell, *Argent,* 91; *Who Was Who in America,* 4: 146.

25. *Beaufort Gazette,* March 26, 1931; *Savannah Morning News,* March 21, 1931.

26. Conant, *Tuxedo Park,* 96; Thorne, *Journal of a Boy's Trip on Horseback, 1848.* The authors are indebted to Landon K. Thorne III for use of this family document.

27. Conant, *Tuxedo Park,* 39, 54–79, 90–91, 96, 98, 297; *Who Was Who in America,* 4: 940; Danielson, *Profits and Politics in Paradise,* 11–13.

28. Lubbock, *Six Decades in Texas,* 1–6.

29. Mackenzie, *Some Data and Other Stories,* vii–xiii; Jones, *Stormy Petrel,* 242–85.

30. Tetzlaff, *Cultivating a New South,* 118; Holland, *Letters and Diary of Laura M. Towne,* 4, 26; Pearson, *Letters from Port Royal,* 26–30; Billington, *Journal of Charlotte Forten,* 107–8, 144, 153, 158–59, 185, 193, 205.

31. Tetzlaff, *Cultivating a New South,* 119–23; Gonzales, *Black Border,* 17, 287–340, 343–48; Macdonald, *Recollections of Juliana,* 5–19; Turner, *Africanisms in the Gullah Dialect,* xiv–xx.

32. *Beaufort Gazette,* June 14, 1912; Maddox, *A Lamp Unto the Lowcountry,* 155; Baker, *Gleams of Truth;* Baker, *Mizpah: A Calendar for 1911; Mizpah,* also a calendar; Baker, *In Mellow Light.*

33. *Beaufort Gazette,* April 5, 1912, March 26, 1914, February 25, June 4, 1915, November 17, 1916.

34. *Beaufort Gazette,* October 1, 1908, September 8, 1910, July 4, 1913, July 16, March 19, 1914, September 8, 1916, November 14, 1919; *Charleston News and Courier,* July 12, 1931.

35. *Beaufort Gazette,* October 24, 1919, January 7, 1926, July 23, 1931, January 26, 1933, December 14, 1934, September 12, 1935; McTeer, *Beaufort, Now and Then,* 128.

36. *Beaufort Gazette,* December 29, 1911, May 3, 1912, March 19, 1914.

37. *Beaufort Gazette,* June 29, 1907, July 13, November 16, 1917; McTeer, *Beaufort, Now and Then,* 129; *Charleston News and Courier,* March 2, 1937.

38. *Stitch in Time,* 89, 127.

39. *Beaufort Gazette,* December 17, December 24, 1931.

40. *Beaufort Gazette,* April 21, 1932; repinted from *New York Evening Graphic* in *Beaufort Gazette,* May 5, 1932; *Dictionary of American Biography,* supp. 5: 452–4; *Stitch in Time,* 218–9.

41. *Beaufort Gazette,* May 12, 1932, October 26, 1933, August 23, August 30, 1934; McTeer, *High Sheriff of the Low Country,* 82–86; *Beaufort, Now and Then,* 131–32.

42. *Stitch in Time,* 218–19.

43. *Beaufort Gazette,* July 13, February 28, 1917, January 25, February 1, 1924, June 28, 1928.

44. *Beaufort Gazette,* October 22, October 29, 1931, September 1, October 20, 1932, January 12, 1933, October 4, 1934; Tedesco, "Edison Marshall," 217–22.

45. *Beaufort Gazette,* May 3, 1928, October 29, 1931, February 22, 1934; *Rochester Times-Union,* April 19, 1928; Bennett, "Kate Gleason's Adventures in a Man's Job," 43, 168–75.

46. *Beaufort Gazette,* April 25, August 1, 1935; Ransom, *Last Trumpeters and Other Stories;* Ransom, *Fishing's Just Luck and Other Stories;* Ransom, *The Woodland Book;* Lahr, "Artificial Respiration," 115–16.

47. *Beaufort Gazette,* June 20, 1935, May 28, June 18, 1936; Spieler, "Beaufort Art Colony Flourished During the 1930s."

48. *Beaufort Gazette,* February 16, 1939; "Francis Parkinson Keyes, 1885–1970," in Garraty and Carnes, *American National Biography,* 12: 645–46.

49. *Beaufort Gazette,* May 16, 1940; Zaidman, "Zora Neale Hurston, 1901–1960," 159–71.

50. *Beaufort Gazette,* April 4, 1940; Spieler; "Tidalholm, Lady Russell and Our Literary Past."

51. *Beaufort Gazette,* October 24, 1940, June 11, 1942, October 20, 1944.

52. Maddox, *Lamp Unto the Lowcountry,* 227; Bain, Flora, and Rubin, *Southern Writers,* 62–65.

53. *Beaufort Gazette,* November 2, November 23, 1939; Kunitz and Haycraft, *Twentieth Century Authors,* 581–82; James and Brown, *Book Review Digest,* 405; Griswold, *Sea Island Lady.*

54. Pinckney, *Hilton Head;* Rowland, Moore, and Rogers, *History of Beaufort County,* 1: 76n; Edgar, *South Carolina: A History,* 497.

55. *Beaufort Gazette,* October 27, 1944; Ethridge and Kopala, *Contemporary Authors,* 687.

56. *Beaufort Gazette,* March 17, 1938, December 26, 1940; Kunitz and Haycraft, *Twentieth-Century Authors,* 7–8; Adams, "My Favorite Town," 356–60.

CHAPTER 13: DEPRESSION AND NEW DEAL

1. Wallace, *South Carolina: A Short History,* 711; *Beaufort Gazette,* May 14, May 28, 1931.

2. *Beaufort Gazette,* June 16, 1934, July 14, 1932, June 1, 1933, July 12, 1934, July 8, 1937.

3. *Beaufort Gazette,* July 12, 1934, January 31, August 1, 1935, January 5, 1939.

4. Trask, *Carolina Trasks,* 93; Trask, "Truck Farming in Beaufort County"; *Beaufort Gazette,* July 21, 1932.

5. *Beaufort Gazette,* December 8, 1932.

6. *Beaufort Gazette,* January 5, 1933, July 18, 1935, April 2, 1936.

7. *Beaufort Gazette,* January 21, 1932, January 5, October 5, 1933.

8. *Beaufort Gazette,* March 3, 1932, January 4, 1937, February 27, 1938.

9. *Beaufort Gazette,* April 13, 1923, March 26, 1936.

10. *Beaufort Gazette,* July 28, August 4, August 18, 1932.

11. *Beaufort Gazette,* March 23, May 18, 1933.

12. *Beaufort Gazette,* March 26, 1936.

13. *Beaufort Gazette,* March 16, 1933.

14. *Beaufort Gazette,* February 9, 1933.

15. Tetzlaff, *Cultivating a New South,* 211–14; *Beaufort Gazette,* October 6, October 13, 1932.

16. *Beaufort Gazette,* February 2, March 15, July 26, August 9, October 11, October 18, November 8, 1912.

17. *Beaufort Gazette,* November 1, 1912.

18. *Beaufort Gazette,* February 10, 1922, September 24, 1925.

19. *Beaufort Gazette,* May 20, 1909, November 1, 1912, January 21, 1915, October 6, 1916, March 30, 1923, March 15, 1934.

20. *Beaufort Gazette,* January 13, 1927.

21. *Beaufort Gazette,* September 25, 1910, August 9, 1912, November 20, 1924; family history provided by H. H. VonHarten and his daughter, anthropologist and historian Laura VonHarten, December 23, 2005.

22. *Beaufort Gazette,* December 1, 1922, January 4, 1924.

23. *Beaufort Gazette,* August 22, 1929, September 3, 1936; Bailey, Morgan, and Taylor, *Biographical Directory of the South Carolina Senate,* 1: 321.

24. *Beaufort Gazette,* June 23, July 21, 1910, June 20, 1913, March 6, 1930, May 3, 1934.

25. Burn, *An Island Named Daufuskie,* 431; *Beaufort Gazette,* May 7, 1908; April 14, 1910.

26. *Beaufort Gazette,* April 14, June 2, September 15, 1910.

27. Von Harten, "Early Days of the Shrimping Industry," 4–7; *Beaufort Gazette,* April 20, 1923.

28. *Beaufort Gazette,* July 4, 1929, March 13, 1930, September 3, 1931, August 4, 1932; Von Harten, "Early Days of the Shrimping Industry," 9.

29. *Beaufort Gazette,* April 5, October 4, 1928, March 6, 1930, August 9, 1934.

30. *Beaufort Gazette,* July 19, October 4, 1928, January 17, 1929, December 12, 1929, March 13, 1930.

31. *Beaufort Gazette,* June 18, 1931, August 17, 1933.

32. *Beaufort Gazette,* February 4, 1932, October 3, 1935, September 10, 1936.

33. *Savannah Morning News,* September 27, September 29, 1935; *Beaufort Gazette,* October 3, 1935.

34. *Beaufort Gazette,* March 19, 1936, January 12, 1939, June 1, 1939, April 24, 1941.

35. *Beaufort Gazette,* January 28, November 24, 1932, March 23, 1933; Hayes, *South Carolina and the New Deal,* 30–31.

36. *Beaufort Gazette,* May 4, 1933; Keyserling, *Doctor K,* 27–31.

37. *Beaufort Gazette,* August 31, September 14, September 21, October 12, 1933; Hayes, *South Carolina and the New Deal,* 89–90.

38. Hayes, *South Carolina and the New Deal,* 39–41; *Beaufort Gazette,* August 24, September 7, October 5, 1933, January 25, May 10, 1934, January 10, 1935.

39. *Beaufort Gazette,* January 24, 1935, February 7, 1935.

40. *Beaufort Gazette,* August 10, September 14, November 23, December 14, 1933, May 31, August 23, 1934.

41. Hayes, *South Carolina and the New Deal,* 52–55; *Beaufort Gazette,* August 10, 1933, October 11, 1934, January 24, 1935.

42. Byrnes, *All in One Lifetime,* 84–85; Hayes, *South Carolina and the New Deal,* 75–84.

43. Hayes, *South Carolina and the New Deal,* 134–35; *Beaufort Gazette,* March 12, 1908, June 9, September 23, 1910, October 4, 1934, October 1, 1936.

44. *Beaufort Gazette,* February 8, 1934, November 21, 1935, March 26, 1936, February 4, 1937.

45. Hayes, *South Carolina and the New Deal,* 58–68; *Beaufort Gazette,* May 2, October 17, November 14, 1935, September 17, 1936, March 10, 1938, February 13, July 24, 1941.

46. *Beaufort Gazette,* February 23, June 29, July 13, 1933, December 19, 1935, April 9, April 16, April 23, 1936, March 31, June 23, July 2, 1938.

47. *Beaufort Gazette,* November 2, November 9, 1939, September 26, 1940.

48. *Beaufort Gazette,* July 21, September 6, September 29, 1938, September 26, 1940, May 1, October 9, 1941, July 23, 1942.

49. *Beaufort Gazette,* July 16, October 15, October 22, 1931.

50. Hayes, *South Carolina and the New Deal,* 93–96; *Beaufort Gazette,* January 26, 1933, September 13, 1936, October 27, 1939, January 12, 1939.

51. *Beaufort Gazette,* June 22, July 6, 1939.

52. *Beaufort Gazette,* August 8, August 29, 1935, August 18, 1938, January 23, 1941.

53. *Beaufort Gazette,* January 3, 1935, October 29, 1936, August 5, 1937, March 10, July 14, 1938; Moore, *South Carolina Highway Department,* 197–98.

54. *Beaufort Gazette,* April 18, 1935.

55. *Beaufort Gazette,* March 11, July 29, 1937, January 26, February 16, 1939.

56. *Beaufort Gazette,* September 21, December 14, 1933, January 25, November 15, 1934. The editorials of E. O. Wilson likely represented more than his own personal opinion. The *Beaufort Gazette,* after 1925, was owned by a consortium of Beaufort businesses and political leaders and operated through the chamber of commerce.

57. *Beaufort Gazette,* November 1, November 8, 1934.

58. Hayes, *South Carolina and the New Deal,* 140–43.

59. *Beaufort Gazette,* December 13, 1934, February 21, 1935.

60. *Beaufort Gazette,* February 28, 1935.

61. *Beaufort Gazette,* May 30, 1935.

62. *Beaufort Gazette,* July 1, 1937; Rogers, *Generations of Lawyers,* 166–69, 326n.

63. Hayes, *South Carolina and the New Deal,* 147–48, 163; *Beaufort Gazette,* April 25, 1935, May 11, 1939.

64. *Beaufort Gazette,* May 11, 1930; reprinted from *Greenville Free Press* in *Beaufort Gazette,* June 29, 1930; *Beaufort Gazette,* July 20, 1939.

65. *Beaufort Gazette,* July 13, 1939.

66. *Beaufort Gazette,* July 1, July 22, 1937, April 20, 1939, April 18, 1940, January 16, 1941.

67. *Beaufort Gazette,* March 31, 1938, June 27, 1940.

68. *Beaufort Gazette,* December 21, 1939.

69. *Beaufort Gazette,* January 2, 1941.

CHAPTER 14: WORLD WAR II AT HOME AND ABROAD

1. *Beaufort Gazette,* March 24, March 31, June 16, December 8, 1932, April 27, May 11, June 8, 1933.

2. *Beaufort Gazette,* September 14, December 7, 1933.

3. *Beaufort Gazette,* August 19, 1937, April 28, 1938, March 16, 1939.

4. *Beaufort Gazette,* May 30, August 8, 1940.

5. *Beaufort Gazette,* September 19, 1940, March 20, 1941; Alvarez, *Parris Island,* 82.

6. Alvarez, *Parris Island,* 85–92.

7. Alvarez, *Parris Island,* 103–10.

8. *Beaufort Gazette,* May 7, 1942; Alvarez, *Parris Island,* 91, 93, 112–13.

9. Alvarez, *Parris Island,* 90.

10. *Beaufort Gazette,* March 3, 1916, April 21, 1927, June 17, 1921.

11. *Beaufort Gazette,* May 23, May 30, June 13, June 20, July 11, November 7, 1919.

12. *Beaufort Gazette,* October 17, 1919, June 4, 1920, June 17, 1921, May 3, June 14, 1928, January 29, June 20, 1929.

13. *Beaufort Gazette,* August 27, 1931, June 2, 1932.

14. *Beaufort Gazette,* May 14, 1925, March 5, 1931.

15. *Beaufort Gazette,* March 7, March 21, 1935, January 12, March 9, 1939.

16. Alvarez, *Parris Island,* 97; *Beaufort Gazette,* April 1, 1943, April 2, April 9, April 22, May 5, May 13, May 20, 1943.

17. Alvarez, *Parris Island,* 96; *Historic Preservation Plan: U.S. Marine Corps Air Station;* Gaddo, "MCAS, Beaufort."

18. Coletta, *United States Navy and Marine Corps Bases,* 49–51; Shettle, *United States Naval Air Stations,* 1: 33; *Beaufort Gazette,* March 18, November 11, December 9, 1943, February 10, 1944.

19. *Beaufort Gazette,* October 3, 1940, May 1, July 10, 1941, January 15, March 26, May 21, 1942.

20. *Beaufort Gazette,* February 26, 1942, February 11, February 18, 1943.

21. *Beaufort Gazette,* April 8, April 9, April 16, June 11, June 28, November 5, 1942, February 11, 1943.

22. *Beaufort Gazette,* January 22, February 5, March 5, April 2, May 21, 1942, January 14, February 11, July 8, August 19, 1943, November 10, 1944.

23. *Beaufort Gazette,* April 15, 1943, August 11, September 22, October 20, 1944.

24. *Beaufort Gazette,* March 4, July 1, July 20, September 16, October 21, 1943, February 10, February 17, June 22, 1944. Since the *Beaufort Gazette* was owned by the Beaufort Press, Inc., and managed by the Beaufort Chamber of Commerce from 1925 to 1948, E. O. Wilson's opinion was reflective of the Beaufort business community.

25. *Beaufort Gazette,* April 23, 1942, January 21, March 4, 1943, February 3, July 13, October 6, 1944.

26. Tetzlaff, *Cultivating a New South,* 211–14; *Beaufort Gazette,* February 9, 1933, January 18, 1934, December 11, 1941, October 29, 1942, January 7, 1943, July 29, 1945, March 30, December 1, 1944.

27. Shettle, *United States Naval Air Stations,* 2: 51; Gaddo, "MCAS, Beaufort," 42.

28. *Beaufort Gazette,* March 24, 1938, September 26, October 17, November 7, November 14, 1940, February 27, 1941, July 16, 1942.

29. *Beaufort Gazette,* September 17, 1942; *Reflections of People, Places and Events,* 30.

30. *Beaufort Gazette,* January 1, 1942; *Official Roster of South Carolina Servicemen,* 1: xxii. A list of Beaufortonians killed in action in World War II concludes this chapter.

31. *Beaufort Gazette,* June 18, 1936, June 11, 1942; *Official Roster of South Carolina Servicemen,* 1: xiv.

32. *Beaufort Gazette,* February 12, 1942; *Official Roster of South Carolina Servicemen,* 3: 2030, 2032.

33. *Beaufort Gazette,* April 16, 1942; *Official Roster of South Carolina Servicemen,* 2: 1029, 1030.

34. *Beaufort Gazette,* May 21, 1942; *Official Roster of South Carolina Servicemen,* 4: 3435, 3436.

35. *Beaufort Gazette,* January 21, 1942; *Official Roster of South Carolina Servicemen,* 4: 3546, 3548; Bailey, Morgan, and Taylor, *Biographical Directory of the South Carolina Senate,* 2: 1388–89.

36. *Beaufort Gazette,* May 28, 1942; *Official Roster of South Carolina Servicemen,* 3: 2382; Andy Kinghorn interview.

37. *Official Roster of South Carolina Servicemen,* 1: 37.

38. *Beaufort Gazette,* November 3, 1944; *Official Roster of South Carolina Servicemen,* 1: 229.

39. *Beaufort Gazette,* December 29, 1944; *Official Roster of South Carolina Servicemen,* 2: 1304, 1305.

40. *Beaufort Gazette,* January 28, 1943; *Official Roster of South Carolina Servicemen,* 3: 2502.

41. *Beaufort Gazette,* February 11, 1943; *Official Roster of South Carolina Servicemen,* 3: 2530.

42. *Beaufort Gazette,* March 4, 1943; *Official Roster of South Carolina Servicemen,* 3: 2415.

43. *Beaufort Gazette,* November 17, 1944; *Official Roster of South Carolina Servicemen,* 2: 1420.

44. *Beaufort Gazette,* February 18, 1943; *Official Roster of South Carolina Servicemen,* 1: 446.

45. *Official Roster of South Carolina Servicemen,* 4: 3121, 3122.

46. *Beaufort Gazette,* January 21, 1943; *Official Roster of South Carolina Servicemen,* 3: 2284.

47. *Beaufort Gazette,* September 1, 1944; *Official Roster of South Carolina Servicemen,* 3: 1905.

48. *Beaufort Gazette,* July 13, 1944; October 6, 1944; *Official Roster of South Carolina Servicemen,* 1: 689, 873; Harrell, "The Quest." Daniel Harrell, Claude "Pecy" Capplemann's stepson, has been researching Capplemann's war record for several years. The authors are grateful to him for sharing his personal papers.

49. *Beaufort Gazette,* January 21, February 18, 1943; *Official Roster of South Carolina Servicemen,* 1: 673.

50. Keyserling, *Doctor K,* 52–78; *Beaufort Gazette,* July 28, September 1, 1944; *Official Roster of South Carolina Servicemen,* 3: 2361.

51. *Beaufort Gazette,* December 16, 1943, June 8, 1944; *Official Roster of South Carolina Servicemen,* 5: 4274.

52. *Beaufort Gazette,* June 3, June 10, June 17, December 16, 1943, July 28, December 29, 1944; *Official Roster of South Carolina Servicemen,* 4: 3289.

53. McGowan, *Gullah Mailman,* xvi; *Beaufort Gazette,* September 1, December 8, 1944; *Official Roster of South Carolina Servicemen,* 4: 2785.

54. *Official Roster of South Carolina Servicemen,* 4: 3220; "Navy Secretary Names Destroyer to Honor World War II African-American Hero." The authors are indebted to Mae Mendoza, assistant librarian at the University of South Carolina Beaufort for sharing her research on the life of William Pinckney.

55. *Official Roster of South Carolina Servicemen,* 1: xv–lxiv; *Beaufort Gazette,* January 1, July 21, October 6, October 13, 1944. The *Official Roster* does not list date or place of death. Those whose hometown is designated "Beaufort Co." lived in unincorporated areas.

CHAPTER 15: THE POST-WAR BOOM IN BEAUFORT COUNTY

1. *Beaufort Gazette,* December 17, 2002; Danielson, *Profits and Politics in Paradise,* 12–13, 14–15, 22–23, 27–29, 40–44; Taylor, *Historic Beaufort County,* 66; Edgar, Bailey, and Moore, *Biographical Directory of the South Carolina House of Representatives,* 1: 577, 581, 586, 590, 602, 609, 613; Moore, *South Carolina Highway Department,* 280. Both authors of this volume have lived in Beaufort County during most of the last half-century. We make no claim of historical objectivity for this concluding chapter. We hope that it provides useful encouragement to the next generation of historians who might undertake to write volume 4 of *The History of Beaufort County.*

2. Danielson, *Profits and Politics in Paradise,* 14, 15; Taylor, *Historic Beaufort County,* 68.

3. Danielson, *Profits and Politics in Paradise,* 14; G. Thomas Upshaw interview.

4. Danielson, *Profits and Politics in Paradise,* 44, 45, 47, 48, 50, 51; Taylor, *Historic Beaufort County,* 78; Hiott, "James Cuthbert Self (1876–1955)," 857–58.

5. Alvarez, *Parris Island,* 133–34, 170–80; Stevens, *Court-Martial at Parris Island,* 1–10, 33, 177–78.

6. Gaddo, "MCAS, Beaufort," 42–45; Alvarez, *Parris Island,* 141–42.

7. Moore, *South Carolina Highway Department,* 197–99; Alvarez, *Parris Island,* 140–41; Bailey, Morgan, and Taylor, *Biographical Directory of the South Carolina Senate,* 2: 1388–99.

8. *Beaufort Gazette,* March 16, April 6, 1923, November 12, 1931, January 19, 1990.

9. Helsley, *Beaufort: A History,* 194–95.

10. Petty, *Growth and Distribution of Population in South Carolina,* 227; "Beaufort County Population Count by Race" and "Beaufort County Census Count, 1990 and 2000"; Helsley, *Beaufort: A History,* 207.

11. Alvarez, *Parris Island,* 127–28; Helsley, *Beaufort: A History,* 197–98; *Beaufort Gazette,* May 16, 2004. The authors are indebted to Margaret Rushton and her students at Beaufort Middle School (formerly Beaufort High School, 1959–1999), who created a timeline of school integration in Beaufort County and personally interviewed many of the original participants. Their 2002 publication, funded by the National Endowment for the Humanities, *Look Back, 1965–1972: Civil Triumph: The Integration of Beaufort High School,* is an excellent summary of those historical events. Because some of the original participants have since died, their interviews are significant contributions to the history of Beaufort County.

12. Goodwine, "Penn Center," 711–12; Helsley, *Beaufort: A History,* 201, 208; Jacoway, *Yankee Missionaries in the South,* 251.

13. Helsley, *Beaufort: A History,* 207–8; Keyserling, *Doctor K,* 95–98.

14. Mitchell, "Joseph William Frazier," 340–41; Helsley, *Beaufort: A History,* 221.

15. *Beaufort Gazette,* June 26, 2006; Hefter, *Hilton Head Island,* 104.

16. Hefter, *Hilton Head Island,* 113–15; Danielson, *Profits and Politics in Paradise,* 53–133; Taylor, *Historic Beaufort County,* 88–89.

17. Danielson, *Profits and Politics in Paradise,* 94–95, 189, 199–208, 213–30, 236; Bailey, Morgan, and Taylor, eds. *Biographical Directory of the South Carolina Senate,* 1: 568–569; Hartsook, "John Carl West," 1014–15.

18. Danielson, *Profits and Politics in Paradise,* 149–56; Edgar, *South Carolina in the Modern Age,* 133; Helsley, *Beaufort: A History,* 209.

19. Danielson, *Profits and Politics in Paradise,* 169, 178–84, 238.

20. Danielson, *Profits and Politics in Paradise,* 157; Taylor, *Historic Beaufort County,* 70–71, 96–97; Miller, *Fripp Island,* 45–57; Behan, *Short History of Callawassie Island,* 184–85.

21. Danielson, *Profits and Politics in Paradise,* 148; Bailey, Morgan, and Taylor, *Biographical Directory of the South Carolina Senate,* 1: 574–75, 692–93, 3: 1649–51; Keyserling, *Against the Tide,* 69–93; Bass, "Harriett Keyserling," 518–19.

22. Helsley and Norris, "Donald Patrick Conroy," 215; Rowland, "John Jakes," 492; Kozak, *Lights, Camera, Beaufort,* 4–21.

Bibliography

MANUSCRIPT, PRINTED PRIMARY, AND ARCHIVAL SOURCES

Alvarez, Eugene. *Parris Island: The Cradle of the Corps; A History of the United States Marine Corps Recruit Depot Parris Island, South Carolina, 1562–1983.* Washington, D.C.: History and Museums Division, Headquarters U.S. Marine Corps, 1983.

Baker, Julia Aldrich. *Mizpah: A Calendar for 1911.* Landon: E. Nister, 1910. Reprint, New York: E. P. Dutton, 1913.

"Beaufort County, 2000." Report provided by Ian Hill, Beaufort County Planning Office.

"Beaufort County Population Count by Race" and "Beaufort County Census Count, 1990 and 2000." Government report. Lowcountry Council of Governments, Yemassee, S.C.

Beaufort County Register of Deeds' Office.

"Beaufort Family: Guerard-Pollitzer." Manuscript provided by Henry C. Chambers, former mayor of Beaufort and great-grandson of Henry C. Pollitzer.

Carolina Plantation Society. *Constitution of the Carolina Plantation Society.* Charleston, S.C.: Privately printed, 1959.

Christensen, Frederick. Diary. South Caroliniana Library, University of South Carolina, Columbia.

Code of Laws of South Carolina, 1902. 2 volumes. Columbia, S.C: The State Co., 1902.

Code of Laws of South Carolina, 1922. 3 volumes. Columbia, S.C.: State Printing Co., 1922.

Danner family genealogy. Courtesy of Ruby Ellis Danner Hrybarrow, Beaufort, South Carolina.

Elliott, Honorable William. *Address Delivered at the Commencement of the Work on the Port Royal Dock.* Carolina Day, June 28, 1891. Charleston, S.C.: Walker, Evans and Cogswell, 1891.

Elliott, Will. Memoir. South Caroliniana Library, University of South Carolina, Columbia.

Fraser, Charles E., to Jim Mozley, William Preacher, John Yelverton, and Christian Smith "Memorandum: Great Stories for the Wilson Ruins," October 26, 2001. Spieler Collection.

Gray family archival material. Provided by Dr. John W. Gray III, Myrtle Bush Farm, Burton, S.C.

Handbook of South Carolina: Resources Institutions and Industries of the State, 1907. Columbia, S.C.: State Department of Agriculture, Commerce and Immigration, by the State Printing Company, 1907.

Hansen, Laura. *A History of the Knights of the Wise Men, St. Helena Island, South Carolina.* Frogmore, S.C.: Penn Center and Sea Island Preservation Project, 1995.

Harrell, Daniel V. "The Quest." Privately assembled manuscript on the World War II career of Lieutenant Colonel Claude M. Cappleman, USMC. Beaufort, S.C.

Historic Preservation Plan: U.S. Marine Corps Air Station, Beaufort, South Carolina. Pamphlet File No. 926., U.S. Marine Corps Museum, Parris Island, S.C., 1989.

Holland, Rupert Sargeant, ed. *Letters and Diary of Laura M. Towne.* New York: Negro Universities Press, 1969.

Hollins, Judith Livingston. "Have You Packed the Purdy? A History of the Hollins Family and Their Migration to South Carolina." Paper submitted to Lawrence S. Rowland's History 409 seminar, University of South Carolina Beaufort, April 28, 1999.

In Memoriam: George Waterhouse, Born in Lyman, Maine, May 16, 1839. Died in Saluda, North Carolina, August 17, 1894. N.p. Book in possession of the authors.

Journal of the Constitutional Convention of the State of South Carolina. Columbia, South Carolina: Charles Calvo Jr., State Printer, 1895.

"Letter from Secretary of War Transmitting a Letter from the Chief of Engineers, Report of Examination of Beaufort River, South Carolina." December 18, 1903. 58th Congress, 2nd. session, Document No. 199. *Congressional Record.* Washington, D.C.: Government Printing Office, 1903.

Liollio Architecture. *A Historic Structure Report: The Old Beaufort College Building.* Pamphlet. Charleston, S.C., 1998.

Look Back, 1965–1972: Civil Triumph; The Integration of Beaufort High School. Margaret Rushton and her students at Beaufort Middle School.

Lynah family archival material. Provided by Charles Lynah, Tybee Island, Georgia.

The Official Roster of South Carolina Servicemen and Servicewomen in World War II, 1941–1945. 5 vols. Columbia, S.C.: Division of General Services, State Budget and Control Board, 1967–1972.

"Prospectus for the Development of Port Royal Harbor and Parris Island into a Great Shipping Port and Railway Terminal, June, 1904." U.S. Marine Corps Museum Collection, Parris Island, S.C.

Reports and Resolutions of the General Assembly of the State of South Carolina 1893. 2 volumes. Columbia, S.C.: R. L. Bryan Company, 1894.

South Carolina Secretary of State Papers, 1878, 1887, 1896, 1898. South Carolina Department of Archives and History, Columbia.

Spieler, Gerhard. "Beaufort County Blacks and History: The Black Role in the History of Beaufort County." Unpublished manuscript in possession of the authors, Beaufort, S.C.

———. "Palmetto Bluff Plantation: A Lowcountry Saga." Research paper prepared for W. F. Grabenbauer, Manager, Palmetto Bluff Lodge, Union Camp Corporation, September 19, 1985.

Spieler, Gerhard, and Lawrence S. Rowland. *A Brief History of the Beaufort Arsenal.* Pamphlet 496. Parris Island, S.C.: Parris Island Museum.

Stockton, Robert P. *The Beaufort Arsenal: An Architectural History.* Charleston 1992. Pamphlet 408, Parris Island Museum, Parris Island, South Carolina.

Thorne, Samuel. *The Journal of a Boy's Trip on Horseback, 1848: Kept by Samuel Thorne.* New York: Privately Printed, 1936.

Tillman, Governor Benjamin R. Papers. South Carolina Department of Archives and History.

Trask, Mary Canada. "Truck Farming in Beaufort County," Unpublished seminar paper presented to Dr. Lawrence S. Rowland's History 410 seminar, University of South Carolina Beaufort, December 4, 1995.

U.S. Department of Defense. "Navy Secretary Names Destroyer to Honor World War II African-American Hero." News release, February 29, 2000.

U.S. Senate. "Removal of the Naval Station, Port Royal, South Carolina." 56th Congress, 2nd session, Senate Document No. 188. *Congressional Record.* Washington, D.C.: Government Printing Office, 1901.

———. "Report to the Hearings before the Committee on Naval Affairs Relative to the Proposed Transfer of the Naval Station from Port Royal, South Carolina to Charleston, South Carolina." 56th Congress, 2nd session, Senate Document No. 156. *Congressional Record.* Washington, D.C.: Government Printing Office, 1901.

VonHarten, Laura. "The Early Days of the Shrimping Industry, 1880–1945." Paper submitted to Lawrence S. Rowland's History 410 seminar, University of South Carolina Beaufort, December 14, 1995.

"VonHarten Family History." Family archival material provided by H. H. "Bubba" VonHarten and Laura VonHarten, December 23, 2005.

Waterhouse, George, to Miss Mary Waterhouse, March 31, 1890. Correspondence of the Waterhouse-Crofut Collection, South Carolina Historical Society.

Wilson Family Archival Material. Provided by Mr. and Mrs. Robert McC. Wilson of Cedar Grove, N.J.

Wynn, Gerald. "History of Troop B, 202nd Cavalry SCANG." Unpublished manuscript, October 1997.

ARTICLES

Adams, Samuel Hopkins. "My Favorite Town." In *Port Royal Under Six Flags.* Edited by Katherine M. Jones. New York: Bobbs-Merrill Company, Inc. 1960.

Bass, Jack. "Harriett Keyserling." In Edgar, *The South Carolina Encyclopedia,* 518–19.

Bennett, Helen Christine. "Kate Gleason's Adventures in a Man's Job." *American Magazine,* March 1928.

Coleman, John B. "My True Life Story." In *Sea Island to City: A Study of St. Helena Islanders in Harlem and Other Urban Centers,* by Clyde Vernon Kiser, New York: Columbia University Press, 1932.

Gaddo, Staff Sergeant Randy. "MCAS, Beaufort, South Carolina" *Leatherneck: Magazine of the Marines,* May 1984, 42–45.

Gelston, Arthur Lewis. "Radical vs. Straightout in Post Reconstruction Beaufort County." *South Carolina Historical Magazine* 75 (October 1974): 225–237.

Goodwine, Marquetta L. "Penn Center." In Edgar, *The South Carolina Encyclopedia,* 711–12.

Hartsook, Herbert I. "John Carl West" In *The South Carolina Encyclopedia,* 1014–15.

Helsley, Alexia Jones and Gene Norris. "Donald Patrick Conroy." In Edgar, *The South Carolina Encyclopedia,* 215.

Hiott, Susan Giaimo. "James Cuthbert Self (1876–1955)." In Edgar, *The South Carolina Encyclopedia,* 857–58.

Lahr, John. "Artificial Respiration: Accentuating the Negative in *The Color Purple* and *Miss Witherspoon.*" *New Yorker,* December 12, 2005, 115–16.

Li, Jian. "A History of the Chinese in Charleston." *South Carolina Historical Magazine* 99 (1998): 34–65.

Mitchell, W. K. "Joseph William Frazier." In Edgar, *The South Carolina Encyclopedia,* 340–41.

Powers, E. Bernard. "Community Evolution and Race Relations in Reconstruction Charleston, S.C." *South Carolina Historical Magazine* 95 (January 1994): 27–46.

Rowland, Lawrence S. "John Jakes." In Edgar, *The South Carolina Encyclopedia,* 492.

Sears, Stephen W. "Getting Right with Robert E. Lee." *American Heritage,* May/June 1991, 58–72.

Shick, Tom W., and Don H. Doyle. "The South Carolina Phosphate Boom and the Stillbirth of the New South. 1867–1920." *South Carolina Historical Magazine* 86 (1985): 1–31.

Spieler, Gerhard. "Beaufort Art Colony Flourished During the 1930s." *Beaufort Gazette,* August 20, 1966.

———. "Black Freemasonry in Beaufort." *Beaufort Gazette,* June 28, 1985.

———. "Maude Odell: From Bay Street to Broadway." *Beaufort Gazette,* August 18, 1998.

———. "Social Societies Helped Blacks Following Their Emancipation." *Beaufort Gazette,* January 31, 1985.

———. "Tidalholm, Lady Russell and Our Literary Past." *Beaufort Gazette,* July 17, 2001.

Tedesco, Joseph S. "Edison Marshall." In *American Short Story Writers, 1910–1945,* 2nd. ser., vol. 102, of *Dictionary of Literary Biography,* edited by Bobby Ellen Kimbel, 217–222. Detroit: Gale Research, 1991.

Washington, Martin. "Life Story of Martin Washington." In Clyde Vernon Kiser, *Sea Island to City: A Study of St. Helena Islanders in Harlem and Other Urban Centers.* New York: Columbia University Press, 1932.

Wolf, Kurt J. "Laura Towne and the Freed People of South Carolina, 1862–1901." *South Carolina Historical Magazine* 98 (October 1997): 375–405.

Zaidman, Laura. "Zora Neal Hurston, 1901–1960." In *American Short Story Writers, 1910–1945,* 1st. ser., vol. 86, of *Dictionary of Literary Biography,* edited by Bobby Ellen Kimbel, 159–71. Detroit, Michigan: Gale Research Inc., 1989.

BOOKS

Bailey, N. Louise, Mary L. Morgan, and Carolyn R. Taylor, eds. *Biographical Directory of the South Carolina Senate, 1776–1986.* 3 vols. Columbia: University of South Carolina Press, 1986.

Bain, Robert, Joseph Flora, and Louis D. Rubin, eds. *Southern Writers: A Biographical Dictionary.* Baton Rouge: Louisiana State University Press, 1979.

Baker, Julia Aldrich. *Gleams of Truth.* Spartanburg, S.C.: Waddell and Band, 1904.

———. *In Mellow Light.* Boston: Christopher Publishing House, 1936.

Barnwell, Stephen B. *A History of an America Family.* Marquette, Mich.: privately printed, 1969.

Bedford, Henry F., and Trevor Colbourn. *The Americans: A Brief History.* New York: Harcourt Brace Jovanovich, 1980.

Behan, William F. *A Short History of Callawassie Island, South Carolina: The Lives and Times of Its Owners and Residents 1711–1985.* New York: iUniverse, 2004.

Billington, Ray Allen, ed. *The Journal of Charlotte L. Forten: A Free Negro in the Slave Era.* New York: Dryden Press, 1953.

Biographical Directory of the American Congress. Washington, D.C: Government Printing Office, 1961.

Burn, Billie. *An Island Named Daufuskie.* Spartanburg, S.C.: The Reprint Company, 1991.

Byrnes, James F. *All in One Lifetime.* New York: Harper Brothers, 1958.

Cole, Nathan. *The Road to Hunting Island.* Charleston, S.C.: Arcadia Publishing, 1997.

Coletta, Paul, ed. *United States Navy and Marine Corps Bases, Domestic.* Westport, Conn: Greenwood Press, 1985.

Conant, Jennet. *Tuxedo Park: A Wall Street Tycoon and the Secret Palace of Science that Changed the Course of World War II.* New York: Simon and Shuster, 2002.

Creel, Margaret W. *A Peculiar People: Slave Religion and Community Culture among the Gullah.* New York: New York University Press, 1988.

Dabbs, Edith M. *Sea Island Diary: A History of St. Helena Island.* Spartanburg, S.C.: The Reprint Company, 1983.

Danielson, Michael N. *Profits and Politics in Paradise: The Development of Hilton Head Island.* Columbia: University of South Carolina Press, 1995.

Dictionary of American Biography. 22 vols. New York, Charles Scribner's Sons, 1935.

Edgar, Walter B. *South Carolina in the Modern Age.* Columbia: University of South Carolina Press, 1992.

———. *South Carolina: A History.* Columbia: University of South Carolina Press, 1998.

———, ed. *The South Carolina Encyclopedia.* Columbia: University of South Carolina Press, 2006.

Edgar, Walter B., N. Louise Bailey, and Alexander Moore, eds. *Biographical Directory of the South Carolina House of Representatives.* 5 vols. Columbia: University of South Carolina Press, 1974–1993.

Elliott, William. *Carolina Sports by Land and Water.* New York: Arno Press for Abercrombie and Fitch Library, 1967.

Ethridge, James, and Barbara Kopala, eds. *Contemporary Authors: A Bio-Bibliographical Guide to Current Authors and Their Works.* 1st revision, vols. 1–4 (combined in 1 volume). Detroit Mich.: Gale Research, 1962, 1963, 1967.

Faunt, Joan Reynolds, Robert E. Rector, David K. Bowden and Walter B. Edgar, eds. *Biographical Directory of the South Carolina House of Representatives, 1692–1973,* 5 vols. Columbia: University of South Carolina Press, 1974.

Ferrell, Mallory Hope. *Argent: Last of the Swamp Rats.* Edmunds, Wash.: Pacific Fast Mail Company, 1994.

Garraty, John A., and Mark C. Carnes, eds. *American National Biography,* 24 vols. New York: Oxford University Press, 1999.

Glenn, Isabella C. *Life on St. Helena Island.* New York: Carlton Press, 1980.

Gonzales, Ambrose Elliott. *The Black Border: Gullah Stories of the Carolina Coast.* Columbia, S.C.: The State Company, 1922.

Griswold, Francis. *A Sea Island Lady.* New York: William Morrow, 1939.

Hayes, Jack Irby, Jr. *South Carolina and the New Deal.* Columbia: University of South Carolina Press, 2001.

Heyward, Duncan Clinch. *Seed from Madagascar.* Chapel Hill: University of North Carolina Press, 1937.

Hefter, Natalie Harvey, ed. *Hilton Head Island: Images of America.* Charleston, S.C.: Arcadia Publishing, 1998.

Hegstrom, Margaret E. *Penn: A History, 1862–1982.* Columbia, S.C.: Office of the Governor, CETA Division, 1982.

Helsley, Alexia Jones. *Beaufort: A History.* Charleston, S.C.: History Press, 2005.

The History of the Parish Church of St. Helena. Columbia, S.C.: R. L. Bryan Company, 1990.

Huggins, Phillip Kenneth. *The South Carolina Dispensary: A Bottle Collector's Atlas and History of the System.* Columbia, S.C.: Sandlapper Publishing Company, 1997.

Jacoway, Elizabeth. *Yankee Missionaries in the South: The Penn School Experiment.* Baton Rouge: Louisiana State University Press, 1980.

James, Mertice M., and Dorothy Brown, eds. *The Book Review Digest, 1939.* Thirty-fifth Annual Culmination, March 1939–February 1940. New York: H.W. Wilson Company, 1940.

Johnson, Allen, ed. *The Dictionary of American Biography.* 10 vols. plus supplements. New York: Charles Scribner and Sons for the American Council of Learned Societies, 1927–1957.

Johnson, Guion Griffis. *A Social History of the Sea Islands: With Special Reference to St. Helena Island, South Carolina.* Chapel Hill: University of North Carolina Press, 1930.

Jones, Katherine M. *Port Royal Under Six Flags.* New York: Bobbs-Merrill, 1960.

Jones, Lewis P. *Stormy Petrel: N. G. Gonzales and His State.* Columbia: University of South Carolina Press, 1973.

Keyserling, Harriett. *Against the Tide: One Woman's Political Struggle.* Columbia: University of South Carolina Press, 1998.

Keyserling, Herbert, M.D. *Doctor K.* Beaufort, S.C. privately printed, 1999.

Kiser, Clyde Vernon. *Sea Island to City: A Study of St. Helena Islanders in Harlem and Other Urban Centers.* New York: Columbia University Press, 1932.

Kozak, Ginnie. *Lights, Camera, Beaufort: Hollywood Comes to the Lowcountry.* 2nd Edition. Beaufort, S.C.: Portsmouth House Press, 1998.

Kunitz, Stanley, and Howard Haycraft, eds. *Twentieth Century Authors: A Biographical Dictionary of Modern Literature.* New York: H.W. Wilson Company, 1942.

Linder, Suzanne C. *Historical Atlas of the Rice Plantations of the Ace Basin—1860.* Columbia: South Carolina Department of Archives and History, 1995.

Loring, Jessica Stevens. *Auldbrass: The Plantation Complex Designed by Frank Lloyd Wright: A Documentary History of Its South Carolina Lands.* Greenville, S.C.: Southern Historical Press, 1992.

Lubbock, Francis Richard. *Six Decades in Texas: Or Memories of Francis Richard Lubbock, Governor of Texas in Wartime; A Personal Experience in Business, War and Politics.* Austin, Tex.: Ben C. Jones, 1900.

Macdonald, Clare I. *Recollections of Juliana: A Sketch in Ebony.* Columbia, S.C.: The State Company, 1924.

Maddox, Annette Milliken. *A Lamp Unto the Lowcountry: The Baptist Church of Beaufort, 1804–2004.* Nashville, Tenn.: Fields Publishing Inc., 2004.

Mackenzie, Sarah Childs, ed. *Some Data and Other Stories of Southern Life,* by Sarah Barnwell Elliott. Bretenahl, Ohio: Seaforth Publications, 1981.

Marsher, William, and Fran. *The Great Sea Island Storm of 1893.* Macon, Ga.: Mercer University Press, 2003.

McGowan, Pierre. *The Gullah Mailman.* Raleigh, N.C.: Pentland Press, 2000.

McNeil, Jim. *Charleston Navy Yard: A Pictorial History.* Charleston, S.C.: Coker Craft Press, 1985.

McTeer, J. E. *Adventures in the Woods and Waters of the Lowcountry,* Beaufort, S.C.: Beaufort Book Company, 1972.

———. *Beaufort, Now and Then.* Beaufort, S.C.: Beaufort Book Company, 1971.

———. *High Sheriff of the Low Country.* Beaufort, S.C.: Beaufort Book Company, 1970.

Miller, Edward A. Jr. *Gullah Statesman: Robert Smalls from Slavery to Congress 1839–1915.* Columbia: University of South Carolina Press, 1995.

Miller, Page Putman. *Fripp Island: A History.* Charleston, S.C.: History Press, 2006.

Moore, John Hammond. *The South Carolina Highway Department, 1917–1987.* Columbia: University of South Carolina Press, 1987.

———. *Columbia and Richland County: A South Carolina Community.* Columbia: University of South Carolina Press, 1993.

Nash, Gary B., et. al. *The American People: Creating a Nation and a Society.* New York: Harper and Row, 1986.

O'Toole, G. J. A. *The Spanish War: An American Epic.* New York: W. W. Norton, 1984.

Outerbridge, David E. *Champion in a Man's World: The Biography of Marion Hollins.* Chelsea, Mich.: Sleeping Bear Press, 1998.

Pazant, Rosalie F. *Never Too Late.* Atlanta, Ga.: Hi-Tech Media, 1992.

Pearson, Elizabeth Ware, ed. *Letters from Port Royal.* New York: Arno, 1969.

Perry, Grace Fox. *Moving Finger of Jasper.* Jasper County, S.C.: Confederate Bicentennial Commission, 1962.

Petty, Julian J. *The Growth and Distribution of Population in South Carolina.* Columbia, S.C.: State Council for Defense, Industrial Development Committee, 1943.

Pinkney, Josephine. *Hilton Head.* New York: Holt and Rinehart, 1941.

Pollitzer, William. *The Gullah People and Their African Heritage.* Athens: University of Georgia Press, 1999.

Powers, Bernard E. *Black Charlestonians: A Social History, 1822–1885.* Fayetteville: University of Arkansas Press, 1995.

Ransom, Elmer Inglesby. *Fishing's Just Luck and Other Stories.* New York: Howell Soskin Publishers, 1945.

———. *The Last Trumpeters and Other Stories.* Athens: University of Georgia Press, 1941.

———. *The Woodland Book.* New York: Howell Soskin Publishers, 1945.

Reflections of People, Places and Events: A Pictorial History of Jasper County. Ridgeland, South Carolina. Jasper County Historical Society, 2000.

Rogers, George C., Jr. *Generations of Lawyers: A History of the South Carolina Bar.* Columbia: University of South Carolina Press, 1992.

Robinson, Carline S., and William R. Dortch. *The Blacks in These Sea Islands: Then and Now.* New York: Vantage Press, 1985.

Rowland, Lawrence, Alexander Moore, and George Rogers. *The History of Beaufort County,* vol. 1, *1514–1861.* Columbia: University of South Carolina Press, 1996.

Shettle, M. L. Jr. *United States Naval Air Stations of World War II.* 2 vols. Bowersville, Ga.: Schaertel Publishing Company, 1995.

Simkins, Francis Butler, and Robert Henley Woody. *South Carolina during Reconstruction.* Chapel Hill: University of North Carolina Press, 1932.

A Stitch in Time: Townsend, Vermont, 1793–2003. Townsend, Vt.: Townsend Historical Society, 2003.

Stevens, John C. *Court Martial at Parris Island: The Ribbon Creek Incident.* Annapolis, Md.: Naval Institute Press, 1999.

Taylor, Michael C. *Historic Beaufort County: An Illustrated History.* San Antonio, Tex.: Historical Publishing Network, 2005.

Tetzlaff, Monica. *Cultivating a New South: Abbie Holmes Christensen and the Politics of Race and Gender 1852–1938.* Columbia: University of South Carolina Press, 2002.

Tindall, George Brown. *South Carolina Negroes, 1877–1900.* Columbia: University of South Carolina Press, 1952.

Trask, Frederick Graham. *The Carolina Trasks: An Informal History.* Columbia, S.C.: R. L. Bryan Company, 1981.

Turner, Lorenzo Dow. *Africanisms in the Gullah Dialect.* Columbia: University of South Carolina Press, 2002.

Underwood, James Lowell. *The Constitution of South Carolina.* 4 vols. Columbia: University of South Carolina Press, 1989.

Wallace, David Duncan. *South Carolina: A Short History.* Columbia: University of South Carolina Press, 1951.

Who Was Who in America. 5 vols. Chicago: Marquis Publishing Company, 1966.

Williams, Rose-Marie Eltzroth, ed. *Railroads and Sawmills: Varnville, South Carolina; 1872–1997; The Making of a Low Country Town in the New South.* Varnville, S.C.: Varnville Community Council and R. L. Bryan Company, 1998.

Wilson, James Grant and John Fiske, eds. *Appleton's Encyclopedia of American Biography.* 6 vols. New York: D. Appleton, 1888.

Woofter, T. J. *Black Yeomanry: Life on St. Helena Island.* New York: Henry Holt, 1930

DISSERTATION

Devlin, George Alfred. "South Carolina and Black Migration, 1865–1940: In Search of the Promised Land." Ph.D. dissertation, University of South Carolina, 1984.

INTERVIEWS

Christensen, Niels, III (1913–2002). Interviewed in Christensen Realty Office, October 3, 2000.

Dukes, Marvin H., Jr., former commodore of the Beaufort Yacht Club. Interviewed in the offices of Dukes, Williams, and Infinger, P.A., August 1, 2002.

Gray, Dr. John W., III. Interviewed at Myrtle Bank Farm, November 22, 2001.

Kinghorn, Andy, son of A. Mills Kinghorn. Interviewed June 29, 2006.

McLeod, C. I., III. Interviewed at Seabrook, S.C., August 3, 2001.

Rhett, Nancy Ricker. Interviewed at Rhett Gallery, March 22, 2005.

Simmons, Theodore. Interviewed at Dale, South Carolina, July 27, 1999.

Upshaw, G. Thomas, president and CEO of Palmetto Electric Co-op. Interviewed by phone, November 6, 2006.

Index